THE AMISH

The Companion to AMERICAN EXPERIENCE PBS.

THE

AMISH

Donald B. Kraybill

Karen M. Johnson-Weiner

Steven M. Nolt

THE JOHNS HOPKINS UNIVERSITY PRESS
Baltimore

© 2013 The Johns Hopkins University Press
All rights reserved. Published 2013
Printed in the United States of America on acid-free paper
2 4 6 8 9 7 5 3

The Johns Hopkins University Press
2715 North Charles Street
Baltimore, Maryland 21218-4363
www.press.jhu.edu

Library of Congress Cataloging-in-Publication Data
Kraybill, Donald B.
The Amish / Donald B. Kraybill, Karen M. Johnson-Weiner, and Steven M. Nolt.
p. cm.
Includes bibliographical references and index.
ISBN 978-1-4214-0914-6 (hardcover) — ISBN 978-1-4214-0915-3 (electronic) —
ISBN 1-4214-0914-3 (hardcover) — ISBN 1-4214-0915-1 (electronic)
1. Amish—Social life and customs. 2. Amish — History. I. Johnson-Weiner, Karen.
II. Nolt, Steven M., 1968– III. Title.
E184.M45K725 2013
289.7′3—dc23   2012035333

A catalog record for this book is available from the British Library.

All Scripture quotations are from the Holy Bible, King James version.

*Special discounts are available for bulk purchases of this book. For more information,
please contact Special Sales at 410-516-6936 or specialsales@press.jhu.edu.*

The Johns Hopkins University Press uses environmentally friendly book materials,
including recycled text paper that is composed of at least 30 percent
post-consumer waste, whenever possible.

For Stephen E. Scott (1948–2011),
friend and colleague whose humility, wit, and patience
reflected the virtues of Old Order life

CONTENTS

Preface   *ix*

Acknowledgments   *xv*

I. ROOTS

CHAPTER 1   Who Are the Amish?   3

CHAPTER 2   European Origins   22

CHAPTER 3   The Story in America   37

II. CULTURAL CONTEXT

CHAPTER 4   Religious Roots   59

CHAPTER 5   Sacred Rituals   77

CHAPTER 6   The Amish Way   97

CHAPTER 7   Symbols and Identity   115

III. SOCIAL ORGANIZATION

CHAPTER 8   Diverse Affiliations   137

CHAPTER 9   Population Patterns   155

CHAPTER 10   Community Organization   171

CHAPTER 11   Gender and Family   193

CHAPTER 12   From Rumspringa to Marriage   212

CHAPTER 13   Social Ties and Community Rhythms   231

CHAPTER 14   Education   250

IV. EXTERNAL TIES

CHAPTER 15   Agriculture   275

CHAPTER 16   Business   291

CHAPTER 17   Technology   312

CHAPTER 18   Health and Healing   335

CHAPTER 19   Government and Civic Relations   352

CHAPTER 20   The Amish in Print   369

CHAPTER 21   Tourism and Media   385

V. THE FUTURE

CHAPTER 22   Pursuits of Happiness   403

APPENDIX A
Related Groups: Mennonites, Brethren, Hutterites   421

APPENDIX B
Key Events in Amish History   423

Notes   425
Bibliography   461
Index   487

PREFACE

Although the Amish are a tiny slice of contemporary American society, they are among its most recognized groups. Pundits and advertisers, cartoonists and Hollywood scriptwriters alike can invoke the Amish with confidence that Americans will recognize these plain-dressing, horse-and-buggy-driving people. Googling "Amish" retrieves millions of results touting Amish products and Amish tourist sites. Hundreds of Amish-themed romance novels penned by non-Amish writers have spilled into the national book market since 2005.

But it was not always this way. Amish people were not always the darlings of the merchants of popular culture. The first group of Amish arrived on American shores aboard the ship *Charming Nancy* in 1737, and for two hundred years they lived quietly amid their rural, non-Amish neighbors. One of many immigrant groups, they stirred little interest among outsiders. That invisibility vanished two centuries later in 1937, when Amish people in eastern Lancaster County, Pennsylvania, publicly protested the local township's plans to demolish one-room schools and construct a consolidated public elementary school. The conflict was so intense that it caught the attention of the *New York Times,* which ran a series of stories on Amish life. Throughout the remainder of the twentieth century, their conflicts with the state continued to generate national visibility, and the Amish soon became noted for their public dissent from the national narrative of technological progress and individual autonomy.

Yet even as mainstream America began to notice the Amish and their rejection of telephones, automobiles, and public grid electricity, it also dismissed them. As the larger society had begun to experience massive change—urbanization, industrialization, consolidation of education, technological advancements, growth of the welfare state, changing gender and family roles, and globalization—it saw the Amish as residual holdovers from nineteenth-century America. To modern Americans, the Amish seemed outmoded and doomed.

In the 1950s, Gertrude Enders Huntington, a young PhD student in anthropology

at Yale University, decided to study an Ohio Amish community for her dissertation research. Sixty years later she recalled that at the time "the Amish . . . were considered
stupid and were universally disliked. They were backward and they impeded progress
for everyone." Her professors "were enthusiastic" about her studying the Amish, she
says, but only because they were certain the Amish were about to disappear. They urged
Huntington to interview them "before they died out." In fact, one of her professors "was
convinced that such a rigid religious orientation was certain to create serious mental illness, which certainly would contribute to the death of their culture."[1]

The Yale professors were wrong. By the dawn of the twenty-first century, the Amish
were thriving in America. In 1900 they had numbered only 6,000, but by 2012 their ranks
had swelled to nearly 275,000, and they had spread into thirty states and the province
of Ontario. Indeed, the population of this distinctive ethnic group, which is still largely
unplugged from the electrical grid, is doubling every twenty years.

The Amish story is compelling because it raises intriguing questions about modern
life, the meaning of progress, and the roots of social well-being. How can an Amish busi-
nessperson with an eighth-grade education develop and manage an innovative manufacturing firm that trades its goods internationally? How do Amish parents raise children
to be productive in modern America while reinforcing the cultural framework that separates them from their mainstream peers?

Our conceptual orientation employs cultural analysis to unpack the web of meanings
that guide social interaction within Amish life—meanings that have shaped its evolving
diversity and identity. We are interested in how humans construct meaning in their social
worlds to explain their behavior and how they draw distinctions and create symbolic
boundaries.

The scholarly literature on the Amish has contributed much to our understanding of
specific topics and particular geographical communities. What is missing—which this
volume provides—is a study of national scope that explores the diverse Amish identities
that have emerged since the late nineteenth century. Our work focuses on the geographic
expansion of the Amish and their growing diversity, changing identities, and new patterns of interaction with the larger society.

In this book we report the research that we have conducted over the past twenty-five
years in a multitude of Amish communities in a dozen states—drinking coffee around
kitchen tables, kneeling with families for evening prayers, listening to stories during the
communal meal after church services, observing youth singings and weddings, and inter-
viewing people in cow barns and carpentry shops and even as we drove them to appointments with their chiropractors.

Our work has used the research methodologies of history, religious studies, sociology, and anthropology, including ethnographic description, participant observation, and
face-to-face interviews. Survey results, archival documents, and an abundance of printed

primary and secondary sources have provided rich data for analysis and interpretation. Because we focus on the Amish experience at the national level, we were not able to delve deeply into any particular geographical community or subgroup of Amish. Nevertheless, we offer detailed evidence from many settlements to illustrate and support our arguments.

Amish people have not stood on the sidelines, watching passively as the rest of the world sped by. Since the late nineteenth century, they have made many choices, taking the initiative to sort out their response to modernization. Although they privilege tradition, they are not antichange or antimodern. Amish religion does emphasize separation from the world, but that is quite different from an ideology that seeks to protest or overturn all things modern. They are not Luddites. Instead, the Amish consider new technologies and adopt only those elements that will sustain their church-communities without erasing the boundaries that separate them from mainstream society.

The central question we pursue throughout this book is this: How has the Amish struggle with modernity modified their religious worldview, cultural patterns, social organization, and interaction with the outside world? As they have wrestled with the forces of progress, Amish communities have, in different ways, been willing to concede some traditions and modify others. While they have staunchly resisted acculturation in such areas as higher education, Social Security participation, and mainline Protestant religious practice, they have yielded in various ways to new technologies, workforce demands, and changes in health care. We investigate how this dynamic struggle has transformed Amish identity and internal diversity. In addition, we trace the Amish journey in the American imagination—from backcountry enclaves to popular culture—and ask what the Amish saga tells us about the American character and the political context that has enabled them to flourish.

Cultural minorities use a variety of strategies to protect their ways of life, and the Amish are no exception. Their stance has been proactive engagement rather than passive acquiescence. In this book we argue that as the Amish grappled with the forces of modernity they employed a three-pronged strategy: *resistance, acceptance,* and *negotiation.* Seeking a balance between social isolation and wholesale accommodation, they have struck cultural compromises that blend aspects of tradition and modernity, trading concessions back and forth in a process of social bargaining.

Some scholars of Amish society have focused on particular topics—conflicts with government, occupational change, businesses, media relations, religion and spirituality.[2] Others have dealt with Amish communities in specific regions or states.[3] Our research stands on the shoulders of John A. Hostetler's *Amish Society,* first published by the Johns Hopkins University Press in 1963 (with later editions in 1968, 1980, and 1993). His groundbreaking work was the first comprehensive scholarly treatment of Amish life, but even its most recent edition (1993) was limited in geographic scope and reflected Amish society as it was in the 1960s and 70s. We extend Hostetler's efforts by tracking the geographical dispersion, numerical growth, cultural diversity, and myriad occupational and technological changes that have transformed Amish life in recent decades.

In short, *The Amish* is the first scholarly synthesis and interpretation of this unique ethnoreligious minority in the twenty-first century. However, this book is not just about the Amish but about America more broadly, because any examination of Amish society illuminates mainstream culture in new and often surprising ways. Clearly, an investigation of Amish life invites us to critically reflect on our own values and practices as well.

One of the challenges we faced as we sifted through stacks of field notes and historical sources was how to narrow our focus, for at every turn we had enough material to expand each chapter into a book of its own. We thus had to select the issues most salient to our argument and give scant if any attention to topics such as diet, singing, dress practices, gardening, and buggy styles.

We have organized our account of Amish society into twenty-two chapters in five sections. After tracing their European origins and immigration to North America (chapters 1–3), we describe the religious foundations that undergird their culture (chapter 4) and then the distinctive rituals that embody Amish faith (chapter 5). We explore key dimensions of Amish values and symbols in chapters 6 and 7. In the following seven chapters (8–14) we describe various aspects of Amish social organization, beginning with the maze of some forty affiliations and then turning to gender, *Rumspringa,* community, and education.

The seven chapters in part IV, which deal with external ties, highlight Amish interactions with the larger society in the areas of agriculture, business, technology, medicine, and the state. We conclude this section by probing the Amish presence in print, tourism, film, and online media. In the final chapter, we explore some of the changes afoot in Amish society, reflect on the outcomes of their struggle with modernity, and ponder their future.

Finally, we want to add a note about words. One of the difficulties we faced in writing this book was finding accurate, yet clear terms to describe the complexity of Amish life. The Amish world has no central bureaucratic structure; its two thousand congregations and forty different affiliations operate somewhat independently and exhibit a wide diversity of cultural practices. A former Catholic who joined the Amish noted that the diversity of Amish groups is similar to his "Roman Catholic heritage and the several hundred types of nuns, brothers, priests, monks. They all have the same faith and doctrines but a great number of differences in their constitutions and garb and practices."[4] When we write about all the horse-and-buggy-driving Amish groups collectively, we use broad phrases such as *Amish world, Amish society, Amish life,* and so on. To denote a particular kind of Amish, we employ the words *affiliation, group,* and sometimes *tribe.*[5] In addition, some affiliations have *subgroups.*

The phrase *Old Order* can be confusing because it has two meanings. It first emerged as a historical label in the 1860s and 1870s in the aftermath of a national schism that produced two Amish branches: the Old Order Amish, who sought to maintain older traditions, and the more progressive Amish Mennonites, who eventually lost their Amish identity as we explain in chapter 3. In the course of the twentieth century, additional divisions within the historic Old Order branch led to new groups, so that by the twenty-first century, the Amish world included diverse affiliations with names such as Andy Weaver, Renno, mainline Old Order, Swartzentruber, and New Order, to mention just a few. Thus, we use *Old Order* at times in its historical sense and at other times to name a particular group within the larger Amish world.

When describing the various Amish groups arrayed between the cultural poles of separation and assimilation, we are loath to use the labels *traditional* and *progressive* for several reasons. These terms present a false dichotomy: even the most modern societies have traditions; and the most traditional ones, far from being static, incorporate some new social elements. Moreover, in American culture the word *progress* is laden with positive assumptions—forward, better, good—despite the fact that some of the repercussions of progress are detrimental if not downright destructive. Nevertheless, some Amish groups are quite open to outside influence, while others cling tenaciously to longstanding traditions. So with some reluctance we use *progressive* and *traditional, liberal* and *conservative, change-minded* and *tradition-minded* to describe an affiliation's degree of separation from the outside world. We also speak of *high* and *low*—two terms used by the Amish themselves—to refer to a group's location on the ladder of assimilation into mainstream society.

The Amish, who speak a German dialect, refer to outsiders who speak English as simply "the English." We use the terms *non-Amish, outsiders,* and *English* interchangeably to refer to people outside Amish society.

Although the story we tell accents Amish diversity, for stylistic reasons and literary ease we sometimes use the phrase *the Amish.* Many Amish voices speak throughout the text. Most of those we interviewed preferred to speak anonymously, and we have honored their requests. However, we have typically identified those who have used their own names in their published writings. All anecdotes, including those that open chapters, come from our fieldwork, and none are composites.

Our goal is to tell the Amish story with the resources of solid scholarship in a style that appeals not only to scholars but also to a broader audience interested in the Amish experience.

§ *Visit www2.etown.edu/amishstudies/ for more information, photos, resources, and updated demographic statistics on Amish society as well as for educational supplements for* The Amish.

ACKNOWLEDGMENTS

Community is a prominent theme in Amish life, so it is appropriate that this book was a collective project, from the research and writing through the editing and production. Consequently, the roster of people and organizations to whom we are grateful is long.

First, we recognize the substantial support of a collaborative research grant from the National Endowment for the Humanities that underwrote much of the research for this book, the development of an Amish Studies website (www2.etown.edu/amishstudies/), and a conference, The Amish in America: New Identities and Diversities, organized by the Young Center in 2007. We acknowledge, however, that the views, findings, and conclusions stated on the website and in this book do not necessarily represent those of the National Endowment for the Humanities. We thank our advisory committee, a group that offered suggestions, criticism, and support for the project during the grant period. The committee consisted of the following colleagues: Herman Bontrager, Jill E. Korbin, Mark L. Louden, Thomas J. Meyers, Stephen E. Scott, Diane Zimmerman Umble, G. C. Waldrep, and David Weaver-Zercher.

Jeff Bach, director of the Young Center at Elizabethtown College, provided space, practical support, and, most importantly, encouragement as we wrote the manuscript. We owe enormous gratitude to our Young Center colleague Cynthia Nolt, whose probing questions helped us to clarify our arguments and whose tireless efforts, keen eyes, and meticulous copyediting skills honed our rough prose at every turn through multiple revisions. Developmental editor Valerie Weaver-Zercher offered helpful suggestions for improving the organization and flow of the text. We also thank her for pointing us to Lipovetsky's work on hypermodernity. A team of capable assistants—Ambre Biehl, Sarah Biedka, Kayla Roush, Lauren Stoltzfus, Elaina Truax, and Julia Ward—aided us in gathering and tabulating data, editing, and fact-checking. The graphics were expertly prepared by Linda Eberly and the maps by Carol Cady.

Stephen E. Scott, research associate at the Young Center, was instrumental in gathering information on Amish affiliations, migrations, and new settlements. His remarkable mastery of the details of Amish life and his friendships in many Amish communities were indispensable for our research. Our gratitude to him is mixed with profound sadness over his sudden death in December 2011.

We thank David Luthy for access to the resources of the Heritage Historical Library and for his counsel and help over the years, which contributed in many ways to this book. We benefited from stimulating conversations with Carl Desportes Bowman at the beginning of the project and especially thank him for alerting us to Bauman's work on liquid modernity. We give special thanks to John Cross and Martha King for their contribution to the chapters on agriculture and health, respectively, and to James Cates and Richard Stevick for helpful critiques of the chapter on *Rumspringa*.

The accuracy of our text was improved greatly by the feedback and critical suggestions of those who generously contributed time to reading a draft of the manuscript. We thank the anonymous peer reviewer selected by our publisher and sixteen Amish readers and other colleagues, including Herman Bontrager, Edsel Burdge, Eli Burkholder, James Cates, Eli Ebersol, Henry Erb, Larry Gretzka, Cephas Kauffman, Linda King, Jill E. Korbin, Orie Lehman, Wilma Lehman, Mark L. Louden, Thomas J. Meyers, Floyd Miller, Levi P. Miller, Lynn Miller, Ben Riehl, Gracia Schlabach, Judith Stavisky, Victor Swartz, David Weaver-Zercher, Marvin Wengerd, Wayne Wengerd, and Erik Wesner.

Most essential to our cultural description were the scores of Amish people who spent time visiting with us, answering questions, and explaining various aspects of their way of life. For their patience and time, we thank them.

It is hard to image a better editor to work with than Greg Nicholl and his superb team at the Johns Hopkins University Press. Their extraordinary enthusiasm, support, and advice at every turn of the publication process were invaluable.

We thank our spouses, Fran, Bruce, and Rachel, for their enduring patience, support, and interest in what was at times an all-consuming project for us.

ABOUT THE MAPS

The ESRI data and maps DVD data used to construct the U.S. state and county boundaries for figures 1.1 and 3.1 were provided by TeleAtlas North America, Inc., Lebanon, NH; and for Canadian geopolitical boundaries by Government of Canada, Natural Resources Canada, Earth Sciences Sector, Geomatics Canada, Surveyor General Branch, Ottawa, Ontario, Canada (Geobase www.geobase.ca/geobase/en/data/index.html and GeoGratis www.geogratis.gc.ca/geogratis/en/index.html).

European data for figure 2.1 was obtained from GADM database of Global Administrative Areas ver. 2.0 www.gadm.org/; and VMap1 from mapAbility.com (www.mapability.com/index1.html?http&&&www.mapability.com/info/vmap0_intro.html).

The maps were prepared by St. Lawrence University Libraries GIS Program using materials from the U.S. National Imagery and Mapping Agency and are reproduced with permission. The constructed maps have neither been endorsed nor authorized by the U.S. National Imagery and Mapping Agency or the U.S. Department of Defense. Map projections are North America Albers Equal Area Conic NAD83 and Geospatial Coordinates WGS84. Amish content information provided by the Young Center of Elizabethtown College.

I

ROOTS

CHAPTER 1

WHO ARE THE AMISH?

Levi and Annie Fisher had a restless night. Earlier on that September day in 1953, a constable had come to their dairy farm and arrested Levi for refusing to send their fourteen-year-old son to ninth grade. Levi and Annie believed that eight grades of school were enough to lead a faithful and productive Amish life. Now Levi was struggling with what to say at his upcoming hearing. Should he pay his fine and send his son to high school, or should he heed his conscience? On September 22, Levi pleaded not guilty and was sentenced to five days in prison, leaving the farm chores in the hands of his family. By January 12, 1954, Levi had been arrested and imprisoned four times. But he was not alone. Authorities near Lancaster, Pennsylvania, had arrested some one hundred Amish people that fall. The national crusade for educational progress in the mid-twentieth century had hit a bump on the back roads of rural America.

A Thriving People

North America is home to hundreds of ethnic and religious groups, each with particular practices that may seem strange to outsiders. Yet even in such diversity, the Amish stand out. In fact, it is difficult to imagine a group more at odds with the plot of America's narrative. As many Americans celebrate their love affair with the automobile, Amish people continue driving horse-drawn buggies.[1] As electronic media have accelerated the pace of communication, Amish churches have resisted telephones and remain unconnected to the Internet. The best Madison Avenue marketing has not enticed Amish families to buy televisions, change their hairstyles, or adopt the household conveniences—from vacuum cleaners to dishwashers—that Americans of all stripes consider necessities. Amish children end their schooling at eighth grade, unmoved by the promises of higher education. Meanwhile, the Amish have refused to fight in America's wars, held at bay the country's social welfare programs, and shown little interest in feminism or other widespread social movements. In a society that celebrates the individual and supports freedom of choice, they insist on submission to God, communal tradition, and the church.

Yet despite the yawning gap between Amish culture and mainstream society, the Amish are thriving. They are doubling in number every eighteen to twenty years and defying the predictions of twentieth-century observers that they would dwindle. From a mere 6,000 in 1900, their population has now grown to some 275,000 across thirty states and the province of Ontario.[2] While more than half live in Pennsylvania, Ohio, and Indiana, growing numbers call Wisconsin, New York, Michigan, Missouri, and Kentucky home.

Although these horse-and-buggy-driving people comprise less than one-tenth of 1 percent of the 315 million Americans, they are widely recognized for their distinctive culture. Fleeting references to "the Amish" appear in cartoons, late-night talk shows, print media, and even in promotions for new fashion. Television programs in the United States and abroad feature vignettes of Amish life. Thousands of online ads hawk the merits of "Amish made" products, and the tourist industry invites visitors to "Amish Country" to explore their curiosity about these unusual Americans. From Amish romance novels to food and furniture, the Amish brand sells. Although the Amish themselves do little to invite such attention other than quietly living in a way the rest of the world finds peculiar, public curiosity about them is flourishing.

So who are the Amish? How are they coping, and why are they thriving in the twenty-first century? And why do people find them so fascinating? Before exploring these questions, we offer a brief overview of Amish society and then turn to the ongoing discourse between the Amish and modernity.

Overview

A Protestant Christian group that reaches back to sixteenth-century Europe, the Amish church emerged in 1693 under the leadership of its namesake, Jakob Ammann (b. 1644).[3] Amish families immigrated to North America between the 1730s and 1850s, and their last European congregation dissolved in 1937. Since that time, Amish people have lived only in the United States and Canada.[4]

The Amish embrace orthodox Christian beliefs, seek to practice the teachings of Jesus in daily life, and baptize only those who voluntarily confess their faith in him and commit to follow the regulations of their church. The children of Amish

writer year (name of the Book) where
it was published

NON FICTION
789.73 krq
the Amish

parents are not members of the church unless they choose to join—typically in their late teens or early twenties. Some 85 percent of Amish youth on average opt for baptism and thereby make a lifelong commitment to the church. Because few outsiders convert to the group, the Amish resemble an ethnoreligious community more than a denomination.

Amish church and community life is anchored in a *church district*—what other Christians might call a congregation or a parish. The district has physical boundaries and consists of twenty to forty Amish families who live among English-speaking neighbors, whom the Amish refer to as "the English." Members of the congregation are bound by frequent—often daily—interaction and regular church attendance. They meet every other Sunday morning for three hours of worship in members' homes or barns, rotating their meetings from one household to another throughout the year.[5] The church district is the locus of ecclesiastical authority and the primary unit of social organization, ensuring that Amish life remains grounded in small-scale, face-to-face interactions.

Church districts that share a common history in a given geographical area constitute a *settlement.* Some settlements, such as the one in Ohio's Holmes County, have more than two hundred districts. Most settlements are much smaller, however, with only a dozen or so districts—or in some cases just one. Often the smaller settlements are newer ones founded by a few families moving to a new location. Robust growth and ongoing migration have produced more than 460 settlements that together claim more than two thousand church districts, as shown in figure 1.1.

To Be or Not to Be Modern

The Amish saga threads through the larger narrative of modernization in America, a story shaped by the development of machine power, technological invention, industrialization, communication, and a rational market economy. The process of modernization transforms societies on two levels: *structure* and *consciousness.* The changes wrought by modernization both revamp the organizational patterns of societies and penetrate human consciousness, altering social values and ways of thinking.[6]

More important for understanding the Amish story than the process of modernization is its consequence: modernity. The salient markers of the modern era are *specialization* of work and social activities, *separation* of time and space, an expanding *diversity* of lifestyles, a *rational* and calculating outlook, an accent on *individualism,* the rise of large *abstract* organizations, and an ever-expanding range of *choices.* In fact, some analysts contend that this last marker—choice—is the most pronounced trait of modernity. From lifestyles to food, from religious practices to hobbies, the indelible imprint of choice is stamped on the fabric of modern life.[7]

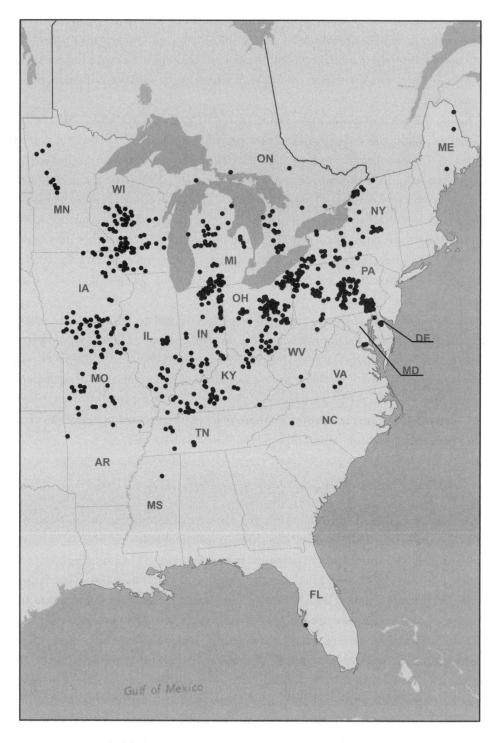

FIGURE 1.1. Amish Communities in North America. Communities are also found in
Colorado, Kansas, Oklahoma, Montana, Nebraska, South Dakota, Texas, and Wyoming.
Map prepared by St. Lawrence University Libraries GIS Program

Although Amish people live in rural areas of North America, many no longer earn their livelihood by farming. *Doyle Yoder*

As we listened to the stories recounted by Amish people, one thing loomed large: their encounter with modernity has been a continuous and complicated struggle. Sorting out how to survive in a modernizing world without losing their religious commitments has not been easy. They have wrestled with how to respond to technological inventions (the car, electricity, television), religious innovations (Sunday school, mission activism, seminary education), and a pervasive scientific outlook that has transformed education, health care, and many other aspects of contemporary life.

Amish people did not tuck themselves away on the back shelf of a country store as the twentieth-century forces of urbanization, industrialization, government, and technology transformed American society in myriad ways. They actively decided what to embrace and what to reject, discerning just how far they could wade into mainstream American life without compromising their religious values.[8] For example, in the 1960s when some state health boards required dairy farms to cool milk in refrigerated bulk tanks, Amish farmers in Lancaster, Pennsylvania, did not retreat from dairying. Instead, they installed the tanks and, in lieu of electricity, used diesel-powered refrigeration units. At the same time, however, the farmers reiterated their traditional stand against selling milk on Sunday—a day the Amish consider divinely ordained for rest—and did not allow commercial dairies to haul their milk on that day.

Amish convictions have perplexed many other Americans, especially government officials, who have struggled with what to do with a people who refuse to go to high school and who insist on traveling by horse and buggy on highways built for cars. What should officials do, for instance, with a people who are a magnet for lucrative tourism yet whose horses' hooves chip away the surface of public roads?

Modernity has indeed shaped Amish society. Yet as the legal system has grappled with how to respond to the convictions of this resilient minority, the Amish have left their distinctive mark on American cultural life as well.[9]

Bargaining with Modernity

Folks who read by lantern light, travel by horse and carriage, and entertain themselves without televisions or iPods are surely stuck in tradition. Or are they? Walk into a booming Amish manufacturing shop and you may see sophisticated equipment powered by air and hydraulic pressure. Visit an Amish dairy farm and you may see an efficient operation using the latest feed supplements, fertilizers, and veterinary practices. Enter a new Amish home and you may find up-to-date bathroom facilities and a spacious kitchen with beautiful wood cabinets and the latest gas appliances. Certainly, the most conservative Amish do not use such items, but stereotypes aside, many Amish people are quite modern in some ways, even as they reject certain trappings of contemporary life.

Their unusual blend of progress and tradition poses interesting questions about how the Amish have coped with the pressures of modern life. Why have they accepted advances in some segments of their lives while staunchly resisting them in others? Throughout the twentieth century, Amish people tenaciously sought to preserve their traditions despite the persistent press of modernity. Although they have obviously benefited from modernization, they remain skeptical of its long-term impact, particularly in the realm of technology. They fear that modernity is a divisive force that might, in time, tear their families and communities asunder. That worry is not an idle one, for some social analysts argue that the pervasive specialization of modern life unglues social bonds and pulls apart the interconnected components of traditional societies.[10]

Cultural minorities use a variety of strategies to protect their ways of life. In order to thrive in America, the Amish have employed a three-pronged strategy in their struggle with modernity: *resistance, acceptance,* and *negotiation.*

To fortify their way of life, the Amish have constructed certain cultural fences of resistance—plain dress, horse-drawn transportation, religious rituals, and a distinctive dialect. They have rejected high school education, public-grid electricity, the Internet, and television. Some forms of resistance—especially the challenge to educational reform in the mid-twentieth century and, more recently, to certain building codes—have been costly, and the Amish have occasionally paid the price of imprisonment.

Had they simply rejected all things modern, however, they would surely have become a fossilized subculture. Instead, they have also reached across their cultural fences and accepted certain advantages of modern life such as detergents, insecticides, high-precision milling machines, in-line skates, and, in some communities, cell phones. By adopting some innovations from the outside world, they have enhanced their lifestyle and increased the productivity of their farms and shops. The Amish have also accepted the imposition of state and federal taxes (income, sales, and real estate) as well as government guidelines regulating food production and safety standards in their businesses.

Some of the choices they faced in modern America required little discussion because the options seemed so obvious. In the eyes of Amish elders, television clearly offered more harm than good. Other choices, fraught with ambiguity, were more difficult because their long-term impact on community life was uncertain. Trying to sort out such murky issues, the Amish have also negotiated with modernity, rejecting some aspects of a particular practice while accepting others. They selectively participate in modern life on their own terms: riding in cars but not owning them, tapping electricity from batteries but not from the public grid, working in retail sales and light manufacturing but not in the professions. This process of bargaining with modernity has enabled them to maintain their ethnic identity and, at the same time, flourish economically.

Seeking a balance between strict isolation and wholesale accommodation, the Amish strike many cultural compromises that blend aspects of tradition and modernity. Concessions are traded back and forth in a process of social bargaining. When the negotiations involve cultural phenomena—values or ways of thinking—we call the process *cultural bargaining*. When patterns of social organization are on the negotiating table, the exchange involves *structural bargaining*—adapting and changing organizational forms and practices.[11]

The negotiating metaphor captures the dynamic process of give-and-take both *within* Amish communities—as factions struggle to agree on acceptable practices—and *between* Amish society and the larger world. It also explains accommodations that may appear inconsistent to outsiders, such as installing propane refrigerators instead of electric ones or using tractors for stationary power at the barn but not for pulling equipment in the fields. These and other adaptations have been hammered out at the metaphorical bargaining table over decades, resulting in diverse ways of being Amish, ways that appear strange to the non-Amish world. Sometimes

Higher Amish groups permit their members to ride in (but not own or operate) motor vehicles for business purposes or long distance travel. This practice illustrates one way such groups have negotiated with modernity. The most traditional Amish groups permit their members to ride in privately owned vehicles only when travel by public transportation (bus or train) or horse and buggy is not feasible. *Daniel Rodriguez*

the Amish have acquiesced to the demands of modernity. At other times the agents of modern life have bent the rules or made special concessions, such as the legal exemption from Social Security granted to the Amish in the United States.

This way of seeing their struggle with modernity distinguishes negotiable issues from nonnegotiable ones and identifies the fault lines of resistance. Our threefold model of resistance, acceptance, and negotiation also underscores the dynamic interaction between Amish society and the larger world, the growing diversity within the Amish world as various subgroups forge different bargains with modern life, and the fact that the outcomes of the deliberations are always uncertain.

The Meltdown of Solid Modernity

Our three-part model is complicated because the process of modernization seems unceasing and modernity itself is a slippery concept. The new products and lifestyles of yesterday are the antiquated ones of today. As sociologist Zygmunt Bauman notes in *Liquid Modernity,* "Modernity means many things, and its arrival and progress can be traced using many and different markers."[12] Moreover, modernity evolves and transforms itself into ever-changing forms. Indeed, two key aspects of present-day modernity are *liquidity* and *speed.*

Bauman argues that modernity has morphed from *solid* to *liquid* forms. The solid forms of late nineteenth- and early twentieth-century modernity, rooted in social norms and structures, limited human freedom and expression. Stable traditions affix people to a particular place or nation-state, often by invoking God's will to bless social hierarchies, including human-made rules about race, gender, caste, and class. Solid modernity provides social stability through slow-to-change bureaucratic institutions and rigid factories such as those created by Henry Ford, where employees each played a specialized role and functioned as components of an assembly line whose only purpose was efficient production.

During the last quarter of the twentieth century, however, the solid forms of modernity began melting into more liquid ones. Transitions from still photos to video, from landline to mobile phones, from a factory-based economy to Internet commerce, from manufacturing to service industries, and from physical books to e-books all signal the meltdown of solid modernity. The World Wide Web, with its vast virtual universe, illustrates the weightless, mobile, ephemeral, ever-changing liquidity of twenty-first-century modernity.

French philosopher Gilles Lipovetsky, in *Hypermodern Times,* makes a convincing case that speed, intensity, and excess typify our supermodern lives. Our hyper-hyper-everything culture that wants more and more, faster and faster, can lead to superficiality, spectacle, and insecurity. Fast food, faster microprocessors, instant downloads, immediate tweets, express mail, extreme sports, hypertext, hyperindividualism, and rushed everything—all produce data overload, excessive choice, and anxiety because we are always short on time and can never keep up.[13]

The speed and fluidity of contemporary modernity complicate Amish negotiations. For example, the solid modernity typified by the landline telephones the Amish resisted in 1910 is unlike the forces of liquid modernity that produced smartphones. Much of the Amish saga is rooted in their resistance to the solid forms of modernity in the first half of the twentieth century: telephones, cars, tractors, and consolidated public schools. How will they fare in a hypermodern world, in which change is instantaneous and temptation lurks not only in the city or in the movie theater but also on handheld devices in backcountry fields? Will the Amish need to shift their coping strategies in order to survive in this swirling sea of fluid modernity?

The ongoing dialogue with modernity has created many struggles *within* Amish society, and on a few occasions unresolved differences spawned new Amish groups.

The factions most determined to resist modernity have found security in their traditional ways, whereas those open to change have been more willing to bargain with the wider world.

Searching for the "Real" Amish

A young Amish child learns that she is different from the outside world. She also discovers that her church district, whose members drive black carriages, has different rules than the church district two miles up the road, whose members drive yellow-topped buggies.

Asked how her church differs from another Amish group in the same area, an Amish storekeeper responds, "Oh, there's hardly any difference between us." Down the road, however, a member of that other group answers the same question this way: "I don't know where to begin. I don't even know how those other [Amish] people can call themselves Amish."

A non-Amish bookstore owner in Easton, Maryland, speaks with annoyance about a new Amish farmers' market that recently opened on the edge of town: "They say they're Amish, but they're not because they use cell phones and ride in vans and have electric lights in their market."

So will the "real" Amish please stand up? In truth, all of these people are genuine Amish. Real Amish are those in Williams County, Ohio, who live in austere houses and flee from all appearances of ostentation; they are also those who reside in sizable, attractive brick homes in Rush County, Indiana. Real Amish women are those bent over quilting frames, and they are those pushing Walmart shopping carts. Authentic Amish men are those wearing two suspenders or one suspender or none, and they are farmers, welding-shop owners, and factory employees building recreational vehicles.

In the early twenty-first century, there are some forty different Amish *affiliations*—clusters of church districts linked by social and spiritual bonds. The congregations in an affiliation usually share the same history or distinctive practices—or some combination of both. Some affiliations have names, such as Swartzentruber Amish, New Order Amish, or Byler Amish, but others are known only by the name of the town or area where their members live. The largest groups have more than a hundred districts, while others have only a few. Tribes such as the Lancaster Amish and the Swiss Amish have congregations in several states, as we describe in chapter 8. In addition, some districts, although not linked to an affiliation, still maintain bonds of fellowship with a few other districts.

Affiliations fall along a continuum of low-to-high traditionalism, as shown in figure 1.2. Amish people refer to the most traditional clusters as "low," meaning that they are near the bottom rung of the ladder of assimilation into modern society and

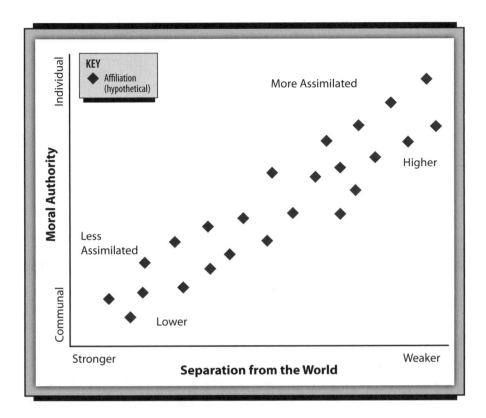

FIGURE 1.2. Amish Affiliations by Moral Authority and Separation from the World

that they resist changes that would pull them up the ladder. In contrast, the more progressive affiliations are dubbed "high" because they are inching up the social ladder and getting ever closer to the outside world. The lowest groups still use outhouses, milk their cows by hand, and hang kerosene lanterns on their buggies at night. The higher ones have LED lights installed on their carriages, use automatic milkers, carry cell phones, and pay third parties to advertise their business wares on the Internet.

Considering the magnitude of difference in Amish life, it is hazardous to speak of "the Amish" as if they were one unified group. Although all Amish people share many religious and cultural values, they express them in diverse ways. Nonetheless, they have some common practices, as shown in table 1.1.

In many settlements, shop owners, mechanics, carpenters, and factory workers are fast replacing the Amish farmer, once the quintessential Amish worker. Differences also mark the world of women's work. Homemaking remains the occupation of many Amish women, but increasing numbers own and manage small businesses.[14] In some groups, construction crews travel to suburban areas for work, but certain traditional affiliations forbid working in suburban locales. Adults in some of the higher affilia-

Table 1.1. Ten Practices Amish Groups Have in Common

Rural residence
German-based dialect
Eighth-grade education
Church services in homes
Small local congregations
Lay ministers
Church-regulated dress
Selective use of technology
Horse-and-buggy transportation
Nonparticipation in the military

tions occasionally join tour groups that travel by bus to scenic sites, something that members of lower churches would never do.

Other differences are harder to see but no less significant. A majority of Amish parents view private schooling as a key ally in passing on their religious values to the next generation, and they defend their schools as on par with public education. But parents in some lower affiliations marginalize formal schooling, contending that the child's real education takes place outside the schoolroom.[15] And in a few areas, some Amish children attend public schools, although only through the eighth grade.[16]

Changes in the larger society also elicit different responses from Amish people. Although some families in Ontario participate in provincial health insurance plans, most do not. Across the continent, Amish appraisals of biomedical and psychological therapies vary widely. Members of some more traditional groups turn to age-old remedies such as wearing copper rings to ward off arthritis and consulting homeopathic healers for health problems. At the same time, members of many liberal tribes see family physicians and undergo state-of-the-art medical procedures.

Despite the differences, all Amish people live in rural areas and use horse-drawn carriages for local travel.[17] They speak a German-based dialect but also learn to speak and write in English. Their worship services are led by lay clergy without theological training. All Amish congregations subscribe to the beliefs codified in the 1632 Dordrecht Confession of Faith and sing a cappella hymns written in the sixteenth century. All wear distinctive clothing, although the patterns and styles vary by affiliation.

Apart from songbooks and benches, Amish church districts own no property, have no church buildings, and lack any traces of the bureaucracy that marks modern institutional life and mainstream religion.[18] There are no national or regional Amish offices, synods, conferences, or even written constitutions that confer ecclesiastical authority or streamline uniformity. The Amish have no theological seminaries, social service agencies, official periodicals, or youth camps. As we explain in chapter 10, the diverse Amish groups are linked together by informal bonds of family, ethnicity, and fellowship.

Our operational definition of *Amish* includes any group that (1) affirms the basic tenets of Amish belief outlined in the 1632 Dordrecht Confession of Faith, including adult baptism, separation from the world, and nonviolence; (2) uses horse-drawn transportation; (3) speaks a German-derived dialect; and (4) considers itself Amish. Most Amish view other "Plain people," such as traditional, plain-dressing Mennonites and Brethren, to be theological kin because their churches share some historical ties, beliefs (such as adult baptism and nonviolence), and a conviction that the church should stand apart from popular culture. For an overview of the non-Amish plain-dressing groups, see Appendix A.

Amish Stories, American Stories

Cultural identity is not a fixed or inherited set of characteristics. The symbols, patterns of behavior, mental habits, and folkways that shape identity are constructed through conversations both with in-group members and with outsiders. Those conversations mark boundaries, but they are porous and dynamic ones. In short, cultural identity is socially constructed through interaction, and its meanings are fluid and ever changing.[19]

As humans we construct narratives—stories that make sense of our experiences, interpret our lives, and offer us an identity. "We tell and retell narratives that themselves come fundamentally to constitute and direct our lives," says sociologist Christian Smith. In telling these stories, we "understand what reality is, who we are, and how we ought to live by locating ourselves within the larger narratives . . . that we hear and tell." Our cultural narratives create identity by reminding us who we are, where we came from, what we are doing, and why.[20]

Some narratives are well-rehearsed and crisply conveyed through television advertisements or campaign speeches—or, among the Amish, through ancient hymns or Sunday morning sermons. More often, though, these narratives, Amish and non-Amish alike, are folded into less articulate and even nonverbal messages, symbols, church regulations, and ordinary practices of daily living. Formal or informal, articulate or not, narratives communicate meanings—through the settings, the parties involved, and the interactions—that shape and reshape cultural identity.

Amish identity emerges as children hear adults offering accounts of why things are the way they are. They learn where Amish people fit in the world, why they do what they do, and how they are different from English people, even from other Amish people. Telling these stories in the flow of daily living animates their lives and provides a distinctive Amish lens for seeing and interpreting the world. Amish identity is not merely the sum of buggies, bonnets, and beards. Rather, identity arises from a process of creating and making meaning, somewhat akin to storytelling.

Amish children grow up immersed in symbols that define their lives in sharp contrast to the outside world. They do not wear the popular clothing styles displayed in store windows. As they travel to town, sleek cars speed past their slow-paced horse-drawn buggy. Even when their destination is the local Burger King, and they place their order in English, they converse with one other in a dialect unknown to other patrons.

All of these patterns of separation and distinction raise an interesting question: Are the Amish Americans? They certainly think so. When we asked an Amish leader that question, he retorted with a tone of irritation, "Of course we are; we live here!" Indeed, the ancestors of most Amish people arrived in America over two centuries ago. Even the most conservative Amish claim the U.S. Constitution's First Amendment in their struggle against laws that they feel infringe on their religious convictions.

Yet the question probes something deeper than the simple affirmative answer. It digs into other layers of inquiry such as these: Have the Amish absorbed core American values? Do they dream the American dream? Do they desire the same things as "the rest of us"? In some ways they seem like outsiders or strangers, even the exotic "other" as people in faraway cultures are sometimes labeled. Have they truly *become* Americans, or do they just live here?

The Amish story bears some similarities to the narratives that shape most other Americans, but it explains reality in ways that are at odds with mainstream American sensibilities. Consider these two quite different cultural narratives: one that reflects how Amish people might tell their story, and one that might be told by many middle-class Americans.[21]

An Amish Story

A long time ago in Europe, our forebears were persecuted because they refused to baptize babies or worship idols in the Catholic Church. Back then the government and the church were mixed up together, and the government tried to tell the church what to do. A lot of our ancestors were burned at the stake or had their heads cut off because they wanted to follow Jesus and live as the Bible says. They thought the Bible was a higher authority than any human government. Like Jesus, our martyrs didn't fight back when they were persecuted. Eventually they came to America to find religious freedom and good farmland.

Our ancestors faced the same basic problems we still do today—pride, disobedience, greed—and if we listen to what they said, we can save ourselves a lot of heartache. They established many good traditions that have helped to preserve our church. We try to stay away from worldly things and not get mixed up with government. But we do pray for elected officials and pay taxes because Jesus said we should.

Over the years our church has made many rules that help guide how we should live. I don't always understand the reasons behind some of the rules, but I know that they hold a lot of wisdom because a person can't always make good decisions on his own. It's better to rely on each other than just on yourself.

I'm amazed by how much the world has changed. The world seems to go so fast these days, and people almost worship sex and money. From what I read in the newspapers, a lot of Americans are lonely, and families are falling apart. We think that having big families and a close-knit church, living in the country, and not using too much technology are the best ways to be content on this earthly journey.

The church helps protect us from the dangers of the world, but we have our problems too. The most important things in life are to obey God, the church, and our parents and to help each other whenever we can so that we can be a light to the world. We are just strangers and pilgrims here because we're just passing through on our way to a heavenly home.

An American Story

Our way of life has always been about freedom. In 1776 Americans decided they didn't want a king telling them what to do or taxing them without their consent, so they started a revolution. The founders of our country believed in liberty, and even though some owned slaves, they created a society that's still a beacon of liberty for the whole world. Unlike other places in the world, people here got rid of superstitions and realized that individuals had a right to think for themselves and should not be controlled by folklore or old traditions that didn't mean anything to them.

Sometime in the twentieth century, women won the right to vote and racial segregation ended, giving everybody equal opportunity and the choice to be whatever they want to be. Anyone can become president. Women can do anything men can do. I can choose my own lifestyle, and I don't have to marry or have children if I don't want to. When I visit a historical museum, I'm amazed at how hard life was for people in the past and I'm grateful that I didn't live back then.

The keys to getting ahead in life are hard work and education. America has the greatest universities in the world. We've put a man on the moon and mapped all our genes. Science and technology have made amazing strides in my lifetime, giving me more choices and control over my life, and I expect those advances will continue. Doctors can treat just about any illness or condition, and I am confident that medical discoveries will keep increasing our life spans.

I can go anywhere I want and move wherever a job or education takes me without having to ask anyone's permission. Anyone can reach me on my cell phone, day or night, no matter where I am. I can listen to my own music without being bothered by anyone else's tastes. I rely on computers and the Internet so much it's hard to remember how I lived before I had them 24/7 in the palm of my hand. From file sharing to social networking, technology is bringing the whole world closer together. I can only imagine all the new things the next generation will be able to do to make things better!

Of course, these stories are oversimplified in order to illustrate the distinct topographies of Amish and American identity and show the deep gulf between the basic contours of these two worldviews. This particular American story may not reflect the experiences of some ethnic minorities or recent immigrants, yet it has been the dominant metanarrative shaping American politics, higher education, and the American self-understanding. And although it is not everyone's story, it is a coercive narrative that the Amish have heard time and again as they faced off with federal officials, school boards, and municipal authorities. In many ways the Amish narrative challenges the optimistic American embrace of progress, raising the question: Exactly what kind of Americans are these Amish?

It is true that they do not fly the American flag, fight in the military, or celebrate the unveiling of new media gadgets. Nor do they hold public office, serve on juries, or assume the civic responsibilities often associated with citizenship.

They do, however, play softball, read local newspapers, pay taxes, and occasionally vote. When it comes to industriousness, stable families, and a yearning for lean government, they exemplify some deeply rooted traditions in American culture. Amish people are like other Americans in other ways as well. Amish parents want the best for their children and worry about whether their children will make good choices. Some Amish teenagers think their parents are too strict, and sometimes they rebel. Amish people seek meaningful work and fulfillment in friendships and community activities. Their deep desires often reflect those of most Americans. However, they have pursued those aspirations in different ways.

Having sojourned here for almost three centuries, often on the fringe of society, the Amish have been shaped by the American experience. They have not emigrated or searched for other homelands because, despite their fears of modernity, North America has offered them ample space to practice their religion.[22] Their practices have sometimes tested the boundaries of religious liberty, but the legal outcomes have helped to preserve the free exercise of religion for their fellow Americans as well.

Young Amish women stand on the beach near Rehoboth, Delaware. Like other Americans, Amish people enjoy the beauty of nature. *Gary Casadei*

The Pursuit of Happiness, Amish Style

The Amish story is compelling because it raises profound and intriguing questions about modern life, the meaning of progress, and the roots of social well-being. How can one-room Amish schools, with only eight grades, devoid of all technology save a battery-operated clock, turn out successful entrepreneurs whose firms gross annual sales of a million dollars? What is the meaning of assimilation and multiculturalism in light of the Amish American experience? How have the nonconforming, peculiar-looking Amish come to feel at home in American society, whether shopping at big-box stores or negotiating legal exemptions from Congress?

In this book, we assess how the Amish have fared in their struggle with modernity. As they wrestled with the forces of progress, what were they willing to concede or negotiate? Even more important, on which issues did they dig in and resist? We explore how the outcomes of their struggle reshaped their identity and added to their internal diversity. In addition, we chronicle the transformation of the Amish in the American imagination—from backward bumpkins to media icons—and ask what the Amish story tells us about the American character and the cultural ethos that offered them such a congenial habitat.

The Amish have employed a strategy—a set of goals and calculated means—as they have grappled with modernity. Theirs has been a stance not only of resistance but also of proactive engagement. Throughout their history they have made choices that have shaped how they live, work, and raise their families. They were not passive when, in 1967, in the midst of concerns over the Vietnam War–era military draft, an informal network of lay leaders formed the National Amish Steering Committee to represent Amish interests to the government. They took action when school consolidation threatened to disrupt their children's education in rural public schools by building one-room schools that now thrive in the Amish world. And the Amish were anything but passive in 2003 when Ohio Amish farmers and business leaders formed Green Field Farms, a corporation that markets Amish-grown organic products in several states.

Lacking knowledge of such Amish initiatives, it is easy for outsiders to imagine them as a static people who live just like their ancestors did 250 years ago. That myth assumes that the Amish have been bystanders—a quiet folk society disengaged from the transformations of modern America. On the contrary, as they were shaped by and contributed to those transformations, they made many choices along the way. As we narrate the Amish story, we pay special attention to their choices—to be or not to be modern, to assimilate or to withdraw—for those decisions and their consequences have shaped the character of the Amish in America.

That their choices have fashioned their destiny as a people raises a fascinating paradox. If choice and its concomitant responsibilities are prized in American culture—if indeed the essence of being American is to have choices—then the Amish can truly claim an American identity. If choice is the ubiquitous mark of modernity, then the Amish, like their neighbors, have been branded with this mark. In fact, their fundamental notion of what it means to be a church community is based on the idea of voluntary adult membership, a concept that reaches back to their religious roots in the sixteenth century. What could be more modern than the notion of choice in religious affiliation?

Yet Amish choices, ironically, restrict the range of individual choice. They have chosen, in other words, to limit choice. Members are not free to dress as they please, buy a car, or pursue higher education. And while individuals can make many choices, the community's collective choices do shrink the scope of individual liberty.

The Declaration of Independence proclaims an American creed in these words: "We hold these truths to be self-evident, that all men are created equal, that they are endowed by their Creator with certain unalienable Rights, that among these are Life, Liberty and the pursuit of Happiness." Do the Amish find happiness in their countercultural way of life? Is it possible to have a meaningful and satisfying life without the latest technology, college degrees, luxury vacations, and an embrace of scientific progress? Might it be that Amish people have outwitted modernity and are as happy as the rest of us in mainstream society?

We will explore these and other questions from both the Amish and American side of the cultural dialogue that has shaped—and continues to shape—Amish life and appraisals of that life. Before doing so, however, we turn to the birth of the Amish church in Europe.

CHAPTER 2

EUROPEAN ORIGINS

No sooner had Dirk Willems escaped from prison than a guard and a sheriff took off in hot pursuit of him. It was 1569 in the Dutch village of Asperen, and Willems had been jailed for joining a radical religious group, the spiritual forebears of the Amish. Now, as he fled those who would torture and perhaps execute him, he made his way safely across a frozen pond. The guard was not so fortunate. He broke through the ice, and as he sank into the frigid water, he called for help. Willems could have considered this an act of divine judgment on his captors and continued his escape. Instead, he stopped, turned around, and went back to rescue his pursuer, believing it was his Christian duty to return good for evil. Unimpressed by Willems' choice, the sheriff had him rearrested. Shortly thereafter, Willems was burned at the stake as a heretic.

A Particular Past

More than 400 years after Dirk Willems' astonishing rescue of his enemy, the Amish continue to tell his story. They recount this tale of the man who saved the life of his enemy in their sermons and school curriculum. It is a story of suffering and martyrdom but also a dramatic reminder of tough ethical choices, religious commitments, and actions that run counter to mainstream expectations. And it is a reminder that Amish society is rooted in a particular past that continues to inform its contemporary identity.

Reminders of heritage abound in Amish life. When church members gather for biweekly church services, they sing from the *Ausbund: das ist, Etliche schöne Christ-*

liche Lieder (True Collection of Some Beautiful Christian Songs), a hymnbook filled with sixteenth- and seventeenth-century lyrics. They listen to sermons peppered with references to ancestral martyrs. Even those Amish who are most reluctant to interact with outsiders or who grumble about intrusive tourism express eagerness to chat with a visitor from Switzerland or Germany, revealing their sense of connection to places "over in the Old Country." Amish interest in the past is also evident in the abundance of genealogy books and memoirs they write, with titles such as *Echoes of the Past* and *Hidden Treasures Handed Down from Our Ancestors Since 1600.*[1] Amish people have a strong sense that history is a reliable guide, and in turn, their history offers clues for understanding their interaction with broader American culture.

Amish roots reach back to the sixteenth-century's Protestant Reformation and, more specifically, to the Radical Reformation that emerged in those tumultuous times. During the first half of the 1500s, many things that Europeans had long taken for granted were in flux. Spanish conquistadors spread stories of a vast "New World" populated by exotic people, plants, and animals, which called into question the European understanding of the world. Meanwhile, huge quantities of Mexican silver captured by these same conquistadors destabilized European economies, sparked inflation, and pushed many peasants to the edge of survival. Compounding a sense of unease, the printing press sped ideas—and rumors—across the continent with stunning speed.

As if such developments were not enough to rattle social stability, vocal religious critics began challenging the Catholic Church, the institution that had long claimed to hold society together on earth and assure one's journey to heaven. Leading reformers such as Martin Luther, Ulrich Zwingli, and John Calvin questioned church doctrine and structure and eventually split with Rome, establishing the Lutheran and Reformed churches. The stage for a more radical reform movement was set.

Radical Anabaptists

The ferment of the 1500s produced other religious dissenters as well, dissenters whose critique of Christendom was deeper than that of the mainstream Protestants. These radicals, who gathered in small groups in German-speaking lands and in the Netherlands, challenged the entire premise of the medieval state-church relationship by arguing that the true church was composed of only those who separated themselves from the corrupt world and obediently followed the teachings of Jesus. This way would not be popular, they warned. Indeed, Jesus had said that his followers would be a "little flock" scorned by "the world."

The radicals rejected the prevailing practice of routinely baptizing all infants, a practice that linked Christianity with citizenship. Instead, they began to baptize one another as a sign of their adult commitment to "take up the cross" of Jesus and live a disciplined life accountable to one another rather than to the state church. As a result, they earned the nickname "Anabaptists" (rebaptizers) and found themselves condemned by both Catholics and mainline Protestants as religious, social, and political revolutionaries.[2]

Almost all Anabaptists were orthodox Christians who affirmed the authority of the Bible and embraced traditional understandings of the Trinity, sin, and God's grace as the basis of salvation. But Anabaptist views of the nature of the church and Christian life set them apart from many other Christians of their day. Anabaptists believed that the true church was an alternative community, distinct from surrounding society and not responsible for enforcing civic morality or acting as a moral prop for the state. Anabaptists expected government to maintain a minimal level of social order, but they also believed that such a worldly task was not a responsibility of the righteous. Instead, church members were to be obedient to Jesus, renouncing violence (even in self-defense) and refusing to swear oaths.

These commitments put Anabaptists at odds with civic and religious leaders, who censured the radicals as subversives who would upend social order and theological truth. Authorities used edicts, legal harassment, imprisonment, and even execution in a vain attempt to stop the spread of the Anabaptist movement. These actions only confirmed the Anabaptists' sense that the world was brutal and immoral and that they were justified in rejecting it.

Between 1527 and 1614, authorities killed as many as twenty-five hundred Anabaptists. Their martyrdom remains a focal point of Amish consciousness. The hymns that form the core of the *Ausbund* were written by Anabaptists jailed in Passau, Bavaria, as they awaited execution. One such hymn intones:

> *When the distressed cry out*
> *To their God on high,*
> *He sustains them*
> *In all their needs.*
> *He does deliver all those*
> *Who are of a broken heart,*
> *Having a contrite spirit...*
> *[Yet] the righteous must suffer much*
> *In this strife with affliction...*
> *[But] God always helps them.*[3]

Other hymns memorialize sixteenth-century martyrs such as Hans Haslibacher, who was beheaded in 1571.

Hundreds of Anabaptists were tortured and put to death for their religious beliefs in the 1500s. Maria van Beckum was burned at the stake in the Netherlands in 1544 because she had been baptized into the Anabaptist faith. She and her sister-in-law Ursula (*at left*) prayed to God to forgive their tormentors. Ursula watched Maria be burned and then stood on the woodpile for her own execution. *Martyrs Mirror Trust: Kauffman Museum, Bethel College/Mennonite Historical Library, Goshen College*

Many Amish households own a thick book about these martyrs entitled *Martyrs Mirror.* More than a thousand pages in length, *Martyrs Mirror* begins with the crucifixion of Jesus, recounts the suffering of the early church under Roman persecution, and culminates in hundreds of pages of Anabaptist martyr stories—including the story of Dirk Willems, who saved his pursuer's life. This hefty book, available in both German and English versions, continues to find a ready Amish market in the twenty-first century.[4] Even though many families do not regularly read aloud from the book because of its somewhat archaic language, its martyr stories are frequently retold and applied in sermons. "We hear about the martyrs almost every time we have church," one middle-aged woman affirmed.

The prominence of the martyrs in Amish memory and the emphasis the Amish give to their self-surrender and reliance on God is significant. At the same time, the martyr stories also cast the state in the role of antagonist and suggest that the world cannot be fully trusted. While other spiritual descendants of the Anabaptists have valorized the Anabaptists' willingness to speak truth to political power or highlighted their penchant for evangelism, the Amish have emphasized martyrdom and obedience to God's will even in the face of stiff opposition.

Martyrdom shaped the Anabaptist movement in specific ways. Persecution contributed to the fact that Anabaptism never had a singular spokesperson or overall leader. Although by 1545, twenty years after its inception, the movement received the nickname "Mennist" or "Mennonite," thanks to the influential writing of Menno Simons, an Anabaptist preacher, Menno never held the same status among Anabaptists as, for example, Luther did among Lutherans. The harassment also flushed Anabaptists out of the urban areas where the movement started and scattered them into rural hideaways. By the mid-1600s, Swiss and German Anabaptists were concentrated in Alpine valleys around the Swiss city of Bern, north through the Rhine Valley, and eastward into parts of Austria and Moravia. Meanwhile, Dutch Mennonites had spawned a string of communities across northern Europe and into Prussia-Poland.

Despite a lack of state authority to enforce religious orthodoxy, as in Lutheran lands, or any central doctrinal authority akin to the Catholic pope, the Anabaptist radicals generally recognized one another as members of the same faith. For example, by the mid-1600s, Dutch Mennonites, who thrived in the relatively tolerant environment of the Netherlands, were occasionally using their political influence to ask the Dutch government to pressure Protestant officials in Switzerland to ease persecution of Swiss Anabaptists. Although such intervention relieved some pressure, waves of legal harassment continued in Switzerland, periodically pushing groups of Swiss Anabaptists to leave for more lenient lands to the north, particularly the Rhine Valley regions of Alsace and the Palatinate where, after the end of the Thirty Years War in 1648, nobles were looking for loyal tenants to restore their war-ravaged estates.[5]

The Anabaptists who left Switzerland for quiet farms to the north may have escaped harassment from Swiss state authorities, but their migration soon produced intense quarreling within their ranks. Seeking solace, they floundered into division.

Jakob Ammann: Infected with Anabaptism

The Swiss and south German Anabaptist worlds of the late 1600s provided the seedbed that germinated the Amish movement.[6] In Switzerland, Anabaptists continued to face round after round of edicts aimed at stamping out their churches. Although Swiss authorities had ended executions in 1614, they repeatedly ordered local officials to hound, imprison, or exile Anabaptists. In a few cases, captured Anabaptists were sold as galley slaves on Adriatic ships, condemned to work themselves to death. Individual mandates saddled Swiss Anabaptists with heavy fines, took away their children's right to inherit property, and banned them from burial in community cemeteries. In an effort to flush out hidden pacifists, one mandate even required Bernese men to appear in public wearing a sidearm, such as a sword.

The Anabaptist world in Switzerland did, however, contain paradoxes. First, despite their outlaw status, Anabaptists, known for their honesty and morality, earned the respect and quiet admiration of their state-church neighbors. An investigation in 1692 even turned up sentiments suggesting that some Reformed Church members regarded Anabaptists as model Christians. Said one woman, "No, indeed, I am not worthy to be [an Anabaptist] … because [they] are a completely holy people."[7] Sympathetic members of the state church, known as the "true-hearted," protected Anabaptists in various ways by providing warnings or hiding places when authorities sent dragnets through rural regions.

Indeed, these friendly neighbors, also known as "half-Anabaptists," irritated the state-church clergy, who preached against the "Anabaptist heresy." In 1693 a Swiss Reformed pastor named Georg Thormann published a thick book denouncing the Anabaptists because so many of his own parishioners thought of them "as saints, as the salt of the earth, as the true and chosen people and the proper core of all Christians." Some of his congregants were even attending Anabaptist worship services on the sly or neglecting Reformed services.[8]

A related paradox was that despite the ongoing persecution Swiss Anabaptism was undergoing something of a religious revival and attracting new converts who, unlike the true-hearted, actually joined the Anabaptists through baptism. Such conversions lay behind Pastor Thormann's frustration because they had been increasing for some time. For example, in June 1680 a Bernese court with jurisdiction over religious matters noted that a resident of the village of Erlenbach had become "infected with the Anabaptist sect." That convert was a tailor named Jakob Ammann.[9]

A son of Michael and Anna (Rupp) Ammann, Jakob Ammann was born in February 1644 near Erlenbach.[10] He married Verena Stüdler and, as an adult, probably lived in the area of Steffisburg. Little information survives about his wife and children, although he had at least one daughter. Ammann likely joined the Anabaptists in 1679, and at some point was ordained a preacher and, later, an elder (bishop) with the authority to baptize and ordain.

It is likely that Ammann's parents also became Anabaptists in the late 1600s, and it is clear that his younger brother, Uli Ammann, converted. Around 1693 Jakob Ammann and his family left Switzerland and moved north, settling in the Alsatian lowlands (present-day France) near the town of Heidolsheim. By 1695 he had moved again, this time up into the Alsatian highlands, near the village of Sainte-Marie-aux-

Mines (also known as Markirch) in the Lièpvre valley. (See fig. 2.1 for the two areas of Amish origin.)

Ammann's move from Switzerland to Alsace was not unusual. During the second half of the seventeenth century, a growing number of Swiss Anabaptists fled harassment by moving north into the Palatinate or Alsace to the estates of nobles happy to trade religious toleration for an obedient and dependent labor force. Tolerant French noblemen who governed the Lièpvre valley and other Alsatian regions welcomed the refugees. In time, Mennonites in Alsace and the Palatinate gained a reputation as skilled and innovative farm managers who invested in livestock and experimented with cattle breeding and land fertilization.[11] The immigrants were not permitted to engage in profitable guild crafts, enter universities, or seek converts, but the freedom they did enjoy was remarkable compared with their situation in Switzerland. By the early 1690s, some fifty-two Anabaptist refugee families were managing estates and mills and comprising up to half the population in some villages.[12]

This Anabaptist diaspora faced new challenges. Back in Switzerland, persecution had provided them with both a sharp sense of alienation from the world and grateful reliance on true-hearted neighbors, whose friendship blurred the lines between the Anabaptist church and the evil world. But in the more tolerant air of Alsace and across the Rhine River in the Palatinate, those old patterns no longer made sense. The new atmosphere of forbearance meant that Anabaptists there did not need to rely on sympathetic state-church allies. It also meant, however, that the Anabaptists themselves would have to be vigilant if they were to remain separate from the world. This difference lay at the heart of Amish origins.

Confrontation and Schism

Soon after arriving in Alsace, Ammann and other Swiss refugees, many from Ammann's home near Steffisburg, became troubled by the conditions they found in the Alsatian Anabaptist congregations. The new arrivals thought that their Alsatian comrades seemed too comfortable with the relative tolerance of the ruling noblemen. Ammann and his supporters soon began calling for a sharper distinction between their church and the state church, which they regarded as corrupt. Anabaptists should not attend state church services, Ammann argued, nor should they think that true-hearted sympathizers were assured of salvation.[13]

At the same time, Ammann advocated certain reforms of church life. He proposed observing the Christian ritual of communion (also known as the Eucharist or Lord's Supper) twice a year instead of annually, the Anabaptist custom at the time. Furthermore, Ammann taught that this special service, which recalls the death of Christ, should include a ritual in which church members washed one another's feet in imi-

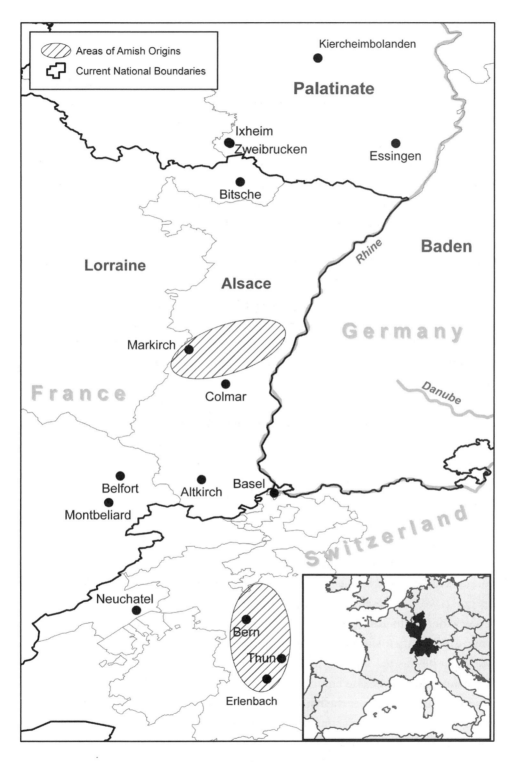

FIGURE 2.1. Areas of Amish Origin in Europe ca. 1700.
Map prepared by St. Lawrence University Libraries GIS Program

tation of Jesus, who had washed his disciples' feet at the Last Supper as a sign of service and humility.

Finally—and most controversially—Ammann insisted that both church membership and church discipline should have clear social implications. If members were expelled because of unrepented sin, other church members should avoid, or shun, the excommunicated members in symbolic ways such as not eating with them. This shunning, known as *Meidung,* was not to be a punishment but rather a lesson, a means of helping the erring members realize the seriousness of their offense against God and the church and encouraging confession and repentance.

Ammann was an articulate spokesperson for a significant Anabaptist lay movement that included preachers such as Ulrich Müller, whose sermons had been attracting converts to Anabaptism in the Bernese Oberland area since the early 1670s. This renewal movement challenged some of the older Swiss Anabaptist traditions by proposing innovations that Jacob Ammann was able to voice in a forceful manner.[14]

Although many Anabaptists in Alsace saw Ammann as a reformer, many others back in the old Swiss communities regarded his reforms as abrupt departures from long-standing custom. In reply, Ammann pointed to the Dordrecht Confession, a sixty-year-old Dutch Anabaptist statement that taught both shunning and the footwashing ritual. These were not innovations, Ammann retorted, but practices that stood on clear biblical and Dutch Mennonite precedent.[15] Ammann and his followers may also have been influenced by Pietism—a renewal movement in German Lutheran and Reformed churches. During the late 1600s, this reformist thinking was spreading through many Protestant communities. Apart from the Anabaptists, Radical Pietists active in the Rhine Valley were also advocating the practice of shunning and even had held up the Dordrecht Confession as a doctrinal blueprint for their members.[16]

In late summer and fall of 1693, Ammann and several supporters traveled from Alsace to Switzerland to impress upon church leaders there the merits of Ammann's reforms. They also chided the Swiss for being too cozy with "the world." The encounters did not go well. Letters documenting the debates suggest that Ammann and his group were aggressive and demanding. The Swiss Anabaptists, particularly their senior elder, Hans Reist, did not help matters when they first delayed meeting with Ammann and then simply dismissed his concerns. At one point, when Reist sent word that he was too busy with his farm work to meet with the Alsatian delegation, Ammann "almost became enraged and immediately placed Hans Reist, along with six other ministers, under the ban as a heretic," leaving others at the gathering "horrified" and pleading for reconciliation. The split only deepened in the weeks that followed.[17]

Efforts to mediate the conflict failed, and by February 1694 a clear breach in fellowship pointed to the emergence of a distinctly "Ammann-ish" group.[18] The two most contested issues remained the spiritual status of sympathetic neighbors (the true-hearted) and the practice of shunning. The Swiss Anabaptists, suffering state harassment, often depended for their very survival on sympathetic neighbors. They were not about to condemn the true-hearted or look for new ways, such as shunning, to call public attention to themselves in the face of persecution.

For his part, Ammann pressed for church renewal from a setting outside of Switzerland in which cultural accommodation and lax discipline seemed to threaten faithful Christian living. Certainly he was not alone in his concern for strict moral reform and rigorous church regulations. Nearly all of the Anabaptist ministers in Alsace supported him, as did several ministers from the Palatinate area of Germany along the Rhine River near the Alsace.

Ammann's Party

Ammann's faction eventually became known as the Amish Mennonites, or simply the Amish. Most of Ammann's Swiss and Palatinate supporters began moving to the Alsatian valley of Sainte-Marie-aux-Mines, where they coalesced into a stronger community. Between 1694 and 1696 alone, some sixty households arrived from the Swiss canton of Bern, and by 1699 Amish families owned many of the valley's farms and were heavily involved in the local timber and sawmill business. The influx changed the region's composition and, over time, stirred some local resentment.

Longtime residents recognized the new group as "the Jakob Ammann Party" or "the Jakob Ammann Group" and readily identified Jakob Ammann as "the Patriarch." In 1698 one Alsatian magistrate called him the "leader of the new Anabaptist sect." Indeed, records reveal that Ammann often witnessed legal documents and represented his people to civil authorities. In 1696, for example, he successfully won for his flock exemption from participating in the militia and from performing a civic duty involving the collection of local taxes, sometimes by force. In both cases, the Amish agreed to pay special taxes in exchange for their exemptions.[19]

At other times Ammann engaged in religious arguments—sometimes quite publicly in the village street—with the Catholic priest from Sainte-Marie-aux-Mines's Saint Louis parish. In several encounters the two men exchanged heated words over reports that an Amish woman was being coerced into converting to Catholicism. In 1701 Ammann represented his people to local officials in a case involving orphaned Amish children. Typically, civil authorities appointed guardians for orphans, but Ammann said his church would take responsibility for its children. The village clerk rejected Ammann's claim, but the Amish apparently appealed to the grand bailiff who, remarkably, sided with them and ordered the clerk to permit the Amish to act "according to their customary procedures."[20]

Nicholas Blank, a member of Jakob Ammann's congregation, owned this homestead near Ste. Marie-aux-Mines in the Alsace region of France in the early 1700s. Inside the barn, Blank's initials are carved into the interior beams, which suggest that very little has changed since Ammann's time. *Donald B. Kraybill*

In September 1712 the congenial political environment ended abruptly when French King Louis XIV ordered the expulsion of Anabaptists from crown lands in Alsace, "with no exceptions … [including] even the oldest who have been there for a long time." Although the tolerant local ruler of Sainte-Marie-aux-Mines protested the eviction, the Amish were dispersed within months.[21] Ammann's community, which had prospered in the Lièpvre valley for almost twenty years, now scattered to isolated enclaves nearby and to the Palatinate, Hesse, Baden, and Bavaria.[22] In these places, officials permitted Amish religious dissent, but typically barred the Amish from buying land. As a result, Amish enterprise shifted, and most households took up work as managers or leaseholders of large estates owned by absentee landlords, where their reputation as skilled farmers served them well.

What happened to Jakob Ammann after 1712 remains unknown, as do the place and date of his death. The only later mention of him is in 1730, when his daughter asked to return to the canton of Bern, Switzerland, telling officials there that her father had died outside the canton.[23]

In the twenty-first century, Amish people have mixed feelings about Ammann.

Most Amish know very little about his life and have never read his writings. Some who have read his letters from 1693 are embarrassed by his rancorous tone and combative style. Contemporary Amish people do not take the same uncompromising stance as Ammann did toward those who, in the 1600s, were called true-hearted. Nowadays the Amish are more inclined to say that only God knows the spiritual state of those outside their church, and that it is no one's place to judge. On the other hand, the Amish have retained key teachings from Ammann's day, notably the practice of church discipline tied to shunning and the conviction that separation from the world is a critical measure of Christian faithfulness. So in that sense, the Amish remain spiritual heirs of a reform movement that Jakob Ammann had advanced.

Dressing the Part

Although distinctive dress is a highly visible element of Amish identity today, clothing was not a prominent issue in the 1693 debates. That did not mean that clothing styles were unimportant to Ammann and the early Amish. In the 1600s in Switzerland and in many other parts of western Europe, clothing was highly regulated. Governments issued detailed "sumptuary laws" that outlined what type of clothing was permissible for members of each social class. Rules in the canton of Bern, for example, forbade gold embellishments, silk lace, ornamental ribbons and pearls, and the use of extra fabric to make unnecessarily wide sleeves or trousers. Officials justified such rules, in part, with religious arguments, warning that God would judge the canton for the sin of haughtiness if Swiss men wore billowing sleeves or shoes that were too pointy.[24]

In such a context, early Amish attitudes toward clothing take on new meaning. Ammann was a tailor, so he was intimately familiar with sumptuary laws and would even have had a hand in enforcing them before he converted to Anabaptism. Tailors could be fined if they made clothing that ran afoul of the laws, and they were obligated to tell customers what kinds of garments they were allowed to wear. In short, restrictions on what people could wear—and in Switzerland, religious reasons for doing so—were not uniquely Anabaptist or Amish concerns but widely shared social norms.

Even so, the Amish apparently were recognizable, to some extent, by the way they dressed. In 1702 an Alsatian Catholic priest named Antoine Rice said the Amish were distinguished by the fact that "the men . . . have a long beard and the men and women wear clothing made only of linen cloth, summer and winter." In contrast, the Anabaptists who had not sided with Ammann had "shorter beards" and dressed "about like the Catholics."[25]

Scholar Mary Ann Miller Bates suggests that early Amish adherence to plain dress may have actually won them some public favor. By scrupulously following laws that required peasants to dress as simply as possible, the Amish appeared to be virtuous citizens, sending a message that the state had nothing to fear from them: they were not social revolutionaries but model subjects. In fact, the Swiss Reformed pastor who had published a lengthy attack on the Anabaptists in 1693 had tried to refute the popular notion that because they dressed simply and obeyed clothing regulations more conscientiously than did state-church members the Anabaptists were moral people.[26]

Although clothing did not figure prominently at the outset, some of Ammann's opponents thought he enforced dress rules too strictly. In a letter written in 1693, Ammann defended himself against the charge that he excommunicated people simply because of what they wore. But he did not back away from his basic conviction that those who want "to be conformed to the world with shaved beard . . . and haughty clothing" should be admonished by the church and banned if they do not change their ways.[27]

In time, one difference that emerged between the Amish and Mennonites was that Mennonites adopted pockets and buttons, while the Amish continued to close their coats with hook-and-eye fasteners. A folk saying about the difference even emerged:

> Die mit Hacken und Ösen wird der Herr erlösen,
> Die mit Knöpfen und Taschen wird der Teufel erhaschen.
> *Those with hooks and eyes, the Lord will save,*
> *Those with buttons and pockets, the devil will snatch.*

The rhyme originated with critics of the Amish, who were poking fun at the perceived Amish obsession with minor details.[28] Yet the saying did capture the way specific dress patterns, rather than a general preference for plainness, eventually helped shape Amish identity.[29] Although distinctively Amish styles of clothing evolved much later in North America, the assumptions underlying Amish views of clothing were present already in the 1600s. The Amish accepted the widely held idea that dress could and should be regulated and that such choices had deeply moral implications. Where the Amish differed from others of the era, however, was in their conviction that the church, not the state, should regulate dress.

A Withering Church in Europe

In one crucial way, the early Amish were very similar to their neighbors. By the 1730s, they were welcoming the opportunity to move to British North America. In 1681 William Penn founded the colony of Pennsylvania as an expression of his Quaker peace principles and commitment to toleration, and he sent agents and advertising into the

Rhine Valley to generate interest in immigration. The possibility that families could buy land for themselves and their offspring made moving to North America attractive for many German households. That Pennsylvania had no militia and granted freedom of worship made it especially appealing to Amish, Mennonites, Radical Pietists, and other religious minorities. Some five hundred Amish immigrated to Pennsylvania in the decades before the American Revolution, making them one small slice of a sizable German trans-Atlantic movement.[30] For a timeline showing Amish lineage, see figure 2.2.

Later arrivals could count on help from those already in North America in getting settled and finding their way around. Amish newcomers often carried church letters from ministers in Europe attesting to their standing in the Amish community and commending them to the church in the New World. Typical was immigrant Christian Schwartzentruber (1793–1875), who left the principality of Waldeck, Germany, in 1819, as part of a second, larger wave of some three thousand Amish emigrants who sailed for North America between 1815 and 1860. Schwartzentruber carried with him a written recommendation from Samuel Brennemann and Jacob Brennemann affirming that he "may . . . be taken in and accepted as a Brother in the Lord and in the congregation."[31] Schwartzentruber settled first among Amish in Somerset County, Pennsylvania, but after marriage moved to Ohio and eventually to Iowa.

The Amish church in Europe withered in the late 1800s. In many ways, emigration undercut the group's ability to endure. Membership likely peaked in 1850, when five thousand members lived in Alsace, with a lesser number in Hesse, the Palatinate, and elsewhere. But the departure of many households and crucial young leadership to North America during the 1800s drained the church's vitality. Two of Bavaria's

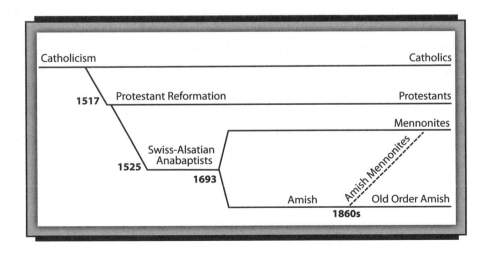

FIGURE 2.2. Anabaptist-Amish Timeline, 1517–1890

three Amish churches, for example, disbanded during that time due to massive emigration to Illinois and Ontario.[32]

The forces of acculturation also levied a toll. The secular principles of the French Revolution had made once-persecuted dissenters into legally recognized citizens, which in turn opened the way for Amish families to join the social mainstream. Genealogical records for the Amish congregations in Hessian Waldeck and Wittgenstein reveal prosperous families who hoped to join more respectable state churches. At the same time, citizenship brought new requirements of universal military service by all males. As those Amish with the strongest peace convictions headed for North America, some of the young men who remained accepted induction into the army. In the 1880s, a Hessian Amish elder, Peter Schlabbach, was even elected to the Prussian legislature. Within a decade, his dwindling congregation had to combine with a neighboring Mennonite church to survive.

During the later 1800s and early 1900s, the few Amish who remained in Europe merged with nearby Mennonite groups, who were undergoing their own process of assimilation. Churches of Amish background in Alsace remained somewhat more traditional, but, especially after World War I, they surrendered practices that might have distinguished them—shunning and the footwashing ritual—and accepted marriages between Amish and non-Amish individuals. In many cases, nationalist influences even led congregations to make peace with military service. In 1937 the last Amish congregation, a small church in the Palatinate village of Ixheim, merged with the Zweibrücken Mennonites, closing the Amish story in Europe. See Appendix B for key dates and events in Amish history.

Some scholars suggest that the demise of the European Amish church was inevitable and that it had more to do with geography than emigration and acculturation. Because the Amish were tenant farmers and leaseholders on scattered estates, they were unable to create close-knit communities like those formed by Amish immigrants in North America. The difficulty of establishing stable communities, these observers argue, explains why the European Amish declined while their American cousins increased.[33] Regardless, the Amish experience in America was hardly free from tension, and the evolution of Amish identity there grew out of a dynamic struggle marked by both social separation and cultural engagement.

CHAPTER 3

The Story in America

The oral tradition of the Amish of Daviess County, Indiana, includes the story that their leaders once preached and prayed in the White House. Sometime in the 1890s, two of the settlement's leaders, Bishop Joe Wittmer (1844–1915) and Minister Peter Wagler (1853–1933), were traveling in the East and had stopped over in Washington, D.C., to change trains. As the two men waited in the grand station hall, an official approached them, asked if they were clergy, and invited them to conduct a chapel service at the White House. The invitation startled the two men, but according to family memory, "after some hesitation they complied with the request. They felt that to do otherwise would be inconsistent with their calling."

Entwined with the American Saga

The story of Joe Wittmer and Peter Wagler praying in the White House is highly unusual in Amish lore, but it underscores the fact that Amish people have never lived in isolation. Whether changing trains in an urban depot in the nineteenth century or supporting volunteer fire companies and marketing furniture to sophisticated urbanites in the twenty-first century, they have always engaged the wider world. The Washington, D.C., encounter also suggests the way mainstream American society has repeatedly approached them—expecting them to act in certain ways or to fulfill popular expectations. All the while, the Amish seek to be true to their "calling" in a world that frequently misunderstands them and shares few of their values.

Like Wittmer and Wagler, who never aimed for the halls of political power, America's Amish have not sought social limelight or national influence. Yet the Amish story has been deeply entwined with the America saga. Despite its European roots, the Amish movement has been a North American phenomenon. The diverse ways of being Amish in the twenty-first century have emerged in an American context in response to American conditions and concerns. Twentieth-century efforts to plant Amish settlements in Honduras and Paraguay proved fruitless, while Amish populations have continued to flourish in the midst of a fast-paced America committed to pluralism and individualism.[1]

Perhaps the most striking aspect of the relationship between the Amish and mainstream Americans has been how the hopes and fears of outsiders have helped to shape Amish identity. Most other Americans—tourists, policy makers, consumers, coworkers, and neighbors—have changed their views of the Amish over the centuries, in concert with the changing mores of mass culture. If American society has been broadly tolerant, its tolerance has had a coercive edge, molding Amish society in subtle but real ways. We view the Amish through the lens of popular opinion at the end of this chapter, but first we explore the early interactions between the Amish and other Americans.

Products of Immigration

Amish interaction with American culture began with immigration, as families arrived in two distinct waves that coincided with major movements of German-speaking Europeans to North America. Between 1736 and 1770, about five hundred Amish arrived through the port of Philadelphia and settled in the southeastern Pennsylvania counties of Berks, Chester, and Lancaster. By 1767 some of these households had moved west into Somerset County, and by 1791 others had purchased farms in Pennsylvania's Kishacoquillas Valley. In the decades that followed, descendants of these eighteenth-century arrivals established a string of communities from eastern Ohio (1809) to southeastern Iowa (1840).[2]

Although Amish immigrants carried distinct religious convictions, they shared many folkways with other Pennsylvania Germans as well as a German dialect that came to be called "Pennsylvania Dutch." The dialect was itself a product of immigration and resettlement as arrivals from various parts of Germany mixed their speechways in North America and produced a dialect that was not precisely the same as anything spoken in Europe. In fact, some scholars consider Pennsylvania Dutch a language rather than a dialect. Throughout the 1800s, Pennsylvania Dutch was the linguistic currency of Lutheran, Reformed Church, and non-religious Pennsylvania Germans alike. By the late twentieth century, however, the most traditional Anabaptist groups were all but alone in holding onto Pennsylvania Dutch, and it became something of a marker, setting its speakers apart.[3]

A second wave of Amish immigrants came to North America roughly between 1815 and 1860.[4] During these years some three thousand Amish left Europe, seeking both economic opportunity and freedom from compulsory military service, which was then becoming more common. Relatively few of these nineteenth-century new-comers settled in Pennsylvania, although some traveled through the state and found temporary shelter among fellow church members there. Louis Jüngerich (1803–1882), who moved from Hesse to Pennsylvania in 1821, wrote to his uncle in Europe that the Amish church in America "works actively" to help those "arriving in this country. Entire families can often find shelter with them. . . . Members of the congregation paid their passage and picked them up from the ports."[5]

With land prices higher in the East, most nineteenth-century Amish quickly headed west. Some arrived in New York City and traveled west from there, but others bypassed the East Coast entirely, taking passage on European cotton ships bound for New Orleans. From there they traveled up the Mississippi River and its tributaries to new homes in Illinois, Indiana, Iowa, Ohio, and Ontario.

In a few cases, Amish from both rounds of immigration settled in the same places and worshiped together. Such was the case in Johnson County, Iowa, and, for a time, in the area that would become known as Nappanee, Indiana. More frequently, however, newer immigrants established communities distinct from those formed by descendants of earlier settlers. Both waves of immigrants recognized one another as Amish, but economic factors and kinship networks largely determined where they settled.

Amishness in an Era of Refinement

Amish immigrants came to North America looking for freedom to practice their faith as well as opportunity to secure land for their children and grandchildren. "We had everything in abundance," an Amish writer mused in 1862, as he considered his people's situation.[6]

Yet the American context posed distinct challenges. Parents and church leaders needed to make sense of life in a restless nation that had little time for tradition and celebrated individual freedom. In the New World, with few established cultural norms, it was not always clear how the church-community would preserve a rigorous moral order. One theme in nineteenth-century Amish history was the interplay between church and family, the two most basic and sometimes competing authorities in Amish society.[7] Parents, more so than the church, were responsible for the training and discipline of children. As Anabaptists, the Amish did not baptize infants or consider them members of the church, even though children routinely attended Sunday worship. Only at baptism did a young adult formally come under church authority.

When church leaders gathered during the early 1800s, they struggled over how to manage churchly responsibility and teenage freedom.[8] An 1837 meeting of ministers in Somerset County, Pennsylvania, for example, criticized parents who dressed unbaptized children in fashionable clothes. Neither were parents to turn a blind eye to teens who "take the liberty to sleep or lie together without any fear or shame." If this happens "with the knowledge of the parents," the ministers announced, "parents shall not go unpunished."[9]

But as Amish elders were discovering, authority in any form—parental or churchly—was a fragile thing in America. Dramatic economic transformations challenged established ways of life, often placing both parents and bishops on the defensive. Coming to America had offered immigrants and their descendants remarkable opportunities to acquire land and take up the trades of their choice. Now the fruits of that enterprise were maturing in a social and political atmosphere that celebrated self-determination and material refinement rather than traditions of simplicity.

The nation's open, risk-taking economy had produced remarkable social mobility, at least among white Americans. Paradoxically, the breakdown of social class distinctions actually made Americans more class conscious, since anyone could aspire to live like an aristocrat so long as he or she convincingly imitated genteel ways. Americans purchased detailed guidebooks based on Renaissance-era manuals for young nobles that promised to teach anyone how to dress, eat, speak, and entertain like a lady or a gentleman. Refined Americans worked long and hard to give the appearance of not having to work at all. Genteel life required genteel surroundings, and even common folk began to outfit their houses with carpets, mirrors, and dishes that they displayed only "for show." Homes became places of retreat rather than centers of production. Work space that once housed the family loom or a craftsman's tools now became a parlor, complete with stuffed furniture purporting a life of leisure.[10]

This revolution of daily life during the first half of the nineteenth century was both far-reaching and profound not only because it changed how thousands of people lived but also because it revised the way they thought about *how* they should live. By 1850, in the wake of this refinement of material and social culture, middle-class respectability was anything but plain. Amish commitments to simple ways, which had not been far from the mainstream in the 1700s, suddenly seemed out of step.

These social transformations were all too obvious to David Beiler (1786–1871), an esteemed bishop in Lancaster, Pennsylvania. Writing in 1862, Beiler was distressed by the "great changes during these [past] sixty years," certain that "whoever has not experienced it . . . can scarcely believe it." Remembering his youth, he wrote that "there was no talk of fine shoes and boots nor did one know anything of light pleasure vehicles." In those days, he noted, wagons were unpainted, and "there were not such splendid houses and barns." Nor did homes feature sofas, writing desks, carpets, and decorative dishes, as had now become fashionable.[11]

Beiler was no petulant elder. His insightful observations track closely with material changes across American society, including ways in which a new consumer culture was displacing household production. "It was customary to hear the spinning wheel hum or sing in almost every farmhouse," Beiler recalled of his childhood, and he mourned that "the large amount of imported goods with which our country is flooded, and also the domestic cotton goods which are to be had at such low price, have almost displaced the home-made materials so that the daughters who now grow up no longer learn to spin." Young men, too, were beginning to work away from home, earning cash to buy fancy harnesses or "strange colored fine store clothes."[12] Although Amish traditionalists such as Beiler had not yet distinguished themselves by rejecting consumer technologies such as the telephone as they would after 1900,[13] they were skeptical of the Industrial Revolution from its earliest days. They recognized the way mechanization displaced family and local communities in favor of distant sources of production and influence.

Amish leaders also found themselves increasingly out of step with the nation's religious tenor. In the same way that the Industrial Revolution championed specialization and efficiency, nineteenth-century Protestant leaders were recasting the relevance of their churches in a society that celebrated growth and change. Religious renewal, America's Protestant elite claimed, required coordinated planning and rational organization. Protestant leaders constructed a host of institutions and enterprises that merged churchly goals with plans to reform and redeem society. Sunday schools, for example, not only taught morality but also produced "better"—more properly refined—citizens. By pouring their energies into special-purpose organizations championing education, publication, and moral uplift, Christians could find their calling in national causes rather than in local concerns or peculiar practices. This agenda was often combined with an emotion-laden revivalism that sought to convert individuals, not to a particular church community, but to a broad moral vision of civic renewal.[14]

David Beiler and other tradition-minded Amish were also concerned about the economic and social transformations reshaping America in the early 1800s. But these changes did not prompt them to join popular Protestant causes of revivalism and reform. Instead, they responded to religious and cultural unsettledness by appealing to the importance of a stable, tradition-guided moral order, which they called the *Ordnung*.

Keeping the Old Order

Ordnung is the German word for "order," but for the nineteenth-century Amish, it had broader implications than the English term may suggest. The Amish notion of

Ordnung was one of *divine* order, of life as it should be lived—tested by tradition, dubious of progress, unaffected by the whims of change. This set of moral guidelines, formulated by the local church and adapted over time, constrained individuality and regulated dress and household furnishings. It stood in contrast to the mainstream emphasis on progress, a competitive economy, individualistic authority, and the religious revivalism of enterprising churches that aimed to redeem America through civic moral crusades.[15]

The role of the Ordnung in guiding Amish church life came sharply into focus after 1862. That year Amish bishops, ministers, and deacons from across the United States and Ontario began a series of annual gatherings to address and resolve disagreements in certain Amish communities. These so-called *Dienerversammlungen* (ministers' meetings) convened each spring from 1862 through 1878 (except in 1877) to consider such issues as the proper way to baptize, how to relate to Mennonites, and how much the church should accept American cultural mores.[16] Was posing for photographs a sign of vanity? Was voting in public elections acceptable for a pacifist group—especially in a nation gripped by civil war? Should the church approve lightning rods, a new technology that might undermine one's trust in God? Could farmers adopt hybrid species such as mules?[17] In short, which offerings on the American cultural menu should the church accept and which should it reject?

As leaders met to discuss, debate, and seek consensus, it became clear that they did not agree on the role of the Ordnung in defining their practices. A majority of those who attended the Dienerversammlungen seemed somewhat open to adapting to the times, and some even welcomed change. Others wished to hold tight to the *alte Ordnung,* the "Old Order," of their forebears.

By 1865 conservative leaders, who had wanted to keep the old practices (Old Order), realized they were being outflanked. That spring, thirty-four tradition-minded ministers caucused in Holmes County, Ohio, a few days before the larger body of ministers met. The traditionalists prepared a manifesto of their commitment to an Old Order way of life and a list of things to purge from Amish communities, including those that "serve to express pomp and pride and lead away from God." The list ranged from "speckled, striped, flowered clothing made according to the style of the world" to "unnecessary, grand household furnishings," and "pompous carriages," as well as commercial insurance and businesses operated "according to the ways of the world." The tradition-respecting leaders concluded that the gate on the pathway to heaven "is portrayed for us as straight, and the way as narrow, but it is not therefore ever closed, but stands open for all repentant souls, and as the Savior says . . . 'Whoever does not forsake all that he has cannot be my disciple.'"[18]

The 1865 ministers' meeting ignored the conservative leaders' overture, and in response the tradition-minded churches withdrew from the national ministers' forum. Change-minded Amish, on the other hand, proceeded down a slow but determined path of greater accommodation to American society. Within two generations, the progress-seeking churches would surrender their distinctive Amish identity and merge with neighboring Mennonites.[19]

Meanwhile, the tradition-minded "Old Order" Amish came to be identified by plainness, simplicity, small-scale farming, and skepticism of the emerging consumer culture. The Old Order Amish also defined *church* in small-scale, local terms, rejecting church buildings, denominational structures, and salaried ministry. These adherents to tradition believed that the Ordnung was the best way to maintain church unity and social balance, and they dismissed modern modes of authority such as science, written constitutions, subjective feelings, and professional expertise. In the 1870s, some of the most obvious markers of acculturation to mainstream religion were revival meetings, Sunday schools, and the use of English in worship services— all of which the Old Orders rejected.[20]

Given the localized authority of the Amish church, the nineteenth-century rift between the change-leaning Amish and the Old Orders was more of a gradual shifting of allegiances than a single schism. One church district's decision to align with the Old Order camp, for example, might prompt a wavering district in another settlement to follow suit—or to bolt for the progressives, depending on the issues and personalities involved. There were Old Order Amish districts in Wayne County, Ohio, as early as 1865, yet the separation of Old Order and progress-minded Amish in eastern Pennsylvania did not occur until 1877. And the sorting out in Ontario continued into the 1890s.

As late as 1912, some lines of fellowship were still fluid, as emerging technological issues were beginning to mark Old Order identity. That year, members of a Johnson County, Iowa, church voted on whether to accept telephones. Back in 1890 the district had constructed a meetinghouse, signaling its openness to pursuing a progressive path. Yet some members still held Old Order sympathies. When the district considered accepting the telephone, all the women voted against it, while the men were divided on the matter. At that point Bishop Jacob F. Swartzentruber (1851–1924), who opposed telephones, declared that the majority had spoken and that phones would be prohibited. That decision produced anything but peace, and a number of change-minded households—in which husbands apparently overruled their wives' convictions—left to form a progressive Amish-Mennonite congregation. Those who remained with Swartzentruber then abandoned their meetinghouse and moved decisively into the Old Order camp.[21]

Old Order Growth and Diversity

During the national ministers' meetings of the 1860s and 1870s, Old Order advocates were in the minority, but that did not mean that the Old Order Amish were in decline. Old Order church districts persisted in many historic Amish communities, and between 1860 and 1920 sixty-two new Old Order settlements emerged in twenty-four states across the country.[22] Many of these new communities, established on marginal farmland with limited access to markets, did not survive the depression of the 1890s or the dust bowl of the 1930s. Others, however, blossomed into thriving Old Order settlements such as those in Arthur, Illinois (begun in 1864), and Geauga County, Ohio (founded in 1886). (See fig. 3.1.)

The growth and spread of the Old Order movement also bred a certain amount of diversity despite—or perhaps because of—the Old Orders' commitment to the Ordnung, which was rooted in local tradition. Unlike the change-minded Amish leaders who had come to dominate the ministers' meetings and who used parliamentary procedure and published minutes to render their rulings, Old Order authority rested on informal oral tradition in each local community. In this way, a commitment to tradition actually worked *against* uniformity because no structures or authorities outside the local area could dictate practice.

For example, the Amish in Somerset County, Pennsylvania, had worshiped in meetinghouses prior to the split between conservatives and progressives, so the Old Order Amish there continued to do so. Meetinghouses were part of the Somerset Ordnung even though Old Orders everywhere else demonstrated fidelity to tradition by *rejecting* church buildings and worshiping in private homes.[23] In each case, the authority of the local Ordnung dictated practice.

Some aspects of a settlement's Ordnung could change, however. For example, in the 1860s, the roofs and sides of Amish buggies in Lancaster, Pennsylvania, were covered with yellow oilcloth, but by the early twentieth century, buggy tops there had uniformly switched to gray as one type of waterproof material had replaced another. Meanwhile, midwestern communities adopted black-covered carriages.[24] Indeed, apart from horse-drawn transportation itself, few aspects of Amish life have ever been permanently fixed, even though individuals are not free to flout local custom.

Although each church district had ecclesial autonomy, leaders often collaborated and deferred to one another in order to restrain change and avoid offending the sensibilities of fellow conservatives. Nonetheless, local choices sometimes proved contentious, and differences emerged within—and not just between—settlements, especially when bishops or ministers disagreed over how to interpret the Ordnung. By the end of the nineteenth century, such differences had occasionally produced new Old Order affiliations, which we explore in chapter 8.

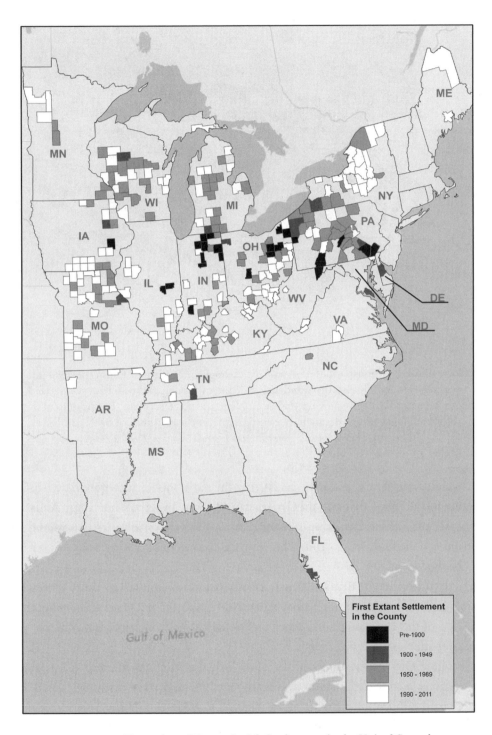

FIGURE 3.1. Expansion of Extant Amish Settlements in the United States by
County and Time Period. Settlements had also been established in Colorado,
Kansas, Oklahoma, Montana, Nebraska, South Dakota, Texas, and Wyoming
by 2011. *Map prepared by St. Lawrence University Libraries GIS Program*

Horse-and-buggy transportation became the distinguishing mark of Amish society in the twentieth century. This northern Indiana–style buggy is equipped with battery-operated lights, turn signals, a slow-moving-vehicle emblem, and a license plate. The buggies of the most traditional groups do not have electric lights, enclosed fronts, or SMV emblems. In Indiana, some county governments license buggies. *Dennis Hughes*

Diversity had its limits, however. During the early 1900s, automobile ownership became the fault line that no Old Orders would cross. In 1927, when some Amish in Somerset and Lancaster Counties bought cars, observers on all sides considered it a step outside the Old Order orbit. The network of churches growing from this schism became known as Beachy Amish, nicknamed for their first bishop, Moses M. Beachy (1874–1946). Although Beachy Amish members have continued to dress somewhat plainly and even retained the Pennsylvania Dutch dialect for a generation or so, their embrace of the car, along with other technological and doctrinal innovations, put them outside the Old Order fence.[25]

Scattered Old Order communities, often linked as much by kinship as by church connections, maintained ties and shared news through two privately issued but widely read publications, Raber's *New American Almanac* and the *Sugarcreek Budget*. Starting in 1930, Deacon John A. Raber (1885–1967), a bookstore owner in Baltic, Ohio, began issuing an annual almanac in German, *Der Neue Amerikanische Calendar* (*The New American Almanac*). Raber's *Almanac* listed Old Order church districts, including all conservative affiliations but not the car-driving Beachy Amish.[26]

Meanwhile, the *Sugarcreek Budget,* which circulated well beyond its Ohio home-town, printed news-filled letters from readers across the country. Readership was never confined to Old Orders, but reading the *Budget* was one way that Old Order readers maintained an Amish consciousness across a scattered faith community. In fact, Old Order letters, printed next to missives from more progressive readers, helped establish and normalize Old Order boundaries. Letters from Old Order "scribes" (as the letter writers became known) reported news of community mem-bers and events, including which households had hosted church services. The letters might even discuss commodity prices—but never the cost of a new car.[27]

Postwar America and the Amish "Mission Movement"

The mid-twentieth century proved to be an especially tumultuous period in Amish history. World War II had dramatically increased Amish exposure to the wider soci-ety and prompted new questions about Amish relations with the world. At the same time, perennial Amish concerns about their mischievous young people took on added urgency in an American society agitated by its own sense of a crisis among its youth.

The Second World War thrust more than seven hundred Amish young men into a whole set of dramatically new experiences. Amish men had long been conscien-tious objectors (COs) to war. But prior to 1940, COs had been fined or jailed—situa-tions that had increased their sense of sectarian aloofness from a hostile state. During World War II, COs—including Amish men—were assigned to alternative labor in civilian service projects ranging from national parks to public psychiatric hospitals.[28] Letters and reports from that time and later reveal how these experiences challenged the church's rising generation. For some, the needs of the world and the possibility of serving others became compelling new opportunities. For others, such experiences energized a commitment to separatism but on new terms. And for many Amish in Pennsylvania, whose generous draft boards had given them farm furloughs in lieu of civilian work assignments, the war years created something of a gulf between their experience and that of their fellow Amish in the Midwest.

The wartime experiences set the stage for a wide-ranging and controversial Amish "mission movement" that swept through many settlements during the late 1940s and 1950s.[29] For a decade or more, a significant number of young Amish men and women quietly but persistently promoted a kind of activism that sought to reform aspects of Amish religious life and encourage Christian service outside the church. Mission movement proponents challenged long-standing practices such as the free-wheeling ways of unbaptized teens and promoted a more introspective devotional life. They also held mission conferences, participated in Mennonite Voluntary Service, distributed evangelical literature to thousands of Amish homes, and funded full-time Amish mission workers in Mississippi, Arkansas, and Ontario. Several dozen attended college to obtain credentials they saw as important for their success in such work. And they did all of these things within the Amish fold despite the growing tension sparked by their actions.

This internal tension was augmented by new external pressures on Amish society. Postwar America was consumed with concerns about child rearing and education, from behavioral psychology to public school reform.[30] States began pressing rural school districts to upgrade and consolidate school facilities and to enforce high school attendance. Meanwhile, Cold War conscription kept a spotlight on Amish young men who claimed conscientious objector status while some of their unbaptized younger brothers ran wild on Saturday nights. Of course, the Amish churches had no authority over those unbaptized teens, but that logic was often lost on English neighbors and state officials. When Amish parents refused to send their children to consolidated public schools or to any school beyond eighth grade—a stubbornness publicized by a series of high-profile confrontations in the 1950s—some outside observers saw parental irresponsibility and a hopelessly backward church out of step with progressive American values.[31]

Crisscrossing pressures complicated the issues as participants on all sides thought the others were jeopardizing the futures of vulnerable youth. Amish parents went to jail rather than send their children to high school, and local officials refused to grant CO status to an Amish man whose younger brother had been arrested for underage drinking.

Such conflicts fed the controversy that soon erupted when the Amish mission movement encouraged youth Bible studies and Sunday schools—stiffening both support and criticism within church circles. Some Amish leaders declared the mission movement's medicine to be worse than the malady. Others saw a greater threat coming from public school superintendents and draft boards in the larger world.

By the early 1960s, many of these tensions had spun themselves out, with profound implications for Amish identity. Almost all mission movement advocates left the Amish fold for Mennonite or Beachy Amish churches. Some of the movement's activities—from founding a nursing home for non-Amish residents in Arkansas to opening schools for aboriginal peoples in Ontario, all of which were more accountable to government than to the church—pressed the limits of Amish patience. Mission movement activists were committed to an assertive, rational, organizational view of the world that was impossible to reconcile with the informal, local, face-to-face character of Amish life. The exit of the activists had profound implications for those who remained in Amish churches. The mission movement's rapid rise and fall sharpened the traditional Amish resolve against evangelistic work and attending college.

Indeed, in the decades that followed, most Amish settlements become more religiously sectarian. Subscribing to magazines from other denominations or attending religious services elsewhere became quite rare.[32]

Sectarian sensibilities were bolstered by the fact that conflicts with public school officials, though not settled everywhere, were moving toward resolution: by the mid-1960s, most states permitted the Amish to open their own schools and end formal education with eighth grade. The rise of Amish schools, the appearance of a decidedly Amish school curriculum, and the publication of Amish devotional materials by the new Amish-affiliated Pathway Publishing Corporation (now Pathway Publishers) further insulated Amish religious life and teaching.[33] By 1970 these changes and Amish reactions to them both diversified and consolidated Amish identity in new ways.

The legacy of these mid-twentieth-century events played out in various ways. In most Amish communities the growing religious and educational separatism emerged alongside a cautious openness to technological change as household economies began tilting away from farming and toward small businesses such as cabinetry or construction. In many places, occupational and technological boundaries were becoming more fluid as religious life and primary schooling became more fixed in tradition.

In other cases, Amish efforts to resolve the tensions of the times produced new groups. Some leaders had privately sympathized with the mission movement's attempts to curb the excesses of rowdy youth. But rather than rallying interest in outward activism, these ministers harnessed the power of the Ordnung itself and incorporated into church discipline things that had previously been considered the prerogative of parents. For example, some districts began enforcing prohibitions on smoking and unsupervised courtship. Between 1953 and 1961, families from various midwestern communities migrated to form new settlements that self-consciously combined such reformist convictions with a conservative commitment to stave off technological change. A different agenda animated the so-called New Order Amish, an affiliation that emerged in the 1960s. Like the mission movement advocates of the previous decade, the nascent New Order affiliation promoted youth Bible study meetings, forbade tobacco, insisted on "clean" living, and described its personal faith with more emotional and individualistic language.

The proliferation of Amish groups, coupled with the continued growth of Amish populations and the multiplication of new settlements, meant that by the late twentieth century the Amish world had become quite complex. Furthermore, the internal complexity had evolved in the midst of shifting popular perceptions of America's Amish.

The Amish in the Public Eye

In 1900 America's Amish population was small—perhaps no more than six thousand—and attracted scant public attention. Observers at the time would have been hard-pressed to imagine the Amish developing a national reputation, let alone becoming national icons.[34] Yet during the course of the twentieth century, this remarkable cultural transformation took place. Without an organized public relations campaign, promotional budget, or celebrity spokesperson, a tiny and publicly self-effacing religious group became widely known. By the 1990s, comedians, cartoonists, and television scriptwriters could include offhand Amish references with the assurance that audiences—even if misinformed about the details of Amish culture—recognized "the Amish."

Of course, that most Americans have come to regard the Amish in certain ways may say more about mainstream society than it does about the Amish themselves. Still, popular understandings have an impact on ordinary Amish life, shaping everything from public policy to tourism. Amish identity in the twentieth century was hewn not only from their own convictions but also from public perceptions. An overview of those perceptions illustrates the changing views of Americans toward these nonconformists in their midst.

Stubborn Traditionalists

Amish people first gained national attention in the 1930s as they became entangled in an effort to resist government involvement in local life. In 1937 Amish parents in one Lancaster County, Pennsylvania, township organized opposition to state consolidation of rural schools and tried to halt the construction of a new building. Since most communities were fighting *for* a share of New Deal dollars, Amish opposition to federal funds was newsworthy, and the Amish cause made the *New York Times*. The image in these stories was of backward and ill-informed people fighting a futile battle against the future. One *New York Times* article characterized Amish life as "drab."[35]

Conflicts heated up as the United States expanded programs that cared for the aged or dictated workplace dress. After 1955 some self-employed Amish farmers stubbornly refused to participate in Social Security. They garnered sympathy from government critics, such as the editors of *Reader's Digest*, and eventually received congressional exemption from the program in 1965. As minority rights and identity politics gained ground during the 1960s and 1970s, the Amish won additional group-based exemptions such as a waiver of Occupational Safety and Health Act mandates requiring the wearing of hard hats on construction sites.[36]

Amish men walk up the steps of the U.S. Supreme Court when the high court considered the *Wisconsin v. Yoder* case in 1972. *Lancaster Newspapers*

In this context, lingering conflicts over compulsory high school attendance found resolution in a U.S. Supreme Court ruling in the 1972 case of *Wisconsin v. Yoder*. Chief Justice Warren Burger wrote in defense of the Amish dissent, legitimating, as one observer put it, "the right not to be modern." This antimodern image was closely tied to the logic of the ruling, since the justices' arguments were based largely on their assumption that, as backward farmers, the Amish had no need for advanced schooling.[37]

By the end of the twentieth century, however, conflicts with the state often conjured popular appraisals of the Amish that were much less sympathetic. Could ultraconservative Amish refuse to immunize their children? Could they persist in using primitive plumbing that undercut public health codes? Local jurisdictions often said no. And when cases of child abuse surfaced, the public was decidedly unsympathetic to the Amish argument that their self-trained counselors and homespun treatment centers were better suited to punish perpetrators and handle victims' needs than were social service professionals, whom the Amish kept at bay.[38]

Technophobes Choosing a Simple Life

Another set of popular images revolved around Amish aversions to the latest forms of technology. As rural electrification, telephone cooperatives, and agricultural mechanization became common in the early twentieth century, the Amish refusal to connect to public utilities and to buy cars began to set them apart from their rural neighbors.[39] After World War II, most Amish refused tractor farming even though agricultural extension agents encouraged them to "get out of the mud" of their bygone traditions. Farming with horses kept their agriculture small-scale, and although many adopted hybrid seeds and chemical fertilizers, their farming remained labor-intensive. More visibly, horse-and-buggy travel marked the Amish as distinctively odd in a nation committed to automobile ownership and constructing a multimillion-dollar interstate highway system.[40] They soon became known as "horse-and-buggy people," studied by sociologists as a folk society frozen in time.

Suddenly, in the 1970s, the image of the Amish as irrelevant relics was flipped upside down. The energy crisis and an emerging environmental movement created an atmosphere in which the Amish were hailed as a people *ahead* of their time. Activists certain that "small is beautiful" applauded the Amish as a people who lived off the grid and did not allow technology to master them. Indeed, some outsiders began to see the Amish as Luddites, opposed to all technology. As such stereotypes gained currency in ensuing decades, observers were shocked or indignant to learn that Amish youth traveled on in-line skates and Amish contractors used cell phones on job sites.[41]

Inadvertently, popular understandings of the Amish as technophobes also created a mystique about Amish products—in effect, an Amish brand—for consumers looking for distinctive goods that bespoke a plain, homespun aesthetic. The appeal of the Amish brand, mostly promoted by English entrepreneurs, fueled Amish small business growth and a boom in Amish-built furniture and other woodcrafts. Ironically, this demand for homemade products often encouraged Amish entrepreneurs to adopt new technologies in an effort to boost production and match consumer appetites.

Objects of Tourist Desire

The consumption of Amish products with their enticing Amish brand was intertwined with Amish-themed tourism. By the mid-1950s, American middle-class tourism was mushrooming. Bus and car tours to Lancaster County, Pennsylvania, promised views of an old-fashioned way of life for northeastern urbanites living in a postwar society undergoing dramatic social change. (See fig. 3.2.)

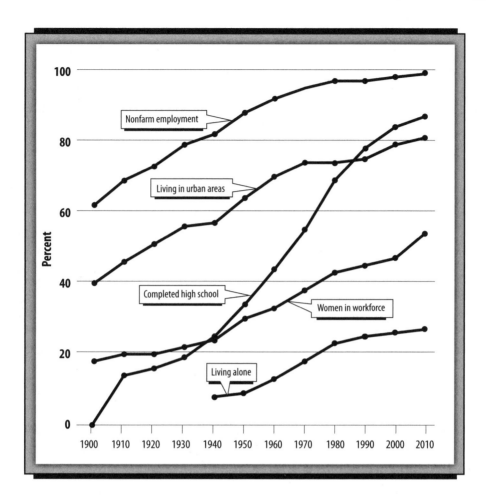

FIGURE 3.2. Twentieth-Century Social Changes in the United States.
Source: U.S. Census Bureau and U.S. Department of Labor

The 1955 Broadway musical *Plain and Fancy,* which mixed Amish family life with a celebration of American self-determination, dramatically boosted tourism. The Amish Farm and House, the first Amish-focused attraction to charge admission, opened east of Lancaster City the same year. Amish tourism in the Midwest picked up in the 1960s with bus tours of Holmes County, Ohio, and the opening of Amish Acres in Nappanee, Indiana, in 1970. Each of these venues mixed images of the Amish as quaint relics with hints that these people might well be the keepers of traditional wisdom in this new atomic age of science and suburbia.[42]

A combination of nostalgia and avant-garde art merged in the 1970s and stirred an interest in Amish quilts. In 1971 the Whitney Museum of American Art in New York City included Amish quilts in an exhibition (and subsequent traveling show), *Abstract Design in American Quilts,* that treated functional handicraft as boldly designed modern art.[43] Collectors began flocking to Amish settlements to buy old quilts, which one scholar dubbed "America's first abstract art."[44] The sudden rush to acquire their quilts birthed a new cottage industry among Amish women and reshaped their quilting tradition as they adapted to demands for contemporary design. "We have to keep up with what colors are fashionable so we can make the changes from one year to the next," said one. Within a few years, Doug Tompkins, founder of the Esprit clothing company, had filled his San Francisco headquarters with Amish quilts and opened the building to Californians eager to glimpse a bit of Amish culture that seemed at once both old-fashioned and cutting edge.[45]

Amish tourism received a further boost in 1985 thanks to the Academy Award–winning feature film *Witness,* starring Harrison Ford.[46] The film's unlikely plot revolved around the clash of cultures that flared when a hardened detective found refuge on an Amish farm. *Witness* presented Amish people as peaceful but naive—sequestered from the world and unfamiliar with modern ways—and helped to spur a steep rise in tourism to Amish communities. In the twenty-five years that followed the film's release, the annual number of visitors to Lancaster County, Pennsylvania, skyrocketed to eleven million.[47]

Media Icons: Rumspringa and Forgiveness

Popular media had been complicit in shaping public perceptions of Amish identity throughout the 1900s, but two events near the turn of the twenty-first century highlighted how Amish Americans had become icons of popular media. In 1998 and again in 2006, high-profile crime stories wove together images of pastoral innocence with hard-edged drama.

In 1998 two Amish-reared young men linked to a Philadelphia-based cocaine distribution ring that was tied to the Pagans motorcycle gang were caught selling drugs to their Amish friends in Lancaster County. This remarkable collage of images made the "Amish drug bust story" a sensation, but it also revealed that some unbaptized Amish teens lived very differently from their parents, a fact that generated intense media interest.[48]

Overnight, *Rumspringa*—the Pennsylvania Dutch term for the years when teenagers "run around" and socialize with their peers before they join the church—found its way into the vocabulary of reporters. Tapping into popular interest in Rumspringa, an independent film entitled *Devil's Playground* tracked drug use among a few Amish teens in northern Indiana. Other media stories focused on alleged child abuse and animal abuse at Amish hands. The theme in this string of exposés was hypocrisy: the Amish had been too good to be true; in fact, they were not very good at all.[49]

In 2006 another crime story propelled public perceptions of the Amish in a different direction. On October 2, a non-Amish man entered an Amish school near Nickel Mines, Pennsylvania, and shot ten girls, five of them fatally, before killing himself. News media swarmed to the crossroads village to cover the horrific shooting in the most idyllic of locations. But within hours, the story of lost innocence shifted to one of bewilderment. Reporters struggled to understand how members of the Amish community almost immediately forgave the shooter and reached out in compassion to members of his family, hugging them at his burial and treating them as fellow victims.

This incident thrust images of the Amish as an unbelievably forgiving people into hundreds of media stories around the world. Many writers saw the Amish as living Christian values that lots of people professed but few practiced. For their part, the Amish were as uncomfortable with this new status as they had been with the drug bust story, though for different reasons. "The news reports have set a high standard for us," one confided. "We don't want to be exalted," another explained. "Now we're under the public eye . . . . We wonder: can we Amish people really be what the public expects of us now?"[50]

These stories demonstrate a fluctuating view of the Amish that, as religion and media scholar David Weaver-Zercher has argued, oscillates between two poles. Americans tend to view the Amish as a "saving remnant"—a simple, pious community living life as it once was and still could be. Yet they also see them as a "fallen people"—the subject of exposés and the butt of jokes that purport to reveal the real and repressed nature of their life. In fact, Weaver-Zercher contends, these seemingly conflicting interpretations almost always go together, reassuring modern observers that they need not feel guilty if they admire, but then quickly dismiss, the Amish way.[51]

By the twenty-first century, Amish identity was, at least in part, tied up with the expectations, fears, and dreams that mainstream Americans projected onto them. In reality, of course, Amish society is much more complex than any of these popular images, even if Amish people cannot entirely escape their influence. It is to the basic building blocks of their community and way of life that we now turn.

II

CULTURAL
CONTEXT

CHAPTER 4

Religious Roots

On a sweltering August Sunday morning, an Ohio Amish congregation gathers for worship on the second floor of a member's barn. The smell of threshed oats and fresh-cut hay fills the modest sanctuary with the scents of summer. The family hosting church has arranged backless wooden benches into twenty-foot-long rows—four rows for the men and boys that face five rows for the women and girls, with an aisle in between. During the three-hour service, members kneel twice on the bare wood floor to pray. Each time the people turn to kneel facing their benches, the host quickly rises and pulls the barn's two twelve-foot-high doors shut with a dramatic clang. When the prayer concludes, he reopens the doors. Asked later by a visitor why the doors had been closed, the elderly bishop replies matter-of-factly, "Because Jesus taught us to pray in private" (Matt. 6:5–6).

Sources of Amish Spirituality

The opening and closing of barn doors on a summer morning offers a glimpse into the interior of Amish religious sensibility. This most simple gesture—fraught with affection for Scripture, humility, and devotion—reveals the community's deeply Christian roots. It also offers a metaphor for the inner religious lives of the Amish, which have garnered much less scholarly and popular attention than the visible emblems of buggies, quilts, and beards.[1] As in other human societies, Amish beliefs become embodied in social practices that, in turn, shape and reproduce their religious views. While their heartfelt commitments may remain concealed by the doors of more visible markers, they permeate all aspects of Amish culture.

Social scientists have long explored the correspondence between religious beliefs and their social contexts. All religions are nested in particular social systems, and the Amish faith is no exception. The themes of humility, obedience, and patience mesh smoothly with the patterns of a small community that expects its members to deny self-interest for the sake of collective goals. The religious ideals and the social system reinforce each other. Beliefs legitimize social practices, which, in turn, create a plausibility structure that gives credibility to spiritual ideas. We begin by examining several of the roots of Amish spirituality and then describe some of the faith commitments that both shape and are shaped by Amish practices.

Ancient Authorities

Amish spirituality is grounded in several sources of inspiration—the Bible, *Martyrs Mirror,* the *Ausbund,* the Dordrecht Confession, and various prayer books and devotional writings. The Amish use Martin Luther's 1534 German translation of the Bible, and when they read the Bible in English, they turn to the 1611 King James Version. Many households own a Bible with the German and English versions printed side by side. Although they rarely use words such as *infallibility* or *inerrancy,* which are popular in fundamentalist Protestant circles, Amish people have an abiding confidence in the Bible as an entirely authoritative guide for daily living.

The Amish give priority to the writings of the New Testament, especially to the teachings of Jesus. Only New Testament texts are read aloud in the church service, and three-quarters of these come from the Gospels of Matthew, Mark, Luke, and John, which recount the life and teaching of Jesus. The Amish especially highlight Jesus's Sermon on the Mount (Matt. 5–7), with its admonitions to be meek, merciful, and pure of heart; to love and forgive enemies; and to trust God's divine providence.

Despite the prominence of the New Testament, the Amish do not neglect the Old Testament. Some of its verses are memorized, and many sermons retell the creation story and the lives of Joseph, Abraham, David, and other Hebrew patriarchs and prophets. Scriptures from both Old and New Testaments are used in the rituals of baptism, communion, ordination, weddings, and funerals.[2] Nevertheless, the Amish hermeneutic—their way of reading and interpreting the Bible—privileges the New Testament and especially the teachings of Jesus.

Selections from the Bible are read in every church service, in daily family devotions, and for personal inspiration. Rather than trying to exegete the meaning of a verse, the Amish, in the words of one person, think the Bible can "interpret itself" if the reader believes and obeys the plain sense of the text. Beyond that, they believe that any interpretation should involve the entire congregation and its leaders. As one man explained, "Amish spirituality is grounded in religious tradition connected to

Members of an Amish congregation in central Pennsylvania gather for Sunday worship in the home of one of the families. This group drives white-topped buggies. *Dennis Hughes*

scriptural commands, and straying outside those boundaries is viewed as 'betrayal of Scripture.' Hence, few go there.'"

Scripture is discussed in informal settings, especially within families, but not in organized Bible study groups because, as one member said, "Bible study groups tend to be divisive rather than edifying or unifying." Critical analysis, especially by individuals, is discouraged for fear that such study might give rise to factions, challenge traditional authority, and sow discord in the congregation.

Unity is best promoted, the Amish contend, when all members hear the same preaching and teaching. Congregations grant considerable authority to preachers to interpret the meaning of Scripture and its application to daily life. But even a minister's interpretation in a sermon is subject to review and possible correction by other preachers at the end of each church service.[3]

A Cornerstone Prayer

The Lord's Prayer, which Jesus taught to his disciples (Matt. 6:9–13), is the cornerstone of Amish devotional liturgy. The words of this petition are uttered in every worship service, wedding, and funeral. Its phrases flash across Amish minds in silent prayer before and after meals, and they are spoken in the kneeling prayers when the family gathers each evening for devotions. Children memorize the Lord's Prayer at an early age, and this prayer, so precious to the Amish, is the final, silent plea at the graveside service.

The Lord's Prayer is central to Amish devotional life in part because Amish people generally do not compose original prayers for public utterance, thinking that doing so would call too much attention to the one praying. Trying to improve on the words of Jesus, in Amish minds, would be a useless act of pride. One young carpenter explained, "It is a well-rounded prayer. We think it has all the basics, and we don't think we can improve on Jesus." A key phrase in this oft-repeated prayer is its pointed reminder of the importance of accepting, without complaint, whatever divine providence brings: "Thy kingdom come, Thy will be done in earth as it is in heaven" (Matt. 6:10). From cradle to grave, "Thy will be done" etches a deep sense of submission into Amish minds.

Martyr Hymns

In their church services, the Amish sing from the *Ausbund,* the oldest Protestant hymnal in continuous use. First printed in 1564, this small but chunky 900-page book contains the words of 140 songs, nearly half of which were written by or about martyrs. For more than a century after its initial publication, officials considered the *Ausbund* a heretical book, and some governments banned and confiscated it. The hymn texts appear in Gothic German script without musical notation. The melodies, half of which were originally folk tunes, have been maintained across the generations through oral transmission as children learned the tunes from their parents. The words and images of these songs keep Amish spirituality anchored in a sixteenth-century world.

Eighteen Articles of Faith

The Amish themselves have never written a formal confession of faith or a systematic doctrinal theology. They show little interest in abstract theological concepts, pointing instead to the practical teachings of Jesus. For the most part, their implicit theology is orally transmitted from older members of the congregation to younger ones.[4] For them, truth and universal principles are not found in papers produced by study commissions, panels, or scholarly research, but rather are found in the life of Jesus, whose example silences debate on lofty theological questions.

Nevertheless, various Anabaptist groups did compose statements of doctrine in the sixteenth and seventeenth centuries, and the Amish have long used one of those, the Dordrecht Confession of Faith. Written by Dutch Mennonites in 1632, the

Dordrecht Confession is a statement of faith organized in eighteen sections called articles—and thus it is often called "the Eighteen Articles." Apart from the Bible, the Dordrecht Confession remains the theological foundation of Amish spirituality. Its articles, especially the one on shunning, were frequently cited in the controversies that produced the Amish church in 1693.

The Eighteen Articles "remain firmly established and accepted" in all Amish churches, according to one Amish historian, and churches use them to instruct baptismal candidates.[5] The articles cover basic topics of Christian doctrine—creation, sin, salvation, baptism, and eternal life. Other sections highlight distinctive Anabaptist themes such as prohibitions of revenge, refusal to swear oaths, the ritual of footwashing, and the practice of church discipline through excommunication and shunning. These articles provide a written bedrock for the oral tradition of Amish spirituality.

Several Amish leaders in the nineteenth and twentieth centuries wrote about doctrine and theology, but these were often private reflections on faith composed for their heirs rather than systematic statements of Christian faith for broad distribution.[6] The closest example to a reformulation of a doctrinal statement is a document produced in 1983 by New Order ministers in Holmes County, Ohio. Yet even that 70-page booklet, its authors insist, "is not intended to replace any former confession of faith."[7]

Prayer Books and Devotional Writings

While the Dordrecht Confession links Amish spirituality to seventeenth-century Dutch Mennonite views, their main prayer book, *Die Ernsthafte Christenpflicht* (The Prayer Book for Earnest Christians), first printed in 1708, reflects the influence of Swiss Anabaptist writers, as well as the sentiments of Pietism. Available in German and English, *Christenpflicht* has enjoyed some sixty North American printings.[8] Again, because the Amish resist composing original prayers for public gatherings, these historic prayers shape the tone of Amish spirituality. Prayers from *Christenpflicht* are read in church services, when the family kneels for evening prayers, and on other devotional occasions.

Lust-Gärtlein, another prayer book, was first compiled in 1736. Its prayers, likely written by Pietist devotional writers, are designated for certain occasions or times of the day, such as the evening or Christmas, or for certain people, such as pregnant women or those who are recently widowed.[9] *Lust-Gärtlein* also contains a section of forty-seven short admonitions translated as "Rules of a Godly Life," which explain how to lead a "God-pleasing life and to attain eternal salvation."[10]

A formative source for Amish spirituality, "Rules of a Godly Life" is widely read on fasting days and used for instructing youth and for private inspiration. Divided into three sections—admonitions for thoughts, words, and deeds—"Rules" expounds on spiritual virtues such as patience, humility, suffering, loving enemies, and discipline.

Members of more progressive Amish groups may also read contemporary devotional material such as *Our Daily Bread,* popular among many Christians; *Beside the Still Waters,* produced by conservative Mennonites; and *Tagliches Manna,* authored by writers from horse-and-buggy churches. Books written by mainstream evangelical Christian authors such as Max Lucado, Rick Warren, and James Dobson are also found in some Amish homes. An Amish man in the Lancaster, Pennsylvania, community estimated that half of his Amish friends under age forty had read Warren's *The Purpose Driven Life.* Such books, however, would rarely be found in conservative settlements.

Two Pillars of Faith

One Amish author calls *discipleship* and *obedience* the twin "unchangeable truths" of the Christian faith.[11] Amish churches embrace basic Christian beliefs, but like other Christians, they also accent certain themes. Unlike modern modes of spirituality that see the spiritual quest as mostly private, the Amish fuse personal faith and communal commitments.[12]

For both the early Anabaptists and the present-day Amish, the paramount question of faith is this: What does it mean to follow Jesus in daily life? This discipleship tradition rests on Jesus's words to his disciples: "If any man will come after me, let him deny himself and take up his cross daily, and follow me" (Luke 9:23). Amish leaders believe that the "most devoted, sincere, and useful Christians" are those "who practice self-denial and sacrifice their own selfish interests and desires in service to God."[13]

For the Anabaptists, the radical commitment to give up selfish desires and follow Jesus requires a voluntary decision confirmed by adult baptism. Although the wording of baptism vows varies slightly from one Amish group to another, all candidates are asked if they will "renounce their own flesh and blood"—in short, deny their selfish desires. On bended knees, they promise to yield themselves to God's will and to covenant with the church to remain steadfast until death.

Obedience, the second pillar of faith, often tops the list when the Amish describe discipleship.[14] An Amish businessman calls obedience "the most important word in the dictionary." Amish faith underscores the importance of obedience to Christ and the church as well as the severe consequence of disobedience: eternal damnation. Disobedience is considered dangerous because it signals self-will and, if not confessed, leads to eternal separation from God. Furthermore, disobedience disrupts the harmony of community, in which yielding to others is paramount.

Obedience to the will of God is the cardinal religious virtue in Amish faith. To highlight the imperative of obedience, leaders frequently cite Scripture passages such as "We ought to obey God rather than men" (Acts 5:29) and "Obey them that have the rule over you" (Heb. 13:17). In the Amish view, genuine spiritual obedience will produce righteousness in daily living. Submission is another way of speaking about obedience. One Amish writer says, "There is probably nothing harder for the flesh than submitting to others."[15]

The theme of obedience undergirds the entire socioreligious system by fusing faith with life, and the individual with the community. "Our brotherhood," writes one New Order minister, is based on "self-denial, submission, and obedience."[16] The emphasis on discipleship and obedience means that Amish faith focuses more on *how* one lives than on *what* one believes. We discuss this theme in more depth in chapter 6.

The Fruits of Faith

Yielding to Divine Providence

Early Anabaptists sometimes used the German word *Gelassenheit* to convey the idea of yielding fully to God's will and forsaking all selfishness.[17] They believed that Christ called them to abandon self-interest and follow his example of suffering, meekness, humility, and service. In the words of an Ohio deacon, "Gelassenheit is the first step to true brotherhood . . . overcoming selfishness . . . renouncing force. . . . The opposite of Gelassenheit is force and manipulation." Furthermore, the church's purpose is "to give this principle bodily form by living it out in everyday life."[18]

Gelassenheit signals a calm surrender to God's will. It echoes the words of Jesus, "Not my will, but Thine be done," spoken as he faced a torturous death. Following his example, Anabaptist martyrs died without fighting back, and their blood has imprinted the virtue of surrender onto the sacred texts of Amish history.

Surrendering to the purposes of divine providence means that one does not quarrel with God but rather accepts suffering with a quiet confidence that God's will, although often concealed from humans in this life, ultimately shapes all events into a larger pattern of good. The Amish community at Nickel Mines, Pennsylvania, exhibited this spirit of acceptance in 2006 when it rejected revenge in response to the shooting of ten girls and expressed confidence that justice was in God's hands.

The mantra "Thy will be done" found in the Lord's Prayer captures the central script of Amish faith: yieldedness to God's will. This stance of Gelassenheit frames the Amish response to daily hardships—a child's illness, a sudden death, a drought, or a job loss. Acceptance of such adversity is not easy, and Amish people readily admit a propensity to anger and disappointment. Yet following Jesus, in their view, means renouncing Satan, denying self, and yielding to God's call again and again. *Thy Will Be Done* is the title of a book chronicling more than a hundred stories of accidental or premature deaths among the Amish, and the theme of Gelassenheit also threads through a collection of first-person accounts of Amish people with disabilities.[19] This resignation to divine providence pervades Amish thinking and action and extends beyond the spiritual realm to other dimensions of Amish life.

Defenseless Disciples

Traditional Anabaptist practice also includes a commitment to forego violence, even in self-defense, in the face of hostility. Christians, the Amish believe, should pray for their persecutors, love their enemies, forgive those who wrong them, and refuse to resist evil with force. This nonviolent stance rests on Jesus's teaching to love enemies and accept injustice without a fight. As indicated by the second part of the title of their martyr book, *The Bloody Theater, or Martyrs Mirror of the Defenseless Christians,* the Amish consider their religious ancestors "defenseless" disciples.

Forgiving others, in the Amish view, is one of Jesus's prominent teachings. And while most Christians emphasize God's forgiveness of sins, Amish people point to the forgiveness clause in the Lord's Prayer that also puts that responsibility back on humans: "Forgive us our debts, *as we forgive* our debtors" (Matt. 6:12).[20] Here, the Amish say, is evidence that the effectiveness of God's grace depends at least in part on the willingness of Christians to forgive others. Indeed, the Amish note, Jesus followed his prayer with a pointed conclusion: If you forgive, you will be forgiven; if you do not forgive, you will not be forgiven (Matt. 6:14–15). Twice a year, prior to each church district's communion service, leaders highlight Jesus's admonition to forgive the wrongs of others seventy-times-seven times—implying that forgiveness should be a daily habit.

Any use of violence is considered disobedience to God. Thus the Amish will not only sit in jail rather than fight in war, they will also absorb hostility rather than file lawsuits, because litigation employs coercive force. Holding public office is also taboo, because a public official may need to use lethal or legal force. Amish people insist that they do not seek adversity or persecution and that suffering does not necessarily bring heavenly rewards. When faced with insult or injustice, they simply believe that Jesus expects them to respond with patience and forgiveness.

Humility, Patience, and Silence

The Amish believe that a humble person, fully yielded to God, submits to others and patiently accepts suffering, and thus Amish leaders urge their people to "patiently bear the cross of Christ without complaining." Humility is welcomed in Amish life as a sign of discipleship, for Jesus described himself as "meek and lowly in heart" (Matt. 11:29) and "humbled himself, and became obedient onto death" (Phil. 2:8). Humility is perfected in "death to self," argues one Amish writer, who places obedience, self-denial, humility, and meekness among the highest Christian duties.[21] This communal stream of spirituality stands in stark relief to more individualistic versions of religious experience.

Humility is expressed in personal spirituality as well as in corporate theological views. The Amish have confidence in God's providence and are content to live with mystery and unanswered questions. Their profound sense of theological humility means that they do not attempt to explain all religious riddles, nor do they seek to speak for God or claim to know God's mind on matters of eternal destiny. Like other aspects of their faith, their theological humility sets them apart from the modern penchant to know, explain, and control. "We should not put a question mark where God puts a period," said one Amish minister.

Patience is one expression of humility and Gelassenheit. Amish spirituality values patient waiting rather than rushing to conclusions and forcing results. Indeed, the perception of time in Amish society, regulated by the changing seasons, is slower than the speeding seconds tracked by digital clocks. Patience is the implicit, invisible message conveyed by every Amish carriage that slowly makes its way along roadways as cars streak past it.

Amish spirituality is also a quiet spirituality. Silence, rather than a boisterous retort or argument, is the common Amish answer to conflict.[22] Amish people are comfortable with silence and feel no need to fill in all the pauses with words. Behavior expresses meaning better than words. A father who lost a daughter in the schoolhouse shooting at Nickel Mines said, "Our forgiveness was what we did, not what we said." A silent prayer opens and closes every meal in Amish homes, and a quiet prayer on bended knees signals humility in church services. When perplexed by an attorney or a bureaucrat, outwitted by a regulation, or cursed by an outsider, the Amish response is often simply silence.

Their example, of course, is Jesus, who remained mute in the face of mocking taunts. This is the silence of nonviolence—of loving the enemy, of "walking the second mile," of humility, and of patience. Such spiritual values, which find little traction in a noise-filled, hyperactive culture, are important for achieving harmony in a collectivist society. It is to that communal body—what one scholar of Amish life called "the redemptive community"—that we now turn.[23]

A Covenant Community

Small and Local

The forces of specialization in contemporary America have pulled many parts of social life asunder. Work, education, leisure, and religion—once lodged at home or in the neighborhood—are dispersed. With abundant religious programming available on television and via the Internet, stay-at-home spiritualists can worship with a virtual community thousands of miles away.

In a radical rejection of these trends, Amish people continue their centuries-old tradition of holding church services in their homes every other Sunday. Their spirituality is grounded in their church district, with physical boundaries marked by roads, streams, and fence lines. The district's twenty to forty families live near each other. A single four-letter word, *Gmay*—a dialect shorthand for *Gemeinde* (community)—refers to this local church-community, both its members and its worship services.

This little community meets together to interpret Scripture and establish guidelines for dress, technology, and leisure. Although a cluster of Gmays may collaborate, each one is the ultimate authority in the lives of its members. Each congregation rules on membership, baptism, ordination, and excommunication. No national delegate body, conference minister, or synod office holds authority over the local Gmay. "We don't have a pope," quipped one Amish man, "just a lot of bishops."

The high view the Amish hold of the Gmay's authority is based on their interpretation of Matthew 18, a passage in which Jesus declares that decisions made by the church are affirmed in heaven. Their Anabaptist forebears rejected Catholic and Protestant views of sacraments, especially the idea that sacred elements in the communion service held the real presence of Christ. The bread and wine used in the service, the Anabaptists argued, were only symbols of Christ's body and blood. For the Anabaptists, the real presence of Christ—the true sacrament—was when Christians gathered for moral discernment in the spirit of Jesus (Matt. 18:18–20). Such a view invests the covenant agreed to by members of each Gmay with considerable divine authority.

In members' meetings, convened at the close of some Sunday services, members might discuss how to assist a family with a major medical bill, approve candidates for baptism, plan for an ordination, restore a wayward member, or endorse guidelines for using new technology. Decisions on these matters carry binding expectations, the Amish believe, because the covenant forged by the Gmay is guided by Jesus's spirit and ratified in heaven.

A Disciplined Life

A communal spirituality that focuses on the daily practice of faith requires common lifestyle understandings for the Gmay. What is striking about Amish religion is how it crisscrosses all dimensions of daily life, from dress codes to the use of technology, from education to political participation. "We must submit to each other in the application of biblical principles that are not specifically spelled out in the scriptures," says one Amish leader.[24]

The common guidelines for Amish life, known as the *Ordnung,* provide a blueprint for expected and forbidden behavior. Although the Ordnung is typically an oral tradition, ministers in some groups keep a written record of it. This body of interpretation—both oral and written—gives guidance on moral issues that are not addressed directly by Scripture as well as practical applications of biblical principles. The Ordnung typically includes guidelines for dress, buggies, technology, home décor, sports, and similar matters. Although leaders recommend guidelines, they are only binding when ratified by the congregation.

In one sense, the Ordnung communicates the collective advice of the Gmay. But it is more than advice. The Ordnung requires obedience because the Amish believe that it flows from the moral discernment of the church, which is blessed by the spirit of Christ and endorsed by heaven. Yet because of its oral and unsystematic character, the Ordnung is pliable and adaptable. A good Ordnung, the Amish say, is readily accepted by members and promotes harmony and unity in the redemptive community. Members who intentionally stray from the guidelines will receive repeated admonitions before they face excommunication. In some cases violators leave the church before it suspends their membership. The Ordnung's central role in providing moral guidance reveals the priority of faithful practice over doctrinal belief in Amish religion.

The Moral Muscle of Tradition

Custom carries a hefty dose of moral authority in Amish society. Regardless of whether the norm involves wearing a particular style of dress, living without public electricity, growing a beard but shaving the mustache, or holding worship services in homes rather than in church buildings, traditions are change-resistant. The Amish believe that tradition carries God's endorsement and that submitting to it is a sign of a humble and godly character. That many people cannot say when or why a particular practice emerged does not bother them. They assume that the church in decades past, under the guidance of God's spirit, deemed it a wise practice for the community's spiritual well-being. A given Gmay may reconsider or change elements of its Ordnung, but its embedded bias leans toward continuity rather than change.[25]

Unlike most mainstream Americans, who have great confidence in analytic reasoning, intellectual rationale, and the latest scientific studies, many Amish people are content to trust the time-tested wisdom woven into the fabric of traditions. There is no impulse to update statements of faith, revise patterns of worship, or write new songs for church services. Tradition is the default response to change. "How thankful we can be," says one writer, "for the many guidelines that have been handed down to us from the church of our forefathers . . . basic principles that have been taught from generation to generation."[26]

Over time, cultural practices have come to carry religious authority as well as social imperative. Dropping the taboo on owning motor vehicles would not only assault the wisdom of ancestors but also shred a central piece of Amish identity. Buying a car, Amish people point out, is the first thing ex-members do when they leave the church.

The covenant community nourishes Amish faith through its teaching, rituals, traditions, and Ordnung. And although these practices provide a reservoir of rich resources, Amish people quickly note that neither the community nor its customs save them. Only faith in Jesus Christ, they say, does that.[27]

A Back Road to Heaven

A "New Birth" or "Born Again"?

The quest for salvation and eternal life is a central theme in Christianity. The Amish view of salvation reflects the communal dimension of their spiritual life. Using a biblical metaphor, they see themselves as strangers and pilgrims in this world, traveling on a heavenward journey along a back country road.

Unlike some Christians, who see religious conversion as resolving an existential crisis, Amish people view conversion as more of a process. True, baptism stands as a critical marker in Amish life—a symbol of the choice to join the disciplined church-community.[28] But salvation itself is more of a turning point on the road to a mature religious commitment. "Salvation is a gradual project," notes one leader, because children grow up observing their elders practicing their faith.[29] They absorb it through social osmosis rather than intellectual inquiry. In the words of one Amish man, "Salvation cannot be reduced to a conversion experience."

Many Christians use the biblical language of "new birth" or being "born again" to describe religious conversion. In what might seem like splitting hairs, the Amish make a distinction between these theological code words. For many Amish, the former phrase suggests a communal understanding of faith, while the latter term signals a highly private understanding. Amish leaders preach about the importance of the "new birth," but they avoid the "born again" label because they associate it with religious groups that accent individual experience and an egocentric view of salvation marked by claims about "my personal relationship with Jesus Christ."

Emotional expressions are somewhat restrained in Amish life. Baptism, for example, stirs emotions but not the verbal exuberance common in some religious circles. In some Protestant churches, crisis conversions locate moral authority in personal experience. This is consistent with an individualistic culture in which subjective feelings are a highly valued authority. However, in a collective society in which the church is a source of moral wisdom, giving too much weight to personal emotions would challenge the collective order.

An overemphasis on the individual, argues one Amish writer, "exalts the feelings and emotions of the individual until they become an end in themselves and an authority to settle all controversy. This appeals to people, because it promises them freedom." The writer argues that "people who overemphasize and are overly dependent on the personal leading of the Holy Spirit have an aversion to Scripture passages that uphold tradition. They will use the Bible freely to support their beliefs. . . . People will do things or go to places because [they say] God told them to do so." Rather than heeding churchly authority, he concludes, "it is more common for people to speak of their own decisions, based on their own discernment as to what is 'God's will.'"[30]

From the Amish viewpoint, a heavy emphasis on a *personal* relationship with God may embolden people to speak of "*my* interpretation of the Bible" or to assert that "God spoke to *me*." Such personal narratives of faith are suspect because they shift moral authority from the community to the private sphere of individual experience.

A Living Hope

The phrases "assurance of salvation," "eternal security," and "once saved, always saved" are code words in some Christian circles that meet with sharp resistance in Amish settings. For some evangelical Protestants, these labels are a mark of religious confidence. Amish people, however, are loath to declare that they have an "assurance of salvation" because for them such assertions presume that human beings can know the future and read the omniscient mind of God.

The Amish prefer to speak of "a living hope": a quiet and calm confidence that God will be a just and merciful judge when they face eternity. This stance, grounded on a deep sense of humility and providential trust, acknowledges that God is the one who ultimately decides such weighty matters.

Amish leaders are also hesitant to endorse any theology that drives a wedge between salvation and ethical practices. Unhitching salvation from ethics would lighten one's responsibility to the Ordnung and make obedience optional—leaving some ethical choices to personal preference. They cite Jesus's teaching that good trees bear good fruit, noting that the true followers of Jesus will be known by their obedience (Matt. 7:17–24). Although they emphasize that salvation comes by confessing that Jesus is the son of God who died for their sins, Amish people also believe that, as his disciples, their lives must exemplify his ethical practices.

Amish understandings of their relationship to God and their relationship to other people are so interconnected that it makes no sense to them to separate ethics from salvation or to speak of one dimension and not the other. In this sense, Amish religion is holistic and organic; beliefs and behavior cannot be divided into distinct categories. This is why bold claims of salvation apart from obedience appear dangerous to them. An exaggerated stress on personal salvation, they say, threatens the entire foundation of communal spirituality and fruits of faithful living. Yet all of this makes the Amish vulnerable to charges from evangelical Protestants that they are seeking to "earn their salvation" or that they are spiritually deceived into thinking that doing "good works" and following human-made rules will save them.

From the Amish perspective, a modest view of salvation resting on a "living hope" encourages members to heed the guidance of the church throughout their lives. Debates about assurance of salvation in Amish circles become animated because they strike at the heart of their entire socioreligious system—the churchly authority vested in the Ordnung. These different understandings of salvation point to the fundamental chasm between Amish views of moral authority and those of evangelical Christians, some of whom believe that few Amish are saved.

The Larger World

Separation from the World

When Amish baptismal candidates kneel and confess their faith in Christ, they renounce three things: the self, the devil, and the world. This triple renunciation names three entities that threaten the well-being of the covenant community. Selfishness leads to pride and disobedience; the cunning devil, with his tricks and deception, lures members astray; and undue affection for the outside world may pollute the purity of the church.

The term *world,* in the Amish mind, refers not to the cosmos but to the values and vices of mass culture. Deep reservations about "worldly" culture appear in biblical texts that Amish leaders cite: "Love not the world, neither the things that are in the world" (1 John 2:15); "Whosoever . . . will be a friend of the world is the enemy of God" (James 4:4); "Wherefore come out from among them, and be ye separate, saith the Lord" (2 Cor. 6:17); and the Apostle Paul's admonition: "Be not conformed to this world" (Rom. 12:2).

A sharp dualism between church and world crystallized in the sixteenth century as Anabaptists were tortured and executed. The words of one early Swiss Anabaptist confession epitomize the deep chasm between the church and the world: "All of those who have fellowship with the dead works of darkness have no part in the light. Thus all who follow the devil and the world have no part with those who are called out of the world into God."[31]

This tenet of faith—*Absonderung,* translated as "nonconformity" or "separation" from the world—means keeping a cautious distance from evil: violence, war, promiscuous sex, abortion, greed, fraud, divorce, drugs, and so on. The Amish affirm Jesus's description in Matthew 7:13–14 of two mutually exclusive ways: a narrow path leading to eternal life and a broad avenue filled with people heedlessly heading toward destruction. Members of their church-community, the Amish say, should seek to follow Jesus on the narrow path. The words of a well-known song in the *Ausbund* etch this belief into Amish consciousness:

> *There are two ways in this time,*
> *The one is narrow, the other broad.*
> *Who now will go the other way,*
> *He will be despised by everyone.*[32]

Reservations about the larger social world run deep in Amish spirituality for two reasons: the religious persecution of their Anabaptist forebears and their belief that Satan governs the rebellious spirit of the present world. Biblical cautions about the world were galvanized into Anabaptist consciousness as hundreds of them lost their heads to the executioner's sword, were burned at the stake, or suffered various kinds of torture.[33] These images and their implications survive in *Martyrs Mirror* stories and *Ausbund* hymns.

Then, too, the worldliness of mass society is dangerous because Satan controls it. Biblical images often cited in sermons depict Satan as a roaring lion masquerading as an angel of light.[34] "Evil companions," according to one writer, "are the devil's dragnet by which he draws many into hell."[35] One Amish minister sees Satan shaping popular culture through music: "Many [non-Amish] are filled from early morning to late night with the satanically inspired music of lust and greed . . . these sounds keep good thinking out of our minds, [which soon] become filled with this garbage, pushing out the good." The writer concludes, "We know that whenever God creates something sacred and good, Satan, in his persistent opposition to God, will, without fail, try to set up a very clever, but worthless, counterfeit."[36]

Nevertheless, although Amish people reject aspects of contemporary culture, they certainly expect to find many non-Amish people in heaven. When asked about the salvation of others, they are quick to repeat the words of Jesus: "Judge not, that ye be not judged" (Matt. 7:1). Because only God knows human hearts, Amish people are loath to speculate on anyone's eternal destiny. What matters is that people—regardless of their church affiliations—keep their baptismal promises and follow the teachings of their particular church. Spending time forecasting the eternal destiny of others, they say, would be trying to do God's work.

Evangelism and Service

The Amish believe that their redemptive community should be a witness—a light in the larger world, as proclaimed by Jesus: "Ye are the light of the world. A city that is set on a hill cannot be hid" (Matt. 5:14).[37] They also echo Christ's teaching that their way of life should not call attention to themselves, but "give glory to your Father in heaven." As one Amish man explained, "We try to let our light shine, but not shine it in the eyes of others." In a gentle critique of noisier evangelistic voices, one leader said, "We want our witness to be a quiet light." The swift Amish forgiveness after the slaying of schoolgirls in 2006 spawned more than two thousand news stories around the world. "That story," observed an Amish farmer, "made more of a witness for us all over the world than anything else we can ever do."

The communal focus of Amish spirituality diverges from evangelistic methods that focus on individual conversion. For the Amish, evangelism often violates humility and rings of a belief that "my religion is better than yours." Furthermore, it downplays the centrality of the church's collective witness. Additionally, mission activities in other cultures would likely bring disruptive changes to long-established church traditions. Although the Amish do not proselytize or try to recruit outsiders, anyone who confesses faith in Jesus Christ and is willing to accept the church's expectations is welcome to join. Still, the number of converts is small.

Although Amish churches do not engage in evangelism efforts or operate mission agencies, some members give financial contributions to non-Amish mission projects. And members of Amish groups serve others outside their community by participating in various Anabaptist service and disaster relief organizations (see chapter 19). In some settlements, Amish people engage in civic activities by serving in volunteer fire companies, donating blood, raising funds for hospice care, and becoming organ donors when they die. All of these activities express humanitarian care for those be-yond the Amish fold.

A Durable Faith

The principles of discipleship, yieldedness, and separation from the world set the tone for Amish religious life. Yet like people everywhere, the Amish experience gaps between ideal values and social realities. Amish people are the first to confess that they too often fail to follow the teachings of Jesus. For some, spirituality has become rote conformity to the rules of the church and lacks heartfelt devotion. Others may dress the part but are not fully committed—"half-Amish," so to speak. They wear plain garb but are worldly at heart. One Amish man admitted, "The only reason I stayed Amish is because I married a lovely Amish girl!"

Indeed, the waters of Amish spirituality are not always tranquil. Crosscurrents beneath the placid surface sometimes challenge traditional views. Voices in some communities call for more engagement in the outside world via service and mission-related activities. Some members who desire a more evangelical emphasis with a born-again experience question the orthodox Amish view. Amish business owners, struggling to compete in the public market, sometimes try to bypass church rules and gain more access to forbidden technology. Greater exposure to the outside world and its unfettered individualism challenges the long-standing Amish values of humility, obedience, and submission.

Yet despite these crosscurrents, Amish faith has been hardy, avoiding the mul-titude of innovations produced by mainstream religion and spirituality in modern America. Amish resistance to higher education, a scientific worldview, analytical study of the Bible, individual-centered religious experience, mission outreach, and church bureaucracy has been staunch. As we explain further in chapter 5, Amish pat-terns of religious ritual have also remained largely untouched by modernity.

For the vast majority, the heart of Amish faith throbs with the quiet rhythms of a deep and genuine spirituality. The final words of "Rules of a Godly Life" sum up the spirit of Amish faith this way:

> *Finally, in your conduct be friendly toward everyone*
> *And a burden to none.*
> *Toward God, live a holy life;*
> *toward yourself, be moderate;*
> *toward your fellow men, be fair;*
> *in life, be modest;*

in your manner, courteous;
in admonition, friendly;
in forgiveness, willing;
in your promises, true;
in your speech, wise;
and out of a pure heart gladly share of the bounties you receive.[38]

CHAPTER 5

SACRED RITUALS

A hush settles over 140 people packed together on backless benches in the basement of an Amish home in Kentucky. Children and adults, wearing their dark Sunday best, have gathered for a three-hour church service. Rising from the men's side, the warbling voice of the Vorsinger—*the man who leads the congregational singing—slices through the silence. He stretches out the first syllable of the first German word of a hymn written by an Anabaptist martyred in 1527. A few seconds later the rest of the voices join in unison:*

> *When Christ with His true teaching*
> *Had gathered a small group,*
> *He said that each one with patience*
> *Should daily bear the cross with Him.*

The Gathered Community
Church at Home

Sunday church services reenact the deep meanings of *Gelassenheit* in the Amish moral order. The sanctuary may be a home, a barn, or a shop, but for three hours it approximates a medieval monastic setting laced with humility, patience, and silence. Like other Amish rituals, the church service blends social structure and cultural values, embodies deep religious beliefs, and reinforces Amish identity.[1] In this chapter we examine a variety of rituals inscribed in Amish religious life, from church services and members' meetings to council meetings, communion, ordination, discipline, and excommunication. We discuss baptism in chapter 12.

Amish people walk to church on a Sunday morning. Those living near the host family walk while others arrive by buggy or bicycle. *Doyle Yoder*

Meeting in a home reinforces the fact that Amish religion is embedded in the material texture of daily life.[2] Each *Gmay* gathers every other week—twenty-six times annually—so that each household hosts church about once a year. As the Gmay is welcomed into each family's home, the congregation has an annual opportunity to appraise a family's compliance with *Ordnung* expectations for home furnishings and appliances. Thus, each household is, in a real sense, open for inspection once a year. Cleaning and preparation begin several weeks in advance. The district's bench wagon, stacked with benches, eating utensils, songbooks, a prayer book, and a Bible, arrives at the home of the host a few days before the meeting.[3] On Friday or Saturday the family reconfigures living or work spaces in their home, shop, or barn and arranges the benches to create a temporary worship space. "I love taking church at our house," one women explained. "I've always enjoyed the excitement and bustle of housecleaning, scrubbing porches, window screens, cleaning out corners, preparing food. It's all a part of our tradition and one I really enjoy."[4]

Services usually begin between eight and nine o'clock in the morning. In order to arrive on time, farm families begin chores early on Sunday mornings. Members walk or arrive by horse and buggy. "You have to pace your horse," explained one man. "You can't be ten minutes late and expect to make it up as you can in a car."

A Simple Sanctuary

Backless benches arranged in two sections—one for men and one for women—face each other. Some traditional groups have a small singers' table for the *Ausbund*s, but most affiliations place the hymnals on the benches in advance. Neither ministers nor members carry Bibles to church.

The term *ministers* refers to the ordained men—typically a bishop, two or three preachers, and a deacon—who lead the congregation. Amish ministers do not preach from a pulpit or behind a lectern but stand on the floor a few feet from their congregants. Church services are conducted in two languages. The hymns, Scripture reading, and prayers are read from old German texts, but ministers preach in Pennsylvania Dutch.[5]

There are no printed worship bulletins, as are often found in other Christian churches, nor are there icons or other religious symbols—no cross, altar, chimes, candles, robes, incense, or stained glass windows. The congregation is the choir, and it sings without organ, piano, or other instrumental accompaniment. With no electricity, video, microphones, or sound system, silence prevails until the singing begins.

The worship service is a common experience for everyone in the district, from small babies to great-grandparents. In a remarkable rejection of religious specialization, there are no nurseries, age-defined Sunday school classes, or programs for special interest groups. In this way, the Amish again emphasize unity and uniformity over individual or subgroup interests.

The striking simplicity stretches beyond worship to the absence of administrative overhead, salaries, offices, technology, facility maintenance, and security systems. The simple gathering in a private home symbolizes a stark reality: the gathered community—not buildings, budgets, performances, or professional staff—is the sacred object blessed by divine presence.

Rites of Deference

Gender, age, and leadership roles shape social interaction. Depending on the setting, the ministers shake hands with the men and women either before or after they enter the assembly area. Women enter the meeting area by age and sit on the women's side. Then the ministers and older laymen enter, followed by the other men in descending age. Role trumps age, as does length of ministerial tenure. A thirty-year-old bishop, for example, enters before an elderly deacon. The ordained men sit together, but the arrangement varies by affiliation.

Seating by gender and age instead of in family units symbolizes accountability to the authority of the church rather than to the ties of kinship. Young children enter

Two brothers place *Ausbund* hymnals on benches in the upper floor of their barn
in preparation for an Amish church service. *Burton Buller*

and sit with their mothers or fathers until around age nine or ten; then boys and girls
join their age and gender cohort. In some groups the unmarried males, called "boys,"
walk by the ministers' row as they enter, shaking the ministers' hands. The boys traditionally enter the room last.

One Amish man recalls the first time he walked in with the boys, as a nine-year-
old. "I well recall how important I felt walking in . . . that first time," Sam Stoltzfus
recollects. "I can also remember well shaking hands with the four ministers, who
looked so reverent with their hats on. . . . Deacon Aaron was last and had such nice
twinkly eyes. . . . There we'd sit, me and Manny Beiler, holding the *Ausbund* hymn
book together. . . . Mom had warned me that if I didn't behave, I'd have to sit with her.
That happened once or so."[6] Because people enter by gender and age in the same
order at each service, an absence is easily noted.

Only men lead singing or speak during the service. In some communities the
bishop opens the service with a few words, while in other churches a song leader
opens the service by calling out the number of the first hymn. As the second line
of the first song begins, the ministers rise and walk to a private room for a consultation, known as *Abrot,* while the congregation continues singing. For twenty minutes

or so the ministers discuss leadership matters and also decide who will preach the sermons that morning.

Ministers usually do not know in advance exactly who will preach. Although they follow an informal rotation, it may be preempted by any visiting minister in attendance, who customarily would be invited to preach. One minister explained that he had "a sermon ready to preach for four months, but I didn't need it because there were always visiting ministers." Conversely, "if you visit another congregation, you always go prepared to preach" because you likely will be asked. In any case, ministers never preach from a prepared text. They may read and think about ideas for a sermon in advance, but sermons are never outlined or written.

The following is the typical order of a church service, although practices vary slightly by settlement and affiliation.

Upon arrival, men and women congregate in separate locations.
New arrivals go around the circle shaking hands.
Entrance into worship areas by gender and age.
Congregational singing (30–40 minutes).
Ministers meet (Abrot) in separate room.
Opening sermon (25–30 minutes).
Silent kneeling prayer.
Scripture reading by a deacon or minister as members stand.
Main sermon (50–75 minutes).
Affirmations (*Zeugnis*) of sermon by ministers or elderly men.
Acceptance of affirmations and prelude to prayer by main preacher.
Main minister reads prayer as members kneel.
Benediction spoken as members stand.
Closing hymn.
Members' meeting (if needed).
Fellowship meal.
Visiting and fellowship.
Departure of most members.
Evening meal (for the host's family, neighbors, and close friends).

A Liturgy of Humility

As ministers begin preaching, they apologize for their limited ability and their unworthiness, and they express the wish that someone else would preach. One minister in Pennsylvania often tells his congregation, "Here I am. I don't know where I'm going [with my sermon], so please pray for me." Through this rite of humility, preachers emphasize that they are merely God's servants, giving themselves up to God's inspiration and guidance. In that sense, preaching itself becomes a ritual act of resignation and submission.

The change-resistant liturgy includes a capella singing in unison, two sermons, Scripture reading, and two kneeling prayers. After the first song is announced, a Vorsinger (song leader), who remains seated, slowly stretches out the first syllable of each line, and the congregation joins on the second word. The lyrics, printed without musical notes, are from the *Ausbund*. The tunes are sung from memory, and voices rise and fall in unison without a discernible rhythm.[7] This slow and melismatic style draws out each syllable over several notes. One song, with four or five verses, may stretch for twenty to thirty minutes. The speed reflects a particular group's degree of cultural assimilation: the more traditional the group, the slower it sings. The ancient German words and the slow methodical tones construct a cadence and a mood reminiscent of a medieval world—one that collides with modern sensibilities attuned to speed and quick transitions.

An Amish writer describes singing as "something we can all help with in our own way. It is not the voice of one person only, or the voice of only people with spe-

---

Das 131. Lied.

Ein geistlich Lied.
In der Weis: „Aus tiefer Noth schrey ich zu dir." (3)

1.

O Gott Vater, wir loben dich,
Und deine Güte preisen:
Die du, o Herr, so gnädiglich,
An uns neu hast bewiesen,
Und hast uns Herr zusammen g'führt,
Uns zu ermahnen durch dein Wort,
Gib uns Genad zu diesem.

2.

Oeffne den Mund, Herr, deiner Knecht,
Gib ihn'n Weißheit darneben,
Daß er dein Wort mög sprechen recht,
Was dient zum frommen Leben,
Und nützlich ist zu deinem Preiß,
Gib uns Hunger nach solcher Speiß,
Das ist unser Begehren.

The first and second verse of *Das Loblied* in German
Gothic script, as it appears in the *Ausbund* hymnal.

cial talent." He concludes, "The individual voices of men and women, the boys and girls, the rich and poor, lift their voices to God. All blend into one expression to our Heavenly Father, from whom all blessings flow, and to the Good Spirit dwelling among us."[8]

The second song in almost every church service is *Das Loblied* ("The Praise Song"), which serves as an Amish anthem of sorts.[9] One young boy had to memorize "the whole 28 lines," with its 140 German words, before his mother would permit him to sit with the older boys in church.[10] On any Sunday the one thousand or so Gmays meeting for worship across the continent sing *Das Loblied.* One member described this common ritual as evoking "a beautiful feeling of unity among all Amish groups." The first verse contains these words:

> *O God Father, we praise You*
> *And Your goodness exalt,*
> *Which You, O Lord, so graciously*
> *Have manifested to us anew,*
> *And have brought us together, Lord,*
> *To admonish us through Your Word,*
> *Grant us grace to this.*[11]

Sermons

The ministers typically return to the assembly during the singing of *Das Loblied.* One minister then preaches an opening sermon of twenty-five to thirty minutes, outlining the biblical theme for the day. After this, another preacher or the deacon reads a chapter of Scripture, followed by a second sermon that usually lasts an hour.[12] As they begin, one member explained, preachers always "earnestly ask the congregation to pray and ask God that He would give His divine message through the minister to his flock . . . on that particular day and time."[13]

Preaching styles vary by affiliation and personality. Some preachers lean against a post in a barn or basement as they preach, while others stand or pace in front of the congregation. Some have a distinctive sing-song cadence to their delivery. Preachers in the most traditional groups do not make direct eye contact with congregants while preaching, whereas in more progressive districts, especially New Order ones, preachers look directly at members of the audience, reflecting greater individual attention.[14] Preaching without notes or an outline, ministers sometimes stop mid-phrase as they ponder what to say. "You never know what will come forth," said one preacher. "Sometimes you are surprised [by what you say] and credit that to the Holy Spirit."

The emotional tone of most sermons is somber and serious, underscoring the eternal consequences of members' earthly journey. Ministers recite Bible stories or events of suffering from *Martyrs Mirror* as well as exemplary stories from daily life to teach honesty, integrity, and virtuous living. Leaders admonish members to avoid temptation and worldliness, practice humility and obedience, and yield to God's will in the midst of trials.

Twice during the service, members turn and kneel for prayer, resting their hands on the bench where they were seated. The first prayer, a silent one, follows the opening sermon. The second prayer, near the end of the service, is read from the *Christenpflicht* prayer book by the main preacher. As part of this prayer, the Lord's Prayer is read in every service. There are no audible, extemporaneous prayers.

A short rite of Zeugnis (testimony) follows the main sermon, when, for a few minutes, the other ministers and sometimes older men offer their endorsement. They draw attention to important themes in the sermon and may, on rare occasions, correct an error or suggest an alternative interpretation. This ritual reminds everyone that the sermon is a communal product, scrutinized by all the leaders of the Gmay.

When members rise from the closing kneeling prayer, they remain standing as the preacher reads a benediction. When the words "Jesus Christ" are spoken, everyone genuflects slightly at the knee, following an old Christian rite (Phil. 2:10). The congregation then sits for a closing hymn, which concludes the service.

Sitting on backless benches for three hours challenges even the most patient souls to remain alert. Most remarkable is how three- and four-year-olds sit still hour after hour. Those under four occupy themselves quietly with handkerchiefs, string, beads, or tiny toys. Some congregations pass a snack for young children midway through the service, but children older than five would likely be embarrassed to take it. One Amish writer, after confessing his struggle to stay awake, offered these suggestions for drowsiness: get enough sleep, sit alert, skip breakfast, drink coffee, or take some No-Doz or Wake-Ups.[15] While it is doubtful that many Amish are using alertness aids other than coffee on Sunday mornings, the writer's advice emphasizes that sitting through a three-hour service is no small feat, even for those who have been doing it their entire lives; it is not unusual for church members to catnap, especially when the meeting space is warm in summertime.

Fellowship

Congregations typically gather for a fellowship meal following the church service.[16] The assembly area is quickly converted into a makeshift dining room, with some benches serving as seats, while others are adjusted to make temporary tables. The hostess and the other women of the Gmay provide a meal following the district's customary menu. The simple fare usually consists of bread, spreads, cheese, pickles, finger foods, cookies, pies, and plenty of coffee. In some traditional groups, bean soup eaten from bowls shared by several people is common. Members usually eat in shifts, with separate tables for the men and women, who eat before the children and youth. Cleanup and visiting continues for several hours until horses and carriages are hitched up for the homeward journey.

The ritual meanings of the church service underscore the key values of Amish spirituality: Gelassenheit, humility, patience, and unity. Dress—especially on Sunday—signals obedience to the collective order. Unison singing unites the congregation in one voice. Kneeling on wood or cement floors shows humility before God. And the fellowship following the service underlines the importance of supporting one other. Performing these rituals together, from the youngest child to the oldest minister, without any display of individual talents, performances, or preferences, minimizes social distinctions. The message is clear: bend to the community, respect the wisdom of the forebears, and hearken to the mysteries of divine providence.

Members' Meetings

At the close of some services, leaders convene a members' meeting to handle business or disciplinary matters. Children and nonmembers are excused from these meetings. Moderated by the bishop, members' meetings operate under two assumptions: that the spirit of Jesus is present and that the decisions are ratified in heaven (Matt. 18:18–20). The bishop may report on plans to raise funds to assist a family struggling with hardships or a large medical bill. If the cost exceeds the capacity of one district, adjoining ones may be asked to contribute. Apart from twice-a-year collections at communion, the deacon or other appointed men may visit each home to solicit voluntary contributions when special financial needs arise. Plans for collections, baptisms, ordinations, and other events are announced at the members' meeting.

Members' meetings also address violations of the Ordnung. These may involve confessions, sanctions, excommunication, or the restoration of repentant sinners.

If sin is confessed, the congregation pardons the penitent and offers forgiveness with God's blessing. In an Amish equivalent of "What happens in Vegas, stays in Vegas," a firm taboo on gossip surrounds members' meetings. Subsequent mention of who confessed what, along with any other tidbits from the meeting, is strictly forbidden. In fact, those who break confidence may find themselves called to confess at the next members' meeting.

Council Meeting

Prelude to Communion

The Amish do not observe Advent or Lent in their church calendar, but they do commemorate Good Friday, Easter, Easter Monday, and Pentecost as well as Whitmonday, Ascension Day, Christmas, and, in some groups, Old Christmas (also known as Three Kings Day or Epiphany). Communion, held twice a year, near Easter and again in October, is the highest moment in their church life.

It is hard to exaggerate the spiritual significance of communion in Amish life. Unlike most Protestant and Catholic observances, which focus on an individual's personal relationship with God, the Amish observance has a communal dimension. For them, communion celebrates the unity of the Gmay as the people of God. Its lengthy prelude, stretching over five Sundays, stresses forgiveness and harmony within the church. The five-Sunday sequence begins with the New Birth Sunday, when the Scripture text is Jesus's discussion of the new birth with Nicodemus (John 3), followed by an off-Sunday, Council Meeting Sunday, another off-Sunday, and finally Holy Communion.

Council Meeting Sunday, which is held two weeks before communion, is known as *Ordnungs Gmay*. This church service, attended only by baptized members, is a time when individuals recommit themselves to upholding the church's guidelines. It is also a time to purge sins and to prepare the Gmay, the body of Christ, for communion. Members examine their lives, confess their faults, forgive others, and repair any breaches of love. Any serious friction, disagreement, or disobedience must be addressed in order to restore tranquility prior to the upcoming communion service. The quest for peace happens throughout the year, but Ordnungs Gmay sets a deadline that prevents discontent from festering on and on.

Requiring harmony before the communion service can proceed reveals a distinctive Amish belief: because communion is a celebration of unity, it would be sacrilegious for a fractured Gmay to engage in the ritual. In fact, if discord prevails, communion may be postponed for weeks or even months.[17] This practice diverges from that of most Christian churches, which rarely if ever postpone communion, since their understanding of the rite focuses on an *individual* transaction between God and the celebrant rather than on the unity of the group.

The Quest for Harmony

Council meetings can be weighty times if dissension is brewing. Troubles may arise from disobedience to scriptural teaching—dishonesty or adultery—or from violations of the Ordnung, such as owning a computer or wearing fashionable clothing. Other woes may revolve around interpersonal disputes among members. Whatever the source, the issues must be resolved before communion.

The cornerstone text for the council meeting is Matthew 18, in which Jesus asserts that only those who humble themselves like children can enter the kingdom of God. The text includes Jesus's admonition to forgive seventy times seven and concludes with a parable that warns that those unwilling to forgive will be punished. This chapter also prescribes a process for resolving interpersonal conflict: members should try to resolve their differences privately, but if that fails, the church must intervene. Those who stubbornly refuse the church's counsel will face excommunication. In Amish eyes, this text authorizes the church to make decisions with grave and eternal consequences. For example, the church will pardon sin if it is confessed to God and the church. This robust view of the church adds a dose of gravity to the Ordnungs Gmay.

In their council meeting sermons, preachers typically rehearse biblical stories, beginning with creation and noting the enmity between the brothers Cain and Abel, God's punishment of disobedience with a great flood, and Abraham's obedience in offering up Isaac as a sacrifice. In the words of a bishop's wife, the sermon is "filled with examples from the Bible. Abraham's devoted loyalty to God, Jacob's meek peacemaking spirit, Joseph's love for his unkind brothers . . . to show what is expected of a true upbuilding church member."[18]

A pivotal story is the defeat of Joshua's army by the people of Ai. Ministers remind the congregation that just as the Israelites' hidden plunder had to be confessed before Joshua's army could be victorious, so too must all hidden sin be brought to public confession. This story and others are used to underscore the reality that "any rebellion or disobedience can turn into a deadly sin," according to one member. Humility, confession, and unity are prominent themes throughout the service. One bishop, casting about for a metaphor that a tech-savvy outsider would understand, said, "The service is like a search engine, looking for sin and bringing forgiveness."

One of the *Ausbund* hymns sung at the Ordnungs Gmay includes these words:

> *You shall love your neighbor as yourself*
> *In joy and in sorrow.*
> *You shall not exercise yourself in sin,*
> *For it is now high time*
> *To begin doing what is right,*
> *To follow Christ Jesus*
> *And look at his example.*[19]

Affirming the Ordnung

Near the end of the council meeting, the bishop reviews the Ordnung by memory and highlights any recent concerns. One bishop reports that instead of going over all the rules on dress he simply says to the women, "You know better than I do what the church expects." He also admonishes congregants about any worrisome practices that he fears may lead them astray.

The service ends as each ordained leader says, from his seat, "I am in unity with the Ordnung, and if communion can be held, I wish to participate in my weakness. If I could be accepted, it would bring me deep joy. If I have offended anyone with words or deeds, I wish to be admonished about it in love, and would also hope to receive it in the same way, and make things right, with the Lord's help." Then each lay member is asked to give his or her verbal assent. According to one member, "Two of the ministers go around, one with the men and one with the women, and give each person opportunity to respond, '*Ich bin einig*' (I'm agreed)." Those who cannot affirm the Ordnung may need to explain their concern. Of course, the bishop and ministers hope to receive a unanimous affirmation.

Reflecting on a council meeting, one woman wrote, "Oh that God might grant us His strength and keep this body of Christian believers from falling away from His will." To prevent a fall, she pleaded, "We need patience and love and compassion for each other. We must treat the one beside us with respect, and watch over his soul with care. . . . Above all, we must be a good example to others."[20] The biannual council meetings not only clarify the moral boundaries of Amish society, but they often ease conflict, promote compliance, and enhance harmony.

The preparation for communion concludes with a day of fasting (*Fastdag*).[21] In some settlements, Fastdag falls on Good Friday in the spring and on October 11, Saint Michael's Day, in the fall.[22] Other communities observe Fastdag on the Sunday between council meeting and communion. Special prayers in *Die Ernsthafte Christenpflicht* help church members prepare for the fast, which one woman described as "going without food in order to spend time in prayer." She added, "Fasting . . . gives us time to pray, teaches us self-discipline, reminds us we can live with a lot less, and helps us appreciate God's gifts."[23] In reality, the fast usually covers only breakfast, or as one member said, "Not eating or drinking between midnight and noon the next day."

Communion

The communion service is called *Gross Gmay*, literally "big church." Despite its somber tone, it is a celebration of unity. The service begins on Sunday morning and continues into the afternoon—in some congregations until as late as 4:00 p.m.—without a formal break. After the singing but before the first sermon, members again pledge their commitment to unity and desire for communion. Following the bishop's lead, each minister and then each member reaffirms his or her peace with God and the Gmay.

During the lunch hour, people quietly leave the assembly in shifts to eat in an adjoining room while the service continues. Some ministers time their sermons so that they are speaking of Christ's crucifixion around 3:00 p.m., the supposed time of Christ's death. The service peaks as the minister retells the suffering of Christ, and the members share the bread and wine.

The bishop breaks apart a loaf of bread and moves through the assembly, row by row, giving a piece to each member, first on the men's side and then on the women's. Then, as the single cup of wine is passed, each member drinks from it. The home-made bread and wine symbolize Christ's body and blood, broken and shed for the sins of the world. When speaking of the bread and wine, the bishop stresses that many grains are ground to become a loaf of bread and many grapes are squeezed to make wine. Members are reminded that "if one grain remains unbroken and whole, it can have no part in the whole . . . if one single berry remains whole; it has no share in the whole . . . and no fellowship with the rest."[24] These metaphors underscore the importance of surrendering one's individual will for unity in the whole body.

The words of a communion hymn summarize the sentiment of the day:

> *Without a doubt this pleases God well,*
> *Where men keep peace, love, and unity.*
> *In that place the Lord kindly gives*
> *Life and blessing forever.*[25]

Three rituals close the Gross Gmay: footwashing, the holy kiss, and almsgiving. The practice of footwashing demonstrates the importance of servanthood and emulates Jesus's washing of the feet of his disciples at the Last Supper: "If I then, your Lord and Master, have washed your feet; ye also ought to wash one another's feet. For I have given you an example, that ye should do as I have done to you" (John 13:14–15). The Dordrecht Confession commends footwashing as a sign of true humility and lowliness. As the congregation sings, members, segregated by sex and arranged in pairs, wash and dry each other's feet, using towels and tubs of warm water that have been placed in the assembly area. One member explained, "You pour water from your cupped hands over each foot three times to signify the Trinity." As a sign of humility, some members stoop rather than kneel to wash one another's feet.[26]

Following the footwashing, the pair offers each other a "holy kiss" and a blessing.

The older person says, "The Lord be with us," and the younger replies, "Amen to peace" (referring to peace with God and the members of the Gmay). The "kiss of peace," mentioned five times in the New Testament, is a fitting capstone for the five-week spiritual journey on which congregations embark twice a year.[27] Having purged sin, reaffirmed the moral order, and renewed their commitment to God and one another, members are rejuvenated for another six months of life together.

Finally, as they leave the meeting area at the conclusion of the Gross Gmay, members place an offering in an alms box or give it to the deacon, who deposits it in an alms account. This is the only time that an offering is collected as part of a church service.[28] As noted earlier, funds for various community needs are collected throughout the year by visits to individual households or in response to public announcements.

Ordination

A Quick Calling

Ordinations, which involve the selection, or "making," of deacons and ministers, usually occur in the late afternoon at the close of a communion service. Ordination is a corporate moment of submission in Amish life, as members of the Gmay yield to God's divine choice. The ninety-minute ritual overflows with suspense because the Amish believe that the holy hand of heaven reaches into the home or barn where the congregation is gathered to select a new shepherd for the flock. No other ritual approaches the emotion-packed experience of ordination, for the new leader will influence the decisions and direction of the group for years, if not decades. The new shepherd will shoulder heavy responsibilities on top of his everyday work. Along with his spouse and children, he will be expected to comply more fully with the Ordnung and to live an exemplary life.

The rite of ordination poignantly demonstrates the Amish view of lay leadership. In many Christian churches, an individual may sense a personal calling for ministry and pursue education to prepare for it. Among the Amish, however, a person never seeks ordination; in fact, doing so would be viewed as vain and would disqualify the person by default. "The calling comes through the church, not the individual," says one writer.[29]

Any member may nominate a candidate, but the Amish believe that God makes the final selection through a procedure of drawing lots (sometimes called casting lots), the same method used in the earliest days of the Christian church (Acts 1:24–26). The voice of the church and God's selection is "far greater authority than something as fickle and unreliable as the feelings of any individual, much less the individual involved," Amish leaders say. Individual initiative has no place in this process. The individual's "part is to submit, to accept, and to humbly bow to the will of God as revealed through the church."[30]

Ordination is remarkably similar across affiliations.[31] Preparation begins when a leadership vacancy arises because of death, disabling illness, or the formation of a new district. Specific plans are announced in advance, and a vote to proceed is taken at the council meeting two weeks prior to the actual ordination. Leaders generally move forward only if the vote is unanimous.

Who Will Be the One?

Both men and women nominate candidates, but only married men are eligible to be candidates—or as the Amish say, "to be in the lot." At baptism, young men pledge to serve in leadership if called by the church. The two weeks leading up to the ordination are a time of soul-searching, anxiety, and contemplation. Members pray for God's guidance as they consider whom to nominate, and eligible men and their families wonder if they will be nominated and how their lives will be changed if they should be ordained. One minister confided that in the week before his ordination he did the math and reckoned there were fifteen eligible men in his district. With "an average of five or six in the lot, I figured I had one in three chances of landing in it," he concluded.

After this lengthy period of preparation, the actual ritual of ordination is remarkably swift. At the end of the daylong communion service, the presiding leaders go to a private room to receive the nominations.[32] Baptized members file past the door, which is slightly ajar, and whisper the name of a candidate. The number of nominations required for candidacy is two or three, depending on local tradition. One man in the lot may have received only two votes, while another may have received a dozen. The size of the candidate pool typically ranges from four to eight. In a survey of 172 ordinations in the Arthur, Illinois, settlement, the largest number of candidates in any lot was twelve. Although most nominees were between ages thirty and forty-five, one man was ordained at age twenty-two and one was chosen when he was fifty-one.[33]

Having tallied the votes and determined the number of candidates, the leaders then prepare a set of *Ausbunds* equal to the number of candidates. Inside the front cover of one book, they place a slip of paper containing a Bible verse (often Acts 1:24 or Proverbs 16:33) and then bind each book with string or a rubber band. The books are shuffled, then brought into the assembled congregation and placed on a table or a bench. All this time, the congregation has been waiting patiently in silent anticipation.

The presiding bishop announces the candidates and asks them to come forward to the table, where they are asked to affirm the foundational beliefs (*Grundsatzen*) of the church. Then the congregation kneels in silent prayer, yielding itself and its corporate future into God's hands. When they arise from prayer, the bishop invites the candidates, in no particular order, to select one of the hymnbooks. After each one has selected an *Ausbund*, the bishop proceeds to open each book, moving from candidate to candidate, with all eyes watching, until the fateful slip of paper appears. At that moment the suspense breaks.

Having located the slip of paper, the bishop announces the chosen man's name and invites him to rise. The bishop reiterates the new shepherd's duties, admonishes him to be faithful to his new calling, and then greets him with a handshake and a holy kiss.[34] After this official rite of ordination, other ministers and fellow nominees follow with their greetings and handshakes as well. The presiding bishop's wife and the wives of other ministers greet the man's spouse in a similar fashion.

News of the divine selection slowly begins to sink into reality. In virtually every case, the man and his spouse and children—having learned only a few minutes earlier that he was even a candidate—are overcome with emotion, as are those who were so narrowly missed by the hand of God. Quiet sobs of surprise and tearful emotion break the silence. "It's a weighty time," says a man who was in the lot three times. "There are no congratulations; it's not a 'Hurray!' type of thing." Asked to describe what it was like when her husband was chosen by lot, the wife of one minister could only say, "It was a very quiet ride home in the buggy that day." A minister who was in the lot for bishop but not selected said, "I dodged a bullet that day."

The speed with which the ordination process occurs is stunning. There is no training, preparation, emotional warm-up, or door of escape. There is also no celebration, only tears, silence, and heartfelt promises of prayer and support. The ninety-minute event transforms the life of the newly ordained man and his family. Clergy receive no compensation for their work apart from occasional gifts. They serve for life unless debilitating illness intervenes or they are silenced for disobedience or moral turpitude. They receive no formal education, and their on-the-job training consists mostly of advice from mentors and personal study. For the most part, Amish leaders earn the blessing and trust of their congregants as they carry out the duties of their role.

Accountability and Discipline

Confession

Like other people, the Amish forget, rebel, fall short, and, for a variety of reasons, stray from their commitments. The rite of confession addresses deviance and restores backsliders to full fellowship. Minor transgressions are handled privately, but serious infractions require a public confession before the Gmay. These can be cathartic moments when, the Amish believe, the power of the corporate church combines with divine presence to forgive and to purge the cancerous growth of sin.

Public confessions occur during members' meetings or council meetings. The procedure varies somewhat by affiliation, the local ethos, and the particulars of each case.[35] In some cases, leaders, offenders, and members have informal discussions about possible atonement and consequences prior to a formal meeting. Transgressions against the moral order (biblical teaching or the Ordnung) are redeemed either by a "freewill" confession initiated by the offender or by a confession requested by church leaders. Calibrated for the circumstances and severity of the offense, confession may take several forms: private or public, either seated or, for the most serious offenses, kneeling.

In a freewill confession, a member voluntarily reports a *Fehla*, or failure, to a minister. The infraction might be a biblical sin—for example, fornication, dishonesty, filing a lawsuit—or a violation of the Ordnung, such as owning banned technology, gambling on horse races, or appearing on television. One man agreed to speak on camera in a Swiss television documentary, thinking it would only be aired in Europe. After learning that the program would also air in his local area, he said, "I went running to my bishop to confess the moment I heard it was going to be shown on PBS." When a wayward member confesses a failure to a church leader, the minister may offer loving counsel and close the issue in private. In more serious cases, the leader may require the offender to make a public confession to the Gmay. Freewill confessions are the least complicated because the wayward person is penitent and cooperative.

Relationships become more strained, however, when violators do not take the initiative to confess. Sometimes ordained leaders become aware of a transgression through personal observation or reports from other members. Following the guidelines of Matthew 18, the bishop typically asks the deacon and a minister to visit the offender privately. If the offense is a minor one that has drawn little attention, and if the member is contrite when confronted, the issue may be resolved privately.

Serious matters that draw public attention typically require a sitting or kneeling confession in the presence of the congregation. In the case of a sitting confession, the bishop explains what happened as the offender remains seated. The offender then responds, "I want to confess that I have failed. I want to make peace and continue in patience with God and the church and in the future to take better care."

For the most serious offenses, the bishop asks the wayward member to come forward and kneel near the ministers in the midst of the congregation. The bishop then may present a remedy agreed upon in advance, or he may ask questions about the offense and whether the offender is sorry and willing to change. He may also give the offender time to explain his or her side of the story. After answering questions or offering explanations or both, the person leaves the room and the bishop presents the

Gmay with a remedy endorsed by the ministers. A vote is taken to see if the members support the proposed remedy.

Excommunication

If the congregation affirms the proposed action, the offender is invited back to the meeting and asked, "Are you willing to take on the discipline of the church?" Depending on the circumstances, the person is then either reinstated or informed that he or she will be excommunicated for two to six weeks. Both temporary and permanent excommunications are known as the *Bann* ("ban" in English). As a sign of remorse, some members volunteer to be placed in the ban. Penitent offenders are eventually restored to fellowship.[36]

Offenders under a temporary ban attend church services and meet with the ministers for admonition during the Abrot at the beginning of worship. When they return to the service, they sit near the ministers in the center of the meeting area. As a sign of sorrow, they sit bent over, with a hand covering their face during the opening sermon. They usually do not participate in the noon meal following the worship service. This short-term exile allows persons under a temporary ban time to reflect on the seriousness of their transgression. Other members may visit them during this time to show their support and encouragement.

At the end of the temporary ban, offenders are invited to make a kneeling confession in a members' meeting, and they are asked several questions: Do you believe the punishment was deserved? Do you sincerely ask patience from God and the church? Finally, do you promise to live more carefully with the Lord's help as you promised at baptism?[37] Sins that are confessed to the church are pardoned and are believed to be erased in the name of God. Those who acknowledge their sin and promise to cooperate with the church are reinstated. The bishop offers them his hand as a sign of their restored fellowship, raises them up from their knees, and gives them a kiss of peace. (In the case of women, the bishop's wife gives the kiss.) The meeting, which concludes with some fitting words of comfort, can be a moment of catharsis and healing in the life of the church.

One young couple, married for several years, asked to be placed in the ban because of guilt about their premarital behavior. Another member described the experience this way: "They asked to be expelled, and so there was this six-week period of repentance. When they were reinstated . . . everybody felt that this couple really wanted to . . . let the church know that they were sorry for what they had done and wanted to lead a better life. Everybody felt so good about it. It was really a healthy thing for the church. It was really a good feeling."

Church leaders confide that stubbornness or rebellious attitudes are more often the cause for discipline than transgression of a rule. For the headstrong who will not submit to the church, the temporary excommunication may lead to full excommunication. Errant members are invited to come to church. "But if they don't come," explains a member, "then the church, you might say, 'subpoenas' them; they must be there in two weeks, and if they don't come then they lose their membership." This places the burden of responsibility on the offender. Wayward souls who are unwilling to confess their transgressions or who deliberately leave the church are excommunicated.

Membership is terminated by a vote (*Rat*) of the congregation. The bishop says, "In the name of the Lord and the church, peace and fellowship was extended to you and also in the name of the Lord and the church, it is now renounced." In most cases, unrepentant ex-members remain in the ban for the rest of their lives and may be subject as well to *Meidung*, or shunning, which we explain in chapter 10. Those who later confess their transgression can be restored to full membership. Although few former members return to the fold, some have been reinstated even after twenty or more years in exile.

Forgiveness and Restoration

Leaders have considerable freedom to improvise with most disciplinary cases. They seek solutions that maintain harmony and preserve the integrity of the Ordnung as well as the authority of leadership. Bishops frequently remind the Gmay that an honorable outcome requires humility, respect, and submission by everyone.

Offenders who are contrite are quickly forgiven and reinstated into the fellowship. The obstinate who challenge the authority of leaders, however, will feel the harsh judgment of the church. A petty, tit-for-tat syndrome sometimes sours the confessional process. In one case, a member pressed for action against a bishop's son who was attending movies and flaunting his car. In due time, the bishop brought revenge by threatening to excommunicate the member for installing a telephone in his barn. The spirit of the process depends on the leadership style of the bishop and the attitude of the out-of-order member.

In general, older bishops counsel leaders to "work with your people" through gentle persuasion. At their ordination, ministers are admonished to handle problems with love and kindness. This discipline process usually involves gradual discernment unless a member deliberately wants to leave the church and, for example, abruptly buys a car, stops attending services, or files for divorce. Such actions will, of course, accelerate the separation process.

Confession in front of the gathered body ritualizes the value of obedience and submission to God and the Gmay. It subverts individualism and heralds the virtues of Gelassenheit. This ritual's cathartic value is that it offers healing, spiritual reunion, and a oneness with the community and the divine that transcends the self. This church-based system of justice restores repentant offenders and offers a healthy process for healing. These rituals, however, are often not adequate to address addictive behaviors tied to alcohol, sex, or domestic abuse. Offenders with serious psychological disorders may sincerely confess again and again to behaviors that the church is not equipped to handle. When this happens, leaders or Amish friends may encourage the offender to find professional treatment, or outside authorities may intervene with results that are disruptive to the community and painful to all involved.[38]

These rituals of worship, ordination, and discipline have successfully withstood the changes and innovations that transformed the larger Christian world in the twentieth and twenty-first centuries. In short, these religious rites show little if any accommodation to or acceptance of outside cultural influences. Such practices, invisible to the public eye, comprise the heart of Amish spirituality as divine presence touches earth, binding decisions are ratified in heaven, the penitent confess on bended knees, and the congregation sings ancient songs of praise.

CHAPTER 6

THE AMISH WAY

In the summer of 2010, an Amish community in Ohio was shocked to learn that Monroe Beachy, an Amish investment manager, had filed for bankruptcy after losing $17 million placed in his confidence by some 2,700 investors, most of whom were Amish. Upset that he had violated church teaching by filing for bankruptcy, Amish investors proposed to the U.S. Bankruptcy Court an alternative church plan to repay creditors. In their plea to the court to dismiss the bankruptcy claim, Amish leaders explained their rationale: "As a Plain Community we have historically believed that the Bible teaches we are strangers and pilgrims upon the earth (Hebrews 11:13-14), and to treat our fellowmen with integrity and respect. We file no claims in court. We are responsible to pay our debts. We purpose to live peaceably with all men, which extends to every aspect of our lives, even into our business life. . . . We will do all in our power to collectively pay this debt rather than file bankruptcy."

A Deep Taproot

The Amish response to Beachy's bankruptcy claim represents an unusual twist in the story of investment fund failures, which usually end with irate investors scrambling to get the highest possible fraction of the reorganized assets. Instead, the Amish plan aimed to distribute the remaining funds based on biblical principles of care for the poor and needy, and it viewed investors as members of a community rather than individuals seeking amends. The plan reveals a distinctive culture, the values of which may appear inscrutable to those outside it. Speaking with us about the distinctive features of Amish life, the owner of a farm equipment company said, "You guys probably call it culture, but I just call it 'the Amish way.'"

Every society has its own way—its particular set of values and practices that shape how people perceive and go about life. Humans are both the producers and the products of culture. We construct and reproduce our way of life, our customs and values; and the culture we create, in turn, shapes our understanding of our social and physical environment.[1]

Gelassenheit is the deep taproot that nourishes the Amish way. A German word that resists easy translation, it roughly means "calmness, acceptance, and yieldedness."[2] In everyday conversation, Amish people more often use a different expression. "We say *geh lessa* all the time," explains one father. "It means to let go, quit trying to figure it out, let it alone." In brief, Gelassenheit is the Amish version of "let it be": stop trying to change things and accept life for what it is. This master disposition, deeply bred into the Amish soul, governs perceptions, emotions, behavior, organizational structure, and even aspects of architecture.[3] Gelassenheit is the seed from which the other cultural values that we examine in this chapter—obedience, humility, plainness, and joy in everyday routines—grow.

As we noted in chapter 4, in the spiritual realm Gelassenheit signals yieldedness to God's will. Paul Kline, a deacon and retired lumberyard owner, summarizes the sweeping implications of Gelassenheit this way:[4]

- Yieldedness, resignation, inner surrender, obedience, and overcoming selfishness;
- Willingness to reject force and manipulation, to suffer, to surrender self-will and arrogant self-assertiveness;
- Expressing humility, plain dress, a plain lifestyle, and obedience to the *Ordnung*.

In practical terms, the submissive posture of Gelassenheit discourages higher education, abstract thinking, competition, and scientific pursuits. The yielded person submits to the authority of God-ordained leaders, respects the wisdom of tradition, and washes the feet of others in a sacred rite of humility.

Although self-surrender seems repressive to modern people, the Amish believe that those who forego personal advancement for the sake of family and community make a redemptive sacrifice that honors God and transforms the church into the body of Christ. "The yielding and submitting is at the core of our faith and relationship with God," said one member.

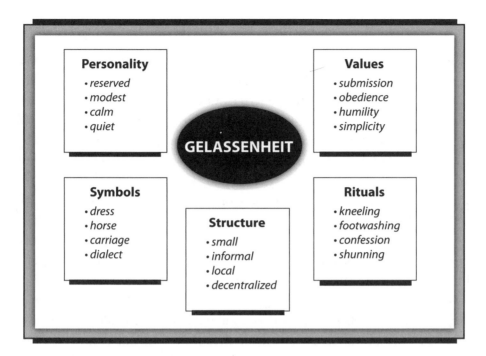

FIGURE 6.1. Five Dimensions of Gelassenheit

Etched into Amish consciousness, Gelassenheit penetrates Amish life from body language to social organization, from personal speech to ethnic symbolism, as shown in figure 6.1. How one smiles, laughs, shakes hands, removes one's hat, and drives one's horse signal Gelassenheit or its absence. A boisterous laugh and a quick retort betray a cocky spirit. Personal features on public display—a dress that is too bright or too short, a hat with a turned-up brim, stockings in a too-thin material, prayer caps loosely tied or even untied, sleeves rolled up—can signal a celebration of the individual spirit rather than a yielding to the community. An aggressive handshake and a curt greeting disclose an assertive self that does not befit Gelassenheit. Rather, a gentle chuckle or hesitation before a response embodies a spirit of humility. Likewise, a slow and thoughtful answer, deference to another's idea, and simple silence are signs of the Amish way.

Gelassenheit transforms personal interests and individual energies into cultural capital that benefits the entire church-community. The cultural grammar of Gelassenheit blends submission to God's will, personal meekness, and small-scale organization. The meek spirit of Gelassenheit unfolds as individuals yield to higher authorities: the will of God, church, elders, parents, community, and tradition.

Taming the Big "I"

Gelassenheit stands in sharp contrast to the bold, assertive individualism of mainstream culture. This core value of the Amish way collides with modernity's penchant for individual achievement. While modern culture cultivates self-determination and personal fulfillment, Gelassenheit breeds a subdued person who discovers fulfillment in the service of community. But rather than pitting the individual against the community, the Amish see the primary opposition as between two social systems: the church, which calls for self-denial, and the world, which exalts the individual.

In a collective society, maintaining harmony and cooperation requires the taming of egos. In an essay entitled "The Big 'I,'" an Amish author insists that "today everyone chooses the lifestyle which best suits his own tastes, and it's no one else's business. Rather, the idea is to live and let live. You let me go and I'll let you go, [and it] brings the opposite of true submission, it brings rebellion, greed, and pride."[5]

Two Pennsylvania Dutch words, *uffgewwe* (to give up) and *unnergewwe* (to give under), capture the relationship between individuals and community. Adults are asked to "give up" things and to "give themselves under" the authority of the church. One member explained, "To give yourself under the church means to yield, to submit." Baptismal candidates sit in a bent posture with their hands covering their faces, signifying their willingness to "give up" self-will and to "give themselves under" the authority of the church. One member, writing to a person facing excommunication, said, "My heart just bleeds for you, all cause you cannot *give yourself up* to church rules and those set above you in the church by God."[6]

For the Amish, self-denial means "sacrificing our own selfish interests and desires in our service to God."[7] One leader writes, "We are part of a group, and as such we must be willing sometimes to make personal sacrifices in order to serve the overall benefit of the group." Regulations may not always seem fair for everyone, he notes, "but that is the price we pay for the privilege of living in a disciplined church . . . a small price indeed."[8]

It would be easy to conclude that losing one's self in Amish society is demeaning or dehumanizing. But bending to the call of community does not necessarily smother individual expression. Within cultural boundaries, creative self-expression flourishes—from quilting patterns and embroidered handkerchiefs to colorful stickers on children's lunch pails, from gardening to hobbies, from farming to crafts. As in other societies, Amish personality styles, preferences, and habits vary. An Amish father explained it this way: "The idea that Amish people give up freedom of choice and let the community make them all the same is a myth. Granted, Amish life has a strong communal dimension, but this doesn't mean individuality necessarily withers away for us. All it means is that we have another source of social strength and collective wisdom to help make choices for the betterment of all and ultimately for the good of self."[9]

He then offered examples of choices he had made that were not dictated by the church. "Choice of jobs is something we make from time to time. When I made the choice to go ask Sweet Nancy for a date and she said yes, we made a consequential and very rewarding choice, for it led to the choice of marriage and beginning a family—something I would not trade for any amount of wealth or status. Buying a home was a major choice. How big, how many acres, what price range? Do we buy acreage and build, or do we buy an existing house? Do we buy at public auction or private? And so on. I could go on and on about a myriad of banal choices we make on a daily basis, like Pepsi or Coke, vanilla or butter pecan, boxers or briefs. You get the idea."

Similar to the ways in which Amish think about the dialectic of self and community, paired oppositions—obedience and disobedience, humility and pride, plainness and luxury, work and idleness—also structure meaning in Amish consciousness. These polarities permeate the training of children, relationships in the community, and interactions with the outside world.

Obedience

Early childhood socialization is crucial to acquire the habits of obedience. Children learn to "give up" and "give in" at an early age. Parents teach uffgewwe, giving up, as they hold a toddler's hands together for prayer before meals to prevent the child from reaching for food.[10] The large size of families teaches young children to wait their turn every day as they yield to siblings—whether sharing toys, bedrooms, or food—and prepares them for living in community. One Amish saying is "The most decent person gives up first." So it is not surprising that Amish children are less likely to use first-person singular pronouns—I, me, mine, myself, my—than non-Amish children.[11]

Parents emphasize the importance of discipline (*die Zucht*) for a child. Incorporating obedience into daily routines makes it a taken-for-granted habit that becomes a powerful means of social control. Children are taught from the Bible: "Obey your parents in the Lord for this is right."[12] "By the time that the child reaches the age of three, the mold has started to form and it is the parents' duty to form it in the way the child should go," a leader noted. "When the child is old enough to stiffen its back and throw back its head in temper, it is old enough to be disciplined in a way that gently breaks that temper." Said one young mother, "Spanking is a given. We start at about a year and a half, and the majority of it is done before they turn five."[13] And a

An Amish brother and sister run an errand for their parents. Children learn the
Amish values of humility and simplicity at an early age. They also learn hard work
and responsibility. Some traditional groups consider ponies to be unnecessary
hobby animals and prohibit them. *Doyle Yoder*

grandfather observed, "The children of parents who teach obedience are much more
likely to remain in the church."

Members are expected to accept church decisions. Spouses typically discuss issues together, but a wife is expected to yield to her husband if they come to an impasse. Ministers defer to bishops and younger bishops to those with seniority. And
even older bishops must yield to the counsel of their peers and the authority of Scripture and tradition, or they may be removed from office.

These rites of surrender are sacrifices for the larger goal of an orderly and unified
community. But while obedience is expected, it is usually couched in a spirit of loving concern throughout the entire social system. Parents are not to discipline children in anger. Only with the congregation's support may a bishop excommunicate
a member in "hopes of winning him back." Calls to obey typically echo concern for
someone's eternal destiny.

Humility

Stooping Low

Humility is one sign of Gelassenheit. "If other people praise you . . . , humble yourself," the Amish learn. "But do not praise yourself, for that is the way of fools who seek vain glory. . . . In suffering be patient, and silence your heart under the mighty hand of God."[14] Amish people frequently cite 1 Peter 5:5: "Yea, all of you be subject one to another, and be clothed with humility: for God resisteth the proud, and giveth grace to the humble." They often point to Jesus, the meek servant, as the model of humility. Pride and humility (*Hochmut* and *Demut*) frame Amish consciousness and articulate the battle line between self-interest and community well-being.[15]

Pride is a religious label for the sinister side of individualism, which the Bible condemns in verses suggesting that God "hates a proud look" (Prov. 6:17) and "resisteth the proud but giveth grace unto the humble" (James 4:6).[16] One Amish publication says it starkly: "Pride . . . seeks the exaltation of the self."[17] The devotional text "Rules of a Godly Life" declares, "No sin [in Scripture] was punished more severely than pride. It changed angels into devils."[18]

One member, writing to another facing censure by the church, pleaded, "Humble yourself and stoop low enough so that you can forgive others. . . . And make peace with the church."[19] High-mindedness is equated with arrogance and worldliness, whereas lowliness reflects humility and weakness—the true spirit of Gelassenheit. Thus, "high" church districts are ones that are higher on a ladder reaching toward the proud outside culture. By contrast, "lower" *Gmays* are plainer ones that hold tighter to tradition.

The presentation of the self is particularly vulnerable to pride, the Amish believe. In an essay entitled "A Proud Look," one bishop wrote, "As the subtle spirit of pride influences people, the pleats are made more figure-flattering, the dresses are shorter, tighter, and lighter. The stockings are more sheer and the shoes more fashionable and less practical."[20] Because the size and prominence of mirrors in a society signal the cultural value attached to the self and appearance, it is not surprising that the mirrors in Amish homes are typically smaller and fewer than those in non-Amish homes and in lower groups are often hidden away in bureau drawers.[21]

Modern society provides a full repertoire of props for making up and presenting a unique self for every occasion. "The primacy of bodily image is the very emblem of postmodern individualism," argues one social analyst.[22] Tattoos, hairstyles, clothing, jewelry, cosmetics, and suntans enable individuals to package and present themselves in unique ways that clamor for attention. Because such self-exaltation defies the Amish way, all cosmetic props are considered signs of pride. Jewelry (including wedding rings and wristwatches) is taboo. Any form of hair styling, fashionable clothing, neon color, or print fabric is also off-limits. Makeup is proscribed, even for the deceased in the casket.

Off Camera

Pride has many faces. The well-known Amish aversion to personal photographs is legitimated by the second of the Bible's Ten Commandments: "Thou shalt not make unto thee any graven image, or any *likeness* of any thing . . ." (Exod. 20:4).[23] In the middle of the nineteenth century, when photography was becoming popular, the Amish applied this biblical injunction against likenesses to photographs of individuals. Discussions of photography surfaced five times in the Amish ministers' meetings held from 1862 to 1878, and attendees agreed that portraits encouraged self-adulation, the exact opposite of self-denial.[24] An 1865 Ohio Ordnung advised members not to "carry hidden photographs made into likeness of men or to hang them on the walls in the house to be seen."[25] A late twentieth-century Daviess County, Indiana, regulation says simply, "No photographs." Grounded in religious objection, the prohibition discourages pride because posing for a photograph is considered self-exalting. In most Amish communities, members who readily pose for photos or face television cameras will be censured by the church.

There is also a deeper cultural meaning beneath this restriction. Photography de-contextualizes; it extracts people from their social context. Moreover, photographic images become objects for study, making the self an object for reflection, which encourages a rational, analytical mindset. In the 1860s, one minister noted that people were tempted to "send their pictures around." Portrait photographs not only challenge the virtue of humility but also disturb the thick social context of Amish life.[26]

If photographs of Amish people are forbidden, why do so many circulate? Media photographs are often snapped with telephoto lenses and without permission. Some Amish permit outsiders to take pictures of farming, business operations, gardens, and home furnishings but not of people, especially not ones in which individual people can be identified. The moral line, for many, is the direct face-on shot, especially if the subject appears to be posing. If someone is photographed from a distance without their consent, the moral burden falls on the photographer, the Amish reason. Some more progressive Amish parents may allow pictures of their children who are not baptized church members. Similarly, unbaptized teens may be more willing to pose, and some might even own cameras until they join the church.

Plainness

Simplicity

The lowly spirit of Gelassenheit denies worldly pleasures and costly entertainment. Purging selfish desires means yielding to the plain standards of Amish dress and accepting restrictions on transportation, technology, and home appliances. When things become too convenient, they border on luxury. In the Amish economy, rags are recycled into carpets, clothing is patched rather than discarded, and toys are passed down to younger children. The exaltation of thrift rests on the belief that the habit of austerity—developed over the decades—produces a wholesome life by stifling vanity and discouraging waste.

"Our Master [Jesus] instructed us to despise things of this world and not permit them to sidetrack us or weigh us down in our journey toward eternity," explains one Amish man. "If we planned to stay here, then it would make sense to accumulate and enjoy all the earthly comforts," but "it just makes sense to travel lightly," since heaven is our destination.[27] An elderly leader writes, "We should not be looking to and depending on the scientists all around us who are still promoting the unproven assumption that BIGGER IS BETTER. This is a mistaken idea. Our goal is to make use of the simple ways of living and retain the faith of our forefathers as handed down to us from the generations who have gone before us! It is entirely in vain to depend on the morals of the world today to take us the route we want to go."[28]

"How can we instill in our children the value of plain life?" one mother asks. "Pray for our children, consistently practice simple living in our homes. Unless we are truly humble, we are not truly plain. We must be willing to be something less than our neighbor across the road. . . . Eventually our children will see that the luxuries and complexities of the world are a hindrance to our faith." Simplicity is "not the key to eternal life, yet we feel plainness is necessary fruit—evidence that we have set our affection on things eternal."[29] She concludes by offering these guidelines to teach children simplicity:

- Keep toys few and simple.
- Dress and name dolls plainly.
- Teach basic, practical sewing skills rather than embroidery and painting.
- Make new out of old, such as hooking, braiding, and sewing rugs.
- Teach that modest clothing is a safeguard in an evil world.
- Encourage them to wear the hidden ornament of a meek and quiet spirit.
- Eat plainly, using homegrown foods rather than luxury or snack foods.
- Remind children "that the trend toward what is bigger, fancier, and more expensive leads rapidly in one direction—away from God."

This modest home in Ethridge, Tennessee, is owned by members of the ultratraditional Joe Troyer Swartzentruber Amish. *Ordnung*, family wealth, and regional economy may influence the architecture, appearance, and plainness of a house. *Erik Wesner*

Frugality

The Amish are consumers, but not conspicuous ones. They are concerned more about usefulness than show, practicality than display, saving than spending. These habits of frugality are rooted in old agrarian traditions as well as in explicit religious values.[30] One expression of thrift is a strong ethic of saving money. In a booklet about "principles for everyday living," a business leader underscores saving as a "spiritual principle for everyday practice" and advises, "Save all that you can. . . . It's not what you earn, but what you save and give that counts . . . every dollar which has been saved will come in handy . . . nobody ever went broke saving money."[31]

One father explained how he teaches his children to save: "When we attend a social function or community event such as an auction or local farm show, or before we take a trip—say, to Washington, D.C.—I hand my children a twenty-dollar bill and tell them, 'This is your allowance for any extra food or souvenirs you want to buy.' Anything they don't spend they are allowed to put in their piggy bank for savings."[32] In many communities, children under the age of twenty-one turn their earnings over to their parents but may keep any "tips" for themselves. One eight-year-old

Amish girl helped her aunts with their summer produce stand and was pleased to have nearly ten dollars in tips by the end of August, although she had no plans to spend the money.

Amish people save money in traditional ways, including savings accounts, certificates of deposit, real estate, and, among some groups, mutual funds. Some Amish communities operate modest savings and loan funds to encourage saving. Instead of banking funds for college, young adults save to buy a home or begin a business. One young adult earned $24,000 a year, saved half of it, and soon bought a small house with almost no mortgage. Another had saved $200,000 by the time he was twenty-eight to invest in a farm.

Amish frugality may seem paradoxical since the impulse to save could border on self-reliance, which counters communal values and dependency on the church. In fact, saving and frugality often have collective expressions, whether that be avoiding purchases or entertainment because of church rules, borrowing money from an Amish-managed mortgage fund, or joining with other households to buy in bulk. A striking example of such thrift is the dozens of Amish-run bulk-food stores and "bent

This professionally landscaped and well-appointed Amish home near Lancaster, Pennsylvania, is similar to nearby English homes. The definition of plainness and simplicity varies widely by settlement and group affiliation. *Daniel Rodriguez*

and dent" stores that market unsold food and dry goods from major chain stores. Open to the public, these retail stores cater to Amish and English customers alike.

Telling the Truth

Integrity is an outgrowth of plainness, a cultural coin with two sides: honesty and trust. Based on Jesus's teaching "Let your yea be yea and your nay be nay" (Matt. 5:37), Amish people believe that truthfulness reflects godliness and lying is a sin. Children are promptly punished for lying. Honesty is so deeply bred into Amish culture that it creates complications for defense attorneys with Amish clients. Rather than accept the assumption of "innocent until proven guilty," most Amish offenders readily admit guilt in court for the sake of a clear conscience. Others refuse to say "with absolute certainty" that particular events or stories are true, because they believe that only God is all-knowing and humans are prone to mistakes—a belief that also proves difficult for the legal system to accept.

For example, when a member of the conservative Andy Weaver affiliation was attacked by a burglar, he told police that, when the intruder had attempted to strangle him, he had gotten a good look at his face. The home invader was convicted and sent to prison, where he died. In response to a lawsuit filed by the convict's family after his death, a reporter contacted the Amish man and asked if he were "absolutely certain" about his testimony. The Amish man replied that, no, he could never be certain; only God could be certain. Not surprisingly, the news report provoked a storm of public criticism of the Amish. Writing about the event later, the Amish man noted, "Once I became aware of the consequence of that answer, I wrote and explained the reason to the newspaper office and the prosecutor. I think that helped settle the issue."[33]

The Amish consider transparency in financial matters to be an expression of integrity. In their oral culture, deals are sealed with a handshake and grounded in trust rather than in legal documents. Attorneys and contracts are used for real estate transactions and major business agreements; nonetheless, a handshake and a verbal promise still certify many transactions. Apart from trust's moral value, social theorists note that high-trust societies function efficiently because they can conduct business more quickly and inexpensively and with fewer legal and contractual fetters.

At some charity auctions organized by Amish auctioneers and attended by both Amish and outsiders, sale managers do not require bidders to register, provide identification, or even pay a financial clerk for products they purchase. Instead, auction-goers receive a pencil and paper and are instructed to record their own purchases, add their total charges at the end of the auction, and then deposit a check or cash in "donation boxes" placed throughout the auction area.[34]

Concern for honesty is also at the root of Amish resistance to bankruptcy. The

Amish view bankruptcy not only as a financial failure but also as a moral affront, because creditors might not be repaid in full. In the words of an Amish statement, "Bankruptcy is morally abhorrent and is not consistent with the values we hold regarding honesty and integrity. It is a dishonorable discharge of debts."[35] Personal and business bankruptcies are very rare. If a business is struggling financially because of mismanagement, changing market conditions, or some other reason, church-appointed trustees will step in and oversee the operation to avoid legal bankruptcy and attempt to ensure that creditors are fully paid.

Joy in Everyday Routines

Family and Nature

Gelassenheit, with its emphasis on obedience, humility, and plainness, may appear to cast a shadow of austerity over Amish life. But the Amish way also provides for personal joy and pleasure. It is not the pleasure of a spa, individual sports, musical accomplishment, or the performing arts. Amish pleasures are rooted in family, nature, and community events, not in individual performance or upscale creature comforts.

Calling his three young children "our little disciples," a father exclaimed, "What a great joy it is to raise God's children."[36] Amish people regularly cite family as the source of innumerable joys, while also acknowledging its challenges. They find fulfillment in family activities—raising children, working together, and gathering with kin. There are countless small joys—sipping homemade root beer on a summer day, smelling freshly baked pies, enjoying a surprise visit from out-of-state friends, watching chicks hatch, and quietly viewing a sunset. Many families spend hours together trying to conquer large jigsaw puzzles. In a variety of activities—from shelling peas to singing for the elderly, from remodeling a kitchen to ice-skating, from quilting to cleaning, from playing table games to pulling weeds, or simply sitting in a circle visiting—many Amish people delight in chatting with family and friends as they work and play. "Visiting is our national sport," one Amish man said with a wink.

Virtually all Amish families have a garden planted with vegetables and often with ornamental flowers. Women, especially, take delight in gardening, arranging winter travel so as to be home at just the right time to start young plants indoors for transplanting outside later in the spring. "What adds more charm to an old farmhouse kitchen than a freshly cut garden bouquet?" one Amish woman asks. "There are always flowers to pick and cut, from spring's daffodils to autumn's chrysanthemums. . . . And they are a pleasure. But they have a deeper value. God created flowers, and he knew that people would need them."[37]

Nature is a source of inspiration and renewal for many Amish people because they believe that the closer they are to nature, the closer they are to God. Whether toiling

Members of a Kentucky Amish community chartered a bus for a sightseeing trip that included a stop at Lookout Mountain, which straddles the Tennessee-Georgia border. *Stephanie A. Richer*

in fields on sultry days, picking cherries, fishing, stargazing, or birding, they enjoy and marvel at the beauty of the created order.

Birding is a popular intergenerational pastime. Some families, equipped with binoculars and bird guides, travel by van or bus to visit migratory sites. Likewise, some families enjoy camping, typically pitching tents on private land rather than in public campgrounds. Men and boys (and occasionally women and girls) who live near the Chesapeake Bay, the Atlantic Ocean, or inland lakes and streams enjoy fishing. Other fishing enthusiasts converge on farm ponds or engage in winter ice fishing.

Hunting, especially for deer, is a popular avocation. Although the Amish consider killing humans a sin, they have few qualms about shooting animals since they are harvesting them for food and protecting gardens and croplands.[38] A West Virginia woman wrote about hearing "shots echoing and re-echoing through the hills" and added, "I rejoice whenever any get shot, but even if there's just one left, it'll get into my garden." Venison is canned, frozen, and smoked for year-round use.[39]

Hunting tales fill the letters submitted by correspondents to December issues of Amish newspapers and periodicals. "Corn husking is finished . . . now we are in the whitetail elimination mode," reads a typical statement. Although hunting is usually a male pastime, some letters point to wider interest: "Three of our granddaughters each got a doe this year in the junior season. They are 12, 13 and 15."

Hunting, like other activities, varies by church affiliation and the dictates of the local Ordnung. While the most conservative groups hunt and fish locally and stocking the larder is enough to justify an enjoyable pastime, others go further afield, lured by big game trophies. Some hire outfitters to guide them on trips to the western Rockies. Outdoor sports shows draw Amish customers, who purchase guns, archery equipment, and other accessories. But hunters in traditional Amish groups forego expensive gear, and some have run afoul of state game laws for refusing to wear bright orange hunting vests, which they consider worldly.

Plain Entertainment

It is rare for Amish people of any sort to attend professional sporting events, although in some Indiana communities young people are regular fans at local public high school basketball games—even though the Amish themselves do not attend high school. When it comes to playing sports, volleyball is the game of choice for all but the most conservative Amish groups. Most view it as the perfect form of Amish athletics: it involves teamwork, cooperation, and a sizable number of players; both men and women can play with little training or expensive equipment. In the higher communities, youth enjoy baseball or basketball pickup games, and in some cases they form teams that are part of organized civic leagues. Sledding and ice skating are favorite pastimes everywhere, and in some communities, ice hockey on a frozen pond. Amish teens and unmarried young adults in more liberal groups also engage in snowmobiling and water skiing.

Few Amish families speak of taking vacations, but some members of liberal groups plan trips that mix recreation with business or family activities. Amish newspapers are replete with accounts of interstate trips by van loads of visitors attending weddings, funerals, or family reunions in other settlements. Such excursions can offer relaxation and opportunities to sightsee along the way.

Although visiting other settlements is quite common, some Amish people also travel to tourist destinations. For example, two or three households may hire a van and driver to take them to see a national park or historic sites on their way to visit, say, an Amish settlement in Colorado or Montana. Some bus operators, in consultation with Amish customers, develop multiday bus tours of scenic areas. Occasionally, Amish people join a commercial bus tour with non-Amish travelers. A few families living on the East Coast take their children to Washington, D.C., to tour the government buildings and visit museums with an eye to education. An Amish man reflecting on a tour of the Holocaust Memorial Museum noted, "It was a profound and moving experience. . . . While we want to appreciate any respite from persecution we get, may we never become the persecutors."[40]

Whether fishing, hosting a community event, or stopping at a state park on the way home from a cousin's wedding, Amish recreation typically reflects the Amish way—collective, informal, simple, participatory, and close to nature.

Reading and Writing

Unconnected to the Internet and without television or video games, many Amish people find joy and pleasure in reading and writing, especially during the slower winter season. In all but the lowest groups, families frequent public libraries. For example, according to staff estimates, Amish people "make up 90 percent of the Geauga County [Ohio] bookmobile patrons."[41] Many households also buy books from the more than one hundred Amish bookstores scattered across the country. Popular titles include biographies, histories, books about nature or travel, and, for children, the Laura Ingalls Wilder series. At least one Amish bookstore in Pennsylvania stocks juvenile books from the American Girl series that have rural settings. Some young women also read Amish-themed romance novels. Karen Kingsbury and Francine Rivers are frequently named authors, as are Janette Oke and evangelical nonfiction writers such as Max Lucado. In general, the church discourages mainstream fiction because of its overt sexual themes, violence, and general portrayal of worldly lifestyles. Many families read local newspapers, trade magazines, and birding, hunting, and fishing magazines, as well as Amish periodicals.[42]

In addition to reading, the Amish practice another old-fashioned art form: writing with pen and paper. Adults and children write letters, cards, and topical essays. Hundreds of "scribes" send reports of community activities to weekly and monthly Amish periodicals. The number of poets writing for Amish publications has increased dramatically in recent years. In the magazine *Family Life,* for example, the yearly number of poems increased from 19 to 90 between 1989 and 2009. The editors noted that "20 years ago there were relatively few poem writers among our people. . . . During the two decades since 1989, a large number of younger and very talented poem writers have come onto the scene. The quality of the poems has kept pace right along with the increase in quantity."[43] In some communities writing poetry or stories is a culturally acceptable form of public self-expression, while in more conservative circles, where Gelassenheit permeates more deeply, poems and stories are shared only among family members.

Art and Crafts

The values of humility and simplicity shape Amish approaches to home décor and artistry. Purely decorative artwork is frowned upon because it lacks a practical use.

Colorful wall calendars, embroidered family registers, and genealogical charts are more likely to hang on Amish walls because these support family life. Practical expressions of creativity include colorful quilt patterns, attractive flower gardens, and artistic lettering in Bibles as well as sturdy toys, dolls, crafts, and furniture designs. Among change-minded groups, schoolroom walls often display pupils' artwork and feature colorful bulletin boards created by Amish teachers.

Many people enjoy making crafts as gifts for family members or to sell to neighbors and tourists. In some communities, older artistic constraints eroded in the 1990s with the rapid rise of tourist markets. Among more conservative Amish groups, however, craft production is still strictly controlled by the Ordnung. For example, some affiliations limit the production of dolls to the tourist market and stipulate that they not have facial features so as to avoid any semblance of a human visage.

Even among the more progressive groups, art that exalts the individual artist is generally unwelcome, although the Amish have historically accepted a handful of folk artists who worked within the cultural boundaries.[44] Susie Riehl, for example, is a self-trained Pennsylvania artist whose works of nature scenes and Amish life devoid of people sell for more than $3,000.[45] Public art shows that call attention to the artist are generally not allowed because they would cultivate pride. One artist explained, "It's okay to paint milk cans, but not to display your work at art shows." The long-standing emphasis on practicality is being eroded in some areas by tourist markets and technology. For example, one man in a liberal group creates and sells digital art.[46] Churches have sometimes granted artists with physical disabilities special freedom to display and market their work because such sales are one means by which disabled persons can support themselves financially.

The Shrinking Edges of Gelassenheit

Gelassenheit remains the deep taproot that nourishes the Amish way, but some of its influence is waning in more liberal groups. Although Amish people have resisted the pressures of individualism and remain accountable to their local Gmay, the extent of that submission is undergoing change in some communities. More openness to individual recognition, for example, is evident in higher groups.

Increased public recognition of individuals includes the use of full names on business cards, listings in public telephone books, and published materials. In the mid-twentieth century, virtually all Amish authors wrote anonymously, refusing to claim personal credit for their ideas or to call too much attention to themselves. Some authors used only their initials, and others included their name but only on an inside title page, not on the book's cover. A growing number of Amish authors now reveal their names. Most of the correspondents reporting activities from their communities in Amish publications sign their names, as do authors writing for other Amish periodicals.

Some Amish authors also use their name in public media. Elizabeth Coblenz (1936–2002) of Geneva, Indiana, began writing "The Amish Cook," a syndicated newspaper column, in 1991. Her essays blended recipes with vignettes of daily Amish life and were carried by over one hundred mainstream newspapers. Although she wrote under her own name, she would not appear in photographs or on television or allow her voice to be taped for radio. After her death, her daughter Lovina Eicher continued the column.[47] Linda Byler, also writing under her real name, has authored a popular series of Amish romance novels, including *Running Around (and Such)*, *When Strawberries Bloom*, and *Big Decisions*.[48]

The very presence of such cultural negotiation points to the fact that the foundations of the Amish way continue to resist the pervasive pressures of liquid modernity. The values we have examined—obedience, humility, plainness, and simplicity—may not seem like powerful engines of resistance against the forces that drive modernity, yet the way these sentiments quietly steer Amish life offers testament to their influence. The public symbols of Amish identity have provided a more visible form of resilience, as we show in the next chapter.

CHAPTER 7

Symbols and Identity

Saloma Miller Furlong, who grew up Amish in Geauga County, Ohio, explains that Amish children at an early age "know that they are Amish and different from English people. The first things that identify them as different from the outside world are the obvious ones, such as plain clothing, traditional dialect, and riding in horse-drawn buggies. Everything about their way of life and their belief system shapes and reinforces this identity from the cradle to the grave—at least for the people who stay within the culture." Even though she left Amish life as a young adult, Furlong says, "that feeling of being fundamentally different has not ever really left me. When I left, I had to 'graft' my Amish identity with my newfound mainstream American identity to become a 'hybrid.' There are some aspects of who I am that shall forever remain shaped by Amish culture."

Mapping the Moral Geography

Humans are social beings with attachments to tribes, ethnic groups, families, teams, friends, neighborhoods, and nations—some by birthright, some by intention. Each of our tribes has its symbols of identity that set it apart from others. National flags, corporate logos, sports jerseys, and job uniforms remind members and nonmembers alike who is on the team and who is not. And our teams, so to speak, have regulations about membership and rules for how to play the game. Amish teams have their own distinctive rules and garb that reflect their moral order. As Furlong's words demonstrate, that moral order persistently reminds its members of who they are and how they should live.

The Amish seek to create church-communities that will help members attain eternal life. "Heaven is our ultimate goal," said a retired businessman. Two key assumptions guide the pursuit of this goal. First, the community must separate itself from the larger world and set guidelines so that individuals do not stray from the pathway to heaven. Second, symbols of separation and norms of conduct create a way of thinking and acting regarding right and wrong, good and bad. In this chapter we explore this Amish moral order and the distinctive symbols that mark its borders.

Amish cultural norms prescribe how to act toward and think about *moral objects*—material items, ideas, and activities. Like other societies, the Amish distinguish between desirable or "clean" moral objects and forbidden or "dirty" ones. Boundaries and labels distinguish between things that purify the community and things that pollute it, between those that build it up and those that tear it down. This code of distinctions implies action toward the moral objects: whether you should use, do, or believe in them, or you should not.[1]

For the Amish, moral objects fall into four distinct territories: *desirable, forbidden, ambiguous,* and *neutral.* Desirable moral objects fill a large landscape that we might call the vestibule of heaven. Here we find obedience, humility, gardening, reading, carpentry, bird watching, dishwashing, and hard work as well as belief in angels, Satan, and divine creation. These desirable beliefs and activities directly or indirectly aid the heaven-bound journey. Obedience to God, parents, and elders directly serves the ultimate goal of Amish life. By teaching children obedience and a healthy work ethic, dishwashing indirectly does the same. All good things, however, are not equally good. For example, while raising vegetables and raising children are both desirable, raising children counts for more. Although they are weighted differently, desirable moral objects for the Amish are those values, practices, and things that clearly contribute to one's heavenward goal.

The forbidden region includes things such as killing people, swearing oaths, adultery, pride, evolution, higher education, divorce, boasting, holding public office, owning a computer, and ordaining women as church leaders. Embracing any of these moral objects, the Amish believe, hinders the mission of their society. Pride signals individualism, which can disrupt communal harmony. Lipstick and any type of jewelry call attention to the self. Holding public office reveals disloyalty to God's kingdom. Many desirable moral objects have a forbidden counterpart: divine creation versus evolution, humility versus pride, and carriages versus cars.

Yet the Amish recognize that moral geography is not so simple that everything can be neatly sorted into categories of clean and sullied; they know that a vast territory exists where the line between virtue and vice is ambiguous. For example, it may

The showroom of an Amish furniture business near Arthur, Illinois, reflects the moral order of that community. Upscale furniture designed for suburban Chicago homes is manufactured with nonelectric machines. Skylights made by an Amish shop illuminate the showroom. Propane gas lamps in the ceiling provide light at night. *Donald B. Kraybill*

be hard to predict the long-term moral consequences of something new. Or some members may want to lift an old taboo while others worry that doing so will be detrimental. A material item such as a fax machine may at once be dangerous and useful, so its use must be controlled. Because greater mobility could tear apart a close-knit community, the use of cars must be restrained and their ownership prohibited.

It is also possible to "purify" some ambiguous things by adapting them—or, as one man put it, "Amishizing" them—so that they mesh with the moral order. Examples include replacing a tractor's rubber tires with steel wheels or the electric motor on a sewing machine with an air motor, or stripping a computer of its Internet connection and video capacities. Morally messy things are also regulated by making a distinction between ownership and access. In some groups owning a riding mower is prohibited, but using one owned by an outside employer is permissible. The ambiguity of these moral objects is often a source of contention within and among Amish groups, at times leading to ecclesial divisions.

A long list of things are considered neutral, meaning that they have little or no moral content or consequence and thus are acceptable. For example, the Amish are not reluctant to own and use eating utensils, soap, spices, shovels, flashlights, and pocket knives. Eating pizza, hunting deer, owning private property, buying and selling with outsiders, and riding on public buses also lie in this amoral territory.[2]

The *location* of a physical item or activity may determine whether it is considered morally acceptable or dangerous. Ornamental Christmas trees have no intrinsic moral value, but they are considered out of place in an Amish home. A minister may speak English in a local restaurant, but preaching in English during a church service would be out of order. Although footwear might not be regulated during the work week, wearing athletic shoes to church would be offensive. Telephones, which some groups accept in the office of a business, are prohibited inside schools.

The moral geography of Amish life varies by affiliation and local congregation. Moral objects that are accepted by some groups and strictly forbidden by others include attending a professional baseball game, serving as a volunteer firefighter, hiring a truck for business, working for a non-Amish employer, smoking tobacco, affixing LED lights to a carriage, and owning a propane refrigerator, cell phone, bicycle, power lawn mower, or chainsaw.

The *Ordnung:* An Oral Map

Navigating the moral terrain of Amish culture requires a map—in fact, two of them: Scripture and the Ordnung. One member explained that the Ten Commandments (Exod. 20:2–17) and Jesus's Sermon on the Mount (Matt. 5–7) "are especially important scriptures" because they "tell us how we should live." Scripture commands honoring parents, loving enemies, and telling the truth. In addition, it clearly states that God forbids murder, adultery, divorce, fornication, hate, and anger.

The Ordnung provides guidance on those issues that Scripture does not clearly or directly address.[3] Containing prescriptions (what one should do) and proscriptions (what one should not do), this oral guidebook applies biblical principles—especially separation from the world—to everyday issues ranging from education to transportation, from dress to technology. For example, it *prescribes* how men and women should wear their hair and their general style of dress. It also *proscribes* owning a television or a car.

The Ordnung regulates private, public, and ceremonial life by oral tradition rather than by written rules.[4] "The people just know it, that's all," said one member. Rather than a packet of rules to memorize, it is the "understood" set of expectations for behavior. Outsiders may perceive it as a list of rules, but the Ordnung is organic, malleable, dynamic, and subject to varied interpretation by leaders. Because it is unwritten, it privileges the memory of older people.

Two Layers

The Ordnung has two layers: implicit and explicit. The *implicit*, below-the-surface layer holds the wisdom of accumulated tradition. Old customs provide moral guidance and become the taken-for-granted way of "our people." "It's just the way we do things," said an Amish man. The deeply entrenched practices governed by the implicit Ordnung do not need debate; they are simply assumed as the Amish way. Examples include not wearing jewelry, men growing beards and shaving their upper lip, traveling by horse and carriage, meeting in homes for worship, and singing without instrumental accompaniment. These practices are fairly stable and need little verbal reinforcement. One woman said, "We're not supposed to wear makeup, but it's something the bishops don't even need to mention. I don't even think they know about makeup. They wouldn't really know how to talk about it." Common sense, in the Amish world, dictates that working as a bartender or selling cars so obviously violates religious principles that no reminders are needed.

By contrast, the *explicit* layer of the Ordnung is discussed in conversations, members' meetings, and council meetings. It addresses emergent issues (e.g., the use of cell phones and computers), challenges to long-standing taboos, leisure activities, and other current concerns. As one Amish man said, the explicit Ordnung speaks to "the issues we must face when the taken-for-granted is no longer taken for granted!" As changes unfold in the larger society, the church must grapple with them. Technological innovations such as calculators and embryo transplants in dairy cows may be permitted or forbidden, depending on the discernment of the local district. Controversial issues—installing phones in shops or using rototillers in gardens—may be accepted by default in some *Gmay*s and never even considered by others. In still others, such issues may fester for years. In the end, the explicit aspects of the Ordnung are ratified by the members of each local district and enforced by its leaders.

Following the Map

In the same way that all children learn the rules of grammar by listening and speaking, Amish youth absorb the Ordnung—the grammar of Amish life—as they observe adults and hear them talk. The Ordnung becomes the taken-for-granted reality—"the way things are"—in the child's mind. In the same way that non-Amish children learn that women, rather than men, wear lipstick and shave their legs, so Amish children learn the expectations of behaving "Amish." In other words, to a child growing up in the world of the Ordnung, wearing a hat or apron wherever one goes is the normal thing to do. The same goes for occupations. For example, asked whether an Amish person could be a real estate agent, a member of a conservative group replied, "Well, it's just unheard of. A child wouldn't even think of it."

Compliance with the Ordnung varies by role, ritual, and circumstance. The higher one's level of authority, the more conservative the expectations. Because ministers and their families are expected to exemplify compliance, they are generally held to stiffer standards. After a man is ordained, he will grow his beard fuller and longer, wear a wider-brimmed hat, and drive a more traditional buggy. His wife will wear more conservative shoes, a larger head covering with wider strings, and a plainer-cut dress. And the couple's children will also feel the social squeeze to comply more fully with Ordnung standards.

For lay members, the regulations are a bit softer and subject to interpretation by local leaders. Single members and couples without children are granted more leniency than parents, who must model exemplary behavior to their children. Although children are immersed in the Ordnung, it is not until baptism that they make a personal vow to uphold it for life. Thus, even though most unbaptized youth comply, they cannot be held accountable to rules they have not promised to obey. Adults who are traveling or living away from home for a few weeks may enjoy more freedom simply because they are beyond the gaze of others in their community. In general, compliance with dress regulations rises at ritual gatherings—church services, council services, ordinations, and especially communion services.

Depending on the community, exceptions may be granted to the elderly and those with disabilities or special health problems; for example, the community may allow those needing to operate home medical equipment access to 120-volt electricity from a portable generator or the public grid. Although self-propelled riding lawn mowers are forbidden in most communities, some do permit electric wheelchairs and scooters for the elderly or disabled. Members working for a non-Amish employer or visiting in an English home may watch television or use a computer, something they otherwise would not do.

Some bishops, either by personal disposition or by local tradition, are more lenient than others in their enforcement of the Ordnung. And of course every congregation has some members who are more devout than others. Those who conform to key visible markers such as dress standards will likely enjoy some "breathing space" in which to maneuver within other regulations.

The moral guidelines may change as the normative order flexes with new issues and new leaders. Most Gmays are reluctant to revise practices long ingrained in the Ordnung, and because changing the Ordnung is so difficult, Amish people are slow to outlaw things at first sight. If a new practice—for example, the use of LED lights, barbecue grills, or trampolines—is seen as harmless, it may drift into use with little ruckus.

At the same time, however, the acceptance of a new practice by a progressive group may derail its use by a lower community that wants to distinguish itself from the "worldly practices" of the higher group. One low affiliation, for example, rejected LED flashlights to avoid the path of a more liberal group that had adopted them. Sometimes, rather than overturn old regulations, members devise ingenious ways to bypass them. Traditional groups in upstate New York, when faced with state milk regulations requiring refrigerated bulk tanks, refused to use electricity on their own properties and instead constructed electrified community milk cooling stations on rented, non-Amish land.

The Ordnung may seem like stuffy legalism even to some Amish people, but for most it is a sacred order that unites the church and separates it from worldly society. One Amish leader said, "A church without Ordnung is just confusion!" An Ordnung is a map that guides members and thus creates order, predictability, clarity of boundaries, and unity in the community. "A respected Ordnung generates peace, love, contentment, equality, and unity," said one minister. "It creates a desire for togetherness and fellowship. It binds marriages; it strengthens family ties to live together, to work together, to worship together, and to commune secluded from the world."[5] For the Amish, bending to the Ordnung, the community's collective wisdom, brings divine blessing and the hope of eternal life.

The customs, regulations, and standards of the Ordnung translate the values of *Gelassenheit*—humility, simplicity, and obedience—into life-shaping traditions. Most importantly, the Ordnung forges identity by articulating the essence of the word *Amish*. Some members may not know the reason for a particular practice because its legitimacy lies not in its original purpose but in its entwinement with Amish identity.

"Our identity, what holds us together," said an older member, "is based on three things: steel wheels [no cars], German, and plain clothing." Saloma Miller Furlong notes some additional practices that shaped her Amish identity: "No telephones. No electricity. Getting spanked for disobeying my parents. Working hard. Good cooking and baking. Gardening. Going barefoot in the summer. No hugging or kissing [in public]. Quiet prayer before and after meals. Washing clothes with a gasoline-powered wringer washer. No financial freedom until age 21."[6] The elder's trilogy of Amish cultural habits—language, dress, and horse-drawn transportation—anchors Amish identity both within the community and beyond. We examine each in turn.

A Trilingual People

Language constructs images of reality in our consciousness and defines the "way things are." It unites those who speak a common tongue and separates them from those who do not. Amish people use three different languages. They speak a German dialect known as Pennsylvania Dutch; they speak, write, and read English; and they read an older form of German that is archaic in German-speaking Europe.[7] They shift from one language to another depending on the mode (speaking, writing, and reading), their linguistic skills, and the cultural context. The Pennsylvania Dutch dialect is spoken among fellow Amish, but speakers switch to English when conversing with outsiders. While most Amish are able to understand German when reading the Bible and other religious texts, they read and write mainly in English.[8]

Pennsylvania Dutch

Not standardized and generally unwritten, Pennsylvania Dutch is the primary *oral* language for all Amish except for a small minority of so-called Swiss Amish who speak a form of Bernese Swiss German.[9] The two dialects are so different that when Swiss German speakers and Pennsylvania Dutch speakers meet, they generally switch to English. "It's like Spanish to us when they talk Swiss so fast to each other. We don't have a clue what they are saying," explained a Pennsylvania Dutch–speaking man from northern Indiana.

Pennsylvania Dutch is not derived from the Dutch language of the Netherlands but is rather a German dialect that evolved in the United States among German-speaking immigrants from the upper Rhine Valley of Germany who settled in southeastern Pennsylvania in the eighteenth century. Only a few hundred of these immigrants were Amish, but by the end of the twentieth century, most of the non-Amish speakers of the dialect had shifted to English, and Pennsylvania Dutch became primarily an Amish and Old Order Mennonite mode of speech.[10] The dialect resembles those spoken in the Palatinate region of Germany, near the city of Mannheim. Linguists have long identified regional variations and speech islands within the dialect as it is spoken by the Amish across North America. Speakers occasionally sprinkle English words—such as *kite, pencil, pacemaker, tractor, refrigerator,* and *computer*—into their sentences. About 15 percent or less of the Pennsylvania Dutch vocabulary is English-derived, and its core grammatical structures remain Palatine German.[11]

Pennsylvania Dutch is the language of family, friendship, play, and intimacy. Most children live in the world of the dialect until they attend school. Although they learn to read, write, and speak English in school, the dialect prevails in friendly banter on many school playgrounds. Most importantly, Pennsylvania Dutch is the language of identity and ethnicity that binds Amish people to a particular community and sets them apart from the English-based, mainstream society.

English

English is the linguistic currency with outsiders. The competence of Amish people to speak, write, and read English varies by training, occupation, intelligence, and frequency of interaction with non-Amish people. Many business owners, for example, develop an extensive English vocabulary related to their line of work. They talk about marketing strategies and use legal terminology with ease. But they may stumble when trying to communicate religious ideas in English, underscoring the importance of the dialect in creating and perpetuating a distinctive worldview.

English is also the default language for writing to other Amish people, whether leaving a note on the kitchen table, sending a sympathy card, or penning a letter for an Amish publication. Some writers occasionally sprinkle German or dialect phrases into their English prose. When writing religious documents, however, leaders typically use German with a smattering of dialect words.

Reading is yet a bit different. Most printed materials—mainstream newspapers, regional newsletters, periodicals, cookbooks, history, and inspirational books—are read in English. Children use English textbooks in Amish schools. Yet key religious documents, including the Bible, some historical texts, prayers, and hymns, are typically read in German. Almost nothing is read in the dialect.

The number of English publications produced and consumed by Amish communities has skyrocketed since 1990. These include weekly newspapers, newsletters, other periodicals, songbooks, cookbooks, devotional books, historical accounts, family histories, and memoirs. Many Amish subscribe to their local daily newspaper and to *Reader's Digest,* as well as to other popular magazines related to their work and hobbies. The abundance of these materials makes English the default literary language because they far outstrip publications written and read in German.

Standard German

If the dialect is the mother tongue and English is the trade language, then old German is the voice of spirituality. The German in Amish religious books and documents reflects the sixteenth-century style of early modern German as the language was becoming standardized for the first time through the influence of Martin Luther's translation of the Bible. Schools teach students to read German in old *fraktur* script so they can read religious texts. Scripture verses, church regulations, religious booklets, and sayings of respected leaders are usually printed in German. A manual for funerals in one settlement uses English to describe how to prepare funeral meals but shifts to German to delineate the order of service and the suggested hymns.[12] Nevertheless, although the Bible, the *Ausbund,* prayer books, and older religious materials are typically read in German, the ability to speak that language varies greatly.

Both the dialect and German provide a tangible connection to Amish heritage, but German has the higher sacred status. Nonetheless, a few lay members would prefer if the prayers and hymns in church services were translated into either English or Pennsylvania Dutch because, in the words of one, "too many young people just don't know what they're singing or what the prayers mean." In more conservative communities, however, this is not a problem because their people have less exposure to the English-speaking world.

Translations

Because some people have difficulty understanding German, a growing number of religious publications have parallel columns of German and English on the same page. Many households have a Bible in which Luther's German translation appears alongside the English of King James.

Several Amish publishers have produced English translations of religious materials. In the 1960s, Pathway Publishers printed *A Devoted Christian's Prayer Book* (with selected prayers from *Die Ernsthafte Christenpflicht*), as well as translations of the Dordrecht Confession and "Rules of a Godly Life." *In Meiner Jugend,* a similar compilation published for youth in 2000, included a new English translation of religious doctrines as well as baptismal and marriage vows. The editor explained that the English translation appears beside the German, not to "replace or supplant the German. Quite the opposite. The English version should be used . . . to clarify the meaning of the German."[13]

An ambitious translation project to present German and English side by side was managed and published in 2000 (and revised in 2008) by an Indiana Amish woman, Mary M. Miller. *Our Heritage, Hope, and Faith* is a 570-page compendium of prayers, songs, and material related to religious ceremonies that encompasses the core of Amish spirituality. Miller compiled it because, she says, "We are not as much at home in the German language as our forefathers were. Therefore it takes more of an effort, yes, a real dedication, to keep the true spirit of these songs, prayers, and our German heritage alive. And to do this we must understand what they are saying."[14]

In a similar project, the Ohio Amish Library published English translations of *Ausbund* hymns to "help us understand more fully what is sung . . . [and] to understand the beliefs and sufferings of the writers."[15] Although these publishers argue that English translations will enhance the comprehension of German not erode it, the need for them suggests a declining competence in reading German in some Amish communities.[16]

Preserving Identity

Many Amish view English as the currency of high culture and worldly society, a language of sophistication at odds with the lowly spirit of Gelassenheit. To use English in prayers or religious services is considered worldly. Some leaders see the growing use of English and worry that some children are learning too much of it too early. One mother in a traditional group noted that her children sometimes speak English at home after they begin school. "Sometimes they do it [speak English] just for fun, but, if they do it regularly, we make them quit."[17] If the dialect dies, the folklore it encodes and carries will also vanish.

"We don't know what language Adam and Eve spoke nor what language is spoken in heaven," one Amish leader notes. Still, he argues that "losing our mother tongue and drifting into the world usually go together." He criticizes people who "think it is demeaning or beneath them to use German or speak Pennsylvania Dutch." Anyone who speaks English at home, he argues, "is putting in a vote to drop a rich heritage . . . [one] that is so great that we can't afford to lose it."[18]

The dialect fortifies Amish identity in several ways. It serves as a social adhesive to bind and unite the community into a world of its own. It creates an alternative worldview that reaches back to the religious roots and martyr past of Amish people. Reading the Bible, *Martyrs Mirror,* and other religious materials in the "original" tongue creates for them a conversation with their sacred history.

The ethnic tongue also separates. Few Amish are ever completely at ease with English. There are moments of hesitation when they grope for an English term or stumble when pronouncing one. It is difficult to tease, dream, and communicate emotions in a foreign language. The dialect provides a prudent way of keeping the world at bay. It modulates interaction with outsiders and stifles intimate ties with non-Amish neighbors. In all these ways, the dialect creates a way of perceiving reality that obstructs the dialogue with modernity. Knowing that the dialect reflects their ethnic identity, the Amish have refused to concede it.

The Garb of Identity and Belonging

Distinctive dress is one yardstick by which to measure the symbolic and real social distance of any minority group from mainstream culture, and it is the most salient symbol of Amish identity.[19] Without plain garb, an Amish person's public ethnic identity would vanish. Even within Amish circles, dress reveals important clues to one's status and compliance. If the central challenge of a collective society is ensuring individual commitment to the group, prescribed dress helps to accomplish that goal. It creates a cultural moat that encloses and separates, and it binds members of

With some age variations, Amish children typically
dress like their parents. The style and color of shirt, vest,
trousers, and hat of both father and son signify their
conservative affiliation. *Doyle Yoder*

the community together and gives them a common identity. A clear countercultural
symbol, plain dress rejects not only designer labels but also the values of consumer
culture.

We have argued that individualism is the deepest value separating Amish culture
from mainstream society. Clothing is surely the most visible mark of that divide. Lipovetsky, in *Empire of Fashion,* contends that the ephemeral world of fashion, with
its celebration of spectacle and superficiality, best typifies modern culture. In contemporary culture, dress expresses personal preference and social status. People use
dress—styles, colors, logos, brand names—to articulate their individuality and manage how they present themselves to others. Self-adornment is a way to stand out, to

be seen, to be recognized. Within Amish society, however, the individual relinquishes the right to use dress as a major tool of self-expression.

Group-prescribed dress signals ethnic membership, submission to the moral order, and yielding of the self to the church. Members don the "company uniform," so to speak, because they always are "on duty" as representatives of their community. Central to both self and group identity, plain garb is the articulation of loyalty and belonging. Dressed in distinctive garb, children learn to act, think, and feel Amish from their birth onward.

Dress is not merely a tool of social control, however; it is a church tradition legitimated by prominent principles in the Bible. Amish elders contend that clothing should reflect the biblical values of humility, modesty, self-denial, simplicity, and separation from the world. Clothing, argues one writer, should be "neat, plain, simple, serviceable, and cover the body."[20] The Amish book *1001 Questions and Answers on the Christian Life* devotes nine pages and forty-three questions and answers to dress—second only to the topic of heaven.[21] Although Amish publications cite numerous Bible verses when making the case for modest and distinctive dress, clothing regulations usually are not tied to specific Scriptures but are simply accepted as "the way our people dress."[22]

An Amish writer, comparing church-prescribed dress to police uniforms, notes, "It is our duty to keep it [plain dress], just as it is a policeman's duty to wear his uniform."[23] Another leader says, "We should not be ashamed to be identified with the church and God. Men of the world are not ashamed of the uniforms they wear . . . let us not be ashamed of our church's Ordnung but voluntarily submit ourselves to it so that the world can see we are a separate and peculiar people."[24]

Amish dress performs a variety of social tasks: (1) it signals that a member has yielded to the collective order; (2) it prevents dress from being used for self-adornment; (3) it promotes equality; (4) it creates a common consciousness that bolsters group identity; (5) it encourages members to "act Amish"; (6) it projects a united public front, which conceals diversity in other areas; and (7) it erects symbolic boundaries around the group.

What Dress Says to Insiders

Dress speaks loudly inside Amish society because Amish people see a direct link between clothing and conviction, between outward appearance and inner piety. Dress is a barometer of Gelassenheit. It shows whether one is obedient or disobedient, humble or proud, modest or haughty, yielded or stubborn. One Amish publication notes, "It is a fact that religion in the heart has something to do with the form of the clothing." Clothe your heart with humility, advises the author, and your body will give evidence.[25]

For the Amish, all cosmetics and jewelry are taboo, including engagement and wedding rings, body rings, tattoos, and wristwatches. Pocket watches are acceptable for both men and women, however, and in some highly traditional groups men and women might wear copper rings, not as jewelry but as a folk remedy to treat arthritis. Women in all groups wear a head covering *(Kapp)*, and all men grow beards, although when they begin varies by affiliation. In some groups men stop shaving after they are baptized, but in most groups marriage marks the point at which a man begins growing a beard. Men may not wear neckties, which are considered needless adornment. Men in most, but not all, affiliations wear suspenders. None wear belts.

Dress provides subtle clues to an individual's conformity to church standards. The width of a hat brim, the length of hair, the size of a head covering, the length of a skirt, and the color of shoes and stockings quietly signal a member's compliance. Subtle variations announce whether one is liberal or conservative, showing off or obeying the church, "crowding the fence" or falling in line. Hair and dress styles indicate church loyalty. Speaking of men, a minister noted, "You can single your people out, your families out, which way they are leaning, by the cut of their hair." "How a child is dressed," said one woman, "gives away the mother's heart." The Amish believe that pleats, ruffles on sleeves, and bow ties at the elbows of young women's dresses speak volumes about the home in which they are raised.

To the outside eye, the Amish may appear to dress alike. Yet a closer glance reveals a mosaic of details that signal important meanings within the culture. The style and color of dress signify social distinctions linked to at least ten dimensions of Amish life: (1) gender, (2) age, (3) marital status, (4) compliance, (5) church membership, (6) social esteem, (7) religious rituals, (8) rites of passage, (9) sacred-profane boundaries, and (10) ethnic-public domains. These cultural patterns clarify roles, identities, and commitments in Amish society.

Team Uniforms

The Amish do not wear only black and white, as some stereotypes suggest, although it is true that most groups reject bright red, yellow, and orange, as well as any flashy color combinations. Colors common in Amish clothing include darker ones such as purple, blue, maroon, green, brown, and gray, as well as black and white. In more progressive groups, children's clothes, especially girls' dresses, are often pastels. Amish clothing is almost always made from solid-colored fabrics rather than prints or patterns. Nonetheless, each of the forty-plus Amish affiliations has its own distinctive styles and colors, sharpening team identities. Stephen Scott, in *Why Do They Dress*

Young Amish women observe a horse auction near Milverton, Ontario. Their dress indicates their church affiliation and their black *Kapps* announce their unmarried status. The distinctive garb also shows their separation from the non-Amish world. *Mark Burr*

That Way?, found some three hundred differences in twenty items of clothing for men and women across fifteen communities.[26]

Worried that losing plain dress will lead to assimilation, one Amish man described how the "undressing" of the Amish might proceed: "It all comes one step at a time. First we can go without bonnets, then the corners come off the caps [head coverings], and then the strings, dresses gradually get shorter and tighter, caps a bit smaller, and somewhere along the line the cape is discarded. The apron, of course, has disappeared long before this. Soon the only place to take anything away from is the dress, bare arms, low necklines, tight bodices and short skirts. This may not all come in one year or in one generation . . . but the passing of the bonnet means big changes are coming."[27] Scott actually identifies nine steps along the pathway to mainstream fashions among midwestern Amish.[28]

The daily acts of dressing are rites of Gelassenheit that signal yieldedness to God and the Ordnung of the church. While the clothing code may seem complicated and constraining, it frees Amish people from the burden of choice. Although some Amish youth press their mothers to buy just the right pastel color so that their shirts or dresses match their friends' clothing, they spend less effort than mainstream teens sorting through their wardrobe each morning and shopping to stay abreast of current fads. They may appear to be obsessed with dress, but, ironically, they have fewer worries about clothing than do most Americans, whose dressing rituals signal obedience to the "Ordnung" of Madison Avenue. Moreover, Amish cultural tastes are regulated by the church, not by fashion designers or trendsetting celebrities. Conformity to ethnic dress standards not only unites them and marks their social turf, but it also frees them from incessant choice.

The Hoofbeats of Tradition

The Social Work of Horses

What visual image could be more countercultural than a horse pulling a buggy through a thicket of traffic? The horse and buggy, prime symbols of Amish identity, protest key values of modern life: speed, power, and mobility. The horse on the road challenges the values embedded in the automobile, and the horse in the field questions the assumptions of high-tech agriculture. The typical Amish farm family has one or two driving horses and six to eight horses or mules for field work. Nonfarm families usually keep a horse or two and a pony in a small barn on their property.

The horse became the default symbol of Amish life as cars became popular with other Americans in the early twentieth century. The horse embodies four key Amish values: tradition, limitation, nature, and sacrifice. First, it heralds the triumph of tradition and signals faithful continuity with the past. The horse offers tangible proof that the Amish have not sold out to the glamour and glitter of hypermodernity. A striking symbol of nonconformity, the horse separates the Amish from the modern world and anchors them in the past. To be content with horse-drawn travel is a sign of commitment to patience and the church. In this way, the horse approximates a sacred symbol.

Second, the horse imposes limits on speed, size, and mobility. Plowing a field with horses takes longer than it does with a tractor; traveling by horse and buggy increases the time fivefold over traveling by car. A horse culture places other limits on social life as well. At best, on level roads, travel is confined to about thirty-five miles a day. By restricting mobility, the horse curtails the geographical size of a settlement and intensifies face-to-face interaction. In short, the horse builds social capital by keeping people together. Horses impose other curbs as well. Amish farmers must yield to nature's clock because horses cannot be used in the fields at night. Using horses or mules for field work slows the pace of work and restricts the number of acres a family can till. Modern farmers with megatractors can cultivate a thousand acres, whereas the typical Amish farmer has fewer than fifty tillable acres. The horse limits the expansionist tendencies of modernity and tempers the pace of Amish life.

Third, the horse preserves a link with nature in the midst of America's high-tech environment. By living close to nature, Amish people believe they come closer to God as they experience the rhythms of the changing seasons and the daily struggle with unpredictable weather. Horse care—birth, death, illness, grazing, excrement, and unpredictable temperaments—brings daily contact with nature. The horse also tethers the Amish to nature by keeping them out of cities. For those Amish working in shops and factories, the horse preserves a critical bond with nature.

Fourth, dependence on the horse requires daily sacrifice, a cogent reminder that identity and tradition supersede convenience in Amish life. Horses must be fed morning and evening. It takes time to hitch and unhitch them. Stables must be cleaned and manure hauled to the fields. Horses must be shoed regularly, they kick and bite, and driving one on hilly country roads is dangerous.

An ever-present sign of tradition, the horse slows things down, imposes limits, and articulates some of the deepest values of Amish life. Riding in a horse-drawn carriage is a visible symbol of identity, unmistakable to insiders and outsiders alike. As does any effective cultural emblem, the horse both integrates and separates as it marks the symbolic boundaries of Amish society.

Assorted Brands of Buggies

While the horse is a badge of identity for all Amish communities, buggies distinguish different affiliations from one another. In *Plain Buggies,* Stephen Scott identifies more than a dozen different carriage styles, including various colors—white, black, brown, yellow, gray.[29]

On the outside at least, the carriage epitomizes a cluster of Amish values—separation, simplicity, frugality, equality, and humility. Clashing with the sleek style of modern cars, the stark, rectangular buggy symbolizes the stalwart nature of Amish society. Its shape and accessories are governed by local tradition rather than by market research or consumer desire. Like the horse, the carriage has spawned an infrastructure of Amish industries that manufacture, repair, and service carriages. Locally produced, the carriage is unaffected by the fluctuation of oil prices and import trends. It is, in short, a cogent statement of Amish values and identity.

Although for the most part the buggy suppresses individual expression among members, for teenagers it is a different story. Some teens, depending on their affiliation, decorate their carriages with stickers and plastic reflectors or add air horns, stereo systems, and CD players run by batteries. One elder complained, "Some have wall-to-wall carpeting, insulated woolly stuff all around the top, a big dashboard, glove compartment, speedometer, clock, CD player, buttons galore, and lights and reflectors all over the place. . . . If they have the money, that's what they do, and

The different colors of these carriage tops (*from left:* white, black, yellow, white)
show the church affiliations of their owners. Three different Amish groups live
close together in Mifflin County, Pennsylvania. *Daniel Rodriguez*

that's pride." Nonetheless, the buggy still stands apart from the high-performance
cars driven by some non-Amish teens.

As a prominent public symbol, the horse and carriage articulates an image of uniformity that conveniently camouflages a multitude of differences in income. A businessman who travels in a hired truck all week supervising a multimillion-dollar enterprise drives his horse to Sunday services. Change-minded Amish who limit the size
of their families and professionally landscape their homes nod with affinity to their
stricter neighbors as their carriages pass on backcountry roads. Whereas in modern
society the car accentuates social status and inequality, for the Amish the carriage
levels social life. Farmers and homemakers, laborers and millionaires alike drop their
trappings of status as they step into similar buggies. And they will all rest in a horse-
drawn hearse on their final trip to the cemetery.

Dialect, dress, and horse and carriage remain potent signs of cultural resistance,
markers that for more than a century have successfully protested modernity, mobility,
and consumption-driven lifestyles. Some Amish groups have acquiesced by accepting various changes—increasing the number of English words in the dialect, using
synthetic fabrics for clothing, and hiring vehicles for certain purposes, for example.

Even so, dialect, dress, and horse-drawn transportation remain robust symbols of integration and separation. Unlike the ceremonial symbols some other American ethnic groups display at cultural festivals, Amish signs of identity shape everyday behavior. They link members together in a common history and a shared resistance to modernity. As badges of ethnicity, they mark boundaries between the church and the world and announce Amish identity to insider and outsider alike. They offer compelling proof that, even while certain changes are unfolding behind the curtain, the Amish are still Amish.

III

SOCIAL ORGANIZATION

CHAPTER 8

DIVERSE
AFFILIATIONS

A barn raising in southern Indiana attracted Amish participants from four settlements in Orange and Washington Counties. Some of the men arrived in enclosed buggies, while others came in open ones. Half of the carriages bore an orange slow-moving-vehicle triangle, but the other half did not. A few of the workers had hired English drivers to bring them to the site—an act that would have violated the consciences of others. Many had long beards, though a few sported tightly trimmed ones. Some of the men wore wide suspenders, others narrow ones, and still others none at all. The majority spoke Pennsylvania Dutch, while the rest conversed in Swiss German. About half of the men enjoyed some tobacco as a workday pleasure, but others refused to smoke or chew on principle and avoided working with those who did.

These men, committed to helping one another, had come together around a common building project as Amish people. Yet their differences in appearance, custom, taboos, and communication were striking reminders of the diversity among the many groups who claim the name Amish.

Our People

Our story so far has focused on the core values and practices of Amish life, even as we have argued that the Amish world is becoming increasingly diverse. In this chapter we explore this variety and its consequences. The tangle of Amish communities with its assortment of *Ordnung* regulations is often a mystery to outsiders—and frequently to the Amish themselves.[1] A member of a liberal affiliation, speaking of a rather conservative Amish group, said, "Now they're a different breed, aren't they?" The history of the various "breeds" is lodged in oral tradition, often making it difficult to unravel. Moreover, the practices of different churches and their connections are fluid because they reflect the ongoing life in organic communities rather than formal organizations.

At the opening of the twentieth century, there were 42 geographically distinct Amish settlements in North America, representing 3 or 4 *affiliations*—groups defined by shared views and practices.[2] By 2012 the number of settlements had swelled to 463, and the number of affiliations had multiplied to more than 40. If the smaller subgroups within some affiliations are counted, the number of identifiable cohorts rises above 65, not including the more than 130 fairly independent congregations that lack a firm relationship to a wider affiliation. Although a multitude of Amish identities cropped up in the twentieth century, members of the 2,000 church districts still broadly recognize one another as Amish, use horse-and-buggy transportation, reject higher education, and speak a Swiss or German dialect, among other practices they have in common.

What exactly is an affiliation? When speaking of their own group, Amish people often talk about "our people" (*unser Leit*) and "our way" of doing things. An *affiliation,* as we define it, is a cluster of two or more districts with at least twenty years of shared history. Affiliated congregations share similar Ordnungs, which specify distinctive *lifestyles* and visible *symbols* that set them apart from other affiliations. These interwoven features create a unique *identity* that is expressed in use of technology and consumer products, style of architecture, levels of income, degree of social isolation, and types of occupation as well as in hairstyles, dress patterns, and carriage color and style. Members of an affiliation have a collective awareness of in-group membership and are known as a distinctive group within Amish society and, sometimes, by non-Amish people.

Despite Ordnungs that are similar, the practices of districts within an affiliation are not uniform in every detail because ecclesial authority rests in each local district. As a general rule, the larger the number of districts in an affiliation, the greater the affiliation's diversity. Thus, in a sizable affiliation, some congregations may permit gasoline-powered garden tillers, central gas lighting in homes, or air-powered sewing machines, whereas others may forbid them. Small affiliations with only a handful of districts are much more likely to have greater uniformity across all districts. As shown in table 8.1, the size of affiliations in 2011 ranged from the expansive Lancaster, Pennsylvania–based tribe, with 291 congregations, to tiny ones such as the two-district group in Kokomo, Indiana, which was founded in 1848, and the four-district Abe Miller group in Tennessee.

Table 8.1. Amish Affiliations Ranked by Number of Church Districts, 2011

Affiliation	Date Established	Origin	States	Settlements	Church Districts
Lancaster	1760	PA	8	37	291
Elkhart–LaGrange	1841	IN	3	9	177
Holmes Old Order	1808	OH	1	2	147
Buchanan/Medford	1914	IA	19	67	140
Geauga I	1886	OH	6	11	113
Swartzentruber	1913	OH	15	43	119
Geauga II	1962	OH	4	27	99
Swiss (Adams)	1850	IN	5	15	86
Troyer	1931	OH	6	17	53
Swiss (Allen)	1852	IN	7	17	46
Dover	1915	DE	10	16	42
Andy Weaver/Dan	1955	OH	1	4	40
Nappanee	1841	IN	1	1	37
New Order–Non-electric	1967	OH	7	13	35
Arthur	1864	IL	2	4	31
New Wilmington	1847	PA	2	6	28
Daviess	1868	IN	1	1	26
Kenton	1953	IN	6	13	25
Ashland	1954	OH	6	9	23
Jamesport/Bloomfield	1953	MO	3	5	20
Michigan-related	1970	MI	3	15	20
Nebraska	1881	PA	2	5	19
Renno	1863	PA	2	4	19
New Order–Electric	1972	PA	6	16	17
Fredericktown	1972	OH	2	4	15
Kalona	1846	IA	1	3	13
Kansas/Oklahoma	1883	KS	3	6	12
Milverton	1824	ON	1	4	12
Missouri/Illinois	1960	MO	2	9	11
Somerset	1772	PA	3	6	10
Tobe Hostetler	1940	OH	1	4	10
Milroy/West Union	1969	IN	3	3	9
Guys Mills/Fredonia	1972	PA	2	4	7
Aylmer	1953	ON	1	3	5
Byler	1849	PA	2	1	5
New Order–Tobe	1967	OH	1	1	5
Abe Miller	1970	TN	2	3	4
New Order Fellowship	1983	OH	3	4	4
Turbotville	1970	PA	1	1	3
Kokomo	1848	IN	1	1	2
Subtotal				**414**	**1,780**
Unclassified				34	133
Grand Total				**448**	**1,913**

Source: Compiled by Stephen Scott from settlement directories, other documents, and informants.

A small number of church districts, including this one near Hutchinson, Kansas, permit the use of tractors for field work. A tractor is also used to pull this homemade school bus, which transports Amish pupils who live too far away to ride their bicycles to school. *Steven M. Nolt*

In short, affiliations are loose federations of like-minded Amish churches. They are in no way highly organized groups with bylaws, articles of incorporation, rules for decision making, or protocols for leadership succession. Shaped by local traditions, their informal organization and degree of cohesion depends on the number of districts in the affiliation, the leadership style of the senior bishops, and how frequently—if at all—leaders within an affiliation meet. All the bishops in small affiliations like Dover, Delaware, and Bloomfield, Iowa, meet twice a year. In contrast, bishops in the large Elkhart–LaGrange affiliation in northern Indiana meet once a year, but attendance is irregular, and some of the ordained men never attend. Regardless of affiliation, bishops will convene special meetings when a major issue is causing *Unfrieden,* or unrest.

Complicating the maze of Amish life is the fact that certain districts may share a distinctive trait that sets them apart from other districts. For example, the five dozen *Gmays* that permit tractors for tilling and harvesting in the field are sometimes lumped together as "Tractor Amish," even though they are not an affiliation but simply districts in various settlements that happen to share this atypical custom.[3]

Researcher Stephen Scott has also identified similar clusters of districts, such as the "Reformist" Amish.[4] These Gmays—roughly twenty, scattered in Ontario, Missouri, Maine, Montana, Minnesota, and Illinois—seek to remain in the Amish mainstream but ardently promote high moral standards for courtship (for example, forbidding dating couples from spending any time alone that might lead to sexual temptation) and strictly prohibit smoking and chewing tobacco. While their approach to such matters is similar to that taken by the New Order Amish, the Reformist churches are much more conservative in dress and technology than the New Orders. Amish-owned Pathway Publishers is the voice of this movement.

Another cluster of districts, the so-called Kenton Amish, began in 1953 when conservative-minded families from the Elkhart–LaGrange settlement in Indiana moved to Kenton, Ohio, to begin a settlement with a "low-tech, high morals Ordnung."[5] The Kenton network of some twenty districts of highly traditional Amish in four states share strict standards on dress and technology. Like the Reformists, the Kenton Amish also insist on rigid moral standards regarding courtship and hold parents responsible for the sexual indiscretions of their children. Scott has identified other clusters with shared similarities, such as Midwest Conservatives, Midwest Mainstream, and various Michigan districts that have religious views similar to the New Orders but without the technological liberties of that group.[6]

Names and Distinctions

The names of affiliations derive from various sources. Some carry the name of a founder (e.g., Tobe Hostetler); some, the location of their origin (e.g., Jamesport, Missouri); and some, a label applied to them by others (e.g., New Order). The names of other tribes stem from the unique circumstances surrounding their founding. For example, the Nebraska Amish of central Pennsylvania's Kishacoquillas Valley (commonly known as "Big Valley") have no connection to Nebraska except that a bishop from that state provided guidance when they organized in 1881.[7] In one unusual case, the label Swartzentruber Amish does not reflect the name of the group's founding bishop, Samuel Yoder, but rather the surname of two brothers whose unflinching views influenced the group's formation.[8]

Some affiliations have nicknames. The Nebraska Amish are often called "white toppers" because the sides and roofs of their carriages are covered with white canvas. And the Andy Weaver tribe, named for its original leader, has been nicknamed the "Dan Gmay" because when the affiliation formed in 1955 the first name of three of its ordained leaders was Dan.[9]

The districts of small affiliations are often clumped together in one settlement, while the districts of some large affiliations, such as Buchanan, Iowa, are spread across many states. In some cases a particular group, such as the Daviess Amish in Daviess County, Indiana, may be the only Amish in the area, making the settlement

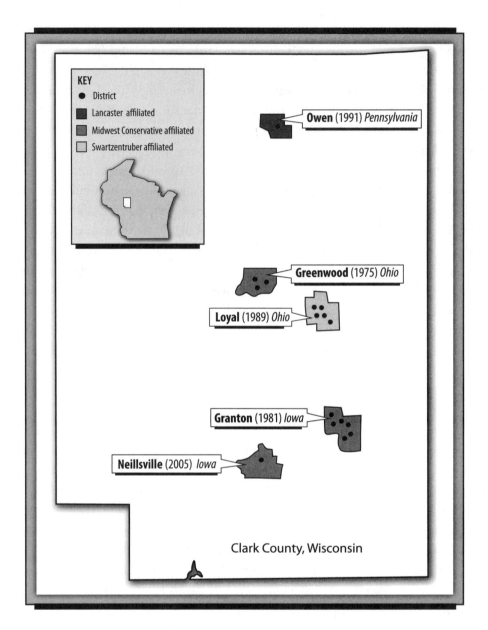

FIGURE 8.1. Five Settlements by Town, Affiliation, Founding
Date, and State of Origin in Clark County, Wisconsin

and the affiliation coterminous. In sharp contrast, a large settlement, such as that in
and around Ohio's Holmes County, can be home to several affiliations.

Many affiliations have geographic offshoots or daughter settlements that have
been established by members migrating to new areas, as illustrated in figure 8.1.
Usually these new communities remain part of the parent affiliation, but not always.

Some daughter settlements eventually develop a separate identity and gradually dissolve their ties to the mother group, but others do not. Even though the Amish in St. Mary's County, Maryland, left Lancaster County, Pennsylvania, in 1943, the St. Mary's leaders still participate in the biannual Lancaster bishops' meeting, as do Lancaster-affiliated bishops from Kentucky, Indiana, and Wisconsin. In contrast, the Lancaster daughter settlement in Romulus, New York, has evolved in a more conservative direction than its parent community.

As we noted in chapter 1, Amish people distinguish between groups based on the restrictiveness of their Ordnungs. In general, low affiliations are more traditional and sectarian, and they draw sharper boundaries with the outside world. Lowness also signals greater humility, less use of English, and less interaction with worldly culture. The higher churches, by contrast, are moving up in the world, becoming more liberal and imbibing more worldly practices.[10]

Amish people in both high and low groups sometimes disparage the opposite type of affiliation with stereotypical comments. For example, one Lancaster deacon, speaking of the Swiss Amish in Indiana, said, "They're just stuck in tradition." Likewise, a progressive Amish person, observing a farmer in a low group milking his cows by hand, said, "It's remarkable how backward some Amish are." Those in lower churches also sense the wide gulf between themselves and their higher brethren. A Swartzentruber bishop, speaking of the more progressive Lancaster tribe, told us, "They're as different from us as you [English] are." This off-hand remark is startling not only because this leader considers his Lancaster brethren as already wading into mainstream society, but also because he perceives such a wide chasm between himself and others who also sing from the *Ausbund* and kneel in humility to wash feet at communion. Because they fear that some of the higher groups soon will—or already have—lost precious Amish practices, the most traditional affiliations see their mission, in part at least, as trying to preserve the old ways of being Amish lest they be lost forever.

It is tempting to impose a linear progression on affiliations and assume that the low ones will eventually evolve along the same path to higher ground. Such a one-dimensional model overlooks the multitude of elements that influence Amish groups as well as the fact that some of the most conservative ones are able to severely retard most changes. Some affiliations simultaneously exhibit liberal traits in certain aspects of community life and conservative behavior in others. For instance, some affiliations that are change-minded in their religious views also have the most restrictive youth practices. Similarly with technology, most New Order districts forbid the use of cell phones, while several Old Order groups accept them. Clearly, while the "low" and "high" distinctions are helpful in sorting out Amish affiliations, they are not an adequate explanation for social change.

A young Amish girl stands on a rail to drive the horses as her father and brother load loose hay onto a wagon. Low affiliations use an old-fashioned, wheel-driven hay loader like this one to place hay on wagons. *Doyle Yoder*

Progressive Amish affiliations permit some state-of-the-art technology. This hay baler collects loose hay on the ground and wraps it tightly into large round bales each weighing several hundred pounds. The baler—designed for a tractor—is powered by a large gasoline engine that is pulled by horses. *Daniel Rodriguez*

How Do Affiliations Emerge?

The histories of some affiliations are rooted in internal divisions, while other affiliations were seeded by migration. In any event, the identity of a group evolves slowly over time and is usually shaped by a mix of two or more of these factors: (1) migration history, (2) ethnicity, (3) distinctive Ordnung practices, (4) local conditions, and (5) internal divisions.[11] The confluence of these historical and sociocultural factors produces the many different brands of Amish life in North America.

Some tribal identities emerged from long-standing relationships established by eighteenth- or nineteenth-century Amish emigrants from Europe. Others were started by migrations within North America after 1900. Families from different areas may move to a new geographical area to establish a community with a distinctive lifestyle, such as a more- or less-liberal Ordnung regarding tobacco use, tractor ownership, pneumatic power in shops, youth activities, or Sunday school.

Ethnicity is a sense of peoplehood created by common cultural customs, language, country of origin, or some amalgam of these things. In the Amish world, the primary ethnic line falls between the Swiss Amish minority and the Pennsylvania Dutch–speaking majority. In the 1850s, the Swiss Amish emigrated from Europe directly to eastern Indiana, although their daughter settlements are now found in several states. They continue to speak a distinctive Swiss-German dialect and share a fairly unique set of surnames and customs. The Pennsylvania Dutch–speaking Amish comprise nearly 94 percent of the Amish world and often hold somewhat negative and stereotyped impressions of the Swiss Amish.[12] (See fig. 8.2.)

Distinctive Ordnung practices related to dress, technology, and modes of interaction with the outside world also shape the identity of affiliations. A clump of districts may develop a particular practice—the use or rejection of bicycles, distinctive haircut styles for men or bonnet size for women—that becomes a key marker and, over several decades, defines its identity.

Local conditions—social, political, religious, economic—also mold the distinctive practices that distinguish an affiliation. The presence of other nearby Amish groups may encourage one group to reject certain forms of technology such as propane lights, tractors, or chainsaws because it wishes to stay behind its change-minded neighbors. Local English industries or urban markets in some regions may entice Amish workers and encourage certain occupations and the development of distinctive lifestyles. In addition, the geographical terrain—from forest to plain—may increase the use of certain technologies, like tractors for field work. These differences may also help to stir unrest, which sometimes plays a role in the birth of affiliations. Certain trigger issues like the acceptance of new technology, the practice of shunning, or support for mission activities may create controversies and produce a schism.

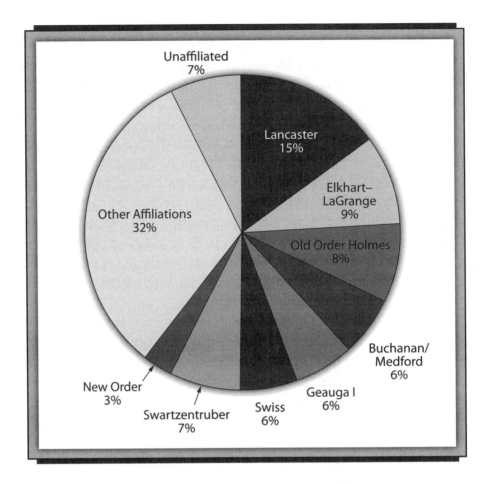

FIGURE 8.2. Proportional Size of Selected Affiliations

Such an event may embed the divisive belief or practice in a group's identity for a long time.

A Sampler of Schisms

Historian Leroy Beachy, writing about the Holmes County settlement, referred to the 1900s as "a seemingly reckless century of division" because the Amish community there splintered into more than thirty separate groups. Many of them no longer bear the Amish name, and some that do refuse to commune with one another.[13] This settlement has experienced remarkable discord, but so have those in other locales, such as the Big Valley in central Pennsylvania.

Every schism has its own set of flammable embers, but the features of Amish society that tend to ignite conflict include (1) social differentiation, (2) decentralized polity, (3) an emphasis on ethics, (4) separation from the world, and (5) leadership styles. A basic axiom of social organization is that size breeds differentiation. In other words, larger affiliations tend to splinter into subunits more quickly than smaller groups. The likelihood of dissent is also compounded because the decentralized church polity ultimately places authority in local congregations. Besides, the Amish-Anabaptist theology of discipleship emphasizes the importance of following Jesus in daily life and stresses mundane practice as much or more than abstract doctrinal belief. Differences in opinion about how best to *practice* everyday faith cannot easily be papered over with vague theological statements.

In addition, applying the principle of separation from the world to daily living is open to dozens of interpretations, especially when it comes to technology. For example, should electricity from public utilities be allowed, and if so, under what circumstances? An Amish person disenchanted with a proliferation of affiliations in his area blamed it on "strife, disagreement, and unrest regarding congregational rules and regulations." As an example, he cited one group that forbids using a chainsaw to cut wood because they see it as "evil, arrogant, proud, and disdainful," while "we have another group that does not detect any spiritual harm in owning and using a chainsaw. . . . So here is a group, there is a group [and] hardly any two groups have the same standards."[14]

Finally, leaders—especially bishops with strong personalities—can sow seeds of discord if they do not yield to fellow leaders or to members of their own Gmay. Some Amish people note that a doctrinal, technological, or dress issue that appears pivotal in a controversy may be a smokescreen for deeper issues—personality conflicts, power struggles, or quarreling of one kind or another among leaders.

Despite the five factors that sometimes enable division, basic Amish religious and cultural values also restrain it. Patience, yielding to others, and submitting to churchly authority and tradition—not schism—are by far the more typical mode of dealing with conflict. Although formally autonomous, church districts frequently defer to one another, trying to forestall change so as not to offend the sensibilities of more conservative leaders, members, or neighboring districts. Nevertheless, schism has been a part of the Amish experience.

Two divisions a half century apart produced two new affiliations that have become opposite poles on the Amish continuum in North America. The Swartzentruber Amish are the most conservative affiliation, and the New Orders are the most liberal. These two wingtips of the Amish world—Swartzentrubers and New Orders—represent 7 percent and 3 percent respectively, leaving the vast number of Amish people in the middle.

Swartzentruber Amish

The Swartzentruber Amish coalesced in 1913 in eastern Ohio around a particular interpretation of church discipline. Although shunning ex-members remained a common Amish commitment, the manner in which it was carried out had come to vary. Traditionally, anyone who was excommunicated was shunned until he or she repented. For those who refused to recant, shunning was lifelong. This traditional view was known as *streng Meidung,* or "strict shunning."

By 1900, however, many midwestern Old Orders were drawing a distinction between how they would shun members excommunicated for defecting to related Anabaptist churches and how they would shun those excommunicated for major sins or persistent disobedience. In either case, the ex-member had reneged on his or her baptismal vow, but some leaders thought that quietly leaving the Amish faith for a conservative Mennonite church was a less serious matter and that shunning in such situations could cease if the person became a faithful member of another Anabaptist group. When most leaders in Holmes County, Ohio, signaled their desire to relax strict shunning along these lines, Bishop Samuel E. Yoder (1872–1932) balked. By 1917 Yoder's church district, which upheld strict shunning no matter what the offense, had broken fellowship with neighboring Amish congregations. A group of Amish mediators from Indiana and Illinois were unable to mend the breach. The disagreement over shunning may well have provoked the division, but historical accounts point to other factors that played a key role.[15]

Beyond retaining strict shunning, the new Swartzentruber group staunchly refused to alter the traditional Ordnung in any way and soon became known for resisting innovation in household technology, farming practices, dress customs, and worship ritual. This traditional tribe eventually launched daughter settlements in Ohio, Tennessee, and New York; by 2012, it had spread to thirteen states and Ontario.

New Order Amish

The New Orders also emerged in Holmes County, though nearly fifty years after the birth of the Swartzentrubers. The roots of this movement go back to the late 1940s and 1950s. During World War II and the Korean and Vietnam Wars, Amish men who were drafted typically declared themselves conscientious objectors and, in lieu of military service, served in Civilian Public Service work camps (during World War II) or as orderlies and maintenance staff in public hospitals and mental institutions, at minimum wage.[16] These experiences exposed them to the outside world and in some cases led them to question their religious tradition. Simultaneously, Mennonites and other Protestant revivalists were active in Holmes County and publicly questioned whether Amish church regulations (Ordnung) were a stumbling block to receiving divine salvation. The confluence of these factors birthed the so-called Amish mission movement (discussed in chapter 3) and caused unrest within Amish ranks and an exodus to churches that were more evangelical.

A number of Amish lay members and a few ministers sympathized with those who were attracted to evangelical religious language and experience but did not want to discard basic Amish beliefs or practices such as horse-drawn transportation, which they saw as a useful discipline for maintaining a simple Christian lifestyle. They began gathering for evening Bible study, and they organized separate youth meetings for their children as an alternative to the sometimes-rowdy Amish youth activities of the time, which could include alcohol consumption and sexual indiscretion.[17]

These developments fomented discontent within the Holmes County settlement, both because detractors claimed the reformers exhibited a "holier-than-thou" attitude and also because the settlement was still unsettled from the recent exodus of members spurred by the midcentury mission movement. Cautious voices feared that the cycle would repeat itself. Tensions were such that in 1963, and again in 1965, Holmes County church leaders invited a group of Amish bishops from other states to resolve the differences, but to no avail. In 1966, fellowship between the Old Order church and the reformers broke down, and the Old Orders dubbed them *New Order* Amish. Forty-five years later, one New Order minister still regrets the label, "because we prefer the name Amish Brotherhood."

By 2012 the New Order movement included four subgroups in some seventy districts in twelve states. One of these subgroups allows public utility electricity in homes and businesses. Generally, New Orders have sought to maintain aspects of plain dress, speak Pennsylvania Dutch, and use horse-drawn transportation. However, they all place more weight on the importance of doctrinal belief, personal religious experience, and a more analytical understanding of Christian faith alongside the Ordnung of their church.

Having largely frozen technological change in 1917, the Swartzentrubers stand in stark contrast to the New Orders. New Order activities, such as Sunday school, youth group Bible studies, and the requirement that teens must be baptized before being allowed to date, as well as conveniences such as tractors in the field, telephones in the home, and airplane travel are all categorically rejected by the Swartzentrubers.

Symbolic Separators

Amish groups, like all human groups, erect signs that set themselves apart from each other. "We don't have ponies or peacocks," said one woman, noting two distinctions between her conservative church and more liberal ones. The following examples illustrate how the symbolic separators of dress and buggies mark the identities of affiliations.

Clothing

A woman's head covering—the closely fitted cap worn almost all the time—announces its wearer's affiliation, because the size, style, and number of pleats vary by group. Most Amish women wear bonnets over their coverings in public. The vast majority wear black bonnets, but the Byler Amish women wear brown bonnets. Swartzentruber women wear scarves over their coverings and under their bonnets, and women in the Nebraska Amish affiliation wear large wide-brimmed, flat-crowned straw hats instead of bonnets.

In change-minded groups, mothers may dress their school-age boys in shirts of various colors, young women have some choice of apron style, and adult women may select various fabrics and colors for their dresses. More conservative communities severely restrict the colors and style of clothing for men and women of all ages.

The style and size of men's hats, the color of their trousers, the width of their suspenders, and the cut of their hair reveal their affiliation—and its degree of traditionalism. Even footwear marks church ties. While some groups permit dark-colored sneakers, more conservative ones insist on black leather shoes, with one requiring that all shoes have distinct heels.[18] The shirt style—pullover or buttoned—and the number of suspenders function like team uniforms in the sense that they announce the affiliation of the members. Although most men wear two suspenders, Renno Amish men in Mifflin County, Pennsylvania, wear only one. And in a few affiliations the men simply button their trousers, using neither belts nor suspenders, as a mark of traditionalism. Nebraska Amish men wear white shirts for everyday activities, but in more progressive groups, men have a greater selection of colors for their shirts.

Buggies

Carriages also signify an affiliation's identity. The style, color, and accessories turn buggies into mobile billboards for their specific tribe. In addition, the design of the buggy body, the size and location of windows and doors, and the type of door (sliding doors or roll-up curtains), lights, brakes, dashboards, sun visors, turn signals, wheel type (steel-banded or rubber-banded), and accessories vary from one group to another.

Several tribes have black-topped buggies, but their distinct body designs, doors, and windows distinguish them from one another. Although members of the Lancaster, Pennsylvania–based affiliation live in several states, they all drive the gray,

Lancaster-style buggy, though sometimes with subtle variation in amenities. Most of the Swiss Amish scattered across several states ride in buggies that have no tops or other enclosures.[19] Riders sit in the open and shield themselves from rain and snow with large umbrellas—though some Swiss districts allow parents to create small enclosures, called "kid boxes," to protect young children from inclement weather.[20]

Many affiliations place flashing red lights on the backs of their carriages to warn surrounding traffic. The Delaware Amish, however, affix large strobe lights on the tops of their buggies. Swartzentruber carriages, in contrast, sport few elements of self-protection and do not even display the bright orange slow-moving-vehicle triangle that most other Amish buggies bear.[21] The carriages of the Swartzentruber and Nebraska tribes carry a kerosene lantern instead of electric lights for nighttime visibility. Even here, there is some difference in practice: one Swartzentruber subgroup's members place lanterns on each side of their buggies, while members of another faction hang only one light at the back of the left side of the buggy.

Groups that are more liberal outfit their buggies with accessories that include LED lights, turn signals, axle-driven alternators to charge batteries, hydraulic brakes, windshield wipers, frost-free windows, clocks, speedometers, and various colors of upholstery. One man confided that he has a battery-powered GPS in his buggy "in case my horse gets lost!" These upscale buggies stand in stark contrast to the roofless Swiss and one-lantern Swartzentruber vehicles.

Although these symbolic separators perform important social functions by marking boundaries and honing identities, some Amish people, especially in liberal groups, question their spiritual value. "I have been taught that we need standards, fences or guard rails to keep our sheep in," said one man. "But why do we all have different kinds of fences or guard rails? . . . Didn't God give us the laws which govern how to build the strongest fences?"[22]

The Ties That Break and Bind

The boundaries between affiliations vary somewhat. Some boundaries are porous, and others are more like stone walls. Some subgroups within affiliations maintain warm fraternal relations with one another, while others do not. Amish people speak about *diening* with another group, as in "we *dien* with the Troyer people." The German word *Diener* is the term used for a minister. It means "servant," so to *dien* with a group means that ministers from both affiliations are welcome to preach (serve) in each other's Sunday services because the two groups are "in fellowship" and have a spiritual affinity that allows them to collaborate on some level.[23]

Ordained leaders of groups that are in fellowship greet one another with a handshake and kiss when they meet, according to admonitions in the New Testament

(Rom. 16:16; 1 Cor. 16:20). The kiss is a visible symbol of an ecclesial bond between two affiliations. In addition, tribes that are in fellowship with one another may look favorably on intermarriage among their young people, and bishops may attend or witness ordinations in one another's congregations. Leaders may also be called in to help mediate disputes in the other affiliation.

There is no template that prescribes who diens with whom. Typically, groups in fellowship have something in common that draws them together—similar views of shunning, salvation, acceptable household technology, or some other issue. Sometimes the links of affinity are long-standing ones, rooted in church polity. For example, historically, the Lancaster Amish, despite being among the most technologically progressive affiliations, dien with the much more traditional Andy Weaver group, which formed in Ohio in 1955. The common bond between the two groups is their shared commitment to strict shunning, which trumps their sharp differences in the use of technology.[24] Not all of the Lancaster districts, however, dien with the Andy Weavers. Although most affiliations share a common understanding of whom they do and do not dien with, final authority to tie or cut bonds of fellowship and to extend or retract invitations to clergy from other groups rests with the local district's ministers. Asked how his church determines who it diens with, a Swiss minister responded, "I don't really know. . . . We would fellowship with a group that keeps the Amish ways . . . with those that have the same 'core values' and keep the *Bann*."

The fellowship relationships are usually symmetrical, but not always. On some occasions a higher congregation will permit a minister from a more conservative group to preach in its church services even though the conservative group would likely not reciprocate. Occasionally, reciprocity happens by mistake. In one case, a minister from an out-of-state New Order church accompanied family members to the funeral of a relative in a much more traditional affiliation. To his surprise, he was asked to preach the funeral sermon. The local ministers knew that the visiting minister was ordained but were not aware that he was from a New Order church. When they discovered it after the funeral, they were annoyed, believing that he should have declared his affiliation and declined to preach out of respect for their more traditional Ordnung. A breach of fellowship can feel especially harsh if a schism occurs within an affiliation and the two new factions break fraternal ties. Such splinters divide families and neighbors, which can create many awkward encounters at funerals, family reunions, and other events.

As evidenced in the barn-raising vignette at the opening of the chapter, members of groups that do not fellowship together may labor together in a neighborly fashion, employ one another in business, and participate in public events such as auctions. The boundaries and rituals of religious distinction usually become more visible in the context of formal church activities.

Table 8.2. Growth of Amish Church Districts in
Selected Affiliations, 1991–2010

Affiliation	1991	2010	% Growth
Swartzentruber[1]	38	103	171
Swiss (Adams) [2]	33	87	163
Daviess	11	26	136
Swiss (Allen)	21	46	119
Geauga I	53	113	113
Lancaster[3]	141	286	102
Milverton	6	12	100
Elkhart–LaGrange[4]	92	173	88
Holmes Old Order	87	147	68
Arthur	18	30	66
Tractor Old Order[5]	25	40	60
New Order[6]	45	69	53
Total of twelve affiliations	**570**	**1,132**	**99**
Total North America	**898**	**1,826**	**103**

Source: Compiled by Stephen Scott from settlement directories, other documents, and informants.

[1]Includes four subgroups, but not the Jacob Hershberger one.
[2]Includes several subgroups.
[3]Includes daughter settlements.
[4]Includes related settlements in Wisconsin and Michigan.
[5]Tractor groups are a classification, not an affiliation.
[6]Includes all groups of New Orders.

Different Rates of Growth

Apart from their different symbolic separators and variation in day-to-day practice, the growth rate of affiliations also varies dramatically, as shown in table 8.2. The growth of church districts in twelve selected affiliations, tracked over a twenty-year period, reveals their rate of expansion. Although the number of districts is not an exact yardstick of population growth, it serves as a proxy—assuming that the number of members per district in each group remained roughly constant from 1991 to 2010.[25]

Although the total number of Amish districts in America increased by 103 percent in the two decades, the growth of the twelve selected groups varied from 53 percent to 171 percent, demonstrating dramatic fluctuations from tribe to tribe. The increase of Swartzentruber districts, for example, outpaced that of New Orders by threefold. What is striking in table 8.2 is that the most traditional, sectarian affiliations (Swartzentruber; Adams County Swiss) are growing much more rapidly than their liberal-minded cousins (Holmes Old Order; Arthur; New Order). Several factors may help to explain these different rates. As we show in chapter 9, the most traditional groups have larger families and fewer defections. These groups draw the sharpest lines of separation from the larger world and curb interaction with outsiders. One way they increase separation is by living in remote rural areas with few urban temptations and less exposure to Amish communities that are more assimilated. Furthermore, the most conservative affiliations customarily practice strict shunning, which may deter members from defecting. In any event, the uneven growth rates, if constant over time, suggest that in coming years the most traditional groups will increase their share of the Amish pie.

The expanding geographical and cultural diversity of the Amish in America poses a fundamental question: What is the social glue—the secret of their sense of solidarity—that bonds Amish people together despite their vast variety? The answer lies in an interplay of internal and external factors that we explore in chapter 10. Before doing that, however, we trace the factors that are producing their population growth.

CHAPTER 9

POPULATION PATTERNS

What thirty-four-year-old David Rapinz missed the most when he joined the Amish in Geauga County, Ohio, was his pilot's license. Giving that up was harder than giving up his TV and car. He tested the Amish waters for four years before kneeling for baptism in 2000. "It was the thing I needed to do in my life," he said. "It's not for everybody. . . . It's a complete lifestyle change . . . [but] that's what I wanted to do. [Until now] I didn't have a church or anything like that." Rapinz married an Amish woman with whom he fell in love before he was baptized. He works as a senior advisor at H&R Block, and when he is at the office, he uses a phone, computer, and e-mail account that are owned by his employer.

Robust Growth

The Amish have enjoyed remarkable growth in the twentieth century. From a meager band of some 6,000 in 1900, their numbers had swelled beyond a quarter million by 2011.[1] Since 1960 the Amish population has doubled about every twenty years. In fact, from 1991 to 2012, their population grew from 123,000 to nearly 274,000, as shown in table 9.1. Despite the social and technological upheavals that have accompanied the twentieth century, the Amish, with their emphasis on separation from the world and their penchant for traditional ways, have thrived.

Only a tiny fraction of this growth has come from converts like Rapinz, however. Groups can grow only by having children or winning converts, and the Amish have grown primarily through natural reproduction rather than evangelism. But produc-

Table 9.1. North American Amish Church Districts and Population, 1901–2012

Year	Church Districts	Estimated Population
1901	63	6,300
1911	60	6,600
1921	83	9,960
1931	110	14,300
1941	154	21,100
1951	202	27,675
1961	269	36,855
1971	367	50,280
1981	569	77,955
1991	898	123,025
2001	1,382	189,335
2012	2,007	273,710

Source: Compiled by Stephen Scott from Raber's *New American Almanac,* 1930–2012; *The Mennonite Year Book,* 1905–1960; and Amish historical documents.

Note: The estimated average number of people per district increased in the twentieth century as follows: 100 in 1901, 110 in 1911, 120 in 1921, 130 in 1931, and 137 in 1941 through 2012.

ing the children is not enough—they must also be persuaded to join their birthright community. The spectacular growth of Amish society is driven not only by sizable families but also by vigorous retention of young people.

Large Families

Families in agrarian societies around the world are large in part because children are an economic asset to the labor demands of farm life. With their own long-standing ties to the soil and rural setting, Amish families are no exception. A recent summary of births and deaths in 300 church districts in 60 settlements across 17 states offers a snapshot of the reproductive power in these communities in a single year: 2,356 births and 203 deaths.[2] The *Gemeinde Register,* a newsletter that serves Ohio Amish communities, reports a similar burst of growth: 886 births and 91 deaths in one year.[3]

Married Amish women on average have about seven children, far exceeding the overall average of 2.1 births to women in the United States.[4] This high reproductive rate fuels the growth of the Amish population. Not only are families large, but almost everyone is producing children. The percentage of unmarried Amish people over 30 years of age is generally below 6 percent, whereas 35 percent of all Americans ages 30 to 34 have never married. The average age of first marriage for Americans, 26.5 years for women and 28.7 years for men, is higher than the average for Amish women (21.1) and men (22.3).[5]

Table 9.2. Average Number of Children Born to
Amish Women by Settlement/Affiliation

Settlement/Affiliation	Women	Children (Mean)
Adams Co., IN	N/A	9.0
Allen Co., IN	N/A	8.0
Arthur, IL	192	5.9
Buchanan, IA	40	10.2
Elkhart–LaGrange, IN	N/A	7.0
Holmes Co., OH		
Old Order	304	6.2
Tobe	59	9.2
Andy Weaver	133	8.0
New Order	143	5.5
Kalona, IA	58	7.5
Lancaster Co., PA	125	7.2
Nappanee, IN	N/A	7.0
Nebraska, PA	120	5.7
St. Mary's Co., MD	45	9.0
Swartzentruber	45	9.3
Wisconsin (all settlements)	245	9.4

Source: Settlement directories; Nolt and Meyers, *Plain Diversity*, 119; and 2010 Lancaster Demographic Study of 18 districts.
Note: Includes all live births to women by the end of their childbearing years (ages 45–65).
N/A = no data available.

Although the overall average is seven children, Amish family size fluctuates by settlement and affiliation, as the data in table 9.2 illustrate. Parents in the rather strict community of Buchanan County, Iowa, for instance, have nearly twice as many children (10.2) as the New Order families in Holmes County, Ohio (5.5). Similarly, researchers Charles Hurst and David McConnell found that 47 percent of the Swartzentruber Amish have nine or more children compared with 25 percent for other Amish in Wayne County, Ohio.[6] The traditional Swiss communities in Adams County, Indiana, have two more children on average than the more liberal Amish living near Nappanee, Indiana. The pattern is clear: the more conservative the community, the higher the number of children.[7]

The traditional *Gelassenheit* mindset—to accept whatever comes, including children, as nature's way, with the blessing of God—that characterizes more conservative communities may help to explain this phenomenon. Couples in more liberal communities, shaped by the modern impulse to control the circumstances of one's life, are more likely to practice family planning, whether by natural or artificial methods. Despite church admonitions against it, strategies for limiting children remain a fairly private matter even in close-knit communities. Indications of family planning in any particular affiliation are apparent not from the number of religious admonitions but from the size of completed families.

The father's leadership status is also associated with some differences in reproduction rates. Two research studies found that the families of ordained leaders tend to have more children on average than ordinary families.[8] This difference may result because leadership nominees are more conservative and, if ordained, may feel compelled to meet community expectations for large families.

Will Family Size Decline?

One of the most sweeping and consequential changes underway in many Amish communities since 1975 is a shift toward nonfarm work. Numerous studies have confirmed that *some* farm families have more children than nonfarm households, with differences ranging from one to three more children.[9] But the association between farming and large families is not always strong. Among the Swiss Amish in Adams County, Indiana, the move away from farming has not reduced family size, nor do the farmers in the Elkhart–LaGrange settlement have large families. Thus, while agriculture as a vocation does not necessarily correlate with family size, the conservatism of a group does.

Comparing general fertility in Europe and North and South America from the eighteenth through the mid-twentieth centuries, historian Walter Nugent found that fertility rates "at first glance" appear "lower in urban-industrial" societies than in rural ones, "but there are too many exceptions for the pattern to hold." In many cases, for example, fertility increased for a generation or two after an industrial revolution and declined gradually only when the implications of urbanization had worked themselves out over time.[10] Seen in that light, it is possible that the long-term impact of Amish occupational change on family size may manifest itself more vividly in the coming years as the children and grandchildren of nonfarmers complete their families.

Even though we might expect that Amish family size will eventually shrink with the decline of farming because children, no longer needed for labor, will become an economic liability, several factors may mitigate such a decline. One is that many Amish people have set up small shops and industries that provide chores and apprenticeships for children; thus, the work of children continues to make a valued contribution to the family economy. Another factor is that the strong moral imperative to reproduce that propels growth in Amish society is not occupation dependent but arises from the enduring power of an oft-cited religious directive in Amish writings and oral lore to "be fruitful and multiply" (Gen. 1:22). An esteemed Amish leader, writing in *Family Life* in 2012, strongly encourages parents to have large families. He cites Solomon's words in Psalm 127 that "children are an heritage of the Lord . . . like arrows in the hand of a mighty man . . . happy is the man that has his quiver full of them."[11] It is morally unacceptable for Amish married couples to decide not to reproduce, and parents rarely delay their first conception. Some couples who are unable to conceive adopt children born to non-Amish parents.

Finally, even though the majority of Amish people now find work outside of agriculture, virtually all of them continue to live in rural areas on small, child-friendly plots that can support sizable families. Thus, even if family size declines somewhat, it is unlikely that Amish families will soon shrink to the two-child American norm. The Amish experience, given the move to small businesses, the biblical imperative to reproduce, and the rural home setting, may counter the idea that industrialization always leads to smaller families.[12]

Seekers and Joiners

Although converts bring new perspectives to Amish communities, they are not a significant source of growth. Only about seventy-five outsiders have joined and remained members of Amish churches since 1950.[13] Some seekers are young adults like seventeen-year-old Kendra, who told us she planned to join the Amish after she graduated from high school. She has lived near an Amish community all of her life, "loves how they live," and has read twenty books about them. A year ago, "I actually came out and told my parents that I am turning Amish," she said. "But they aren't too happy about me joining . . . I've been just taking it slow. . . . I just have to wait two more years!"[14]

Emily, a non-Amish youth from Maryland, decided not to wait that long and was baptized into a Lancaster County *Gmay* as a seventeen-year-old. "Her parents," reported one Amish observer, "were bewildered [at first] . . . but now they seem to accept it better." Her father admitted, "It's kind of unbelievable. . . . But there's lots of worse things she could have done."[15] Within a few months she left, though, because she had discovered that "the Amish aren't perfect."

More typical are married seekers with children who become disenchanted with hypermodernity and are drawn to the slower pace of Amish life. A project manager in the IT industry, hoping to move his family to an Amish community, told us, "This is not a passing interest." He continued, "We are not obnoxious tourists. We are earnestly considering this path and . . . are looking for Amish subgroups that are on the conservative side but not quite Old Order. We need to find a group that is fine with indoor plumbing and with having our horses shod by a farrier versus doing it all ourselves. We are absolutely open to living by the customs and rules (the *Ordnung*). I know that sounds ironic as I sit writing you an electronic e-mail. At some point I would abandon the use of computers."[16]

After some seekers test-drive Amish life for a few weeks or even years, they discover the difficulty of driving across the cultural bridge to Amish land and shift into reverse. Others continue their journey by living in an Amish community and participating in church and community activities for several years until they eventually request baptism. Some seekers who do not take the big step nevertheless remain closely involved with their new-found Amish friends. A retired Pennsylvania state trooper who considered becoming Amish lived in a small bungalow near Amish families for several years and then decided to join a car-driving Amish Mennonite congregation so that he could continue providing taxi service for his horse-and-buggy neighbors.

Bill and Tricia Moser switched from mainstream to Amish life in the late 1990s in Michigan. He was an architect, and she was an occupational therapist. After becoming disenchanted with the militarism of their local Protestant church, they moved to an Amish community and eventually joined. "I'd been thinking for a long time that I wanted to shrink my world, create a life where work, recreation, family, and religion were all one, a whole, not so fragmented," Bill explained. After living in an Amish community, he discovered, "This was the vision I had . . . their work, their religion and life all integrated together." The Mosers' new congregation went through some difficult struggles, leading the couple to consider leaving. But their children, by then accustomed to Amish ways, declared, "If you do that, you will be doing it without us."[17] So they stayed.

A convert himself to the plain-dressing Old Order River Brethren, Stephen Scott received frequent inquiries from people contemplating joining an Amish community. Some of them had done careful research and held a reasonable understanding of Amish membership requirements. Others did not. Scott recalled a telephone call from a man who wanted to join an Amish group that does not "have electricity and lives like cave people." After Scott explained the challenges of Amish life, the caller said, "I have one more question: Do they use toilet paper?"[18]

Based on many conversations with people prospecting for an Amish home, Scott identifies four types of seekers. *Checklist* seekers want a church that meets certain specifications. One young man wanted a horse-and-buggy church that would hire him as a youth pastor and also allow him to play gospel songs on a steel guitar. These folks, says Scott, often become "wandering saints who never find a perfect church." *Cultural* seekers, imagining that the Amish live a Little-House-on-the-Prairie type of life, are enchanted more by pioneer agriculture than by the religious aspects of Amish life. By contrast, *spiritual utopian* seekers, yearning for a church that replicates true

New Testament Christianity, hope to find it in an Amish community. Finally, *stability* hunters often come with emotional issues stemming from dysfunctional families and hopes that their problems will be solved in the stable context of an Amish community.[19]

Some who join Amish communities have been long-time critics of modern society and sometimes transfer their criticism to the Amish. Converts in general tend to be especially zealous in keeping Amish traditions and regulations. They can become discouraged by the inconsistencies of Amish life and the weak convictions of some birthright Amish who chafe at church regulations. One Amish historian estimates that half of the converts eventually drop out.[20]

Converts hail from various Protestant, Catholic, and non-religious backgrounds. One newcomer arrived with Mormon credentials, and a few have come from Mennonite roots. Since the early 1990s, two Amish congregations near Aylmer, Ontario, have incorporated into their fellowship some twenty Russian Mennonites whose ancestors migrated to Canada in the late nineteenth century.[21] About half of these newcomers were single men who married Amish women.

This Canadian example illustrates two patterns about newcomers. First, regardless of settlement, about half of them arrive already married, and most of the others are English men who marry Amish women. Becoming Amish seems to hold more attraction for English men than for English women, although in a few cases English women dating Amish men have joined and then married. Second, joiners tend to cluster in certain communities. The large Lancaster County affiliation, for example, has had only two converts since 1900 (both of whom later left), whereas the smaller settlement in Geauga County, Ohio, counts at least half a dozen newcomers in its ranks.[22]

A few converts have been ordained as ministers or asked to fill other leadership roles.[23] Baptized in 1966, Catholic-raised David Luthy soon began working for the Amish-run Pathway Publishers in Aylmer, Ontario, and married an Amish woman in 1971. Eventually Luthy became director of the Heritage Historical Library, which holds an extensive collection of Amish historical materials.

Non-traditional Amish surnames such as Alexander, Coletti, Engbretson, Jones, Johnson, Theil, and Vendley now appear in Amish directories amid the traditional Stoltzfuses, Millers, Yoders, and Waglers. Some of the transplants gather periodically for a "converts' reunion."[24] Even after many years of living in Amish communities, however, some converts never fully assimilate. One man who was baptized into a conservative group admits that he never got used to "their German coldness. I'm Italian and we hug each other."[25]

Retention and Defection

In addition to the small influx of converts and high birth rates, the growth of the Amish population is also fueled by the retention of many of its young people. Most of those who defect do so before baptism, but a few leave later in life. Exit patterns vary by historical time period, affiliation, settlement, father's occupation and ordination, family dynamics, and attendance at Amish schools. The rates reported here combine both pre- and post-baptism defections. Although retention rates in some settlements can be calculated by using family information from settlement directories, an exact national composite rate is elusive because of incomplete records.

Fluctuating Rates

The historical evidence shows a decline in defection in some Amish communities in the last half of the twentieth century. Defection in Geauga County, Ohio, for example, dropped from 30 percent for those born during the 1920s to 5 percent for those born in the 1960s. Similarly, the exit of people from the Elkhart–LaGrange community in northern Indiana dipped from 21 percent for those born in the 1930s to 10 percent for those born in the 1950s. The loss of Amish-born people in Nappanee, Indiana, dropped from 55 percent in the 1920s to 16 percent in the 1970s.[26]

That retention increased at the very time that Amish people moved into nonfarm work and accelerated their contact with the outside world might seem paradoxical, but two other factors help to explain the trend. The stronger retention rates coincided with the end of the military draft and the rise of Amish schools. Both of these factors insulated children and young people from outside influences. Some eighteen-year-old Amish men performing their alternative to military service in city hospitals in the 1950s and 60s never returned home. Moreover, the shift to nonfarm work mostly pertains to married men, who would be less likely to leave the Amish fold because of exposure to the outside world than would twelve-year-olds attending public schools or single young men working in urban areas.

Three or more generations ago, most Amish children spent their formative years in public schools surrounded by non-Amish peers, only to spend their adult working lives in agricultural relationships with mostly Amish neighbors. For twenty-first-century youth, the reverse is true: during childhood they attend an Amish school surrounded by ethnic peers and then spend their adult lives working with non-Amish coworkers, customers, clients, and suppliers. So while it may seem paradoxical that retention rates rose as farming declined, the paradox fades in the face of these factors.

Our study of more than 11,000 children born in the Holmes County settlement before 1980 shows a clear link between defection and affiliation, as shown in table 9.3.

Table 9.3. Amish Defection Rates by Affiliation in the
Holmes County, Ohio, Settlement

Affiliation	Children	Defectors	Defection Rate (%)
New Order Christian Fellowship	286	196	68.5
New Order	1,010	408	40.4
Old Order	7,817	1,964	25.1
New Order Tobe	216	42	19.4
Old Order Tobe	671	41	6.1
Andy Weaver	1,246	33	2.6
Total	**11,246**	**2,684**	**23.9**

Source: Compiled by Stephen Scott from *Ohio Amish Directory, Holmes County and Vicinity, 2010*.
Note: Number of children includes all those born before 1980 except "special needs children." Excludes Troyer and Swartzentruber affiliations.

In general, the more conservative the Ordnung, the higher the retention. The New Order defection rate (40.4 percent) is fifteen times higher than that of the more traditional Andy Weaver group (2.6 percent). Nolt and Meyers found this same pattern in northern Indiana even when they compared districts within the same affiliation. The most liberal cluster of districts had lost 31 percent of its youth compared with only 7 percent in a more traditional cluster.[27]

It is difficult to generalize, however, because the defection rate even among liberal affiliations varies, depending on the group, its setting, and its practices. The defection rates of three sizable progressive affiliations—the Old Orders in Holmes County, the Lancaster County Amish, and the Geauga County Amish—are 25 percent, 16 percent, and 5 percent, respectively. These differences likely show the impact of geographical context—people leaving the Holmes County Old Order group have a half dozen or so nearby Amish or Amish-related alternatives, whereas the Lancaster and Geauga dropouts have no Amish groups and few car-driving churches with Amish ties nearby.[28] Similarly, defection in the Swartzentruber community in rural upper New York State is lower than in some other Swartzentruber settlements in which youth have exposure and easy access to more liberal Amish groups and, in some cases, help from ex-Amish organizations that assist those who want to leave.[29]

Thus, a particular affiliation with daughter settlements in different states may have different rates of retention in the various settlements. A young woman who ran away from a Swartzentruber settlement in Missouri counted sixteen people (six before baptism and ten after) who left her fifty-family community over a six-year period.[30] "There is a big variation in defection between Swartzentruber communities," she notes, with rates as high as 25 percent in some communities and as low as 5 percent in others.

Retention rates are sometimes higher in families where the household head is a farmer and/or ordained.[31] This may result from a more conservative outlook in general rather than farming or ordination per se. "Conservative thinkers," said one leader, "are more likely to be ordained and to have offspring that think like dad does." In general, males tend to defect at higher rates than females, and those attending public schools at higher rates than their peers in Amish schools.[32] Finally, defections cluster somewhat in certain families. In one study, 39 percent of the families with children who defected lost three or more.[33]

These social factors that sway the likelihood of defection underscore the impossibility of calculating an exact composite rate. Nonetheless, based on evidence from numerous settlements and affiliations, we estimate that on average about 85 percent of Amish-born children will join and remain lifelong members of an Amish community.

Who Leaves and Why

Whether one leaves the Amish before or after baptism makes a big difference because the church respects one's choice to be baptized or not to be. Youth who leave before making that pledge will not be punished officially, although in certain affiliations they may be ostracized by friends and family. In all groups, however, those who exit after baptism will be excommunicated and face some form of shunning, because they have broken their lifelong vow to uphold the teachings of the church.

Some unbaptized youth who decide to leave but fear the reaction of their family may choose to vanish in the night. Others gradually drift away from the church-community as they develop outside interests and social ties. Many continue to relate to their extended family and Amish friends throughout their lives, even attending church services occasionally. Others move out of the orbit of Amish life, returning home only for funerals and weddings. We explore the decisions that youth face regarding baptism and church membership in chapter 12.

Youth who choose not to join the church may make that decision for several reasons: a dysfunctional family environment, educational and/or occupational aspirations beyond the Amish realm, or romantic ties with an English person that pull them out of the community. Growing up in a family with sexual or domestic abuse or an overly strict or incompetent parent may cause a child to flee Amish life. Saloma Miller Furlong, in *Why I Left the Amish,* points to some of these reasons for her departure. Family troubles as well as an outside romance pushed and pulled Ruth Irene Garrett away from her Iowa Amish community, as she explains in *Crossing Over: One Woman's Escape from Amish Life.*[34]

Other youth, like Ira Wagler, who left and returned to his Iowa community a half dozen times before finally leaving, simply become restless within the bounds of Amish life and enjoy exploring the larger world. Still others, often from more liberal families, set their minds on becoming pilots, musicians, or doctors and leave to pursue the necessary education. Wayne Weaver, who left Amish life to pursue medicine and become a physician, tells his story in *Dust between My Toes*. Similarly, Andy Yoder of Sugarcreek, Ohio, completed college and entered medical school. "My parents have been wonderful, welcoming me home when I am not in school," he says. "I love the Amish culture and never thought I would leave it . . . but I always enjoyed school and dreamed of going to high school and college."[35]

Some rebellious Amish youth who leave the community engage in activities that are offensive to their birthright culture. For example, "Emma the Amish model" appeared on the New American Pinup website selling underwear in a provocative pose. The Amish Outlaws, a band consisting of four ex-Amish and two "honorary Amish" men, play all sorts of music in full Amish attire at various East Coast venues.

Adult church members who leave are typically married and twenty-five to fifty years of age, and they usually exit for different reasons than do youth. Common reasons for abandoning Amish life in adulthood include (1) a desire for a more intense "born again" religious experience, (2) freedom to own more technology—especially a car, (3) dissatisfaction with the leadership and regulations of the Gmay, (4) a preference for speaking English in church services, and (5) involvement in mission activities. In some cases, all of these factors blend together.

Despite their exit from Amish life, former members often point to positive Amish values such as a strong work ethic; helping one another with emergencies, finances, and work; not relying on government or insurance companies for help; being accountable to each other; and taking care of the elderly. Some adults who leave, like youth who run away from dysfunctional families, carry pain and bitterness for years. Others, with the passage of time and maturity, develop an appreciation for some of the values of Amish life. People like Wayne Weaver and Andy Yoder still carry a deep respect for their Amish heritage. One study of former members of Amish and Beachy Amish (car-driving) churches who had completed at least a bachelor's degree and entered a profession found that, without exception, they embrace many of the religious and cultural values of their Amish heritage in their lives in the modern world.[36]

Tough Love

Leaving the Amish is quite different from dropping out of a mainstream American church, where the only consequence might be a call from a staff member for an exit interview. Excommunication and shunning (*Bann und Meidung*) are long-standing Amish practices related to the termination of membership and the treatment of former members. Because the Amish believe that baptism and church membership are not just a private spiritual matter, forfeiting one's membership carries significant social consequences. Rituals of shaming remind everyone of the breach and encourage the wayward one's return into the fellowship.[37] One sociologist contends that reintegrative shaming, like shunning, is more of a deterrent to deviance in the larger society than the threat of formal punishment.[38]

Amish people offer several reasons for the practice of shunning, also known as social avoidance.[39] They note that more than a half dozen New Testament passages endorse it.[40] In 1 Corinthians 5, the Apostle Paul urges church members to clean out the "old leaven" of "malice and wickedness" before they eat the Lord's Supper (v. 8). In a pointed admonition, Paul tells the Corinthian church to remove a wicked person from its midst and "deliver such an one unto Satan" so that his or her spirit will eventually be saved (1 Cor. 5:5).[41]

Article 17 of the Dordrecht Confession of Faith, the early seventeenth-century Anabaptist statement that the Amish use for baptismal candidates, explicitly advocates social avoidance on biblical grounds. Shunning reminds offenders of the seriousness of defaulting on their baptismal vows with the hope that they will confess their errors and return to the church. Ex-members are not enemies of the church, leaders are quick to note, but brothers and sisters who must be treated with love. The Dordrecht Confession explains that members should not consider transgressors "as enemies, but admonish them as brethren in order to bring them to knowledge, repentance, and sorrow for their sins so that they may be reconciled to God and His church and consequently be received and taken in again."[42]

As we noted in chapter 8, since the early twentieth century Amish communities have made a distinction between those that practice strict shunning (*streng Meidung*), which is lifelong (unless the offender repents), and a more lenient form that makes it easier to lift the ban on a former member. The stricter style requires transgressors to confess their error to the congregation that excommunicated them. More lenient affiliations will cease shunning if the wayward person joins a plain-dressing, nonresistant Amish Mennonite or Mennonite church. Regardless of how it is terminated, the practical application of shunning varies from family to family and from affiliation to affiliation, with traditional ones being harsher than liberal ones.

Shunning does not necessarily mean severing all social ties—members may, for example, converse with ex-members—but it does restrict certain types of interaction. Shunning is an asymmetrical, one-way relationship. Members are permitted to help and visit offenders, but offenders are not granted the dignity of aiding a member. Members may shake hands with offenders but not accept anything—gifts, payments, or money—directly from their hands. According to the ritual formula in more conservative groups, the offender should place such items on a table or counter, and the member should pick them up without a direct transaction. Also forbidden are accepting rides in an offender's car and eating at the same table with an ex-member. Sometimes, for public meals within the community, a different tablecloth or several inches of separation between tables mark the boundary between present and former members. Because these are *group* rites of shaming—not acts of personal animosity— their importance swells in social settings. For example, a more liberal family might, in the privacy of their home, welcome an ex-member to their table but refuse to eat with the same person at a wedding or funeral meal or similar public gathering.

"Remember," said a farmer, "we still help ex-members. If an ex-member's barn burns down, we go and help to rebuild it. We will help them if their wife is sick. . . . [But] generally we don't invite them to social events or to weddings or to things like school meetings." Members are expected to shun ex-members within their own family circle, even an excommunicated spouse. Members who refuse to do so, especially in public settings, may need to confess their disobedience, and if unwilling, they too may face the sting of shunning.

"Shunning and spanking go side by side," an Amish mother explained. "We love our children. When we spank them, it's a discipline to help them control their minds. When spanking, we don't get angry at them, and the same is true for shunning." For the Amish, healthy churches, like good parents, are responsible to administer discipline with love. Parents and churches both seek to protect those under their care from their own frailties.

The Amish believe that they have a divine responsibility to hold accountable those who break their baptismal vows, to remind them of what the Amish consider the eternal consequences of their negligence, and to preserve the purity of the church. In the Amish view, shunning is a form of tough love for backsliders. An elderly bishop called it "the last dose of medicine that you can give to a sinner. It either works for life or death." Another leader explained that a church without shunning "is like a house without doors or walls, where the people just walk in and out as they please." And, one bishop told us that shunning helps to maintain the integrity of church membership because "it helps to keep our church intact" by removing rebellious and disobedient spirits who would stir up dissension.

Although the church views shunning as a tough form of Christian love, Amish leaders, like officials in other churches, are susceptible to abusing power—wielding their authority in oppressive ways. A domineering leader may at times use excommunication and shunning as a tool of retaliation.[43]

Some ex-members understandably become bitter toward the church and denounce shunning as an unloving practice. The tough love often feels harsh to those who are expelled, and some of them remain embittered for life. Many others make a more or less smooth transition to the outside world and leave any bitterness behind.

Ex-members can, however, return to the fold anytime and receive pardon—upon confession of their deviance. "I have a brother who is excommunicated," explained one person. "But the back door is always open. He can come back if he wants to, but it's up to him." Although most ex-members never return, a few do.

Explaining Amish Growth

As we noted in the preface, the growth of Amish society in North America since the mid-twentieth century surprised many scholars who were predicting its demise. The ability of this distinctive community not merely to survive but to thrive in the midst of a hypermodern society begs for an explanation (see fig. 9.1). Given the birth and defection rates cited in this chapter, the solution to the puzzle of Amish growth may seem obvious: high birth rates and strong retention.

While those two metrics help us understand Amish growth, they do not explain it entirely. A compelling explanation requires a systemic view of Amish society as a holistic system of interconnected beliefs, practices, and institutions working in tandem to sustain itself, arresting assimilation into mainstream society and, at the same time, creating a viable and attractive community that young people are willing to claim as their own as they move toward adulthood. Such an explanation explores the conditions (beliefs and practices) that support and encourage large families and the factors that create lifelong commitments to Amish ways. Numerous sociocultural factors contribute to the vitality, and hence the growth, of Amish life.

A system of distinctive symbols (dress, language, and carriage)—articulated publicly in daily life—marks the visible boundaries of Amish culture, as we described in chapter 7. These signs and their associated rituals create a clear and robust identity that builds solidarity within the community and clarifies its separation from the outside world.

The decentralized structure of Amish society places ecclesial authority in small, close-knit congregations that hold members accountable to one another and to the Ordnung of their community. Membership in a geographically bounded community tempers individualism, increases social control, and builds commitments to core practices. By limiting mobility, horse-drawn transportation supports this small-scale, face-to-face community. In addition, a horse-based culture requires rural environs and keeps Amish communities outside urban areas, which threaten Amish sensibilities.

We proposed in chapter 1 that when Amish groups have faced new developments in American society, they have negotiated with modernity—rejecting things that would hinder their way of life, accepting helpful things, and adapting certain practices and technologies to minimize their harm. These negotiations are especially evident in the areas of social interaction with the outside world, technology, and education.

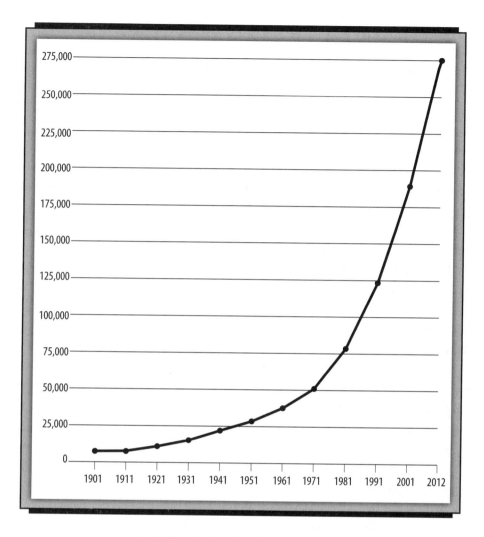

FIGURE 9.1. Amish Population Growth in North America, 1901–2012.
Source: Raber's New American Almanac, *1930–2012;* The Mennonite
Year Book, *1905–1960; Amish historical documents.*

Although all Amish people uphold the principle of separation from the world, the various groups do not apply it in the same way. In the economic sphere, all affiliations engage in trade with the outside world, but they vary the conditions under which it occurs. Some groups maintain separation from the world by emphasizing small, family-based farming, while others permit members to develop entrepreneurial businesses that use advanced technology, creative advertising, and competitive marketing. The most traditional groups do not permit members to work in non-Amish factories or engage in construction work in suburban areas. The development not only of trade but of Amish businesses themselves is, of course, essential to the economic viability of Amish society.

Amish affiliations also differ in how they apply the principle of separation to social interaction with outsiders. Lower groups restrict how and when their members relate to non-Amish people and popular culture much more than liberal groups do. Nevertheless, all Amish affiliations do separate themselves from the larger society in both symbolic and practical ways. All groups prohibit marriage to outsiders unless they have joined the Amish church. This practice of *endogamy* (marriage within the group) reduces the intrusion of outside influences, increases homogeneity, and deters people from leaving the community. Endogamy also makes it easier to socialize children into an Amish worldview because they are not exposed to competing religious traditions within their family.

In the realm of formal education, the church has also declined to negotiate. The rejection of high school and higher education limits access to educational credentials and thus to professional jobs that would place members directly into mainstream culture and encourage more mobility, which could eventually erode the solidarity of Gmays. The ordination of lay ministers without formal training reduces the analytical and theological speculation that could erode long-standing Amish beliefs and convictions. The rise of Amish private schools after 1950 has been a key development for socializing Amish youth with like-minded peers and curtailing not only outside friendships but also competing worldviews that might undermine Amish religious ideology.

When it comes to social discourse with public media, the Amish draw a sharp line by rejecting the ownership of television and access to the Internet, at least at home. Such selective adaptations welcome positive influences while rejecting those that would be detrimental to core Amish beliefs and practices.

Finally, that decisions about these everyday matters are made in the context of the church and are seen as expressions of deep conviction creates a sacred canopy over all of Amish life. This religious canopy legitimates the entire social system, endowing practices and customs with a sacred authority that impedes social change.

These and other aspects of Amish life cohere to bolster its growth. Working in concert, these factors fortify beliefs about the importance of marriage, child bearing, and large families. They also protect Amish life from individualistic values that would threaten if not upend traditional family practices. Similarly, these elements create a distinctive and productive society that socializes youth into an Amish worldview that satisfies their longing for meaning and belonging so that, in the end, four out of five claim this society as their own.

CHAPTER 10

COMMUNITY ORGANIZATION

The Single Boys' Gathering, open to "unmarried men aged 21 to 101," is one of many annual "reunions" for Amish people with similar interests. The 2011 reunion, held near Nappanee, Indiana, drew over 160 church members from 19 settlements in 10 states. The event opened Friday evening with a talk by a local minister and continued with visiting around a bonfire. Saturday events included a tour of the area, softball, volleyball, a hog roast, and poetry readings. As a fundraiser, participants shelled out $50 to $100 apiece for a mug with the Single Boys' Gathering logo featuring the profile of a young man seated by a campfire in the woods. A poster in their gathering place featured an Oscar Wilde quote: "Rich bachelors should be heavily taxed. It is not fair that some men should be happier than others."

Social Architecture

To the outside eye, the stark symbols of dialect, distinctive dress, and horse-drawn transportation place the Amish beyond the orbit of mainstream society.[1] Hidden beneath these signs, however, is an even more striking rejection of modernity: the absence of bureaucracy. In his study of modernization, German sociologist Max Weber (1864–1920) traces a shift from *traditional* views of authority legitimated by custom, religion, and personal relationships to *rational* models of authority anchored in impersonal laws, regulations, and organizations. The rise of rational authority— embodied especially in bureaucracies such as governments, factories, banks, hospitals, and universities—is the biggest difference between premodern and modern societies.[2] Unlike traditional forms of authority, modern organizations gain their clout from written policies, contracts, paid officials, specialized roles, hierarchies of rank, and employee expertise. Although the rational calculation embedded in bureaucracies promotes efficiency, Weber worried that its rigidity and mechanistic rules could create an "iron cage" that would fetter human freedom.

The Amish world is remarkably free of bureaucracy and its rational modes of authority. But although corporate-style organizations are absent, Amish society is hardly disorganized. Its building blocks include geographic settlements, nuclear and extended families (chapter 11), church districts, and affiliations (chapter 8). In this chapter we explore the architecture of Amish social structure, focusing on church districts, leadership, formation of new settlements, and emergence of non-bureaucratic organizations.

The entire Amish social system, rooted in more than two thousand church districts, is linked by informal webs of kin and friendship, homespun committees, and loosely coupled networks. Largely cut off from the Internet, mass communication, and rapid transit, Amish life revolves around local affairs. The social architecture of Amish society is *informal, small,* and *compact.* These features dramatically diverge from the bureaucratic design of postindustrial societies. Amish social structure embodies a *Gelassenheit* style, a structural humility unlike the centralized systems of authority that consolidate modern expressions of power.

Informal

To the modern observer, the organization of Amish society may seem loose, fuzzy, and amorphous. There are no national or regional headquarters, annual conventions, or organizational charts—and certainly not an executive director or a marketing department to promote Amish interests. Kitchens, shops, and at-home offices provide space for committees, organized as need arises, whose officers and members work without pay. This nebulous structure confounds outsiders seeking information on official Amish opinions and policies.

With few contractual and formal relationships, Amish life is bonded by informal ties, family networks, common traditions, uniform symbols, and a shared caution of the outside world. The informality expresses itself through face-to-face interaction on a first-name basis and with an awareness of each person's position in an extended family system rather than in a role-defined organizational flow chart. When people first meet, they do not introduce themselves by stating their occupation, as middle-class Americans might, but try to ascertain whether and how they might be related. Oral communication takes precedence over written, and meetings of ordained leaders rarely generate many records. Organizational procedures are dictated by oral tradition and collective memory, not by policy manuals. Congregations across a given settlement are loosely coupled by family ties and the friendships of leaders rather than by bylaws, charters, or formal policies.

Small-Scale

From egos to organizational units, Gelassenheit prefers small-scale things. Meeting in homes for worship limits the size of congregations. Small schools provide a personalized education, and small farms are preferable to large ones. Large manufacturing operations are often frowned upon because big operations draw attention to their owners, generate excessive wealth, and establish a power base that threatens the informality of Amish society.

An Amish businessman explained, "My people look at a large business as a sign of greed."[3] Another Amish man put it this way: "Our discipline thrives with a small group. Once you get into that big superstructure, it seems to gather momentum and you can't stop it." Amish people sense that, in the long run, the modern impulse for large-scale things could damage the intimate character of their community. In the words of one Amish carpenter, "Bigness ruins everything." Indeed, a commitment to human-scale units may provide a psychological boost to individuals because they are known intimately by others in their small church-community and do not vanish in a crowd.

Compact

Interpersonal relationships in Amish society are enmeshed in what social scientists call a "high-context culture," one in which things are left largely unsaid and members learn by doing and by interacting with others.[4] In this dense environment of overlapping relationships, members of the community know the same people—their siblings, parents, grandparents, cousins, employers, friends, neighbors, ministers—as well as the occupations, hobbies, and social reputations of those people. "Everybody knows everything about everyone else," said one woman. A grandfather agreed: "In our communities we can't hide anything, not in church, not on the farm, not in our community. After a couple gets married all the women are watching to see when the young bride is expecting [a baby]. When the older women see she is, they set a chair for her at church so she doesn't have to sit on a [backless] bench. And then everyone knows. And when she sees the chair, she often blushes. The whole neighborhood knows everything because everything is so transparent. We can't hide anything from anyone."

Work, play, child rearing, education, and worship are not as sharply separated in Amish life as they are in mainstream society. In modern society, for example, customers entering a pharmacy expect to know only that the pharmacist has been trained and licensed by the proper authorities, represented by framed certificates on the pharmacy wall. Customers judge only the pharmacist's professional credentials, not the pharmacist's character as a parent, spouse, or church member. Nor do most customers care—or know about—the pharmacist's life outside of the pharmacy. For the Amish, however, public and private roles are not split; the same circle of people interacts in family, neighborhood, church, and work. People know and relate to one another in many different roles simultaneously—as a relative, neighbor, coworker, and fellow church member.

One leader described these thick, crisscrossing networks when he asked, "What is more scriptural than the closely knit Christian community, living together, working together, worshiping together, with its own church and its own schools? Here the members know each other, work with and care for each other, every day of the week."[5] In a high-context culture, gossip and small talk become informal means of social control, leading one member to declare, "The Amish grapevine is faster than the Internet."

Districts

The twenty to forty Amish families who live near each other form a church district known as the *Gmay*—the primary social unit beyond the family. These districts are the pillars of the entire social system. As districts grow in membership, they divide, guaranteeing that all districts remain roughly the same size. In settlements with sparse population, a district may stretch twelve miles from side to side, but where the Amish population is dense, the span may shrink to a mile or so, and families are able to walk to services. Ironically, the rise of Amish businesses has brought people closer geographically, since they live on smaller plots of land.

Roads, streams, township lines, and other markers form a district's boundaries. Like members of a traditional parish, the Amish must participate in the district that encircles their home. If residents of one district want to join another Gmay, they must move into its territory. Because there are no church buildings, the homes of members become the gathering sites not only for worship but also for socializing (see fig. 10.1).

Because extended families live so close, often some members of a district are related to one another. Kinship networks are dense with many repeated surnames. For example, one district in northern New York contains a large number of Millers, some more closely related than others. The large Lancaster settlement has 176 women named Mary Stoltzfus. The abundance of similar names generates nicknames based on physical traits, personal habits, or unusual incidents. The nicknames tend to follow patriarchal lines across several generations. One woman said, "I'm a Bootah.

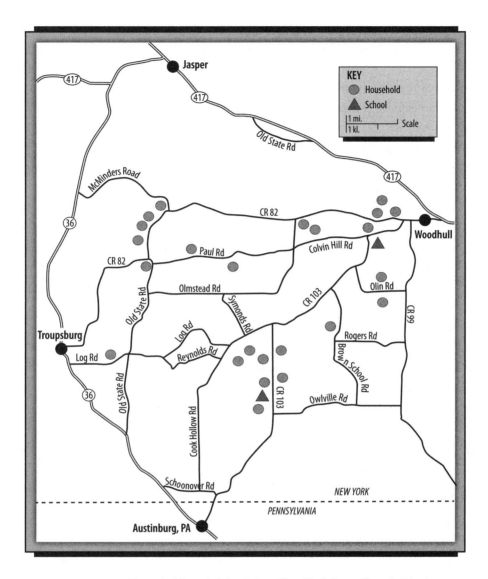

FIGURE 10.1. Households and Schools in a New York State Church District

That goes way back to my great-grandparents. When they got their marriage license, the clerk wasn't too bright, and she wrote their names 'Bootah' (butter) instead of Beiler. So ever since we've been the Bootahs."[6]

The church district is the social and ceremonial unit of the Amish world. Sunday worship services, baptisms, weddings, and funerals take place within the Gmay, as do many fellowship meals, work parties, and social activities. In short, the Gmay is church, family, factory, club, and precinct, all packaged together in a neighborhood parish.

Districts select and ordain their own leaders—typically a bishop, two or three ministers, and a deacon. The leaders (all males) are viewed as servants of both God and the congregation. In fact, their German title, *Diener,* translates literally as "servant." Leaders have no professional credentials or special training, and they serve for life without pay, earning their own living by farming, carpentry, or other occupation.

A bishop serves as the spiritual head of a district or, in certain affiliations, of two neighboring districts. He officiates at baptisms, weddings, communions, funerals, and members' meetings. As the spiritual head of the leadership team and the symbol of church authority, the bishop interprets and enforces church regulations. If disobedience or conflict arises, he is responsible for resolving it. Family and church networks are often entangled in controversies of one sort or another and require delicate diplomacy.

The minister, or preacher, fills the second leadership role in the district. A congregation usually has two or three preachers, depending on their age and health. One of them serves as the lead minister, working closely with the bishop to give spiritual direction to the congregation. Apart from their general leadership roles, the ministers' primary responsibility is preaching on Sunday mornings.

Each congregation also has a deacon, whose public duties include reading Scripture and prayers in worship services, depending on local custom. The deacon supervises an alms fund and attends to the material needs of families in the district. (Individual congregations own no land or buildings and have no assets other than the alms fund.) The deacon also assists with baptism and communion and carries responsibility for reproving wayward members. At the request of the bishop, the deacon, often accompanied by a minister, visits members who may have violated the *Ordnung* and reports back to the bishop, who may then initiate a process of church discipline.

Leadership

As we discussed in chapter 5, Amish leaders are selected by drawing lots. This may seem like a game of chance to outsiders, but for the Amish, this mystery-filled rite, a combination of democracy and God's will, gives all church members a voice in the selection of new leaders while conferring divine blessing and legitimacy on church authority. Without a search committee or rounds of potentially divisive voting, the Gmay quickly finds a qualified leader who is well-known to his fellow congregants.

Despite their belief in divinely sanctioned leadership, the Amish are well aware that their leaders are fallible human beings. If a particular leader annexes more authority than he should or in some way violates the stewardship of his office, he may be silenced by his congregation. In the vast majority of cases, however, Amish leaders earn the trust of their congregants as they carry out the duties of their role. "Remember, the bishop didn't ask for this job," said a member. "Most of them are more like a governor than a ruler."

Patterns of leadership and authority vary by settlement and affiliation. In some affiliations the bishops meet on a regular basis once or twice a year to consult with one another; leaders in other groups meet only when urgent matters require it. Among the ethnically Swiss Amish congregations, the bishop often exercises a heavier hand than in the non-Swiss affiliations. Paradoxically, in some cultures, hierarchical structures and rituals help maintain and facilitate egalitarian relationships across the society.[7] This is true in Amish society, but in most but not all cases, the leadership seniority is a soft hierarchy based on age and tenure. This informal hierarchy undergirds the authority structure among the bishops. A young minister explained that "the oldest ones have priority." Young ministers often go to an older bishop for advice. "And he will not hesitate to give his opinion, based on Scripture. Then he will conclude and say, 'Don't do it that way just because I told you, go home and work with your church.' So it is not a dictatorship by any means."

A bishop carries heavy responsibilities and exerts wide influence over the life of the Gmay. His personality and views shape the ethos of the congregation. Diverse views and styles of bishops lead to diverse interpretations of the Ordnung. Some bishops are dominant and heavy-handed, while others are gentle and gracious. Certain bishops hold authority tightly in their own hands, while others consult widely before making decisions. For example, one Swartzentruber woman blamed a recent schism in her community on a new bishop, noting her own father's deathbed warning that if that man "ever got the reins," there'd be no stopping him. On the other hand, a young Amish teacher in a progressive Indiana settlement said that he has lived under three different bishops and has not yet experienced a harsh one. "People are people, and styles and interpretations will vary," he said. "But I think it is safe to say there are many more George Washingtons out there than Fidel Castros."

A bishop has considerable latitude in deciding what he brings to the congregation for a vote. Because he controls the agenda, he can stall or expedite an issue. The power of lay members is curbed somewhat because there is no open agenda or the opportunity for motions from the floor in members' meetings.

Although bishops have considerable clout, several checks and balances restrain their reach. First, they need the unanimous consent of the congregation to proceed with most proposed actions.[8] Second, a bishop's attempt to promote or obstruct a proposed action—to discipline an erring member, change the Ordnung, or accept a new practice—will only be effective if the ministers support it. Long-term stalemates may arise if the other leaders and the bishop disagree on a matter. An additional check on a bishop's muscle is the sentiment of the bishops in nearby districts. Leaders within the same affiliation try to balance forbearance and respect, and they usually seek to cooperate while still respecting one another's autonomy. If one bishop allows bicycles, cell phones, or even LED flashlights, and neighboring bishops do not, the decision will stir ill will toward the permissive leader.

Relatives on the ministry team can also bring complications. If, for example, several of a bishop's adult children and cousins strongly favor or oppose an issue, it may influence how he proceeds—or it may divide the family.[9] Occasionally, a father and son may be bishop and minister in the same district, or two brothers may be chosen to serve as minister and deacon. One bishop in Illinois found himself squeezed between his own brother, who wanted to start a Sunday school, and the affiliation's elder bishop, who strongly opposed it.

If a bishop and his congregation face an impasse, or if he is accused of immorality or a serious abuse of power, three outside bishops will mediate the situation and seek a resolution, which could include removing him from office. Bishops of isolated districts that are not closely affiliated with other Gmays are the most vulnerable to abuse of power because they have the fewest external checks.[10] Observing one such district, a professional working with one of its members noted that "the insular and non-hierarchical nature of Amish groups means that a few people 'in power' in a particular group can destroy lives if they so choose."[11] The first district to form in a settlement may be isolated geographically for a number of years until it grows, but it will likely maintain fraternal links to other districts, which helps to reduce the risk of dysfunctional leadership.

Settlements

Popping Up Like Mushrooms

The expanding North American Amish population has seeded more than five hundred new settlements since 1900, and the number continues to rise. In fact, nearly 40 percent (176) of present-day settlements were started since 2000 (see fig. 10.2). When different Amish affiliations establish new communities in the same geographical area, they are considered separate settlements.[12] Minimally, a settlement must include three households.[13]

New communities have emerged in Iowa, Illinois, Kentucky, Minnesota, Missouri, and Ontario, which already had long-established settlements, as well as in states without previous Amish communities such as Arkansas, Maine, Nebraska, and South Dakota. Regardless of state, new settlements are distinctly rural. Over half of those founded after 1990 were started in rural counties without a town or city of 10,000 people and without obvious ties to nearby metropolitan areas.[14]

The years 2006 to 2007 marked a record in settlement expansion, with forty-eight new communities—the highest number ever for a two-year period—averaging a new

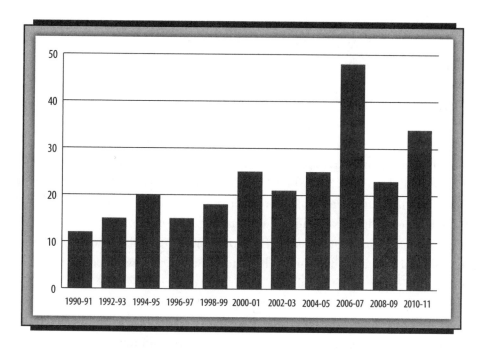

FIGURE 10.2. Number of New Settlements, 1990–2011.
Source: Migration reports in the Diary *and other Amish publications.*

one nearly every other week. An Amish correspondent writing in *Die Botschaft* said the new settlements were "popping up like mushrooms." Another writer enthused, "If the new settlements keep on sprouting up like they have the last 10 years, then in a few years we will be able to hitch old dobbin to the buggy and travel from one to the other." Still another correspondent confessed that the avalanche of new communities simply "befuddles" him as he tries to "remember them all and who's moving where. It is kind of hard for our own brains to keep up."[15] In 2010 explorers hunting for land even went to Alaska and Mexico—well beyond the reach of their traditional home-lands. For now, at least, the Amish have remained focused on finding available acres in the contiguous United States.[16]

The sharp spike in new settlements masks three important realities. First, about half (235) of all settlements have just one church district, and these one-district settle-ments account for only 10 percent of the entire Amish population. Second, it may take a decade or more for a new venture to develop stable roots. Third, a number of these new settlements are likely to falter and disband within several years.

By 2012 Amish settlements in the United States were found as far west as Montana, as far south as Texas and Florida, and as far northeast as Maine. Although the one-district settlements may not be geographically close to other Amish people, they usu-ally have fraternal relationships with other Amish groups and may receive ministerial help from their home community. For example, Swartzentruber ministers from upstate New York regularly make the long bus ride to their newest daughter settlement in Maine to conduct church services for young districts that have not yet ordained their own ministers.

Fading Like Flowers

Although Amish people have planted more than five hundred new settlements since 1900, not all of them have flourished. Amish historian David Luthy has documented the deaths of 144 settlements in North America in the twentieth century. Seven were in Canada, one was in Mexico (1923–1929), and one was in Honduras (1968–1979). In addition, a small Amish settlement in Paraguay (1967–1978) failed. Some other settlements did not fold as communities, but they lost their Amish identity when their members joined Mennonite or similar car-driving churches. To date, the Amish have abandoned all their settlements in seven states (Alabama, California, Georgia, New Mexico, Oregon, South Carolina, and Vermont) and never returned. On the other hand, three settlements in Colorado died between 1914 and 1920, but Amish settlers returned eighty years later, in 2000.[17]

Settlements may disband for reasons that include poor land, undesirable weather, conflicts with government regulations (state or local), church controversies within the community, and the inability to attract new members. If a newly planted settlement does not recruit a dozen families within a few years, prospective settlers may assume it has problems and shy away from it. Even communities that grow larger and exist for a decade or more may still wither at some point because of other adverse circumstances.[18]

Amish historian Joseph Stoll has also argued that a central feature of Amish society—lack of centralized and coordinated authority—also contributes to settlement failure. New communities are generally established as grassroots ventures led by a small number of families, not organized or commissioned by centralized church leadership. Stoll explains that the "system of starting new settlements" does not always work, "because . . . we really don't have any system. All too often a few random families, because of some common dissatisfaction, band together haphazardly to start a new settlement."[19] New Order leaders have sometimes encouraged members to start new settlements as a means of spreading an Amish witness, but this motive is not typical in other groups.

A study by Joseph Donnermeyer and Elizabeth Cooksey found that the survival rate of new settlements before and after 1950 jumped from 23 percent to 68 percent, suggesting that new settlers may be learning from past mistakes.[20] Moreover, they discovered that the survival rate for new communities was highest in counties that already had an Amish community. In some cases, members of the existing settlement help the newcomers or at least have paved the way by acquainting neighbors and civic leaders with Amish ways.

For Amish households, the process of establishing a successful new settlement involves a host of practical concerns that include finding specialized products such as the naphtha gas that some groups use for indoor lighting or securing services such as horseshoeing that might not be available in the new location. The practical realities of new settlements sometimes force districts to modify their Ordnung or else spend more time and money to obtain products and services that were readily available back home.[21] Building schools and finding non-Amish drivers to provide occasional "taxi" service for extended trips are all part of the difficult work of establishing a durable new settlement.[22]

Amish on the Move

Although most families remain rooted in the area where they were born and raised, others move within their home state or to other states. Each year a steady stream of Amish families moves across state lines, and a few cross the United States–Canada border. Some Amish people migrate to start or join a new settlement, while others simply move from one established settlement to another. Interstate Amish migrants travel by rented vans or commercial buses, transporting their household goods, equipment, and animals by commercial haulers.

Amish writer Joseph Stoll notes the "rolling stone" syndrome of some people who "are nomads by nature. Although they may be ever so well-meaning and spiritually concerned, their gypsy-like traits do have an unsettling effect on the permanence of a new settlement."[23] Jacob K. "Oregon Jake" Miller may hold the distinction for being the most mobile Amish man ever. Born in Somerset County, Pennsylvania, in 1852, Miller lived in eight different states and moved twelve different times, always by train. He lived in Oregon three times, once in California, Illinois, Ohio, Virginia, and twice in Delaware, where he lived in retirement after 1921.[24]

In some ways, Oregon Jake is an anomaly—hence, his notoriety in Amish circles to this day—but his experience is also a reminder that mobility is not an uncommon thing. Indeed, some 2,350 Amish households—about 12,000 people—moved across state lines in the five-year period from 2006 through 2010.[25] This number does not include migrations within a state. Table 10.1 shows the interstate gains and losses of ten states in that five-year period. States with large, long-established settlements are more likely to be net losers because some of their families are fleeing urban encroachment upon older communities. The impact of a gain or loss on a state's Amish community clearly depends on the overall size of that state's Amish population.

Table 10.1. Amish Household Migration Gains and Losses by State, 2006–2010

State	Number of Households		
	Gain	Loss	Net Change
Top 5 Gaining States			
New York	344	113	+231
Kentucky	259	169	+90
Illinois	136	63	+73
Kansas	87	17	+70
Virginia	56	11	+44
Top 5 Losing States			
Pennsylvania	132	447	−315
Wisconsin	217	301	−84
Delaware	6	87	−81
Ohio	219	288	−69
Michigan	113	166	−53

Source: Migration reports in the *Diary* and other Amish publications.
Note: Intrastate migrations are not included.

Four states in table 10.1 show a net gain of 70 or more immigrant Amish families over the five-year period. New York, surpassing other states with 344 new households, had the largest net gain (231 families), followed by Kentucky (90), Illinois (73), and Kansas (70). The three states with the highest net loss of households were Pennsylvania (315), Wisconsin (84), and Delaware (81). Wisconsin welcomed 217 new immigrant families in the five-year period, but it also lost 301 families, yielding a net deficit of 84 households. Pennsylvania, home to the largest Amish population in 2011 (61,270), welcomed 132 families from other states but lost 447 households, for a net loss of 315 families. For a state such as Delaware, with a slim Amish population (1,350), the loss of 81 families (about 400 people) over five years is a more severe blow than for Amish-heavy states such as Ohio or Pennsylvania.

Whether setting out to start a new community or joining an established one, migration involves both push and pull factors. Push factors nudging people to leave their homes may include (1) suburban congestion and sprawl, (2) high land prices, (3) tourism and other outside intrusions, (4) disputes with municipal authorities over issues such as zoning, (5) weak regional economies, (6) occupational changes (closing of markets, jobs, factories), and (7) church-related troubles or disputes.

Conversely, other forces may tug families toward new locations. These enticements may include (1) fertile farmland at reasonable prices; (2) nonfarm work in specialized occupations; (3) rural isolation that supports a traditional, family-based lifestyle; (4) social and physical environments (climate, governments, services, economy) hospitable to the Amish way of life; (5) new markets for Amish-made products; (6) a new church-community with certain practices such as supervised youth activities, more or fewer restrictions on technology, or rules against using tobacco; and (7) proximity to family or other Amish groups. Other reasons may be as ambiguous as "the call of the west," as a Colorado immigrant described his motive for moving from Ohio.

The decision to move is often a conservative choice. For example, when confronting a lack of farmland, Amish people may need to either move or accept the changes that come with increasing participation in the local economy. In such cases the conservative-minded households are often the ones that decide to move rather than change their lifestyles—or their Ordnung—to adapt to new economic conditions. This has happened in Lancaster County, where the growth of microenterprises and work in suburban farmers' markets provide considerable employment. Some of those hoping to avoid such work and maintain more traditional farm lives have packed their bags. Similarly, some conservative-minded members of long-established communities, unhappy with youth activities or Ordnung changes, move to avoid offensive practices. For example, appalled by what they saw as behavioral problems and lack of discipline among the young folk in their Ashland, Ohio, community, several families began a new settlement in New York's Mohawk Valley. The choice to stay or to move carries many repercussions for occupation and family life.

At other times, moving has been an economic survival strategy. In the early 1980s, the sharp downturn in the midwestern farm economy prompted more than forty families to move to Stephenville, Texas, where they took jobs as laborers in large English agribusinesses. Viewing their time in Texas as a temporary sojourn to accumulate needed capital, none of the Amish purchased land. By 1993 the settlement had folded because all the households had moved either back to their original settlements or to the sort of older settlements from which they had come.[26]

Flashpoints

When Amish people plant new settlements, long-time English residents may welcome them or be somewhat indifferent to their arrival. Occasionally, locals resist or resent Amish newcomers. In 2011, a year after arriving in Tripp, South Dakota, Amish people faced the ire of residents upset by horse manure on local roads. Business owners complained to city officials, and one garage owner, tired of manure from the streets sticking to the tires of his customers' vehicles, called the situation "pathetic." A month later, residents of Todd County, Minnesota, were grumbling to their board of commissioners about "big piles of horse poop" in the grocery store parking lot and horseshoes destroying the shoulders of their roads. Over the years municipalities in several states have discussed the idea of using various types of "diapers" on horses to keep their droppings off roadways.[27]

Other flashpoints with horse-drawn transportation have involved the refusal of Swartzentruber Amish to attach the orange slow-moving-vehicle emblems to the backs of their carriages, making them more difficult to see, according to some non-Amish neighbors. Although many states accommodate the Swartzentrubers by permitting silver reflective tape instead of the orange triangles, Swartzentrubers who established new settlements in Pennsylvania in 1997 and Kentucky in 2002 were fined and jailed until the issue was resolved through judicial or legislative action.[28]

The growing Amish population in Cortland County, New York, created a stir when Amish parents refused to send their children on regular school buses where they would be exposed to the dress and technology of non-Amish students. The school district, required by state law to transport private school students, refused to run special buses for the Amish. School board president Lloyd Parker said, "It's divided this community big-time. There's pro-Amish and anti-Amish people." Just two years earlier, as Amish emigrants from Pennsylvania had begun buying run-down farms in the region and bringing new energy and optimism to an otherwise declining rural region, locals had welcomed the Amish as an economic asset. "Farms are being used," said an enthused neighbor. "There's cows. There's people building instead of things falling in on themselves."[29] In the wake of the school bus controversy, however, some locals criticized the Amish as aloof and an economic drag on local school budgets.

Long-established settlements normally develop amicable relationships with nearby residents and civic leaders. Irritations and controversies most typically flare during the first decade of newly planted communities as Amish people iron out any wrinkles with their new neighbors. In declining rural regions, Amish migrants can spark economic revitalization. In 1989, for example, an agricultural extension agent in Parke County, Indiana, helped to persuade families from Lancaster County, Pennsylvania, to begin a new settlement. Parke County had faced a farming crisis until the Lancaster Amish bought land and revived the dairy industry. County businesses even vied for Amish cash by installing horse-hitching rails, and the state welcomed the newcomers by installing road signs warning motorists of horse-drawn vehicles.[30]

Similarly, Otsego County in New York's Mohawk Valley actively recruited Amish families from Pennsylvania to spur economic development. Hartwick Planning Board member Orrin Higgins promoted Otsego County at auctions in Lancaster County by distributing a one-page flier listing farms for sale. He envisioned that, by moving to Otsego County, the Amish could keep their farming heritage and the county would keep its rural character intact. In his words, "It would be a plus for our community if we could encourage these people to move in."[31] By 2002, the county had two Amish settlements.

Table 10.2. Amish Population by State and Province, 2012

State/Province	Settlements	Church Districts	Estimated Population
Ohio	54	474	63,990
Pennsylvania	55	431	63,785
Indiana	22	335	47,235
Wisconsin	48	127	16,255
New York	46	109	14,715
Michigan	38	98	12,935
Missouri	41	91	10,645
Kentucky	35	72	9,000
Iowa	22	58	8,175
Illinois	18	50	7,000
Ontario	15	38	5,130
Minnesota	15	28	3,520
Tennessee	6	17	2,120
Kansas	7	12	1,620
Maryland	3	12	1,620
Delaware	1	10	1,500
Oklahoma	4	7	945
Colorado	4	6	810
Montana	4	5	675
Virginia	4	6	450
Maine	5	5	375
Nebraska	4	4	300
West Virginia	3	3	225
Arkansas	2	2	150
Other states*	7	7	525
Total	**463**	**2,007**	**273,700**

Source: Raber's *New American Almanac,* settlement directories, and Amish publications.

Note: Population estimates are based on state-sensitive averages of the estimated number of people per district. The actual population may vary from the estimates.

*The following seven states each have one settlement and one district: Florida, Idaho, Mississippi, North Carolina, South Dakota, Texas, and Wyoming.

Bird's Eye View

Although Amish people have moved into thirty states and the province of Ontario, 98 percent of them remain in the eastern half of North America (Missouri, Iowa, Minnesota, and states east of the Mississippi River, as well as Ontario). And 93 percent live in just ten states. Table 10.2 shows the big picture of Amish settlements and populations by state and province in 2012. Additionally, although there are some 460 settlements, nearly half (48 percent) of the Amish population resides in the twelve largest settlements, as seen in table 10.3.

Table 10.3. The Twelve Largest Amish Settlements, 2012

Settlement	State	Church Districts	Estimated Population
Holmes County	Ohio	246	31,980
Lancaster County	Pennsylvania	188	31,020
Elkhart–LaGrange	Indiana	154	21,560
Geauga County	Ohio	94	13,255
Adams County	Indiana	50	7,200
Nappanee	Indiana	41	5,455
Arthur	Illinois	29	4,060
Daviess County	Indiana	27	3,805
Mifflin County	Pennsylvania	26	3,120
Allen County	Indiana	19	2,735
New Wilmington	Pennsylvania	19	2,415
Indiana County	Pennsylvania	18	2,395

Source: Raber's *New American Almanac,* settlement directories, and Amish publications.

Note: The average number of people per district varies by settlement. Holmes County, for example, has 130 per district, while Lancaster County averages 165.

Emerging Organizations

The rapid expansion of Amish settlements makes the absence of bureaucracy and the persistence of small-scale community life in Amish society all the more striking. A remarkable number of special-purpose groups and networks that provide some order and coherence to Amish life beyond the local Gmay are emerging. With no national bureaucratic structure, Amish society is loosely linked through networks of leaders, periodic gatherings, committees, and informal organizations that span local districts and often include people from many settlements and affiliations.

None of the associations or committees report to Amish bishops, nor do ordained officials appoint lay people to them. Simply put, there are no church-owned or church-operated agencies or institutions. When lay members form local committees to tackle particular tasks, such as promoting buggy safety or planning teacher-training meetings, they usually consult with ordained leaders. Ministers, who often attend meetings as quiet monitors, are asked for advice or their blessing on various projects. In general, ministers and bishops rarely initiate new ventures or serve on committees, although they may give tacit approval to them. Yet all Amish organizations, including Amish-owned businesses, exist under the sacred canopy of the Amish faith and reflect its basic values and standards.

Table 10.4 shows a sample of different networks and organizations, varying from loosely coordinated annual gatherings to well-organized commercial operations. The development of mutual aid associations in the late nineteenth century and pri-

**Table 10.4. A Sampler of Amish Networks,
Committees, and Organizations**

Mutual Aid Associations	**Health**
Fire and storm aid	People Helpers
Hospital aid	Special needs groups
Liability aid	Mental health centers*
Revolving loan funds	Birth centers*
	Medical clinics*
Education	
Schools	**Special Interests**
Book societies	Historical libraries
	Historical associations
Government Liaison	Hobby networks
National Steering Committee	Trade reunions
State steering committees	Horse Progress Days*
Safety committees	
	Businesses
Aid to Outsiders	Publishers
Disaster aid	Bookstores
Old Colony Mennonite Support	Retail stores
Benefit auctions	Manufacturing
	Agriculture

* Collaborative projects with, or operated by, non-Amish partners

vate schools in the mid-twentieth century were the first institution-building efforts
(see chapter 14). Since 1975, the development of Amish organizations and networks
has picked up speed. Some of the regional and national networks assist local projects
such as private schools, while other associations serve individuals with special needs
or interests. A number of associations have newsletters and annual gatherings, often
called reunions. Many of these organizations are Amish-developed and directed.
Others are hybrids, partnerships of one kind or another with outsiders. Because all
Amish organizations are largely voluntary, members of some affiliations, especially
the more liberal ones, participate in them much more than members of traditional
groups do.

Mutual Aid Associations

Amish people believe that church membership entails accountability to and for each
other, including financial assistance to fellow members facing high medical bills or
property loss. Leaders discourage commercial insurance plans that would undercut
this religious duty within the community. Numerous mutual aid programs ensure aid
in the face of fire or storm damage or high health care costs. Fire and storm aid plans,

the earliest type of Amish associations, emerged in the late nineteenth century (1872 in Ontario and 1885 in Pennsylvania).[32]

Mutual aid associations vary in their scope and organization, and they may encompass a few districts, an entire settlement, or an interstate affiliation. Some of these programs require an annual premium, while others—especially in the more traditional groups—collect funds only in response to specific needs. ("Assessment by need after the fire," explained one member.) If the burden is too heavy for a single district, adjoining Gmays help each other. Manual labor for cleanup and rebuilding is freely given by members whenever disaster strikes. Remarkably, common to all these aid programs is their ability to address major needs without bureaucratic red tape, paid employees, underwriters, offices, computers, threat of lawsuits, or profits. Unlike commercial insurance, the transaction and administrative costs of Amish "insurance" are virtually nil. Volunteer assessors and aid plan directors operate from their kitchen desks during evening hours and can rely on the cooperation and ready payment from members without fear of litigation.

Caught between the rising costs of hospitalization and their reluctance to accept commercial or government-provided health insurance (Medicare or Ontario Health), Amish communities have devised various ways to assist families with major medical expenses. Some settlements have informal community-based "insurance" plans, while conservative communities rely on more traditional forms of support. Medical costs are covered in three basic ways: (1) spontaneous collections and benefit meals or auctions, (2) organized Amish hospital aid, (3) and negotiated discounts with hospitals. We describe these in chapter 18.

In the 1960s, some Amish businessmen began purchasing commercial liability insurance to protect themselves from outside lawsuits. Amish churches have had a long-standing opposition to any worldly insurance programs because they undermine mutual aid and use the force of law. To provide liability protection without using commercial insurance, some settlements established liability aid and product liability programs. Participation is voluntary, and members of the plan make a small annual contribution that fluctuates with the level of need.[33]

A handful of informal revolving loan funds, akin to old-style community savings and loan agencies, provide loans to qualifying families. Some Amish people put money into the fund at a miniscule rate of interest so that other church members can apply for low-interest mortgages for home or farm. The directors of the different funds in various settlements hold an annual meeting. Most of the funds shy away from providing loans to commercial Amish businesses, which usually acquire bank loans if they need capital. The policies of these financial assistance programs vary by state because of different state regulations.

Schools, Government, and Civic Aid

Although individual schools are operated by a board of fathers who act as trustees, most settlements have a school or "book" committee that offers advice on textbooks, prepares guidelines for operating the schools, and serves as a liaison with state departments of education. The school committees may also sponsor periodic local or regional training workshops for teachers. In chapter 14 we trace the development of Amish schools.

In 1967, during the Vietnam War's military draft, Amish leaders from several states formed the National Amish Steering Committee to act as a broker between the Amish and Selective Service officers managing conscription and conscientious objection. After the draft ended, the Steering Committee continued to act as a liaison with the federal government and eventually spawned and coordinated state-level steering committees to serve as go-betweens with local and state officials. The national and state steering committees function as self-perpetuating bodies outside the formal structure of the church (see chapter 19). Because the National Amish Steering Committee must interact with the epitome of bureaucracy in the United States—the apparatus of the federal government—it has assumed the most complex structure of any Amish organization apart from businesses. Yet even the Steering Committee operates from a private home office with volunteer labor.

In response to accidents on homesteads, farms, shops, and public roads, certain Amish communities formed safety committees in the 1990s to encourage safety training and compliance with government safety standards. These committees maintain a close relationship with local, state, and federal officials and hold training meetings, workshops, and field days to educate Amish people about hazards and safety precautions. A number of Amish disaster aid organizations recruit Amish volunteers to assist in cleanup and rebuilding projects outside the Amish community following tornadoes, hurricanes, and floods. We elaborate on these efforts in chapter 19.

Health

A variety of Amish networks and organizations focus on physical and mental health issues. For example, People Helpers formed in 1995 to assist the caregivers of those with mental illness. Eventually it expanded and now holds educational meetings about mental illness and makes referrals to professional caregivers. Similarly, an organization called Family Helpers plans activities and workshops to promote healthy marriages.

Several groups of Amish people in different states have developed homespun residential treatment centers for people with depression and related issues, including sexual abuse and addiction. In addition, several professional medical centers have developed close partnerships with Amish groups for the treatment of mental illness and clinical care of children with unique hereditary illnesses (see chapter 18).

A plethora of support groups focus on special health interests. Since 1963, individuals with various disabilities have met at the Annual Handicapped Gathering. Eventually, specialized reunions spun off from this gathering to extend emotional support and provide information and resources to individuals and families dealing with cerebral palsy, polio, blindness, multiple sclerosis, and deafness. A similar gathering, the Sudden Death Reunion, is held annually for families who have recently lost a loved one through an accident or other unexpected means.

Special Interest Networks

Some Amish communities have small, informal historical libraries located in a home or as part of a bookstore. Other libraries have their own building and volunteers. The Heritage Historical Library in Aylmer, Ontario, has a vast collection of Amish materials. Amish historians gather for a two-day meeting every other year in a different settlement.

Like the Single Boys' reunion mentioned in this chapter's opening, the National Single Girls' Gathering meets for two days each year. Other special interest groups have emerged around hobbies such as birding and have occasional local, regional, or national meetings. Horse Progress Days, which showcases new horse-drawn equipment as well as other new technology for shop and home, rotates from state to state each year and attracts upwards of 10,000 attendees.

As more Amish people entered nonfarm occupations in the last quarter of the twentieth century, special occupational groups emerged, and many of them hold periodic reunions. These Amish versions of trade conventions are favorite times to meet old friends and share expertise and knowledge about tools, products, and markets. Accountants, auctioneers, harness makers, machine shop operators, produce farmers, shed builders, income tax preparers, and quilters are some of the occupational groups that hold such gatherings. Although participants in all these special interest gatherings come from multiple affiliations, few people from the most traditional groups attend.

What Holds Them Together?

Our survey of districts, leadership, settlements, associations, and emerging organizations reveals an informal, small, and compact social architecture that embodies the

Thousands of people gather for Horse Progress Days, an event that rotates from state to state each year. Amish manufacturers and English workhorse enthusiasts demonstrate the latest horse-drawn equipment. *Daniel Rodriguez*

spirit of Gelassenheit. Grounded in the ecclesial authority of individual congregations, the social networks spanning the Amish world create bonds of fellowship that transcend geography and affiliation. These associations arose spontaneously without centralized or national direction in order to address needs beyond the capacity of local communities.

The architecture of Amish life remains largely untouched by the bureaucratic mentality that permeates much of the corporate world. The Amish aversion to bureaucracy stands as a stalwart example of their rejection of the structural realities of modernity. Amish beliefs about separation from the world and their predilection for locally based, small-scale, decentralized social units—church, schools, businesses—arrest, or at least retard, the growth of bureaucratic structures.

Without the organizational fixtures of solid modernity, how do Amish people sustain and understand their identity? Asked what holds Amish people across America together, one northern Indiana bishop thought for some time and then ventured, "We have the Eighteen Articles [the 1632 Dordrecht Confession], and the horse and buggy, and beyond that we interpret it in the church." In the absence of modern organizational glue, Amish identity hinges on the interplay of shared religious markers and symbolic separators. The religious markers, especially the Dordrecht Confession and its teaching on shunning, are anchored in the past, while the symbolic separators, such as the horse and carriage, create new meanings in contemporary society. To accept car culture, Amish people assert, would push them beyond the Amish pale. On the other hand, simply buying a buggy does not make anyone Amish. The symbolic separators, they believe, must coincide with membership in a church that collectively embraces a particular past and gives those symbolic separators their spiritual potency.

The absence of modern structural identity also means, as the bishop suggested, that identity in the Amish world will be contested. It will not fall within the neat lines of an organizational flow chart or a uniform set of bylaws but will be interpreted and applied differently in nearly two thousand local church districts. Traditional forms of unity, in essence, work against modern modes of uniformity.

And yet, as we shall see, the forces of modernity do play a role in the formulation of Amish identity, creating and affirming boundaries for the Amish via commercial images and public policy. Each time a marketing label features a buggy silhouette with the words "Amish made" or government officials formulate a legal exemption for "the Amish," outsiders are rarifying and reaffirming an identity with which insiders must live. Modernity, in other words, is always close at hand.

In fact, although most Amish people spend little time in sociologist Max Weber's iron cage of bureaucracy—absent as they are from the corporate world, higher education, the military, and government welfare programs—they increasingly find themselves standing in bureaucracy's doorway. For example, Amish employees of sizable English-owned industries as well as Amish entrepreneurs who own larger firms face aspects of modern organizational life on a regular basis. A variety of regulatory agencies dealing with zoning, environmental resources, labor, and safety issues now touch not only businesses but also homeowners who may, for example, want to add a grandparents' apartment to their home. As an Amish deli shop owner put it, "The state health department's Ordnung is much more burdensome than my church's."

While their ideology rejects bigness, more and more Amish people, especially those operating businesses, are increasingly exposed to the logic and rationality of bureaucratic life, and that exposure may affect how they think about their church and community. What we can say with some certainty, however, is that modernity has held little sway over Amish family and gender roles. In the next chapter we explore the family, the basic social unit that ranks second only to the church in its prominence in Amish society.

CHAPTER 11

GENDER AND FAMILY

Gathering in the cellar of a home to make sausage after butchering a pig, Katie and Susie picked cooked meat off of the bones. Susie's husband, Pete, joined them, and next to each was a little pile of salt. "We like to eat a little too," confided Katie, dipping a small piece of pork in the salt. Her husband, Andy, had wrapped his hair and beard in a Kopduche, or head scarf, causing great hilarity and teasing about the new "woman in the group." The women criticized Andy for some of the spices he was adding and his mixing techniques, so his daughter fried some of the sausage he had mixed so that everyone could test it. Katie and Susie pronounced it flat and sent Andy back to try a new blend.

Casting Roles

In the Amish world, gender is constructed in the context of community, legitimated by religion and tradition, and reinforced in daily interaction. One's role is defined by one's place in the family and the church-community, and one's identity is ensconced in relationships with others and shaped by the obligations these relationships entail. When an Amish child enters the world, his or her life is in many ways already mapped out. The label "another dishwasher" or "a little woodchopper" may greet the arrival of a new baby, and little girls learn to be Amish in ways different from little boys. As they sit on the boys' or girls' side of the kitchen table every day, small children begin to learn about gender and the ways it forms their place in their community.

The term *patriarchal*—in its anthropological and sociological sense—is an apt description of gender relations in Amish society: the male is the head of the family, and men occupy all visible leadership roles. Amish writer Joseph Stoll argues that "Scripture very clearly places the man in a position of responsibility as the head of the household, and his wife in a position of subjection."[1] Yet as we see in the opening vignette, that label does not capture the fullness and nuance of gender roles. For Amish people, subordination means neither inequality nor lack of importance. Outsiders' assumptions about rigid patriarchal frameworks obscure the many ways in which Amish women's agency is respected, affirmed, and operative. Gender relations in Amish life reflect a "soft" patriarchy, whose sinews stiffen and relax in different situations.[2]

The family is the primary social unit in Amish society. When Amish people report the size of their *Gmay,* they note the number of households, not the number of individuals. The Amish view of biblical roles—"The head of every man is Christ; and the head of the woman is the man; and the head of Christ is God" (1 Cor. 11:3)—means that, to them, male is dominant over female, older over younger, and parent over child.

The family is the church in microcosm, reflecting and reinforcing the social architecture of the church. The father serves as the head of the family just as the ministers lead the congregation. The mother is to support the father in every way she can. Together they raise their children in the church, a task that, according to one Amish publication, "must be more important . . . than our work or our leisure."[3]

Anthropologist Gertrude Enders Huntington observes that Amish people pass through six distinct stages of socialization: infancy, early childhood, school age, adolescence, adulthood, and old age.[4] Examining each stage with an eye toward how gender is constructed illuminates family life and the various scaffolds that support it.

Infancy

Because the Amish do not proselytize, the growth of their communities depends on having an abundance of children. Given the importance of the family, it is not surprising that babies are welcomed. Children are expected and cherished, and those with physical or mental disabilities are considered special gifts from heaven. In some communities, infertile couples adopt children or provide foster care for non-Amish children through social service agencies.[5]

Where babies are born varies widely across settlements.[6] In some communities most children are born in hospitals, while in other settlements birth centers have become common (see chapter 18), and in still others, births take place in the home. Available options, family preference, and tradition all influence birthing practices. Local custom determines who will help with childbirth. In ultraconservative communities, a woman in labor is likely to be attended by her mother and mother-in-law at home, although she may go to a hospital in an emergency. In other settlements, obstetricians or certified nurse midwives deliver the babies, while yet other groups turn to unlicensed Amish and English midwives. (The non-Amish midwives typically have a medical doctor on call to provide backup services if needed.) Midwives may deliver the babies at the mother's home or provide a "delivery room" in their own home or at a birth center. Some mothers deliver their first child in a hospital but then use a birth center or home delivery for the others. When births occur at home, the fathers often assist.

Midwives, Amish and non-Amish, work as neighbors helping neighbors, and they often have a special relationship with those they help. "Grandma Sue," an Amish midwife who practiced in different settlements and delivered well over two hundred Amish babies, laughed at one child's remark that "Sue always seems to find out about our baby before we children do." Some parents told their inquisitive children that Grandma Sue brought the baby, leading one child to wonder, "How many babies does Sue have that she doesn't want?" New mothers-to-be learn the lore of maternity through word of mouth, midwives, and the wisdom of older women rather than through birthing classes, books, or online sources.

Infants are welcomed as new members of the community and are seldom left alone. Until they are older or another child comes along, they sleep in the same room as their parents and typically take their naps in the main living area or in the kitchen. They are brought to the table at mealtimes and to church services on Sunday. People of all ages delight in infants, and even their youngest siblings hold them, play with them, and attempt to cheer them when they cry. The Amish view a new child as a gift from God, blameless and vulnerable, and see caring for their offspring as the parents' God-given duty.

Early Childhood

Amish homes are not child-centered. Children learn early that they have responsibilities and are expected to obey their elders. Sixteenth-century Anabaptist leader Menno Simons argued that parents have a moral responsibility to watch over the souls of their children, for "this is the chief and most important care of the godly, that their children may fear God, do good, and be saved." He contended that although worldly parents might desire for their children "that which is earthly and perishable, such as money, honor, fame and wealth," true Christians have a duty to "bring them up in the nurture and admonition of the Lord."[7]

A widely held maxim in Amish society is that children reflect the teaching they receive from their parents. In the words of one woman, "If you raise your children right, they won't leave the Amish." Thus, parents feel strong social and religious

These Amish parents with their young child are visiting Cadillac Mountain in
Acadia National Park, Bar Harbor, Maine. *Michael Cohn*

pressures to steer their children toward the church. With no formal institutions for
religious education—no Sunday schools, church camps, or Bible schools—the burden of a child's spiritual formation falls on parental shoulders. Biblical teaching en-
joins parents to "train up" their children to honor, respect, and obey their parents.
The words of the fifth commandment, "Honor thy father and thy mother," are heard
frequently in Amish circles.[8]

As soon as children are old enough to be disciplined, about the age they start to
walk, they are old enough to begin learning their roles in the community.[9] And, as
befits a community in which the church and one's role as a Christian are most important, the first lessons of the preschool stage involve obedience to God. Writing
in *Family Life,* one mother recounted the time she decided that "our one-year-old
should learn to be more quiet during family prayer." As she tells the story, "When
prayer was finished, I gave him a slap on his seat, which started him crying in rebellion. I spanked and talked to him until I felt my strength and heart faltering and failing me in accomplishing the needed discipline." The payoff came, she says, when on
"the next Sunday, I had such a different child in church. Then I wondered why I had
put it off so long, thinking it was just a minor thing."[10]

Socialization into the community begins early. The little girl who has worn a *Kapp*
(head covering) since birth will protest its removal by the time she is two. Preschool-

ers "playing church" sit quietly on benches for ten or fifteen minutes at a stretch, replicating the behavior they see on Sundays. In myriad ways, young children imitate and practice adult behavior.

There are few obvious gender differences in the treatment of young children. Although Amish parents, like their non-Amish counterparts, are likely to hand babies gendered toys—a truck to a boy, a toy purse to a girl—little boys carry dolls, little girls roll toy trucks back and forth, and toddlers play together regardless of sex. Depending on who is available and what work is pressing at home, a brother is just as likely to be told to watch his younger siblings as a sister.

School Age

In the third stage of socialization, beginning at age six or seven when they start attending school, Amish children are called "scholars." Even then, their home plays the primary role in preparing them for an Amish life. When children are not in school, they are with their families, doing chores with their parents, siblings, and grandparents. In so doing, they learn the practical skills that will enable them to earn a living, keep a home, and raise a family.

Generally, girls help their mothers and boys help their fathers, but work is not rigidly gendered. Far more important than their specific tasks is that they learn to be obedient, work hard, and do their best. Thus, if there are no "big boys" around, a girl will take over some of the outside barn or shop chores. Similarly, younger boys may be pressed into service around the house, watching younger siblings, cleaning, helping with dishes, or working in the vegetable garden. If they have no sisters, the boys take turns washing and drying the dishes for as long as they live at home.

In school as at home, boys and girls work and play together, and on the playground, girls swing the baseball bat just as enthusiastically as the boys on the mixed-gender teams. Throughout their years in school, boys and girls continue to study the same lessons, but by the time they reach the older grades, sharper gender differences emerge in the choice of games and other activities. Sometimes the distinctions are subtle. In Swartzentruber schools, for example, children are often given printed pictures to color following the Friday spelling test. Girls receive pictures with flowers or home scenes, while boys are given pictures with puppies, horses, or barn life. The gender differences were quite striking at recess in one school, where the children built "teepees" together, but then, while the boys played hunting, the girls pretended to cook stew over a campfire. In real life, girls may clean the schoolroom on Friday afternoons while boys fill the wood box.

As children get older, dress clearly marks gender. In the plainest communities, boy babies usually wear dresses and can be distinguished from girl babies only by their

Two Amish mothers and their eight children enjoy the delights of wading in a stream. Young children learn communal habits as they grow up surrounded by extended family and community. *Doyle Yoder*

lack of a head covering—and even this difference is hidden outdoors, because both wear bonnets. Once they are toilet trained, however, little boys start wearing pants, and their dress mirrors that of their fathers. Girls' dress marks two stages. Little girls wear pinafore-style aprons that button in the back over long-waisted dresses that also button in the back. At puberty they adopt adult-style "front shut dresses" and capes (a bodice worn over the main dress). In more traditional groups, dress can signal an in-between stage: preteen girls wear crossed capes instead of the aprons they have worn since birth. Only after completing school, at age fourteen, do they begin to dress as adult women. In other church-communities, girls are wearing adult-style dresses by the seventh grade.[11]

Adolescence

Between the ages of fourteen and sixteen or seventeen, after finishing eighth grade and before joining *die Youngie* (young folks), Amish teens begin to assume adult roles but without adult responsibilities. Psychologist Richard Stevick calls this brief, two-year period "the quiet years."[12] Teens begin life in "the real world," moving beyond the less-valued school studies into more tangible work activity.

During this period, children begin practicing adult roles and, depending on the family, may even assume adult tasks. For example, girls begin to take a greater part in meal preparation and learn to make head coverings and clothing, while boys take charge of livestock or a particular job in a shop. Some young teens may also begin to "hire out," working for Amish neighbors or family members. A girl may care for her young nieces or nephews at a married sister's house, while a boy might work at his older brother's sawmill, furniture shop, or market stand. Immersed full-time in work, Amish adolescents experience intensive vocational training.

The teenage years also mark a new relationship with family and church, for at sixteen or seventeen years of age, teens join the Youngie. At this point, they gain more autonomy, and the peer group becomes much more important. This period, called *Rumspringa* (see chapter 12), is the bridge from childhood to adulthood. During this transition, teens ponder the most important decisions of their lives: whether to become baptized and join the church and whether and whom to marry.

There is typically little sex education, and despite growing up around animals, children in the most conservative affiliations are often uninformed about reproduction. One Swartzentruber man was surprised to learn—after he got married—that women had menstrual cycles. Boys may be used to their sisters being "sick" at regular intervals, but it is never discussed. Nor will parents explain to boys or young girls who have not reached puberty why their older sisters will not participate in canning or baking at particular times of the month.[13] In contrast, most members of the more progressive groups are fully aware of menstruation and sexual reproduction issues.

Adulthood

At Home

Gender roles are fully realized in marriage, when spouses seal an eternal and holy bond of matrimony. Divorce, considered a sin, is forbidden in Amish society. One of the "Ten Rules for a Successful Marriage" published in two regional Amish newsletters is "never, never, never even think of divorce as a solution for your marriage problems."[14] The taboo on divorce is so strong that if one partner leaves the Amish, remarriage for the remaining one may only occur after the death of the wayward spouse. Remarriage is quite common among widows and widowers, however.

Amish marriages are grounded more in respect than in romance, and affection is typically displayed only in private. Yet this is another of the ten rules: "Keep your love as romantic as possible. Appreciate each other. Express that appreciation in actual love and affection in the home."[15] Some husbands in communities more open to change acknowledge Valentine's Day with a bouquet of flowers or a card. Although hugging in social gatherings is rare and discouraged, an Amish woman suggested in a cookbook she compiled that hugging is good for a healthy marriage.[16]

The Amish draw on the Bible for their understanding of appropriate gender roles. They cite the New Testament proclamation, "Wives, submit yourselves unto your own husbands, as unto the Lord. For the husband is the head of the wife, even as Christ is the head of the church: and he is the savior of the body. Therefore as the church is subject unto Christ, so let the wives be to their own husbands in every thing" (Eph. 5:22–24). A guide for Christian living published by Pathway Publishers cites Scripture (1 Pet. 3:1) to argue that, as a "keeper at home," a wife should not be "seeking employment outside the home, or seeking fulfillment in a 'career.'"[17]

Guided by these religious beliefs, the husband, with the help of his wife, takes the lead in providing for the spiritual and material welfare of the home. An Amish man is the public face of his family, the spokesperson to the outside world, and he ostensibly makes the final decisions, while his wife remains in the background. Because the public face of Amish life is what the world sees, it is not surprising that the popular image of Amish life is one of ironclad patriarchy.

Yet the term *patriarchy* obscures a more complicated gender reality. Within the family, hierarchy is seldom absolute, and many Amish marriages are characterized by mutual support and an equality that is also based in Scripture. After all, one preacher insisted, "Doesn't it say in Galatians, 'There is no such thing as . . . male and female, for you are all one person in Christ Jesus'?" Ultimately, a woman's equality as a Christian often overrules her subordination to men in the earthly hierarchy. As one scholar puts it, "Amish marriage must be 'in the Lord': that is, with a co-religionist." This means that "an individual's first duty is to God (as represented by the church-community), and one's second responsibility is to one's spouse."[18] If a husband makes a decision, his wife is expected to yield to it—but not if that places her in conflict with the *Ordnung*. Such an action by a husband would be considered very improper.

In the privacy of the home, the softer side of patriarchy appears because the Amish see marriage as "a partnership in the Lord and the basis of a family whose function [is] to produce willing, responsible members of the believing family."[19] In Amish eyes, both parents play important roles—the wife watches over the children and runs the house, while the husband takes the lead in earning an income and dealing with outside issues. As one Amish man put it, "The husband is the King and his wife, the Queen." In other words, within the family, the husband and the wife share responsibility and are mutually dependent on each other.[20]

This partnership is largely unseen by outsiders. More significantly, mainstream notions of gender equality, which assume equal access to all *public* roles, prevent many non-Amish people from seeing the power Amish women exercise in their communities. Yet, as an Old Order bishop writes, "Who would say that a mother's role is of less importance in eternity than a father's? Although women are not called to be leaders or set in places above men, their work is of equal worth before God."[21]

Similarly, Amish-born Louise Stoltzfus recounts how a visiting minister once asked a congregation, "Who has the most important role in the church?" In response, he answered, "Not the deacon, the minister or the bishop; it is the mothers with babies on their laps who have the most important task in our church." Stoltzfus concludes, "It was a special blessing to hear a church leader give colloquial voice, during what is usually a formal presentation, to this fundamental truth of Amish faith and understanding. The family is central. To be a mother is a high and holy calling."[22]

Women participate in the religious, political, and economic decision making in their family and Gmay. Indeed, husbands often defer to their wives' opinions and expertise, and many spouses jointly hold mortgages and bank accounts and make major decisions together. Thus, despite the patriarchal language that locates women in a position of subjugation, their role is frequently akin to that of a partner. The index of wives' names in some Amish directories is titled "Marriage Partners." One Amish housewife goes further: "If you listen to the men speaking, they say, 'This is what my mother did.' Mothers rule the world."

Although Amish work is gendered, the boundaries between "men's work" and "women's work" are permeable. Men hold and care for young children during the church service. Women help in the shop, barn, or field as needed. Men and women work side-by-side preparing food at weddings and charity auctions. For large public events, men take the lead in making ice cream and barbecuing chicken. Men also help with the vegetable garden, preparing it for planting and seeding, weeding, and harvesting. That said, certain activities show little crossover: welding and diesel repair are men's work, cross-stitching and canning are women's.

Despite the broad cultural patterns of gender roles and family norms, the equation of power in Amish families, as in those of their non-Amish counterparts, varies with the personalities of the spouses. In some households, the husband functions as the leader in all things. In others, the wife dominates family dynamics, although she may defer to her husband in public settings. In still others, the spouses are more equally balanced. As in all human societies, some Amish marriages are dysfunctional, and these couples may or may not accept outside help to resolve their troubles.[23]

In the Church-Community

Within the church, as within the family, men and women occupy separate domains that often overlap. In public life, the patriarchal nature of Amish society is more obvious. Only men serve as ministers and bishops, so all church functions—preaching, praying in public, administering communion, leading members' meetings and council meetings—lie solidly within their sphere.

Women, however, share responsibility for the well-being of the community. Although men have the obvious leadership roles, women prepare the home in which the congregation worships. Marilyn Lehman, who grew up Amish in LaGrange County, Indiana, contends that when women prepare the home and food for the fellowship meal after church, they transform the space "from ordinary to ceremonial." Furthermore, she argues, the collective work done by women—the wife, her sisters, her daughters, and nearby female neighbors—is "as vital to the creation and maintenance of community as it is to the preparation of space for ceremony." Women's collective work creates and undergirds the ceremonial space that supports the Sunday morning worship.[24]

As church members, women have a voice and a vote in church decision making and thus some constraint on men's exercise of power. Women join with men to decide when a new minister is needed, and they also nominate candidates for ordination. Women, like men, are responsible for maintaining the Ordnung, and they too have a vote when it is reaffirmed. When asked whether the ministers would listen if she had a disagreement with the Ordnung, one young woman answered, "Of course—they would have to!" As Louise Stoltzfus puts it, "Women are very free to say what's on their minds."[25] On the other hand, said one man, "Women are *not* free to say what's on their minds in a church meeting and do so at the risk of making a confession for being out of their place. At the same time, women have a tremendous influence in the community and in private conversations with their 'leader husbands' that are very instrumental . . . to maintaining the peace and harmony of the congregation."[26]

Outside of the Gmay, men also fill the leadership roles on local Amish school boards and on settlement-wide committees involving safety, fire and storm insurance, loan funds, trusteeships for failing businesses, government relations, and mental health. Women take the lead in organizing more informal gatherings—weddings, funerals, reunions—especially those aspects pertaining to food.

Women, like men, are obliged to obey God and refrain from worldly things. As a woman in an ultratraditional community put it, at the baptism ceremony "the Amish way is that the men have to go ahead of the women, but the women get baptized just as well as the men do." In short, the Amish notion of the church as the body of Christ in which male and female are spiritual equals requires and honors the participation of both, although they participate in different ways.

Old Age

The relationships Amish couples establish as adults carry them through to the final stage, when they become simply "old folks." In their retirement years, parents move to a *Dawdyhaus,* a small apartment or cottage adjacent to the main house of one of their married children, and turn their business or farm over to others. Because offspring are eager to assume ownership of the business or farm and the older folks are needed to help them, it is not unusual for retirement to begin in the fifties.

Retirement might mean that husband and wife slow down, but nonetheless both continue many of the chores that occupied them when they were raising children. They generally remain financially independent, funded in their golden years by income from the sale of their farm or business, proceeds from an auction of extra furniture and no-longer-needed machinery, personal savings, and their part-time labor. Remaining physically, socially, and emotionally close to their children and grandchildren, they lead independent lives, and their wisdom is valued.

With very few exceptions, the Amish make no use of retirement centers or nursing homes. If a parent needs long-term assistance with the activities of daily living, adult children take turns providing it. In some cases an infirm parent who needs continuous care rotates from home to home, spending several weeks in each one. Otherwise, adult children may take turns providing care in the Dawdyhaus.

The Extended Family

It is difficult to exaggerate the importance of the extended family in Amish society. Mary, a typical thirty-five-year-old married woman, is ensconced in a thick family network of some 250 people that includes grandparents, parents, aunts and uncles, siblings and their spouses, first cousins and their spouses, and a similar clutch of relatives on her husband's side. The majority live within fifteen miles of Mary's home, and some live within just a mile. Some are members of her church district. Her extended family provides care, support, and wisdom for all stages of life—from pregnancy to how to dress the deceased for burial. They offer recipes, childcare, and homespun remedies for common ailments. This pool of knowledge is a reservoir of cultural capital, an oral how-to manual for fixing problems from marital discord to depression.

When men and women marry, they retain ties to their extended families as well as to other members of their community. Same-sex siblings play a particularly important role, especially for women. Only daughters surpass sisters in importance, and women draw on the emotional and practical support of their female relatives in a variety of ways.

A woman is usually helped after she gives birth by her mother. If there are no older girls in the home, an unmarried sister or a niece may move in to help care for the newborn and assume household chores for a while. Only if no relative is available will a neighbor be called on to supply an unmarried daughter to help out. Sisters and married daughters provide labor and support when a family readies the house for church services. This task, which fills two or more weeks preceding the gathering, involves cleaning everything and even laying new shelf paper or repainting rooms. At weddings, aunts and married sisters of the bride are often invited to share the honor of cooking, and unmarried sisters wait on tables.

Singles

Single men and women rarely live alone but are instead integrated into the extended family network. Singles are treated with respect and participate in the life of the church-community, but because the bulk of activities are family oriented, a single person can sometimes feel "like an oddball," in the words of one single woman.[27] Because getting married and having children is such an esteemed goal in Amish society, singles sometimes feel marginalized. On the other hand, one single woman declared, "I don't feel second class." Some singles pursue careers such as teaching, craft making, or running small businesses, earning the admiration of others in the community.

Individuals rarely choose to remain single or childless. In one settlement, only 7 percent of those thirty to seventy-five years of age had never married.[28] Marriage is the ritualized step into Amish adulthood, leaving singles in a liminal space for a number of years until they realize that marriage will likely elude them. The ambivalence of their status is rehearsed at the start of every church service as they continue to walk into the service and sit with the unmarried "boys" or "girls." Eventually, usually in their thirties, they begin to sit with the married men or women.

A gathering of single Amish women, which rotates from community to community across the United States, is held every year. In some settlements, singles organize evening and weekend social events. A higher female birthrate, a higher rate of male defection from the church, and the restriction that marriage be between fellow church members results in more single Amish women than men. Single adult women often live with and care for their aging parents. They may also develop especially close relationships with their sisters, nieces, and nephews.

Sexuality

The Amish strongly oppose extramarital and premarital sex. Their reliance on Scripture, the importance of the family, and the welfare of their communities both inform and preserve the Amish view that sexual expression belongs within marriage. "We're still very Victorian in this sphere," noted one man. Although Amish sexual standards may be more concrete and specific than those of some cultures, the Amish do not claim exemption from lust or sexual desire. "We all have temptations until we die," a seventy-six-year-old grandfather said. "When I see women half-dressed on the street, they look tempting, and my mind goes to the ditch." Yet oft-heard calls for holy living and moral purity reinforce Amish sexual mores, as do sanctions against those who transgress them.

Sexual Transgressions

Premarital sex occurs with greater frequency in some communities than in others, and undoubtedly some courting couples who engage in sex use natural or artificial birth control to avoid pregnancy. Transgressors are expected to confess to the church regardless of whether pregnancy results. As one woman put it, "If you commit adultery or fornication, you go tell the ministers. That's how they find out. Usually people are so ashamed that they request their membership be put aside [in a temporary excommunication]."

Men and women hold equal responsibility to confess fornication, but the expectation for confession varies in different groups. In some groups, after a public confession and a short period of excommunication, the wayward couple is completely forgiven and restored into full fellowship. After noting how rigorously some other communities punish premarital sex offenders, one woman added, "In our church, they're in the *Bann* just over one church Sunday. If a girl gets pregnant, we say, 'That's too bad,' and then we move on." In other Gmays, the excommunication might last as long as six weeks.

In most churches, couples who conceive before marriage are disgraced in several ways. In addition to a public confession before the Gmay and an excommunication of two to six weeks, wedding festivities may be shortened, fewer guests invited, and the ceremony held on a different day of the week than customary or ahead of the regular wedding season to accommodate the impending birth. These public changes shame the couple and their parents and help to discourage premarital intercourse.

If both partners are baptized Amish members, they almost always marry and try to have the wedding before the baby arrives. Amish people unequivocally consider abortion to be a sin. If the father is not Amish, the pregnant woman might leave and marry the father outside the church, or she might remain in the community and raise the child as a single parent, or she might even arrange for an Amish couple to adopt the child. Church members tend to be more forgiving of the premarital pregnancy of an Amish couple than that of an Amish woman and a non-Amish man.

Sexual Orientation

The Amish consider homosexual activity a sin.[29] Because they are not exposed to much television or other mass media, some Amish people are not familiar with the terms *gay* and *lesbian* or public discourse on the topic, although others learn about same-sex issues when they read local newspapers.

No systematic research has measured the prevalence of homosexuality among the Amish. Some Amish people privately express same-sex inclinations, but they tend to keep their desires under cover. Those with homosexual inclinations who are married may feel dissatisfied and unhappy, but they nevertheless continue in their marriage, yielding their personal yearnings to the expectations of their church. In short, a de facto "don't ask, don't tell" policy seems to prevail. "The Silent Struggle," an anonymous essay on homosexuality that appeared in the Amish publication *Family Life,* never mentions the word *homosexuality.* The essayist notes, "Many [people] have been this way since childhood; no one knows why. And our plain society keeps these people hidden, pretending there is no problem, offering no help." The writer goes on to advise, "Do not enter marriage just to be socially acceptable; you will hardly be happy and it would be unfair to your partner." He or she summarizes by saying that "there is hope" that people can change via God's power, yet also suggests that not everyone will or can change sexual orientation, and that it is God's will that such people accept remaining single.[30]

Homosexual practice that becomes known must be confessed publicly in church. Most of the confessions are made by men, perhaps because women may be able to carry on affairs more discreetly than men.[31] Some who claim a homosexual identity seek out others in the community with a similar inclination or look for counselors to help them claim a heterosexual identity. Some individuals leave the Amish community because they realize it is impossible to live as an openly gay or lesbian person in Amish society, but such cases are relatively rare.

Abuse and Violence

Sexual Abuse

No systematic or evidence-based studies have documented the extent of sexual abuse in Amish families. Nevertheless, anecdotal evidence and legal charges against some individuals indicate that Amish society, like other societies, experiences sexual abuse. In some cases, ex-Amish people point to sexual abuse as one reason for leaving the community.

Sexual violations occur both inside the nuclear family and within the extended family or neighborhood. Typical cases involve teenage boys or adult men abusing young women who are not baptized or married. The size of extended families and the high density of Amish communities provide a large pool of potential victims for perpetrators. Compared to those in small-family societies, male Amish predators have easy access to many possible victims—sisters, nieces, granddaughters, and neighbors.

A clinician notes, "The majority of Amish offenders with whom I have counseled are hapless individuals who experience inappropriate sexual desires and act on victims of convenience. A few are truly predatory and need to be treated as such, but the majority are conscience-ridden and struggling with what they are doing, experiencing a compulsive desire they realize is wrong, and even revolted by their own behavior."[32]

The Amish church forbids sexual abuse and considers it a sin. When a case of sexual abuse becomes public knowledge inside the community, the offender typically makes a public confession and then is placed in the Bann for several weeks. This shaming ritual is rarely adequate to terminate compulsive abuse; offenders with a serious psychological disorder and addiction may continue abusing victims until halted by other interventions.

Amish people prefer to deal with abusers inside their own church-based system of discipline rather than report them to outside authorities. However, their religious practices of forgiveness and pardon coupled with social shaming do not always provide the necessary therapy for sex addicts or adequate protection for victims. Despite their aversion to informing civil authorities, some members have reported cases of abuse to outside authorities and cooperated with law enforcement officials. Some Amish offenders have served extensive prison sentences, and others have undergone treatment in Amish-operated mental health centers.[33]

Several cultural factors make it challenging to report sexual abuse to outside authorities, and some victims and Amish people who know of the abuse do not know how to report it. Sex education is not included in the school curriculum, and some youth do not understand inappropriate sexual advances or know what to do if violations occur. Because Amish people have less exposure to and interaction with social service agencies, counseling, and health care professionals, outside experts are less likely to learn of or detect abuse in Amish clients.

Abuse is typically reported to church leaders, who are always male. Because the church, family, and community are knit together and the authority structure is patriarchal, male leaders may not be sensitive to the needs of female victims. Men may minimize the acts of a male perpetrator or blame female victims for the violations. Moreover, female victims may face intimidation and scorn within their family and community if the abuse they report leads to imprisonment of the perpetrator. Furthermore, church leaders, with their limited knowledge of addictions and treatment therapies, do not always realize that church discipline is inadequate to address serious psychological disorders, which need much more than "a prayer and some help from above," as one Amish man put it.

Numerous outside professionals have worked in tandem with Amish people to address the problem of abuse and to provide treatment. Despite the complications of reporting and responding to abuse, some Amish people have actively sought to raise awareness of it and to support victims and their families. In Ohio, an outside social services agency prepared a booklet about sexual abuse entitled *Strong Families, Safe Children,* which was widely distributed in Amish communities by church leaders.[34] Two other booklets, *Healing from Sexual Sin* and *Walk in the Light,* were written by Amish people. *Healing* offers help for those who struggle with sexual issues, and *Walk* contains an explicit discussion of the psychological damage related to sexual abuse, suggests ways to prevent it, and gives advice on what to do when it occurs. One woman who experienced sexual abuse wrote a book about her story that was sold within and beyond the Amish community.[35] An Amish periodical, *Family Life,* has published numerous articles on abuse in an effort to inform families and assist victims.[36]

Domestic Violence

Although the Amish religion emphasizes peaceful and nonviolent living, anecdotal evidence, reports of counselors, and concerns of church leaders point to the presence of some domestic violence in Amish communities. The same issues that impede reporting sexual abuse to outside authorities also obstruct reporting domestic violence.

Some leaders have demonstrated concern about violence in their communities. *Family Life,* for example, published an article on the topic in the mid-1990s.[37] In one settlement, a group of Amish women calling themselves the Sewing Circle collected stories of domestic violence and printed them in a booklet to raise awareness of the problem. Their purpose was "to encourage Plain People who are victims of domestic violence to know that there is hope and healing for their pain. . . . We reached out from our own abuse and found people who responded; and in their response was hope. In turn . . . we are offering the same hope that was offered to us."[38]

The incidence of violence and abuse in Amish communities likely varies across affiliations. In one study, which included interviews with 288 randomly selected Amish women of childbearing age, only two participants (less than 1 percent) reported that "a spouse or boyfriend had pushed, grabbed, shoved, or slapped them" in the past twelve months. None of the Amish women reported that they had been kicked, beaten, threatened with a gun, or forced to have sex in the previous year. In comparison, 7 percent of non-Amish women of similar age in the same study had suffered violence at the hands of a spouse or boyfriend.[39] A police officer who has investigated numerous cases of sexual abuse in one Amish settlement says she was "never called to investigate any cases of domestic violence," although, of course, some cases may never have been reported.

Changing Society, Changing Roles

Stereotypical Amish family life unfolds on a small, family-owned farm. As partners, the husband and wife perform distinct tasks but recognize each other's contributions to the well-being of the family. Eating three meals a day together, with their sons and daughters seated on separate sides of the table in order of age, the parents know that the labor of all is critical to the well-being and economic productivity of their household.

This pattern, considered ideal by many Amish people, remains stable in many communities. In others, however, it has vanished as men and some women have begun leaving home before sunrise for work at a factory, construction site, or market stand. As communities change, so do family and gender relations. The economic value of children and the social worth of the mother who births and cares for them reflect somewhat their contribution to the family economy.[40] For example, Amish wives whose husbands work as day laborers "make a smaller contribution to the subsistence and to the economic survival of their family, which may affect both their self-esteem and status in the community."[41] In addition, children have less economic merit in the families of factory and construction-crew workers than they do in farm families and families with home-based shops, who need their labor.[42]

Perhaps most importantly, when men work away from home, the traditional family structure is disrupted. Wives lose the support of their husbands during the day and must care for children alone. One grandmother grumbled that her son-in-law did not eat breakfast or lunch with the family because he worked in carpentry for a non-Amish employer, leaving his wife alone with six children, the oldest of whom was a first-grader.

As Amish communities adopt different patterns of work, their family routines change in ways that mirror the transformation of American society from 1850 to 1950. Industrialization and the rise of wage labor had a major impact on gender and family relations as men and unmarried children left the family home or farm for outside employment. As a result, the woman as housewife and homemaker played a subordinate role in the economic well-being of family and community.

Likewise, the growth of nonfarm employment in Amish society will, in time, reorder gender and social relationships. Some scholars assert that the traditional Amish farm family is "the prototype of the pre-industrial capitalist family" in which

Amish men and women work side by side preparing food for a benefit sale.
Women do the bulk of cooking in their homes, but men sometimes assist with
large community dinners. *Dennis Hughes*

women's work in the home, essential to the economic well-being of the family, is seen
as a calling and gives her prestige. With the spread of nonfarm work, however, even
women's decision-making power within the community may decline as the financial
base changes.[43] On the other hand, Amish women who have more disposable
income from their own small businesses may exert new forms of influence in their
community.

Outside employment and entrepreneurship weaken the kind of marital partnership
fostered by farming. Whereas husbands and wives almost always hold joint legal
ownership of farmland, when a husband starts a business, his wife is rarely a co-
owner.[44] And when either spouse receives a regular wage, it disrupts the balance of
power found in farm partnerships in which the monthly milk check, the seasonal
produce sales, or the annual tobacco check symbolize the productive effort of the
entire family.

A major development since 1980 is the growing number of women who own and
operate small businesses—roadside produce stands, quilt shops, market stands,
bookstores, fabric shops, greenhouses, and the like. These ventures have given

greater voice and agency as well as financial muscle to women. We explore this shift in our discussion of the rise of business in chapter 16.

Some of the marks of individuation in modern societies include the choice of marriage partners, the option of divorce, the choice to remain single or to be childless, and a blurring of male and female occupational roles. The Amish have fervently resisted all of these trends. Couples must marry within the church and marry for life, and they are expected to have children. Very few married women, even those owning businesses, work away from home full time while their children are young.

Yet economic and occupational change is slowly creating ever more diversity in the Amish world. While more traditional groups endorse the complementary roles of men and women working together on the family farm, affiliations that are more open to change permit men greater occupational options, offer women more opportunity to work outside the home, and allow couples to exercise more control over the number of children they conceive.

The construction of gender and family in Amish society is clearly more complicated than the term *patriarchy* suggests. As members of the Gmay, men and women promise to yield their lives to God and accept their gendered roles when they choose to be baptized. To embrace *Gelassenheit*—to trust in God completely—levels men and women yet recognizes specific gender obligations in ways that promote family stability and the well-being of others over self-will and individual achievement.

Traditional gender expectations, the power of extended families, the importance of lifelong marriage, the rejection of divorce, the taboo on extramarital, premarital, and homosexual sexual activity, the high value bestowed on childbearing, and the overwhelming priority of family commitments over personal careers—all demonstrate the staunch Amish resistance to the transformation of gender roles and marital patterns that occurred in twentieth-century America. Nevertheless, modest adaptations of traditional gender and family roles show that Amish society is not completely cordoned off from the advances of modernity. The behavior of some youth during Rumspringa, the topic of chapter 12, offers even more evidence of that fact.

CHAPTER 12

FROM RUMSPRINGA
TO MARRIAGE

On June 24, 1998, federal agents arrested two Amish-raised young men in Lancaster County, Pennsylvania, and charged them with intent to distribute cocaine for a drug ring tied to the Pagans motorcycle gang in Philadelphia. Within hours, the event was a major news story far from the local police blotter. From the New York Times *to Australian Broadcasting and hundreds of points in between, the story received extensive coverage. Eventually the indicted young men were each sentenced to a year in prison. But before they began their jail time, both requested baptism and joined the Amish church, taking a step their parents had long wished for.*

Myths and Reality

Linked to black-jacketed bikers and illicit drugs, the drug bust story piqued public curiosity and revealed to outsiders a surprising aspect of Amish life: teenagers are allowed some autonomy before joining the church as young adults. The Amish call this period *Rumspringa*, literally translated as "running around" but best understood as the time when youth socialize with their peers. Few Americans had ever heard the word before the drug story broke, but in the weeks and years that followed, Rumspringa became one of the most recognized aspects of Amish life, both real and mythologized.

The notion that a traditional group trying to avoid a modern world teeming with temptation would allow its youth to explore that very world captured the American imagination. How could a separatist church be so tolerant of the exploits of its youth? One political philosopher even pondered why an illiberal group like the Amish had developed such a liberal policy of membership.[1] Stern indoctrination, if not brainwashing, was what many outsiders expected to find in Amish life—not choice, not freedom, and certainly not drugs.

This baffling paradox prompted numerous journalistic and artistic ventures. For example, filmmaker Lucy Walker found four Amish teens willing to describe their wild, drug-laced parties on camera. *Devil's Playground,* Walker's 2002 documentary, featured the wildest of the wild in Rumspringa. In 2004, UPN's reality series *Amish in the City* turned its lens on Rumspringa with six episodes showing Amish youth interacting with urban teens in a California beach house.[2] Several television series, including *ER* and *Judging Amy,* focused on Rumspringa, as did an Oprah Winfrey show. For several months in 2009, a dark comedy-drama entitled *Rumspringa* played off Broadway, and within a year, interest in Rumspringa had spread to England, as British TV broadcast *The World's Squarest Teenagers.* In 2012, TLC's nine-episode reality series *Breaking Amish* followed four young Amish adults and one Mennonite "in their pursuit to chase big dreams in the Big Apple."[3]

Rumspringa is much more nuanced and varied than these media productions suggest, however.[4] Teens do enjoy a measure of freedom before settling down, being baptized, getting married, and becoming adult members of the community. During this time they face the two most crucial decisions of their lives: whether to join the church, and if and whom to marry.

Rumspringa, an exciting adventure and at times a period of inner turmoil, commences at age sixteen—or seventeen in more traditional groups—and continues until marriage. It is a time when *die Youngie,* or "young folks," socialize with their Amish peers. With few exceptions, young adolescents eagerly count the days until they are old enough to join the young folks. In some communities, a boy receives his first carriage so he can drive to youth activities alone. Most important, courtship begins during Rumspringa, as youth embark on a social life in which their peer group plays a new and dominant role. Because popular media and programs like *Devil's Playground* and *Amish in the City* have created and perpetrated a number of untruths and half-truths, we examine both the myths and the realities they often obscure.

Myth One: Amish youth are breaking church regulations. In fact, although they have been immersed in Amish culture and have worn the distinctive garb of their community since birth, they are not church members—and thus are not required to submit to church regulations—until they choose baptism. Rumspringa is an ambiguous time, a liminal period when youth are betwixt and between the supervision of their parents and the authority of the church.[5]

Myth Two: Parents encourage their children to explore the outside world.[6] Some pundits say that the church has established a cultural "time out" for that purpose, but that is simply false. As an Amish woman in southwestern Michigan explains, "Rumspringa, the way people talk about it, is a lie. What group of parents that love their children would say, 'Go out and do whatever you want and then decide whether you want to be like we raised you'?" It is true that Rumspringa is a rite of passage that starts at about sixteen years of age when youth begin to socialize with their friends on weekends. It is also true that parents in certain communities tolerate more rowdiness on the road to adulthood than do some other parents. But no Amish church ever designed a tradition to encourage its youth to explore the larger world, nor does any church urge them to imbibe popular culture. Some parents dread the time and pray diligently that their offspring will not make foolish choices that could hound them forever.

Myth Three: Rumspringa-age youth leave home and live in cities for a few years. In fact, virtually all unbaptized Amish teens continue living at home and spend their Rumspringa years under their parents' roof. The only thing that changes after they join the Youngie is that their social life becomes more independent from that of their family. Although living and often working at home, they are now able to keep their peer-based activities somewhat private.

Myth Four: Youth who break church rules during Rumspringa are shunned for life. On the contrary, parents may punish deviant youth, but the church only has authority to excommunicate and shun baptized members who violate regulations. Unbaptized youth who run away or are rebellious may be labeled "yankovers" or "jerkovers" and severely scorned and ostracized by their family and community, especially in the more traditional groups, but the church does not and cannot shun them.

Myth Five: Rumspringa is all about deciding whether or not to be Amish. For a few youth this is true, but as one Amish father said, "The main purpose of Rumspringa is courtship; it's a time to find a mate." The decision to join the church becomes an existential crisis for a few, but the overwhelming majority of youth expect to join the church and do not struggle with the decision. Youth in higher groups grapple more with the choice—especially if it involves giving up cars, televisions, or other possessions—than youth in lower affiliations.

Myth Six: Rumspringa ends with baptism. In fact, Rumspringa ends with marriage, which signals adulthood. This is when boys become men and girls women in Amish culture. For some, marriage comes shortly after baptism; others begin dating after baptism, and still others date both before and after baptism. The unmarried may run around with the Rumspringa "boys and girls" until their early thirties. Two twenty-six-year-old "girls" in one community "still go with die Youngie," according to one man. "As they get older they go to [Sunday evening] singings more sporadi-

A young Amish man who plays on a baseball team in a local civic league changes into his uniform shirt under the back lid of his buggy. During Rumspringa, some youth engage in activities that are unacceptable for adult church members. *Dennis Hughes*

cally and then stop going. It's an individual choice." Unmarried baptized youth who violate church regulations while still running around will face church discipline like any other church member.

Myth Seven: Rumspringa is similar in all Amish communities. In fact, the type of Rumspringa activities varies among settlements and even within an individual settlement. The degree of parental oversight and involvement with youth activities as well as the amount of contact young people have with mainstream culture is quite uneven. In some communities Rumspringa activities take place in homes under watchful adult eyes. In large settlements, where the number of Rumspringa-age youth may surpass a thousand, and in communities adjacent to urban areas, "running around" may involve peers whom parents do not know and activities that are worldlier.

To make sweeping generalizations about Rumspringa is simply hazardous. An Amish leader in Canada, referring to wild Rumspringa parties, wrote, "We know nothing of such a practice in the thirty-five church districts in Ontario. Nor is it known in *many* Amish settlements elsewhere."[7] Sensational media accounts imply that all Amish youth experiment with drugs, engage in premarital sex, and flock to drinking parties. Some youth do these things, but most do not. In many communities, there are no wild parties; instead, youth gather to sing German hymns on Sunday nights, and rarely is there mischief worthy of a headline. In other communities, some youth own cars, hit the party scene, and give their parents anxious nights. In still others, teens ride in buggies, play volleyball, and hit hockey pucks on local ponds. Rumspringa comes in many forms and is shaped by local tradition, community size, family reputation, and the church-community's values.

Singings

Sunday evening singings are the most common and oldest youth activities, dating back to the nineteenth century or even earlier.[8] Traditionally, singings were held in the home that hosted the church service earlier that day. More recently in many places, singings are hosted by another family in the church district.[9] In some areas, the gathering—held in a home, barn, shop, or outdoors in pleasant weather—is preceded by volleyball, card or table games, and a meal or picnic, depending on the season and local custom. Singings are a prime youth activity across all communities, but the format and practices vary.

Regardless of the details, the Sunday evening singing is the big event of the week for most youth. For some it is more about fraternizing, courtship, and fun than singing. The Youngie learn to know each other and develop their social skills as well as their identities during the pre- and post-singing banter.

Teens often share a carriage ride to the singings with their siblings, friends, or a neighbor. In some communities, dating couples may arrive together, while some unattached boys—hoping to escort a girl home—come alone. The size of the group varies from twenty to two hundred, depending on the settlement. The singing, which may last for one and a half to three hours, begins with religious songs in German. In less traditional communities, the group usually switches to faster tunes, including English gospel songs. Typically, the host family serves water midway through the evening, and a light snack and beverages at the end.

There is no moderator or song leader. Youth call out the page number of a hymn or just begin leading it, since the words and tunes of hymns are well known. In some groups, the girls may do most of the singing while the boys listen, joke, or tease one another. In certain settlements, boys stay outside to smoke and drink beer some of the time. The singing may conclude with birthday songs or a thank-you song for the host family.

Informal visiting, inside or outside, often stretches for an hour or longer after the singing ends. This is also the time when rowdy groups might engage in mischief of one type or another. Considerable speculation focuses on who will ride home with whom—signaling the beginning or end of a romance. One Amish person who attended a singing after a wedding season joked that the local young people were "bravely going on after losing nine couples to Cupid's arrows" in recent months.[10]

While singings are the central ritual of Rumspringa for the most conservative groups, in more progressive communities they are only one of many social activities. In some settlements youth socialize at sporting events such as hockey, volleyball, and softball games as much, if not more, than at singings.

"Gangs"

Although the Amish sometimes use the English words *crowds* or *gangs* to refer to the Youngie, these youth groups should not to be confused with violent street gangs. There were few Amish gangs before the mid-twentieth century. Distinct groups emerged as settlements grew larger and the abundant number of youth could not all gather in one place. The structure of the groups varies greatly, resulting in many different versions of Rumspringa.

Small affiliations with only a few church districts may have just one crowd that includes all their youth. In sharp contrast, large settlements may have two or three dozen groups with a hundred or so members in each. Such gangs typically attract youth from many different *Gmay*s. In settlements with many groups, teens select one by simply showing up for an activity. Some switch groups, but more typically they stay with the same gang until they marry. In the Lancaster settlement, young men and women who join a crowd in the same year form a "buddy bunch," segregated by gender. These clusters may simply hang out, or they may hold their own events apart from those organized by the full group.

Psychologist Richard Stevick distinguishes between peer-centered and adult-centered gangs.[11] Those in smaller communities tend to be adult-centered because, with only a few groups, parents usually know what their offspring are doing, which makes it difficult to hide deviant behavior. In some communities, parents chaperone youth events fairly closely. Groups in large settlements that cover a big area typically are peer-centered, and their anonymity helps the Youngie evade parental oversight. The most notorious parties, as well as drug and alcohol abuse, almost always occur

Volleyball is the sport of choice for many Amish young people. At some youth gatherings, a dozen teams play at the same time. The various styles of dress and headgear reflect the different church affiliations of the players in this particular game. *Doyle Yoder*

in the larger settlements.[12] Members of some peer-based gangs buy cameras, radios, DVD players, televisions, or even cars, and then store them at the homes of non-Amish neighbors or in a clubhouse rented by their group.[13] Small clusters of friends may take long-distance trips to go snow or water skiing, fishing, big game hunting, or snowmobiling. The number, size, and type of parties range from small nonalcoholic ones featuring volleyball games to large gatherings with hired bands and alcohol that draw several hundred people from several states. Some of the parties get quite rowdy. A twenty-five-year-old woman who abandoned Amish life lamented, "Once I turned sixteen, you partied, you drank, you got drunk, and you woke up the next morning and you thought, 'Gosh, what did I do last night?'"[14]

In communities in which the young people have greater access to non-Amish society and may even work for outside employers, those pressing the boundaries might wear Amish clothing and ride in slow-paced carriages during the week but dress "English" and cruise in sporty cars on the weekend. On Saturday nights, they may listen to hard rock music and watch movies, and then eight hours later snooze in church during the slow songs of the *Ausbund*. Such Youngie live in a different world on the weekends when they step into Rumspringa.

The gangs in the larger settlements have different identities. For example, the Amish settlement in northern Indiana has about a dozen crowds, each of which attracts from two hundred to five hundred young people.[15] The larger groups have half a dozen subgroups that meet periodically. The gangs have distinct reputations and names, such as Topekas, Whassups, High Clintons, Low Clintons, Easties, and Barrens. The large Lancaster, Pennsylvania, settlement has some forty groups, with thirty to 150 members, with names like Shotguns, Broncos, Mustangs, Dominos, Eagles, Hummingbirds, Swans, and Quakers. Groups are fluid, and they frequently form and dissolve. According to one Amish observer, some thirty-five new gangs formed in the Lancaster area over a ten-year period. Some withered, others morphed into different groups, and still others were fresh start-ups.[16]

Not surprisingly, when multiple groups emerge, each develops its own identity and reputation. So-called "slow" groups tend to be more traditional in dress and behavior. Members of the "faster" gangs press the boundaries of acceptable Amish behavior by driving cars, using drugs and alcohol, visiting bars, and playing video games. For example, in one settlement with nearly a dozen groups, Amish informants identified the distinguishing traits of two of them—the Scavengers, and Rangers.[17] The Scavengers, they said, were "old school" because they drink Budweiser and smoke Marlboro Reds. Very few of them drive cars. One informant considers the Scavengers conservative and strict because they wear Amish clothing, play volleyball and softball, and attract large groups to their singings.

The Rangers, on the other hand, try to mimic the English way of life by driving cars, wearing fashionable clothing, bowling, and watching movies. Sometimes they get together just to show off their cars. Many wear name-brand clothes, such as Abercrombie, Hollister, Buckle, Billabong, and Hurley, and some occasionally wear Goth or hip-hop clothing. They are not very involved in church activities, and most delay baptism until their early or mid-twenties. The Rangers play basketball and softball and hold volleyball tournaments. A Rangers subgroup does some extreme sports such as wakeboarding and snowboarding.

In large church communities with diverse gangs, most youth anticipate their sixteenth birthday with an eye on a particular group. The choice of group matters because members generally choose marital partners and long-term friends through gang connections. Teens may choose a gang through the nudging of their parents, in reaction to it, or in response to invitations by peers, siblings, or cousins. Teens in the same family may join different crowds. Some preteens even know the names, reputations, and markers of each group: the type of haircut, the tilt of hats, the color of suspenders, and the style of buttons on boys' shirts. For girls, the hem length, brightness of dress materials, use of straight pins or buttons, and thickness of stockings can signal group identity. Such symbols locate a particular crowd on the reputation grid of the region.

In some Amish settlements young men play pickup football at social gatherings. Women rarely play, and some adults consider football a worldly sport to be avoided. *Daniel Rodriguez*

A group's ethos, whether docile or rowdy, will shape teen behavior, including their likelihood of joining the church. Group selection is not just a teenage matter. It keeps some parents awake at night because they, better than their children, grasp its long-term consequences. A father described his son's choice of a gang as "one of the severest trials I went through in my lifetime—that [my son] wouldn't get sucked into the bad crowd." Parents who try to persuade a daughter or son to join a particular group realize that if they push too hard, their efforts may backfire.

Whether youth groups are adult-centered or peer-centered depends not only on community size, but more importantly, according to Stevick, on "a community's local history, tradition, and moral beliefs."[18] Although the peer-adult difference historically reflects the size of the settlement, that distinction has been diluted somewhat by the rise of adult-supervised youth groups in the twenty-first century. The front-page, drug-bust headlines in 1998 spurred some parents to establish parent-supervised groups in the large Lancaster settlement. Twelve years later, over half of the groups in that area had parental direction. The guidelines for one parent-centric group include the following stipulations:

- Dress shall conform to church standards.
- Singings and other activities will be supervised by two or three sets of parents.
- Parents, with input from teenagers, will determine the place and time of singings and what games will be played.
- The singing will begin at 7:00 p.m. and end by 9:00 p.m.
- Youth will leave the singing before 10:00 p.m. and arrive at home by midnight.
- Smoking is prohibited at the suppers and singings.[19]

A group of parents in the Old Order affiliation in Holmes County, Ohio, also established supervised youth groups for their offspring. Even some smaller, more traditional settlements have reasserted stricter behavioral guidelines, and parents are often present at singings and similar gatherings. One father noted, "Sometimes after church [the youth] may get together and play games. They sing every Sunday. There's a 1:00 a.m. curfew." An adult couple must also accompany the young people on any trips. All of these changes underscore the growing influence of parental guidance during Rumspringa in some communities.

Courtship

As with Rumspringa, courtship varies across groups and settlements, but there are some typical patterns.[20] All Amish groups practice endogamy—marriage within the group—which means that the bride and groom must be church members in fellowshipping congregations before they marry.[21] Although the church does not arrange marriages, the church membership requirement means that it does sanction them. Most, but not all, dating partners come from the same Amish affiliation.

Courtship is energized by the fact that marriage and having children are highly valued in Amish society. It is rare for a person to choose to remain unmarried or for married couples to decide not to have children. Apart from baptism, marriage is the most important rite of passage; it signals the step from girl to woman, boy to man. Marriage, not baptism, is the doorway to adulthood.

Dating never begins before age sixteen, and some youth wait until they are seventeen or eighteen. A few affiliations, especially the New Order Amish, permit only those who are baptized to date. This lowers the age of baptism and marriage and increases the church's control over dating.

Traditionally, secrecy surrounded courtship, and even parents did not always know whom their children were dating. The wider community would only learn about romances when wedding plans were "published," or announced in church, two weeks before the wedding. Although secrecy still shrouds dating in more conservative communities, the veil has lifted elsewhere. Yet, although it is often known when a boy and girl are dating, couples try to keep their plans quiet despite widespread speculation about when they will be published.

As in past generations, youth most often find partners at Sunday evening singings. The boy always takes the initiative. Dating partners in more traditional settlements may learn to know each other at social or work frolics. A boy may express his interest to a particular girl in advance by sending her a card or letter. Or he may ask a friend or relative to alert her of his interest so that she is not surprised when he asks to walk with her or take her home after a singing. In a growing number of communities, prospective partners become acquainted by texting prior to the first date. Traditionally, the initial date happened at a singing, but that too is changing in some areas.

Courting usually proceeds at youth gatherings or at the girl's home. A boy will travel by horse and buggy—or, depending on the *Ordnung* of his church, by bicycle or in-line skates—to see his girlfriend. If she lives in another settlement or some distance away, he may need to take a bus or hire a driver.

Some leaders say the sole purpose of dating should be to search for a spouse. In such communities, boys are permitted to date only one girl. But in other communities a boy may date several girls—one at a time—in the course of a year. When a couple begins dating, they typically see each other only every other week at the girl's home and otherwise communicate by letters. In some settlements, though, teens have cell phones and call or text their boyfriend or girlfriend throughout the week. They may also hang out together during the week and attend parties together on weekends. At the other extreme, a dating Swartzentruber Amish couple will not be seen as a couple in public until after their engagement has been announced two weeks before the wedding.

The Amish oppose premarital sex. Nevertheless, some dating couples do engage in it—the rate certainly varies by community—and undoubtedly some use birth control. As noted in chapter 11, transgressors are expected to confess their sin before the Gmay.

An old courtship practice, which the Amish and other immigrants brought from Europe, is known variously as bed courtship, bedding, or bundling. In this practice the dating couple spends much of the night together in bed, clothed but ostensibly without sexual relations. This was the traditional practice in most Amish communities until the mid-twentieth century. Since then, the practice has sharply declined, and it likely persists in fewer than 10 percent of Amish groups. It provoked considerable debate in some areas, and opposition to it was a factor in the formation of the New Order Amish movement in the 1960s.[22]

Most, but not all, Swartzentruber groups have retained bed courtship, and parents ensure that their Rumspringa-age daughters have a private bedroom, at least on weekends. When the young man and woman arrive at the girl's house, they go quietly to her bedroom and lie together, fully dressed, on her bed until long past midnight. Swartzentruber girls will remove their outer dress, keeping on the "courting" or under dress, which is "never sheer, low cut, or otherwise suggestive."[23] According to one Swartzentruber woman, "Under dresses can be almost any color, but not white or pink or yellow. Girls just make it so it's new and not worn out." Often the young man's male friends and the young woman's sisters—members of the Youngie but not yet dating—try to "drop in" on the couple, but they must do so quietly so as not to disturb the rest of the family.[24]

The Andy Weaver affiliation in Holmes County, Ohio, allows bed courtship, but some parents discourage it in favor of "chair courtship." In some districts, this means that the young woman sits in her boyfriend's lap as the two occupy a single chair, leading an elder to lament, "Lap-sitting chair courtship . . . causes a lot of problems." In his Gmay, families with daughters about to join the young folks invest in a wide chair so the couple can sit side by side. Noting that this purchase often elicits comments about a possible wedding, one mother said with a smile, "Sometimes we parents just say we're getting a little wider in our old age." Her husband added that the couple "[could] put two regular chairs beside each other, but it's just not as comfortable."

The diversity of courtship practices among the Amish illustrates the variety of ways in which local communities define proper behavior for finding and dating one's future spouse. Across affiliations, however, chastity remains the goal for unmarried teens.

Identity and Autonomy

Rumspringa is a liminal time fraught with ambiguity for Amish youth, who are neither Amish nor English, neither children nor adults. They live at home, but their locus of external control shifts from parents to peers. In a culture that stresses submission to adult authority, teens are especially vulnerable to peer influence.

Developmental psychologists contend that the teenage search for identity and autonomy requires a successful resolution for a stable adulthood. Western models of psychological development assume that identity is self-constructed and that autonomy—especially independence—is a virtue. Similarly, modernity prizes self-esteem and self-actualization. But the construction of identity and the search for autonomy are different in collective societies such as the Amish. One Amish man flatly rejected the notion that modern adult identities are self-constructed by noting that "all kinds of cultural influences shape identity everywhere."

Stevick argues that, while identity and autonomy are independent and complementary psychological states in mainstream culture, in Amish society they are in more tension.[25] Some adolescents step into Rumspringa with little anticipatory socialization as they explore questions of identity and autonomy: Who am I? What do I believe?[26] For a few Amish youth, the exploration results in ambivalence about self, faith, family, and morality, but that is of course true for mainstream teens as well.

An Amish child's identity is both collective and personal, but the group identity is especially prominent in interactions with outsiders. Dressed in the garb of their tribe, children grow up with a keen awareness of being different from outsiders. The experience of riding in a carriage, subject to curious stares, crystallizes a sharp sense of Amish identity. One's personal identity is further shaped by one's niche in the thick web of a large extended family. At the same time, however, personal identity is somewhat blurred because playmates dress similarly and engage in the same cultural practices. Moreover, the importance of cooperation, obedience, and humility— not autonomy—are highlighted in hundreds of ways for children before they turn sixteen.

The highly communal nature of Amish identity formation places some youth at risk during Rumspringa. In one change-minded settlement in which dozens of youth drive cars and pickup trucks, local officials use the acronym DWA (Driving While Amish). Police engage in Amish profiling—stopping cars carrying Amish teenagers for DUI checks. With little orientation to the dangers of drugs and alcohol, some teens sink into abuse. Growing up sequestered, those needing help may have little knowledge of social services or how to access them. In 2002 the Amish Youth Vision Project began to work with court-assigned offenders in northern Indiana. Over a three-year period (2006 to 2008), 185 Amish youth participated in a series of eight weekly alcohol and drug education classes.[27] All of them had been arrested for alcohol consumption or possession or both and were assigned to the program as a condition of their probation. In addition to alcohol, some participants had problems with nicotine and marijuana, and a handful had used methamphetamines. In this community, as in some others, alcohol was the drug of choice among Amish youth. Two-thirds of the participants in the program were male.

Regardless of the settlement, young men have greater freedom to challenge traditional mores during Rumspringa than young women do. As Stevick notes, boys are often more overt in flouting community dress standards and more likely to own cars or trucks, use alcohol, and engage in other rebellious activities.[28] This is true in even the most isolated communities. A young Swartzentruber male working away from home, for example, recharged his forbidden cell phone at an outdoor electrical socket in a strip mall—something a young woman in his church-community would never do.

Big Questions

The Rumspringa experience has several layers: psychological, religious, and social. It is a psychological journey in self-understanding, a search for identity that fits within the contours of Amish society. On the religious level it brings youth face-to-face with spiritual questions. Will they embrace Amish understandings of Christian faith? Anxiety about one's salvation and eternal destiny may expedite this choice. In the end, the ultimate question is whether to be Amish—to join the church, marry, and accept the church's authority for the rest of one's life.

The religious and social layers blend together, since the confession of Christian faith and the promise to surrender one's life to the church are woven into the baptismal vows. For some youth the emphasis is on personal faith; for others it is on accepting the church's authority. In any event, they are two sides of the same baptismal coin.

Most youth process the big questions in one of three ways. First, the vast majority embark on Rumspringa assuming they will join the church. For them, rather than a crucible of crisis, the teenage years are a time of greater freedom, a time to socialize with friends, find a spouse, and simply have some fun.

Second, a few youth set their sights on leaving the Amish long before Rumspringa. Perhaps they dream of becoming an airplane pilot or a nurse and know that those occupations require advanced schooling. Or, unable to imagine being bridled by church regulations the rest of their lives, they think that leaving will expand their personal freedom. Still others plan to exit as a way of coping with painful or dysfunctional family situations. Those who reject baptism will not face excommunication or shunning, and whether or not such a decision ruptures their family ties depends a great deal on the attitude of their parents and church-community.

For a few in the middle—unsure about joining or leaving—Rumspringa presents a real dilemma. They count the benefits and liabilities at night before drifting off to sleep. A forty-year-old man who ultimately did join the church reflected on his decision: "The thought of stepping into a somewhat foreign culture looked far more difficult and less rewarding than submitting to the expectations of the Ordnung simply because I was already used to them."[29] Ira Wagler, who made the opposite choice, explained his journey this way: "I had every intention of returning and settling down . . . but it didn't happen. In fact, it pretty much went just like the preachers always claimed it would. Once the 'world' gets its grip on you, the probability of return recedes into impossibility. One can weep and wail and repent at leisure, but it will be too late. You can't go back."[30]

In one midwestern settlement, sociologist Denise Reiling found that youth decided to join or leave the church "in relative isolation, without much discussion or deliberation with others." Some considered defection "a very serious sin, and as such, involving others in the deliberation would exacerbate the offense." Defection carries a stigma because it dishonors parents, rejects the religious teaching of the church, and, in the eyes of some, could lead to eternal damnation.[31]

The Amish believe there is an age of moral accountability in the late teens when young people become responsible for the eternal consequences of their behavior. Until that time, babies and children who die go straight into the "arms of Jesus." Likewise, those who confess faith in Jesus at baptism have a living hope of a heavenly home. But what about those in Rumspringa who have not yet been baptized? They are seen as standing in the doorway, neither in nor out. What if they die in an accident while running around? Or if Jesus returns to earth before they confess their faith in him? "Someday, somebody's children are going to be in that state and Jesus is coming," one twenty-five-year-old Amish man said. "That is my greatest concern. . . . But that's a risk we've all had to take to get to be Amish, passing through that period."[32]

Some Rumspringa youth also worry that they risk eternal damnation if they are not baptized into the Amish church, even if they join another church. Although the Amish respect other Christian traditions and do endorse adult choice, they strongly encourage their children by word and example to accept the faith in which they were raised. Indeed, members in some communities would say defection may lead to hell. Consequently, some youth who ponder leaving may undergo an intense spiritual struggle about their eternal destiny.[33]

Such youth face a culturally constructed dilemma. On the one hand, their heritage promises freedom of choice. Indeed, they will not be formally punished or shunned if they leave. On the other hand, if they abandon the Amish way, they will dishonor their parents, and some fear they may be headed toward fire and brimstone.[34] To add to the weighty decision, they know that if they are baptized and join the church, the vows they declare before God and the congregation will carry serious consequences for life and eternity. It is better, candidates are told, not to make a vow than to make one and break it later.

Baptism

Baptism is the most important rite in Amish life. It signals an individual's confession of Christian faith and willingness to submit to the authority of the Amish church until death. The entire sociocultural system rests on two foundational understandings: (1) the church is a voluntary body comprised of those who make an adult decision to embrace Christian faith; and (2) upon baptism, the church has the authority to enforce collective guidelines for its members' conduct. Thus, baptism is a monumental commitment with everlasting consequences. Baptismal candidates are reminded that their Anabaptist forebears who knelt for this ordinance risked torture, imprisonment, and even death. Nonetheless, as we reported in chapter 10, at least 85 percent of youth who are raised Amish take this monumental step.

The typical age at baptism ranges from seventeen to the early twenties. Women tend to be baptized at a slightly younger age than men. Candidates attend a series of instruction classes before baptism, which occurs once a year or every other year depending on the affiliation. The number and the format of the catechism sessions vary by settlement, but the baptismal candidates typically meet with the bishop and ministers to review the Eighteen Articles of the Dordrecht Confession. At the wrap-up session the ministers emphasize the weight of the decision and remind young men that by accepting baptism they are also consenting to serve as leaders if the church and God should ever call them.

The Dordrecht Confession describes worthy candidates for baptism as those who "bring forth genuine fruits of repentance, amend their lives, believe the Gospel, depart from evil and do good, cease from wrong and forsake sin, putting . . . on true righteousness and holiness."[35] The statement makes it clear that the act of baptism cannot save anyone and that only faith and a spiritual new birth can lead to salvation. As they kneel on the floor, the candidates renounce self, the devil, and the world, and promise to obey Christ and the church for the rest of their lives.

The rite of baptism follows the second of two sermons that are part of a regular church service. The candidates sit in a front row in a bent posture during the morning sermons—a sign of their yieldedness to God and willingness to submit to the authority of the church. The sermons typically include Old Testament stories related to water—Noah's ark and the children of Israel crossing the Red Sea—as well as New Testament teachings on the new birth and examples of baptism.

The bishop then invites the candidates to kneel and asks the four baptismal questions:

1. Can you also confess with the eunuch [described in Acts 8:37]: Yes, I believe that Jesus Christ is the Son of God? Answer: *Yes, I believe that Jesus is the Son of God.*
2. Do you also recognize this to be a Christian order, church and fellowship under which you now submit yourselves? Answer: *Yes.*
3. Do you renounce the world, the devil with all his subtle ways, as well as your own flesh and blood, and desire to serve Jesus Christ alone, who died on the cross for you? Answer: *Yes.*

4. Do you also promise before God and His church that you will support these teachings and regulations [Ordnung] with the Lord's help, faithfully attend the services of the church, help to counsel and work in it, and not to forsake it, whether it leads you to life or to death? Answer: *Yes.*[36]

After each candidate responds with yes, she or he remains kneeling as the congregation rises. The bishop reads a baptismal prayer from the prayer book that includes these lines: "They renounce the devil, the world, and their own flesh and blood. . . . They desire to live only for Jesus Christ. . . . They consent and gladly agree to place their faith in the holy Gospel and to give themselves in full obedience to it. . . . May they be enabled by Thy power to strive against and overcome sin, the world, the devil, and hell so that they may be crowned as heavenly kings."[37]

Following the prayer, the congregation is seated again while the deacon, who has provided a small pail of water and a cup, pours a small amount of water into the bishop's cupped hands, which rest on the head of a kneeling applicant. The bishop releases the water, baptizing the young person in the name of the Father, the Son, and the Holy Ghost. The bishop then invites the person to rise and, if he is male, offers two signs of fellowship—a handshake and a kiss of peace. The bishop's wife does likewise if the newly baptized person is female. The ritual is repeated for each baptismal candidate. Finally, the bishop concludes by telling them, "You are no longer guests and strangers, but workers and members in this sacred and godly fellowship."[38] In his concluding admonition, the bishop urges the congregation to be faithful and obedient, and other ministers offer words of affirmation as well. After they attend their first communion, the newly baptized will hold all the rights and responsibilities of membership.

The Riddle of Rumspringa

Why do the overwhelming majority of Amish youth choose baptism into the Amish faith? Observers who have seen popular representations of Rumspringa sometimes wonder how Amish-raised youth can reject the taste of the American life they have sampled and pledge themselves to their distinctive birthright faith.

The answer lies in the fact that numerous socioreligious forces funnel youth toward the church. Parents and leaders have reminded them that the Amish faith, which they have absorbed since childhood, is important for eternal salvation. They have also been taught to honor and respect their parents, so to veer away at this point would shame and dishonor them. For many youth, their embrace of Amish ways reflects a deep and sincere spiritual commitment.

Peer pressure is another potent factor. This, of course, is why many parents hope that their offspring will join a youth group that encourages church membership. Romantic ties can also matter. One Amish man openly admitted that "the only thing that brought me to the Church was a pretty Amish girl." Girls often join the church before boys, and girls in courtship exert a strong tug over their prospective spouses.

Economic opportunities, especially for males, may also nudge youth toward baptism. The opportunity to take over a business or a farm, or to secure employment in an aunt's greenhouse or an uncle's shop, may add incentive. Finally, their childhood immersion in Amish culture, membership in a large extended family, and firsthand knowledge of the benefits of communal support in hard times make joining their birthright church the easiest and most comfortable option. Obviously, a different mix of these factors comes into play for every individual.

The riddle of Rumspringa persists, however. Why does a religious tradition that emphasizes separation from the world and the transience of this life allow its young folks some freedom during Rumspringa? Because of their theological commitment to voluntary adult baptism, Amish parents and church elders have little leeway. Besides, by providing an exit door, Rumspringa screens out prospective members who do not fit the Amish ethos—those most likely to later become malcontents in the church. Filtering them out in advance grants them the freedom to explore other ways of life, and it is easier for church leaders to maintain harmony within the community with them gone.

Moreover, Rumspringa provides a form of social vaccination, a small dose of the outside culture that prevents members from being "stricken" by it later. During Rumspringa some teens learn that, although some green grass grows on the other side of the Amish cultural fence, plenty of weeds sprout there as well. Furthermore, those who return home and "repent from a misspent youth . . . become stalwart defenders of Amish tradition, having experienced the bankrupt, empty life of 'doing your own thing,'" according to one Amish leader.

Is the choice to be or not to be Amish a real choice? There is freedom to leave the community without impunity; otherwise there would be few, if any, defectors. The host of forces corralling youth toward church membership, however, suggests that the choice may be a perceived one as much as a real one. In fact, even the most rowdy youth typically explore the outside world with an Amish peer group, ensuring that even their deviant behavior is undertaken in Amish company. Those on Facebook, for example, have mostly Amish friends, insulating them somewhat, despite their foray into popular social media.

Moreover, even for youth in the most progressive communities, the cultural chasm between Amish life and mainstream society is deep and wide and not easily crossed. To take the leap is like plunging into a foreign culture with its own language, values, and practices. For those in conservative communities with limited interaction with outsiders, the gap is even wider, and they have fewer skills with which to make the crossing.

Finally, although the religious principle of voluntarism is foundational, the informal social pressures from parents, peers, and extended family are intense. These prods to embrace the faith mitigate somewhat the claim of an entirely free, unfettered choice. Vigorous retention is essential for any endogamous group to grow, so such prompts are understandable. Women are somewhat more likely than young men to join the church; nevertheless, some of them also struggle with the decision. Saloma Furlong, who grew up in Geauga County, Ohio, and defected after baptism, says, "When I was nineteen, there were subtle hints and outright suggestions that I should be baptized and join the church. I was unsure about joining church because I didn't know if I could be sincere about it and be a good Amish person. And deep down, I knew that if I did join and then left the Amish, I would be shunned for the rest of my life. . . . In the end I did not have a choice. If I hadn't joined that summer, the expectations for [the] next summer would have only become more intense."[39]

So, although baptism might, for some youth, be less of an actual choice than a presumed rite of passage, the perception of choice is important. Those who join the church may someday need to remind themselves—should they become restless—that they indeed had a choice, and that it was their decision to join. Baptism, then, becomes a signpost of their commitment, a reminder that they have chosen this life for themselves. This signpost fortifies adult commitment to the church and increases the willingness of members to build the community as well as to yield to its demands.

Thus, despite the many myths that encircle it, Rumspringa is a time for youth not only to sort out their identities but to prepare for the lifelong commitments that await them. We explore the obligations and rewards of those commitments in chapter 13.

CHAPTER 13

SOCIAL TIES AND COMMUNITY RHYTHMS

The Beiler family lost a twenty-year-old son in a tragic snowmobile accident in 2005. On the first Sunday after the funeral, thirty-two families visited them to offer support and share their grief, and an average of twenty-five visitors a day came over the next two weeks. In addition, in the eight weeks following their son's death, they received over six hundred sympathy cards and letters as well as bouquets of flowers from Amish friends near and far. Such an outpouring of care is not unusual after a death—especially the unexpected one of a young person.

The Web of Community

Beneath the bonnets and buggies of the Amish world lies a human community woven together by resilient threads of duty and care, friendship and family.[1] This deep and enduring sense of belonging is undoubtedly what draws many outsiders to the Amish way of life. Spontaneous visiting, social gatherings, shared labor, and distinctive rituals create solidarity and generate social capital. Much like financial capital, the social version provides resources that can be accrued, compounded, and drawn upon—in this case, for the well-being of the community and the benefit of individual members. Social capital includes networks of relationships, rituals, extended family ties, and long-standing social traditions.[2] Combined with the cultural capital of shared values and knowledge, social capital enables communities to mobilize resources to raise a barn or orchestrate a meal for four hundred people (see fig. 13.1).

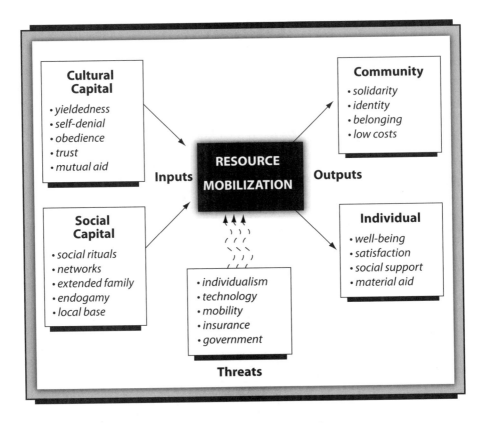

FIGURE 13.1. Cultural and Social Capital Resources

An Amish man described it this way: "There's much caring and sharing in times of need, helping together to raise barns and in funeral and wedding arrangements, to plant and harvest crops if a farmer is laid up. . . . Much of this caring is done at a moment's notice, when the neighbors see the crops need to be tended."[3]

Many activities in the Amish life cycle create and expend social capital. Some of the church decrees over the years, such as forbidding motor vehicles, have helped to preserve the social capital that energizes community by reinforcing small-scale, slower-paced ways of life. From weddings to funerals, from visiting to bidding at auctions, the everyday rhythms of community build solidarity and shape Amish identity.

Weddings

Weddings signal the passage to adulthood in Amish society. Next to baptism and communion, the wedding is the most important ritual enactment because it underscores the importance of marriage and its potential for procreation, which is crucial for community growth. The energy, excitement, and festivity surrounding a wedding signal its significance.[4] Although weddings vary from community to community, some practices span all of them. Unlike the unique, customized ceremonies crafted by mainstream couples in the twenty-first century, Amish weddings, like all Amish rituals, are regulated by the community, not by the individual participants. As one observer notes, the simplicity of Amish weddings reinforces the values of relationships, community, and faith, rather than calling attention to fashion, style, and lavish expense.[5]

Weddings are usually held on weekdays, although in communities with many factory workers some weddings are held on Saturdays to accommodate work schedules. Some settlements hold weddings throughout the year, but others observe a wedding "season" in the spring and fall. Still others hold weddings on Tuesdays and Thursdays following the autumn harvest. In a sample of 1,087 weddings in five states and Ontario, only 3 percent were held during December, January, and February. Thirty-seven percent occurred in May and June, and the rest were scattered across other months, with regional variations. The average age of marriage is 21.1 for women and 22.3 for men. Except in Ontario, the grooms are, on average, older than the brides.[6]

In settlements with a wedding season, it is not unusual for people to be invited to a handful of weddings within several days. Friends and family from out of state may travel by train, van, or bus to participate. Guests at one wedding in Delaware came from nine different settlements stretching from Texas to Ontario.[7] A Pennsylvania woman, writing in an Amish publication, said, "Our community had a round of weddings, ten in all, and now we are leaving for two more in Kentucky."[8]

The wedding ceremony is held in the house, shop, or other building at the home of the bride or a relative. The reception may be held at the same place as the ceremony, but in some communities, it is hosted elsewhere. There is never a rehearsal because the well-known ritual steps require no practice.[9] Photographs, gowns, veils, rings, and tuxedos are missing. The music consists of slow-paced *Ausbund* hymns sung a cappella by the congregation.

Two couples who accompany the bride and groom constitute the wedding party. Although they wear new clothing, it is the same style that they wear to church. The bride and her two attendants wear the same color dresses, typically some shade of blue. The three women wear white capes and aprons over their dresses.[10] The three men wear black suit coats and white shirts, as they do for church. Before and after the service, the groom wears the wide-brimmed hat customary for adult men.

The five-minute wedding ceremony comes at the end of a three-hour service that otherwise follows the order of a typical church service. While the congregation sings several hymns, the couple meets privately with the ministers for about forty minutes. During this time they receive admonitions and blessings as they embark on their marital journey.

The wedding vows vary slightly among different Amish affiliations, but regardless of their wording, the promises, which seal an eternal and holy bond, are said in solemn tones. The vows in the Lancaster settlement include these questions:

1. Do you promise . . . that if he/she should be afflicted with bodily weakness, sickness, or some similar circumstance that you will care for him/her as is fitting a Christian husband/wife? Answer: *Yes.*
2. Do you also solemnly promise with one another that you will love and bear and be patient with each other, and shall not separate from each other until the dear God shall part you from each other through death? Answer: *Yes.*[11]

After making their vows, the couple returns to their seats without a kiss or any other display of affection. The bishop offers a prayer for them and then invites other ministers to offer words of blessing. The service concludes with a kneeling prayer, after which the festivities begin.[12]

Despite the sober tone of the ceremony, the day is a happy one, with food, fellowship, and fun for some three to five hundred invited guests. In many communities a large noon meal follows the nuptials, after which singing and games continue until an evening supper. The revelry may then drift toward midnight. In a few communities in which the evening activities have turned into boisterous parties, the church has instituted "day weddings," which end without evening meals or late-night celebrations. Other communities expect wedding days to include a few pranks targeting the couple, such as hiding their horse's harness, placing their carriage on top of a shed, or putting flour between the sheets of their bed. Tossing the groom over a fence or placing a broomstick across a doorway to see if the bride steps over it (suggesting the new wife "won't pick up a broom"!) is customary in some locales.[13]

To orchestrate such a large gathering and prepare two meals for several hundred people without a catering service requires an enormous outpouring of free labor. Each community has its own ways of sharing the burden of preparation. In some areas, the bride's mother and family are responsible for planning the meal, while someone else coordinates the events on the day itself; in other communities, the bride's family is more directly involved in all preparations. In Swartzentruber communities the parents of the bride and groom do not even attend the wedding ceremony because they are helping to cook and set up the tables for the meal.

In every community, members of the local district provide food, prepare the facilities, and assume various roles throughout the day—as cooks, ushers, waiters, dishwashers, table setters, and hostlers who care for the horses. Some communities have wedding trailers equipped with propane-powered refrigerators and stoves as well as storage areas for food and utensils. The trailers are towed by truck or tractor to the

In her bedroom, a young Amish woman in New York State displays her wedding dress (*on the right*), which she made. Next to it is the matching dress and shirt she made for herself and her fiancé to wear the day their wedding plans were announced in church. The color and style of wedding dresses varies by affiliation. *Karen M. Johnson-Weiner*

wedding site. Groups that do not permit such refrigeration follow a schedule of food preparation during the week leading up the wedding day: cakes on one day, pies on another, potatoes peeled on Wednesday, and so forth. Most communities have a customary wedding meal, but the menu varies by locale.[14]

An evening highlight in some communities occurs when the youth pair up as couples to enter the dining area after the adults have eaten. In some settlements, partners are assigned by the bride, either at the request of the boys or by convenience. In other locales the boys walk by the single girls, each inviting a girl to sit with him at the meal. Guests scan the lineup looking for new romantic pairs appearing in public for the first time. More singing, games, and, in some groups, square dancing follow the evening meal.

Wedding gifts are practical and often include items such as dish towels, storage containers, and canning jars. In many communities, the bride and groom receive separate gifts; a wife might give the new bride a saucepan, while her husband presents the groom with a set of pliers. New couples receive their gifts at the wedding in some communities, but in others they receive them later, as they visit family and friends.

Newlyweds do not take a honeymoon. In some communities, they spend their first night at the bride's home and help to clean up the house the next day. Some couples move to their new home shortly after the wedding, but in other areas the bride and groom live with parents for several weeks before setting up house on their own. In certain groups, newly married couples visit relatives for several weeks, often staying overnight, depending on the distance.

With the wedding behind them, the newly married hold full adult status as they participate in community life. Soon they will help with the weddings of others, a way of replenishing the goodwill—repaying their social capital debt—into the Amish reservoir.

Visiting, Writing, and Holidays
Thick Social Ties

Visiting is the social glue that binds the Amish community with informal ties of trust and respect. Much of the visiting occurs spontaneously when friends drop by unannounced. Other fraternizing happens at reunions, auctions, quilting parties, work parties, picnics, holiday gatherings, meals after church, weddings, and funerals. Visiting may mean extended conversations after church, stopping by someone's house on the way to the store, joining in a work party or quilting bee, or catching up during a bus ride. Visitors may arrive without notice to spend the night with friends in another community. Regardless of the venue, visiting is a means of recharging the networks of social capital. It strengthens the bonds of obligation between individuals in the community.

Interpersonal relationships in Amish society are enmeshed in a thick social context, unlike the amorphous ties of cyberspace. Relationships cut across affiliation boundaries, often highlighting similarities such as the same birthday, common hobbies, or shared heartbreak. One young wife who had just suffered a miscarriage welcomed a visit from an older woman in a neighboring church district who had had the same experience. A schoolteacher and her daughter enjoyed visiting with teachers in another community and exchanging ideas for bulletin boards. An older woman waited impatiently for her "twin"—a woman from another settlement who happened to share the same birthday—to arrive for a visit. They had been pen pals for years but had only met face-to-face once, years before. Her husband was looking forward to taking the twin's spouse fishing.

Visitors make demands, often showing up unannounced for a meal or lodging and expecting their hosts to take them around to visit others in the area. But visitors are

Two Old Order Mennonite women (*center* in light dress and *far right*) join Amish women for a quilting party in an Amish home in a progressive settlement. *Shirley Wenger*

not guests in the sense that hosts are expected to entertain them. They often join in the housework—helping to sew, preparing meals, and assisting with farm chores. In return, the hosting family receives news, entertainment, and companionship. And the connections between families and friends are reinforced, benefiting everyone involved.

Extended family reunions, common in Amish society, are frequently daylong events in the summer. In addition, families gather for birthdays, anniversaries, and other special occasions. For scattered families, these events involve considerable travel. One couple in Wisconsin were surprised on their anniversary when their children and grandchildren arrived by chartered bus from another Wisconsin settlement and others came by van from Minnesota, Illinois, and Iowa.[15] First cousins, who may number fifty or more in a family, sometimes charter a bus together for a special day trip to a scenic site or state park.

Writing

When traveling is not convenient, letter writing serves as a substitute for visiting. Participants in old-fashioned circle letters add their epistle to a packet that circulates among others with similar interests or needs. Without easy access to telephones or e-mail, Amish people use circle letters to provide information and affirmation for those who suffer similar afflictions, disabilities, or accidents. Examples of such "circles" include couples dealing with infertility, open heart surgery patients, parents of children killed in accidents, and individuals with a particular illness such as muscular dystrophy.

Many other circle letter writers focus on shared circumstances—ministers who were ordained in the same season and year, parents of twins, parents who have only boys or only girls, and those with the same birthday, to name a few. Letters flow to relatives or old *Rumspringa* friends who have moved away. The letters build bonds of care and support that crisscross region and affiliation. Announcements in an Amish newspaper for a new circle letter may invite, for example, anyone by the name of Lavina, men born in July 1956, or girls who enjoy making greeting cards.

A less personal form of bonding occurs among readers who follow the endless stories by correspondents ("scribes") who write columns for *Die Botschaft,* the *Budget,* the *Diary,* and *Plain Interests,* all of which have national circulation. Writing in English, the scribes offer detailed accounts of local happenings—church services, accidents, visiting, harvesting, travel, medical problems—as well as wisdom, jokes, and much more, for Amish audiences across the country. Regional newsletters such as *Gemeinde Register* (Ohio), *Die Blatt* (Indiana), and the *Grapevine* (Iowa) keep people informed of events in their area. Reunions, circle letters, and newspapers not only disperse information, but they also build solidarity and confirm identity in Amish communities across North America.

Holidays

Visiting also marks holidays. Depending on the community, the Amish may or may not recognize Martin Luther King Day, President's Day, Memorial Day, Fourth of July, and Labor Day. Most, however, observe Thanksgiving and New Year's Day. Their sacred days stretch back to European custom. In addition to Christmas and Easter, the Amish celebrate Good Friday, Easter Monday, Pentecost, Whitmonday (Pentecost Monday), and Ascension Day. Some eastern settlements observe a second day of Christmas on December 26, and many midwestern Amish celebrate Old Christmas, also known as Epiphany or Three Kings Day, on January 6.

Second Christmas, Easter Monday, Pentecost Monday, and Ascension Day are festive times for visiting and relaxing. Amish businesses close on these days, and people dress in Sunday clothes to visit with friends, families, or old Rumspringa chums. Youth attend special outings, and some adults plan van or bus trips to other settlements over these holidays.

Extended families typically gather for a day of eating and visiting during the Christmas season. With families spread across many states, some travel long distances for the gathering. An Iowa grandmother explained that her family had held their family Christmas celebration at her daughter's house in Wisconsin on Thanksgiving. "Our children and grandchildren left Iowa in two vans to go to Wisconsin. Others came there by train. . . . All 41 slept in the same house. With 22 grandchildren under 10, there is no dull moment."[16]

For more conservative groups, Easter Monday and Pentecost Monday are traditionally days for going fishing. In eastern Pennsylvania, fishing is also a favorite activity on Ascension Day. Traditionally, Ascension Day was a fasting day, meaning families did not eat breakfast, spent the morning in quiet reading and reflection, and went visiting in the afternoon. In more traditional groups this pattern continues, but in more progressive communities, the entire day may be spent visiting. One Lancaster man described it this way: "The day is for visiting and starts early for young and old alike. Uncles, cousins, and families congregate. Youth groups plan outings—softball and volleyball. Charter buses take youth and married folks to other communities 150 miles away to visit [and] relax." He estimates that on Ascension Day about half of his people "are on the move . . . and with about six per buggy that's 1,800 horses clip clopping down the roads. So drive carefully those of you driving Detroit and imported vehicles. We appreciate it."[17]

Frolics and Fun

Amish gatherings tap and replenish social capital. Frolics—one-day work projects that blend volunteer labor and fellowship—are a time when a specific family benefits from the communal goodwill accrued in the social bank. Unlike modern societies, which segregate work and play, the Amish often mix them together. Although *frolic* means merriment, the Amish use it to describe a "work party" that exemplifies the joy of shared labor.

Frolics are commonplace and may involve building a new pig barn, adding a room or apartment to a house, or building a storage shed at a school.[18] Other frolics center on cleaning up after a storm or fire, harvesting vegetables, or painting a house to ready it for new inhabitants.

Banter and good humor abound as families gather to help a neighbor move, work crews clean up after a flood, friends gather to fix up a house for newlyweds, or parents prepare a school for a new year. Depending on the project, men and women attend frolics together or separately. Some activities follow gender roles. Shelling peas, quilting, and baking Christmas cookies typically fall to women. When men gather for a construction frolic or to clean up debris after a storm, women come along to prepare a meal.

A barn raising demonstrates the power of cultural and social capital. The work is gendered—men construct the barn while women prepare a large meal for up to two hundred people. Barn raisings are fast disappearing in communities with few farmers. *Doyle Yoder*

Some communities have a family tradition called "sisters day," during which adult sisters meet for a frolic in one of their homes. Sometimes they preserve vegetables, quilt, bake, or clean. "Oftentimes," said one woman, "we take our sewing and just talk while the children play." Some sisters sew clothing that is distributed to refugees in other countries through Mennonite Central Committee or Christian Aid Ministries. Sister gatherings can provide an opportunity for siblings to catch up with one another's lives, especially after they have begun helping their own children and caring for their grandchildren.

Peer groups from Rumspringa days often meet in adulthood as well. The women might get together once a month for a small frolic or a quilting party, much like a sisters day. An elderly woman wrote in *Die Botschaft,* "Last Wednesday our buddy group of six ladies were together at Reuben Lapps. Anna had the table all set with her pretty dishes for a tea party. We had a fun day catching up on each other's lives."[19] At other times throughout the year, couples who met during Rumspringa may gather for a Christmas singing, a picnic, or to sing for folks who are homebound.

One man we know complained that the women are always "going away too much. They're just not home enough." But if the women are away too much, the men are just as guilty. Especially in the late winter and early spring, men are often found at auctions. A favorite place to visit with friends and neighbors, auctions also combine work and play. One might have to wait all day to bid on a washing machine, a horse, or a drill press to get a "good buy." In addition to seasonal auctions, charity auctions and equipment sales are held throughout the year. These events are filled with chatter, food, the excitement of endless bidding, and the auctioneer's sing-song call. Auctions, the Amish equivalent of a parade or fair, provide fun, fellowship, and a bit of work throughout the year.

Snowbirds

One distinctive center of recreation and visiting is Pinecraft, Florida, a winter haven for many older Amish "snowbirds" fleeing south, especially those from more liberal affiliations.[20] On the outskirts of Sarasota on Florida's Gulf Coast, Pinecraft first attracted Amish in the late 1920s when a handful of families, mostly from Ohio, bought land there to try celery farming. By 1931 a group of nearly thirty year-round residents, both Amish and Mennonites, comprised the Pinecraft community, and their presence attracted winter visitors—often relatives or friends who went south to visit and enjoy a few weeks of warmer weather. A few of the visitors built cottages, but most were short-term visitors who stayed with locals or in guesthouses. By the winter of 1939–1940, the village included about fifty Amish households hailing from nine states—nearly half from Ohio, followed by Indiana and Pennsylvania.[21]

In the decades that followed, more and more winter visitors spiked the growth of the village. By the turn of the twenty-first century, Pinecraft was hosting nearly four thousand snowbirds a week during January and February.[22] Ten busloads of Amish, mostly older adults, arrive each week, and then the buses depart with homebound loads. One bus company based in Millersburg, Ohio, delivers 4,000 to 4,500 passengers each year, two-thirds of whom are Amish. Buses from Indiana, Pennsylvania, and beyond also bring Amish travelers. Although some visitors stay only two or three weeks, others have purchased cottages and spend the entire winter, typically arriving after fall communion in October and returning home for spring communion in March or April. Some youth rent condos at Siesta Key and rarely visit Pinecraft.

Pinecraft has more than five hundred small houses and apartments, the majority Amish-owned, but their high prices tilts home ownership toward the wealthy.[23] The local Amish church claims some fifty households, but only about twenty are year-round residents. Although the small, permanent congregation is considered a New Order church, it does not have a firm affiliation with other New Order groups. Some snowbirds who were uncomfortable attending the New Order church established two more conservative church services that are held during the winter months.

Pinecraft is in *Ordnung* limbo because, other than the handful of permanent residents, people are away from the watchful eye of their home districts. The Pinecraft "understanding" permits such things as microwaves, appliances, and air conditioning, but not computers, TVs, DVD players, and radios. Because municipal law bans horses, most people pedal around town in large three-wheel tricycles or bicycles. No one drives a car, although increasing numbers have battery-powered bicycles or three-wheeled motorized carts. Many Amish men do not wear their traditional hats or suspenders, and some make other minor changes to their wardrobe while in Florida.

Time in Pinecraft is filled with visiting, and many residents do so over meals in local diners. The back room of Troyer's Dutch Heritage Restaurant is especially popular. Here non-Amish, Amish, and former Amish share tables—without separate spaces for the shunned. "Ninety-five percent of the people in this room, including the waitresses, can speak Pennsylvania Dutch," declared an Amish grandfather enthusiastically. Pinecraft provides a site for rekindling old friendships but also for forging new social ties that transcend the geographic settlements up north.

After breakfast, many men fish from the shore at South Lido Beach or in the nearby bay. Others charter deep sea fishing boats, paying $150 or more per person. Older men play shuffleboard at Pinecraft Park or neighborhood courts. Another popular pastime is bocce, and a few people even try their hand at golf. Throughout the day, women gather for quilting bees and conversation. When the weather is warm, young people, families, and even older couples take the half-hour bus ride to the beach at Siesta Key. Few adults engage in mixed-sex bathing, but young people often do.

For adults, the main event during most evenings is visiting or playing games in one another's homes. In house after house in Pinecraft, people gather around tables to play dominoes or Scrabble or just to visit. Most adults regard Sunday as a day of worship, rest, and visiting, and everyone attends one of the three church services in the morning.

Reflecting on the Ordnung in this cultural limbo, Richard Stevick notes, "If 'lax' is not the word for Pinecraft, 'relaxed' certainly is."[24] The rule is simply "What happens in Florida stays in Florida." While technically accountable to their hometown Ordnung back in Ohio or elsewhere, snowbirds and their back-home bishops usually observe a "don't ask, don't tell" rule.

A disproportionate number of snowbirds in Pinecraft, noted one Amish man, "are in the entrepreneurial class." Few farmers can manage a Florida getaway, and few members of highly conservative affiliations show up. For the more traditional Amish, with limited finances and stricter Ordnungs, the wintertime activities of their home communities cannot easily be left behind. Those in more tradition-minded communities who travel are likely to visit family in other communities, not to vacation in the sunny South.

Sounds of Solidarity

Singing is a popular group activity. Families often sing when they worship at home on their district's off-Sunday. Children attending Amish schools sing during their daily opening exercises and for Christmas programs, family days, and special visitors. Young people's gatherings and weddings feature abundant singing. Small groups of adults sing to cheer the sick or homebound, and singing also occurs at family gatherings and frolics.

Historically, three features of Amish singing—German words, unison voices, and lack of instrumental accompaniment—have underscored the community's distinctive identity. Until the mid-twentieth century, the bulk of Amish singing was in German. Since then, more English songs have entered the repertoire in many communities, and now much of the singing outside of church, especially in higher groups, is in English. Nonetheless, German songs remain standard fare in all church-related services as well as in the informal gatherings of the lowest communities.

For many generations, *die Youngie* have listened to and sung popular songs of their day. One Swiss Amish girl in New York, busy putting together a small collection of English gospel tunes to share with other young people, notes that the group "usually sings in German for at least an hour, and then we might sing in English." Swiss Amish families, especially in Adams County, Indiana, have also maintained a folk tradition of yodeling.[25]

Heartland Hymns, a collection of 526 hymns published by a Pennsylvania Amish couple in 2005, was intended for use by family and community gatherings outside Sunday morning worship. It illustrates the growing blend of old German hymns and English songs among more progressive groups. Eighty-nine percent of the hymns are in English, the remainder in German or in both languages. Most of the German songs are translations of English hymns such as "Sweet Hour of Prayer" and "Savior, like a Shepherd Lead Us." A large number might be classified as country gospel, including "Keep on the Sunny Side of Life," "The Cabin on the Hill," "Daddy's Hands," and similar titles. Unlike the *Ausbund,* which includes no musical notation since its unison tunes are passed on orally from one generation to the next, virtually all of the *Heartland Hymns* have musical scores and shaped notes for four-part harmony. The popularity of this book and ones like it signals a growing use of English songs and harmony in family and informal gatherings among change-minded Amish people.[26]

Unison singing, however, continues to be the unchallenged standard in church services everywhere. Singing in parts is forbidden for Sunday services because it draws attention to the musical skills of certain singers, divides the unity of the *Gmay,* and distracts from the meaning of the words. More importantly, part singing may discourage less capable singers and pave the way for special music groups that perform for an audience. Musicologist Hilde Binford has noted that "singing for the Amish has never been a question of singing the pitches accurately or 'in tune.' What has been important is that *everyone* sing, from the special children, including the severely disabled and deaf, to the elderly and infirm. They look to the martyrs who sang on their way to death and believe that all should sing what is in their hearts."[27] Singing not only builds bridges to their Anabaptist past, but it also reinforces the equality and vibrancy of the Amish community.

The church firmly discourages musical instruments, fearing their use would encourage performance, show off individual talents, and distort a true spirit of worship. In more liberal communities, Rumspringa youth sometimes create or hire instrumental bands for their parties and dances. The harmonica and, in some communities, the guitar have become acceptable in private and family settings over the years. Although pianos are not found in Amish homes, some of the most change-minded families use battery-powered portable keyboards to accompany singing in private settings. Acknowledging the use of instruments in the Old Testament, one Amish publication anchors the church's objections to them on their "notable absence" in the example of Jesus and the apostles. Moreover, "musical instruments tend to distract from the spirit of simplicity which is consistent with New Testament teaching."[28] Accompanied by instruments or not, singing builds group solidarity in Amish society.

Rhythms of Care

Mutual aid runs deep in the Amish soul because church membership carries the responsibility to care for the material and social needs of fellow members. An Amish farmer in Ohio summarizes the assumptions of mutual responsibility this way: "When I am plowing in the spring, I can often see five or six other teams in nearby fields, and I know if I was sick they would all be here plowing my field." When disaster strikes in the form of illness, flood, or fire, the community rallies quickly to help the family in need. This commitment is grounded in the biblical injunction to "bear ye one another's burdens, and so fulfill the law of Christ" (Gal. 6:2).

The legendary tradition of barn raising illustrates how cultural and social capital is mobilized for a need within the community. When a barn is struck by lightning and bursts into flames, everyone in the church-community knows exactly what will happen in the next three days. Neighbors immediately drop their work to help with the cleanup while the debris still smolders. In the next days about a hundred men will erect a new barn, and dozens of women will prepare food to sustain them. A festive spirit infuses some levity into an otherwise tragic situation. "Barn raisings are for us what the World Series are for you," one Amish man says.[29]

The recovery effort swings into action without the deliberations of insurance adjusters, lawyers, and contractors. It happens spontaneously because the barn-raising habit is so tightly woven in the texture of Amish life. Everyone donates their time, knowing that their house or shop may be the next to erupt in flames. This simple but powerful tradition exemplifies the social and cultural capital—the taken-for-granted rituals and values of mutual obligation that stabilize Amish society.

In more conservative communities, barn raisings are a common response not only when fire destroys an existing structure but whenever a young couple needs a new barn or house or an established family can afford to upgrade. But with the decline of farming in many settlements, some children have never attended a barn raising. "Benefit auctions for medical expenses are the new version of barn raisings," one member asserted. Although barn raisings are the traditional symbol of communal care, many other forms of mutual aid also flourish. As more Amish move into nonfarm jobs and as the community interacts more closely with the outside world, new patterns of aid are emerging. These changes have created different ways in which twenty-first-century children in the various communities are socialized into the Amish way and interact with the non-Amish world.

In large settlements, benefit auctions are widely used to assist members with special needs. These charity sales of donated crafts, quilts, furniture, and food are organized to aid families with excessive medical bills or a special need such as a paraple-

Table 13.1. Community Events in the Bloomfield, Iowa, Amish Settlement

Blood drives	Produce walks—touring greenhouses
Visiting medical practitioner	Special Ed. meeting (Canadian speaker)
Visiting chiropractor	Pasture walk—sharing ideas on grazing
Visiting horse chiropractor	Southern Iowa Driving Horse Sale
Trip to health mines in Montana	Sudden death meeting for parents
Cardiovascular screenings	Old Order history meeting
Safety awareness meeting	Produce growers meeting
Financial stewardship meeting	Shaklee health products meeting
Bloomfield Dairy Day	Iowa Amish school meetings
Hillview School reunion	Produce auction investors meeting
High-density grazing seminar	Sewing for relief projects
Pancake Day at Graber's Country Store	

Source: The Grapevine, January 2008 to October 2008.

gic child. Annual benefit auctions also pump funds into organizations that serve the Amish community, such as the Clinic for Special Children in Pennsylvania. In northern Indiana, chicken barbecue or sandwich sales are popular means of raising money for special needs.

From frolics to benefit auctions, the community surrounds its members with care, and in the process recharges its pool of goodwill. In so doing, it distinguishes itself from the broader society, where needy individuals often have to haggle with lawyers and insurance providers to solve their problems. Examples of the rhythms of community life in one settlement (shown in table 13.1) are similar to those in many other communities across the country.

In addition to organized efforts, there are many spontaneous and informal expressions of mutual care. A mother with four young children noted that, whenever she needs a babysitter, she can drop off her children with any one of her three cousins living nearby. Neighbors and extended family members provide endless hours of birthing care, child care, and elder care. This network also pitches in to help with farm and house chores if someone is injured or ill.

Letters and cards to the bereaved or ill—many sent by individuals who are not even acquaintances—also express care. Amish newspapers and newsletters announce "showers" that request cards or scrapbook pages for those who have lost a loved one or are depressed, injured, recuperating from surgery, or struggling financially.[30] People of all ages are recipients of such showers, and they in turn often respond publicly. A man who had broken his ankle wrote a letter in *Die Botschaft* thanking "all the people for sending me encouraging letters, cards, sunshine boxes, groceries, money, gifts, meals brought in, and the boys that hauled the wood."[31]

The community also offers emotional support to those who are grieving. In some settlements, following the death of a spouse, parent, sibling, or child, a bereaved woman signals her mourning by wearing a black dress in public settings for several months or more than a year depending on local custom. This rite of dress reminds and invites the community to respond to the bereaved in thoughtful ways. Families who have lost a loved one will typically receive Sunday afternoon and evening visits from friends for several months. Although such visiting gradually declines, it often continues for a year.

Passing On

When a member of the community dies, neighbors and friends are there to support the bereaved family.[32] The rites of farewell in Amish society are the ultimate enactment of enduring values—the final statement of surrender and yieldedness to God's will. They also are the final payout of social capital for the deceased. Although customs vary across the country, all Amish funerals profoundly declare simplicity, equality, community, and separation from the world.[33]

Funerals are nonworldly in every way. Plain and simple in their ritual enactments, without flowers or elaborate caskets, they are held in a barn, home, shop, or tent at the home of the deceased or a relative, never at a funeral home or church building. They downplay individuality, personal achievement, status, and wealth. Eulogies are absent. All praise goes to God, not the deceased. Regardless of status in life, the deceased is dressed in simple clothes, laid out in a coffin identical to that used for all funerals in the community, transported in the same horse-pulled hearse, and buried in a hand-dug grave in a cemetery that is on the edge of a field, where the grave markers are all of similar size. These practices place everyone on equal footing as they enter the eternal community.

Licensed funeral directors play a minimal role. For the most traditional groups, they only fill out the necessary state-required papers. For many affiliations, however, a mortician embalms the body, typically at the mortuary (or very occasionally at the home), and then returns it to the home within a few hours. Very few if any cosmetic enhancements are made, even in the case of accidents. Some morticians add fluids to improve body color, but they almost never use surface cosmetics. In some settlements, the mortician dresses the body, but in others, family members or friends of the same sex dress the body at home. Local custom dictates the color of dress. Some deceased are dressed in their best church clothing, others are dressed in black, and still others wear white garments, symbolizing passage into a new life beyond.

Regardless of locale, neighbors and friends in the church district assume shop, barn, and household chores, freeing the immediate family from daily tasks. They will continue to help the family until the funeral has been held. Designated individuals lead and supervise the extensive logistics for seating and feeding three to six hundred people as well as for accommodating a large number of horses and carriages.[34] In some communities, the family extends invitations to limit the number of guests, but most funerals are open to the entire community. Sometimes members of different Amish affiliations as well as outsiders also attend.[35]

Sometime before the funeral, the deceased is placed in a simple wood coffin constructed by an Amish carpenter. In large settlements, coffin makers keep various sizes in stock, but in smaller or lower communities, a coffin maker builds to order. Regardless of the cause of death, caskets are open for viewing prior to the funeral. With some exceptions, it is customary to have four formal viewings: one for the family and guests during the multiday visitation, one for the family in a private service the day of the funeral, one for guests at the end of the funeral, and a final one for those who attend the graveside service.

In all settlements, friends and relatives visit the family and view the body at the home over a two-day period before the funeral. They come by the dozens, if not hundreds, and "visit together—it's almost a social affair," said one person. The reality of death is not hidden or shielded, even from young children. One man, carrying his toddler and holding his preschool son by the hand, brought them in to see the body of a young boy killed in a logging accident.

The old tradition of a wake, in which several people stayed with the body throughout the night, has largely, but not entirely, disappeared. In Arthur, Illinois, and in some traditional communities, for example, two or three family members sit quietly, day and night, by the body, which is laid out on a bed in a room off the main living room. The constant presence of friends, neighbors, and distant family members at the home reminds the bereaved that, in their grief, they are surrounded by community. As newcomers arrive to join those who arrived earlier, they shake hands with everyone present, extending the same greeting to neighbors as to bereaved family members. This serves as a quiet sign that all are in mourning and that the whole church-community has suffered a loss. One widower, recounting the ways the church supported him during his wife's death, repeatedly asked, "Where else could you ever get support like that?"

Members dig the grave by hand in a nearby family or community cemetery and arrange church benches for several hundred guests in a home, the upper floor of a barn, or a shop. Funeral services are typically held on the morning of the third day after the death, but rarely on Sundays. Sometimes more mourners arrive than can be accommodated in a single house or barn, requiring concurrent services in different buildings. The funeral service for an elderly bishop in New York was held in four homes, with all mourners coming together for the final outdoor viewing. Hundreds stood quietly until all attenders, followed by the immediate family, had filed by the open casket.

In some communities, a short private service is held with the immediate family before the public funeral. Then, during a simple public service, ministers read hymns, Scripture passages, and prayers, and deliver several sermons. Singing is part of the service in some areas but not in others. Funerals are typically conducted in Pennsylvania Dutch, but high groups incorporate some English as a courtesy to non-Amish neighbors and friends in attendance.[36]

The style of hearse varies by affiliation, but it is always pulled by horses and leads a long procession of buggies to a nearby burial ground, often on the edge of a pasture. A brief viewing (in some settlements) and a short graveside service mark the burial. Pallbearers lower the coffin, and family members shovel soil into the grave as a hymn is read or sung. The final benediction is the Lord's Prayer. This venerable petition, "Thy will be done," memorized in childhood and repeated thousands of times in life, now seals the transit to eternal life.

A funeral meal for guests and family members, prepared by the local district and other friends, may be served before or after the burial. "They will feed you and your horse," explained one mortician who has long served Amish clients.

The Amish accept death in graceful ways, observed one funeral director. Comparing them to other people with whom he has worked, he said, "The Amish are more reserved, quieter, and subdued at death. There are some tears, but no loud crying or wailing, just a lot of silent crying." A painful separation laced with grief, death is received in the spirit of *Gelassenheit*—as the ultimate surrender to God's higher ways. The bereaved allow tears to flow, but the sobs are restrained as people submit quietly to divine purpose.

This sampler of the rhythms of Amish community demonstrates the many ways in which cultural and social capital are mobilized to assist individuals and bolster the common good. These resources enable the Amish to prosper in many ways—from financial and social strength to emotional well-being. Their solidarity results in part from their success in thwarting the forces of modernity that threaten to diminish social capital and dissolve the bonds of community.

Although some communal customs have changed over the decades, many Amish practices have quietly resisted the tendrils of modernity that could erode community. Not all the resistance has been quiet, however. Amish people displayed a very public and forthright protest to the expansion of formal education in the twentieth century, a story we explore in the next chapter.

CHAPTER 14

Education

In May 1991 Lucian Niemeyer received an invitation to visit an Amish school. A recently retired business executive from Philadelphia, Pennsylvania, Niemeyer had started making regular visits to Lancaster County and, along the way, had forged friendships with members of the Amish settlement there. That morning, after observing the classroom and its thirty-two students from a back-row seat, Niemeyer's eyes filled with tears. As he wiped them with his handkerchief, he confided apologetically to a friend, "I can't believe it. This is the way it should be. It's amazing to see it right here in the midst of our modern commotion."

The Demise of the Little Red Schoolhouse

When Niemeyer visited Clear Valley School, he wept to see a scene long gone from public schools. There was the nineteen-year-old teacher, Lydia, and her seventeen-year-old assistant, Erma, skillfully teaching almost three dozen first through eighth graders in a one-room school. Colorful chalk drawings of rural scenes filled one side of the blackboard. Individual posters, each with a pupil's name, were fastened to one wall. Pink streamers hung from the ceiling, and seventeen straw hats hung from pegs on the back wall. The open windows offered the students a view of cows and horses in a nearby pasture.

After Lydia read Psalms 100, the pupils repeated the Lord's Prayer and sang a German hymn, followed by an English one. Then the work began. Lydia taught clusters of students from two grades at a time, sometimes at their seats and other times at the blackboard. The first and second graders practiced math with flash cards while the seventh and eighth graders calculated percentages and the diameter of a circle. Other students quietly helped one another in an orderly way. Five or six hands would shoot up whenever Lydia posed a question. When students completed their worksheets properly, Erma pasted smiley faces on them.

A visitor might assume that Clear Valley School was an ancient Amish institution. In fact, it was founded in 1962 as the Amish began establishing their own schools by repackaging old-fashioned public education in an Amish box.

The story of Amish education offers a compelling demonstration of Amish resistance to key educational trends of the twentieth century, including school consolidation, busing of children to centralized schools outside their local communities, an extended school year, and additional years of compulsory education. The resistance was so stiff that hundreds of parents were imprisoned.

Until 1950 virtually all Amish parents sent their children to small, rural public schools, where they studied with non-Amish peers and teachers. In some areas Amish fathers served on local school boards. As long as such public schools were small, under local control, and following a traditional curriculum, Amish parents had no objections.[1]

In the course of the twentieth century, elementary and secondary education in the United States was transformed in profound ways. In 1913 about half of America's schoolchildren attended a single-teacher school. Fifty years later the portion had tumbled to 1 percent.[2] As a result of massive consolidation, several small schools morphed into one large district that required busing students. In a single decade (1918–1928), one-room schools across the nation closed at the rate of 4,000 per year. Meanwhile, states were setting new standards for teacher education, and legislatures were increasing the length of the school year and the number of required years. Science and technology, as well as physical education, became prominent parts of the curriculum.

These changes in the first half of the century were propelled by urbanization, new standards for pedagogy, a growing national commitment to compulsory education, paved roads and motor vehicles that permitted busing, and, above all, an ideology of progress that promoted schooling for citizenship in a democratic society.

A Long, Contentious Struggle

Three changes in particular kindled the Amish response: the consolidation of small schools into large units, the growing emphasis on high school education, and the enforcement of compulsory attendance laws. The Amish reaction varied by region because educational laws were state-based. The first recorded clash occurred in 1914 in Geauga County, Ohio, when three Amish fathers were fined for refusing to send their children to ninth grade.[3] In 1921 eleven fathers were jailed in northern Indiana for withdrawing their children from ninth grade, and more were imprisoned three years later.[4]

Beginning in 1937, the battle over schools ensued in Pennsylvania, Ohio, Indiana, Iowa, and Kansas. By the late 1960s, it had spread to Wisconsin. Dozens of Amish parents were arrested and served short stints in prison. In one Pennsylvania township alone, more than 125 parents were arrested, some of them as many as five times. Several conflicts became bitter, pitting Amish people against their non-Amish neighbors.

Two controversies, one in Pennsylvania in 1937 and the other in Iowa in 1965, catapulted the Amish struggle into the national spotlight. Amish families in East Lampeter Township, near Smoketown, Pennsylvania, protested plans to replace ten one-room schools with a single consolidated elementary school building. In November 1937, with the blessing of their bishops, the Delegation for Common Sense Schooling presented a 130-foot scroll-like petition with three thousand signatures from Amish and non-Amish neighbors to state officials asking to be exempt from a new law that stretched the school year to nine months and raised the age when children could leave school with a work permit to fifteen. The petitioners argued that they would only send their children to public schools "with a free conscience" if the schooling were limited to eight months a year, terminated after the "low grades," and taught "the truth" in a one-room schoolhouse.[5]

The brouhaha in Pennsylvania caught the attention of the *New York Times*, which published twenty-three articles about the Amish between March 1937 and December 1938, many of them tracking the East Lampeter conflict. In the previous twenty years, the *Times* had published only five articles about the Amish.[6]

Nearly thirty years later, a school conflict near Hazleton, Iowa, sparked another blitz of national media attention when a photo of Amish children scampering into a cornfield to avoid being bused to a consolidated school hit the press. This image stirred public sympathies across the country, including those of a Lutheran pastor who lived in Michigan. Reverend William C. Lindholm eventually founded the National Committee for Amish Religious Freedom—a group of scholars, religious leaders, and lawyers that helped take the Amish cause to the U.S. Supreme Court.

Amish Objections

Why were these quiet people willing to face prison, lobby legislators, and circulate petitions? In short, because they wanted to retain control of their children's education and because they objected to the new compulsory attendance rules that lengthened the school year and mandated some high school. "We have what we want, so why fool with it?" asked one Amish father. Four educational themes permeated their protests: mode, curriculum, control, and consequences.

Mode. The Amish distinguish between schooling ("book learning"), which teaches skills, and education (wisdom), which inculcates values. Although they permit children to be schooled by "outsiders," they have never allowed them to be "educated by the world."[7] Schooling is necessary for children to acquire the factual knowledge of reading, writing, and speaking English, and the mathematical skills necessary to run a business, farm, or household. At the same time, the Amish have always stressed the limits of book learning and argued for practical training and learning by doing, guided by example and experience. Book learning, they feared, would lead their youth away from manual work. Beyond eighth grade they wanted an Amish equivalent of apprenticeships supervised by parents. A frequent Amish refrain is that they are not opposed to schooling, but they consider advanced formal schooling unnecessary.

Curriculum. Amish parents argued that high schools lauded "worldly wisdom," a phrase they borrowed from *Martyrs Mirror,* and that worldly wisdom clashed with the "wisdom from above." They cited Scriptures suggesting that human wisdom is foolishness in the eyes of God (1 Cor. 1:18–28) and that too much knowledge makes people proud (1 Cor. 8:1). Moreover, Amish people insisted that the worldly emphasis on individual achievement, along with a curriculum that included evolutionary biology and sex education, would spoil their children (Col. 2:8). "When you have too much education you become strong, arrogant, and lose your humility. If you get high-minded then the honor goes to you instead of God," said a retired business owner.

Control. The Amish wanted schools controlled by the local community or their church. They believed that God had charged parents with the responsibility of nurturing and training their children and that that responsibility could not be passed off to a distant state bureaucracy. They wanted trustworthy teachers who were known in the community and sympathetic to Amish values and rural ways. Amish leaders refused, in their words, to just "hand our children over" to professional educators. Parents repeatedly pleaded for a continuation of the one-room school within walking distance from home.

Consequences. The paramount fear of Amish parents was that modern education would lead youth away from their faith and undermine the church. The wisdom of the world, said Amish sages, "makes you restless, wanting to leap and jump and not knowing where you will land."[8] Too much association with worldly friends, they worried, would corrupt their youth and lead to marriage and other intimate associations with outsiders.

For the Amish, the church-community depends on a practical education in which wisdom is acquired through sharing labor, learning responsibility, interacting with elders, doing chores, and listening to conversations around the kitchen table. While schooling prepares children to write letters, read newspapers, and do the arithmetic to pay bills, an education prepares them "to live for others, to use [their] talents in service to God and Man, to live an upright and obedient life, and to prepare for the life to come."[9]

An "Explosion" of Amish Schools

The Amish began building their own schools in response to the educational changes and the arrests of parents.[10] Their first private school was founded in 1925 when the state of Delaware announced plans to abolish one-room schools and limit the number of elementary grades to six.[11] By 1938 a second school was operating in Delaware and two schools had started in Pennsylvania.

These four schools were the only ones established before World War II.[12] The real "explosion," to use the term of an Amish periodical, occurred after 1950, as the forces of consolidation reached into more isolated rural areas. Fifty-nine Amish schools started in the 1950s. The decade of 1956–1965 saw nearly ten new schools each year, so that by 1970 Amish schools in fourteen states and Ontario were educating nearly 10,000 pupils.[13]

Writing in 1963, a leader noted, "The art of teaching, unknown in Amish circles a generation ago, has really caught fire among us. . . . Most of our teachers do a lot of self-study, burning gallons of midnight oil to make themselves better teachers. Many have taken subjects by correspondence."[14]

The growth of the Amish school movement, as shown in figure 14.1, was propelled by energetic advocates in various settlements and *Blackboard Bulletin,* an Amish-edited periodical that offered teachers practical classroom advice. Building their own schools led to state-wide and even national cooperation in the establishment of curriculum, the preparation of school textbooks, and teacher training.

The rise of Amish schools solved the issue of public school consolidation, but not compulsory attendance laws. Those conflicts were worked out on a state-by-state basis, sometimes amicably and other times not. Pennsylvania found a face-saving solution in 1955 when officials and Amish leaders negotiated a vocational school program. This arrangement permitted pupils to leave school when they turned fourteen or had completed the eighth grade, provided they kept a journal of their vocational duties and attended a half-day of classes once a week until they turned fifteen, at which time they qualified for a work permit. The state could say that Amish pupils were still in school, and Amish parents could have fourteen- and fifteen-year-olds where they wanted them—at home.[15]

Although some other states adopted a version of the Pennsylvania compromise,

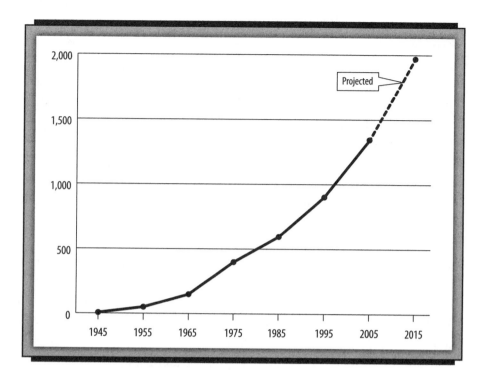

FIGURE 14.1. Growth of Amish Schools, 1945–2015. *Source:* Blackboard Bulletin.

the plan was not accepted everywhere. Ultimately, litigation resulting from a conflict in Wisconsin ended up before the U.S. Supreme Court, which in 1972 ruled in *Wisconsin v. Yoder* that "enforcement of the State's requirement of compulsory formal education after the eighth grade would infringe upon the free exercise of . . . [Amish] religious beliefs."[16]

Although the high court's decision settled the legitimacy of Amish schools and schooling for the most part, the school movement was already well established, with some three hundred schools. And although testimony in the case focused on the threat of public education for the Amish, the practical consequence of *Yoder* was to permit Amish youth to enter apprenticeships when they turned fourteen. By 1985, thirteen years after the Supreme Court decision, the number of Amish schools had doubled to nearly six hundred.

The Structure of Amish Schooling

Organization

In 2012 about 55,000 Amish pupils were being taught by 3,000 teachers in 2,000 private Amish schools in North America.[17] Schools are built when a new settlement forms and, most frequently, as local church districts grow. Depending on the number of young families, a *Gmay* may have its own school or schools, or two or three different districts may send their children to the same school. About twenty to thirty students attend each one-room school, forty to sixty if the school is a larger building.

Typically, three or five school directors—usually fathers appointed by parents—are responsible for managing one or two local Amish schools.[18] The directors recruit and hire teachers, set educational policies, maintain facilities, and manage school finances. Regional school meetings, held annually, provide training and guidance for school directors, teachers, and some church leaders.[19] The one- or two-day event includes presentations and discussions on pertinent topics for teachers and school directors.[20]

Several different models are used to finance schools. In some church districts all households pay a "school tax," but in other places, only the parents of currently enrolled students pay tuition. In still other communities, these two approaches are combined. Some schools offer a discount for multiple children from the same family.

School budgets vary, but in recent years the annual budget for a typical Amish school in eastern Pennsylvania was slightly over $22,000. This included $13,000 in compensation for a teacher and her aide, plus $3,300 for their transportation because they lived far away and hired an English neighbor to drive them. The annual cost per pupil was $738. The nearby public school district's per pupil cost was $10,016.[21] In the smaller schools of the most conservative communities, the cost is far less, for teachers are paid less and walk or travel by buggy to work. In any case, in addition to financing their private schools, Amish property owners pay public school taxes.

Teachers

Teachers are typically young, single Amish women who begin teaching at about eighteen years of age. Generally, they are selected for their academic accomplishment, ability to manage a classroom, and embodiment of Amish values. A handful of teachers are men, and very occasionally an Amish school board will hire a non-Amish teacher. The preparation of teachers varies by affiliation, region, and state requirements. In the most conservative settlements, teachers enter the classroom with little or no training. For example, one Swartzentruber Amish teacher, in talking about her preparation for teaching, noted that as a student she had seen good teachers and bad ones, so when she started teaching, she just tried to follow the example of the good ones.

The bulk of the preparation for those who do receive training occurs in the special meetings for new teachers that are held in some regions, in informal mentorships with seasoned teachers, and in the study of teacher's manuals and textbooks available from Amish bookstores. Because almost all teachers are themselves graduates of an Amish school, they approach their role by seeking to replicate the school experience they had. In some progressive settlements, new teachers take correspondence courses and pass the GED High School Equivalency Test or the Standardized 12th Grade Achievement Test.

The turnover rate is fairly high, because after four or five years in the classroom many young women leave teaching for marriage. A few single women make a career of teaching, but for the most part, teachers change regularly. Indeed, one school director notes that there are "two things people never want to hear: taxes are going up and the teacher has a boyfriend."

Curriculum

Curriculum varies by region, state, and affiliation.[22] Regional Amish educational committees generally maintain contact with their respective state departments of education to file attendance reports and keep tabs on any new regulatory statutes. Several Amish publishers provide textbooks, teaching manuals, and workbooks that are culturally relevant for Amish schools. The largest is Pathway Publishers, located in Aylmer, Ontario, which also publishes the monthly *Blackboard Bulletin* and many other resources for teachers. Schools typically maintain a small library, but teachers and pupils in the higher groups often use the resources of their local public library.

Education for children with disabilities and special needs—psychological, mental, physical—is provided in various ways: classes in public schools or in regular Amish schools, special Amish schools, mobile therapists funded by local public school systems, or some combination of these. As the Amish school movement matured, a parallel "special school" movement emerged in the 1970s and 80s.[23] The first Amish special schools were established in Pennsylvania in 1975, in Indiana in 1983, and in Illinois in 1983. By 2012 many Amish communities had developed schools and educational programs for special needs students. Some of the annual teachers meetings devote sessions to teaching students with special needs.

Religion

Outsiders are often surprised to learn that Amish schools do not explicitly teach religion. Although religious values permeate the school day, the curriculum does not include religion courses or Bible study.[24] In fact, an explicit study of religion in school would cause several problems. It would shift authority for religious interpretation away from church and family, from male leaders to young single women, and from the community to the individual pupil. It could also cultivate an inquiring independence, which might spur critical-thinking youth to later challenge church authority. Finally, in Amish life, the Bible is to be accepted, not studied or dissected. An Amish leader put it this way: "With us, our religion is *inseparable* with a day's work, a night's rest, a meal, or any other practice; therefore, our education can much less be *separated* from our religious practices."[25]

Nonetheless, some change-oriented communities do see their schools as reinforcing church teaching. An Amish bishop told a group of Indiana teachers, "God is the foundation of Amish education. The closer one adheres to God's word and God's principles when administering a system of teaching honor, respect, and discipline, the greater one's probability of success." He noted further that there can be "no neutral position with respect to good and evil. . . . [O]ur allegiance is with one or the other, and this is as true within the classroom as anywhere else."[26] Such Amish see their schools as vital to the well-being of the church.

The Diversity of Schooling

As more Amish schools were established, they developed along paths that reflect the diversity of their communities. In choosing to build or not build a school and in deciding which subjects to teach, which textbooks to use, and how the school day should be structured, local communities reinforce their particular identity and draw boundaries between themselves and the world, and other Amish groups.[27]

Traditional Schools

The Swartzentruber Amish, who represent about 7 percent of the Amish world, have the most traditional schools. The austere architecture of their schoolhouses—simple rectangular buildings without basements, closets, or indoor plumbing—reveal their strict notions of humility and simplicity. The exterior is generally unpainted wood, and the particleboard walls and floor inside are painted in typical Swartzentruber white and battleship gray. These one-room schools, heated by a wood stove, often have a wire strung from the stovepipe to the wall as a drying rack for wet mittens in the winter.

Students enter the classroom through an attached woodshed or perhaps directly from an outside door. Each window has a dark curtain that is tied to one side for illumination, and there are no lights, not even kerosene or propane lamps. The teacher's desk, near the blackboard, faces the rows of children's desks. A bench or a row of chairs in the front of the room marks where children sit when the teacher is "taking their class." Schools do not have designated playgrounds. Instead, during recess

Swartzentruber Amish children in Ohio leave the traditional-style Woodland School and head home for evening chores. *Doyle Yoder*

students play ball games or fox and geese in a surrounding meadow that may well be used for grazing cattle during the summer.

The role of the teacher illustrates how such schools reflect and reinforce the affiliation's values. Swartzentruber teachers receive little or no training and do not expect to teach for more than a year or two, even if they enjoy it. School directors in these settlements often pay teachers as little as five dollars a day, nudging even those who enjoy teaching to give it up for marriage.

Swartzentruber schools provide children the basic literacy and math skills necessary in their highly traditional church-community. Parents do not often visit the school or pay much attention to school activities. There are no special school programs for parents and friends at holiday time. Schools, in short, are not very important in Swartzentruber life.

Indeed, these change-resistant Amish simply perpetuate the most basic educational practices of early twentieth-century rural public education. They use the same texts as their great-grandparents, including nineteenth-century *McGuffey Readers,* the 1919 *Essentials of English Spelling,* and the *Strayer-Upton Arithmetic Series* from the 1930s. Kept in print by Amish print shops, these textbooks immerse children in an early twentieth-century world, and shield them from modern events, technological advances, and religious and cultural pluralism. The language of instruction uses a simple, archaic vocabulary so that pupils can engage in basic interaction with non-Amish neighbors, but it screens them from too much worldly vocabulary and knowledge.[28]

Because the Swartzentrubers esteem old practices, change comes slowly in their schools. In fact, when they do make changes, they tend to step back in time rather than adopt any "modernisms" incongruent with their way of life. Children study German once a week in order to read the Bible and the *Ausbund*, but they do not study history, geography, or health—subjects that their great-grandparents would have studied when they attended public schools in the 1940s.[29]

This restricted curriculum reinforces the cultural isolation of the Swartzentruber community. Furthermore, their schools underscore the value of submission by remaining subordinate to church and family life. Teachers occasionally cancel classes for activities in the local neighborhood such as weddings or silo fillings. Parents sometimes keep scholars home to help with pressing chores, and even the teacher might send a substitute in her place so that she can participate in a quilting bee or help her family get ready for church.

Finally, pedagogy emphasizes rote learning over questioning in Swartzentruber schools, and children are not encouraged to work ahead or do extra lessons if they have finished the day's tasks. At the same time, children learn early that working hard is more important than good grades. The teacher may record perfect scores on spelling tests, but she does not display them where others can see them, nor is there competition between students to see who can do the best. One young child, having just finished first grade, responded to an acknowledgement of her good English with "I'm an easy learner," a matter-of-fact statement meant to dismiss praise.

Change-Oriented Schools

The schools of more progressive groups are quite different from those of the Swartzentrubers. The buildings themselves are larger and more elaborate. In northern Indiana, for example, most schoolhouses have two classrooms and a basement that serves as a play area in inclement weather or as a classroom where children can work in groups to practice spelling words or read with a visiting parent. Some of these schools have indoor plumbing, and some have an attached apartment where the teacher lives. Their amenities include bookshelves, a small library, a battery-run copy machine, and pressurized gas lanterns. The outside landscaping is tidy, with a crushed stone driveway, a ball diamond, playground equipment, and a painted fence marking the school boundaries. In higher communities, teachers are paid fifty dollars a day plus any transportation costs. Monthly teachers meetings and special summer institutes provide venues to meet and learn from more experienced teachers.

In some settlements, schools are a center of Amish life. Parents and other community members stop by regularly, often bringing along younger siblings or visiting relatives. Visitors are welcomed with special songs, guest books, and bulletin boards. Schools present holiday programs and invite the entire church-community. Teachers might take children on field trips to local museums and invite parents to give talks or help with projects. Mothers regularly treat the schoolchildren to hot lunches or special snacks. A letter in the *Budget* reported that one teacher was surprised when her mother and sisters "walked in the school house with ice cream and cake." The letter writer noted that "another hot meal" had been brought in a week earlier.[30] Several schools in his community have "monotony breakers," one Illinois writer reported. For one of these, pupils brought their lunches in unusual containers that included "a breadbox, a toy wheelbarrow, feed bag, and tea kettle."[31]

These higher affiliations want schools to prepare their children for an Amish life, but one that is quite different from that of the Swartzentrubers. As one parent asserted, "Times change, and so education must change for the times." These schools educate children to interact with the world, while at the same time teaching them to remain separate from it. As one Ohio teacher put it, "We expect our schools to provide a basic education for our children, [one] that is essential to our way of living and also to be able to communicate and make a living in the outside world."

Schools in more liberal communities recognize change in the dominant society and try to mediate access to it, even preparing children for work outside their communities. In addition to English, German, and arithmetic, children study geography, American history, and some art, but they do so with textbooks produced by Pathway Publishers. Such texts help children acquire the language and other skills they might need for employment in English businesses, but they do it in ways that reinforce Amish values and behaviors. Teachers also expose pupils to a variety of cultures outside the boundaries of their church-communities. For example, one teacher in Indiana posted a map of the world that announced "five-and-a-half billion people live in more than 175 independent countries on six of the seven continents."[32]

One school in Lancaster County has colorful streamers hanging from the ceiling and student artwork on the walls. A large poster showing a stylish baseball batter proclaims, "The task ahead of you is never as great as the power within you." The small print reads, "Be strong in the Lord and in His mighty power" (Eph. 6:10). Another poster says, "Shoot for the moon. Even if you miss, you will land among the stars." A

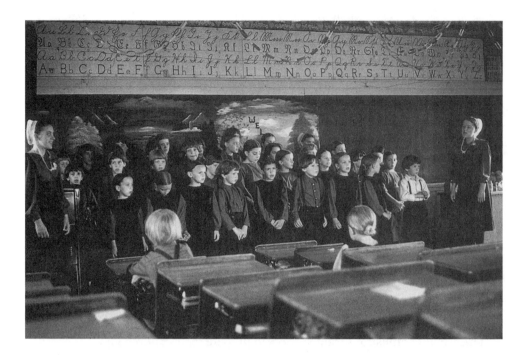

Children in a progressive Amish school practice singing for a parents' program later that day. The teacher's aide (*left*) and the teacher (*right*) direct the singing. Colored chalk drawings are on the blackboard. The two children in the foreground are preschool visitors. *Lucian Niemeyer*

large professionally printed map of the solar system hangs on another wall. The dust jackets of several books, including *You Are Special* by popular evangelical writer Max Lucado, are stapled on a bulletin board to encourage reading.

Students study the parts of speech—nouns, pronouns, verbs, adjectives, adverbs, prepositions, conjunctions, and interjections—as well as long and short vowels. Their academic subjects include reading, history, health, arithmetic, German, and English. Teachers may organize competitive exercises where three or four students race from the back door to the blackboard to be the first to write the answer to a question. Some schools in progressive affiliations even use textbooks from conservative Mennonite publishers that encourage evangelism of outsiders.

Schools in some liberal communities are preparing Amish children to compete economically with their English counterparts on a playing field that may be only marginally in the Amish world, if at all. This refashioning of what it means to be Amish is shocking to the most conservative groups.

Though Amish people do not agree on what constitutes a good Amish education, they are certain that a public high school education would harm their way of life.

Virtually all Amish children end formal schooling with eighth grade, although a few continue studying on their own to obtain a GED or take occasional correspondence courses.

The Outcomes of Amish Schooling
Academic

Evidence from testing of students in Iowa and northern Indiana shows that eighth grade pupils in Amish schools in progressive communities scored more than one grade level above the national standard on the Iowa Tests of Basic Skills. These tests measure basic skills from third to eighth grade, including reading (vocabulary and comprehension), language (word analysis, spelling, capitalization, punctuation, and usage), and mathematics (concepts, problems, and computations). A composite score measures student performance for comparative purposes. Amish third and fourth graders scored slightly below the national average, but fourth graders began to match the standard and eighth graders exceeded it. (See tables 14.1 and 14.2 for details.)[33] This evidence suggests that Amish school students in higher communities are proficient in reading and writing English, and in basic math skills. There is no available evidence that indicates the skill levels of students in the most traditional Amish schools.

Are comparisons with national standards important? They are based on the assumption that if Amish pupils do not measure up to English pupils, the Amish school system is inferior. An Amish educational committee in northern Indiana thinks the standardized tests are helpful to "reveal our weak spots and point out [what] we need to work on."[34] "If somehow in the future, through negligence on our part, another school case [such as *Yoder*] should develop, which could well be expected, then we might lose all that we have struggled and worked for in the last fifty-five years. Therefore, our goal should be striving for improvement."[35]

Amish schools do not teach basic science or technology. Instead, most emphasize an appreciation for nature within a worldview of divine creation. An Amish farmer said, "They tell me that in college you have to *pull everything apart*, analyze it, and try to build it up from a scientific standpoint. That runs counter to what we've been taught on mother's knee" (emphasis added). Amish schools do not teach critical and reflective thinking skills aimed at developing individual autonomy. Teachers do not intentionally suppress independent thought nor do they cultivate or privilege it. Abstract and analytical modes of thought are not encouraged because they would breed impatience with the slow pace of Amish life and erode the authority of tradition.

There certainly are Amish students who, at their own initiative, pursue intel-

Table 14.1. Scores of Iowa Amish Students on the Iowa Tests of Basic Skills in 2009

Grade	National Norm	Johnson County, Iowa (12 Amish schools)	Difference	Davis County, Iowa (12 Amish schools)	Difference
3	3.5	3.2	−.3	3.1	−4
4	4.5	4.4	−.1	4.0	−.5
5	5.5	5.3	−.2	4.8	−.7
6	6.5	6.4	−.1	7.0	.5
7	7.5	7.5	0	8.3	.8
8	8.5	9.6	1.1	10.6	2.1

Source: Iowa Amish school leaders.

Note: The national norm for each grade is established by tests administered in the fifth month of that grade. The difference shows Amish variation from the national norm. For example, Amish eighth graders in Johnson County schools scored at the ninth-grade, six-month level, which is one year and one month above the national norm.

Table 14.2. Scores of Indiana Amish Students on the Iowa Tests of Basic Skills in 2011

Grade	National Norm	Northern Indiana (79 Amish Schools*)	Difference
3	3.35	3.5	.15
4	4.35	4.7	.35
5	5.35	6.0	.65
6	6.35	7.0	.65
7	7.35	8.1	.75
8	8.35	9.8	1.45

Source: Northern Indiana Amish school leaders.

Note: The national norm for each grade is established by tests administered at the three-and-a-half-month point of that grade. The difference shows Amish variation from the national norm. For example, Amish eighth graders scored at the ninth-grade, eight-month level.

*Total of 2,300 students.

lectually challenging questions, but Amish schools do not promote such traits in their curriculum or ethos. Intellectual curiosity is especially threatening in the more traditional groups. Some Amish students who pursue academic interests become self-taught scholars within their communities, while others leave the community for greater intellectual freedom.

Social

Not only do Amish schools teach basic skills and transmit cultural values, but they also perform significant social functions. They control the flow of ideas, build ethnic ties, and mediate relationships with outsiders—all of which enhance dependence on the church-community. Amish schools insulate children from rival explanations of reality and help to keep Amish ideology intact. By propagating ideas and values that undergird the ethnic social system, the schools reproduce the values and structures of Amish society.

Despite their limitations, Amish schools have ably passed on the traditions of faith to new generations. Indeed, schools are key to the growth and vitality of Amish life. Cloistered schools may not stretch Amish awareness of the outside world, but they provide secure settings for the psychosocial development of children and instill in them a deep sense of identity and attachment to their community.

Each school is also a symbol of collective Amish identity and of the community's commitment to a particular kind of education. Moreover, Amish affiliations define and separate themselves from other Amish groups by the type of schools they construct and support. Schools thus symbolize not only separation from the dominant society but also internal differentiation. They are institutions of identity and diversity. Perhaps most importantly, they mediate the access of their youth to the outside world by their choice of textbooks, the subjects they teach, and the prominence of English.

Amish Children in Public Schools

Although Amish schools quickly became the most common site of formal education in Amish society during the second half of the twentieth century, not all Amish children attend such schools. In a handful of communities, some Amish children attend schools run by Old Order Mennonites, and in a few others, Amish children attend public schools (but only through the eighth grade).[36] Amish parents who support public schooling generally live in older settlements with long-standing patterns of collaboration with civic authorities. When families start a new settlement, they usually begin their own school instead of turning to the unknown public ones.

Serious debates within Amish communities about the merits of private versus public schools were typical in the mid-twentieth century. Public school sympathizers thought elementary-age children would benefit by mingling with non-Amish peers and developing local friendships. Similarly, some Amish parents now send their children to public schools so they "learn to get along in the world."[37] An Amish woman in southwestern Michigan echoes those sentiments regarding her own children: "If they grow up Amish, go to the Amish church, go to the Amish school, and only see other Amish, they won't know anything about the world."[38]

Besides, when Amish people make up a sizable proportion of the general population—and a large share of the school-age population—as in St. Joseph County, Michigan, or eastern Holmes County, Ohio—public schools might be sensitive to Amish preferences. In such places, Amish students in public schools feel secure because they have ample Amish peers and teachers who respect Amish parental wishes.[39] In Holmes County, for example, Amish children in public schools see that English children are different, which reinforces ethnic boundaries. A former Ohio Amish teacher notes that he went to a public school as a child and that he and his fellow Amish students "were aware that we were different and had to be." Although the Amish in Arthur, Illinois, have seventeen private schools, about 10 percent of their children attend public schools. Those in public schools are mixed with non-Amish in the first six grades, but they are placed in Amish-only classrooms for seventh and eighth grade, when their non-Amish peers transfer to the local junior high school.

Various factors play into a decision to send a child to public school. A family in Michigan, for example, sent their children to a nearby public school because traveling to the Amish school required crossing a dangerous highway by buggy. Conflict within an Amish school or community may also motivate parents to send their children to public school. When different Amish affiliations live side by side, sending children to public school may be easier than dealing with competing church regulations and expectations in a single one-room school. It may be difficult for parents to explain to their private-schooled children why they cannot do or have the same things as their classmates from a different Amish affiliation.[40]

A few Amish parents consider Amish schools inferior to public ones. One former teacher thinks that since the Amish won the right to establish their own schools, some communities have become lax in their attention to education standards. He notes that, when some settlements established teacher training meetings, "in [my] community they felt it wasn't necessary. We've hired teachers that weren't qualified and the schools suffered." Finally, some parents admit to sending their children to public schools simply because they are tuition-free.

A growing reliance on the Internet and other technologies in public education has pushed more and more Amish families into private schools, however. In 1978 about half the Amish children in the Nappanee, Indiana, settlement attended public schools, but by 2002 only one in five did.[41] An Amish leader in Indiana put it this way: "Amish are stubborn. And back in 1967 the public schools were not all that bad. Local schools were ninety-five percent Amish. . . . The teachers were teaching sound doctrine—no evolution or computers. As long as things were like that, we didn't need our own schools. [But] as public schools changed and became more worldly, more [parents] sent their kids to parochial schools."[42]

It Takes a Tribe
Homeschooling

Given their long-standing belief that parents hold the primary responsibility to educate their children, why do Amish people frown on homeschooling? Their objection reveals their assumptions about the necessity of community-based education.

Amish leaders strongly discourage homeschooling for several reasons. Their system of private schools was well-established and maturing as the homeschooling movement arose in the 1980s. Private schools are important agencies to promote inter-family cooperation and reinforcement of community values and practices. In the school context, young children learn the skills of collaboration, cooperation, and the importance of fitting in with a group larger than their family. In this way, Amish schools socialize students for adult life in a collective ethnic community.

Leaders fear that households that educate their own children will become too independent and self-sufficient and thus troublesome in a church-community that values unity. In addition, teaching generally falls to the mother, who is already responsible for handling many daily chores for her large family. Church restrictions on transportation, telephone, and Internet use also limit access to educational resources for homeschool teachers.

Making a case against homeschooling, one Amish educational leader said, "We all need the help of others in shaping our children's character. We all need the church and the community to enable our children to develop and to be able to function with others." A good school, he argues, "can help children learn to live in harmony with a diversity of talents and personalities."[43] Some groups are so opposed to homeschooling that they have excommunicated families that insisted on teaching their own children.[44]

Apprenticeship

The secret of Amish education lies in the power of informal apprenticeship after eighth grade. This aspect of Amish socialization is rarely described in the scholarly literature.[45] Yet apprenticeship, as much if not more than schools, explains how Amish youth learn the skills, attitudes, and habits that prepare them for productive lives in Amish society as well as in the broader world.

The informal apprenticeship system is, by default, custom tailored for each person. Nonetheless, it produces young adults who are equipped with technical, trade, entrepreneurial, managerial, homemaking, and agricultural skills appropriate to their church-community as well as the work habits that provide a solid foundation for life, as the following examples illustrate:

- A fourteen-year-old girl manages her mother's small quilt shop adjacent to their home on Saturdays, evenings, and during the summer. She greets visitors, explains the various fabrics, and handles the sales.
- An eighteen-year-old boy takes over the management of his father's wood-working shop. He is authorized to hire, fire, and supervise the five other employees—all of whom are older, some in their fifties and sixties.
- A fourteen-year-old boy, employed in the family hydraulic equipment business, travels by hired taxi ten miles away to repair broken hydraulics on an Amish farm.
- A ten-year-old girl serves as a receptionist on Saturday mornings for the family's retail furniture business. When not greeting customers, she files orders and computes financial statements with a small calculator.

In lower communities, children routinely work as hired help for Amish neighbors. One ten-year-old girl helped her aunt care for a toddler and a newborn, doing a range of chores from diapering the baby to preparing strawberries for canning. Her eight-year-old cousin helped an Amish neighbor run the farm stand—sorting produce, bagging groceries, and carrying purchases to shoppers' cars. A young boy may work part-time for a neighbor, helping to milk cows or goats, or clean up an uncle's shop on Saturday mornings.

Children whose parents work away from home are responsible for small enterprises such as raising pets, cleanup and repair projects, and gardening. A twelve-year-old girl understands how to provide child care for younger siblings or neighbors, how to bake a dozen loaves of bread, and when and how to plant strawberries. Children learn to work, and work hard, at an early age, preparing them to run their own homes, farms, or businesses.

Beyond on-the-job learning, one Amish man explained that any "technical training that is needed can be had. It is not uncommon to go to a local tech school for training on installing solar panels or accounting and so forth." Other skills are self-taught. An Amish employee at an English factory said, "All our Amish engineers have only eight grades. But still they do OK. They built a new computerized router to cut holes in PVC dimension stock and outsourced the software writing. But they weren't happy with it, so they will write their own next time, and I tell you, they will accomplish this. Hey, education is caught not taught. You can't teach someone something they don't want to know, and conversely you can't keep them in the dark to stop them from learning what they need or want to."[46]

Ending formal schooling by the age of fourteen provides youth with at least two years of apprenticeship before they begin regular employment. Typically, young people receiving outside income turn most of it over to their parents until they reach age eighteen (twenty-one in some groups) or marry. In return, parents cover the child's debts, room, board, and clothing. Some young people work a short time in several jobs until they discover the work they most enjoy. Through apprenticeship, youth acquire skills and habits of mind that support an enterprising society.

Different Worlds, Different Aims

Iowa Amish teacher Samuel D. Guengerich argued in 1897 that "the righteousness which counts before God is neither sought nor found in the public or free schools; they are intended only to impart worldly knowledge, to ensure earthly success, and to make good citizens for the state."[47] Guengerich captured the Amish critique of public education in a single sentence. A state-devised education does not "count before God" because it is designed to "ensure earthly success," and "make good citizens for the state." Guengerich wanted an Amish education that would "count" in the eyes of God, one that made good members for his church-community.

Six decades later, minister Joseph Stoll echoed Amish anxiety about the threat of cultural assimilation: "How can we parents expect our children to grow up untainted by the world if we voluntarily send them into a worldly environment, where they associate with worldly companions, and are taught by men and women not of our faith six hours a day, five days a week, for the greater part of the year?"[48] Indeed, an aim of public education is to integrate students from diverse cultural backgrounds into a common civic culture. Moreover, with its ideological content and compulsory attendance laws, public education is the most intruding arm of the state in the private lives of citizens.

Both Guengerich and Stoll understood that schooling is not a neutral enterprise. They knew that all education—public or private—involves the cultural transmission of particular values, beliefs, and dispositions. "All teaching," says political scientist Rob Reich, "is a value-laden enterprise. Schools are ethically charged places. . . . Teachers cannot help transmitting certain values to students. . . . Curriculum construction is a process of exclusion as well as inclusion. . . . [In addition,] the so-called hidden curriculum of the school culture and role modeling of the adults, makes neutrality impossible."[49]

State-sponsored education aims to impart academic knowledge as well as to cultivate civic skills and dispositions for good citizenship. American public education champions self-actualization, individual rights, and the freedom to construct one's life without the restraints of tradition. Public education also promotes citizenship and a sense of allegiance to the ideals of equality and freedom.

Amish parents sensed that public education, as it evolved in the twentieth century, would likely separate children from their traditions and cherished values. Professional specialists—educated in worldly universities—would encourage Amish youth to maximize their potential by pursuing more education to "liberate" themselves from the shackles of parochialism. In a setting that champions individuality, Amish youth would become self-confident, arrogant, independent, and proud. By stirring aspirations and raising occupational hopes, teachers would steer Amish youth away from farm and family or at least would encourage restlessness. These outcomes of public education are antithetical to core Amish values of *Gelassenheit,* self-denial, humility, separation from the world, nonparticipation in politics, and a lifelong allegiance to the Amish church.

In contrast, Amish schools are designed to prepare youth for a successful life in the Amish community, not in mainstream society. By all accounts, Amish schools meet their objectives well by producing hard-working, self-motivated individuals who are adept at practical skills. Amish schools are not designed to set students on a track to become physical therapists, nuclear scientists, jazz musicians, ballet dancers, psychotherapists, or politicians. They do, however, provide a basic education for the entrepreneurs of some 12,000 Amish-owned small businesses in North America.

Amish schooling and apprenticeship gives even those who leave the Amish world a solid set of employable skills in the public job market. Moreover, Amish schools also affirm qualities some secular educators are once again coming to appreciate. They offer small-scale, community-based instruction that emphasizes individual responsibility and discipline. Amish children learn to take responsibility for their actions and to behave in a disciplined manner. They are accountable to their teachers and to their parents, and the schools themselves are accountable to a clearly defined, community-based authority.[50]

Advocates of personal autonomy may cringe at the limits of an Amish education. In response, one Amish man said, "Some people argue that Amish kids will never be a Picasso, Mozart, Einstein, etc. Whenever I hear that row, the thought crosses my mind that those people were not the products of an American education either. . . . What I am trying to say is that we don't feel deprived because of only having an eighth grade education. And why spend all that time and money for a Cadillac when a pony cart will do just fine."

The rejection of automobiles and public utility electricity in the first half of the twentieth century shaped Amish identity in profound ways. But the decision to operate private schools had an even deeper influence because the Amish were controlling the ideology that would shape the socialization of their children and exercising agency in organizing their own schools. Paradoxically, the sharper cultural separation embodied in their private school system developed at the same time that the Amish were becoming more entangled in the larger market economy. In chapters 15 through 17 we explore the entanglements resulting from their changing agricultural practices and their foray into business.

IV

EXTERNAL TIES

CHAPTER 15

AGRICULTURE

In January 2001, Amish minister and farmer Rob Schlabach was worried about the precarious state of farming in Holmes County, Ohio. Fifteen years earlier the Amish owners of seven farms adjoining his had all earned their primary income from farming. Now only three of those families relied on agriculture. The families on the other farms still lived on the land, but they held off-farm jobs. "The common comradeship of working together with neighboring farms is getting scarce," he noted, "and the farming skills that have been passed from generation to generation are now breaking up and disappearing. How sad! Plain People are having problems remaining a simple 'people of the land.'" The shift from farming had produced new patterns of work. Schlabach lamented the weekend mentality of "Saturdays off for fun" and the fact that more Amish people were now interested in leisure, play, traveling, and shopping. "All of these are earmarks of the industrial lifestyle, and sad to say, it looks like that is where we are headed."

Faith, Family, and Farming

The Amish have had a long love affair with the land, even calling farming "a religious tenet" and considering the tilling of soil a divine duty God directed in the Garden of Eden (Gen. 3:21). This spiritual connection to the soil is also rooted in the Amish experience in Europe in the seventeenth and eighteenth centuries, where they and their Anabaptist ancestors had a reputation as innovative farmers known for their land stewardship and animal husbandry.[1]

Over the generations, the Amish have developed a strong conviction that the small family farm is the best place to raise children in the faith. One Amish publication flatly declares that farming "is the most ideal occupation for Christian families." The author concedes that "not everyone must be a farmer, only that it is the most ideal." Agriculture is revered because "farming allows us to be part of the cycle of life, death, and renewal that God planned in his wisdom. In our daily contact with creation, we cannot help but stand in awe and wonder of God."[2] Equally important is the shared nature of family farming, in which "my work" and "your work" become blurred into "our work," and children grow up learning to do chores and accept responsibility. This litany of praise for farming as the best vocation for family life and child rearing is reiterated dozens if not hundreds of times in Amish writings.[3]

Until the mid-twentieth century, Amish farming generally matched the pre-industrial image of a small family operation where wife, husband, and children work together as producers.[4] In 1950 more than 90 percent of Amish households received their primary income from farming. Rob Schlabach's lament of farming's decline describes a trend that began to accelerate in the last quarter of the twentieth century. That crisis, in turn, reenergized traditional as well as new agricultural practices in the first decade of the twenty-first century. The story of Amish farming in America has three chapters—pre-1950, 1950–2000, and early twenty-first century—each marked by particular features.

Modest and Diversified before 1950

When the first Amish arrived in America, tilling, planting, and harvesting were done with hand tools and the power of oxen. Horses came into general use only after 1800. In the course of the nineteenth century, many aspects of field work—tilling, seeding, weeding, and harvesting—became mechanized with horse-drawn equipment. Large stationary steam engines powered threshing machines, sawmills, and grain mills. Prior to 1900, the farm technology of the Amish was similar to that of their English neighbors, and in some cases Amish farmers were among the first in their communities to adopt new machinery.[5] Divergence from mainstream agriculture did not become a prominent feature of Amish farming until the first half of the twentieth century.

Typical late nineteenth–century Amish farms were small, diversified enterprises heavily reliant on family labor. The 1880 census, for example, revealed that Amish families in Johnson County, Iowa, produced modest amounts of corn, wheat, hogs, and cattle, just as their non-Amish neighbors did. The Amish households, however, churned much more butter. Because butter making was a task of women and children, its production points to intensive family labor. Despite being small and diversified, Amish farms were tied to local markets and not simply engaged in subsistence agriculture. Cash crops were common. They varied by region and included tobacco in eastern Pennsylvania and commercial peppermint in northern Indiana.[6]

The use of tractors and other engine-powered field equipment in the first half of the twentieth century revolutionized agricultural production in mainstream America.[7] Machine power in the field and electrification in the barn increased output and the scale of farming. In the words of Amish farmer Gideon Fisher, "The world of inventions made a greater change after 1900 than it did in all the years [until then]," due to the advent of "monstrous equipment."[8] Although most Amish had stayed abreast of new farm technology in the nineteenth century, they largely froze their turn-of-the-century farming methods for the next five decades. Their resistance to the new engine-powered equipment was rooted in a fear that it would lead to large-scale mechanized farming that would destroy the pattern of family farms that had anchored Amish society for decades.[9]

A few Amish people flirted with the new technology. The tractor was the most contentious issue, and in several settlements in the 1930s and 1940s Amish farmers began using tractors to plow and power field equipment, only to have their churches forbid them. In the Arthur, Illinois, settlement in the early 1940s, for example, three of the five bishops were sympathetic to using tractors. Unable to find a consensus on their own, they asked bishops from other settlements to help them mediate the issue, which resulted in a taboo on the tractor. A few settlements in Iowa, Kansas, and Oklahoma did approve tractors for field work, but the vast majority of Amish settlements across the country rejected them.[10] Some groups, while banning tractors in the field, allowed them as stationary sources of power around the barn. In such cases the tractor functioned much like a nineteenth-century steam engine, running threshing machines and feed grinders in the farmyard. Until about 1950 the forces of tradition, with a few exceptions, had triumphed by forbidding the use of tractors and engine-powered machines for field work. Those restrictions began to change somewhat in the last half of the century, as we show in chapter 17.

In short, the scale, style, and technology of Amish farming in the first half of the twentieth century remained static. Amish people opted out of the massive mechanization in American agriculture. Amish farmers continued using horse-drawn machinery and retained their small, diversified, family-based farming operations.

The Big Squeeze: 1950–2000

If Amish agriculture changed little during the first half of the century, the second half brought a turbulent time of adaptation, crisis, and decline. By the mid-twentieth century, the mechanization of American agriculture and its growing corporate scale made it difficult for small Amish farmers to thrive. The *Ordnung* that governed farm-

This small, traditional Swartzentruber Amish farm is located in Pontotoc County near Randolph, Mississippi. In many progressive communities, other types of water pumps have replaced windmills. *Erin Jaffe*

ing practices into the 1950s had been shaped by the traditional family farm, and a half century of Amish life was now wrapped into that Ordnung so that any modifications of the taken-for-granted regulations threatened Amish identity. In every settlement and affiliation across the country, the farming Ordnung was under intense strain as it met the revolutionary changes in agriculture.

The most traditional groups continued to cling to small, non-mechanized family farms, while higher groups began adopting and adapting technology to boost their agricultural productivity while staying within the bounds of the Ordnung. For example, since Amish farmers were now unable to purchase horse-drawn machinery from commercial suppliers, who had switched entirely to tractor sales, they turned to building horse-drawn equipment of their own. Moreover, they began modifying large factory-built machines—designed for tractors—so that they could be powered instead by small gasoline engines and pulled by horses.

Changes at the Barn

Although the struggle over the tractor was settled in the first half of the century, the battle over barn technology erupted after 1950. This struggle—involving how to operate a profitable dairy without electricity—focused on two technologies: mechanical milkers and bulk cooling tanks for the milk. The old-style method involved milking cows by hand and chilling milk in large cans in cold water. This labor-intensive milking ritual basically limited herd size to about a dozen cows and required transporting the milk to a local creamery once a day.

After 1940 the growing availability of vacuum milkers powered by electricity made it possible to greatly expand herd sizes. Then, in the 1950s and 1960s, state health regulations for handling and chilling milk made a sharp distinction between Grade A milk for direct consumption and Grade B milk used for making cheese. Grade A, which brought a much higher price, could not be transported in cans and chilled in water but required rapid cooling in bulk refrigeration tanks typically powered by electricity.

The lower Amish groups resisted any innovation in dairying and settled for selling their milk as Grade B to cheese plants. In some of their settlements, in fact, new cheese factories were established for or by Amish people so they could continue to operate their old-style dairies. In Wisconsin, at least half a dozen cheese plants still serve primarily Amish communities. In Conewango Valley, New York, a cheese producer provides a market for Amish milk and a place of employment for members of the Troyer Amish affiliation who live there.[11] When a cheese plant in northern New York closed in 2008, the region's staunchly electric-resistant Swartzentruber Amish, who had relied on the plant as an outlet for their Grade B milk, suddenly had to devise a way to meet Grade A requirements. They agreed to build cooling stations with bulk refrigeration tanks on land owned and electrified by English neighbors. The arrangement, which allowed them to ship Grade A milk without electrifying their own farms, was permitted only in districts that had no access to a cheese plant.[12]

Debates about using vacuum milkers and bulk cooling tanks continued into the twenty-first century in some communities. Those that adopted mechanical milkers and bulk tanks powered their milking systems and refrigeration units with a diesel engine located in a shed adjacent to the barn as well as with the help of 12-volt electricity from batteries. Communities often adopted milkers and bulk tanks at about the same time, but not always. For example, in 2002 sixteen of eighty-one districts in Geauga County, Ohio, permitted bulk tanks, but only seven permitted milking machines.

Adopting new farm technology highlighted the way the Ordnung governing farming was especially resistant to change. One Ohio bishop explained it like this: "All of our farm work is visible to the community, unlike industrial work hidden in a factory or shop." Because farming is so public, the Ordnung is transparent, and "people can see what you are doing, what tools and equipment you are using and what practices you are following so you can receive advice and counsel from the community." Shop

A young Amish woman cleans a vacuum milker beside a stainless steel bulk tank
in the milk house of her family's large dairy. Vacuum milkers and bulk tanks were often
controversial in Amish settlements because they required electricity and diesel power.
The most traditional farmers continue to milk their small herds by hand and
haul their milk in large cans. *Daniel Rodriguez*

owners, in contrast, often faced fewer restrictions when adopting new technology
because their enterprises were new and unburdened by generations of tradition.

Some farmers complained that an inflexible farming Ordnung was actually pushing young families into nonfarm employment and suggested that, if church leaders
wanted to save the family farm, the Ordnung would need to be relaxed. In 2002 dairy
farmers in Lancaster County, Pennsylvania, pleaded with their bishops for permission to use horse-drawn harvesters, rather than old-fashioned corn binders, to cut
corn for silage. After noting that the prices of all of their supplies, equipment, and
cows had risen, they declared, "We have no choice; we *have* to have a lot more cows."
They warned that, if change was not forthcoming, farmers would be forced to "rent
out all their ground and buy all their feed. . . . This will bring a big change for our way
of life."[13] The bishops were not sympathetic to the farmers' pleas.

Some communities did relax their farming Ordnung, but the results did not necessarily save the family farm. In the 1970s, the Arthur, Illinois, Amish shifted to large

laying hen, hog, or cattle feeding operations on smaller plots of land.[14] But volatile commodity prices and environmental regulation of animal waste soon rendered this model as problematic as traditional farming. By the 1980s, Amish people in all but the most conservative communities were shifting away from the timeworn path of the plow.

Leaving the Plows Behind

Beginning in the 1940s, small numbers of Amish men began to find employment off the farm. As early as the 1960s, some household heads in the Nappanee, Indiana, settlement chose to take nearby industrial jobs and rent their land to non-Amish neighbors. During the 1980s, a combination of economic and demographic pressures squeezed many large Amish settlements and spiked nonfarm work.

On the one hand, due to large families and high retention rates, Amish communities were experiencing a population explosion: there were simply too many babies for too few acres. On the other hand, in most historic Amish settlements those acres were skyrocketing in price as suburbanization and rising real estate taxes pushed farming out of the financial reach of many young families. Escalating prices for hybrid seeds, fertilizer, equipment, and veterinary bills all conspired to make farming an expensive enterprise, even on a small scale. At the turn of the twenty-first century, buying a farm, equipment, and cattle for a dairy operation could cost $2 million dollars in some regions. As shown in table 15.1, many young families, sizing up their options, decided that farming was not possible—or that the much smaller investment needed to start a shop or retail store was more attractive.

By the 1990s, in all but the most conservative communities, Amish farming was in a slump if not a crisis. Geauga County, Ohio, for example, lost 26 percent of its 208 dairy farms in the seven-year period from 1990 to 1997.[15] One Amish writer ruefully noted that "the morale among farmers reached its lowest ebb in the mid-to-late 1990s. Many had the attitude that farming was only for the simple-minded or for those too stubborn to acknowledge the times in which we live."[16]

Growing Diversity in Contemporary Farming

Despite the farm crisis of the late 1900s, thousands of Amish families were still in agriculture at the dawn of the twenty-first century. In fact, although the percentage of Amish farmers has declined sharply, the rapid Amish population growth means that the actual number of families that are farming is still increasing, albeit slowly. In many cases, households committed to farming left communities plagued by high real estate prices for more sparsely populated areas where land was more affordable and they

Table 15.1. Percent of Amish Household Heads Whose Primary Occupation Is Farming

Region	%
Ashland, OH	50
Bloomfield, IA	44
Missouri	43
Wisconsin	41
Buchanan County, IA	38
Lancaster, PA	36
New Order*	33
Michigan	32
Lawrence County, PA	28
Jasper/Woodhull, NY	25
Adams and Jay Counties, IN	23
Arthur, IL	21
Clymer, NY	20
Holmes County, OH	17
Elkhart–LaGrange, IN	14
Delaware	12
Geauga County, OH	7
Spartansburg, PA	1

Source: Settlement directories published between 2006 and 2010.

Note: Data collected on heads of households born after 1940. Farming includes commercial animal husbandry related to deer, dogs, rabbits, fish, and hatcheries, and also orchards, produce, and greenhouses, but not forestry and lumbering. These are minimum estimates because they exclude household heads who farm only part-time.

*New Order is an affiliation.

could farm profitably. For example, Vernon and Ida Borntreger, their five children, and two other families moved from Tennessee to Fulton County, Arkansas, in 2009 to begin a new settlement where the Borntregers now grow produce. "It's something that we can do as a family," explained Vernon.[17] Similarly, a woman in western New York noted that families had moved to her settlement so they could continue farming: "I think the men want to be home earning their own money. In my opinion, if the men are home, they can help raise the children."

Small family farms remain the dominant source of livelihood for the lowest groups such as the Nebraska, Swartzentruber, and Troyer Amish. With strict restrictions on technology, they continue to operate small, low-tech family farms much as they have for decades, with a dozen or so cows for milking, supplemented by some swine and poultry. These labor-intensive operations rely on horse power and rarely permit internal combustion power in the fields, although some use gasoline engines on sprayers or for power to fill silos or operate stationary hay balers. Farmers milk their dairy cows by hand and sell their Grade B milk, chilled in cans, to cheese plants. Children work side-by-side with their parents and dream of owning their own farms someday. Although these farms are small in scope, their economic well-being fluctuates somewhat with the larger economy. Amish farms are insulated from the worst economic vacillations, however, because costs are low and labor is supplied by family members. To provide an economic cushion, some families establish small home businesses such as craft production to provide work during the slower winter months.

At the other end of the continuum are larger, relatively high-tech Amish farms whose dairy herds range from forty to eighty cows. These dairies use vacuum milkers, chill their milk in bulk refrigeration tanks, and sell it as Grade A. The cows are bred by artificial insemination, non-Amish veterinarians use antibiotics to treat the herd, and the farmers track the individual productivity of each cow. Agronomists advise these farmers on soil fertility and the use of seeds, fertilizers, pesticides, and insecticides. Engine-powered equipment, pulled by horses or by tractors in a few districts, is used to till, plant, and harvest crops. These larger Amish farms are substantial financial operations whose fortunes rise and fall with commercial feed costs and regional market prices. Yet even they are small compared with the scale of commercial agribusinesses. There are, of course, many variations of Amish farms between the small family operations and the larger ones described here.

Crops vary by type and size of operation and region of the country. Common crops include corn, wheat, spelt, clover, barley, alfalfa, and a variety of hay and grasses for grazing. Tobacco is grown in some Pennsylvania, Kentucky, Maryland, and Wisconsin communities. The type of livestock—chickens, hogs, goats, cows, beef cattle—also varies by region. Many Amish farms focus on dairying. In Wisconsin eight in ten Amish farmers milk cows, while in Michigan 60 percent and in Minnesota almost half do. Professor John A. Cross estimates that there are more than ten thousand Amish dairy farms in the United States and that they constitute about one-eighth of the nation's dairy farms. Cross expects that the Amish share will increase to one-fifth by 2015, yet because of the small size of their operations, they will produce a far smaller proportion of the nation's milk.[18]

Rebooting Agriculture for the Future

In order to keep a solid footing on the shifting landscape of agricultural life, Amish farmers are finding new strategies for survival. Many farm families survive economically by supplementing their income with sideline earnings from other sources, especially as multi-generation families pool their resources. In one case a husband and

Amish people in some regions tap maple syrup and sell it commercially as part of their farming and/or lumber operations. *Karen M. Johnson-Weiner*

wife with several children share the bulk of the farm work with help from a grand-father, while an unmarried brother-in-law operates a small furniture shop in a ret-rofitted corn barn. Meanwhile, a sister operates a small fabric store adjacent to the house, the grandmother takes in work as a seamstress, and several of the teenage children raise guinea pigs for sale to a local pet store.

Beyond this sort of creative combination of resources and labor, a growing num-ber of households have sought to revitalize agriculture by launching new ventures such as cheese making, produce auctions, organic farming, intensive grazing, green-houses, and other enterprises that promise to give rural life a second wind.[19]

Produce Farming and Auctions

Traditionally, all Amish families had gardens to supply food for their families, and many sold produce at farmers' markets in nearby towns or at roadside stands near their homes for supplemental income. In the late twentieth century, however, pro-duce farming for wholesale markets became a viable option and expanded rapidly. Produce auctions gave such endeavors a major boost. The first Amish-organized auction was established near the town of Leola in Lancaster County, Pennsylvania, in 1985. Other auction houses followed, and by 2010 Amish and Old Order Mennonite settlements across America were operating more than sixty auctions in numerous states. Farmers bring their produce by horse-drawn wagons or hired trucks to an auction building that is open several days a week from March to November.

At a typical Amish-operated auction, wholesale buyers from local food stores, restaurants, and even large grocery chains bid on cantaloupes, watermelons, sweet corn, tomatoes, peppers, zucchini, cucumbers, pumpkins, apples, broccoli, carrots, cauliflower, cabbage, herbs, and many varieties of flowers. A local board of directors owns and operates the auction and hires staff (some of them non-Amish). The auctions offer growers a dependable nearby outlet for their products at competitive prices that fluctuate with supply and demand. Some but not all of the produce sold on auction is organically grown. A monthly newsletter, *Truck Patch News,* and two regional gatherings of several hundred growers have bolstered the movement.[20]

Fewer than ten acres of land are needed for produce farming, and the profit per acre is much higher than conventional Amish crop farming. One family that grows an acre of grape tomatoes earns an average of $39,000 a year before labor costs. Although the crop is labor intensive, the cash outlay for labor is low because family members perform the work.[21] In some states, agricultural extension agents have promoted Amish produce farming. For example, in Missouri, where Amish and Mennonite farmers raise 10 percent of the state's fresh vegetables, extension agents conducted four workshops on growing practices that can improve production and reduce toxic damage. More than two hundred Amish and Mennonite growers attended the workshops.[22]

One mother explained how produce farming is a perfect fit with child rearing: "Raising produce is rewarding if you can get the whole family involved. Even preschoolers can help a lot. Four- and five-year-olds can fill flats with pro-mix in the greenhouse. Once they get tired of that, they can help transplant seedlings out of trays into plug flats. . . . A lot can be done in a short time with one adult and three willing little helpers. . . . The produce patch is a good place to catch up on family news, whether we're planting, weeding, or harvesting, it's a fun place to be."[23]

Organic Farming

Although many observers assume that all Amish farms are organic, most are not. During the last half of the twentieth century, the majority of Amish farmers used chemical fertilizers on their land and also killed insects, fungus, and weeds with commercial chemicals. Why did the nature-loving Amish accept chemical farming? One reason was their gradual adoption of hybrid seed corn, despite strong objections from some conservative leaders. Seed and fertilizer salespeople pitched the benefits of chemical fertilization, and some of the most profit-oriented Amish farmers even hired consultants to test their soil and advise them on the use of fertilizer, herbicides, and insecticides.

Not everyone was comfortable with these developments. In 1990 the Amish periodical *Family Life* published a three-part series, "Poisoning the Earth," in which an Amish organic advocate lamented "how readily the usually cautious and conservative small scale Amish and Mennonite farmers accepted this radical departure [use of chemicals] from the traditional" ways of farming.[24] The articles went on to argue for a return to organic production. During the 1990s, a small but increasing number of farms—including some larger dairies—adopted organic methods.[25] In 1997 Ohio had no certified organic dairies, but a few years later there were over one hundred, and 90 percent of them were Amish and Old Order Mennonite.

The shift to organic methods was driven by premium prices for organic products as well as by greater awareness in some Amish communities that, in the words of one farmer, "it was the right thing to do because it fit our beliefs." One convert to organic ways explained that he began to question chemicalized farming and asked himself, "Is this what God expects of us farmers? Should we spray pesticides to kill weeds and insects?"[26] Although he also believed that organic farming was more profitable, he grounded his choice in his religious convictions.

An organic dairy farmer described some of the hurdles to achieving organic certification: no synthetic or chemical fertilizers, no chemically treated seeds for the past three years, no antibiotics, no hormones, and thirty to forty pages of paperwork completed annually for inspection by a certifier. The rules seem complicated at first, he notes, and adds that organic farming is serious business, not an "idyllic vision" for "long-haired, sandaled hippies."[27]

Organic products are sold at the farm, at roadside stands, to small-town grocery stores, and to organic wholesalers who market products for growers. In addition, some Amish-driven marketing ventures have emerged. Twenty Amish leaders in the Holmes County area of Ohio organized Green Field Farms in 2003. Membership in the cooperative is limited to people who use horse-and-buggy transportation. Its purpose is "to oversee the development of profitable markets for agricultural products of our plain communities, and the building of a local economy to support and enable our farmers to thrive."[28] Green Field Farms markets organic products such as eggs, milk, and vegetables. Another example is Lancaster Farm Fresh Cooperative in Lancaster County, Pennsylvania.[29] This organic cooperative distributes a wide assortment of vegetables as well as cream, yogurt, and honey produced by some eighty Amish farms to consumers as far away as New York, Philadelphia, and Baltimore. Farm Fresh has wholesale accounts and also sells directly to individuals who purchase shares in a Community Supported Agriculture (CSA) program. Each retail shareholder receives a weekly summer delivery of organic produce that includes ninety-five varieties of vegetables and fruits.

Intensive Grazing

Intensive rotational grazing is another growing edge in contemporary Amish agriculture. In a rotational grazing system, farmers regularly move cattle from one pasture to another, maximizing cows' access to fresh grass and evenly distributing animal manure across all pastureland. Intensive grazing also minimizes the need to supplement the cows' diet with grain. Most farmers who employ intensive rotational grazing do not milk their cows in the winter months, and they start a new lactation cycle in the spring when the grass returns. This method does not require heavy tillage equipment to plow, till, and harvest feed crops because the main crop is grass. Per-cow milk production is lower than conventional dairies, but so are machinery, labor, and fuel costs. Although grazing is eco-friendly and sustainable, the initial costs (including land) are more expensive than produce farming because rotational grazing requires more acres.

In *Grass-Based Dairy Farming*, fifteen Amish farmers explain their enthusiasm for this method: "We, in the spirit of good land stewardship, are managers of the primary plant of God's creation—grass. We harvest this grass in the most ecologically correct manner we can by our cooperation with the laws of nature and dictates of the bovine species. We then sell her milk as a reward for our stewardship and gain the satisfaction of providing for our families and our communities in a manner that violates neither the earth nor those that tread upon it." The authors argue that grass-based farming "fits our way of life, our values, and our goals, increases rather than depletes the farm's resources, and attracts our children to the farming way of life."[30]

New Ventures

Some other agriculture-related ventures include operating greenhouses, raising animals and birds for pet stores, and raising game animals to sell for hunting on large ranches.[31] In Missouri, a fish farm provides income for one Amish household. In several states, farmers have developed goat dairies to sell milk for cheese because much less land is needed to support a herd of goats than a herd of cows.

In some settlements, greenhouses are especially popular for raising vegetable plants as well as flowers for retail or produce auction sale. Greenhouses are a family-friendly business that require little land and offer a range of tasks that can safely involve the work of even small children. As one woman put it, families want "something they can do out of their home" and noted that her sister could run her new greenhouse "right on the farm."

Raising dogs, rabbits, or guinea pigs for wholesalers who sell them to pet stores provides another source of income in some settlements. In addition to extra cash for the family, these enterprises also often provide experience for children who are learning to work and manage a small business. In other cases, especially with dogs, large-scale breeders may rely on the business for their primary income. In some settlements, Amish breeders have been accused of running "puppy mills" that do not provide proper care for their animals. Although such charges may have been accurate in some cases, those operating registered kennels must meet their state's regulations and pass inspections.

Ecological Sustainability

Although no systematic studies have measured the environmental impact of Amish farming methods, several research projects and ample ethnographic evidence suggests that they minimize ecological harm.[32] Amish farmers use less fossil fuel than non-Amish farmers because they use manual labor, horse power, and manure, and they do not rely on public grid electricity. Amish commitments to small-scale, labor-intensive farming and values such as frugality, simplicity, humility, patience, and modesty combine to reduce ecological injury.

Nevertheless, many Amish farmers use some nonrenewable energy—when running small diesel engines to power hydraulic and pneumatic equipment for dairy operations, for example. Others use gasoline engines on field machinery or to operate elevators, chainsaws, and feed mixers. In addition, Amish manure-handling practices in some communities have increased erosion and water pollution in streams. Furthermore, some households do not properly dispose of the many batteries they use.

Amish lifestyle and technology decisions typically are driven by long-standing Amish values related to family, community, tradition, and separation from the world, rather than by philosophical concepts about sustainability and ecological preservation. Paradoxically, however, even though Amish farm technology and practices are not driven by environmental concerns, Amish values and way of life tend to mitigate environmental harm. In her study of Amish agricultural sustainability, Martine Vonk concludes: "Amish diversified, labor-intensive agriculture is not entirely sustainable in the ecological sense, but certainly has aspects that lead to a low environmental impact."[33]

Since 2000 a growing ecological awareness and concern, prompted by national trends, has emerged in some Amish communities. The resurgence of produce farming, organic products, and rotational grazing has raised the sustainability banner. The 110 members of Green Field Farms in Ohio, for example, describe themselves as "a co-op dedicated to sustainable agriculture." The farmers promoting grazing are explicitly committed to sustainability, environmental friendliness, and reducing fossil fuel consumption. Similarly, the magazine *Farming: People, Land, and Community,* launched in 2001 by several Amish people with the assistance of non-Amish friends, including writer Wendell Berry, has provided a forum for promoting the revitalization of small farms, organic and produce farming, and intensive grazing. The periodical provides practical information "for small-scale diversified farmers" in a way "that offers new perspectives and reasons to hope."[34]

One of *Farming*'s principal writers has been David Kline, an Ohio Amish bishop, naturalist, and author who was a vocal advocate for green issues long before they were trendy in American life.[35] Kline often quotes the words of another bishop: "We should live as if Jesus would return today, and . . . take care of the land as if he would not be coming for 1,000 years."[36]

Historian Steven Stoll notes that the agribusiness industry largely considers Amish farming "nice and good" but irrelevant. The Amish initiatives that support sustainability, Stoll argues, offer hope in the face of an agricultural industry that "tends to destroy the very systems it depends on by polluting and over fertilizing lakes and rivers, by causing soil erosion, by radically simplifying biological diversity, and by requiring the constant combustion of fossil fuels."[37]

Happy Off the Farm?

Because agriculture has been the heart of Amish life for several centuries, it is not surprising that the multitude of changes since 1950 have prompted controversy within Amish circles. Already by the 1980s the growth of outside employment was stirring lively debate about the "lunch pail problem," which arose when fathers carried their lunch to work instead of working on the farm and eating the noon meal with their families. At the same time, some Amish voices claimed that the idyllic view of farming was exactly that: too idyllic. In an essay entitled "Not Everyone Can Be a Farmer," the wife of a shop worker wrote that, despite not living on a farm, "We are a happy family," even though she shoulders more responsibilities for child care with her husband's absence during the day. "Farming," she concluded, "is not the answer to all our problems." More important for her is finding "time for our families and for those better things in life . . . that will count in eternity."[38]

This essay sparked many responses, with writers agreeing that "not everything about farming is desirable." A nonfarm woman confessed, "I have no longing to be a farmer's wife . . . we are content being a happy family." A woman calling herself a "happy day-laborer's wife" wrote that nonfarmers are "left feeling guilty and some-what sinful as if we were on the wrong path somehow," and she noted that "neither Jesus nor his disciples were farmers."[39]

The exchange makes clear that, despite the dramatic shift away from farming in recent decades, some people need to defend their decision to leave the farm even though their off-farm work largely remains in rural settings. In subtle ways, the emotional tie to the land remains strong—so strong, in fact, that some small business owners have returned to the farm. It's not unusual for a successful Amish entrepreneur to sell a business and return to working the soil. One Lancaster Amish man, Elam Beiler, founded a solar business in 1995 that used the sun's rays to recharge batteries for lights on buggies. His company gradually expanded into non-Amish markets, and by 2010 annual sales were $20 million. That year Beiler turned over the management to a non-Amish CEO and moved to Indiana to buy farmland and begin farming with his sons.[40] At the other end of the spectrum, a Swartzentruber Amish man sold his sawmill to his brother and bought a farm when he realized that his sons were becoming quite comfortable speaking English with his non-Amish customers.

The massive transformation of American agriculture—from small scale, low-tech family farms to computerized mega-operations focused on high volume and efficiency and requiring a huge capital investment—has threatened the traditional Amish way of life and its social fabric. Confronted with this new reality, Amish farmers found it difficult to compete without surrendering their family-based operations. As a member of a conservative Andy Weaver group noted, "There are pressures [today that] our forefathers never experienced. The difficulty and cost of farming . . . will influence the Amish a few generations down the road."

The Amish struggle with modern agriculture in twentieth-century America is filled with examples of unflinching resistance, adaptation, and acceptance as Amish people negotiated their way through the rapidly changing maze of American agribusiness. It is also a saga of growing cultural diversity among Amish affiliations and communities across the continent. One of the most consequential outcomes of this struggle has been the growing number of Amish families working off the farm. That is the story to which we now turn.

CHAPTER 16

BUSINESS

As dawn breaks over St. Mary's County, Maryland, Aaron Hertzler and two other Amish men jump into a Ford Explorer driven by an English neighbor. Pulling a trailer filled with tools, they head north to the outskirts of Washington, D.C., where they spend the day installing shingles on a new roof. They use electric tools, listen to their favorite country music on a small radio, and eat lunch with non-Amish subcontractors working on the same building. Back home, Aaron's wife cares for their three preschool children until he returns at about 6:00 p.m. Unless it rains, Aaron follows a similar routine every day of the week except Sunday.

Lunch Pail Work

Many Amish people in communities across North America follow routines similar to that of Aaron Hertzler. Three days a week an Amish woman in Lancaster County rises at 4:00 a.m. to travel by rented van with several other women to Dover, Delaware, where she operates a candy and jelly stand at a farmers' market. In Geauga County, Ohio, east of Cleveland, several members of an Amish household spend their days working in a rubber extruding plant. Near Arthur, Illinois, a van transports eight members of an Amish and English carpentry crew sixty miles to the outskirts of Springfield, where the men spend the day building an addition onto a large home.[1]

These examples demonstrate the occupational realities of many in the Amish world, since some two-thirds of households receive their primary income from non-farm work both inside and outside of their communities. Many work in one of the approximately twelve thousand Amish-owned businesses, while others are employed in non-Amish retail stores, offices, restaurants, factories, or construction firms.[2] These jobs provide new sources of income for Amish people even as the work weaves them more tightly into regional and national economies and challenges Amish convictions about separation from the world. Although sizable numbers of Amish people work for English firms, the most traditional groups have stridently resisted most forms of outside employment. Some permit members to do wage labor for Amish businesses outside their own group, but generally not for English employers.

This diversity of employment is a late twentieth-century phenomenon. Few Amish worked for outside employers before World War II. In 1950 some northern Indiana men were working in factories building travel trailers and boats. Those numbers rose in the 1960s as recreational vehicle plants opened in the region and tapped Amish labor. In many of those factories, the Amish eventually outnumbered the English, creating quasi-Amish workplaces. By the turn of the twenty-first century, nearly 70 percent of Amish men under thirty-five years of age in the Elkhart–LaGrange area of Indiana were working in non-Amish factories, while the proportion that were farming had plummeted to 7 percent.[3]

Building luxury motor homes that they would never purchase does not seem to trouble the Amish. Their church-community is more concerned with how its members spend their paychecks than with the products they produce. Working in outside firms is also the norm in the Nappanee, Indiana, and Geauga County, Ohio, settlements. In these communities, Amish hands work on assembly lines turning out campers, travel trailers, and prefabricated homes; labor with hot-rubber-extruding equipment; and mass-produce furniture and cabinets. Near Yoder, Kansas, Amish employees build cabinetry for corporate jets. In eastern Ohio, they work in large English-owned factories that manufacture garage doors.[4] Rarely do the Amish comprise the entire labor force of a single factory. Amish, Mexican, and Yemeni workers staff a Japanese-managed firm in northern Indiana, for example. In some factories, Amish employees form a subculture—speaking Pennsylvania Dutch more than English as they discuss their off-work lives with their Amish coworkers during breaks.

Occasionally, church leaders have tried to channel occupational change. In the 1950s, a number of men in the Arthur, Illinois, community obtained driver's licenses so they could operate trucks for their non-Amish employers. Fearing this would lead to car ownership, bishops strongly urged members to end outside employment and instead develop their own businesses. The church-dictated change in Arthur was an exception to the rule, however, because employment patterns in most Amish communities change with little formal direction from church leaders.

Local economic and demographic contexts often shape choices. Yet the mere presence of outside jobs in rural communities is not always enough to lure Amish workers. Objections to union membership or contracts that require high school credentials tarnish the appeal of some industries. In north-central Indiana and in Geauga County, Ohio, Amish men are heavily engaged in factory work because non-union shops are common in those locations, and English employers waive company preferences for high school graduates. In contrast, industrial jobs abound in the factory city of Kokomo, Indiana, but local Amish avoid them because the workers are unionized or the employers hire only high school graduates.

In those places where Amish men do gravitate to industrial employment, they find it appealing because the factory makes few demands of off-duty workers. Amish employees see their work as a means to an end, a way to make a living, rather than a source of identity in the way that mainstream Americans might. Few Amish women work in factories, but those who do leave their jobs when they marry. Although Amish men of various ages punch industrial time clocks, younger men—age thirty-five and under—are more firmly ensconced in industry. Furthermore, some men in their fifties exit the factory for less stressful work in small shops or other sideline jobs.[5]

Unlike farming, most outside jobs offer a predictable income. But they also have a down side. All the profits stay in English pockets, and the social ethos is not always conducive to Amish values and practices. Although some employers are willing to let Amish workers take time off for community activities, a rigid production schedule can make this difficult. Moreover, non-Amish employers are required to deduct Social Security taxes from Amish paychecks, tempting Amish workers to later claim some returns, despite the church's opposition. Outside employers also typically offer commercial health insurance and pension benefits, which can undercut the church's long-held conviction that members should help one another bear the burdens of medical costs and care for the elderly. Another consequence of high-paying jobs in English factories is that they force Amish-owned business to dramatically increase wages in order to attract Amish employees.

Finally, when Amish employees are heavily clustered in a particular industry, they risk widespread layoffs if that sector of the economy contracts. During the national recession of 2008–2009, for example, the recreational vehicle industry was hit severely, and hundreds of northern Indiana Amish men were left out of work. For months, households lived from their savings, turned to relatives for support, or, in a few cases, took the unprecedented step of applying for public unemployment assistance. By late 2009 most of the region's manufacturers had begun to rehire, but some former factory employees had other ideas. As Mervin Lehman, an Amish man from Shipshewana, explained, "Our eyes were opened in this recession. All our eggs were in one basket, and we can't have that. So we need to diversify [and] . . . open small businesses." After Lehman was laid off from his factory job in 2008, he started making handcrafted mattresses in his garage. By 2011 his infant business, Heartland Mattress LLC, had "expanded the garage to a 3,600-square-foot manufacturing facility and small showroom." The business is a family affair, with Mervin's wife, Naomi, managing the accounts and their sixteen-year-old daughter helping Mervin stitch queen-size mattresses that sell for $279 to $1,399.[6]

An Amish Industrial Revolution

Heartland Mattress represents the most common Amish alternative to farming: small business entrepreneurship. The Amish stayed on the sidelines of the American Industrial Revolution for a century (1875–1975) by perpetuating a small-farm lifestyle. Nevertheless, in the last quarter of the twentieth century, many Amish communities experienced an industrial revolution of their own (e.g., see fig. 16.1). It was hardly an upheaval by the standards of automated mass production, yet Amish people set up hundreds of their own businesses and hired their fellow Amish as workers.[7]

The foray into businesses was spurred by several factors: the rising cost of land, livestock, and equipment; the decreasing profitability of small-scale agriculture; and the growth of the Amish population. In some settlements there were simply too many Amish and not enough land.

The rise of Amish-owned businesses was a bargain with modernity. The Amish in many areas said, in essence, "We will leave the farm, but instead of punching time clocks in outside factories, we will build our own microenterprises where we can control the terms and conditions of our work and pocket the profits of our toil." This family-friendly bargain meant that many shops could be based at or near home, where grandparents, parents, and children could work together as a productive unit.

Nonfarm work had another appealing incentive. Setting up a farming operation in some settlements could cost a young couple upwards of $2 million dollars in land, animals, and equipment. By contrast, a few thousand dollars was enough to prime and nurture a small business. Working as a laborer in an English factory or an Amish shop required only a lunch box and the cost of transportation, of course. In several settlements, advocates of home-based businesses organized revolving loan funds to supply seed money for Amish microenterprises. The aim, one supporter said, is "getting fathers established at home so they won't have to work away."

Amish-owned businesses have proliferated much more rapidly in some settlements than in others. But even in newer communities, ostensibly established by migrants looking for farmland, many households start small shops. Most Amish businesses are owned by single proprietors, although some are organized as small partnerships or limited liability corporations. The estimated twelve thousand enterprises can be sorted into two broad types: cottage industries that focus on stability and small businesses that pursue profit and growth.[8]

The cottage industries, with fewer than five employees, are usually family-related,

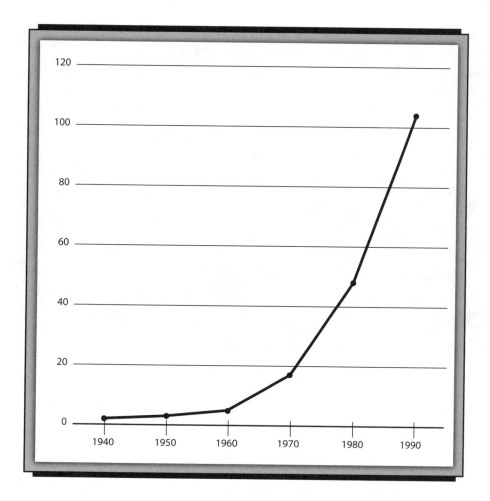

FIGURE 16.1. Rise of Amish Businesses in Thirteen Districts of the Lancaster Settlement, 1940–1990. *Source: Kraybill and Nolt, 2004, 37.*

home-based operations such as small engine repair shops, greenhouses, cabinet shops, quilt shops, carriage or bicycle shops, auction companies, small retail stores, and so on. The owners of these businesses are content with providing a modest income for family members and perhaps a few other employees. Preserving traditional values and keeping the family together, rather than making a profit, are the primary goals of cottage industries. These family-based operations have a custodial and non-entrepreneurial bent that reflects the traditional Amish values of humility and modesty. They are successful, by Amish standards, simply because they provide a stable income for family members and neighbors who work together at or near their homes.

By contrast, growth-oriented small businesses typically have five to thirty employees. They require more investment capital, generate larger sales, and have owners who are more entrepreneurial. As Erik Wesner has shown, these owners, unlike own-

This small Amish business is a sawmill operation in northern New York State. The young family lives in the white "skid house" that can be moved from one site to another. As a family becomes stable economically, they may build a permanent home or acquire a farm or other business. *Donald B. Kraybill*

ers of cottage industries, are more competitive, take more risks, experiment more, articulate a vision for growth, emphasize efficiency and productivity, and seek profits to reinvest in their businesses.[9] Sales volumes range widely, but it is not unusual for larger firms to have annual revenues well above $10 million.

Small or large, many Amish businesses engage in mobile work that most often involves construction-related trades or retail sales at farmers' markets. Construction crews—typically involved in carpentry, excavation, roofing, and other building trades—take a wide range of commercial and residential jobs, from new construction to remodeling. They build, finish, or do subcontract work on barns, industrial buildings, single-family homes, apartment complexes, restaurants, and stores—even structures associated with Amish-themed tourism. Around Dover, Delaware, many Amish men work in masonry and related trades, ironically contributing to the suburban sprawl that has prompted many Amish families to move away. In other parts of the country, some work crews commute two or more hours one way, sleeping overnight in local motels when necessary.

Amish people sell their products in markets in many regions of the country. In the eastern seaboard region from northern New Jersey to the Baltimore-Washington metropolitan area, Amish vendors and workers operate dozens of farmers' markets, and some Amish entrepreneurs even own or lease large buildings and rent market stands to fellow Amish and non-Amish retailers. Other Amish sellers of products such as baked goods, deli items, produce, and preserves rent stands in English-owned markets. Like construction crews, some vendors travel only a few miles, while others travel several hours one way or stay overnight, depending on the distance.

Clearly, although church leaders may have hoped the rise of Amish businesses would eliminate lunch pails, many Amish workers still spend their days far from home and family. Fathers and mothers may work separately from each other in jobs that remove one parent from the homestead, introducing sharp distinctions between the lives of husbands, wives, and children.

The Power of the *Ordnung*

Differences in the Ordnung from one settlement or affiliation to another have produced a diverse pattern of Amish participation in nonfarm employment. The Swiss Amish of Indiana, Missouri, Ohio, New York, and Pennsylvania, for example, prefer mobile construction work because their Ordnungs severely restrict technology in home shops. About 65 percent of male breadwinners in the Adams County, Indiana, settlement, an ethnically Swiss settlement, work in construction away from home and under the more permissive canopy of English work sites.[10]

In all Amish groups, technology rules are usually more lax for those who work away from home. Like a factory employee, a market standholder or subcontractor works on alien turf, usually serving non-Amish customers. By sharply separating their work from their home, mobile workers in many groups are freer to use an array of electrical tools.

The Ordnung also limits or expands the range of entrepreneurial options, depending on the particular affiliation. Some ultraconservative groups require those engaged in carpentry to accept only jobs within buggy-driving distance of home. Amish construction companies in higher communities, however, often have at least one English employee or co-owner who supplies a truck or van. Prohibitions on electric generators in some affiliations have eliminated the possibility of starting welding or machine shops, channeling entrepreneurs into starting woodworking establishments that can operate without electricity.

A flexible Ordnung in liberal settlements allows hydraulic and pneumatic power, electric generators, forklift tractors, cell phones, and third-party access to computers, websites, and e-mail. These technologies permit sizable shops to produce vast quantities of kitchen cabinets, household furniture, farm machinery, and fabricated plastic products, to name just a few. At the other end of the spectrum, traditional groups restrict shop power to a small gas engine that spins a line shaft to operate belt-driven machines, severely reducing their capacity. Moreover, prohibitions on electric inverters and, in some cases, even battery-powered calculators, also diminish output. Such restrictions nudge conservative shops toward making crafts such as wooden baskets that favor intensive handwork over volume.

Products and Services

The diversity and vitality of Amish-owned enterprises is astonishing to many outsiders. *Plain Communities Business Exchange,* a monthly trade newspaper "serving plain communities everywhere," according to its masthead, chronicles business activities and trade shows, and includes advice columns as well as advertisements from suppliers, wholesalers, and retailers of Amish products across the continent.[11] A 400-page business directory produced in one settlement features dozens of four-color ads for Amish firms selling products ranging from solar panels and office furniture to manure spreaders and playground equipment.[12] Likewise, the annual directory of *Amish Woodworkers of America* is filled with color ads for furniture and a listing of hundreds of shops and manufacturing companies in nine states, with a heavy concentration in Ohio and Indiana. The directory aims to help "Amish woodworkers from all over the United States network among each other, buy and sell products across state lines and compete against foreign competition."[13]

Dominant types of Amish businesses include furniture making, farm equipment manufacturing, and construction firms specializing in residential or commercial buildings, as well as related trades such as roofing, plumbing, and painting. Amish retail stores that sell food, clothing, crafts, hardware, equipment, and tools—purchased wholesale from Amish and non-Amish sources—also comprise a sizable segment of business activity. A large number of Amish products are sold through national networks of dealers and wholesalers (Amish and English) who market them across the country.

Some Amish businesses are linked to the global economy. One Amish entrepreneur, for example, buys hand-braided rye straw from China and distributes it to Amish hat makers in at least a dozen states. An Amish inventor of LED lighting fixtures for Amish use relies on Chinese factories to manufacture his products. And European buyers purchase small-scale farm equipment produced by Amish shops.

Small shops in Colorado, Missouri, Maine, Kentucky, Wisconsin—and other places where the Amish are found—make and sell a wide range of goods to both Amish and English customers. Some entrepreneurs operate cleaning or food service businesses. From dry goods stores and welding shops to leather products and furniture making,

Amish enterprises involve male and female entrepreneurs. Table 16.1 offers a sample of the hundreds of types of Amish-owned businesses and services.

The following descriptions illustrate in more detail the broad range of enterprising activities in which Amish people are involved:

- An innovative precision machine shop near Fort Wayne, Indiana, makes brass fittings and couplings for major industrial clients as well as decorative items for gift shops across the country.
- Two unmarried sisters in New York run a thriving stand selling produce and quilts. Their business is built on face-to-face interaction, yet their quilts have been shipped internationally.
- In Pennsylvania, a woman who enjoys flowers, meeting people, and business, developed a booming dried flower enterprise. She sells the flowers and other gift items in a retail store on her property and through mail order.
- A large firm in Ohio manufactures horse-drawn equipment that is sold to both Amish people and non-Amish horse enthusiasts around the world.
- Without using a cell phone or e-mail, an Amish man developed a food retail business with $1.8 million in sales, using mail order and a national network of distributors.[14]
- An Indiana couple started a bakery in their home. Their operation grew rapidly, and their products soon found their way to downtown Chicago. Although they sold the company to English neighbors who opened two retail outlets in the Windy City, the Amish couple still runs the day-to-day operations.[15]
- East of Kalona, Iowa, an Amish man operates a large "bent and dent" store for both Amish and non-Amish patrons. The store sells heavily discounted bulk-sized dry and canned foods that have been removed from the shelves of grocery chains because of damage to the containers or soon-to-expire "sell by" dates.[16]

Local conditions often shape the direction and limits of off-farm work. Proximity to major markets or interstate highways may invite certain types of business, as might the historical tradition of a particular settlement. Long-term relationships with non-Amish neighbors also can provide technical expertise, offer ready customers, and garner civic support for Amish enterprises. Then, too, nearby industrial jobs or tourist traffic may open some economic doors while closing others.

Such factors alone, however, do not fully explain the various types of nonfarm enterprises. The literal landscape, coupled with the contours of the regional econ-

Table 16.1. A Sampler of Amish Businesses

Construction
Residential
Commercial
Log houses
Storage sheds
Metal buildings

Crafts
Folk art
Hats
Quilts
Toys
Baskets

Food Production
Baked goods
Deli products
Health foods
Jams and candies

Installation
Air pumps and systems
Fence installation
Floor covering
Storm windows and glass
Solar systems

Machine and Metal
Hydraulic systems
Machinery assembly
Machinery manufacturing
Machinery repair
Welding and fabricating

Manufacturing
Carriages
Doors (home and garage)
Lanterns and lighting
Vinyl products

Retail Operations
Books
Bulk foods
Clothing and footwear
Dry goods

Farm supplies
Farmers' markets
Garden supplies
Greenhouses
Groceries
Hardware
Household appliances
Quilts and crafts
Roadside stands

Services
Accounting
Auctioneering
Battery and electrical work
Butchering
Clock and watch repair
Engine repair
Horse shoeing
Leather and harness
Printing
Sewing
Spray painting
Tent rentals
Upholstery
Tombstone engraving
Tree trimming

Trades
Carriage restoration
Foundry
Masonry
Plumbing
Roofing and siding
Painting
Tin fabrication

Woodworking
Cabinetry
Furniture (household)
Furniture (lawn)
Kitchens
Hardwood lumber
Sawmills

omy, also plays a decisive role. Marginal farmland and local economies that foster wood-related businesses encourage the development of sawmills, furniture-making businesses, and other lumber-related work. In western Pennsylvania, for example, a regional economy oriented toward forestry and connected to suppliers of wood products has provided wholesale outlets for remote communities far from urban retail markets.

A loose friendship network that crisscrosses settlements and affiliations supports and energizes Amish enterprises. Since 1981 Amish woodworkers have gathered annually to discuss the latest developments in cabinetry, millwork, and furniture making. Accountants, harness and buggy makers, machine shop operators, and quilters hold similar gatherings.[17] Unlike trade shows that convene in hotels or convention centers, these events, often referred to as reunions, rotate among Amish communities, and attendees board in local homes. Participants often bring their families, because the multi-day gatherings can wrap work, vacation, travel, and reunion into a single trip.

Cultural Resources and Restraints

One way of conceptualizing Amish businesses is to see them as the outcome of a tension between *resources* and *restraints* in Amish society, as shown in figure 16.2. Amish cultural values both invigorate and obstruct microenterprises. Resources in the Amish social capital reservoir include a rigorous work ethic, a frugality that minimizes overhead costs, a pool of ethnic labor, entrepreneurial skills forged on the farm, large extended families, and a distinctive "Amish" brand that makes their products attractive. These assets, similar across settlements, supply ample social and cultural capital for the formation and success of Amish businesses.[18]

Other factors, at least at first blush, thwart business success. Cultural restraints on litigation, public electricity, motor vehicle and computer ownership, sales on Sunday, formal education, and commercial insurance, as well as the values of *Gelassenheit*—humility, modesty, smallness, and deference to others—stifle the ability of Amish businesses to be competitive. These cultural factors can retard the entrepreneurial spirit and impede business development.

The interplay between cultural resources and restraints varies from place to place, demonstrating the decisive role of local conditions in shaping commercial activities. Nonetheless, Amish enterprises are negotiated outcomes—compromises between energizing assets and cultural restraints.

But this is not the end of the story. As microenterprises grow and flourish, they affect traditional beliefs and practices, altering the very values that birthed them in the first place. The new material realities—businesses fostered by Amish values—

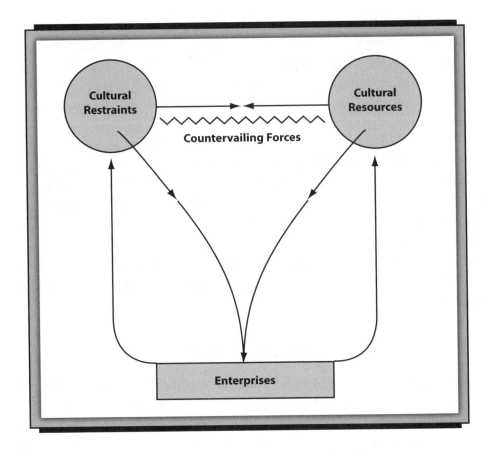

FIGURE 16.2. An Interactive Model of Amish Businesses

are now revising long-entrenched views about individualism, gender roles, social equality, rationality, and separation from the world. In short, this mini-industrial revolution is transforming Amish life in ways that will produce significant long-term consequences.

Failure and Success

Failure

The story of Amish-owned businesses is a remarkable tale of business neophytes without high school diplomas launching successful enterprises that have flourished despite many technological limits and cultural obstacles. All evidence points to a failure rate for Amish businesses that is below 10 percent, far lower than the 50 percent and higher estimates for mainstream small-business failures.[19] The low Amish default rate is even more remarkable because it includes some business closures related to retirement or migration.

Amish informants confirm that there are very few business failures. An accountant for dozens of businesses said, "I can't think of any that have failed in our local four or five districts over the past fifteen years." Likewise, an Amish leader in another settlement, familiar with hundreds of businesses, estimated that fewer than 10 percent fail in the first five years.

Non-Amish professionals who work closely with Amish owners concur. An attorney for hundreds of Amish limited liability companies said, "I don't know of any Amish business foreclosures in our community. There are sales and transfers to other individuals, but not typical liquidations." Likewise, a certified public accountant with dozens of Amish clients estimates that 90 to 95 percent of businesses survive beyond five years, a rate that he calls "significantly high." An official at a bank that has $125 million in loans to Amish small businesses puts their failure/closure rate well below 10 percent. "In the last ten years we never had any of our Amish clients go into foreclosure, nor have we had to force a sale," he said.

Commenting on businesses in his settlement, one Amish elder noted, "I don't know of any that filed for bankruptcy. That would be very discouraged and unheard of here." Yet, although bankruptcy is rare, some businesses do disappear because of financial pressure. Several Amish construction companies folded during the 2008–2009 recession because of the weak housing market. Other small contractors were "on life support and some are owed substantial sums [from non-Amish customers]," which are unlikely to be paid," according to one financial advisor. Some enterprises, such as sawmills and furniture manufacturers, eased production, shortened their work week, or furloughed employees during the recession. One consultant noted that, although low-tech sawmills have been a favorite Amish industry, "now they're in a major funk. Yet, I know of no mill that has shut down and not paid creditors." Because most Amish businesses are small and have low debt leverage, they can, as one English observer put it, "adjust very quickly to downsizing and market flux."

Reasons for business failure include inept management, flimsy products, inadequate capital, changing markets, and tepid product promotion. Some Amish-owned businesses close because they are victims of unscrupulous companies that subcontract with them to produce products and then default on payment, banking on the fact that the Amish will not sue. One conservative Amish farm family in upstate New York accepted a contract to attach baskets to lacrosse sticks. Paid by the unit, they assembled an average of 1,000 sticks each week until the distributer went bankrupt, owing the family several thousand dollars.

When an Amish business does falter to the point of failure, the church may step in to help. Generally, three trustees are appointed to nurse the operation back to profitability or, if necessary, sell it. The local *Gmay* appoints a trustee, the owner in trouble invites a trustee, and those two select a third one. The trio forms a temporary management team that provides advice and, if necessary, assumes power of attorney and executes corrective measures to rehabilitate the business. This church-based "insurance" provides a form of mutual aid for ailing businesses and underscores the fact that ultimately they exist under the wing of the church.

Success

Why have Amish businesses enjoyed abundant success? Both internal and external factors help to explain their robust growth. Certainly the hardy Amish work ethic and embrace of frugality and austerity are key reasons. Moreover, Amish businesses draw on a readily available pool of ethnic and family labor with shared values and worldview. Limited overhead costs also enhance profitability. Many Amish businesses do not provide commercial health insurance or pension plans for their Amish employees because those needs are covered individually or by the Amish community.

In addition, cultural restraints may, ironically, turn into advantages. The taboo on high school, for example, limits men to three career tracks: farming, business ownership, and wage labor. So the would-be surgeons, pilots, teachers, engineers, and software gurus become entrepreneurs in the Amish world. The lid on formal education has also spurred Amish-style vocational training that immerses youth in informal apprenticeships for lifelong technical, manufacturing, and management positions.

Furthermore, the insistence on small-scale operations keeps businesses small, allowing other Amish entrepreneurs to run similar operations in a limited market region. It is not uncommon for owners of growing businesses to divide their firms or spin off certain product lines to adult children or other employees in order to keep a business within culturally acceptable limits. Such strategic downsizing means that, instead of a handful of large factories that concentrate business wealth in the hands of a few, hundreds of owners enjoy the delights of entrepreneurship. Even those who are employees rather than business owners are close to the action and part of a small-team effort.

Surprisingly, the technological constraints on telephones, public grid electricity, and motor vehicles have also become resources. Communicating by postal mail instead of e-mail, answering phones only at certain hours, and using compressed air instead of electricity accentuate the uniqueness of Amish wares and add cachet for customers wanting a distinctive product.

External factors also favor Amish commerce. For example, on religious grounds, self-employed Amish business owners and their Amish employees are exempt from paying into Social Security (or tapping its benefits). Some states also exempt Amish businesses from participation in workers' compensation because private church aid covers the costs of members' job-related injuries. Such exemptions reduce payroll costs for Amish owners and increase their businesses' profitability.

The strength of regional economies and markets can also help to boost profits. Amish communities located within reach of Chicago, Cleveland, Washington, D.C., and Philadelphia benefit from urban markets hungry for Amish products ranging from food to furniture. Amish-themed tourist markets in the larger settlements attract millions of visitors who relish Amish-made products.

That the Amish are recognizable as a distinctive people also benefits their businesses. The mystique of Amish life creates a branding effect so potent that some English companies use a buggy logo or phrases like "Amish Country" to sell non-Amish products. Like the label *Starbucks* or the golden arches of McDonalds, the word *Amish* and the horse-and-buggy emblem perform magic in the marketplace. Similarly, Amish dress standards, which restrict a member's freedom of choice, also announce the presence of Amish workers at job sites. A federal exemption from the hardhat rule at construction sites—in deference to church tradition—spotlights traditional ethnic headgear and offers eye-catching on-site advertising at no cost.

What does the Amish label mean? It stirs nostalgic feelings for the past—images of early Americana, small neighborhoods, and strong families—and it suggests durable products handcrafted with care by hardworking people. Accurate or not, these meanings embedded in the Amish brand capture the imaginations of consumers. From furniture to food, Amish-made or Amish-associated products carry implied stories of America's past and of the values of an exotic people who have spurned the modern world. Regardless of its veracity, the Amish brand stokes sentiments that entice consumers.

Gender at Work

Women in all settlements work as employees and entrepreneurs. Although some women work full time, many more have part-time jobs performing cleaning services for English neighbors or working in restaurants, farmers' markets, and other businesses owned by Amish or non-Amish people. At least 15 percent of Amish-owned businesses in Lancaster County are owned by women.[20] As growing children assume more household chores, a mother might begin a small at-home shop for sideline income, as one woman did by starting a small bulk-foods store in her basement. When women start businesses, they typically enter traditionally female occupations: cleaning, baking, sewing, and gardening. This gendered pattern is extending in new directions as some Amish women have become Pampered Chef consultants. Female-owned businesses target either Amish or outside markets, or often both.

An Amish woman in a progressive settlement displays Christmas items in the dried flower shop she owns. An air-powered ceiling fan (*left*) and a propane light (*center*) are attached to the ceiling. The cash register is battery powered. *Daniel Rodriguez*

In many settlements, women have roadside stands selling produce, baked goods, and craft items. In eastern Cattaraugus County, New York, 37 of the 108 Amish shops in a county brochure reflect traditional women's work—quilts, baked goods, jams and jellies. If a woman's stand prospers, her husband may use it to sell his wood-working crafts. Businesses such as one offering "quilts, wall hangings, pillows, fruits, vegetables in season, maple syrup, & buggy shop" are likely a joint effort of husband and wife.

One woman bakes cookies in her home for a local restaurant. "Christmas is in high gear at the restaurant," she wrote. "I work—2 days a week. We've been doing Christmas cookies, all kinds. If I understood right, we have 800 doz. . . . I've frosted enough trees and stars to do it in my sleep!" An Amish woman in southeastern Michigan began cleaning houses and then expanded her cleaning service to include businesses, among them several automobile dealerships. Regardless of their specialty, women entrepreneurs contribute significantly to the economic well-being of their families.[21] Entering business gives women more access to money and resources and also to the outside world. Women are gaining economic power, perhaps expanding their influence within their own families and communities as well. Some of the Amish business owners in Lancaster County, for example, now employ their husbands.[22]

On the other hand, changing patterns of employment may actually restrict the role of women in Amish life. Some leaders fret because young fathers employed away from home are unable to work with their offspring or teach them occupational skills and thus mothers must carry a greater burden for child supervision. Furthermore, when married women remain at home while their husbands work outside, the sharp separation between the public realm of men's labor and the private world of family turns the "two kingdoms" of Amish religion into gendered domains.[23]

As wage employment outside the community becomes more common for men, it may increase the power of patriarchy in male-female relationships.[24] Men become able to engage in secular activities that women, at home with the children, cannot. One young woman noted, for example, that her father often stops for coffee in town, but her mother is seldom able to go away. In addition, wage labor provides men with a tangible regular income and a defined work day, while women, occupied with the never-ending tasks of child rearing, cooking, and cleaning, are less able to point to concrete accomplishments. Thus, it is still unclear exactly how changing work patterns will transform gender roles.

Tradition and Transformation
Unchanging Traditions

Even as occupational change is transforming Amish society in significant ways, many components of Amish life remain stable. New employment venues have not lured Amish people into high school or college, and the line between automobile use and ownership remains firm. Using new technologies in English factories or on construction sites may actually cement, rather than dilute, Amish notions of separateness because these encounters with the fruits of modernity occur on alien turf.

Nor is the family—that keystone of Amish society—necessarily harmed by changing work habits. Sociologist Thomas J. Meyers has shown that there is little difference in the number of children born to the families of farmers, factory workers, and shop owners in northern Indiana. Nor in that same settlement are defection rates different for children of farm and nonfarm families. Likewise, Lawrence Greksa and Jill Korbin found that Amish farm families in Geauga County, Ohio, had slightly *higher* rates of defection than families with fathers employed in shops, factories, or construction. Indeed, greater differences emerge among settlements than among the occupational segments within a settlement. Gender, public school attendance, proximity to town, and the Ordnung of their Gmay may all be more influential in an Amish teen's decision for or against church membership than her or his father's occupation.[25]

Work Transforming Culture

Yet economic shifts do have profound implications for Amish life—the use of time, family relationships, access to capital and consumer goods, interaction with the wider world, and one's sense of self. Increasingly common are church districts with no farmers, vanloads of men working on construction sites miles away from home, and business advertising that mocks the traditional value of humility. While none of the new occupational ventures signals the end of Amish society, they are certainly changing it. These changes bring a host of potential problems and possibilities to be faced by Amish communities as they decide what to preserve and what to concede.

A major consequence of nonfarm employment for both business owners and wage earners is disposable income. Although, in Amish eyes, wealth should not be conspicuously displayed, it nonetheless produces inequality. When firms have grown too large, some church communities have encouraged or occasionally forced owners to sell them to English buyers. But the end result, ironically, can be an ex-owner with now even more money and free time. The Ordnung and community concerns guide how some of that money is spent—channeling portions of it into underwriting Amish school buildings or funding land trusts that provide first mortgages for newly married couples—but the dollars are also used for landscaping, concrete driveways, eating out, second buggies, big-game hunting trips, and motorboats.

Another byproduct of working away from home is leisure time. Unlike farming or small cottage industries, manufacturing and construction jobs have limited hours. Greater discretionary time brings new leisure activities such as fishing, boating, shopping at the local Walmart, traveling, and playing sports—and more time to spend on them. Free time for the children of parents working away from home is also an issue, because the families of day laborers often live on small tracts that may include a horse stable and a tiny pasture, but hardly enough room for a large garden or other outdoor chores to keep young ones busy and out of mischief.

Traditional notions of church-based mutual aid may also change with the rise of nonfarm employment. Amish employees in English businesses must pay into the Social Security system. Although the church discourages them from collecting government benefits, they are legally free to do so, and anecdotal evidence suggests that some retired factory workers, in fact, do collect.[26] Some Amish businesses assist with employee health insurance (Amish or commercial) and provide retirement funds through 401(k) saving accounts. These developments do not spell an end to traditional mutual aid, but they do suggest that in some communities individuals are taking responsibility for functions that have long been the obligation of the entire church.

Amish business owners operate farmers' markets in urban areas on the East Coast. The market in Annapolis, Maryland, is on the first floor of a large cinema in an upscale shopping area. *Donald B. Kraybill*

Cottage industries can also bring technological changes into the heart of Amish life. For example, in higher communities at-home businesses often have a telephone on the property (although not in the house), which can disrupt the normal routine of family life. If the enterprise is a retail business catering to non-Amish customers, there may be more conversations in English than would ever occur in the home of a farmer or even a factory worker. For precisely such reasons, some conservative communities want to keep home-based enterprises quite small or forbid them altogether.

Furthermore, trying to grow a business larger requires calculation and strategic planning skills. Consciously trying to please customers and thinking about how to make products more attractive and expand market share is a hallmark of successful entrepreneurship. Developing new products, boosting production efficiencies, and pursuing new markets require a rationality that challenges traditional sources of church-based authority.

Most importantly, businesses have created a three-tiered society. The Amish have never advocated absolute socioeconomic equality because, as one member noted, "There have always been a few wealthy Amish." Nevertheless, the traditional farm economy placed everyone on a fairly equal socioeconomic level. All of that has changed. Commercial ventures have sorted Amish society into traditional farmers, business owners, and day laborers. The farmers have collateral wealth in their land, but often have little cash at hand. In general, farm families tend to be more conservative, reflecting plainer, more traditional values. Day laborers in shops and on farms have a steady cash flow and may enjoy a comfortable standard of living in the Amish economy, but they generally do not have significant wealth.

Business owners, however, represent a commercial class new to Amish society. As bright, astute managers, some of them question traditional ways and press for change. Through self-motivation and experience, they have become proficient entrepreneurs. They understand the larger social system and interact easily with outside suppliers, technicians, business colleagues, customers, attorneys, and credit officers, from whom they have learned marketing strategies and profit ratios. They walk a tightrope between traditional Amish culture and the pressure for profit in a competitive world. Indeed, some church leaders worry that the pursuit of profit may be an ugly worm inside the rosy apple of success, and some believe that prosperity is as dangerous as persecution. "Pride and prosperity could do us in," said one elder, and he wonders whether the church can motivate the commercial class to use its resources for community enhancement rather than for self-indulgence.

If the move away from farming is changing Amish society from within, it is also reshaping relations with the larger world of neighbors, local government, media, and public opinion. Amish entrepreneurs who want to establish small businesses on farms may clash with agricultural zoning rules in some settlements, giving local officials contradictory signals: that they want to preserve farmland while building shops on it. Some municipalities proactively engage Amish businesspeople in discussions about proposed commercial zoning or other ordinances in order to preempt potential conflicts. At the same time, the desire to escape government regulation has motivated some Amish to move to less-populated places with few zoning restrictions, where locals welcome them as a force for economic revitalization.

Amish firms in rural economies create jobs and turn out taxable products without demanding government start-up loans or other public perks—an economic fact not lost on many civic leaders. In some depressed areas new Amish settlements have pumped up land values, increased tax revenue, and seeded new businesses. Amish enterprises are closely tied to tourism in some regions, which also pleases those with economic development interests. Although English entrepreneurs dominate Amish-themed tourism in all areas, Amish people are, of course, a vital piece of the puzzle. In all these ways, Amish entrepreneurs have gained a reputation as an economic asset among local and state officials almost everywhere.

Neither Separation nor Assimilation

Their stunning success in entrepreneurship, construction, and factory work has tied Amish people into the mainstream economy as never before. These developments are transforming their traditional way of life in ways that will reverberate across generations. The rise of nonfarm employment may at first glance suggest that these separatists have assimilated into American society and lost their cultural soul. Clearly, nothing unmasks the myth of Amish isolation like an examination of Amish involvement in nonfarm work. On the other hand, nothing better illustrates the resilient and dynamic character of their separatist culture. Amish enterprises demonstrate the interplay of continuity and change that mark the Amish journey in the modern world. Willing to adapt to changing times, the Amish are also keenly committed to drawing lines of distinction and making choices driven by religious and cultural criteria. If anything, Amish success in the world of work has helped to cement their claim that avoiding the lures of high school and college will not leave them destitute.

Regardless of how the Amish steer their way through the turbulent economic currents of the twenty-first century—in cottage industries, at job sites, in factories, or at urban farmers' markets—they will negotiate with cultural resources aplenty. The future will surely challenge Amish communities as they struggle to maintain a tradition of separation while engaging the world in new ways. Their capacity to renegotiate their identity in the midst of liquid modernity and technological innovation will be vital to their survival and success.

CHAPTER 17

TECHNOLOGY

Prohibited from using electric clothes dryers, Amish families have always air-dried their laundry by hanging it outdoors. In 2007 an Amish hardware store in Charm, Ohio, bought European-manufactured, electricity-powered stainless steel spin dryers and modified them to run by compressed air. The spinners were an instant hit with Amish customers, and the store began importing "container loads" of spinners from across the Atlantic. Amish shops in other states soon got into the act, making and selling their own customized versions of the clothing spinner. "They make the clothes so dry you can wear them right away on a hot day!" one Amish man exclaimed. An Amish woman called the spinner "the best thing since sliced bread!"

Technologically Impaired?

Limits on technology are the signature mark of twenty-first century Amish identity. Riding in horse-drawn buggies and living unplugged from the public grid unmistakably separate Amish people from mainstream Americans. In his 1996 satirical music video "Amish Paradise," singer "Weird Al" Yankovic calls the Amish "technologically impaired."[1] Other observers have called them Luddites, presuming they are anti-technology like the followers of Ned Ludd, a legendary nineteenth-century British activist who opposed new technology at the dawn of the Industrial Revolution out of a desire to protect cottage industries.[2]

Yet the Amish do not categorically condemn technology in Luddite fashion, as the clothes spinner example clearly illustrates. Nor are they technologically naive. Rather, Amish communities selectively sort out what might help or harm them. They categorically prohibit some technology—television, for example. Yet most groups accept the newest binoculars and camping gear without reservation. More significantly, the Amish *modify* and *adapt* technology in creative ways to fit their cultural values and social goals. Amish technologies are diverse, complicated, and ever-changing.[3]

Amish identity was not closely linked to technology in the nineteenth century because Amish farm and household technologies were similar to those of their rural neighbors. In fact, some Amish farmers were among the first in their regions to purchase new styles of horse-drawn machinery. Although church leaders who attended the national Amish ministers' meetings from 1862 to 1878 expressed concerns about consumer goods, musical instruments, and photographs, they did not discuss technology itself. Distinctive Amish responses to technology began to emerge only in the twentieth century as the fruits of the late Industrial Revolution—driven by electrification and advanced transportation—moved into rural America. The telephone was the first item to receive a cool reception in Amish communities, but as cars, tractors, radios, televisions, and computers rolled off assembly lines, they too were rejected.[4]

The Amish story reveals the struggle of a small religious group as it tried to cushion the jolt of technological development. Yet, even as the Amish have sought to moderate technology's impact on human interaction and social organization, they raise broader questions about technological determinism: Can humans tame technology, or does it control our destiny?[5] In the words of technology writer Kevin Kelly, "Has the enormity and cleverness of our creation overwhelmed our ability to control or guide it?"[6]

The Amish, arguably more than any other group in America, have tried to domesticate technology so that its potent force does not overwhelm or cripple their culture. Their effort has been moderately successful for more than a century, but only because it has been a collective project. The Amish offer a profound example of one group's deliberate attempts to modulate the pervasive power of technology to shape the character of individual and corporate life.

Deep Assumptions

A Religious Canopy

Several deep assumptions inform and frame Amish views of technology. Unlike life in highly differentiated modern societies, Amish life remains under the religious canopy of the local *Gmay*. Thus it is the church-community, not the individual, that makes major choices about technology. This does not mean that the church makes decisions for families in every regard, but it does provide guidelines—and sometimes specific directives—for technological practice. A district might permit propane-powered refrigerators, for example, but the type, size, and model are left up to each household.

Technology guidelines are dictated by tradition and the *Ordnung*. Decisions made in members' meetings carry authority because they are sanctioned by the church and therefore, the Amish believe, endorsed in heaven. In contrast to mainstream society, in which individuals make decisions about technology based on personal preferences, the ultimate authority in Amish society lies in the church-community. With more than two thousand congregations, this means there are dozens of different Amish practices related to any particular technology.

Separation from the World

As we noted in chapter 4, the Amish believe that the church should keep some social distance from the larger society. Technology can reach across this divide in two ways. First, many forms of technology can directly expose Amish people to the values and lifestyles of the larger culture. In the early twentieth century, the telephone, for example, established a direct tie to the outside world. Later developments—public grid electricity, radio, television, and the Internet—all offered easy access to popular culture.

In addition, some forms of technology, while not direct conduits to the larger world, can modify the lifestyle and social structure of Amish society. For instance, an appliance like a dishwasher diminishes the value of collective work. A car increases mobility and might eventually unravel the fabric of relationships in the local Gmay. Using large tractors for field work could expand the size of Amish farms and lead to profit-driven agribusiness. The Amish fear that, in the long run, technologies such as these will not only change their traditional way of life but pave the way for its disintegration.

Dangerous But Not Wrong

In the Amish mind, technology itself is not considered sinful or immoral. Like a knife, which can cut bread or kill someone, tools can be used to help or to harm, to build up or to tear down communities. "A car is not immoral," said one bishop, "it's what it will do to our community—it's about the next generation." Their fundamental fear is that a particular technology will alter the bonds of community over time. "What will it lead to next?" Amish people often ask. They do not contend that anyone who drives a car is going to hell, but they are leery that car ownership could eventually demolish their community.

An Amish leader explains the assumption of moral neutrality this way: "We do not consider modern inventions to be evil in and of themselves. A car, or even a television set, is a material thing—made of plastic, wood, or metal. It is the use of it that is wrong." Misuse of technology carries moral risk. The same man continues, "The moral decay of these last days has gone hand in hand with lifestyle changes made possible by modern technologies. The connection between the two needs to be examined with care." Finally, he says, "When our possessions become the master and we the servants, we are in bondage."[7]

Responses to Technology

Amish communities have dealt with technology in five ways: rejection, acceptance, adaptation, invention, and distinguishing between ownership and access. Amish affiliations vary in their mode of response. The most traditional groups reject more, adapt less, and invent less than liberal churches. The Swartzentrubers, for example, virtually froze their technology practices after they formed in 1913. In fact, one of their bishops said, "I can count the new devices on six fingers." In sharp contrast, other Amish affiliations accepted or adapted hundreds of state-of-the-art technologies as the twentieth century unfolded.

Rejection

The decisive Amish *no* to both the car and public grid electricity within the last century has helped to preserve the pre-industrial character of their life.[8] Those decisions slowed the pace of change, shaped Amish identity, and stymied social discourse with mass culture. The Amish have been most adamant, however, in their rejection of communication and entertainment technology. Radio, television, video, smartphones, and the Internet are disallowed because they could transmit the vices of modern culture directly into Amish homes. One leader condemns television with these words: "Satan has, no doubt, used it more effectively to bring about the state of the modern world than any other tool which has been produced. Satan's plan is working—men have been given the rope, and they are absorbed in hanging themselves."[9] The ban on television is rarely contested because it makes practical as well as religious sense to keep a healthy distance from what the Amish see as the moral acids of modernity that are delivered by television.

Acceptance

Progress-minded groups have accepted many nonelectric technologies—lawn mowers, chain saws, farm machinery, milking machines, gas grills, children's toys, detergents, and pesticides. A host of factory-fresh air-powered and battery-operated tools have been warmly received by many Amish groups. Battery-powered cash registers, word processors, scales, and copy machines are used in many communities, and battery-powered LED lights are used on many buggies and in homes and shops. State-of-the-art archery, hunting, and volleyball equipment as well as in-line skates are common in many places. Of course, in the more traditional settlements, most new technological gadgets, including LED lights, are not welcome.

Adaptation

Because technology options are not always clear choices between rejection and acceptance, the Amish often tinker with devices to disarm their potential harm to the community or refashion them in ways that mesh with Amish values.[10] These modifications are cultural compromises that enable communities to tame the power of certain technologies so that they can use them. The tinkering is evidence of a culture of innovation that exists within a community of restraints.[11]

Such adaptations in the home include using small air motors to operate sewing machines and food processors, air pumps to pull water out of wells, and propane gas to power stoves and refrigerators and to heat water. Modifications on the farm include using battery-powered agitators to stir milk in large stainless steel tanks and diesel engines to operate vacuum milkers. In addition, the rubber tires on tractors are replaced with steel wheels to render the tractors unusable for highway transportation, and farm machines—designed to be pulled and powered by tractors—are retrofitted with gasoline engines so the machines can be pulled by horses.

Some Amish groups permit battery-powered word processors but not computers. With the help of non-Amish computer technicians, one Old Order Mennonite inventor developed what he called a Classic Word Processor—a modified computer with a Linux operating system, a small monitor, and word processing and spreadsheet software, but no capabilities for e-mail, Internet access, video games, or other interactive media. The operating system restricts the addition of third-party software. Because standard computers are off-limits for Amish firms, the Classic Word Processor is a boon to business owners for managing inventory, payroll, and accounting. The device exemplifies how the community domesticates technology by adapting it for its own purposes. Several competing Amish-modified "computers" are now also available.

Invention and Innovation

Amish mechanics and self-taught engineers are quite resourceful. Early in the twentieth century, an Amish man invented a threshing machine governor to control the speed of the conveyor feeding sheaves of wheat into the machine.[12] If the engine began to stall because there were too many sheaves going into the thresher, the governor slowed the conveyor belt to prevent the engine from choking. Decades later, another inventor built small compressed air motors to operate large cooling fans and water pumps, and yet another made a battery-powered pollinator for tomato plants.

A team of Amish inventors solved a problem faced by families who use propane gas to fuel stoves, refrigerators, and portable lights. Stoves and refrigerators connected to outside propane tanks use gas at a psi (pounds per square inch) that is too low to fuel propane lamps. Amish "engineers" worked on the problem for six years until they were able to create a lamp in 2002 that would burn brightly and quietly even though it used gas at the same pressure as stoves and refrigerators.[13] Thus, all the gas fixtures in a home could draw on the same propane source, eliminating the need for separate propane canisters for portable lamps. This invention also made it possible to connect wall-mounted lamps to a central gas distribution system.

Ownership versus Access

In their struggle to harness technology, the Amish have also drawn a distinction between *ownership* and *access*. This demarcation grants access to the power of technology without placing it completely in the hands of individuals, thereby preserving historic boundaries around Amish identity while harvesting some of the fruits of progress. The distinction developed early in the twentieth century when the Amish confronted the telephone. The church forbade the installation of telephones in homes, but most communities permitted the *use* of public telephones for business and emergency calls.

The Amish took a similar approach to transportation. Even as they rejected the private ownership of motor vehicles beginning in the 1920s, some communities permitted the hiring of "taxis"—vehicles owned and operated by non-Amish drivers—for transportation to distant weddings, funerals, reunions, and for some business trips.

The line between use and ownership applies to self-propelled machines, electricity, computers, and office equipment. A man who works as a groundskeeper for a local motel is permitted to operate the motel's riding lawn mower but not to buy his own. The proprietor of a quilt shop may use electric lights because she rents the building from a non-Amish neighbor. Another Amish woman works as the receptionist at a real estate office, where she operates the computer on a regular basis, but she cannot have one at home. Some Amish business owners hire neighbors or third-party vendors to provide computer services, website operations, and e-mail service for their businesses. Contractors may lease specialized equipment for construction jobs as needed.

These hybrid practices illustrate how distinguishing ownership from use enables access to technology without granting unfettered access. The most traditional groups, however, rarely permit access to any "dangerous" technology that they would not own.

To the outside eye, these practices might appear inconsistent—and the traditionalists would agree. Yet the more liberal communities contend that the distinction between use and ownership provides access to needed technological power while reminding everyone about the boundaries, the dangers, and the church's oversight.

A Spectrum of Restraint

The guidelines for technology use not only vary among affiliations but also within them. Most groups have a spectrum of restraint stretching across six sites of Amish life: school, home, farm, shop, away-from-home jobs, and work for outsiders. Restrictions on technology are most severe in Amish schools and most relaxed in work for non-Amish employers. Overall, households have more restrictions than farms, and shops have more than construction sites.

Schools

Apart from a battery-powered clock, a stove for heating, and a hand-operated pump, most schools have few technological accessories—no calculators, computers, science laboratories, telephones, and in many areas, not even indoor plumbing. School technology varies by church affiliation. Although some schools have copy machines and indoor plumbing, the technology is generally more limited than in the homes of the school's students.

This minimalist approach ensures that schools send a clear message to students: technology is not important! Such a countercultural statement differs starkly from education in modern society, in which schools scramble to stay abreast of the ever-accelerating pace of new technology. In the Amish world, technological competence is simply not considered critical for one's vocation or life satisfaction. Thus, the school provides a protected setting, undisturbed by technological intrusion, for nurturing children in Amish ways.

Home

The periodic use of Amish homes for church services, weddings, and funerals underscores their sacredness. Home life undergirds and nurtures the entire social system.

**Table 17.1. Amish Household Technology in
Traditional and Progressive Affiliations**

Technology	Traditional	Progressive
Water	Gravity flow	Pressurized
Hot water	Heated on stove	Propane heater
Bathroom	Outhouse	Modern indoor bathroom
Kitchen stove	Wood or kerosene	Propane gas
Refrigeration	Ice box or none	Propane refrigeration
Freezer	None	Propane freezer
Food processor	None	Compressed air
Sewing machine	Treadle power	Compressed air or electric*
Washing machine	Gasoline engine	Compressed air
Clothes dryer	None	Spinner
House heat	Wood stove	Propane stove
House lights†	Kerosene lanterns	Propane wall fixtures
Clocks	Wind up	Battery powered
Telephone	None	Landline†† or cell
Reading lights	None	Battery or solar powered

*From inverter or generator.
†About twenty New Order congregations permit connections to the public electric grid.
††On the property but outside the house.

In pre-industrial fashion, the home is the site of most social functions, including birthing, family meals, religious services, childcare, family prayers, and, for many Amish families, work. Because the home is the hub of Amish life, leaders are careful to protect it from worldly influences. Excessive technologies are not welcomed there because they would expose Amish people, particularly children, to the dubious influences of mass culture and would also disrupt the natural ebb and flow of family life.

Silence and sociability are two striking features in Amish homes. Apart from the chatter of parents and children around the big kitchen table or in the wide-open living area, Amish homes are quiet. There is no noise from dishwashers, televisions, computer games, air conditioners, or sound systems. And that is the way the home should be, say Amish people: an island of sanity insulated from noisy and distracting technological intrusions. Without the laptops, video games, televisions, or iPods with earbuds that can isolate individuals in non-Amish families from each other in the evenings, Amish people at home often engage in conversation, games, or household tasks together.

The range of technology in homes varies considerably by subgroup (see table 17.1). In the most traditional settings, women cook on wood or kerosene stoves, and food is either cooled in an icebox or there is no refrigeration at all. In higher communities, propane refrigerators and freezers as well as state-of-the-art gas stoves are

The most traditional Amish homes use wood stoves for cooking and heating water, and do not have pressurized water systems or indoor plumbing. This mother of twin boys cooks and bakes with a wood stove. She is a member of the Nebraska Amish affiliation, which is located in central Pennsylvania. *Donald B. Kraybill*

widely used. In lieu of automatic washers, Amish families use old-style wringer washers powered by gas engines or air motors. Without electric dryers, clothing is dried on outside lines, indoor racks, or in spinners powered by compressed air. Food processors and mixers, powered by compressed air, are found in some homes. But compared to many American homes laden with a myriad of entertainment devices (TVs, DVD players, radios, iPods, computers, game consoles) and personal care items (hair dryers, electric shavers, curling irons), even the most progressive Amish homes are Spartan.

Farm

More technology is employed in barns and in fields than in homes. Even so, Amish farms are much smaller and technologically leaner than those of their English neighbors. With few exceptions, Amish farms do not tap electricity from the public grid

This New Order Amish home in Ohio has indoor plumbing and beautiful cabinetry, which is typical of the more liberal groups. A skylight in the ceiling illuminates the kitchen even on cloudy days. Propane gas powers the refrigerator, the stove, and the iron on the counter. Electricity, from a battery via an inverter, runs the fan. *Daniel Rodriguez*

or use self-propelled equipment in the fields.[14] The differences between the lowest and highest Amish farms, however, are substantial. A traditional farm may have one small gasoline engine (power unit) to operate a corn chopper that grinds and blows silage into a small silo at the barn. Half a dozen cows are milked by hand, and milk is chilled by cold water. In contrast, a more progressive Amish farmer may milk eighty cows with automatic milkers and chill the milk in a large, temperature-controlled bulk tank. On such a farm, a diesel engine provides the power to operate a variety of equipment in the barn. A tractor provides motorized power for work such as grinding feed and filling the silo. In the fields, horses pull highly mechanized equipment powered by gasoline engines.

Shop

Although the levels of production technology vary by subgroup, all affiliations permit more technology for business than for farming. There are several reasons for this difference. The farm Ordnung that emerged over the last century is woven into Amish identity, making it more resistant to change. Conversely, because the emergence of machine shops in the 1970s was largely a new phenomenon, there was little historical Ordnung pertaining to commercial enterprises. As a result, Amish business owners and small manufacturers in progressive settlements experimented, creating innovations that eventually were grafted into the Ordnung. Finally, while farm technologies—especially outdoor ones—are visible and therefore open to community surveillance, innovations inside shops and stores can sometimes hide under the community's collective radar.

Operating without public electricity, Amish businesses have to innovate to compete in the marketplace. Shops in more liberal communities typically have a diesel engine that operates alternators to charge batteries, generators to make electricity, hydraulic pumps to operate large machinery, and compressed air pumps to power air-driven motors. Without using computers, some Amish technicians have rigged homespun systems to automate drilling, machining, and the assembly of some products.

Mobile Work

Mobile Amish workers have considerable flexibility with technology because their jobs take them away from home and often out of the church-community itself. Construction crews typically need electric power, so they plug into public utilities or bring portable generators to building sites to power their electric tools, even though most churches forbid using them at home. Contractors in some settlements lease backhoes, hydraulic lifts, and other equipment that they otherwise could not use.

Amish construction crews also need daily access to vehicles for hauling tools and for long distance travel. An English employee may provide and drive a truck, or a business may lease one and have an English employee or an unbaptized Amish youth drive it. Some companies contract with outside drivers to provide a vehicle and driver as needed. In liberal groups, business owners who travel to work sites are permitted to have a cell phone to coordinate their work; however, some districts have a hard-to-enforce policy: at night the phone is supposed to remain turned off and in the truck! Progressive communities grant families who operate stands at farmers' markets in urban areas greater access to electricity, cell phones, vehicles, and other technologies because the market stands are in rented spaces far from home.

On the other hand, mobile workers in the strictest communities continue to rely on horse-and-buggy transportation, which limits how far they can travel. Yet because they are using traditional technologies, they have less overhead and charge cheaper rates, sometimes irritating English contractors and, occasionally, those from more progressive Amish communities.[15]

Outside Employment

Amish people working for non-Amish employers have the most access to technology. One of the reasons that the lower groups object to members working for outsiders is that they would be exposed to so much technology. Some affiliations permit outside employment, but discourage members from using computers or the Internet on the job. In the large Elkhart–LaGrange settlement in northern Indiana, hundreds of church members work in large recreational vehicle factories where they operate all types of high-tech equipment. The long-standing distinction between owning and using technology makes this possible.

Just Leave a Message

In the first decade of the twentieth century, some Amish people installed telephones in their homes, only to be asked by their churches to remove them.[16] The telephone troubled Amish waters for several reasons. The early phone system made use of party lines, which enabled participants to eavesdrop on others' conversations. Moreover, the phone wires literally tied Amish residences to those outside the church-community, a visual violation of separation from the world. It permitted outsiders easy access to Amish homes, and its ringing disrupted the normal rhythms of family life and church services.

Deeper issues were also at stake, however. Telephone talk threatened face-to-face conversation, the social glue of Amish society. Visiting involves not only words but also the cultural cues of body language and dress, especially pertinent in Amish culture, which mediate the presentation of the self. Phone conversations strip these two crucial elements of Amish discourse—nonverbal signs and social context—as voices are extracted from context, bodies, and appearance.

By the 1910s, a telephone taboo was in effect in most Amish communities. Although phones in homes were prohibited, most affiliations permitted members to use public phones for emergencies—one of the earliest distinctions between ownership and access. High communities eventually made many accommodations as the phone inched closer to the house. By midcentury, some groups permitted "community phone shanties" at the end of a farm lane or another accessible site so that several families could place calls and receive messages. By the turn of the twenty-first century, phones were accepted in New Order homes. Some other progressive church-communities allowed families to install a phone in an outside shanty, barn, shop, or retail store—and even in the basement of their house.

The rise of Amish businesses added pressure to expand phone use. Some churches have permitted phone booths several yards away from offices, others have allowed them adjacent to offices but outside the buildings, and still others have permitted phones inside offices. Business owners without an office phone typically visit their outside phone booth once or twice a day to take and return messages. Some list a time when they are available for live conversations. "Call between 6:45 and 7:00 p.m. or leave a message" instructs an advertisement for an Amish-owned concrete business in Lancaster, Pennsylvania.

Although members of some ultraconservative Amish groups shy away from any direct use of a telephone and prefer to ask an outside person to make calls on their behalf, others use their English neighbors' phones. Some neighbors even allow Amish businesses to share their phone number, in effect providing an answering service for emergency messages from far-flung family members. Many Amish churches welcomed answering machines and voice-mail service as a means of exchanging messages on community phone lines.

By the mid-1990s, cell phones began making an end run around the long-standing no-phone-in-the-home tradition. To the literalists, cell phones did not violate the Ordnung because they were wireless and not physically installed in houses. They were handy for contractors on job sites to coordinate subcontractors. Easy to conceal, they were also difficult to suppress. Moreover, young people who acquired them during *Rumspringa* found them hard to discard after baptism. As cell phones became widespread in some communities, leaders despaired of being able to ban them. Yet they worried that cell phones with cameras and Internet access would open the door to moral depravity, and they threatened to recall them. Still, some people welcomed this new technology that so conveniently sidestepped the old taboo on telephones in homes.

No Love for the Car

During the nineteenth century, the Amish used many forms of public transportation—ships, trolleys, and trains—and these generated no controversy in the twentieth century. With the exception of airplane travel, which all Amish except some New Order districts reject, public transportation has been uncontroversial. Not so the individual mobility promised by the automobile, however.

During the twentieth century, most Americans fell in love with the car—with its power, speed, convenience, and control—and they found it exhilarating to drive. But not the Amish. For Amish leaders trying to keep their congregations intact and sequestered from urban influence, the car was a threat. They feared its speed and easy mobility would decimate their close-knit church-communities whose social ties traditionally drew strength from face-to-face visiting and physical proximity.

Spurning the car, the icon of modernity, illustrates the fortitude of Amish resistance. Although Amish people have made accommodations, such as riding in motor vehicles, horse-drawn transportation remains a cogent protest against the creeping influence of all things modern and, as we have argued, it's *the* defining feature of Amish identity. "When people leave the Amish," said one member, "the first thing they do is buy a car."

One Amish leader explains the harm that cars would cause, arguing that (1) they are luxury and status symbols designed for style, speed, comfort, and convenience; (2) they ruin tightly woven communities where members live, work, worship, and care for each other; (3) they make it too easy to travel to cities; (4) they bring moral decay as people work and live away from their families; and (5) they are dangerous because of their speed. Moral temptations, he proposes, increase in direct relation to speed. Finally, he argues that members must consider the overall harm that cars would have on the church, not just their harm to one individual.[17]

An Amish publication contends that "the free use of it [the car] will lead us to where we don't want to go" and then reiterates how the car pulls families apart, increases the temptation to travel into cities, and detaches families from their local churches. It concludes, "Cities are designed for cars, time is marked by them, and men are known and judged by the automobiles they drive."[18]

All affiliations forbid baptized members from owning or operating a motor vehicle and from obtaining a driver's license for personal use. In more progressive communities, unbaptized young men may own a car during Rumspringa, but they must sell it upon joining the church. A handful of settlements at one time permitted baptized members to obtain licenses if they had to drive trucks for their English employers, but such cases are very rare.[19]

With a few exceptions such as forklifts in shops, self-propelled power implements (harvesters, combines, riding mowers, and garden tractors) are also taboo for fear they might eventually justify car driving or car ownership. Nevertheless, in another example of the distinction between use and ownership, many affiliations permit members to ride in hired vehicles owned and operated by non-Amish people. Some business owners hire English drivers with vehicles on a regular basis or employ them on work crews, to provide labor as well as daily transportation for the business. Long-distance travel by bus, train, or hired vans is part of the life of most Amish communities. Although the most conservative groups permit traveling by public bus or train, their members may ride in private cars only if no public transportation is available.

Shunning the car has helped to preserve the social fabric of local congregations, which is crucial to the success of Amish society. Horse-drawn transportation tethers Amish people to rural areas and grounds their social interaction in their church-community, which in turn reinforces their home-centered way of life.

Unplugged?

One Amish authority declares that electricity and the car are the two technologies that wreaked the greatest havoc on rural life in the twentieth century. The writer explains that "the unlimited use of electric current puts a world of power and convenience at our fingertips that is not good for us. This is especially true of household appliances." He then argues that "push button electric lighting and central heat disperse family throughout the house in evenings instead of encouraging togetherness and communication."[20]

As electrification reached into rural areas in the 1920s and 1930s, Amish communities independently and gradually decided not to tap into the public grid. Like the telephone, the grid was a direct connection to the outside world. Moreover, the early uses of electricity were more applicable to homes than to farming operations, so church leaders considered electricity unnecessary and were leery that conveniences and appliances would eventually follow. The advent of radio in the 1920s was an early warning of how electricity could bring worldly ideas directly into the home, and the rapid introduction of television into American living rooms in the 1950s (see fig. 17.1) underscored for the Amish the wisdom of the taboo on electricity. Putting the grid off-limits effectively buffered them from the avalanche of gadgets that spilled into American life in the twentieth century: radios, televisions, vacuum cleaners, air conditioners, electric lights, dishwashers, and much more.

No Amish communities, however, ban electricity entirely. The Amish had been tapping 12-volt direct current from batteries before 120-volt alternating current became available from public utility wires. The distinction between battery and grid current gelled in the course of the last century and continues to shape Amish choices and patterns of innovation. Even the most traditional churches use battery-powered flashlights, and many affiliations permit battery power for small lights, fans, shavers, and toys in their homes, for lights on their buggies, and for other applications. The long-standing preference for batteries took a surprising twist in the late twentieth century when American manufacturers produced a flood of battery-powered tools

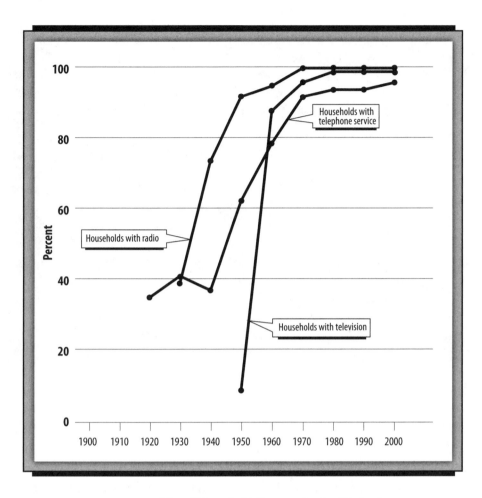

FIGURE 17.1. Rise of Household Communication Technology
in the United States, 1900–2000. *Source: U.S. Census Bureau,
Statistical Abstract of The United States: 2003, No. HS-42.*

for home and shop. Progressive Amish groups welcomed these new tools because they fit within traditional guidelines and boosted manufacturing productivity.

Some people in more lenient communities also invert 12-volt electricity from batteries into 120-volt current in order to operate cash registers, copy machines, word processors, light bulbs, coffeemakers, and fans. Nevertheless, the multitude of electrical gadgets and entertainment devices in mainstream society are simply absent from Amish homes.

The emergence of Amish manufacturing shops in the 1970s and 1980s presented a new challenge: Could large equipment be powered without electricity? With the traditional method—the only one permitted by conservative groups—saws, sanders,

This office copier uses direct current from a 12-volt battery (*left*), which is transformed by the inverter (*above the battery*) into 120-volt alternating current that operates the machine. A propane canister on rollers (*upper right*) provides fuel for a portable gas light. *Doyle Yoder*

and drills are powered by a belt spun by an engine. In higher groups, however, Amish mechanics have created alternative energy sources by using diesel engines to operate pumps and compress air (pneumatic) and oil (hydraulic) for power, as shown in figure 17.2. Nowadays, Amish technicians remove the electric motors from tools such as saws, sanders, and metal cutters and replace them with either air or oil motors. The compressed air and pressurized oil are distributed by hoses or pipes to a wide array of equipment. Compressed air is used in some communities to pump water, power sewing machines, and operate old-style wringer washers and high-speed spinners to wash and dry clothing. This so-called "Amish electricity" has boosted productivity in shops and added convenience to some homes. Amish technicians have also created circuit boards, with air and 12-volt electric switches, to control repetitive movements (that mimic computers) in machines.

A curious thing happened in the early years of the twenty-first century: many Amish people joined the environmental movement and began tapping into "God's Grid." They found that solar power, with its direct tie to nature and no wires to the outside world, fit perfectly with their values. Amish entrepreneurs started constructing, selling, and installing solar technology for Amish and non-Amish customers

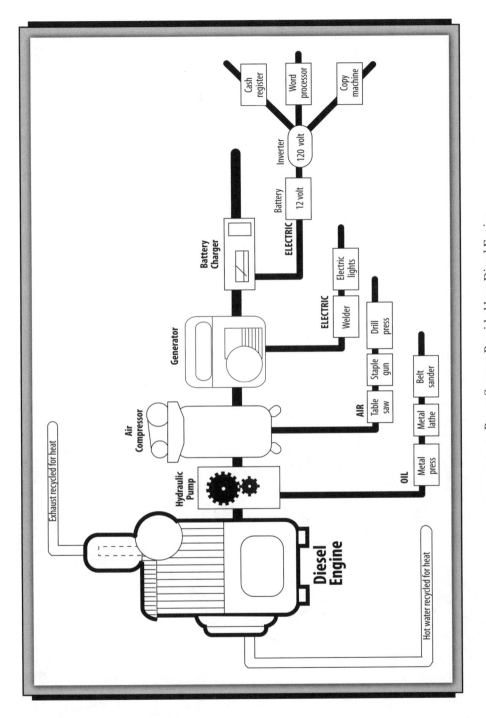

FIGURE 17.2. Power Sources Provided by a Diesel Engine

alike. The story actually began in the 1980s when some Amish farmers used solar chargers to electrify cattle fences. Later, the Amish began using solar panels on the rooftops of carriage sheds to charge the batteries that powered buggy lights. Solar power is now used in many communities to charge batteries for reading lamps, fans, copy machines, sewing machines, light bulbs, word processors, and water pumps. Solar-generated electricity is also used to power tiny drill presses, solder guns, and other small electrical tools.

Amish solar installations are typically small-scale rather than full-size systems that power an entire home. Nevertheless, one solar shop owner who sells to English clients explained with great enthusiasm how a sizable solar panel can provide all the energy needed for the lights, small appliances, and even the refrigerator and washer in a home. The electricity from the solar panel flows into a battery pack, then to an inverter for conversion to 120 volt, and then to an electric wire distribution system throughout the house. On a cloudy day a small gasoline engine runs an electric generator for backup. Solar power offers, in short, the possibility of full electrification for an Amish house. For some Amish elders, that notion conjures up a frightening scenario leading to video games, big screen televisions, computers, and the Internet—all

Amish technicians remove the electric motors from many machines and install pneumatic (pressurized air) or hydraulic (pressurized oil) motors. This "Amish electricity" enables manufacturing operations to function without public grid electricity. *Doyle Yoder*

the things that they have sought to avoid. Yet Amish use of solar power will likely continue to grow, and change-minded churches will need to strike a balance between acceptable uses and those that could link them directly to mass culture.

Negotiating Change

An Amish author writing about the inventions of the last century says, "We have decided their potential for harm outweighs their benefit, and have taken measures to restrict their availability to us."[21] The Amish have tried to tame technology or at least keep what they consider its most pernicious effects at bay. Their technology choices baffle outsiders, who find the lines the Amish draw to be contradictory and inconsistent. However, from an Amish perspective, technology decisions are ways of coping with worldly forces that threaten the integrity of their community.

New technology enters the Amish community when early adopters begin experimenting with outside devices—installing a propane refrigerator, a fax machine, or an inverter to run a word processor on 120-volt electricity. Their experiments typically result in one of these five outcomes within the community:

1. Swift rejection with little discussion and consideration
2. Limited use over several months or years and eventual rejection
3. Creeping use as well as dissent and gradual acceptance by default
4. Growing use with little dissent and rapid acceptance
5. Modification to make the technology fit the moral order

Because acceptance of a particular technology typically happens gradually by default, communities rarely take specific action to adopt a new item. Formal decisions usually involve rejection. With more than two thousand church districts, each having the authority to accept or reject an innovation, there are a multitude of possible outcomes for any one technology, and liberal churches typically allow innovations that more traditional groups never even consider.

Decisions about technology may pertain to just one church district or to an entire affiliation. In any case, decisions emerge within a dynamic matrix of sociocultural forces, and a single factor will rarely explain a particular outcome. Some of the pertinent regulators include the following:

1. *Economic Impact.* New technologies related to "making a living" are more acceptable than those involving pleasure, convenience, or leisure. Thus, a motor on a hay mower in the field is more acceptable than one on a lawn mower.

2. *Visibility.* Invisible changes are more acceptable than visible ones. Using fiberglass in the construction of buggies is easier to introduce than changing the external color of the carriage itself.

3. *Relation to the Ordnung.* New items that overturn existing Ordnung are more difficult than those that are free from previous rules or that can be grafted on to present regulations. Because it is new technology, accepting a string trimmer may be easier than accepting a push power mower that has been forbidden for forty years.

4. *Symbolic Ties.* Changes unrelated to key emblems of ethnic identity— horse, buggy, and dress—are more acceptable than ones that threaten sacred symbols. Likewise, changes linked to negative, "worldly" markers are less acceptable than those without such ties. A word processor with a small screen, for example, would likely be more acceptable than a computer with a large monitor resembling a television.

5. *External Connections.* Technologies that open avenues of influence from mainstream culture and outsiders are less acceptable than those that do not.

None of these factors operates in isolation. Practical matters or internal church politics may also shape decisions, but these five factors silently inform the collective decision making. Change becomes especially controversial when both positive and negative forces intersect. The use of the Internet is contentious because, although it involves making a living, it also blends work and leisure and offers a direct connection to the outside world. Moreover, the willingness of one group to innovate may impede change in another group that wishes to distinguish itself as more conservative. One group's adoption of LED lights, for example, may harden another community's resolve against them.

The response to some new technologies involves mild rejection followed by negotiations that may stretch over a decade and end in various compromises—telephones not in the house but outside, tractors not in the field but at the barn, electricity tapped from batteries but not the public grid, car ownership forbidden but riding in vehicles allowed, and so on. These negotiated adaptations may appear odd to outsiders, but seen through Amish lenses, they are sincere attempts to harness the power of technology for good purposes while curbing its ill effects. An Amish leader, cringing at his neighbor's charge that practices such as riding in cars are inconsistent and even hypocritical, argues that "limiting or restricting something . . . is the very essence of a disciplined life. It can be the hallmark of prudence, wisdom, and responsibility." Table salt, he notes, must be used in moderation: too much can kill.[22]

The Amish Default: Go Slow, Be Careful

When a corporation announces a new smartphone, consumers line up early to snatch up the new product. The modern assumption is "newer is better, faster, and cool." Technology is often consumed without consideration for its longer term impact on the human community. The Amish default response, in contrast, is "go slow, be careful, and check with the community." The Amish in general are late adopters—sometimes decades later—if they adopt at all. More often they are adapters who tinker with the technology.[23]

One Amish writer summarizes their view this way: "Plain people do not oppose *all* new ideas and practices. There is a need to choose only those that will be of genuine benefit, and to reject those that break down the values we uphold. This would apply to modern appliances and household gadgets, many of which have the potential to change our family- and community-oriented way of life in ways we may not realize until the damage has been done."[24]

This strategic, rational, forward-looking analysis challenges the myth that the Amish are backward, naive, old-fashioned Luddites. Instead, they show a remarkable sensitivity to the cost-benefit impact of technology on human relationships, families, and communities. Few if any of them have read about technology's embedded bias—that it changes human perceptions and behavior—but they sense it intuitively.[25]

The influence and interconnectedness of their community and their religion has made it possible for the Amish to restrain technology. In their struggle with technology, the Amish make an assumption that rankles modern values: individuals are not wise enough to make private choices about technology. Individuals, the Amish contend, need guidance and direction from a community to make wise choices. Any success they have had in restraining technology is due to this collective effort.

But not just any community will do. Theirs is a religiously grounded one, which means that technological regulations decided by the church are invested with considerable moral clout. In other words, technological practices are seen not just as human customs but as ones that carry divine legitimacy. Despite this blessing of heaven, Amish people would readily agree that some choices create new problems, and many would concede that their use of technology may at times be inconsistent. Nevertheless, they remain engaged in a communal discourse about technology's impact on their collective life. Surely, that is more than many other people can say.

The Amish saga poses interesting questions about the ability of humans to restrain technology—to assure that technology serves people and not vice versa. Keeping the telephone outside the house symbolizes the community's control over it while permitting limited access without intrusions into family life. Such arrangements are an attempt to master technology without becoming enslaved to it. Although the Amish have successfully tamed some of the technological achievements of solid modernity for more than a century—the car, electricity, tractors, and computers—their future success remains uncertain in the fluid context of liquid modernity. Resisting the ephemeral and ubiquitous nature of technology in a wireless cyber world will surely test the fiber of their religious convictions, as will the world of health care, to which we turn next.

CHAPTER 18

HEALTH AND HEALING

"Are you the biggest loser?" Liz Allgyer asked readers of Die Botschaft *in March 2008. Allgyer, an Amish woman living east of Lancaster, Pennsylvania, was sponsoring a weight loss group for Amish women in her area because she was sure that "in the midst of [autumn] weddings and holidays" people had overeaten, perhaps gaining "five to twelve pounds." When she talks with her friends, Allgyer noted, "the topic of weight loss always comes up." So for twelve weeks the challenge was on to "weigh-in" and "get healthy."*

The Cultural Context

Amish views of health and healing reveal a fascinating interchange between a traditional culture and modern values, as shown in the story above. Liz Allgyer borrowed ideas from well-known self-help programs in wider society—including the name of a then-popular NBC reality show—even as she tailored her comments to Amish readers aware of the frequent feasting during Lancaster's fall wedding season. When it comes to personal health and medical care, Amish culture often mixes rural American customs and mainstream techniques. The Amish discourse about health care shows sharp divides between Amish affiliations and reveals how some groups have accommodated to modernity while others have not.

The Amish bring a distinctive cultural outlook to their conversation with medicine. Their naturalistic worldview places primacy on the will of God, and some of their practices reflect early twentieth-century rural traditions. Those who attend Amish schools may study "health" from an Old Order textbook that emphasizes

God's role in creating and sustaining the world. Only the few Amish students who attend public schools study science in a systematic fashion, and because Amish youth leave school after the eighth grade, they often have only rudimentary knowledge of nature, disease, and the human body.

When Amish patients interact with Western medical systems, they enter clinics and hospitals where the doctors and nurses who care for them do not share their understandings of nature, illness, and personal hygiene. Some Amish people distrust modern medicine because it is such a foreign and inexplicable world, and they opt out of mainstream medical care and pharmaceutical treatments. Ironically, although they may not understand genetics, many Amish people, because of their involvement in animal husbandry, understand heritability much better than many other Americans.

The Amish inhabit a sacred world filled with the spirit of God, who intervenes to bring about certain outcomes, and Satan, who seeks to distort God's plans. They see nature as God's handiwork and think that the more one embraces nature, the closer one walks with God. Likewise, because the body is a natural organism, the more one treats its ills with natural remedies, the more one is in tune with the mysteries of God's intents.

The Amish see modern attempts to explain and control nature, especially scientific techniques to control the body and prolong life—goals most non-Amish patients embrace—as sometimes obstructing the will of God. The *Gelassenheit* disposition to accept whatever comes means that Amish people are reluctant to hinder divine providence.

Such a stance may seem fatalistic to modern sensibilities. But if the Amish embraced a fatalistic worldview, they would never see a doctor or do anything to enhance their health. However, Amish people want to be healthy, and they want to avoid sickness and injury.[1] They consult health care providers and use vitamins and homeopathic remedies. Many take prescription drugs and have high-tech surgical interventions because they believe these measures may heal them or prevent illness. Yet in general, Amish people are more willing to stop interventions earlier and resist invasive therapies than the general population because, while they long for healing, they also have a profound respect for God's will. This means taking modest steps toward healing sick bodies, giving preference to natural remedies, setting common sense limits, and believing that in the end their bodies are in God's hands.

Navigating Health Care

It is risky to generalize about Amish behavior, and health care is no exception. A diversity of perspectives and practices reigns across affiliations as well as within them. Some Amish people wear copper rings to ward off arthritis, go to unlicensed Amish "doctors" for care, and have their teeth pulled to avoid the need for future dental care, while members of other Amish groups dismiss such practices as foolhardy. Some households see a doctor only in emergencies; others go regularly to a family physician. Certain families would not consider open-heart surgery for a loved one, but others, sometimes even in the same *Gmay,* would welcome it.

Issues such as trust, friendship, and personal demeanor weigh heavily in the choice of health care providers. The rural family physician, who has a personal relationship with patients or even makes house calls, is the ideal doctor in Amish eyes because such an easygoing, high touch, low-tech style perfectly fits their values. For these reasons many Amish people will go to chiropractors before medical doctors and may even travel to Mexico for treatments in clinics whose chatty doctors and staff do not rush them through examinations. With limited schooling and English as a second language, Amish people can easily be intimidated by the often impersonal, jargon-filled, high-tech world of hospitals, with their frenetic pace and baffling bureaucracy.[2]

No official Amish pronouncements regulate health care. Choices are molded by tradition, extended family, ordained leaders, and informal conversations in the church-community. When his cardiologist advised seventy-nine-year-old Yonie Esh to have his heart valve replaced, his first thought was, "No way. At my age what's the use?" But then his children "sort of talked me into it," he said, and after reading the Bible, he decided to "give myself up to the surgery."[3] Unlike Esh, a seventy-five-year-old bishop with heart disease in a very traditional group refused any medicine or surgical interventions although doctors repeatedly told him he would die without them—and he did.

Extraordinary interventions for a premature baby or an elderly person rarely occur among the Amish, in part because of cost, but also because of a reluctance to interfere with God's will. Few families want to keep a loved one on life support for more than a few days. Blood transfusions are acceptable, and some Amish people are regular blood donors. Elective abortions require no discussion because they are categorically considered wrong. Likewise, in vitro fertilization would rarely if ever be considered, although less expensive and less invasive fertility treatments are sometimes used. Decisions about how to treat heart disease, cancer, and other serious maladies are in the hands of family and friends, and like other people, Amish families do not always agree on how to proceed.

For religious reasons and because they are frugal, few Amish people have commercial health insurance, and most pay their health care bills with cash. Some Amish employees in English-owned industries do participate in company health plans. The Amish were exempted from the 2010 Patient Protection and Affordable Care Act, which mandates health insurance coverage, because of their religious objections to receiving government aid.[4]

Sometimes cost and convenience limit access to health care. Typically, Amish people have easier access to general practitioners who live nearby than to specialists in urban areas, which require hiring a driver. Although they may not understand the intricate economics of the health care system, Amish patients do know that a fifteen-minute visit with a doctor and a few tests might result in a bill of several hundred dollars or more. The accelerating costs of health care in the twenty-first century have levied a heavy burden on Amish communities, and some expensive procedures are simply rejected. Cautions about modern medicine and its cost lead some Amish people to use it as a last resort, which may at times create medical complications and actually increase the cost.

Perhaps as a result of the high cost, the Amish have become shrewd consumers of particular kinds of health care, especially for emergencies. For example, one family in upstate New York telephoned neighbors to find someone who could drive an injured boy with a "cut finger" to the emergency room. The family wanted the boy to go to a hospital in Ontario rather than to the closest one in New York because the Canadian hospital was much cheaper. Furthermore, the boy's father explained, if the Ontario hospital didn't have a surgeon, patients could transfer to "a teaching hospital with doctors on call for different kinds of emergencies." He also advised not calling ahead, because if you do, he said, "they might tell you that they can't help you and send you elsewhere. If you just show up, then they have to take you."[5] Despite his limited knowledge of modern medicine, this man had learned how to navigate the health care system for his advantage.

Amish people routinely meet with health care providers to work out payment plans and to negotiate lower rates for cash payment. Some Amish communities have forged agreements with hospitals for significant health care discounts. In some locations hospitals compete for Amish patients because they pay cash, bypass insurance regulations, and almost never file malpractice lawsuits.

Many hospitals no longer try to accommodate self-pay patients, however, because hospitals negotiate reduced rates with the government and insurance companies. As a result, Amish patients are sometimes charged higher rates for the same treatment than the hospital receives from insurance companies. Hospitals in areas with large Amish populations are generally better than hospitals in areas with smaller Amish populations at recognizing this problem, but it varies regionally and even among patients in the same hospital.

Many liberal communities have Amish-style "health insurance" plans with premiums and high deductibles; after these are paid, the plan pays some but not all of the expenses. These informal church-aid plans are run entirely by volunteers. Other Amish groups help needy families through voluntary contributions. Typically, it is the job of the deacon to collect or supervise the collection of contributions and, in some settlements, to make financial arrangements with medical care providers. In northern Indiana, one deacon volunteer works full time advising Amish people about where they can obtain the best value for professional health care and reviewing their medical bills. Although the Amish emphasize personal responsibility, each individual also knows that, upon joining the church, he or she has accepted responsibility for sharing the burdens of the other community members.[6]

Resources for Health Care

Amish people tap resources in four systems of care when they seek treatment for physical and mental ailments: folk, alternative, standard, and church-community. Often they use a combination of resources from these four systems. The use of each type of care varies widely by family, affiliation, and settlement. An Amish person may, for example, seek mental health care from a self-trained Amish counselor (folk system), travel to Mexico for cancer treatment (alternative system), go to a state-of-the-art hospital for a knee replacement (standard system), and receive visits and financial support while recuperating (church-community system). The lower groups rely primarily on the folk and alternative systems, using standard care only for emergencies. At the other end of the spectrum, some families in higher groups rarely if ever visit folk practitioners and routinely use the resources of modern medicine alongside homeopathy. All Amish people, however, tap the resources of their church-community.

Extended families are large and provide rich health care resources as well as advice and recommendations. A typical thirty-five-year-old married person is embedded in an extended family system of more than two hundred people. In addition to this dense family network, friends in the Gmay and larger church-community also stand ready to help. Thus, Amish people are rarely alone when they face illness, accident, suffering, or grief. The family system may at times offer erroneous advice or worthless treatment, but its empathic, loving intent meets emotional needs that the modern health care system may be ill-equipped to address.

Folk Resources

Amish people, in general, have a high respect for traditional remedies.[7] The kinship system preserves the wisdom of past generations—knowledge for delivering a baby, tips on toilet-training a child, advice for coping with stress or caring for an injury, and so on. They will often try a traditional herbal concoction for burns before going to a doctor. Although they do turn to doctors and hospitals for emergencies such as broken legs and clogged arteries, Amish people rarely see a physician for a cold or simple illness, believing that patience, hot tea, and a homemade remedy are the best cure. *Die Botschaft* includes a weekly column about home remedies that have been passed along for generations. For example, one treatment for poison ivy suggests rubbing the inflamed skin with water into which a blacksmith has dipped horseshoes, and another suggests using a warm vinegar-water soak. Coltsfoot tea is suggested for chest congestion, and hot lemonade for a head cold.

Beliefs about "drawing pain" off of others may involve family members as well as others. "Mothers can't draw pain off their own children," one woman asserted, in explaining an old practice of an ultraconservative group. In other words, those with ailing offspring must seek help from others. Attempting to relieve one dying elderly woman's pain, several men joined hands in a line. The first laid his hand on the woman, while the last held a wire that went into a tub of water. The pain passed through the men and into the tub. In another case that required six men to draw pain off a suffering child, a woman noted that the water in the bucket "became thick with the pain." One woman implicitly linked medical help to more general social support by noting that, because she is good at drawing pain, other women give her the fussy babies to hold so that she can calm them.[8] This ritual of care, which brings great comfort to the sick and a sense of solidarity to those trying to mitigate the suffering, is only practiced in the most traditional groups. Members of some higher groups consider it witchcraft.

Various Amish folk practitioners provide services designed to promote healing. Perhaps the most curious of these to modern minds is sympathy healing, also known as *brauche,* or powwowing. These "arts" were typical of German immigrants to southeastern Pennsylvania in the eighteenth century.[9] Folk practitioners use incantations and charms that have special powers to detect and purge illness in the body. A woman *braucher* explained that after she "finds the sore" with her hands, "I let it [the pain] out, shake a little, blink my eyes." One of her male patients described her reaction to finding his pain spot: "She threw her head around, her eyes rolled in her head, and she emitted a series of staccato popping sounds."[10]

The secret skills are learned or transferred from older brauchers—often of the opposite sex. Many Amish people view brauche as a form of witchcraft and shy away from it. An Amish cousin of a female "healer" believes that her cousin's art comes from the devil, and an Amish man in the same settlement declared that "the church forbids it [powwowing]."[11]

Members of more liberal groups rarely use brauchers, but in the mid-1980s in northern Indiana, Amish people identified fifteen self-taught Amish folk healers. Patients said they sought out healers to treat small children, keep costs down, and avoid using drugs, and also because they were convenient.[12] In some cases healers have a dispensary of herbs, supplements, and other homespun remedies. Their services, typically based at their home, are advertised only by word of mouth.

In addition to the traditional brauchers, a handful of Amish "doctors" practice other healing arts. These healers, who do not have professional training or state certification, include dentists, physical therapists, chiropractors, and midwives. Many sidestep state regulations by accepting donations from patients rather than charging for services. Some of these mavericks have run afoul of state regulations governing medical practice. Solomon J. Wickey, originally from Berne, Indiana, was known as an iridologist who could diagnose patients' ills by looking in the irises of their eyes. In the 1980s, he was charged with practicing medicine without a license. Wickey eventually agreed to refrain from offering patients formal diagnoses, but he was allowed to recommend remedies and nutritional supplements.[13]

In a 1989 legal case that terminated his career, Amish "chiropractor" Joseph W. Helmuth of Elkhart County, Indiana, faced not only the sanction of the state but the ire of professional chiropractors and the censure of the church. Helmuth had provided chiropractic treatments and physical therapy to an estimated six thousand people over sixteen years. He eventually pleaded guilty to practicing chiropractic treatment without a license, but he was permitted to provide some treatments with, in his words, "certain restrictions which I will try to accept." The church censured him, not for his practice but for hiring a lawyer to defend him in court.[14]

Perhaps the most well-known Amish health expert in the twenty-first century is John Keim, who is widely sought after for his knowledge of treating burns, among other ailments. The author of *Burn Aid,* Keim provides step-by-step instructions for applying his B & W salve, a mixture of honey, lanolin, olive oil, wheat germ oil, aloe vera gel, beeswax, comfrey root, myrrh, and other ingredients, to burn wounds with a dressing of burdock leaves. Anecdotal Amish sources praise the effectiveness of this treatment, and some hospitals endorse it; however, it has not been tested in clinical trials.[15]

Outside observers might wonder how Amish people can believe in folk remedies. For Amish and English alike, the answer is quite simple: when you suffer, you turn to someone like yourself who has experienced the same pain and found an antidote. From an Amish perspective, it is far easier to believe what one's aunt heard from her friend's sister than in what a doctor one does not know says about a drug made by a nameless researcher in a large, profit-driven pharmaceutical corporation.

Alternative Resources

Amish people also rely on many services in the alternative health systems that are provided by non-Amish vendors and practitioners. These resources, available to the larger American public as well, include homeopathic treatments, unlicensed midwives, acupuncture, patent medicines, natural supplements, and many other remedies sold and promoted on the public market. Reflexology, the application of pressure to different areas of the foot to bring about relief from various ailments, is common in some communities. Some Amish people have come to rely on the "healing" properties of essential oils as well as periodic cleansing routines and formulas to detoxify their bodies. It is also fairly common for Amish people to travel by train, bus, or hired van to Mexican clinics, which operate outside of U.S. medical regulations, for dentistry, face surgery, and treatment of cancer, leukemia, hernias, ulcers, and chronic infections. One family, for example, made three separate three-month-long trips.[16]

A study that compared the use of alternative medicine between Amish people and their rural neighbors in Ohio found that 90 percent or more in both groups had used some forms of alternative treatments. The use of chiropractic therapy and reflexology was higher, however, among the Amish. Non-Amish people were more likely to name a medical doctor as the health care professional that they see most often.[17]

Amish health practices from samples of two progressive settlements (Holmes County, Ohio, and Lancaster County, Pennsylvania) are summarized in table 18.1.[18] Among the participants in both areas, about 90 percent report using chiropractic therapy and also seeing a medical doctor, 40 percent or more have used reflexology, and over 80 percent use dietary supplements. In Lancaster County, 38 percent have used tinctures, oils, or dilutions; 50 percent have used cleansing and detox regimes; and 8 percent have traveled to Mexico for medical treatment. Only two people in the combined settlements have used powwowing as a treatment. About one-third of the subjects in both studies report that the health professional they see most often is a chiropractor.

One reason Amish people seek help from alternative providers is that such providers often replicate the high-touch, low-tech, informal ethos of the familial system. Medical professionals have noted that the Amish are often reluctant to talk about their reliance on alternative medicine, partly because of English disdain for folk remedies and partly because they are wary of providing too much information to outsiders. This makes it difficult to assess the scope of Amish use of alternative treatments. Thus, in the words of one study, health professionals must recognize that their "ethical mandate to provide health care that meets the beliefs of the individual may outweigh the mandate to provide the most advanced care for the body."[19]

Many natural-remedy providers aggressively target Amish communities with services and products ranging from miracle supplements, body cleansing regimes, and cranial and body manipulation to home visits by unlicensed chiropractors. Both Amish and English vendors hawk their natural remedies via meetings, direct mail, and color advertisements and notices in Amish publications and newsletters. Typical of the health claims reinforced by religion are these by this Amish distributor:

Table 18.1. Health Care Practices in Two Amish Settlements

	Lancaster Co., PA N=112		Holmes Co., OH N=134	
	%	N	%	N
Have Ever Used:				
Chiropractic therapy	92	103	87	117
Massage therapy	26	29	38	51
Reflexology	41	46	45	60
Acupuncture therapy	4	4	7	9
Tinctures, oils, dilutions	38	43	N/A	N/A
Cleanses or detoxes	50	56	N/A	N/A
Yoga	4	4	3	4
Powwowing	0	0	2	3
Prayer for healing	52	58	75	101
Meditation for healing	15	17	10	14
Dietary supplements	82	92	87	116
Treatment in Mexico	8	9	N/A	N/A
Medical doctor	88	98	99	132
Nurse practitioner	23	26	10	13
Physician assistant	20	22	11	15
Most Often Use:				
Chiropractor	38	42	36	48
Doctor	37	41	59	79

Source: Ohio data from Reiter et al., "Complementary and Alternative Medicine Use"; Pennsylvania data from King and Kraybill, "Exploratory Study of Amish Health Care."

N/A = no data available

"Essential Nutrients have helped so many people with great results. The products are all natural and come from plants which God has provided! Ninety-five percent of all chronic and degenerative diseases can be prevented or reversed with Yongevity products. If you wish to live healthier, happier, with less pain . . . , call [retailer]. May God bless you with better health!"[20] Filled with glowing testimonials, such promotions offer antidotes for stress, infertility, hormone imbalance, thyroid and adrenal issues, joint pain, arthritis, menstrual cramps, bulging veins, colon toxins, heart disease, sinus infection, fatigue, bedwetting, depression, cancer, and virtually any other imaginable malady.

Standard Resources

The standard system of health care includes professionally trained doctors, midwives, dentists, optometrists, psychologists, and other professionals as well as prescription medicine and clinically tested procedures at major hospitals. As noted above, all Amish use some standard health care, but they typically use less than their English neighbors, with some Amish only calling on their local physicians or hospitals in emergencies.

Beyond routine illnesses and emergencies, Amish people use mainstream health care for these and other treatments and procedures: cochlear implants; chemotherapy, radiation, and surgery for cancer; skin grafting for burns; cleft lip and palate surgery; kidney and bone marrow transplants; heart, bone, and cataract surgery; and hip and knee replacements. As these examples show, despite their inclination for natural remedies, Amish people in more progressive affiliations willingly use state-of-the-art medical care; those in more traditional groups are hesitant.[21]

Immunization, birthing, and refusal of treatment are three aspects of standard care that are points of contention between the most traditional Amish and outside authorities as well as within the Amish world. (See Flashpoints, page 345.)

Church-Community Resources

Visiting is a frequent and valued antidote to illness in Amish society. The infirm receive many visits, as do the elderly and those who are grieving a death. Card showers, announced in Amish publications, are also widely used to show love for those suffering illness or accident, and the cards sometimes include small gifts of money to defray medical bills. One announcement invited readers to have a "thinking of you and cheer up shower" for a sixty-four-year-old woman who had recently broken her leg and been diagnosed with bone cancer. Another invitation asked readers to "fill the mailbox" of a ten-year-old with congenital cerebral palsy.

Circle letters are a common way of connecting with others who have experienced a similar illness such as heart disease or breast cancer, or those who have lost children through sudden deaths like drowning. The letters may circulate to eight or ten people who each add a page before mailing it on. Periodic regional or country-wide gatherings for people with certain disabilities or diseases are also an important source of support that stretches far beyond the family circle. All of these expressions of care—from church aid programs to voluntary offerings, from an aunt's advice to a card shower—show the deep reserves of social capital available to support bodily health and emotional well-being.

A religious resource that some people turn to when facing a serious illness is anointing with oil, a ritual described in the Bible (James 5:14). Ordained ministers perform it in the individual's home, not as a last rite but as a sign of the ill person's complete and unconditional surrender and acceptance of God's providential will.[22]

When it comes to dying, the Amish prefer to die at home surrounded by family. With a profound belief in a heavenly hereafter, they consider death a natural prelude to eternal life. They see little need for taking extraordinary measures to prolong life with expensive treatments that may do little to improve the person's condition and may even obstruct God's will. If an adult is unable to make decisions, the family takes over, secure in the knowledge that, by acting in accordance with the teachings of their church, they will make appropriate decisions. Some settlements make extensive use of hospice services, while others do not.[23] When death is near, family and friends sit in vigil around the bed of their loved one. When a person dies, friends and neighbors prepare the body, build the coffin, dig the grave, and stay to mourn.

Flashpoints

Immunization

In the Amish world, the question of vaccination drives a complicated conversation about human volition, responsibility, providence, and the role of government. Although immunizations against such diseases as polio, measles, mumps, and rubella are required for children entering school, parents can be exempted on religious grounds.[24] This decision is generally a family decision and not a church matter. A diversity of opinion persists on whether to vaccinate or not.[25] In 1991 correspondents for the *Budget* estimated the number of people in their communities who had vaccinated their children, and the responses demonstrated the diversity of opinion on this subject. For example, one correspondent reported that 90 percent of parents in his community had had their children vaccinated. Then he noted, "We would not want to deny that there may have been cases where shots have caused adverse effects or even possibly death, but our feeling is that there would probably be much more sicknesses, paralysis, and deaths if no one took them."[26]

In contrast, a correspondent from another community reported that no families had gotten vaccinations. "I feel we should put our trust in God rather than the technology of the world," he said. "I think God put these diseases here for a purpose to chasten us sometimes."[27] One person said that her family opposed vaccinations because they viewed them "as a form of insurance," and, she asked, "Why vaccinate for a disease that isn't even present in a child's body?"[28] Most Amish who refuse immunization see it as putting their faith in science rather than trusting in God.

Even within a single church district or family, members may have different understandings. One mother of four said that she had had her first child vaccinated because her own mother had insisted. Her mother-in-law had objected to vaccinating the second child, however, so that child had only received some of the inoculations. In contrast, a Kentucky letter writer to *Family Life* noted, "We can think that our children will not get these diseases unless God wills, but are we doing our part if we purposefully neglect a preventive measure?"[29] A 2007 study of progressive Amish parents in Holmes County found that only 14 percent had not vaccinated their children. Reflecting the views of non-Amish critics of vaccination, most of them had refused because of concern about adverse effects rather than for religious reasons.[30]

Some outbreaks of poliomyelitis, whooping cough, measles, and rubella have been disproportionately high in Amish communities.[31] For example, in 2005 four cases of polio among the Amish in Minnesota were the first known cases of the polio virus in the United States in twenty-six years.[32] Such outbreaks often stir anger and resentment among English neighbors who think that their children are threatened by what they consider Amish negligence. For their part, Amish people are sometimes willing to vaccinate their children when they realize that noncompliance may endanger the health of others. Although many Amish people have shown greater openness to immunizations in the twenty-first century, pockets of resistance still persist.

Birthing

Many Amish people are ambivalent about government attempts to regulate who may assist families with childbirth and where it should occur. This contentious issue has left a trail of prosecutions of unlicensed midwives serving the Amish in several states for violating regulations regarding childbirth.[33] In a few cases Amish people have even protested by taking their objections and placards to public rallies in support of English birth attendants.

To certain Amish people, some state laws appear to infringe on the choice to have home births. One man lamented, "The State of Ohio is making it very unhandy for midwives who help people do home birthing. These midwives can no longer verify pregnancies or live births. They say that only licensed nurses and doctors can do verification. . . . It is an attempt by the state to shut down home birthing."[34]

Some Amish communities have developed birth centers that commingle professional care and an Amish ethos—a negotiated compromise between home-based and hospital births. One Amish midwife in Ohio transformed her practice into the Mount Eaton Care Center, operated by certified physicians and nurses who are sensitive to Amish ways and who deliver babies in a comfortable, low-tech setting.[35] Various settlements have birth centers that serve Amish families—the Middlefield Care Center in Geauga County, Ohio, and the New Eden Care Center near Shipshewana, Indiana, are two examples. The location of these centers makes it easy for friends and relatives to visit by buggy and bring meals and gifts to the new mothers. "Grandparents sometimes have more than one grandchild at the birthing center at the same time!" noted one doctor. "There is an obvious feeling of pride and community at the center."[36]

With birth centers such as these, expectant mothers are offered the possibility of quality medical care in a setting that is sympathetic to their cultural and religious values.[37] The staff and midwives at such centers know that the women have been running their households up to the time of labor and will return to their work within a day or two after birth. They also know that they may have used raspberry tea to relieve nausea and labor pain or black cohosh root to reduce pain during delivery.[38] These culturally sensitive centers relax some of the routines followed in hospitals and welcome the entire family (including older siblings) immediately after the birth, offering Amish women a hybrid between a hospital and a home birth that grants families greater control over this significant life event. Birth centers are not an Amish invention, however—nearly three hundred of them offer similar services in main-stream society.[39] Nevertheless, those serving Amish families are especially sensitive to Amish cultural issues and preferences.

The Right to Refuse Care

Amish confidence in God's will, their preference for natural forms of healing, and their reservations about scientific interventions have led a few families to refuse treat-ment—pitting them against state regulations and, when it involves children, raising complicated legal issues regarding child rights and parental rights. Those instances of boycotting treatment are usually guided not by official church regulations but by family preference, with or without the counsel of church leaders. Many, but not all, of the cases of refusing care have involved foregoing chemotherapy or radiation for various types of cancer.[40]

One non-cancer example occurred in 2008, when a New York judge ruled that Swartzentruber parents had neglected their infant son by failing to agree to a surgical procedure to implant a shunt in his heart. The father and the boy's bishop testified that their religious beliefs precluded open-heart surgery because "it stops the heart." The court ordered the surgery against the parents' wishes, finding that their son's physical condition "has been impaired or is in imminent danger of being impaired as a result of the failure of his parent . . . to exercise a minimum degree of care," in sup-plying the child with "adequate . . . medical, dental, optometric or surgical care."[41] When a child's death is preventable, it can challenge medical and legal protocols as well as the Amish community itself. Some Amish people worry that, by privileging the standards of modern western medicine, the state may impose on their religious beliefs and curtail the ability of parents to make health care decisions—including end-of-life decisions—for their offspring.

Mental Health Care

Even some liberal Amish who embrace standard medical care are slow to see mental health as a medical issue and view psychotherapy as a questionable exercise in abstracting thoughts and feelings from soul and spirit. Likewise, Amish culture, with its bias against subjective, personal reflection, typically resists talk therapy with professionals because one-on-one counseling introduces an outside, non-church authority (the therapist) into the mix and focuses on the desires of the individual client apart from the wisdom of the church-community. One Amish person said, "Some counselors just blame religion for your problem." Families and leaders may be wary of mental health professionals who have, in some cases, encouraged defection by suggesting that leaving a confining religious community is the path to self-fulfillment. Members of lower affiliations may believe that confession before the Gmay is the only "therapy" necessary.[42]

Nonetheless, a growing number of Amish people now accept mental illness as a medical issue and view depression and anxiety as physical ailments, treatable at least in part with drugs. "Our brains work by using chemicals, like a battery," one Amish publication explained in 2000. "How do we know this? When you take antihistamines for hay fever you become drowsy because it is the same chemical used by the brain that regulates alertness."[43] Since 1990 more than a dozen essays in *Family Life*, as well as growing contact between Amish people and health care providers, have spurred a major redefinition of mental illnesses as medical rather than spiritual ailments.[44]

One result of the mushrooming interest in mental illness was the formation of an informal lay counselor network known as People Helpers in 1995. Regional People Helpers meetings sometimes feature educational presentations by non-Amish psychologists; however, most of the speakers are Amish ministers who offer practical advice on topics such as disciplining children and recognizing depression. In 1997 a new network known as Family Helpers launched an annual marriage meeting in Ohio to promote healthy marriages and reduce marital conflict and abuse. The meeting draws several hundred participants each year.[45]

Since 1999 a handful of communities have opened Amish-operated mental health treatment centers in Michigan, Ohio, and Pennsylvania. These provide services for men, women, and couples in a religious atmosphere. Participants engage in Bible study, group sessions, and physical work. Lay Amish counselors administer medications and arrange for visits to off-site therapists and psychiatrists.[46]

Like the hybrid care modeled by Amish birth centers, some psychiatric centers combine a professional standard of care and Amish sensibilities. In 2002, Rest Haven, an Amish-constructed facility, opened on the campus of Oaklawn, a community-based mental health center in Indiana. Rest Haven houses up to sixteen patients—eight men and eight women—at a time. The medical and counseling staff from Oaklawn conducts group and individual therapy at Rest Haven. An Amish board sets the center's cultural boundaries, which permit electricity but not televisions, computers, or telephones in patient rooms. Volunteer house parents from Amish settlements across the country oversee the kitchen and laundry and lead residents in morning and evening devotions. In 2005 a similar facility, known as Green Pastures, opened in conjunction with Philhaven, a behavioral health care center in Mount Gretna, Pennsylvania. In its first five years this facility served nearly one thousand patients from twenty-seven states and provinces. Fifty-nine percent were Amish, with the remainder coming from other Plain groups.[47]

The emergence of Amish-related and Amish-operated organizations from birth centers to homespun mental health treatment centers illustrates a structural negotiation with modernity—new organizational forms that reflect aspects of formal organizations with a distinctive Amish imprint.

Genetics and Medical Research

The Amish are ideal subjects for genetic research because their exceptional genealogical records, small number of founders, and large families make it possible to trace hereditary traits across centuries and continents. These characteristics of Amish populations and their unique lifestyle have stimulated an unusual amount of scientific research on health and illness in their communities. Although some Amish question or resist mainstream medical treatments, many gladly help to advance scientific research. Households in many settlements willingly cooperate with health professionals who combine clinical services with gathering DNA samples and other data for scientific studies.

Amish populations have a limited gene pool due to their small number of founders and the fact that few converts have joined their communities. These characteristics mean that Amish people have a higher incidence of certain types of genetic disorders than that found in the general population. The types of disorders vary in different settlements. At the same time, a restricted gene pool also provides a protective buffer, so some hereditary diseases in the larger society appear much less frequently or not at all in Amish families.

Professor Victor A. McKusick, a pioneer in the field of medical genetics, began researching Amish genetics in the 1960s. His work was greatly advanced in 1989 when Dr. D. Holmes Morton cofounded the Clinic for Special Children near Strasburg, Pennsylvania, to provide diagnostic and comprehensive medical care for Amish and Mennonite children with inherited genetic diseases.[48] In its practice of genomic medicine, this nonprofit organization blends clinical care with research on metabolic disorders by applying the knowledge of genetics to the everyday practice of medicine. Since its inception, physicians and scientists at the clinic have worked to identify the molecular basis for common disorders in the Amish and Mennonite population and are able to test for some 120 genetic conditions.[49] Using these new understandings of heritable diseases, the clinic provides diagnostic services and comprehensive outpatient care for more than two thousand patients in several states at the remarkably low cost of $800 per person.[50]

A similar clinic serving Amish people in Ohio and eight other states, Das Deutsch Center, was initiated by Dr. Heng Wang in 2000 in Middlefield, Ohio.[51] Providing state-of-the-art clinical care and diagnostic testing, the Center's professional staff has identified and treated more than seventy rare and genetic disorders, some of which are distinctive to the Geauga County settlement.

These two clinics also serve non-Amish children with rare inherited diseases. With collaborating scholars, the researchers of these clinics have published dozens of articles that advance scientific knowledge of metabolic disorders. The clinical care and scientific advances of these two clinics have spurred Amish and Mennonite communities in other areas to establish similar ventures.[52]

Since 1995 Dr. Alan R. Shuldiner of the University of Maryland has conducted scientific investigations involving more than six thousand Amish adults who have participated to advance the understanding of various diseases as well as to receive free medical evaluations and screenings for common diseases.[53] The research staff and Amish liaisons at Shuldiner's Amish Research Clinic have investigated a variety of health issues, including obesity, longevity, blood pressure, osteoporosis, mood disorders, and diabetes. The clinic's research team has produced dozens of scientific articles reporting findings that yield new health information that will benefit Amish and English patients alike.[54] Amish participants in genetics studies often express deep satisfaction that their cooperation in these studies will help thousands of non-Amish doctors and patients.[55]

Health Care as Burden and Gift

Few topics unveil the diversity of Amish views toward modern science and their understanding of divine providence as well as health care practices. Members in some affiliations staunchly resist standard care, believing that they should accept whatever comes as God's will and therefore making widespread use of folk remedies and alternative medicine. Other people accept organ transplants, heart surgery, and knee replacements, and readily participate in scientific studies to advance knowledge about the human genome. Clearly, when it comes to using science to fix illness and ailments, Amish people are scattered across the continuum from resistance to acceptance.

No matter where along the spectrum a particular Amish household falls, health care can be both a burden and a gift. If illness and the medical expenses it engenders become too great for a single person or family to shoulder, the church will spring into action with emotional, physical, and financial support. Caring for the physical needs of others, including the elderly and the disabled, is understood by Amish people as a Christian duty described in the Bible as "bearing one another's burdens" (Gal. 6:2). In their words, such care is simply "being Amish."

In addition to health care, this particular way of being Amish in the world also comes to bear on Amish interactions with the state, civic society, and charitable organizations, which we explore in the following chapter.

CHAPTER 19

Government and
Civic Relations

In November 2011, Jacob U. Gingerich sent a handwritten letter to 138 members of the Kentucky legislature. Earlier in the year Gingerich, a member of the Swartzentruber Amish affiliation, had spent two weeks in prison for driving a buggy without a fluorescent orange slow-moving-vehicle (SMV) triangle. As Gingerich explained in his letter, the SMV's triangular shape represents the Christian trinity, and his church considers affixing such a symbol as a "badge for our protection" to be a pagan talisman. As well, his church "forbids . . . bright, loud and gaudy colors. . . . It is our religious belief to abide by the law of the land, as long as it does not interfere with our religion." Gingerich hoped that Kentucky would adopt laws similar to those in at least eleven other states that permit buggy owners to use lanterns and outline their carriages in reflective silver tape rather than affix the SMV triangle, which "we cannot in good conscious [sic] use."

Subjects and Citizens

The conflict over SMV triangles in Kentucky reflects key elements of Amish interaction with the state. Gingerich's humbly worded petition, mirroring the spirit of *Gelassenheit* and using an old-fashioned medium of communication to address the most bureaucratic structures of the state, shows the cultural gap between Amish and mainstream ways. Journalists following the story noted that "in a high tech world of iPads and smart phones," Gingerich's handwritten letters caught the attention of legislators, who in 2012 took steps to amend Kentucky's highway code along the lines Gingerich suggested.[1]

The confrontation in Kentucky reveals how Amish encounters with the state combine a spirit of deference with an insistence that faith should not budge in the face of governmental power. God has "ordained that there should be a secular government . . . to protect the good and punish the evil," one influential Amish text intones. But if government "asks us to do something that the Bible forbids . . . our first loyalty must always be to God."[2] In addition, this discord points to the diversity of Amish practices since the vast majority of Amish have no problem with the SMV and quietly wonder why the Swartzentrubers so adamantly oppose it. A more liberal Amish man, for example, after reading in his local newspaper about the SMV dispute in Kentucky, wrote a letter to the editor calling the actions of his Kentucky brethren a "disgrace," because the Bible "teaches us to submit to the ordinances of man."[3]

Despite such diversity—or perhaps because of it—Amish struggles with the state also shed light on the nature of the modern nation-state, its understanding of minority rights, its treatment of dissenters, its expansive regulatory power, and its reliance on the courts to settle disputes that elected officials cannot or will not touch.[4]

At first blush, Amish understandings of government might seem like a bundle of contradictions. The Amish appreciate civic order, legal property ownership, and other fruits of a functional state. "We have much to be thankful for to live in a land of religious freedom," one writer affirms. Yet the Amish will not fight to defend the state, participate in the military, or serve on juries. On the one hand, they affirm that God has ordained government, but on the other hand, they assert that this does not "mean God is pleased with all governments," especially those that are "corrupt" and "doing the opposite of what they are ordained for." Yet Amish people also believe they have no "right to resist a corrupt government," protest against it, or try to change it. Instead, they conclude, "We should express our gratitude, live in quiet obedience, and pray for our rulers"—and, following Jesus's example in Matthew 17:24–27, pay taxes.[5]

Amish relations with the state are complicated by their refusal to initiate litigation or use the law aggressively to defend themselves. They view such acts as coercion, which violates the nonresistant teachings of Jesus to love enemies and avoid retaliation. A transgression of this deeply held belief will trigger excommunication in most Amish affiliations. This noncombative stance of Gelassenheit handicaps them somewhat in a system of law that assumes that litigation is often necessary to obtain justice. On some occasions Amish people will reluctantly sign on as plaintiffs in lawsuits prepared by sympathetic third parties.[6]

This seeming ambivalence makes more sense if we understand that the Amish, like their European forebears, see their relationship to the state as that of subjects rather than citizens. *Subjects* are people who petition for privileges and negotiate certain obligations in return. In contrast, *citizens* believe that they have rights and responsibilities common to all citizens. Unlike subjects, who live under the authority and patronage of a ruler, citizens actually comprise the state itself. Citizens possess rights without asking for them and have responsibilities whether they want them or not. Citizenship is, in theory, universal in its protections and its demands. Citizens engage one another as political equals in electoral campaigns and support the state through public and military service. Subjects do not assume that all people should be treated equally but rather that each group of people should arrange its own distinct privileges and duties with the powers that be. In this sense, subjects can simultaneously be grateful for government and see it as something quite foreign to their daily lives.

When the Amish first began to settle in colonial North America, they started moving toward citizen-style participation in public life. They eagerly obtained North American land titles and worked with the provincial government to secure their real estate rights. Yet after more than two and a half centuries of life in the United States, even though Amish people have absorbed some elements of democratic citizenship, their subject-like orientation remains striking. In a face-off with government, they often respond by appealing to the highest executive authority and asking for some dispensation, even if the matter might better be solved, from a political perspective, through judicial or bureaucratic channels. For example, responding to a Pennsylvania law that raised the age for compulsory school attendance, Amish petitioners wrote "To Our Men in Authority," clearly stating that they objected to the law, but concluding, "We beg your pardon for bringing all this before you, and worrying you, and bringing you a serious problem."[7] The petition was hardly a model of modern citizen activism. When Amish issues of religious liberty have made it into the courts or the halls of Congress, they have almost always been presented by sympathetic outsiders.[8]

Encounters with the Law

The overriding narrative of Amish encounters with the state is one of principled obedience. The Amish do not object to paying sales tax or having a lawyer draw up a will. Likewise, Amish violations of criminal law are rare. Before the 1930s, few Amish conflicts took on legal dimensions, and the state generally resolved them in favor of the church. In 1917, for example, Jacob Schmucker, excommunicated in Geauga County, Ohio, sued the settlement's leaders because his shunning "prevented [church] members . . . from continuing to work with" him or enter into "contracts" with him, and it "interfered with the domestic tranquility" of his life. In this and similar cases involving shunning, the courts have ruled in favor of the church and avoided overturning or otherwise becoming involved in matters of church discipline.[9]

During the twentieth century, however, the rise of what scholars call the "warfare state" and the "welfare state" have dramatically expanded and strengthened the power of government to define and regulate more closely matters of public safety and security and intervene more directly in citizens' lives. These developments boosted the number of Amish conflicts with the state. Amish people who speak to government officials, such as Jacob Gingerich, who objected to using an SMV triangle, express a sincere desire to obey all laws that do not conflict with church teaching, but laws and administrative regulations increasingly deal with matters of daily life that have long been governed by the *Ordnung.* Religious liberty in the United States is constitutionally the right to worship and engage in private religious rituals unhindered. The public implications of religion, on the other hand, are less clear because they must be balanced against competing claims of public good. For example, conscientious objection from military service, even when an expression of religious conviction, is not a constitutional right but an allowance granted by Congress as the legislature seeks to draw a line between private faith and public responsibility.[10] For the Amish, however, the distinction between private devotion and public practice is not persuasive because the wide sweep of their faith covers both dimensions.

Amish entanglements with the law can be sorted into several categories.[11] The first consists of clear violations of the law, such as child abuse or disregard for federal environmental protection regulations, which do not turn on questions of religious liberty.[12] If an Amish teenager is arrested for underage drinking, for example, or an Amish business is denied a noise variance, the Amish do not expect any special consideration because they are Amish. In fact, in those cases in which an Amish or Amish-reared individual is arrested for a crime, he or she typically reacts with church-inspired humility and immediately confesses everything—to the consternation of the defense attorneys.

In the second category are regulations that do not appear to outsiders to pertain to religious matters but are in fact intrusive for some Amish groups. Examples include zoning laws that prohibit adding a *Dawdyhaus* for grandparents, building codes that require electrical wiring in new homes, extraordinary medical interventions on young children, child labor laws, state mandates for Amish businesses to participate in workers' compensation plans, and municipal regulations that prohibit stabling horses on small plots of land.

A third set of encounters are those involving more obvious claims of religious liberty or matters of serious church conviction, such as conscientious objection during wartime and Amish prohibitions of photo identification.

Some conflicts between the Amish and the state arouse the interest and patronage of outsiders—principally religious liberty advocates and civil libertarians—who take up Amish causes and engage in vigorous litigation on their behalf. High-profile clashes over public school attendance laws during the 1960s and conflicts over local zoning laws in the early twenty-first century have received such outside attention and support.

Standing Up to the State

The earliest Amish claims of religious exemption stem from their pacifist refusal to participate in the military. Amish nonresistance was tested by the American Revolution, and years later dozens of Amish men used all available means to win exemption from conscription during the Civil War. During World War I, when there were few provisions for conscientious objectors (COs), Amish men often reported to military induction camps when they were drafted and quietly insisted that they would not serve as combatants or noncombatants under any form of military authority. Some camp commanders ignored Amish COs or sent them home on farm furloughs, while others used harsh physical punishment and psychological harassment to try to crack—unsuccessfully, it turned out—their commitment. Stories that portray "nonresistance under test" as a heroic stance continue to circulate in Amish communities.[13]

During the Second World War, the U.S. government permitted COs to perform alternative civilian service in hospitals, forestry, and national parks, in lieu of military assignment. In those years and the Cold War decades that followed, Amish men who were drafted overwhelmingly declared themselves conscientious objectors and typically were assigned to alternative service in understaffed city hospitals. Amish men who were drafted during that period remain deeply grateful for the CO provisions and frequently cite the government's respect for COs as an example of the religious liberty they enjoy.[14]

If Amish relations with the Department of Defense proved conciliatory, those with the Internal Revenue Service (IRS) during the 1950s were confrontational. In 1955 Congress extended Social Security provisions to include self-employed farmers, effectively bringing the Amish—who at that time were almost all farmers—within the bounds of the system for the first time.[15] Amish leaders viewed the nation's old-age pensions and benefits for orphans and the disabled as a secular insurance program that undercut the church's practice of caring for its own members, and they refused to cooperate. From the Amish perspective, resisting Social Security did not contradict the Bible's injunction to pay taxes (Matt. 17:24–27) because they saw Social Security as a form of insurance and not as a tax. "If we do not pay Social Security, does this not give us an excuse to refrain from filing [income taxes]?" asked one Amish primer, before offering a clear *no:* "If our income is large enough that the law requires us to file, then by all means we ought to do so." Objection to Social Security ran deeper than the taboo on insurance and was rooted in the Amish sense of separation from the state. The same booklet explained, "Every time we accept a handout from the government we become obligated to it" and soon "why should we not fight its wars?"[16] For the Amish, conscientious objection to war and to Social Security were twin issues.

IRS agents began garnisheeing money from Amish bank accounts, but some Amish simply closed their accounts. In a dramatic move in 1958, the government foreclosed on several farms to recover lost Social Security funds. During the next two years, the IRS forcibly collected from 130 Amish households. The confrontation that received the most attention occurred in 1961 when federal officials placed a lien on the workhorses of Valentine Y. Byler of New Wilmington, Pennsylvania. Later in springtime, agents arrived at Byler's farm while he was plowing, unhitched three of his horses and led them away as confiscated property. *Reader's Digest* magazine published Byler's story as an account of federal power run amok.[17] Byler sued for damages, but his church forced him to withdraw the suit because it mocked the spirit of nonresistance.

In 1965 Congress exempted self-employed Amish from the Medicare program and from Social Security. Until 1988 Amish employers and employees were still liable for all Social Security taxes, but then Congress expanded the exemption to include Amish who work for Amish employers. Amish employed by English employers, however, must contribute fully to Social Security, even though many refuse to draw benefits to which they are entitled.[18]

Negotiation and Litigation

The confrontation over Byler's horses may be among the most dramatic Amish-state collisions, but high-profile conflicts toggle between quiet behind-the-scenes negotiation and third-party litigation. Such approaches became the dominant pattern in the late twentieth and early twenty-first centuries. Amish negotiation has been led by the National Amish Steering Committee, a group of laymen that, since 1967, has served as the primary liaison for Amish concerns to government.

Quiet Negotiation

The Steering Committee emerged amid growing Amish frustration with alternative service assignments that Mennonites had negotiated with the military on behalf of the Amish. Although Amish leaders embraced alternative service, they were not keen on urban work assignments in major metropolitan hospitals that mission-minded Mennonites had arranged for COs. Amish people preferred rural assignments or farm furloughs.[19] In 1966 Amish leaders from several states meeting in Indiana confirmed that "practically all church leaders . . . agreed that the present . . . system of so many of our boys going to the hospital [urban employment] is proving very unsatisfactory and harmful to our Amish Churches."[20] A delegation of Amish people went to Washington, D.C., to meet with the Mennonite staff member who represented their concerns to the National Service Board for Religious Objectors.

Afterward, the Amish group noted that "the Old Order Amish are following too closely in the steps of the Mennonites, which is undermining our Amish way of life."[21] Subsequently, the Amish delegates went directly to federal Selective Service officials and asked for farm deferments, stating that they would rather have their young men go to prison than work for two years in the city.[22] After some quiet give and take, Selective Service accepted the proposal and directed that Amish draftees be assigned to farm labor.

Although the men who met with military leaders in Washington were standing up for traditional Amish convictions, their direct, unified approach to negotiation was new. In their highly decentralized church, local districts had no mechanism for ratifying the delegation's work. But attendees at an ad hoc meeting of parents and bishops from midwestern and Pennsylvania settlements encouraged the group of Washington "delegates" to transform itself into a permanent body that would represent Amish concerns to government officials. Soon dubbed the Amish Steering Committee, the group selected a secretary and a treasurer, both from Swiss settlements in Indiana, and chose Andrew Kinsinger (1920–1995) as chair. Kinsinger's Lancaster residence placed him in geographic proximity to Washington, D.C., making him the natural contact with federal officials.[23]

The Steering Committee thus became a permanent fixture and gradually expanded to include a "committee man" from each state or cluster of states with Amish populations. The national group meets twice a year, rotating gatherings from one settlement to another. Committee men are not compensated for their work, and when they decide to retire, they find their own replacement. In time, the Steering Committee structure spawned the appointment of additional representatives for local settlements who channel grassroots concerns to the national committee and who explain new agreements with government officials to their hometown constituents.

The formation of the Steering Committee was a negotiated concession to the forces of modern bureaucracy—a response to the state's assumption that Amish people should act and speak as a unified interest group. Federal and state agencies did not want to hear from hundreds of individual church districts. They wanted one Amish spokesperson. Amish church polity could not provide such a singular voice because one unified church did not exist, but the Steering Committee did offer a loose network that could articulate the most widely shared Amish views. Even so, the Steering Committee has always been composed of laymen, never bishops or ministers. Thus, the committee could never, in any formal sense, speak for the church. It could, however, voice Amish concerns and in unobtrusive ways hammer out amiable resolutions with government officials.[24] With the end of the military draft, the Steering Committee's work broadened into a wide range of issues. For example, in the early 1970s, the committee quietly negotiated an exemption from the hard-hat requirement in the new Occupational Safety and Health Act, allowing Amish construction workers to wear their church-stipulated straw hats or knit caps instead.[25]

Third-Party Litigation

Alongside the evolution of an Amish liaison group committed to behind-the-scenes negotiation, conflicts with the state sometimes took a more litigious turn as third-party civil liberties groups pressed lawsuits on Amish behalf. The role of outside advocates was never more prominent than in the Supreme Court case of *Wisconsin v. Yoder et al.* involving the refusal of Amish parents to send their children to high school. By the mid-1960s, most states with larger Amish populations had struck some sort of compromise that balanced state truancy law and Amish objections to high school education (see chapter 14). Yet resolution was elusive in Iowa, Kansas, and Wisconsin, and protracted disputes in those states drew the attention of William C. Lindholm, a Lutheran pastor in Michigan. He spearheaded the National Committee for Amish Religious Freedom (NCARF), which included lawyers, academics, and Christian and Jewish religious leaders.[26]

By the time NCARF formed, conflicts in Iowa had cooled, but in the fall of 1968, Wisconsin authorities arrested three Green County fathers for keeping their children out of high school. Lindholm engaged a Harrisburg, Pennsylvania, attorney, William Bentley Ball, to prepare a legal defense for the three men. In the spring of 1969, NCARF lost its case in Wisconsin's lower courts, but it pressed its appeal through the state judicial system and eventually to the U.S. Supreme Court.[27] In 1972 Chief Justice Warren Burger handed down the high court's unanimous opinion, ruling that the state could not deny the Amish the right to practice their faith even if it precluded certified high school work.[28]

In recent years, third party litigation on behalf of Amish concerns has included cases involving New York state building codes. The Becket Fund for Religious Liberty, a Washington, D.C.–based law firm, has challenged the codes requiring, among other things, smoke detectors, which Swartzentruber Amish residents of the state oppose because they believe such devices betray a lack of faith in God.[29] The first of these conflicts began in 2006 when Swartzentrubers in a new settlement near Morristown, New York, were refused building permits because they would not install smoke detectors.[30] The town's newly hired code enforcement officer began issuing tickets after the Amish started to build without permits. Eventually, the case became a federal lawsuit based on the Amish claim that Morristown was violating their First Amendment rights. As the lawyers for the Amish argued, complying with the requirements of the building code would force the Swartzentrubers in Morristown to change their Ordnung, thrusting them into conflict with other church districts. Furthermore, they argued, "a home that is built in accordance with architect-certified plans or with electronic smoke detectors will be unable to host [church]." Thus the building code violating their Ordnung would have prohibited Swartzentrubers from building homes that could be used as houses of worship.[31]

Third-party litigation is not common, but it often involves high-stakes contests and attracts media attention because advocacy groups for the Amish understand the value of public opinion and are not restrained by humility like their Amish clients.

Stubborn Subjects and Ambivalent Citizens

The spirit of submission cuts both ways when it comes to government relations. On the one hand, Amish people do not clamor for rights or ask for financial entitlements. Yet when they believe a matter of conscience is at stake, they can be remarkably stubborn subjects. As the range of Amish conflicts with the state has grown over the years, it has followed some clear patterns. The Swartzentrubers and the conservative Swiss Amish have scuffled with local zoning officials over ordinances that limit the number of households on single parcels of land or restrict outhouses. Other issues such as tighter photo identification requirements since September 11, 2001, affect groups across the gamut of Amish life. Obtaining a passport to visit relatives in Ontario or simply opening a bank account was already difficult for those without driver's licenses even before states stopped issuing non-photo identity cards. The National Amish Steering Committee typically takes up matters like photo identity that represent broad Amish interests rather than ones like zoning that affect only a small slice of their constituency.[32]

In recent decades, the federal government has been more accommodating of the Amish than state governments have been, likely because at a national level the Amish are such a tiny group and any special treatment is not so politically costly. In 2004, for example, Congress loosened child labor laws to allow fourteen- to seventeen-year-old Amish children to work in many aspects of family businesses.[33] Likewise, the 2010 Patient Protection and Affordable Care Act allowed the Amish to forego purchasing commercial health insurance, as noted in chapter 18. In contrast, local officials responsible for municipal affairs in areas with a sizable percentage—perhaps even a plurality—of Amish have sometimes been the most inflexible because bending zoning, land use, or sanitation rules for the Amish could set problematic precedents. In addition, local officials may not have the staff or budget to deal with complex, exemption-laden ordinances, may not know First Amendment protections, or, in some cases, may even harbor an anti-Amish bias.

Interestingly, local politics can engender citizen-like behavior from some Amish in long-established settlements with progressive outlooks. Although they will not serve on juries or hold public office, many take an interest in local civic affairs. In some settlements, Amish leaders have amicable relationships with municipal officials, who informally consult with them on pending zoning regulations and other matters of mutual interest. Although they decline serving in prominent offices, liberal-minded Amish sometimes will accept appointments on the planning or zoning commissions of rural townships.[34]

Members of Amish communities will also attend public meetings when issues pertinent to them are percolating. In January 2011, for example, Amish men and women helped pack the hearing room at the LaGrange County, Indiana, municipal building and petitioned the county's Alcoholic Beverage and Tobacco Board to deny an alcohol permit requested by a convenience store in the village of Shipshewana. Amish and other town residents wanted to keep the village dry. Although none of the Amish spoke during the time for public comment, Shipshewana Town Manager Sheryl Kelly told a journalist that "their influences really do represent the community."[35]

Amish awareness of and interest in state and national politics often hinges on access to mass media. In late 2007, a sixty-seven-year-old self-employed bishop in the Kalona, Iowa, settlement, conversant on many matters, had not heard of Barack Obama despite intense media coverage of that state's upcoming presidential caucuses. In contrast, an Amish contractor in Maryland whose English driver tunes the truck's radio to daytime talk shows may be quite familiar with current issues as interpreted by political pundits. Amish entrepreneurs who affiliate with the National Federation of Independent Businesses receive that group's voter guide.[36]

Republican Party efforts to register Pennsylvania and Ohio Amish voters for the 2004 presidential election—and the Amish response—illustrate the ambivalent sense of citizenship many Amish people hold. Although church rules do not forbid voting, most Amish refrain from it. "By voting, we become a part of the powers instead of being subject to them," one influential Amish publication explained, adding, "We have enough to do to keep the church in order; let the world run the government" and "If we don't want the government to tell us how to conduct our church affairs, we had better not tell them how to run the government."[37] Amish people who do vote are more likely to do so in local elections than in presidential ones because they worry that voting for the commander-in-chief will compromise their position as conscientious objectors.

Nevertheless, prior to the 2004 presidential election some Amish people in eastern Pennsylvania had caught the contagion of what one Amish man called "Bush Fever," because a local Republican leader with Amish connections led vigorous voter registration efforts in Amish communities. In both Holmes County, Ohio, and Lancaster County, Pennsylvania, 13 percent of Amish adults cast ballots. This unusually high rate of voting in these two settlements was an anomaly not only because it was a presidential election but also because Amish voters were propelled, ironically, by a moral vision for the outside society—opposition to abortion and gay rights—that was of little concern within Amish society itself.[38]

Civic Participation

Although most Amish remain aloof from national politics, many do see themselves as members of local communities and carry a certain sense of civic responsibility. Such commitments are more common in older settlements where Amish people have long-standing neighborly ties. Most Amish consider living a quiet and peaceable life that does not burden the larger society as their way of being good Americans. Nevertheless, Amish contributions to civic life can be much more participatory.

In the Lancaster settlement, for example, Amish people serve as volunteer emergency medical technicians on local ambulance crews.[39] Most volunteer fire companies serving rural areas also have Amish members. Indeed, some companies would hardly function without Amish firefighters, whose flexible work schedule and rural employment allow them to drop everything and respond quickly to alarms. Although Amish firefighters do not drive the fire trucks, they use the latest firefighting technology and serve as elected officers of fire companies. Amish households participate avidly in fire company fund-raising efforts. Women make chicken corn soup and men barbeque chicken for benefit dinners and public auctions and otherwise give generously to fire company treasuries. Even the most conservative Amish may donate items to fund-raising auctions benefiting local volunteer fire companies.

Participating in local fire companies is less common in some areas, but Amish households often contribute to other community causes. An advertisement for a Habitat for Humanity fund-raising auction in northern Indiana featured Amish-donated items such as quilts and furniture as well as items for Amish bidders, including a "buggy with all the extras (heater, fenders, etc.)."[40] In communities where Amish families make use of hospice or grief counseling centers, Amish people express their gratitude by supporting their fund-raisers. Amish people in many settlements also donate blood to public health agencies. The annual blood drive in one Ohio community offers Amish participants a chance to win a buggy. The idea was proposed by an Amish man who serves on the board of his local Red Cross chapter.[41]

This young Amish man serves as the assistant chief of a
local volunteer fire company in Pennsylvania. Here he observes
Amish people preparing equipment to be sold at an auction
to raise funds for the fire company. Involvement in such a role
requires the use of high-tech communications such as the two-
way radio on his belt. *Daniel Rodriguez*

The Amish are reluctant to join service clubs such as Rotary or Kiwanis that might
compete with their churchly commitments. Occasionally, however, individuals do
partner with such groups. This happened during the 2009 Christmas season in Har-
lan, Indiana, where shoppers noticed a pair of Salvation Army bell ringers in "long,
plain dresses and white cotton bonnets" who "moved about with the help of white
canes." Sisters Emma and Naomi Miller, who were blind, were serving with a youth
program associated with Lions Clubs International, a group known for programs
that serve the blind. "[My parents] think it's fine," Emma told a journalist, "but when
I talk to my grandpa and grandma, they don't know what to think sometimes. But

Thousands of people (Amish and English) attend an annual benefit auction for a local fire company. Amish people play a key role in organizing the event each year. The horse auction in the foreground is one of many auctions occurring simultaneously. *Daniel Rodriguez*

they excuse me because I'm blind." That Christmas the sisters raised more money for the Salvation Army than any other pair of ringers. They did so, however, on their own terms, refusing to pose for pictures or wear the insignia vests of the Lions Club, which was helping the women obtain a guide dog.[42]

Charitable Work

Beyond their contributions to civic life, Amish people also engage in charitable work through church-related organizations. Most Amish charitable work takes place through agencies managed by Mennonites or car-driving Beachy Amish. Since the 1950s, Amish men and women have participated in the work of Mennonite Disaster Service (MDS), an organization somewhat akin to the Red Cross that provides immediate relief and long-term rebuilding for Americans in the wake of floods, tornados, hurricanes, and other natural catastrophes. In 1992, responding to devastation in Florida from Hurricane Andrew, a coalition of Amish and conservative Mennonites organized Disaster Response Services (DRS).[43] Like MDS, its Mennonite counterpart, DRS provides volunteer cleanup and rebuilding for mostly lower-income households selected by local aid agencies. But DRS only accepts volunteers who wear plain garb, a reaction against the more liberal ethos of some MDS units in which, as one person noted, volunteers might "find themselves working on a roof next to women in very revealing clothing," which would not be "a consistent witness." Nonetheless, Amish volunteers from many settlements still participate in MDS. In the wake of Hurricane Katrina's Gulf Coast destruction in 2005, an outpouring of hundreds of Amish volunteers from across the country donated thousands of hours in cleanup.[44]

Amish charity gravitates toward practical projects, such as sending food relief to famine-stricken parts of the world or financing well-drilling in poor countries, rather than complex economic development projects or highly technical medical missions. Historically, many Amish communities have generously supported the work of Mennonite Central Committee (MCC), an international relief agency whose global efforts mushroomed after World War II. Each year, for example, Amish men and women contribute to MCC directly by canning thousands of tons of turkey for distribution in overseas schools and refugee camps and volunteering in MCC warehouses packing clothing, health, and educational supplies for worldwide distribution. Amish churches, especially in Pennsylvania, actively support MCC's annual "relief sale" auctions, which sometimes include the sale of a new home built with Amish-donated labor and materials. Amish women in eastern Lancaster County converted a tobacco barn into the Buena Vista Sewing Room, where they quilt, roll bandages, and pack clothing for MCC's global distribution.[45]

In the Midwest, Amish contributions more often flow toward Christian Aid Ministries (CAM), an international relief organization begun in 1981 in Holmes County by an Ohio businessman who was then a member of the New Order Amish.[46] CAM's constituency is largely plain-dressing Mennonites and Beachy Amish, but many Amish people also contribute time or money to CAM, which bills itself as "a trustworthy, efficient channel for Amish, Mennonite, and other conservative Anabaptist groups" seeking to "minister to physical and spiritual needs around the world."[47] In 2011 CAM operated directly in thirty-four countries—eight of which hosted permanent office facilities, schools, or orphanages—and distributed nearly 90,000 food parcels, more than 2.2 million Bibles and other books, some 56,000 pounds of seeds, and almost 26,000 comforters.[48] Amish volunteers are highly involved in CAM's warehouses in Kalona, Iowa; Shipshewana, Indiana; and elsewhere. Giving to CAM and to MCC reflects the evolving Amish economy. A shift away from farming, in which wealth was lodged in land and commodities, to small businesses and self-employment increased financial liquidity, making cash donations more common.

Some Amish people also engage in public service through the Conservative Anabaptist Service Program (CASP). In 2011, for example, a team of twenty-one Amish workers did reconstruction work at a Lake Michigan Recreation Area operated by the U.S. Forest Service. CASP was developed as a government-approved option for alternative service for conscientious objectors if a military draft is renewed.[49]

Amish donors, bidders, and auctioneers are central to the success of a network of Haiti Benefit Auctions hosted in a number of midwestern Amish settlements and in Sarasota, Florida, and eastern Pennsylvania. These auctions annually raise significant contributions for several conservative Mennonite mission agencies that operate projects in Haiti.[50]

Financial support for these organizations points to some of the practical limits of Amish charitable work. Although many Amish contribute regularly to Beachy Amish and Mennonite overseas projects through CAM and other avenues, almost no Amish serve as individual missionaries or aid workers. Virtually all Amish churches prohibit air travel, and Amish theology has long been skeptical of verbal evangelism unaccompanied by the corporate witness of an entire community. Some New Order Amish, who are allowed to fly and whose theology is more open to mission work, have served in overseas assignments, often with CAM or with Master's International Ministries in Ukraine.[51]

One uniquely Amish transnational project is a partnership between Amish schoolteachers from the United States and highly traditional, plain-dressing Old Colony Mennonites who live in northern Mexico and are descended from Russo-German immigrants. This project circumvents Amish dictates against evangelism and air travel: the relationship does not involve proselytizing, and the Amish can travel to Mexico by train or bus.

The partnership began in the mid-1990s when an Amish delegation visited Mexico and met with Old Colony Mennonite leaders. The Mennonites had struggled with poverty, and their schools were inadequate; the Amish visitors saw an opportunity to help a group that was ethnically and theologically similar to their own. These contacts evolved into the Old Colony Support Committee, which draws on donations and volunteers from Amish settlements in Pennsylvania, Ohio, Kentucky, Michigan, Indiana, and Montana to place Amish teachers in Old Colony schools where they head up classrooms and train Mennonite teachers. About two hundred Amish teachers and support staff have served in Mexico, with many of them returning multiple times for four- to six-month terms. Virtually all the teachers are single women whose written reports and "prayer cards" are distributed to Amish supporters, giving them a status akin to missionaries in other traditions. The Old Colony Support Committee provides a quarterly newsletter but remains quintessentially Amish—it has no office or paid staff and holds its low-key annual meetings in members' homes.[52]

The American Oyster

In his 1972 opinion in *Wisconsin v. Yoder,* U.S. Supreme Court Chief Justice Warren Burger wrote, "We must not forget that in the Middle Ages important values of the civilization of the western world were preserved by members of religious orders who isolated themselves from all worldly influences against great obstacles. There can be no assumption that today's majority is 'right' and the Amish and others like them are 'wrong.' A way of life that is odd or even erratic but interferes with no rights or interests of others is not to be condemned because it is different."[53] Burger's sentiment—that the Amish have something to teach other Americans about dissent and democracy—has been echoed by many civil libertarians and religious freedom advocates over the past forty years.

Law professor Garrett Epps, although appreciative of the *Yoder* decision, has wondered if Americans fully understand what the Amish encounter with the state really means. The United States has permitted only a limited degree of religious diversity, Epps notes, because the country tends to transform religious traditions "until they take on a particular American character"—one marked by individual belief, voluntary choice, and universal values—that makes them all pale versions of one another.

The Amish, however, refuse to fit into this American mold, persisting in their un-American style of a collective faith and particular way of life. "Their struggle is for their own survival as a community, not for the liberty of society as a whole," Epps argues. They refuse "to simply become yet another American faith competing in the free market" of denominations, which James Madison and other founders of the nation imagined. As such, the Amish have become like a grain of sand in the American oyster—a minority group that has "resisted . . . the majority's hostility" and acted as an "irritant that cannot be absorbed or digested" but might yet "be transformed into a pearl."[54]

Whether Americans recognize that pearl, and how they value the Amish irritant, may say more about the nature of American democracy than do the words of Justice Burger, who elsewhere in his opinion suggested that the Amish represent the best of American values. In actuality, the Amish stand in sharp contrast to a prized American value like individualism.

Amish encounters with government and their engagement with civic life more broadly reveal the diverse and contested nature of Amish society. Outsiders both scorn them and rally to their defense. Some partisan activists, bemused by constituents who act like subjects rather than citizens, use the Amish for political gain. The impersonal and bureaucratic nature of government requires that Amish people speak with one voice, but even the National Amish Steering Committee refuses to negotiate on behalf of everyone who claims the Amish name. Clearly, the Amish do not speak with one voice. In fact they publish in many voices, as we shall learn in the next chapter.

CHAPTER 20

THE AMISH IN PRINT

In 1975 a small group of Amish leaders led by Ezra Wagler, a deacon in Bowling Green, Missouri, launched a weekly correspondence newspaper entitled Die Botschaft *exclusively for horse-and-buggy-driving readers. The paper is composed of reader-submitted letters that recount the often mundane events of life in dozens of settlements across North America. Subscribers can remain abreast of births and deaths, track the weather, and learn who hosted church services in any number of communities. Innocuous as such material might seem, the content of the paper is not left to chance. A five-member board of deacons monitors* Die Botschaft's *content and advertising, overseeing "what is acceptable to be printed and who is acceptable as writers." Explicit guidelines prohibit "murder or love poems or stories" and "letters of religious discussion or criticism." Similar restrictions apply to advertisements: "No photos of people in ads," "No books on positive thinking or how to get smart," "No Mysteries, War, and Love stories."*

Amish Identity in a World of Print

The extent to which Amish people read and write often surprises outside observers. Despite skepticism about higher education, the Amish have prolific writers, and every large settlement—and some smaller ones—include Amish printers and publishers. Amish authors create a diverse array of works, ranging from professionally published books such as *The Amazing Story of the Ausbund,* written by a minster in the Lancaster, Pennsylvania, settlement and sold publicly, to "On the Beutiful [*sic*]

Country Days," a collection of original poetry photocopied by a fifteen-year-old girl for her friends and relatives. Some parents pen reminiscences for their children and grandchildren, others write and publish stories of personal grief to help console and encourage those similarly afflicted, and still others compile family genealogies or submit articles and poems to one of the many Amish-edited periodicals.

For some Amish authors, writing provides a personal creative outlet, even if it is an anonymous one. In the humble spirit of *Gelassenheit,* many works are published without the author's name. But that feature of Amish authorship points to what is often its larger purpose: supporting the values of the community. Publications as diverse as memoirs, doctrinal works, and cookbooks all reinforce community ties and traditions. For example, *The Amazing Story of the Ausbund* was published in the hope that "the churches of our days may be reminded of things we should be learning from history. We may be standing in greater danger of losing out on many of the beliefs and practices of the early Christians and the first Anabaptists than most of us realize."[1]

Cookbooks also connect communities and perpetuate traditions. *Cooking with the Horse & Buggy People,* a collection of recipes from the large Holmes County, Ohio, settlement, subtly communicates the separation from mainstream society by providing treatments for ailments that would send some non-Amish people to the nearest hospital. There are folk remedies for whooping cough, snake bites, and—alarmingly—"mad dog" bites, as well as a "spring tonic" that combines sulfur, cream of tartar, and Epsom salts in a jar of water. By preserving Amish culinary practices in writing, cookbooks help to transmit a particularly Amish food culture.

But the Amish are not the only ones who use print to reinforce particular notions of Amishness. Non-Amish novelists have employed Amish characters and settings in hundreds of books and short stories. Some writers present the Amish as simple folk who have rejected all technology and are somehow more "real" and honest than most Americans, while others present their own form of morality tale by focusing on what they perceive to be Amish imperfections and shortcomings. The authors of Amish-themed romance novels blend rurality and religion with very chaste romance in ways that have lured millions of readers.[2] The growing corpus of Amish literature produced by both Amish and non-Amish writers warrants attention for the ways it mediates and even constructs Amish identity.

Publishing for Amish Purposes

Amish writing and publishing are not new phenomena. Reformation-era Anabaptist literature such as the *Ausbund* hymns and the *Martyrs Mirror* account of church history continues to inform Amish life. In the late 1800s, Iowa schoolteacher Samuel D. Guengerich edited *Herold der Wahrheit,* a periodical to which many midwestern

Amish households subscribed. Yet writing and publishing remained tangential to Amish life until the mid-twentieth century. The massive outpouring of print within Amish society in the half century since 1960 shows a gradual shift from a German-based oral discourse to an English-based print one. This movement from orality to text-based literacy reveals the influence of modernity's press toward formality and abstraction. Moreover, the plethora of Amish-produced publications offers new ways of formulating and thickening Amish ties across increasingly diverse affiliations.

Producing Schoolbooks

Publishing that was distinctly Amish came into its own because of the need for textbooks and other materials for the emerging network of Amish schools. Initially, many Amish school directors, desiring to maintain a traditional public school curriculum, simply bought discarded texts from neighboring rural public schools. As the number of Amish schools mushroomed, however, there were not enough cast-off books to supply the Amish demand. Moreover, textbook companies continued to revise their titles, and Amish parents grew uncomfortable with the newer versions. The best solution, it seemed, was for the Amish to begin producing their own books.

The first sizable Amish publisher, Gordonville Print Shop, was already an established printing company in central Lancaster County, Pennsylvania, when Andrew S. Kinsinger bought the business in 1957 from its non-Amish owner. A year later, Kinsinger became the first chair of the Old Order Book Society of Pennsylvania, a group that had formed to acquire textbooks for Amish schools. For Kinsinger, using the printshop to produce textbooks specifically for Amish (and Old Order Mennonite) schools was a logical step. In 1958 Gordonville Print Shop obtained the rights to several out-of-print public school textbook series and began to reprint them. Twenty years later, the printshop was employing "four to six people working in the print room" and offered "a full line of books, workbooks, record sheets . . . as well as a full line of supplies . . . for the schools."[3] Under the direction of the Old Order Book Society, Gordonville continues to supply schools in the most conservative Amish communities with textbooks that were standard in public schools several generations ago.[4]

Although the Gordonville books assured parents that their children were learning from the same texts they themselves had used, some leaders in the Amish school movement hoped that private schooling would play a more active role in preparing children for Amish life, and for that task they needed books written specifically for Amish readers. In the summer of 1963, Joseph Stoll and David Wagler discussed publishing school books while threshing oats on their Aylmer, Ontario, farms. Wagler had just started a mail order bookstore and was getting requests for out-of-print books. The men talked about reprinting titles, but soon the conversation turned to writing and publishing "some of our own." As Stoll recalled, "There was some question about who would be the printer. We turned it over to Jacob Eicher [then a minister], who said, 'I can't write or sell books, but I can run machinery.'"[5]

The following spring, Stoll, Wagler, and Eicher incorporated Pathway Publishing Corporation (now Pathway Publishers) and began writing and publishing a line of new textbooks specifically for Amish students. The first of these Pathway Readers appeared four years later, in 1968. Unlike the old public school texts reprinted by Gordonville, the Pathway Readers intentionally reinforce contemporary Amish identity. Many of the fiction and nonfiction stories, particularly in the books for younger children, are set in Amish families and communities, with little reference to mainstream society. The reading books for the upper grades do include some selections by non-Amish authors, but they have been carefully chosen to reinforce Amish values.

In 1995 a former Pathway editor, Delbert Farmwald, and his wife, Linda, started a third Amish publishing company, Study Time, in LaGrange County, Indiana. Farmwald had become dissatisfied with the textbooks available for teaching arithmetic in Amish schools. Many schools were still using the Strayer-Upton series first published in the 1930s and kept in print by Gordonville Print Shop.[6]

Intertwining Amish life and Anabaptist heritage with world events, Study Time mathematics books are designed to prepare Amish children for daily interaction with the broader, outside world. The few illustrations in the texts present the world that children see, with backhoes and dump trucks as well as horses and baskets of corn, while the math problems reinforce Amish ways of dealing with that world. The series draws on American and world history for its problems. Students calculate the average number of patents issued per year from 1500 to 2000, for example, and determine the proportion of volcanoes that are active in Japan.

Study Time editors want their textbooks to encourage students to think for themselves, but at the same time prepare them for eternal life. For example, in a note printed inside the front cover of the arithmetic books, the editors assert that "it is obvious that numbers, facts, and their calculating procedures are so orderly, so accurate, and so consistently dependable that the Author [God] of this entire system of concepts must have been infinitely greater and wiser and keener than the human mind."

Study Time also publishes a number of other titles, including a geography textbook. In a break with tradition, it also produces a multivolume preschool activity set designed to prepare preschoolers for deskwork and the English language. Although the most conservative Amish parents would see little use for such materials, some parents in more progressive communities begin school-like activities in their homes before their children enter school.

Getting Amish Authors into Print

Alongside the production of schoolbooks has been the development, especially since the 1960s, of an Amish literature—books written by the Amish for the Amish—designed to both entertain and instruct. Pathway Publishers has been a leader in providing such books for all ages. Pathway's first hardcover book, *Worth Dying For,* was, in fact, not a textbook but rather a story of religious persecution in the days prior to the Reformation. Published in 1964, *Worth Dying For* represented Wagler's dream of producing "sound reading materials" that would supplant the kinds of reading matter finding its way into Amish homes that, in the eyes of Wagler, too often taught "a false kind of religion which is contrary to the faith of our fathers in such vital points as nonresistance and non-conformity to the world."[7] Another early Pathway title was *The Mighty Whirlwind,* which recounted the experiences of those who lived through the tornadoes that struck northern Indiana on Palm Sunday in 1965. The book included captivating first-person Amish accounts of the storms and their aftermath, along with reflections on divine providence.

Pathway now offers a wide variety of titles for many ages, including autobiographies, novels, and children's books. Historical works include *How the Dordrecht Confession Came Down to Us,* a booklet by minister Joseph Stoll, and David Luthy's *The Amish in America: Settlements that Failed, 1840–1960.* The Benjie and Becky books, a series popular with children, recount the adventures of five-year-old Benjie and nine-year-old Becky—and always end with clear moral lessons. Other books also present the joys and struggles of Amish life, reinforcing through engaging stories the values underpinning the Amish world. For example, in one Pathway book, *The Girl in the Mirror,* young Emma Bontrager, born to a father who is crippled, must learn to work hard and accept what life brings cheerfully and unselfishly. As the book's anonymous author notes in the foreword, "It is my sincere wish and prayer that every young reader will be able to identify with the girl in the story and be led to realize that there are more important things in life than living for 'self.'"[8]

Amish-authored stories are often difficult to classify unambiguously as fiction or nonfiction. For Amish readers and writers, nonfiction (books that are true) and realistic fiction (books that *could* be true) hold more appeal than, say, science fiction or fantasy. Much Amish writing appears to be autobiographical, and even when it is not, it could be. As the author of *The Girl in the Mirror* notes, "Though the characters are entirely fictitious, the problems are not."[9] Because such works of realistic fiction focus on real-life situations, they teach values important in Amish life: helping others, following church teachings, and giving up one's selfish desires in order to lead a life of service to family and church.

A Plethora of Periodicals

Stories with similar lessons are a mainstay of the monthly magazines that Pathway issues. The oldest of these, predating the publishing house itself, is *Blackboard Bulletin,* a magazine for teachers. Pathway also publishes *Family Life,* which first appeared in December 1967, and *Young Companion* for teens. These periodicals provide original stories, articles, poetry, letters, and news as well as reprinted items the editors think would appeal to their readers. Attesting to the growth of Amish interest in writing, the *Family Life* editor reminded readers in 2012 that "years ago there was a shortage of material for our papers. . . . Today we receive far more manuscripts than we can possibly use."[10] The Pathway publications offer specific instruction on how to practice Amish values and faith from a particular perspective. Yet despite their wide distribution, they are unwelcome in the homes of some of the most conservative affiliations. The reason for this, according to founder and editor Joseph Stoll, is that the books may have "too much religion. They [conservatives] might be afraid of Pathway influence. There's the threat of more progressive influence."[11]

Although Pathway periodicals are well known, they are hardly alone. For example, the *Diary of the Old Order Churches* (often simply referred to as "the *Diary*") has been published monthly in Lancaster County, Pennsylvania, since 1969. Each issue includes letters from Amish writers in twenty or more states, with news of baptisms, ordinations, and households moving from one settlement to another. The most distinctive features are special interest columns for "sky watchers," bird watchers, mathematicians, and historians, and "The Hausfrau Diary" for housewives.

The *Diary*'s topical columns presaged a flurry of new topical or regionally focused periodicals that began during the 1990s and early 2000s.[12] For example, *School Echoes,* published in Elkhart County, Indiana, since 2001, is a monthly magazine that includes commentaries and advice from teachers, short articles written by children, word puzzles, and line drawings for children to color. Other special interest publications include *Life's Special Sunbeams,* published monthly for parents of special needs children, and *Ladies Journal,* first published in 2010, which offers "inspiration and encouragement by women of faith." *Plain Communities Business Exchange* appears monthly, and *Von das Schlacht Haus* (From the Slaughter House) comes out nine times a year. Other publications are more general. *Plain Interests,* first issued in 2001, has found wide readership with its historical reminiscences and articles on health, gardening, and everyday topics. In 2012, one Amish publisher counted at least

Table 20.1. Sampler of Amish Publications

Correspondence Newspapers
The Budget (weekly)
Die Botschaft (weekly)
The Diary (monthly)

Regional Newsletters
Der Kierche Brief (Ashland, OH)
Die Bote (LaFarge, WI)
Der Gemeinde Brief (Burton, OH)
The Grapevine (IA)
Lancaster Gemeinde Brief (Lancaster, PA)
Gemeinde Register (Sugarcreek, OH)
Die Blatt (IN, MI, WI)
Plain Connections (WI, MN)

Religious Periodicals
Family Life (monthly for all ages)
Young Companion (monthly for teens)
Beside the Still Waters (monthly devotional)
Tagliches Manna (monthly devotional)

Topical Periodicals
Blackboard Bulletin (monthly)
School Echoes (monthly)
Life's Special Sunbeams (monthly)
Ladies Journal (bimonthly)
Nature Trails (monthly)
Plain Communities Business Exchange (monthly)
Farming (quarterly)
Buggy Builders Bulletin (quarterly)
Truck Patch News (monthly)

fifty Amish subscription publications.[13] A sampler of publications appears in table 20.1.

Perhaps most notable has been the growth in the number of church newsletters, which include community announcements, listings of where church services were held the previous Sunday, which ministers preached, and who will host services on upcoming Sundays. Many newsletters also post classified advertisements and the telephone numbers of non-Amish drivers who provide taxi service.

Inscribing Community

While church newsletters and specialized periodicals present many facets of the Amish world, two widely read correspondence newspapers, the *Budget* and *Die Botschaft*, transcend differences in geography and even *Ordnung*, to some degree, thereby fostering a broad, inclusive sense of Amish communities grounded in common conversations.[14] These weekly newspapers have no screaming headlines or paid writers. Instead, like the *Diary* and the church newsletters, they rely on correspondents—referred to as "scribes"—from various settlements to write letters (in English) relaying local events, which the editors then publish in a straightforward, multi-column format without any photos, editing, or commentary. A typical issue of *Die Botschaft* contains 747 letters from 683 communities in 25 states and Ontario.[15]

The news in these papers focuses on family and community. With the exception of comments on the weather, in fact, many of the reports cover similar content. There is little in the letter from a Kentucky scribe that makes it particularly Kentuckian. Indeed, at any particular time, many scribes write about similar things: church services, accidents, planting, harvesting, visiting, hunting, weddings, burials, and births. "Our church services at Robert A. Troyer's yesterday was well attended with many visitors," reported one scribe from Baltic, Ohio, before listing a dozen of the visitors. Two columns to the left, another Ohio writer noted that they "were blessed with a beautiful day after the area received 3 or more inches of rain" and that "John and Ruth Raber say 'It's a boy.' They have named him Bruce. . . . Grands are Abe J. C. Rabers and Wayne M. Millers."[16]

The similarity in content from letter to letter reinforces the notion that the individual settlements do, indeed, form a larger community. The formulaic organization of the letters further contributes to the sense of oneness. Each begins with a comment on the weather or seasonal activities, followed by church news and life events. If Amish correspondence papers seem strikingly different from social media outlets such as Facebook, they are not. Both these imagined communities—created without face-to-face interaction—bear important similarities. As with online interest groups, the subjects about which Amish scribes write—and those they avoid—combine to create a world of insider knowledge, assumed taboos, and a shared sense of a larger Plain society. For example, letters casually referring to buggy transportation and advertisements selling driving harnesses and offering taxi services normalize the absence of driver's licenses.

Women apparently comprise a majority of the correspondents in the *Budget* and *Die Botschaft*. One study found that 46 percent of *Budget* letters were signed with a woman's name, and another third were signed ambiguously with the name of a married couple or family. An analysis of letters signed by couples or families, as well as anecdotal reports, suggests that a sizable majority of them are also written by women. Less than a fifth of the letters in both newspapers were submitted by men alone.[17]

Although the two papers foster an interstate sense of Amish unity, they have nurtured different perceptions of Amish worlds. The *Budget*, begun in the nineteenth century and published by a non-Amish firm in Sugarcreek, Ohio, has never enforced tight control over the content of letters. Correspondents represent an array of Amish and Mennonite groups, though many have roots in or some connection to eastern Ohio even if they live elsewhere. Thus, the *Budget* includes letters by ex-Amish, notices for evangelical books and audio recordings, and business advertisements with close-up photographs of people.

By the 1970s, such ads, along with letters from former Amish that seemed to encourage defection, were too much for some conservative readers. In response, they launched *Die Botschaft* in 1975, with much sharper editorial guidelines and restrictions to minimize offense to traditionalists. When the English editor of *Die Botschaft* allowed an advertisement for cell phones in late 2003, for example, the board of Amish deacons that monitors the paper intervened to discontinue it.[18] Although some *Botschaft* readers had cell phones—and the advertiser was a Lancaster firm with Amish accounts—the Amish advisers to *Die Botschaft* were uncomfortable because they wanted the paper to present a more explicitly traditional identity.[19] By about the 1990s, *Die Botschaft* had probably surpassed the *Budget* in number of Amish readers, though not in total number of subscribers. Despite their differences, both papers construct and reinforce Amish commonalities amid persistent diversity.

Coming at the very time that television and video images were increasingly driving the discourse of mainstream society, the photo-less, black-and-white, old-fashioned design of correspondence newspapers like *Die Botschaft* drew a bold boundary between Amish life and the rise of a YouTube culture. The upswing of Amish publications also documents the growing disparity within Amish worlds both in content and format—from the black-and-white plainness of *Buggy Builders Bulletin* to the glossy, four-color, professional design of *Ladies Journal,* which began in 2010.

Amish writing and publishing, in all its forms, strengthens community cohesion across time and space by emphasizing values that unite even disparate Amish groups. The flourishing of Amish print culture since the middle of the twentieth century represents a significant cultural shift, one with the potential to mold Amish identity in a variety of ways.[20]

Fictional Portrayals for the Rest of Us

Amish writers for the *Budget* and *Die Botschaft* are not the only people inventing Amish worlds through print. Non-Amish fiction writers also construct Amish images that often have more to do with the popular desires and cultural needs of wider American society than with any single Amish community in particular.[21] Some onlookers see a quaint, simple folk practicing traditional values of a pioneer past where time moves more slowly but faith is stronger. For others, the Amish are an example of a history best left behind or a suffocating conformity out of sync with America's celebration of individual freedom. All of these images are communicated and per-petuated by outside authors who have turned out hundreds of Amish-themed short stories and novels, including mysteries, romances, science fiction, and children's books—works that carry messages that are, in their own ways, as didactic as any Amish-published book of religious doctrine.

Exotic But Pure Relics of the Past

For many Americans, the Amish are, as Malcolm Chase and Christopher Shaw put it, "talismans that link us concretely with the past."[22] A common theme over the years has been the Amish as exotics. Young readers encountered it in the 1955 Nancy Drew adventure *The Witch Tree Symbol*. It emerges too in the story of sixteen-year-old Texas teenager Leah, the heroine in Lurlene McDaniel's 1990s trilogy *Angels Watching Over Me, Lifted Up By Angels,* and *Until Angels Close My Eyes,* as Leah finds first love with a young Amish man named Ethan. The Amish even act in old-fashioned ways when they participate in contemporary crime stories, from Tamar Myers's Pennsylvania Dutch mysteries and the Ohio Amish mysteries of P. L. Gaus to *Plain Truth* by acclaimed novelist Jodi Picoult.

From these books, outside readers learn that all Amish ride in buggies and lack electricity and that all the women make quilts and all the men build barns. Readers also learn that these exotic people dress so similarly that they are hard to tell apart. Nancy Drew encounters "an Amish woman, wearing a black dress that reached the top of her high shoes, a black bonnet, and a white shoulder kerchief and apron" and is surprised to see that she is young.[23] Meribah, the nineteenth-century Amish pro-tagonist in Kathryn Lasky's novel *Beyond the Divide,* wonders "what it would feel like to wear a colorful dress." Instead, "her gray gown and cap" mark her as "one of those pee-culiar sorts with the weird religion and funny talk."[24]

And in these books, the Amish *do* talk funny. Some speak English in a blend of unvoiced consonants and superlative compounds—the *chust wonderful-gut* (just wonderfully good) of Beverly Lewis's protagonists—while others, like Nancy Drew's young Amish friend Henner, speak mixed-up English: "Oh, Nancy . . . you kept us from being dead already yet."[25] McDaniel's Ethan sets himself apart from other seventeen-year-olds by his archaic language, but by the second volume of the trilogy, Leah finds Ethan's speech musical and wonders at his "quaint" use of words.

Living in an old-fashioned, tech-free zone, the Amish of popular novels dem-onstrate the simplicity and stability of the past.[26] They are variously quirky, simple, naive folk, yet they are wise in their simplicity. McDaniel's Leah is amazed by Ethan's "naiveté and unworldliness," and Ethan's brother Eli characterizes the Amish as "liv-ing in the eighteenth century."[27] Although Freni, the cook in Myers's *Parsley, Sage,*

Rosemary & Crime, is "not as strict as some of her brethren," she finds "everything about the outside world . . . an enigma" and believes that "even a quick stop at McDonald's is enough to jeopardize one's soul."[28]

These books offer an Amish world that is "uncomplicated" and full of "large Amish houses and barns, *Daadihauses,* grape arbors, and watering troughs."[29] Nancy Drew and her friends encountered "methodically planned, beautiful farm country," in which "they saw straight green fields of corn, as well as potatoes and tobacco." And they were charmed by "weedless vegetable gardens . . . surrounded by neat borders of flowers—cockscomb, begonia, and geranium . . . in profusion."[30] In short, these novels invite readers to visit an imagined world—uncomplicated by sophistication, yet seemingly healthier than their own.

Saviors of the World

Another genre of Amish-themed fiction presents the Amish as a counterbalance to the terror and uncertainty of a future in which science determines all. In the midst of a pervasive technology that is obscure to ordinary people, the Amish guard the secrets that can enable human survival. For example, science fiction author Allen Kim Lang theorized in 1962 that cultures reverse technologically as humans engage in interplanetary colonization. Amish settlers are thus ideal colonizers because they can help other space travelers develop survival skills for recovery. In Lang's short story "Blind Man's Lantern," Amish newlyweds Aaron and Martha Stoltzfoos journey to the planet Murna in search of farmland that is scarce on overpopulated and overdeveloped Earth. In return for their land, the Stoltzfooses are supposed to help an earlier set of space travelers take the planet "back toward the machine age." Martha is a scientist, but she uses a microscope "designed to work by lamplight, as the worldly vanity of electric light would ill suit an Old Order bacteriologist."[31]

Other science fiction writers have used the Amish to represent the antithesis of science and progress—in short, to represent humanity's saviors. In Isaac Asimov's *Foundation's Edge,* the Hamish, an agrarian folk farming in the ruins of the galactic capitol, hide important secrets. In Greg Bear's Nebula Award–winning work *Moving Mars,* a visiting Martian seeks out the Amish, "who had finally accepted the use of computers, but not thinkers [artificial intelligence computers]."[32]

Science fiction writers are not the only authors who find in the Amish a powerful antidote to modernity's alienation from nature. In Barbara Workinger's 2002 mystery *In Dutch Again,* big city journalist Ian Hunter is enthralled by the assertion of Amish dairy farmer Daniel that "it took many children to work the farms since the Amish didn't use modern farm machinery but relied on horses."

"Your people are real ecologists," Ian commented.

"We believe we are stewards of the Lord's land. We may use it, but not abuse it."[33] Daniel's eighteen-year-old son's new buggy prominently displays a bumper sticker: "Milk, naturally!" For Workinger, the Amish are rational folk who make sane, healthy, and correct decisions in the midst of a nature-abusing society.

Strict Sectarians

Yet even the pastoral scenes that feed the nostalgia for a simpler life warn readers that living in an Amish sanctuary comes at the expense of values that outsiders hold dear. Some Amish-themed novels make clear that, despite any superficial resemblance to the American pioneers, the Amish are not rugged individualists committed to democratic ideals of personal freedom and equality, but rather they are uneasy, often frightened members of rigidly authoritarian, overly conformist, isolated and isolating settlements. The simplest of pleasures is suspect in the Amish world. In Beverly Lewis's *The Shunning*, the young Amish girl Katie must be constantly on guard lest she hum forbidden tunes.

Whereas the dominant society values individuality, the Amish of many popular novels suppress it. In Gaus's *Blood of the Prodigal*, Jeremiah Miller feels guilty for getting up early to enjoy the dawn, worried that this "could give him a sense of identity separate from the others."[34] Katie's psychiatrist in Picoult's *Plain Truth* asserts, "To the Amish, there's no room for deviation from the norm. . . . If you don't fit in, the consequences are psychologically tragic."[35]

In these novels, the failure to fit in, to suppress individual difference, invariably leads to excommunication and shunning. With few exceptions, books by non-Amish authors present shunning as a final, unforgiving, and (for the outside audience) inconceivable act that destroys the life of the one who is shunned.[36] Lewis's protagonist in *The Shunning* "could remember her Mammi Essie telling about a man who had been shunned for using tractor power. None of the People could so much as speak to him or eat with him, lest they be shunned too. 'It's like a death in the family,' Essie told her."[37] These stories typically minimize the role of baptism, church membership, disobedience, and confession, which are integral to understanding shunning, and they overplay its strictness. Gaus and Lewis both present characters who are banned without ever having joined the church in the first place. Nancy Drew and her friends are shunned by the Amish Kreutz family, which refuses to talk further with them—something Amish people would never do to English people.

For non-Amish readers, these works demonstrate the dangers of traditionalism. McDaniel's Leah wants to ask Ethan why his family keeps watch over the body of his little sister before the funeral but "decided he probably didn't know. He rarely knew the why of their customs, only that it was always done that way."[38] Lasky's Meribah finds her life "defined not by herself but by others."[39] In fact, these popular novels imply that the Amish are a dour, supercilious bunch, eager to purge from their ranks those who ask too many questions or assert themselves.

Chaste Romantics

Novelist Helen Reimensnyder Martin first brought Amish romance to the literary world in 1905 with *Sabina: A Story of the Amish.* Over the next century, occasional Amish love stories appeared in print, but it wasn't until 1997, when Beverly Lewis's *The Shunning* appeared on the market, that Amish romance fiction—their front covers branded with petite Amish maidens alongside buggies or barns—emerged as a distinctive genre. Even as late as 2003, Amish-themed romance fiction was sparse, with novels appearing at the rate of one or two a year. Suddenly, in 2007, a burst of seventeen "bonnet novels" appeared on retail bookshelves, and the numbers skyrocketed to forty-five new titles a year by 2010 and then to more than one a week (eighty-five) in 2012. By 2010 a trinity of Amish romance novelists—Beverly Lewis, Wanda Brunstetter, and Cindy Woodsmall—had sold more than twenty million books. More than half of these were written by Lewis, whose success crowned her the godmother of this genre.[40]

The trio was not alone. At least forty other authors had two or more Amish love stories on their resumés as well. Written largely by evangelical Christian women for evangelical readers, Amish romance novels deliver an inspiring evangelical message of personal faith in Jesus, a chaste romance, and, in some cases, a critique of Amish faith. One Amish woman lamented, "Too often they have glaring inaccuracies and ludicrous plots and a disproportionate amount of widowers and Englishers wooing Amish maidens."[41] Yet "bonnet fiction" has influenced the lives of many readers. One Methodist grandmother, discussing how reading it has changed her life, said, "I don't paint my nails as often, go shopping, or watch TV nearly as much as I used to."[42]

The sudden success of Amish romance fiction raises the question: Why did interest in Amish romance, lying largely dormant for a century, suddenly explode after 2006? Valerie Weaver-Zercher tackles that question in *Thrill of the Chaste.* Among other factors, she points to the vast media coverage of Amish forgiveness in 2006 and the economic recession of 2008–2009. The swift Amish forgiveness of the gunman who shot ten young girls in the Nickel Mines Amish School stirred new interest in Amish spirituality. As bad times are wont to do, the recession pulled people back to the traditional values of parsimony, frugality, and simplicity, which the Amish seemed to emulate.

Other factors may be even more responsible for the popularity of Amish romance fiction. Hypermodernity, which many readers experience as an out-of-control pace

A special shelf for Amish romance fiction in retail stores such as Walmart signals the financial significance of this genre. *Valerie Weaver-Zercher*

of life, leads many to look for narratives about communities they perceive as "slower," even as, ironically, hypermodern publishing and marketing strategies make possible the rapid-fire production of novels about such communities. Also, a gnawing disenchantment among evangelical Christians with what they consider the hyper-sexualized quality of much of popular culture increases the appeal of Amish romance fiction. As Weaver-Zercher cogently argues, the romance-laden but sex-free nature of Amish fiction provides evangelical readers with both a safe haven from the wanton sexual encounters of many mainstream romance novels and a reinforcement of the cultural values of sexual fidelity and chastity that they cherish.

While other books mock, disdain, or merely question the group's separatist life-style, some of the bonnet novels question, if not critique, the very religious beliefs that undergird Amish society. The covert message woven throughout much of the Amish romance fiction is that, despite the essential goodness of Amish life vis-à-vis mainstream American culture, Amish people are not truly Christians unless they have an evangelical-style "born again" conversion.[43]

One New Order preacher wishes that Amish romance literature "could be obliter-ated" because he is concerned that the excessive publicity might be "a means to our demise."[44] Even though a few Amish leaders such as this one have spoken out against these novels, some Amish bookstores sell them, and there is evidence that they are being read in many Amish communities, especially by young teens.[45]

Other Mediators of Amish Stories

Novelists are not the only English writers sketching images of Amish life. An abundance of Amish-themed children's storybooks, coloring books, and Christmas books written by English authors for English readers have been published, especially since the last quarter of the twentieth century. Alongside these are literature aimed at tourists, photographic essays, and cookbooks, all mixing fact and fiction as they construct imagined views of a multitude of Amish worlds that appeal to audiences ranging from children at play to cooks at work in the kitchen.

Other writers using print to mediate the Amish to the outside world include the dozens if not hundreds of scholars and practitioners serving Amish people, as the citations in this book attest. Despite their commitments to impartiality and detachment, these mediators bring their own assumptions and biases—conscious or not— to their interpretations of the Amish worlds they construct. The historians have limited written sources, the informants used by anthropologists often represent only one point on the Amish spectrum, and the sociologists selectively gather data to advance theories about Amish life that they hope to prove. One of the special complications for researchers conducting fieldwork and doing long-term studies of Amish life is the fear of losing access to their subjects if their analyses are too critical.[46] As we noted in the preface, by focusing on certain topics to the exclusion of others in this book, we too may be offering a lopsided view of Amish life.

Ex-Amish authors provide still other accounts of Amish life—what it was like to grow up Amish, the emotional struggle over joining the church, or the experience of excommunication.[47] Those who left before joining or as children when their families departed describe Amish life at arm's length. Regardless of their former spot in Amish society, ex-Amish people tell personal stories, narratives that were formed by caring or abusive parents, and exits from Amish life that are variously smooth or harsh.

Finally, depictions of Amish worlds also come from those further afield—from writers and translators outside of North America—adding still other images of Amish life. Counting both translations and original works, fifty-six nonfiction books on Amish topics have been published in languages other than English, including Dutch, French, German, Italian, Japanese, Korean, Polish, and Swedish. Interestingly, the twenty-eight titles in Japanese equal the total number of titles in all other non-English languages.[48] In addition, dozens of Amish romance novels have been translated into other languages.

The sheer number of images of the Amish now available in print evinces both the expansion of print culture among the Amish themselves and the rising cachet of the Amish among outside readers. Mediated versions of Amish society vary greatly in the extent to which they approximate reality, and despite their best intentions to faithfully represent the Amish in published form, Amish and English writers alike fabricate particular versions of Amishness. All of these depictions of Amish life are transformed into commodities that are traded on commercial as well as cultural markets.

The plethora of print-based Amish images is surpassed only by those cropping up in late-night talk shows, circulating in cyberspace, and being purveyed by the marketers of Amish-related products. In the next chapter we explore how representations of Amish ways are commodified through various forms of geographic and virtual tourism.

CHAPTER 21

TOURISM AND MEDIA

Amish families began moving to the rural community of Parke County, Indiana, during the early 1990s, putting down roots and establishing a new settlement. Soon one Amish woman began selling pies and other baked goods through a country store in the village of Bellmore. Sales were modest until the store owner began advertising the items as Amish-made—a move that greatly boosted sales. Uneasy with this merchandizing plan, the woman asked the storekeeper to remove the sign, which he reluctantly did, and sales slumped. Parke County had a well-established tourism industry centering on its claim to be the "covered bridge capital of the world," and visitors could easily integrate the Amish newcomers into that bucolic image. But the Amish were not sure how or if they wanted to be part of that picture.

Searching for the Simple Life in Amish Country

One of the greatest ironies of Amish life is that a people committed to remaining separate from the world have attracted so much attention from it. For many North Americans—indeed, for visitors from around the world—Amish communities are must-see travel destinations. The three largest settlements alone (in Pennsylvania, Ohio, and Indiana) draw some nineteen million tourists and generate more than $2 billion dollars a year.[1] Simply put, the Amish attract tourists, and the dollars they bring enrich entrepreneurial pockets and regional economies alike. Moreover, tourism has profoundly shaped Amish society itself.

Amish-themed tourism draws on and creates popular images of the Amish—images that might not always match the actual lives of Amish people and with which the

Amish might not be entirely comfortable. The myriad representations of Amish life reflect in many ways the hopes and anxieties of mainstream Americans as much as, if sometimes not more than, the realities of Plain living. Regardless, such depictions, mediated by tourist enterprises and popular media, have entered the arena in which the Amish negotiate their identity in twenty-first-century North America.

Curiosity about the Amish is part of the larger American fascination with its own past that has given rise to a booming industry in heritage tourism. Spurred initially by the development in the 1920s and 1930s of such sites as Colonial Williamsburg in Virginia, Greenfield Village in Michigan, and Old Sturbridge Village near Boston, Massachusetts, heritage tourism is "traveling to experience the places, artifacts and activities that authentically represent the stories and people of the past and present."[2] In traveling to well-known Amish settlements such as Lancaster County, Pennsylvania; Holmes County, Ohio; Shipshewana, Indiana; or Kalona, Iowa, visitors find living links to the past in the horse-drawn buggies, bonnets, straw hats, and close-knit communities.[3] Many twenty-first-century North Americans see the Amish as living examples of a simpler, older time in which families stayed together, mothers stayed home with children, and children grew up to be like their parents. For mainstream America, the Amish demonstrate the stability and traditional values of a pioneer past that many see as vanishing.[4]

Religion scholar David Weaver-Zercher links the growing interest in all things Amish to the American search for the simple life: "The simple living ideal has long functioned in American life as a serviceable reform ideology, challenging material excess, technological progress, and mass consumption."[5] Whereas in the early part of the twentieth century, tourists sought craft products that a generation before had been neither special nor mass-produced, nowadays visitors seek the simple life—unhurried, old-fashioned, safe—in communities that seem the antithesis of their own.

Non-Amish entrepreneurs have responded by creating symbolic Amish houses and even small villages that fulfill the nostalgic yearnings of tourists for a pioneer yesteryear. These representations of Amish farms, schools, and homes, sometimes with reenactors in Amish-like dress, help visitors imagine not only real Amish life but also the American past of their expectations. The "Amish" in these staged representations are clean, orderly, and very moral. Without TVs, video games, or disturbing posters on the walls of children's bedrooms, their "homes" eschew the obvious consumerism of twenty-first-century American life. The Amish family, as presented for the tourist eye, works together, and the children are picturesque and obedient, seen but not heard. As one writer put it, "The seemingly simple way of life of the Amish is envied by members of mainstream society who are 'plugged in' but would really like to unplug."[6]

Amish-centric tourism is a twentieth-century phenomenon motivated by the grow-

ing divergence between Amish society and American life. The 1936 publication of
Henner's Lydia, a popular children's book by Marguerite de Angeli, helped to channel the national yearning for the simple life toward Amish society.[7] *Henner's Lydia*
is filled with appealing illustrations of Amish folk engaged in everyday tasks such
as sewing, plowing, walking to school, and caring for animals. It tells the story of a
young Amish girl who takes a trip to the city to work at the market, sees many strange
things, but is glad to come home to the safe embrace of her family. The tourists Lydia
encounters at the market wonder at "homemade" apple butter, and Lydia marvels
at "boughten" food. The chasm between Lydia's small Amish community and the
larger English world was already, in the 1930s, large enough that mainstream readers
were eager for fictional bridges across it.

Widely reported Amish protests of public school consolidation further reinforced
their image as old-fashioned traditionalists resisting the intrusion of modernity into
their quiet communities. Yet while the *New York Times* and other publications characterized Plain life as "drab," "odd," or, at best, "quaint," the public began noting
Amish devotion to faith, tradition, family values, and simplicity. And while many
Americans in the 1960s witnessed a world in which generations seemed alienated
from each other and individuals feared losing control in an ever complicated modern society, Amish children were still working with their parents, doing their chores,
and attending one-room schools. Besides, as mainstream divorce rates increased, the
Amish continued to marry for life. Amish people—satisfied to stay at home in a world
in which everyone else was moving up and moving on—soon became exotic and
fascinating.

The exotic nature of Amish life helps to explain its power to entice visitors, because
the appeal of a tourist destination rests on its difference from ordinary life.[8] In one of
the earliest tour brochures, the 1961 *Meet your Amish Neighbors,* Alma Kaufman and
Flair Travel Consultants invited clients to meet the Amish, whose "insistence upon
living 17th century lives in 20th century America keeps puzzling their neighbors."
The brochure adds that "climaxing the tour you will visit an Amish home where the
lady of the house will serve cookies fresh from the oven. Then you board your bus for
the return to Wooster [Ohio], your mind full of memories of people who have found
happiness in a simple way of life."[9]

The search for the simple life in "Amish Country" is aided by opportunities to experience the smells and sights of a bygone society. A recent guide to the Amish community in Perth, Ontario, for example, suggests that visitors "slow down and take a
traditional horse-and-buggy ride to see the country as [the Amish] do."[10] A similar
refrain in the *2012 Holmes County Map and Visitors' Guide* offers visitors "authentic
tastes, goods, and culture . . . charming bed and breakfasts, friendly people and scenic
drives" and a "comfortable pace." Inviting tourists into an old-time world with a pic-

ture of a young Amish couple in a horse-drawn wagon, a Pennsylvania visitors' guide declares "America Starts Here." The text, underscoring "the simple, timeless pleasures," is overlaid with the phrase "Plain and Simple" in larger print. Other states use similar text and images to market Amish Country and tourist-oriented businesses.[11]

In brief, as the Amish retained horse-and-buggy travel in the first half of the twentieth century, mainstream Americans took to the automobile. And as expressways opened up rural regions to tourism in postwar America, tourists began making their way to Amish farmsteads in search of the simple life.[12] The outsiders' growing curiosity about their exotic fellow Americans provided an opportunity for non-Amish entrepreneurs to begin transforming the images, practices, and artifacts of Amish life into commodities for public consumption.

Tourist Sites as Theater

The emergence of Amish-themed tours, tourist sites, and eateries in the mid-twentieth century created a challenge for both Amish people and enterprising entrepreneurs. The Amish faced the quandary of how to be hospitable to visitors yet retain the boundaries of their communities, even as the visitors increasingly yearned not only for information but also for access to "real" Amish life. The entrepreneurs who catered to tourists had to keep the boundaries intact, because the sharper the difference between Amish culture and the outside world, the greater the appeal of Amish Country as a tourist destination.

This conundrum of the tourist site operator—making Amish life accessible to tourists but not so accessible that all boundaries would dissolve—was resolved somewhat by creating tourist experiences that took on quasi-theatrical features. Like many social rituals, tourist presentations can be viewed as performances with actors, scripts, costumes, and audiences. The theatrical features of Amish-themed tourism include real Amish people backstage, and tours, guides, and costumed actors performing on stage for the visitors. Tourism entrepreneurs stage productions (artifacts, exhibits, presentations, tours, experiences) and sometimes orchestrate brief, but controlled, backstage encounters with Amish people. This staged authenticity offers tourists a glimpse of authentic Amish culture while politely keeping them from slipping backstage for unsupervised contact with real Amish people.[13] The staged performances also protect Amish people from what otherwise would be an unwelcome intrusion of hordes of visitors on their properties and into their daily lives.

The tourist is encouraged to be "a passive consumer . . . through pamphlets, museums, tours, films, dramatic presentations, lectures, and demonstrations."[14] In the end, few visitors have direct access to Amish people apart from those selling their wares to outsiders. Even Amish-operated roadside stands and retail outlets are staged in ways that prevent tourists from intruding backstage. Visitors are regularly reminded through signs and pamphlets to respect Amish privacy and refrain from photographing them. Staged attractions, guided tours, and "authentic Amish" activities like buggy rides satisfy the tourist need to meet the "other" without ever engaging real Amish people in daily life.

An Ohio publication, *Hearts & Hands: The Official Travel Planner of Amish Country*, offers a good example of the theater that awaits visitors to Amish communities. The brochure presents itself as "a starting point" to the "hidden treasures of Amish Country," where tourists can "Meet the people. Taste the food. Take something authentic home." There are maps for self-guided tours, but at the same time the planner subtly encourages tourists not to go it alone because "professional tours provide a much more meaningful tour.... Dinner in an Amish home is an experience not to be missed, [but] this can only be booked through our local operators."[15]

In Lancaster County, visitors may tour the sights in air-conditioned vans or buses. Amish Country Tours offers them a "shuttle tour of the out-of-the-way backroads and country lanes, where [they]'ll experience the work and family ethic of the Amish."[16] Such ventures invite the tourist to safely embrace Amish life. For example, Amish Impressions at the Red Caboose asks visitors whether they have "ever wondered what it would be like to be Amish for one day," and encourages them to "make it happen.... Our motto is 'Picture yourself Amish.' It is here that you can dress in real Amish clothing and have your picture taken in one of our three Amish country scenes and even outside in a corn field (weather permitting)."[17] A few miles away, the Amish Experience Theater invites visitors to witness "the dramatic tale of an Amish family's effort to preserve a lifestyle and culture" and then to enjoy a "unique, intimate visit to three Amish properties—a farm at milking time to observe how the Amish milk cows and cool milk without electricity, a home 'cottage industry' to hear about and observe a unique handcraft, and a visit to an Amish family for an informal chat right in their home."[18]

Although tourism came later to midwestern communities than to Pennsylvania, Amish-themed attractions now also punctuate America's heartland. Amishville, in Berne, Indiana, opened in 1968 with an Amish tour guide, and Amish Acres, which includes a staged representation of Amish life, opened in Nappanee, Indiana, two years later. *Amish Backroads,* a guide to LaGrange County, Indiana, assures visitors that "there is no better place to acquaint yourself with the Amish Culture, craftsmanship and genuine friendliness than our backroads. Experience this simple way of life by driving at your own leisurely pace and discover what makes LaGrange County special."[19] Similarly, Iowa tourism officials invite visitors to the community of Kalona, "a place where buggies travel the highways next to cars, Amish farmers work the land with horse-drawn equipment."[20]

Whether in Arthur, Illinois, or Harmony, Minnesota, Amish tourism enriches regional economies, especially those in the settlements that attract millions of visitors. In Lancaster County, for example, the Amish are a key magnet for eleven million tourists who spend nearly $2 billion dollars in a tourism industry that employs 22,000 people. The three largest centers of Amish tourism (Lancaster County, Pennsylvania; Holmes County, Ohio; and Elkhart County, Indiana) draw nineteen million visitors annually—235 tourists for every Amish person living in those areas. The tourism industry in these communities creates a combined total of 33,000 jobs.[21] Although tourism provides a viable alternative to manufacturing or heavy industry for members of the non-Amish community, the demands of visitors can also be threatening. An editor of Wooster, Ohio's *Daily Record* lamented, "Tiny hamlets like Berlin, which once reposed lazily on summer afternoons, recalling the charm, atmosphere, and pace of bygone days, have been overrun with throngs of tourists."[22]

Yet judging by the number of people who pass through official visitor center turnstiles, tourists appreciate the performances staged for them by those who appear to be in the know, enjoying the Amish worlds constructed for them. As one researcher put it, "Instead of directly observing an attraction," tourists often "find themselves merely seeking to confirm" what authorities have "deemed sight-worthy."[23] Tourism involves encountering a world different from one's own, and that can be unsettling. But in the constructed settings of Amish Country, both real and virtual, the tourist remains in control. The visitor can indulge in nostalgia for the simple life, enjoy a break from the "real world," and leave with a bit of Amishness in the form of memories, photos, and souvenirs.

Despite the magnitude of Amish tourism, surprisingly little evidence-based knowledge exists about who the visitors are, why they come, how they experience their visit, and what reflections they carry home with them.[24] Various scholars have speculated that tourists in general are seeking a temporary escape from the tensions of hypermodern life, searching for authenticity and meaning, hoping to learn about and experience different cultures, or simply engaging in recreation.[25] Without evidence, it is not clear which if any of these explanations best interpret the motivations of visitors to Amish Country or how they experience what they encounter there.

Some may return home convinced of the superiority of mainstream life and relieved that they can travel by car and have access to the Internet, others may leave with both respect and ambivalence about Amish life, and still others may admire it enough to try adopting some Amish traits into their own lives—taking more time for family, watching less television, or attending religious services more frequently.

In any event, tourism allows some visitors to taste Amish life but leave reassured that there really is no place like home and that home can supply all one needs. In *Selling the Amish: The Tourism of Nostalgia,* Susan L. Trollinger argues that the tourist ultimately finds assurance that life can be better. The writer of the *Christian Homekeeper™ Blog* notes that she and her family lived in a "Conservative Amish community" for a while and so experienced all of the "godly attributes . . . and foibles" of the Amish; nevertheless, she realized that women can find the life they seek "right where they are."[26]

Most tourists perceive that their access to authentic Amish life is limited and that what they experience in Amish Country is closer to theater than to real life. Still, they likely leave knowing that having attended a production of Amishness is better than not having gone at all.

Amish Participation in Tourism

Although the Amish did not actively seek the attention of visitors, they have not remained entirely aloof from them. Especially in those settlements with sizable tourist industries, some Amish people participate and benefit significantly from tourism by creating products specifically for tourist markets and in some cases operating sizable retail operations that target visitors. A few Amish families serve family-style meals in their homes for groups of ten to forty visitors, and other households rent small apartments to visitors. Even in more remote settlements, hand-lettered "For Sale" signs on Amish properties along backcountry roads offer tourists sundry products: homemade rugs, root beer, tomatoes, doghouses, eggs, and fishing worms.

While many Amish businesses cater to the tourist trade, the nature of their participation depends on the community. The more conservative Amish groups may restrict interaction with tourists to local farm stands, but others develop or participate in businesses that cater specifically to tourists. In western New York, for example, tourist maps of the region identify shops in conservative Amish communities where visitors can find lawn furniture, produce, maple syrup, and quilts.[27] Operated from outbuildings on family farms, these small businesses offer products grown or produced on-site, keeping family members employed close to home, allowing children to work with their parents, and enabling parents to control the interaction between children and outsiders.

Not far away, in the more progressive Clymer, New York, community, the interaction is different. An "Amish Map" for western Chautauqua County highlights much larger businesses. An Amish harness maker in the community made more than seven hundred harnesses in eleven years: "I had a big shed with nothing in it. My harnesses were wearing out, and there was no one to fix them. So . . . I got me a sewing machine." In addition to making harnesses to order for Amish and English customers, this shop offers grooming supplies, gloves, liniments, and, in an upstairs room, a variety of black and natural-color straw hats. Not far from the harness shop

An Amish woman works in the kitchen of a non-Amish restaurant that caters to tourists.
Women in more traditional groups would not be employed in commercial tourist
businesses in this way. *Burton Buller*

is a bulk-foods store serving Amish and tourists alike. In addition to staples, the store
sells packaged foods, toys, books, school supplies, fabrics, and ready-made Amish
clothing.

Other Amish businesses in the Clymer area clearly cater to the tourist market. One
household runs a craft store and offers buggy rides, while another has an "Amish
family-style restaurant by reservation," and a third gives quilting demonstrations by
appointment. Many Amish people in Holmes County, Ohio, are similarly invested
in tourism. Charles Hurst and David McConnell argue that "manufacturing, tourism, and agriculture form the interconnected core of industries in the county," and
according to one of their Amish informants, "those three here in Holmes County
cannot exist without each other."[28]

The tourist trade offers other opportunities as well—opportunities that some
Amish and Mennonite people consider ways to witness about their faith to outsiders
seeking fulfillment or meaning in life. In several states with sizable settlements of
Mennonites and Amish, Mennonites have established information and interpretative centers to educate visitors about Anabaptist history and beliefs and about the
customs of local Amish and Mennonite communities. Amish people have actively

participated in and supported the programs of two Mennonite interpretative centers: Amish and Mennonite Heritage Center in Berlin, Ohio, and Menno-Hof in Shipshewana, Indiana.

In 1967, three Mennonite businessmen in Berne, Indiana, saw in a recently vacated Amish farmstead both "an educational opportunity" and "a worthwhile business venture." They had little difficulty convincing a young Amish farmer, David Schwartz, to move to the farm and open the property for tours. Within a year of its opening, Amishville was getting rave reviews from travel writers. "We are a humble people," Schwartz explained, and "do not intend to go against our religion by opening an Amish farm to the public." Yet he felt "this is right, that the people ought to know more about Amish ways and we can help do this at Amishville. We will create a better understanding—we feel we are accomplishing something in behalf of the Amish community."[29]

Other Amish participants in the tourism industry echo Schwartz's insistence on the educational importance of such enterprises. As one Lancaster County resident wrote, "Sometimes it would be easy to be resentful about all the tourists clogging our roads and asking us questions, especially when we are in a hurry or busy. But let's remember that we are showing whether we are just Amish or also Christian by the way we treat our fellow humans. After all, if we visited an Indian reservation, would we be less curious?"[30]

Although Amish tradition does not sanction active proselytizing, at least some members find in tourism the opportunity for public witness and a subtle preaching of Christian values. As one Amish minister put it, "Living a good example has led more people to Christ than any amount of talking has ever done."[31]

Not all Amish are cheerful participants in the tourism industry, however. Writing in 1989, an Amish man from Shipshewana, Indiana, complained in a note to the Amish newspaper the *Budget* about the construction of "another new building to promote and accommodate tourism. Many residents are getting quite perturbed at the continuous rush to develop more projects to lure tourists and yearn for good old days when the town was nice and quiet." With all the visitors "during the summer, town officials have problems with traffic and parking and the sewer system is so overloaded that they have to open the gates and let her run." In his view, "the town is so overrun with tourists it seems like a herd of animals," but, he acknowledged, "others call all of this progress."[32]

Writing from Ohio, another *Budget* correspondent wrote that "tourists still flood into Holmes [County] and continue to do so until the fall scenery is past. It's rather ridiculous that our area has become somewhat of a showcase of the world, and even more ridiculous what people do to get some of the tourist's money; such as advertising 'Amish' water." Just as bad were "Amish brand foods from New Castle, PA—

Amish hot dogs, sausage, turkey, chicken, bologna, and kielbasa. Maybe someday the tourists will come to realize Amish and non-Amish foods are identical."[33]

For other Amish people, the problem with tourism is not the inconvenience of being put on display but the fact that the entire enterprise symbolizes worldly pleasures. Said one Amish woman, "We are serving as a tool to lure tourists to Lancaster County. Personally, I do not feel any resentment against tourists, but . . . we are opposed to having our souls marketed by having our sacred beliefs and traditions stolen from us and then distributed to the tourists, and sometimes having them mocked."[34]

Summarizing conversations with more than a dozen Lancaster County Amish people about tourism, filmmaker Dirk Eitzen recounts, "While all of them said they find tourists and tourist traffic annoying at times, most of them also felt that tourism has had, on balance, a positive impact on their own community because of the economic benefits it has brought."[35]

Virtual Tourism

If tourism means observing a performance of Amish life, then the stay-at-home tourist can also participate vicariously in Amish worlds through the lens of a camera held by someone else. To design productions that interpret created Amish worlds, filmmakers—like tourists—struggle to get backstage for scenes of real Amish life. In fact, Amish people are much more averse to speaking on camera than they are to chatting with a tourist: those who grant on-camera interviews risk excommunication. Thus, video producers, like tourists, are often limited to scenes of Amish countryside, interiors of peopleless homes, and activities caught by a distant telephoto lens. Otherwise, even "documentary" productions must turn to ex-Amish people, unbaptized youth, actors, or the faceless voices of actual Amish people.

Produced by American Experience for PBS in 2012, *The Amish* used authentic Amish voices to narrate the film. The director faced a formidable challenge: how to fill the screen for two hours trying to cover a subject that did not want to be covered. Mark Samels, executive producer of American Experience, acknowledged, "In our 23 years, with almost 300 films completed, this was the most difficult one that we've ever made."[36]

Film images, like staged Amish-themed attractions, often perpetuate mainstream stereotypes, play on consumer nostalgia, and reinforce American notions about the authenticity, innocence, and joy of country living. Documentary film maker Eitzen notes that "people watch movies, even nonfiction movies, for the *experience,* that is, for the emotional payoff."[37]

Indeed, "experience" is a catchword on DVD covers, particularly those of documentary films, many of which read like tourist brochures for visits to Amish Country.

For example, the jacket text for the documentary *The Amish: How They Survive* invites the viewer to "go inside an Amish home. Experience moments of Amish life as told by the Amish themselves." Similarly, the jacket text for *The Amish: Back Roads to Heaven* invites the viewer to "experience Amish farm life, family life, business enterprises, childhood, school, worship, horse culture, business practices, barn raising . . . and more." Like Amish-themed tourist attractions, these films carefully craft a portrait of Amish life that emphasizes its peacefulness, lack of technology, sense of community, and distance from the modern world.

Even the most controversial of Amish documentaries, *Devil's Playground*, which features deviant Amish teens engaged in reckless drug and alcohol use—ostensibly demonstrating that Amish life is not nearly as innocent as many imagine—succeeds by juxtaposing mainstream society with pastoral Amish lifestyles. The young people in *Devil's Playground* act like stereotypical modern teenagers, living wild lives and disappointing their parents. These actions seem outrageous and worthy of a documentary only because they run counter to depictions of Amish behavior that viewers expect to see. "Which path will they choose?" asks the DVD jacket, suggesting that the young people at the center of the film must choose between a wild English life and a somber one that virtual tourists expect of Amish youth.

Hollywood too has catered to tourist expectations in portrayals of Amish life. For example, although barn raisings are no longer common in Amish settlements with waning numbers of farmers, no film about the Amish is complete without an elaborate barn raising scene. Indeed, this ritual is prominent in Peter Weir's 1985 Hollywood film *Witness,* which contrasts gritty city life with the serenity of the Amish world. Weir juxtaposes images of pastoral Amish society with its fields of waving grain and spotless, quiet farmhouse interiors with nighttime scenes of inner city bars and violent criminal confrontations. There is murder and mayhem in the modern world, but as the barn raising demonstrates, there is cooperation—even between rivals—in the Amish one, where all work together for one another. Similarly, in the 1997 film *For Richer or Poorer,* a real estate developer and his estranged wife, on the lam from the Internal Revenue Service, find redemption in Amish farm life. The images of Amish life—milking cows, chopping wood, and cooking, all on a neat, flowered farmstead nestled in a fertile valley—prove an antidote to the rampant, fast-paced consumerism of a hypermodern world for viewer and film protagonist alike.[38]

If geographic tourism provided a twentieth-century portal into Amish life in particular communities, television offers a more expansive one in this century. The televised visits, despite claims of being documentaries, are also staged representations that show a producer's artistic selections of certain slices of Amish life that rarely portray its complexity and nuance. These "documentaries" of television tourism, reality series, and talk shows—with the exception of the Amish narrators in *The Amish*—all show unbaptized youth in Rumspringa, ex-Amish people, actors, or in a few cases, members of other plain-dressing Anabaptist groups. With rare exceptions, bona fide adult-baptized, horse-and-buggy-driving Amish people have firmly resisted the enticements of dozens of film producers who hoped to capture their faces on camera. One production company even embedded five teams of people for several weeks in different Amish settlements, scouring communities for willing subjects.

The string of twenty-first-century televised excursions into Amish Country includes *Devil's Playground* (2002) and UPN's six-episode reality series *Amish in the City*, which traced the reactions of five Amish teens who lived with English teens in California in the summer of 2004 (see chapter 12). In 2008 ABC's "Primetime: The Outsiders" tracked a group of Ohio teens in Rumspringa in what was billed as a rare and unprecedented glimpse of Amish life. A follow-up show a year later updated viewers on the exploits of the youth. *Amish Grace,* a fictional account of the story of Amish forgiveness following the 2006 shooting at the Nickel Mines Amish School, which aired in March 2010, was the Lifetime Movie Network's most highly viewed film based on a real-life story.

Meanwhile, across the Atlantic, the BBC in London, which had joined the hunt for the elusive Amish, aired two documentaries—*Trouble in Amish Paradise* (2009) and *Leaving Amish Paradise* (2010)—that followed the departure of two disgruntled families from Lancaster's Amish community. British television's Channel Four produced a four-episode reality show, *Amish: The World's Squarest Teens,* in 2010. This UK version of *Amish in the City* enticed five midwestern Amish youth to explore London and its environs with some British teens. The BBC sequel, *Living with the Amish* (2011), brought six British youth to the United States to live in "Amish" homes.

With ex-Amish people and an assortment of actors, National Geographic aired *Amish at the Altar* in 2010 and followed it with a ten-part series in 2012, *Amish: Out of Order,* in which formerly Amish people interpret many aspects of Amish culture. In the fall of 2012, TLC launched a nine-episode reality television series, *Breaking Amish,* which followed five young adults (four Amish and one Mennonite) as they left their home communities and explored New York City. From daytime talk shows such as Oprah and Anderson Cooper to hundreds of YouTube videos and an assortment of productions for television, Amish youth and ex-Amish people became the guides for cyber-tourism in Amish Country in the twenty-first century.

Regardless of medium, accuracy, or content, Amish-themed "documentaries" and shows have received high scores for viewership and offered millions of people glimpses, however skewed, into Amish culture. Why do these excursions draw millions of viewers? It is the "A word," explains Daniel Laikind of Stick Figure Productions, who produced many of these programs. "The public appears to have a never-ending fascination with the Amish . . . simply because they are different . . . [and] represent a way of life we wish we could live. It is a type of fantasy."[39]

Ironically, the deeply held Amish virtues of humility and modesty that restrain them from seeking or participating in publicity only increases Amish otherness—making them bigger game and more attractive targets for the producers who relentlessly pursue them. Their aversion to publicity underscores their diametric difference from the multitude of other Americans who seek to promote themselves and their projects in the hopes of basking in the limelight that the Amish so dread.

One twenty-first-century form of virtual Amish tourism is the blog, which offers commentary, images, film, and audio clips of the Amish and Amish life to anyone, anywhere in the world, who searches for "Amish" on the Internet.[40] Visitors to blogs often leave comments and even engage in lengthy "conversations" with the blogger and other readers. Some blogs have question-and-answer sections that allow newcomers to query the blogger and seasoned visitors to respond with their own anecdotes and expertise. Like a group on a tour bus, blog visitors share their tourist experience in the company of others.

Many blogs are, in fact, maintained by the same tourist agencies and enterprises that depend on tourism. Clicking on *The Amish Blog,* for example, will bring the virtual explorer to a website maintained by the "Pennsylvania Dutch Country Welcome Center" in Lancaster County.[41] Moving past the blog options to "Lancaster PA home" provides a list of all the attractions offered to those who actually visit Lancaster. Other blogs support Amish-themed products. The popular syndicated column "The Amish Cook" is featured in *The Amish Cook from Oasis Newsfeatures,* a blog sponsored by the publisher of the column's print version.[42]

Still other blogs are established and maintained by individuals. Perhaps the most well-known is *Amish America,* a blog by author and researcher Erik Wesner, who visits Amish communities and posts his observations and his interviews with scholars and authors on Amish-related topics.[43] Some Amish-themed blogs, however, are less about the Amish than they are about a set of political views that the blogger links to the Amish. For example, the *Amish Internet Blog* describes itself as "promoting farm and country life with commentary about Amish issues."[44] It opens, however, with a list of pending legislation that the blogger identifies as "leftist" or "liberal" or impinging on American freedom.

Facebook has increasingly become a site of virtual tourism for people to connect around Amish-themed issues. "Amish Life: Celebrating the Simple Joy of All Things Amish" is a Facebook page billed as "an online community for all things Amish. Join the conversation and share your recipes, recommendations, and photos."[45] The page is actually sponsored by Zondervan, a Christian publisher that uses the page as a marketing tool for its Amish fiction. Viewers who "like" the page aren't necessarily aware of that, of course, which underscores the virtual convergence of commercial and educational interests.

A few Amish people participate in the blogosphere. Several ex-Amish operate blogs and actively interact with their readers, answering questions and explaining various facets of Amish life.[46] Even some church members collaborate with bloggers or those who maintain tourist websites by answering questions posed by readers. The anonymous Amish respondents participate in order to provide accurate information on Amish life. Although Amish people rarely have any way to militate against the construction of Amishness in a virtual world with no boundaries, their participation in blogging and the promotion of Amish values by non-Amish bloggers may increase the volume of their voice in the blogosphere.

Virtual tourism often spurs the real thing. Eitzen observes that "*Witness* turned out to be a huge box office success, reviving and arguably boosting a stagnant tourist industry."[47] Brad Igou, president of the Amish Experience at Plain & Fancy Farm in Lancaster County, notes, "The movie really put Lancaster County and the Amish culture out to a mass audience to a degree that had never been done before."[48] In recent years, the line between virtual and actual tourism has blurred. In 2005, on the twentieth anniversary of the release of *Witness,* Igou organized a tour of key sites in the film, including Intercourse, where the fictional detective John Book punched a tourist bully, and the farmhouse where Book hid out. This was followed in 2010 by another "*Witness* tour" that allowed visitors to see and photograph the farmhouse "as well as see Amish craftsmen completing a new farmhouse for the family," a real-life variation on the barn-raising scene in the film.[49] Igou explained, "Our tour recognizes that many people have become interested in Amish culture by watching a Hollywood movie and [this] gives them a chance to go beyond the movie and see how the Amish live here today."[50]

Who's Looking at Whom?

Some might see the willing participation of Amish families in the tourist industry as a cultural contradiction. Certainly, participation in the tourist industry has its dangers, as Douglas Turco warned in his study of Amish tourism: "Cultural tourism, by its very nature, is invasive, requiring host and guest cultures to interact. Amish youth, seeing their non-Amish counterparts wearing designer clothes and headphones plugged into portable compact disc players, while playing games like *Tomb Raider* on handheld computers, cannot help but be intrigued." Turco went on to argue that by "commodifying their culture for tourism, the Amish seem to be giving mainstream society more of what it wants, while moving closer to the same societal flaws."[51]

Whether tourism ultimately benefits or harms Amish culture remains open for debate. Although it may erode and pollute Amishness by bringing Amish people into closer contact with the English world, tourism may also confirm a visitor's sense of superiority. Trollinger suggests that although tourists to Amish Country are attracted by coherent representations of the Amish that are reassuring and "authentic," ultimately their visit reinforces their own sense of cultural superiority.[52] The same is true for the virtual tourist, since films, like vacations, must end, and just as the tourist is generally happy to resume a "normal" life after the stress of vacation, the film viewer can be content with his or her own life after a virtual visit to the Amish world.

A key scene in *Witness* contrasts the boorish behavior of a bully tourist with the Amish farmer he picks on. The farmer, true to his pacifist values, will not fight back. The viewer can admire the striking "otherness" of such a response yet be reassured that Amish ideals are not practical because, in the end, the farmer needs the fugitive Philadelphia detective, who is wearing Amish clothing, to punch the bully. Like the detective, the virtual tourist returns to the real, non-Amish world convinced that force and aggression win out over pacifism.

If tourists find their own non-Amish identities reinforced by such experiences, Amish people may also have their values reaffirmed by interacting with tourists. Sociologist John A. Hostetler argued several decades ago that Amish people and tourist enterprises may both benefit by preserving clear boundaries between them.[53] Tourism creates expectations for Amish behavior, and the words and images on tourist billboards reinforce the boundaries of Amish culture for the Amish themselves. Exposure to and participation in tourism may strengthen Amish identity by reminding Amish people of how different they are from the worldly visitors in their midst.[54]

Similarly, encounters with tourists may provide Amish people with "an insight into human problems in the outside world" and make them more content with their own culture. Deepak Chhabra considers the Amish response to tourism "negotiated reciprocity" because the Amish neither completely protect themselves from invading tourists nor acquiesce to their needs.[55] The Amish have negotiated an arrangement that allows them to benefit economically from the Amish brand and at the same time guard their distinctive lifestyle.

By constructing Amish people as a "saving remnant" that preserve values and traditions that are disappearing in America, tourism may also help to bolster their separatist values in mainstream society.[56] For example, in response to congressional hearings on child labor legislation that threatened to restrict Amish children from the workplace, Hannah Lapp, writing in the *Wall Street Journal,* argued that, instead of requiring the Amish to obey child labor laws, the Labor Department "would do better to study Amish child-labor practices as a guide to solving problems in child-spoiling mainstream society."[57] Similarly, in his analysis of the U.S. Supreme Court's decision in *Wisconsin v. Yoder*, which allowed Amish children to forego high school,

Shawn F. Peters suggests that Amish piety ostensibly had little bearing on the legal questions, but "it clearly struck a chord with the straitlaced [Chief Justice Warren] Burger," who "gushed that 'the Amish communities singularly parallel and reflect many of the virtues of Jefferson's ideal of the "sturdy yeoman" who would form the basis of . . . a democratic society.'"[58]

The ambivalence of Amish people toward tourism and their role in it underscores the ambiguity of their relationship with modernity and popular culture. It also exemplifies the diverse responses of different Amish affiliations as they struggle to live in twenty-first-century America without fully embracing it. These factors highlight, as theorist Darya Maoz suggests, the ways in which the Amish gaze and the tourist gaze "exist, affect and feed each other and the encounter they produce."[59] Clearly, the jury is still out on exactly how Amish-themed tourism changes both the viewer and the viewed as both sides pursue their own paths to happiness.

V

THE FUTURE

CHAPTER 22

PURSUITS OF HAPPINESS

Asked how a book on the Amish in America should end, one fifteen-year-old New York Amish boy responded, "They lived happily ever after."

"Amen," added his older sister. "They lived happily ever after. Amen."

The authors of *Abundance: The Future Is Better Than You Think* agree with the Amish teens.[1] They predict that the Amish—and the rest of us—will live happily ever after because we are on the cusp of a host of technological innovations. The world's nine billion people will drink clean water, eat healthy foods, live in decent homes, tap endless sources of energy, pursue free education, and be able to get, with a mere drop of their blood, a medical diagnosis anywhere in the world within a few minutes. All these miracles from the hands of technology will arrive, the authors claim, within the next twenty-five years.

We cannot know if these predictions will pan out, but we do know that in the future the Amish will live in a very different world than the one they inhabited in the last century. If horse-drawn transportation seems archaic today, it may look prehistoric a half century from now. How the Amish will fare in the face of a hypermodernity driven ever faster by technology is impossible to forecast. We can predict, however, that the Amish pursuit of happiness will encompass much more than technological innovation. But before turning to these issues, we recap how the Amish have grappled with the twentieth-century versions of solid modernity.

Shunning the Great Separator

We can read the Amish struggle with modernity as simply a protest against technology. On a deeper level, however, it has been a campaign to keep small-scale social units—based on kinship, neighborhood, and ethnicity—from being eroded by the currents of change that decontextualize people by sweeping them out of geographic communities.[2] Fearing that riptides beneath modernity's smooth surface would, in time, set their people adrift, the Amish have tenaciously tried to preserve their small, intimate congregations. Just as industrialization displaced work from the home and scattered the functions of education, work, worship, and leisure across several social spheres, modernity, which has been called the "great separator," severs the connections among family, community, and place.[3] The Amish response to certain new technologies reveals their fear of such fragmentation. Their aversion to photographs of individuals, telephones, automobiles, radio, and television is a protest against the decontextualization that divorces individuals from their social contexts or at least weakens communal ties.

Amish people found the idea of viewing a person out of context, unhitched from his or her local moorings, virtually idolatrous—a conviction that led to their taboo on photographs. Likewise, they resisted telephones, which separated voices from bodies, clothing, and social surroundings. The car, a super-decontextualizer, promised to obliterate geographical boundaries, expand social horizons, and free individuals from the parochialisms of local life. In Amish eyes, however, this all-American marvel was not a delight but a bulldozer that would upend every meaningful relationship. Likewise, television screens, with their flickering images of actors in make-believe settings, were, for the Amish, no more than optical illusions that intruded into the private spaces of homes and turned members of interactive communities into passive viewers.

To be sure, the technology associated with liquid forms of modernity has some interactive elements. The most popular media are "social" media, and the age of Facebook has multiplied the number of "friends" one may claim around the globe. Yet these forms of interactivity continue to decontextualize even as they promise greater connection. Modernization divides whole systems—psychological, social, and organizational—into discrete parts and then separates them in the name of efficiency and productivity. The trademark of Amish culture is its tightly woven community in which all the strands of social life from birth to death are bundled into a single moral order. To be Amish is to have a particular place in a thick web of church, community, and family ties. Such a web could only be preserved, the Amish thought, by protecting themselves from the process of modernization that threatened to tear their lives asunder. Survival, in short, required separating from the great separator.

Their separatist impulse was shaped, of course, by their Christian conviction that they are mere strangers and pilgrims passing through this world on their way to heaven. The penchant to remain separate motivated them to create sociocultural defenses that help to explain their cultural survival. Only by being a separate people have they been able to preserve the integrity of their local enclaves.

Bargaining Outcomes

In chapter 1 we proposed that the Amish fared well in their struggle with modernity because they were so adept at negotiating with it. We employed this bargaining metaphor as a broad interpretive tool and also as a heuristic device to describe actual negotiations. Throughout the twentieth century, Amish leaders protected nonnegotiable elements of their culture from outside forces, yet they were willing to concede other things to the press of progress. In addition, they put a multitude of issues on the bargaining table—trading back and forth with the agents of progress until they struck a cultural compromise. The Amish brought certain assets to the table: they had economic clout—significant value to tourist-heavy areas as well as to business and agricultural economies in rural areas. Furthermore, some of their religious practices were protected by the First Amendment.

The Amish saga, however, is not a monocultural story with a single grand narrative. Amish affiliations and church districts have bargained in different ways over different issues, producing an assortment of story lines that defy generalization. Some groups have focused on resistance, while others have been more open to adaption and change. Swartzentruber Amish, for example, will sit in jail rather than place triangular slow-moving-vehicle emblems on their buggies, yet their co-religionists in Delaware have no qualms about placing flashing strobe lights on the tops of their buggies. Meanwhile, Lancaster County officials plan to place electronic signs along some roads to warn of slow-moving vehicles, and the Amish there do not protest. Clearly, the account of Amish bargaining is a collection of short stories with different characters and sundry resolutions, some satisfying Amish expectations and others disappointing them.

Amish negotiations with modernity generally result in one of three outcomes: retaining nonnegotiables, making concessions, or devising adaptations.

Nonnegotiables

Despite innumerable differences, Amish groups uniformly have resisted certain aspects of modernity, regardless of region or affiliation. With a few exceptions, the nonnegotiable issues noted below remain untarnished by modernity.

Most scholars point to individuation and choice as key earmarks of modernity—and the Amish restrain both.[4] Amish people of all stripes reject contemporary notions of individualism. Although members in all affiliations have the freedom to express certain preferences and individual differences, their baptismal vows restrict unfettered individualism. Amish people do have a choice regarding church membership, but a decision to join sharply constricts their subsequent range of choices. In short, the subordination of individual liberty to collective goals remains intact.

The Amish have staunchly avoided urban life, resisting the centrifugal forces of mobility that would pull them away from home. Amish groups have also stalled cultural assimilation by retaining distinctive emblems of separation—notably dress, language, and horse-and-buggy transportation. Their religious belief in separation from the world has enabled them to avert excessive consumerism in the areas of personal technology, household furnishings, leisure, dress, and the fads of popular culture.

Separation from the world also limits both participation in the political system (except, in some cases, voting) and the receipt of financial support from government coffers. Almost all Amish avoid U.S. federal programs such as Social Security, Medicare, and Medicaid, and those living in Ontario generally do not participate in the Canadian health care system. Moreover, Amish people have remained firm in their conscientious objection to participating in war.

The Amish have opposed large centralized, bureaucratic structures in their communities and have persistently rejected the dominant forms of Protestant Christian religious institutions—Sunday schools, church agencies, seminaries, and even church buildings. Sacred ritual is typically one of the last things to crumble when any religious tradition faces pressure to change. The Amish have constructed a fortress around their most sacred areas of faith—including music, worship, weddings, funerals, and selection of leaders—keeping them safe from outside influences. They have avoided ecumenical dialogue, formal theological training, and anglicizing their worship as well as many other popular religious currents.

In twentieth-century America, Amish communities also built a dike against social movements that would have transformed their lives in dramatic ways. Bucking the tides of popular cultural change, they preserved traditional gender roles, large families, and endogamy. They remain insulated from feminism, divorce, pluralism, multiculturalism, and inclusivism.

In a dramatic *no* to the American embrace of formal education, they do not permit high school and higher education, including study in the fields of engineering, medicine, art, music, and theater. Although they selectively use and adapt much technology, they have categorically spurned television, digital media, and ownership of motor vehicles.

Their resistance has included ideological commitments and sociocultural practices as well as distinctive patterns of social organization. These immutable mainstays of Amish life have withstood the press of progress—at least for now.

Concessions

Despite drawing sharp lines of cultural separation from mainstream society, Amish people readily engage in economic interchange. Far from being self-sufficient, they buy and sell goods in regional, national, and international markets. Although Amish-style capitalism constrains the size of businesses, the power of individuals, and the use of litigation to protect entrepreneurial interests in the marketplace, Amish people do seek profits and do not spurn competition. However, the success of Amish "capitalism" owes as much to accumulated social capital as it does to maximized financial capital.

As we noted in chapter 17, the Amish are not Luddites who abhor technology. Even though they view technological innovation as a threat, they use many basic technologies and judiciously vet new ones according to their potential to help or harm the church-community. The technologies that are accepted or rejected vary by affiliation and district.

Heeding New Testament Scriptures, the Amish pay taxes and obey government regulations insofar as they do not violate their religious conscience. If drafted for military service, they will perform alternative service as designated by the government.

Although the Amish generally avoid the American culture of consumption, even ultraconservative Amish people buy commercial products such as flashlights, hand soap, pesticides, cheese curls, soft drinks, chips, and pizza. The extent of consumerism varies across the gamut of Amish people, from those who rarely shop to those who push carts down the aisles of Walmart and Costco on a regular basis.

Adaptations

A third outcome of the bargaining is cultural compromise. These agreements reflect a mixture of old and new, typically involve some give-and-take on both sides, and embody a delicate balance between tradition and modernity. Such adaptation is seen, for example, in distinctions between access and ownership of motor vehicles and in the rise of Amish businesses, which are located halfway between farm work and outside factory work.

While many aspects of Amish agriculture reflect the small family farms of early twentieth-century America, farmers in more liberal groups have adapted many practices of modern agriculture, although none of them have large corporate-style operations. The move into off-farm occupations—another adaptation—is a major foray into the outside world. Those working in English businesses spend many hours in English environments, albeit often surrounded by Amish coworkers. Amish women and men who operate their own businesses have many links to people in the English world, yet they still operate under the canopy of the church. And as we have seen, the growth of Amish-produced publications attests to a growing comfort with speaking, writing, and reading in English, which constitutes still another adaptation.

Over the last century the Amish have developed a growing dependence on the use of outside professionals—physicians, dentists, optometrists, lawyers, veterinarians, agronomists, and business advisors, among others. The "use them but don't produce them" principle captures the compromise of tapping the services of outside professionals while limiting their own people's education so that they cannot enter those ranks.

As we have documented, Amish people seem to enjoy tinkering with technology, from household appliances to farm and business equipment. Amish mechanics have created endless adaptations to fit technology to the moral order of their churches. Establishing a firewall between using and owning technology can provide access to motor vehicles and the Internet but still keep some distance from the technology.

Finally, Amish bargaining with government agencies has increased at the local, state, and federal levels, especially since the founding of the National Amish Steering Committee in 1967. Negotiations over zoning regulations are common in some of the older settlements where Amish leaders have well-established relationships with government officials. The bargaining does not always go as smoothly in newer settlements, however. Whether in new or older communities, the negotiations we have chronicled have focused largely on the solid forms of twentieth-century modernity, which are gradually dissolving. Successful bargaining with the liquid modernity of twenty-first-century America may be an entirely different matter.

A Precarious Future

The Yale professors in the mid-1950s who predicted the demise of the Amish could never have imagined that twenty-first-century Amish would be thriving in settlements stretching from Maine to Texas and Colorado. Aware of such dubious projections only six decades ago, we are loath to make any long-term forecasts about the Amish future. We do, however, offer some short-term observations on challenges facing the Amish in the decades to come.

Survival in an iPad World

If the home is a fitting metaphor for pre-industrial society, and if Henry Ford's factory symbolizes the modern world, the Internet best captures the realities of liquid modernity. Amish resistance to progress in the twentieth century focused on the solid structures of cities, factories, consolidated schools, and mechanical gadgets—cameras, computers, cars, tractors, and telephones. In the twenty-first century, however, many of the cultural borders around those objects have become blurred and fuzzy. In the past, Amish interactions with modernity involved distinctions between sacred and secular, work and leisure, community and self—distinctions that are disappearing in the digital world.

When Apple introduced its first iPad in 2010, it sold a million of them in thirty days. Two years later, three million of a new version were gobbled up in three days.[5] With each new smartphone app or Twitter scandal, the Amish seem ever more quaint and hopelessly out of touch. How will a traditional people fare in a hypermodern world in which new technology rolls out at an ever-faster pace? Will the negotiation strategies that served them well in the past century be sufficient to sustain them in an iPad world?

Liquid modernity raises new challenges for religious separatists. In the era of solid modernity, the worldly threats were specific and clear. Visible telephone and electric lines were easily banned from Amish homes. With smartphones and iPads, the old boundaries have evaporated, and these devices, oblivious to all borders, are difficult to control because they can be concealed under a bed or in a closet or even carried to a cornfield. Because television is a purveyor of entertainment, it is not difficult for the Amish to declare it outside the bounds of acceptability. But the iPad and similar devices merge media with diverse purposes—from leisure to work, religion to pornography—in one small gadget. Such convergence across cultural boundaries erodes the old borders drawn by Amish churches.

The fixed lines in Amish culture that held solid modernity at bay for so long are now beginning to dissolve. Digital devices are more unpredictable and dangerous than automobiles ever were because, instead of taking an individual out into the world, the new gadgets bring the entire world, with all its temptations and resources, to the individual. What does separation from the world look like when you can hold the world in your pocket?

Internal Tensions

To those on the outside, life in the Amish world seems unchanging. But that slow-paced appearance is something of an illusion. Many issues, in fact, provoke debate in

The boy on the left shows his younger brother how to send text messages on a cell phone. Amish youth in higher affiliations often text their friends, a practice that is forbidden in traditional communities. *Daniel Rodriguez*

Amish communities about how to live in a hypermodern world. Four topics currently discussed in Amish circles will likely spur transformations in Amish society in the near future: the role of business, the impact of technology, relations with government, and theological shifts.

"Business is business and church is church," said one Amish businessman. Echoing this radical departure from tradition, another entrepreneur wondered aloud, "Why doesn't the church just stick to church things on Sunday and let businesses alone during the week?" These simple comments unmask one of the biggest challenges facing progressive affiliations: will local congregations be able to keep Amish businesses within the Amish pasture, or will these new enterprises, like young colts, jump the fence?

Historically, *Ordnung* regulations applied to all realms of life, including all business endeavors. But the desire to be unbridled by church regulations is growing, and it represents one of the most serious challenges to the Amish world. Some businesses, for example, purchase commercial health insurance for their employees. Others are tempted to litigate to protect their financial interests. Still others are tired of technological restrictions that curtail profits. Ironically, the growth spurt of Amish-owned businesses that kept people out of English factories may, in the long run, break down the restraining fences of the Amish corral.

Discussions of technology are also stirring up strife. In the world of liquid and hypermodernity, Amish people are exposed to state-of-the-art technology, whether through the televisions of hospital waiting rooms, the GPS units guiding their taxi drivers, the latest equipment in their shops, or the cell phones in their pockets. Heated debates about technology are occurring in almost all Amish tribes, from disputes over the use of LED flashlights in ultraconservative groups to the adoption of public electricity in more liberal ones.

Despite long-standing declarations about a strict separation of church and state, Amish entanglements with government—not just through negotiations via the Steering Committee, but through other channels as well—are increasing. Some Amish employees in English factories collect Social Security as well as Medicare and disability benefits. Occasionally, families whose children have disabilities access government-sponsored educational programs provided through public schools. Farmers in some groups accept agricultural price supports and collect environmental preservation funds from government agencies. All of these examples, however limited, show the growing acceptance by some Amish of the reach of government into their lives and communities.

Theological changes that subvert deeply entrenched Amish understandings of Christian faith are also afoot. Some Amish people are using evangelical Protestant language to describe their faith, which may prove to be particularly problematic because it represents a shift in moral authority from the *group* to the *individual.* Evangelical faith privileges the subjective authority of the individual over communal authority (Ordnung), separates salvation from ethics, and encourages a customized personal spirituality with thinner communal links.

A related issue involves supporting missionary programs that go beyond local charity and civic activities, such as serving in volunteer fire companies and doing reconstruction after natural disasters. Although Amish churches have not established mission agencies, some members of more liberal affiliations contribute financially to mission programs operated by Beachy Amish churches, conservative Mennonite groups, or independent evangelical agencies. Clearly, these individual Amish contributors are sympathetic to evangelical endeavors even though their own churches do not endorse them in a formal way.

Proliferating Brands of Amishness

Amish population growth and geographical sprawl will likely spawn greater diversity, producing an evolving number of Amish identities, propelled in part by congregation-based ecclesial authority. With some two thousand *Gmays,* there are already nearly that many different ways of being Amish, and the diversity of Amish identities will surely multiply in the future. The proliferation of diversity is not necessarily a threat to Amish life, but it will continue to confront their communities as well as baffle outsiders seeking an easy definition of what it means to be Amish.

The diversity in the Amish world reflects the issues and concerns that drive Amish communities to resist or adopt new technologies and to their different ways of interacting with outsiders. In its own way, each Gmay grapples with how to adapt to changing technology, government regulations, and mainstream social mores that encroach on Amish practice. Moreover, each district has to contend with its own internal struggles whenever its members cannot agree on how to respond to external challenges.

Many Amish youth in the highest groups are up to date on the latest electronic gadgets and Hollywood goings-on, and even the most conservative Amish families feel increasingly squeezed by the intruding world. Growing diversity means parents in different communities face different challenges as Amish children grow up in different Amish worlds. While their peers in Lancaster County or Elkhart–LaGrange are on Facebook, teens in ultraconservative groups may be unsure how to use a cell phone. Before baptism, liberal Amish youth drive cars and dress like the English, while their conservative peers engage in bed courtship and continue to sing slow German songs at youth gatherings. One Amish man lamented the growing differences between Amish affiliations as evidence of disobedience and the imminent return of Christ: "There are so many different groups now. This tells you the end is near."

If the Amish population continues to grow at its present rate, it will produce more remote rural settlements with traditional practices like butchering and barn raisings at the same time that those activities are vanishing in the communities that have a shrinking agricultural base. Another consequence of the growing diversity may be that the most liberal Amish will be less likely to support their ultraconservative brethren when they refuse to install smoke detectors or affix slow-moving-vehicle emblems on their carriages. The affiliations at the opposite extremes of the Amish spectrum use each other to define themselves. Commenting on the wide gap between Amish tribes, one Swartzentruber bishop confessed that the Lancaster County Amish are as different from his own people as his non-Amish neighbors.

For mainstream Americans, the growing diversity of the Amish world and the expansion of Amish settlements will likely spawn local conflicts related to horse-drawn transportation, zoning, building permits, child labor, and competition between Amish and English contractors. Hollywood stereotypes simply cannot begin to prepare locals for an influx of new Amish neighbors who settle nearby. Local people may be disappointed when their Amish neighbors do not fit the stereotypes—or annoyed when they do. In any case, the growing diversity among and within Amish affiliations poses a challenge for the future.

Will Amish Cars Fly?

In a playful essay about the future of Amish society in the year 2100, Brad Igou speculates that, while the rest of the world flies about in airmobiles, the Amish will be driving rebuilt cars left over from the mid-2000s.[6] We agree that Amish cars likely will not fly, but more importantly, we think that Igou is onto a key point about the Amish future and how they adapt: that is, that Amish identity is ever evolving as their practices change. Amish practices in the twentieth century generally lagged behind those of mainstream North America, creating sharp differences that defined in public ways what it meant to be Amish. When American farmers added rubber on the wheels of their tractors, the Amish retained steel wheels. When vacuum milking machines entered American barns in the 1940s, the Amish were slow to adopt them. Only a few settlements had accepted vacuum milkers in the 1950s, while others waited until the 1990s, and a few others still continue milking by hand in the twenty-first century. Although the Amish may be late adopters, they do nonetheless adopt—and even more often adapt—modern practices. So if airmobiles ever do fly in the skies, the Amish might be driving Amish-adapted cars while sporting a new but distinctive identity.

Airmobiles or not, Amish identities will evolve as the twenty-first century unfolds, and this evolution may hold some challenges. We noted in chapter 8 that the more traditional communities are the fastest growing ones and that they will likely become a larger slice of the Amish pie in the future. In addition, some of the more liberal affiliations may reduce the most conspicuous signs of Amishness and define their identity more by personal faith and private religious ritual within their church-communities. This raises a key question: Will horse-drawn transportation remain the litmus test of what it means to be Amish? The answer is likely yes for those groups who seek cultural separation and rural isolation, but perhaps others will develop new forms of Amish identity. A change-minded Amish bishop recently confided, "We probably made a mistake when we didn't accept the car," a harbinger that some churches may eventually trade in their horses for cars and cross the historic line of Amish identity.

In 2002, the Miller family left their Amish church in Wisconsin for an Amish community in Montana. Seven years later they moved to Idaho with their nine children. "We've kind of come out of the box," explained Mrs. Miller. Out of the Amish box, they have joined the world of regular clothes, DVDs, cars, and computers. Yet, she says, "We're not trying to throw everything away. We're trying to keep family first, that's really, really important for me and my husband."[7] Millions of other Americans would say the same thing. But any semblance of Amish identity for families like the Millers will fade fast without the support of a broader Amish community. Because they live by themselves, the Millers' attempt to shrink parts of their Amish identity while holding onto other parts may not be as easy as they hope.

All human groups have their flags—their symbols of identity—although some are more prominent than others. So despite all the variants of Amish life, particular affiliations will still retain an Amish identity in one way or another. Yet a critical question remains: Will the commercial hype affixed to them in the twenty-first century alter Amish identities? Will Amish people begin to think of themselves mostly through the images created by the marketplace—as merely the makers of buggies, furniture, and quilts? Such a relationship could create an economic dependence in which Amish people become captive to producing what the market demands. If that happens, their unique cultural practices will be perpetuated more because their economic survival requires it and less because their faith commends it. If so, these sectarian separatists may be staking their very survival on the admiration of a world they were taught to despise.

American Ties That Bind

We have emphasized the otherness of Amish life as expressed in their public symbols of identity. Yet the Amish are tax-paying citizens who contribute to the national economy and appeal to the First Amendment to protect their religious practices. The Amish and English are, in many ways, interdependent, a fact that cannot be ignored in any speculation about Amish futures.

Amish people often rely on their non-Amish neighbors for a variety of small favors, from access to a home freezer to use of a phone to a ride to the local hospital in an emergency. They shop in non-Amish stores, and some sell food and crafts to tourists at roadside stands. The Amish use commercial banks, eat in English restaurants, buy medicines from local pharmacies, and distribute products from their shops across the country. In the more progressive communities, Amish people work for outside employers. In short, Amish people rely on the outside world for their economic well-being.

A more profound link exists, however, between the Amish and their non-Amish neighbors. Even as the Amish interact with the secular world, they reject it, and in doing so, they define themselves. Being Amish means rejecting the lifestyles of the English world. In that sense, the Amish need the English so that they know who they are *not*.

But the English need the Amish too. While the Amish define themselves in opposition to "the world," their worldly neighbors often look to the Amish for inspiration on how to live a simpler, more unadorned life. In their rejection of cars, televisions, and other trappings of technology, the Amish seem somehow more authentic and unvarnished than outsiders and are frequently referred to as models of resistance to modernity. As a result, the Amish have, ironically, become part of modern American popular culture, the stuff of fiction by writers as diverse as Carolyn Keene, P. L. Gaus, Beverly Lewis, and Jodi Picoult.

The Amish have spurned mainstream lifestyles, but we cannot reject them. They are fellow citizens, acknowledged and accepted, even as they try to separate themselves from us. Accepting and accommodating the Amish and other plain-dressing Anabaptist groups has become an expression of the American commitment to religious freedom, free speech, cultural diversity, and even religious values. Just as Amish churches need us to set the worldly norms they reject, we need them as fellow citizens, for they reinforce our notions of the American character and our legal and cultural commitment to religious liberty, freedom, and the right to be different.

Much of Amish survival and growth can be attributed to their deft ability to negotiate with modernity, but that is only half of the story. They have also flourished in America because of American tolerance of dissenters, respect for minority rights, and First Amendment protection of religious practice without state intrusion. By serving as a test case for religious liberty, the Amish have helped to define the American character.

Thus, the English and Amish exist in a kind of symbiotic relationship, a mutualism in which each is necessary for the other to thrive. As noted earlier, legal scholar Garrett Epps calls the Amish a persistent grain of sand in the American oyster. What they seek, he says, "is not the right to remain the same, but the right to change at their own pace and in their own season. . . . They remain irreducibly other, stubbornly themselves. We have tried and failed to absorb and Americanize the Amish and we should be grateful that we failed."[8]

The Amish and the Modern Soul

Several headlines in North American newspapers during the thirty years from 1888 to 1918 tell the tale of turn-of-the-century public perceptions of the Amish:

A Queer Religious Sect
A Queer People and Their Ways
Odd in Many Ways: They Are a Strange People[9]

Images of Amish people as backward and ignorant continued into the mid-1900s and then shifted toward more positive representations after 1960. The development of tourism and the Amish defense of rural one-room schools may have helped revise their popular image.[10] The widely viewed feature film *Witness* in 1985, and seven years later, *Vogue* magazine's fourteen-page, full-color spread of new fashions, photographed in Lancaster County and titled "The Great Plain," pointed to the rise of the Amish in popular culture.[11] In 2011 the *New York Times,* in an article titled "Amish Fashion Week," reported that Dior Homme was featuring "soft, draped, plain, [clothing with] the boys wearing flat, wide-brimmed hats . . . a sudden flashback to Alexander Godunov as an Amish dreamboat farmer in *Witness.*"[12] And the website Trend Hunter suggested in November 2011 that "Amish-inspired fashions are taking the world by storm."[13]

Rather than denigrating Amish people or calling them odd and archaic, twenty-first-century North Americans are now welcoming their look, their difference, and their novelty.[14] In the tolerant ethos of liquid modernity, Amish ways are not generally scorned but instead are seen as interesting expressions of cultural diversity that deserve at least minimal respect. Plain people, whose martyr ancestors centuries ago were torched for their religious beliefs, now have become objects of public curiosity and admiration. And in an ironic twist of history, both the automobile and the television, forbidden by the Amish in order to keep the world at bay, now bring outsiders by the millions into real and virtual Amish Country.

Some visitors hope to discover in the Amish a genuine connection to their imagined American past. Others, troubled by the pace and stress of contemporary life, want to explore the wholeness that seems to grace Plain communities. Still others are charmed by a people who have had the stubborn courage to temper the forces of modernity. The enthusiasts of liquid modernity affirm the Amish, buy their goods, and emulate their fashion, however loosely. Visitors are uncertain, however, whether the Amish are viable prototypes for contemporary living or cultural leftovers of yore.

Why are we so intrigued by the Amish? They are, of course, different, but mere difference is not enough to explain the extent to which they absorb us. Is it their courage to buck the tide of progress that wins our admiration? Are we drawn to their sense of place, their strength of identity, their apparent security, and even their sense of confidence? Their presumed slower pace of life attracts those of us living harried and frenzied lives. Do we admire their ability to fashion a humane system that seems to meet basic human needs in a satisfying way? In the midst of a fragmented world, their sense of wholeness lures and inspires us. For whatever reason, they seem to have discovered an alternate way to fill some of the longings of the human heart.

The Amish might have been ahead of the times in their critique of modernity, but they are not postmodernists, even though they bask in its tolerance. In many ways, they repudiate the chorus of postmodern themes—relativism, consumerism, inclusiveness, and the pleasures of spectacle. As we have shown, they heed ancient

Flavor is a Japanese bakery that sells "Amish Country" pastries based on authentic Amish recipes as well as other baked goods. This Japanese saleswoman, dressed in "Amish" garb, offers samples to customers in the transit terminal at Nagoya, Japan. *Donald B. Kraybill*

religious authorities, contend for communal constraints, and erect walls of separation—all of which defy postmodern sensitivities. So why, ironically, are we fascinated by a people who eschew many of the values that most of us cherish—individualism, inclusivity, tolerance, choice, and diversity? Most of the things the Amish reject, says one scholar, "are the precise things that Americans cherish . . . and that have made our country great and wealthy."[15]

How is it that we are captivated by a people whose ways we also may find troublesome, even offensive? We are annoyed by folks who limit education, reject evolution, dismiss gender equality, curb personal freedom, and stifle personal achievement and artistic expression. Amish pleas for yielding to community feel oppressive, sexist, and suffocating by some contemporary standards. Their exclusivity and church-prescribed uniformity irritate our penchant for diversity and pluralism. Likewise, their unwavering commitment to permanence in marriage and church vows offends our inclinations for experimentation and change. Their fidelity to tradition—conforming to church regulations, driving similar carriages, dressing alike—also nags us. Are these folks, we wonder, mere puppets of their culture, controlled by the strings of religious tradition?

The rigidity of their moral order seems to squelch the human spirit and squander human potential. Consider the hundreds of potential pilots, chemists, nurses, lawyers, playwrights, and violinists who instead cultivate crops, wash dishes, and pound nails in Amish shops. Certainly it would be a dark and dismal world if everyone joined the Amish and shunned science, higher education, open inquiry, and artistic creativity.

Amish ways indeed trouble the modern soul. Their communal constraints have crafted a secure cultural home without the aid of higher education. They rely very little on government safety nets, yet the homeless and uninsured are missing from their ranks. Widows and orphans, the destitute and the disabled, receive respect and care within their community. Their spontaneous, humane social security efforts spring into action in the face of fire, disability, sickness, senility, and death. Drug abuse and poverty are rare. Youth are occasionally arrested for disturbing the peace or driving under the influence, but violent crime is virtually nil. Divorce is unheard of, and the elderly grow old within a caring circle of family and friends.

As in any society there are unhappy marriages, cantankerous personalities, family feuds, and cases of sexual abuse. As one grandmother noted, "We have our good ones and our bad ones, just like other people." But all things considered, Amish quality-of-life indicators are remarkably robust. "Which society," asked one Amish father pensively, "has the most lonely and homeless people?" In Amish society, youthful teachers master the craft of teaching without the benefit of high school—let alone college. Amish eight-grade private schools produce thousands of entrepreneurs who are able to develop and manage thriving businesses. Work pulses with meaning, human dignity, and a delight in artisanship. Extended family networks provide care throughout the life cycle. Ironically, Amish people seem to be in charge of their destiny with little strategic planning or effort.

Most troubling of all is the possibility that, despite our abundance of high-tech gadgets, leisure time, and national efforts to control things and dominate the world, the Amish pursuit of happiness might produce more satisfied—even happier—lives than the rest of us experience. Despite all our comfort and convenience seeking, the possibility that these homespun folks are happier bothers at least some of us. It seems that in some uncanny way the Amish may have outwitted us—or perhaps even outwitted modernity itself.

Amish ways trouble us because they challenge our assumptions about bigness, progress, diversity, education, freedom, individual dignity, and tradition. They propose that tolerance and individualism may have to yield if they spoil the virtues of an orderly community. The upside-down values of Amish life esteem tradition more than change, lift communal goals above personal ones, acclaim work over consumption, and place personal sacrifice above achievement. They raise doubts about whether the mantra of hypermodernity—more, newer, bigger, faster, and more powerful—necessarily means better.

The Amish suggest that firm limits and clear boundaries may best preserve human dignity over the generations. It is possible, or at last worth trying, the Amish argue, to tame technology, to control the size of things, to bridle bureaucracy, and to hold things to a humane scale. In short, they contend that living with modest humility in a well-ordered and bounded community offers one road to happiness and well-being.

APPENDIX A

Related Groups

Mennonites, Brethren, Hutterites

The Amish share historical roots and theological traits with other Christian groups that descend from the Anabaptist movement of sixteenth-century Europe. The largest related family of churches is the *Mennonites,* whose name comes from an influential Anabaptist leader, Menno Simons (c. 1496–1561). By the late 1600s, Mennonite communities existed in Switzerland and South Germany and also across northern Europe from the Netherlands to what is today Poland. In 1693, the Amish emerged as a distinct group within the Swiss–South German wing of the Mennonite world. In the 1700s, Swiss–South German Mennonites and Amish began immigrating to North America, where they often settled in adjacent but separate communities.

In the twenty-first century, the North American Mennonite world includes dozens of subgroups that roughly divide into two types: traditional and assimilated. Members of assimilated churches participate in many aspects of mainstream culture. They pursue higher education, live in urban areas, engage in professions, use up-to-date technology, and wear contemporary clothing.

There are two types of plain-dressing traditional Mennonites of Swiss–South German background: those who use horse-and-buggy transportation, and those who drive cars. The horse-and-buggy-driving *Old Order Mennonites,* including the Groffdale Conference, or "Wenger" Mennonites, and the Stauffer Mennonites, speak Pennsylvania Dutch and are sometimes confused with the Amish. Several physical markers distinguish the two groups. For example, unlike the Amish, the Old Order Mennonite men do not wear beards, and the fabrics worn by Old Order Mennonite women typically have patterns and designs in contrast to the solid fabrics of Amish women. Old Order Mennonites worship in simple church meetinghouses, unlike the Amish, who meet for worship in private homes.

Numerous groups of traditional Mennonites, including the Wisler Mennonites and the Weaverland Conference, or "Horning" Mennonites, drive cars. They live mostly in rural areas, generally do not speak Pennsylvania Dutch, wear somewhat plain dress, and rarely attend college. They use electricity but typically place some restrictions on television and online access.

The *Old Colony Mennonites* are a conservative Mennonite group descended from the Dutch–North German wing of the Mennonite movement. Old Colony Mennonites live in Canada and in half a dozen Latin American nations, from Mexico to Argentina. Many Old Colony Mennonites drive cars or trucks, but some 60,000 Old Colony Mennonites in Bolivia continue to drive horse and buggy. The Old Colony Mennonites dress in distinctive, plain garb and speak a Low German dialect that is different from Pennsylvania Dutch.

The *Beachy Amish* and the so-called *Amish Mennonites* are groups that emerged in the twentieth century from Amish roots. Despite their names and history, these churches lie outside the contemporary Amish orbit because their members drive cars and use a wide range of consumer technology, and few speak Pennsylvania Dutch. These groups typically engage in vigorous evangelism and mission work and have gained many converts of non-Amish background. Male members wear closely trimmed beards, and women wear small head coverings. Members of some of these groups pursue higher education.

Two other groups are easily confused with the Amish: the *Old German Baptist Brethren* and the *Old Order River Brethren.* Members of these two groups are often misidentified as Amish because their distinctive clothing closely resembles Amish dress and because Brethren men also grow full beards. Both groups drive cars, use electricity, and permit higher education and use of the Internet. They do not speak a German dialect. These Brethren churches trace their history both to the Anabaptist movement of the 1500s and to the Protestant Pietist renewal movement of the 1600s.

The *Hutterites,* who practice economic communalism, branched from the Anabaptist movement in 1528 in Europe. They reject private property and base their communalism on practices of the early Christian church. Some 50,000 Hutterites live in 500 rural communes in the northern plains states and the Canadian Prairie Provinces. They follow traditional religious practices, wear distinctive garb, and speak an Austrian-German dialect. Unlike the Amish, however, they use the most advanced farm technology and motor vehicles, all of which are communally owned.

Four other groups are sometimes mistakenly associated with the Amish: the *Quakers,* the *Amana Colonies,* the *Moravians,* and the *Shakers.* None of these four groups have any direct historical or religious connections to the Amish. Several of these groups, at least in their past, have had some beliefs and practices—pacifism, plain dress, simplicity of lifestyle, separation from the larger society—that resemble Amish ways and have led to understandable confusion.

FOR FURTHER READING

Rod Janzen and Max Stanton. *The Hutterites in North America.* Baltimore: Johns Hopkins University Press, 2010.

Donald B. Kraybill. *Concise Encyclopedia of Amish, Brethren, Hutterites, and Mennonites.* Baltimore: Johns Hopkins University Press, 2010.

Donald B. Kraybill and Carl F. Bowman. *On the Backroad to Heaven.* Baltimore: Johns Hopkins University Press, 2001.

Donald B. Kraybill and James P. Hurd. *Horse-and-Buggy Mennonites: Hoofbeats of Humility in a Postmodern World.* University Park: Pennsylvania State University Press, 2006.

Royden Loewen and Steven M. Nolt. *Seeking Places of Peace. A Global Mennonite History: North America.* Intercourse, PA: Good Books; Kitchener, ON: Pandora Press, 2012.

Stephen E. Scott. *An Introduction to Old Order and Conservative Mennonite Groups.* Intercourse, PA: Good Books, 1996.

Global Anabaptist-Mennonite Encyclopedia Online. www.gameo.org/.

APPENDIX B

Key Events in Amish History

1517	Protestant Reformation initiated by Martin Luther in Wittenberg, Germany.
1525	Anabaptist movement begins in Zurich, Switzerland.
1632	A meeting of Mennonite ministers endorses the Dordrecht Confession of Faith in Dordrecht, Holland.
1693	The Amish movement coalesces in Switzerland and in Alsace, France.
1730s–1770s	The first wave of Amish immigrate to North America.
1815–1860s	The second wave of Amish immigrate to North America.
1862–1878	Continent-wide Amish ministers meetings (*Dienerversammlungen*) are held to confirm Amish unity, but the meetings result in division. A distinct Old Order movement emerges after 1865.
1890	*The Budget,* a correspondence newspaper, begins publication, linking Amish communities over a wide region.
1900–1920s	Social and technological changes—especially the telephone and automobile—challenge Amish church-communities.
1913	Swartzentruber Amish emerge in Ohio as a distinctive conservative group, one of many affiliations that form over the course of the twentieth century.
1925	The first Amish private school, Apple Grove, is founded in Dover, Delaware.
1927	A division in Pennsylvania's Somerset County settlement leads eventually to the formation of the Beachy Amish Church, which adopts both the telephone and the automobile.
1937	Amish in Lancaster, Pennsylvania, protest an extended school year, an increase of the age when children may leave school, and school consolidation, which draws national media attention.
1937	Last Amish church in Europe closes.
1940s	World War II and the years following bring many social and economic changes that would challenge Amish communities in the second half of the twentieth century.

1948	Old Order Book Society forms to provide textbooks for Amish private schools.
1940s–1950s	So-called Amish mission movement energizes many Amish young people to engage in outward-looking religious activism, but they soon exit the church.
1955	Popular Broadway musical *Plain and Fancy* helps generate Amish tourism.
1950s–1960s	The number of Amish schools increases, as do conflicts between Amish parents and public school officials in some states.
1957	*The Blackboard Bulletin* magazine for teachers is established to promote the development of Amish private schools.
1964	Pathway Publishing Company is incorporated by Amish people as a nonprofit organization.
1965	Self-employed Amish receive exemption from Social Security (Amish employees of Amish employers gain exemption in 1988).
1966	New Order Amish group emerges in Ohio.
1967	National Amish Steering Committee forms as liaison to federal government, initially to address military conscription, but soon deals with other issues.
1967	Lutheran pastor Reverend William Lindholm organizes the National Committee for Amish Religious Freedom to provide legal assistance to Amish people challenging school attendance laws.
1972	U.S. Supreme Court case *Wisconsin v. Yoder et al.* legitimates Amish exemption from high school education.
1975	*Die Botschaft* begins publication, featuring letters from Old Order correspondents only.
1970s–1980s	Many Amish people seek nonfarm employment and develop Amish-owned business.
1985	Paramount Pictures' film *Witness* boosts popular interest in Amish.
2006	A shooting at the Nickel Mines Amish School attracts worldwide media attention.

NOTES

PREFACE

1. Gertrude Enders Huntington's lecture at the Pennsylvania State University, Nov. 5, 2009. Unpublished manuscript in Donald Kraybill's files.

2. See Kraybill, *Amish and the State;* Kraybill and Nolt, *Amish Enterprise;* Kraybill, Nolt, and Weaver-Zercher, *Amish Way;* Scott and Pellman, *Living without Electricity;* Umble, *Holding the Line;* Umble and Weaver-Zercher, *Amish and the Media;* Wesner, *Success Made Simple.*

3. See Dawley, *Amish in Wisconsin;* O. Gingerich, *Amish of Canada;* Huntington, *Amish in Michigan;* Hurst and McConnell, *Amish Paradox* (Holmes County, Ohio); Johnson-Weiner, *New York Amish;* Nolt and Meyers, *Plain Diversity* (Indiana); Schwieder and Schwieder, *Peculiar People* (Iowa).

4. Letter to Donald Kraybill, Jan. 9, 2012.

5. For a discussion of tribes in twenty-first-century America, see Watters, *Urban Tribes.*

CHAPTER 1. WHO ARE THE AMISH?

Epigraph: C. Lapp, *Pennsylvania School History,* 410–90.

1. See Seiler, *Republic of Drivers,* for a deft discussion of the links between car driving and other American cultural values.

2. "Amish Population by State (2012)." Young Center for Anabaptist and Pietist Studies, Elizabethtown College. http://www2.etown.edu/amishstudies/Population_by_State_2012.asp.

3. The date of Ammann's death is unknown, as noted in chapter 2.

4. For more details on the Amish sojourn in Europe, see Nolt, *History of the Amish.* The Canadian Amish have always lived in Ontario, except for a few families in British Columbia from 1969–1972. Small Amish settlements existed briefly in Mexico (1923–1929), Paraguay (1967–1978), and Honduras (1968–1979).

5. Most New Order congregations meet for Sunday school on the Sunday when they do not hold worship services, as do a small number of other Amish congregations.

6. The literature on modernization is voluminous. For an overview, consult these essays in *International Encyclopedia of the Social and Behavioral Sciences:* "Modernity: Anthropological Aspects" (9944–49); "Modernity: History of the Concept" (9949–54); "Modernization and Modernity in History" (9954–61). Although various dimensions and analytical frames are used to interpret modernity, we are most interested in its consequences for small tradition-oriented groups such as the Amish. On the various interpretations of modernity pertinent to the Amish story, see Wagner, *Modernity as Experience and Interpretation;* Giddens, *Consequences of Modernity;*

and Berger, Berger, and Kellner, *Homeless Mind.* Taylor, *Modern Social Imaginaries,* investigates how modernization shapes plural conceptions of moral order. Lears's *Rebirth of a Nation* and C. Fischer's *Made in America* offer cogent analyses of modernization in America.

7. See Berger, *Facing Up to Modernity,* and C. Fischer, *Made in America.*

8. Olshan, "Modernity," argues persuasively that the Amish were not passive bystanders to modernization.

9. See Epps, "Amish and the American Oyster."

10. See Bellah et al., *Habits of the Heart;* Berger, *Facing Up to Modernity;* and Giddens, *Consequences of Modernity.*

11. Kraybill first employs the notion of the Amish negotiating with modernity in *Riddle of Amish Culture,* 23–24. For a collection of essays on the topic, see Kraybill and Olshan, *Amish Struggle with Modernity.*

12. Bauman, *Liquid Modernity,* 8. Some analysts tag the late twentieth-century shift as "postmodern," "late modern," "supermodern," or "hypermodern." For example, see Harvey, *Condition of Postmodernity.* We find Bauman's account of liquid modernity not only descriptive but persuasive and incisive.

13. Lipovetsky, *Hypermodern Times,* 29–52. We thank Valerie Weaver-Zercher, who uses Lipovetsky's concept of hypermodernity in *Thrill of the Chaste,* for pointing us to his work.

14. One Amish woman in Indiana lists her occupation in the settlement directory as "Mary Kay Consultant" (*Indiana Amish Directory,* 722). On the emergence of Amish-owned businesses, see Kraybill and Nolt, *Amish Enterprise.*

15. Johnson-Weiner, *Train Up a Child,* 70–71.

16. Ibid., on various approaches to private schooling. On public, private, and home schooling, see McConnell and Hurst, "No 'Rip Van Winkles' Here."

17. The one exception is Pinecraft, a village in the suburbs of Sarasota, Florida. This favorite wintertime vacation spot does not accommodate horses. (See chapter 13.)

18. A handful of districts (mostly New Order) have simple, plain church buildings.

19. Berger and Luckmann, *Social Construction of Reality,* esp. 129–83. Overviews of social science constructs of identity are offered in *International Encyclopedia of the Social and Behavioral Sciences:* "Identity in Anthropology" (7154–59); "Identity: Social" (7166–70).

20. C. Smith, *Moral, Believing Animals,* 64, 67.

21. These are hypothetical narratives based on the many narrative examples in C. Smith, *Moral, Believing Animals,* 67–76.

22. In this regard, the Amish story stands in sharp contrast to that of culturally conservative Old Colony Mennonites, whose story has been one of migration away from modernizing North American society and a search for homes in remote locations within Latin America. See Loewen, "To the Ends of the Earth."

CHAPTER 2. EUROPEAN ORIGINS

Epigraph: Braght, *Martyrs Mirror,* 741–42. For a collection of various reproductions and uses of the *Martyrs Mirror* etching of Willems, see Luthy, *Dirk Willems.*

1. Yoder and Yoder, *Echoes of the Past,* and A. King, *Hidden Treasures.*

2. Surveys of the Anabaptist movement include Snyder, *Anabaptist History and Theology* and *Following in the Footsteps of Christ;* and J. Weaver, *Becoming Anabaptist.*

3. From stanzas 13 and 14 of song 126 in the *Ausbund.* This English translation is from *Songs of the Ausbund,* 1:322. See G. Peters, *Earliest Hymns of the Ausbund,* for other translations. See also Blank, *Amazing Story of the Ausbund.* The vast majority of Amish continue to sing from the *Ausbund* on Sunday mornings. A few settlements use one of two songbooks compiled in America,

either *Eine Unparteiische Lieder-Sammlung zum Gebrauch beim Oeffentlichen Gottesdienst und der Häuslichen Erbauung* or *Unparteiische Liedersammlung zum Gebrauch beim Oeffentlichen Gottesdienst und zur Häuslichen Erbauung,* both of which include *Ausbund* hymns. For a full description of these and three other German hymnals, see G. Schlabach, *Now Thank We.*

4. *Martyrs Mirror* was first published in the Netherlands in the Dutch language in 1660. For an English translation, see Braght, *The Bloody Theater or Martyrs Mirror of the Defenseless Christians.* An Amish publisher has issued a study guide for *Martyrs Mirror*: Lowry, *Martyrs' Mirror Made Plain.*

5. Séguy, "French Anabaptists," and Müller, *History of the Bernese Anabaptists,* 215–37.

6. Much of the discussion that follows draws on Furner, "Repression and Survival of Anabaptism." See also Müller, *History of the Bernese Anabaptists,* for an Amish-published history of these events.

7. Müller, *History of the Bernese Anabaptists,* 140. So loyal were these Reformed Church members to their Anabaptist neighbors that in some cases Bern officials resorted to holding leading citizens of rural villages hostage in order to force locals to divulge information about Anabaptists' whereabouts.

8. Quoted in Roth, *Letters of the Amish Division,* 8.

9. Hüppi, "Identifying Jacob Ammann."

10. This discussion is based on the most recent research on Ammann in Baecher, "Patriarche"; Hüppi, "Identifying Jacob Ammann"; and Furner, "On the Trail of Jacob Ammann."

11. Séguy, "Religion and Agricultural Success."

12. Séguy, "Bernese Anabaptists"; Baecher, "Patriarche," 147.

13. Nolt, *History of the Amish,* 27–50, narrates the Amish division of 1693. Primary sources documenting the schism are in Roth, *Letters of the Amish Division.*

14. Leroy Beachy, *Unser Leit,* 1:25–110.

15. Ammann pointed to Rom. 16:17; 1 Cor. 5:9–11; 2 Thess. 3:6, 14–15; 2 Tim. 3:2–5; and Titus 3:10. The 1632 Dordrecht Confession remains the Amish doctrinal statement to this day. The text is most readily available in Leith, *Creeds of the Churches,* 292–308; an Amish-published translation appears in *In Meiner Jugend,* 8–61. For a recent Amish interpretation of the Dordrecht Confession, see J. Stoll, *How the Dordrecht Confession Came Down to Us.*

16. Research connecting Pietist convictions with Ammann's ideas is summarized in Meier, *Origin of the Schwarzenau Brethren,* 23–24, 56–61, 97, 115, 143, and *"Golden Apples in Silver Bowls."*

17. Roth, *Letters of the Amish Division,* 24, 118.

18. Nolt, *History of the Amish,* 41–46, summarizes the fruitless efforts for reconciliation between the Ammann and Reist factions, which continued through 1711.

19. Baecher, "Patriarche," 151–52.

20. Ibid., 152–54.

21. Baecher, "1712," 6. Baecher's careful archival research points to local economic greed as a motivation for the expulsion order. Certain local figures engineered the king's intervention into Alsatian affairs in order to force the Anabaptists to sell their land holdings at bargain prices to these same local figures. Christian III, Palatine Count of Birkenfeld and Lord of Ribeaupierre, who had welcomed Anabaptists to the area (as had his father and great-uncle before him), was upset by the expulsion order but was unable to stop a royal edict.

22. The "isolated enclaves" included territories near the Lièpvre valley but outside French royal sovereignty, such as Salm, Lorraine, and Montbéliard.

23. Hüppi, "Identifying Jacob Ammann," 330–32.

24. Vincent, *Costume and Conduct.* See Luthy, "Clothing and Conduct in Swiss Laws," for an Amish discussion of sumptuary laws and Amish understandings of plain dress.

25. Quoted in Baecher, "Patriarche," 151.

26. Bates, "Insubordinate Anabaptists."

27. Roth, *Letters of the Amish Division,* 43. In a 1697 letter to friends in Alsace, prominent North German Mennonite elder and ship owner Gerhard Roosen (1612–1711) of Hamburg criticized Ammann for his strictness regarding matters of dress; apparently, word of Amish teaching that had filtered north emphasized clothing regulation; see Roth, *Letters of the Amish Division,* 68–70.

28. Quoted in Bates, "Insubordinate Anabaptists," 531, with citations to folkloric sources.

29. See S. Scott, *Why Do They Dress That Way?,* and M. Gingerich, *Mennonite Attire through Four Centuries.*

30. Nolt, *History of the Amish,* 61–65, 107–17, summarizes Amish emigration from Europe in the 1700s and 1800s.

31. Schmidt-Lange, "Roast Bear?," 9, 15.

32. Nolt, *History of the Amish,* 221–27.

33. J. Hostetler, "Old World Extinction," 212–19.

CHAPTER 3. THE STORY IN AMERICA

Epigraph: J. Stoll, *Amish in Daviess County,* 119–20.

1. An eighth-grade Amish textbook by Uria Byler, *Our Better Country,* paints an image of an accepting American homeland against a background of Old World persecution. Small Old Order Amish settlements existed in Fernheim, Paraguay, from 1967 to 1978, and in Guaimaca, Honduras, from 1968 to 1979.

2. Nolt, *History of the Amish,* 72–95.

3. The dialect is sometimes known as "Pennsylvania German," but we will use the more colloquial designation. Notes 7 and 8 of chapter 7 explain the origin of the dialect and introduce the extensive body of literature on Pennsylvania Dutch.

4. Nolt, *History of the Amish,* 113–26.

5. Levine, Roy, and Smucker, "View of Jüngerich," 5–6.

6. Bishop David Beiler, quoted in J. Umble, "Memoirs of an Amish Bishop."

7. See, for example, Reschly, *Amish on the Iowa Prairie,* 64–86.

8. The Amish church as a whole had no protocols for regular meetings of bishops and ministers. Rather, ordained men in a given region met on occasion to share common concerns, as evidenced by surviving reports from gatherings between 1809 and 1861, all of which are listed in Yoder and Estes, *Proceedings of the Amish Ministers' Meetings,* 401–3.

9. Bender, "Some Early American Disciplines," 95.

10. On the cultural developments discussed here, see Bushman, *Refinement of America.*

11. J. Umble, "Memoirs of an Amish Bishop," 101–2.

12. Ibid.

13. In some cases, nineteenth-century Amish farmers were among the first in their neighborhoods to employ new technologies. Bishop Joseph Wittmer is remembered not only for his invitation to pray at the White House but also as the owner of the first sawmill powered by steam in Daviess County, Indiana (J. Stoll, *Amish in Daviess County,* 116).

14. See C. Foster, *Errand of Mercy,* and Johnson, *Redeeming America.*

15. Nolt, *History of the Amish,* 159–60. The Amish were one of many groups that were uncomfortable with the scientific and technological advances of the late nineteenth century, as noted by Lears in *No Place of Grace.*

16. Nolt, *History of the Amish,* 160–92.

17. Yoder and Estes, *Proceedings of the Amish Ministers' Meetings,* 6, 34, 36–37, 51, 63, 97, 259.

18. Ibid., 258–60.

19. Nolt, *History of the Amish,* 189–221.

20. P. Yoder, *Tradition and Transition,* 261–87. For descriptions of Old Order movements among Mennonites and Brethren, see B. Hostetler, "Formation of Old Orders." The origin of the term Old Order Amish is somewhat obscure. In 1862, at the first *Dienerversammlungen,* tradition-minded leader "Klein" Moses Miller (1811–1897) appealed to those present to "come under the old order" (*müssten unter die alte Ordnung kommon*) (Yoder and Estes, *Proceedings of the Amish Ministers' Meetings,* 6), and the term Old Order thereafter became associated with the conservative cause. However, in the decades after the Dienerversammlungen most tradition-minded Amish referred to themselves simply as *die alt Amisch* (the Old Amish) rather than Old Order Amish. English-language Mennonite publications from the early 1900s began using Old Order Amish as a standard label for the group, and by the 1940s, if not earlier, Amish people had adopted the name Old Order Amish or Old Order Amish Mennonite when speaking of themselves in English. In the Pennsylvania Dutch dialect, however, the Amish have always called themselves *die alt Amisch Gmay* (the Old Amish Church).

21. M. Gingerich, *Mennonites in Iowa,* 311–14. On Pennsylvania Old Order Amish rejection of telephones in 1909, see D. Umble, *Holding the Line.* For context, see R. Kline, *Consumers in the Country,* 23–54.

22. Data from Luthy, *Amish in America* and *Amish Settlements: 2008.* These new settlements were in Alabama, Arizona, California, Delaware, Georgia, Illinois, Indiana, Iowa, Kansas, Michigan, Minnesota, Mississippi, Missouri, Montana, Nebraska, North Carolina, North Dakota, Ohio, Oklahoma, Oregon, Tennessee, Texas, Virginia, and Wisconsin. Thirteen have persisted; forty-nine have failed, most within a few decades of their founding.

23. Luthy, "Amish Meetinghouses."

24. Gibbons, *Pennsylvania Dutch and Other Essays,* 62; S. Scott, *Plain Buggies,* 50–79.

25. E. Yoder, *Beachy Amish Mennonite Fellowship Churches.* On wider debates about the car in early twentieth-century rural life, see R. Kline, *Consumers in the Country,* 57–79.

26. Luthy, "Bibliographical and Research Notes: History of Raber's Bookstore." Since 1970 the almanac has been published in both German and English.

27. Nolt, "Inscribing Community."

28. Nolt, *History of the Amish,* 266–73, 287–90.

29. Nolt, "Amish 'Mission Movement.'"

30. Patterson, *Grand Expectations,* 77–81, 237, 343, 369–74.

31. Nolt, *History of the Amish,* 294–304.

32. Nolt, "Amish 'Mission Movement.'"

33. Johnson-Weiner, "Publish or Perish," 206–13.

34. Old Order values stood in sharp contrast to those that animated American society at the turn of the twentieth century; see Lears, *Rebirth of a Nation.*

35. Kraybill, *Riddle of Amish Culture,* 164–71; D. Weaver-Zercher, *Amish in the American Imagination,* 60–78; "Amishmen Battle to Keep Drab Life," *New York Times,* Aug. 15, 1937.

36. Kraybill, *Amish and the State,* 125–43; C. Hall, "Revolt of the Plain People."

37. A. Keim, *Compulsory Education and the Amish;* Kraybill, *Amish and the State,* 109–23. See also S. Peters, *Yoder Case.*

38. See, for example, Labi, "Gentle People."

39. R. Kline, *Consumers in the Country.*

40. Ladd, *Autophobia;* Lee, "Plain People of Pennsylvania"; Nolt, *History of the Amish,* 292–93; and Shover, *First Majority, Last Minority.*

41. David Chen, "Amish Going Modern, Sort of, About Skating," *New York Times,* Aug. 11, 1996; Rheingold, "Look Who's Talking."

42. Luthy, "Origin and Growth of Amish Tourism"; D. Weaver-Zercher, *Amish in the American Imagination*, 82–121.

43. The original show included one c. 1900 Lancaster Amish quilt; the traveling exhibit included several Amish quilts.

44. Hughes, *American Visions*, 43–44.

45. J. Smucker, "Destination Amish Quilt Country," and *Amish Quilts*, chap. 6.

46. D. Weaver-Zercher, *Amish in the American Imagination*, 152–80.

47. Data provided in June 2012 by staff of the Pennsylvania Dutch Convention and Visitors Bureau (phone conversation, June 7, 2012).

48. D. Umble, "Wicked Truth"; Goldstein, "Party On, Amos."

49. *Devil's Playground;* Ariel Leve, "Back to the Future," *Sunday Times Magazine* (London), Jan. 30, 2005, 20–27.

50. Kraybill, Nolt, and Weaver-Zercher, *Amish Grace*, 49–50.

51. D. Weaver-Zercher, *Amish in the American Imagination*, 185–96.

CHAPTER 4. RELIGIOUS ROOTS

1. For an exception, see Kraybill, Nolt, and Weaver-Zercher, *Amish Way*.

2. The key Old Testament passages that shape the Amish narrative of Hebrew history are printed in ministers' manuals such as *Handbuch für Bischof.* The Scripture readings and hymns for various ceremonies are available to all members in M. Miller, *Our Heritage, Hope, and Faith.*

3. This practice is based on Matthew 18:16: "But if he will not hear thee, then take with thee one or two more, that in the mouth of two or three witnesses every word may be established."

4. Oyer, "Is There an Amish Theology?," provides one scholar's sketch of the contours of an Amish theology. See also Kraybill, Nolt, and Weaver-Zercher, *Amish Way.*

5. J. Stoll, *How the Dordrecht Confession Came Down*, 33, provides a history and use of this confession of faith by the Amish.

6. Examples include David Beiler's writings, especially *True Christianity.* Thoughtful analyses of Beiler's theology are provided by T. Schlabach, *Peace, Faith, Nation*, 212–14, and J. Weaver, *Keeping Salvation Ethical.* Other nineteenth-century Amish writers include David A. Troyer, *Writings of David A. Troyer*, and Daniel E. Mast, *Lessons in the Sermon on the Mount* and *Salvation Full and Free.* Since the mid-twentieth century, considerable theological writing from New Order Amish authors has been published by Amish Brotherhood Publications (a New Order publisher in Ohio).

7. *Truth in Word and Work*, 4. Another resource for Amish beliefs, *1001 Questions and Answers on the Christian Life*, consists of short answers to questions with Scripture texts on sixty-three topics. This handbook and many other religious texts reflecting Amish views are published by Pathway Publishers.

8. For an English translation of selected prayers from *Die Ernsthafte Christenpflicht*, see *A Devoted Christian's Prayer Book.* Leonard Gross, in the preface of *Prayer Book for Earnest Christians* (an English translation), provides a history of *Christenpflicht.* German and English versions of the prayers appear side by side in *Our Fervent Prayers* published by Mary M. Miller, an Amish woman.

9. *Neu vermehrtes geistliches Lust-Gärtlein*, 34–45, 51–53, 63–65, 90, 105–107, 186–87. For a history of this prayer book, see Luthy, "History of the *Lust-Gärtlein* Prayerbook."

10. "Rules of a Godly Life," 65. For quotations from "Rules," we use the Amish translation that appears in *In Meiner Jugend*, 65–103.

11. E. Kline, *Theology of the Will of Man*, 3. For an excellent source on the early Anabaptist view of discipleship, consult Snyder, *Following in the Footsteps of Christ*, 138–58.

12. Raber, "Following Christ in Truth," 11.

13. *1001 Questions,* 76–77.

14. E. Kline, *Theology of the Will of Man,* 3.

15. Raber, "Following Christ in Truth," 10.

16. E. Kline, *Theology of the Will of Man,* 3.

17. For an example of late medieval spiritualist views of *Gelassenheit,* see Birkel and Bach, *Genius of the Transcendent,* 95–123. For the sixteenth-century Anabaptist view of Gelassenheit, see Snyder, *Following in the Footsteps of Christ,* 163–68.

18. P. Kline, "Gelassenheit." These notes later appeared, with minor changes, as "Gelassenheit" in M. Schlabach, *Message Mem'ries.*

19. Chupp and Chupp, *Thy Will Be Done; Beyond the Valley.*

20. Emphasis added.

21. *1001 Questions,* 78, 82.

22. John A. Hostetler identified silence as a key aspect of Amish spirituality in *Amish Society,* 387–90, and in "Silence and Survival Strategies."

23. The meaning of this term, frequently used by John A. Hostetler, is analyzed in Kraybill, "Redemptive Community." See also J. Hostetler, "Amish as a Redemptive Community."

24. Raber, "Following Christ in Truth," 11.

25. For an interpretation of the meaning of tradition, see Bronner, *Explaining Traditions.* For a collection of Amish traditions and wisdom, see J. Hostetler, *Amish Roots.*

26. C. Stoll, "According to the Title Deed," 8.

27. Ibid., 9; Raber, "Following Christ in Truth," 10–13.

28. "Some Questions about Baptism" provides an Amish synopsis of key Anabaptist views of baptism.

29. This observation comes from an Old Order Mennonite leader.

30. "Beware of an Unbalanced Gospel," 12.

31. J. Yoder, *Schleitheim Confession,* 11.

32. *Songs of the Ausbund,* 1:315.

33. Braght, *Martyrs Mirror.* For an excellent overview of Anabaptist martyrdom, see Gregory, *Salvation at Stake,* chap. 6.

34. 1 Peter 5:8 and 2 Cor. 11:14.

35. "Rules of a Godly Life," 89.

36. Blank, *Amazing Story of the Ausbund,* 45–46.

37. For an Amish view of mission work, see the booklet *Church and Mission Work* and Troyer, *Writings of David A. Troyer,* 121–23.

38. "Rules of a Godly Life," 103.

CHAPTER 5. SACRED RITUALS

Epigraph: The hymn is from *Ausbund,* song 7, pp. 46–48; English translation in *Songs of the Ausbund,* 1:56–58.

1. Some sections of this chapter are adapted from Kraybill, *Riddle of Amish Culture,* 111–41.

2. For more on religion and material culture, see McDannell, *Material Christianity.*

3. Not all settlements have bench wagons; in Swartzentruber communities, for example, the benches are transported on an ordinary flatbed wagon. The *Ausbund*s are transported in a wooden box with the benches. Ministers typically use the Bible that travels with the wagon or one provided by the host; however, some New Order ministers carry a small New Testament in their coat pocket, which they use when preaching.

4. L. Byler, "Mrs. Gid," 55.

5. Ministers preach in Swiss German in the Swiss affiliations. See chapter 7 for more on language practices.

6. S. Stoltzfus, "Going in with the Boys," 32.

7. Musicologists call this style of music "free rhythm," but the rhythm is hard to detect by those unfamiliar with such singing. See Durnbaugh, "Amish Singing Style."

8. Blank, *Amazing Story of the Ausbund*, 47.

9. David Luthy notes a few exceptions in a January 9, 2012, letter to Donald Kraybill. *Das Loblied* is not sung on a regular basis in the Daviess County, Indiana, settlement, and in some Swiss settlements it is the *first* song at services for weddings, council meeting, and communion.

10. S. Stoltzfus, "Going in with the Boys," 32.

11. *Songs of the Ausbund*, 1:328–29.

12. Despite slight variations in the lectionary by affiliation, all the Scripture readings are from the New Testament, with a heavy use of Matthew's Gospel in the first quarter of the year.

13. Personal communication to Donald Kraybill, March 8, 2012.

14. Acknowledging that both preacher and congregants are submitting themselves to God as one body, more traditional ministers make little direct eye contact with other church members while preaching. Change-minded preachers, who look in the eyes of members when they preach, are accenting their special role as God's servants.

15. C. Kauffman, "Staying Awake in Church," 7–9.

16. The Dover, Delaware, settlement has a noon fellowship meal for the extended family of the host, not the entire congregation.

17. In the nineteenth century, the Amish settlement in Union County, Pennsylvania, held communion only once between 1873 and 1880 due to profound and unresolved conflict. In the early 1980s, churches of the ultraconservative Swartzentruber affiliation went seven years without communion, a period of turmoil that ended in schism. These sorts of situations are rare, but point to the seriousness with which Amish churches take the collective dimension of communion.

18. "The Church," 12.

19. M. Miller, *Our Heritage, Hope, and Faith*, 252.

20. "The Church," 14.

21. Members are encouraged to read Isaiah 58 on *Fastdag*.

22. Michael, an angel mentioned in the biblical books of Daniel and Revelation, was honored by the Catholic Church each October 11, which became known as Michaelmas or Old St. Michael's Day. In Germany, taxes were due on this day; it also marked the end of the harvest and was something of a rural holiday.

23. M. Miller, *Our Heritage, Hope, and Faith*, 79.

24. *Handbuch für Bischof*, 33. A listing of Scriptures and hymns typically used in the communion service appears in M. Miller, *Our Heritage, Hope, and Faith*, 272–300.

25. Verse three of *Ausbund*, song 84, pp. 449–50, translated in M. Miller, *Our Heritage, Hope, and Faith*, 291.

26. "Most Humble Position?"

27. The kiss is mentioned in Rom. 16:16, 1 Cor. 16:20, 2 Cor. 13:12, 1 Thess. 5:26, and 1 Peter 5:14. For an Amish interpretation of it, see "Christian Greeting." Ministers in all groups greet each other with the kiss and also use it to seal rites such as baptism and ordination. In some groups, lay members of the same gender greet each other with the kiss, but in other affiliations they perform the rite only at the close of the footwashing ritual.

28. For a brief statement opposing public display of alms, see "Public Alms," 8.

29. M. Beachy, "Decided by Lot"; E. Stoll, "Ordaining by Lot"; D. Wagler, "Ordinations in the Church," 35.

30. E. Stoll, "Preparing for an Ordination," 9.

31. Luthy describes ordination procedures and variations in "Survey of Amish Ordination Customs." P. Yoder, *Tradition and Transition*, 60–64, gives a history of the ritual. M. Miller, *Our Heritage, Hope, and Faith*, 301–13, provides the typical hymns, Scriptures, and prayers used in the service.

32. Some New Order churches and a few other groups hold a separate preordination service, during which candidates are nominated, a few days before the ordination service. The logistics of nomination vary somewhat by region and affiliation. In Geauga County, Ohio, for instance, the leaders sit by an open window while members file by outside, whispering the name of their nominee through the window.

33. *Illinois Directory*, 32–34.

34. In the ordination of a bishop, the candidate kneels on the floor as the supervising bishop gives the charge while two others place their right hands on the candidate's head.

35. Procedures for confession are outlined in *Handbuch für Bischof*. M. Miller, *Our Heritage, Hope, and Faith*, 376–92, provides resources for the reinstatement of a fallen member.

36. The length of the temporary ban varies by local custom, affiliation, and the circumstances.

37. Complete wording appears in M. Miller, *Our Heritage, Hope, and Faith*, 378–79.

38. We discuss mental health and views about counseling in chapter 18.

CHAPTER 6. THE AMISH WAY

Epigraph: A & M Trustee Committee, "Plain Community Alternative." See also Randy Ludlow, "Amish Demand to Judge Their Own," *Columbus [OH] Dispatch*, Dec. 12, 2010.

1. Sections of this chapter are adapted from Kraybill, *Riddle of Amish Culture*, chap. 2. Debate about the definition of culture has a long history in both anthropology and sociology. One aspect of that discussion focuses on whether culture *motivates* people to act or if its primary function is to *justify* past actions. We understand culture as doing both. For a persuasive argument for the dual-process model, see Vaisey, "Motivation and Justification."

2. Sandra Cronk, in her 1977 doctoral dissertation, "Gelassenheit: The Rites of the Redemptive Process," was the first scholar to identify Gelassenheit in Old Order communities. Donald Kraybill, in *Riddle of Amish Culture*, used the concept to interpret Amish culture. Numerous Amish and Old Order Mennonite writers have warmly invoked the concept since Cronk introduced it: E. Kline, *Theology of the Will of Man*, 3; P. Kline, "Gelassenheit"; Martin, *Distinctive Teachings*, 45–72; and Joseph Miller, "Peculiar Beauty of *Gelassenheit*."

3. We are indebted to Bourdieu, *Outline of a Theory of Practice*, as well as Swartz, *Culture and Power*, for understanding Gelassenheit as a master disposition in Amish life. In Bourdieu's terms, Gelassenheit is *habitus*—a habit-forming, transposable disposition that blends perceptions and action, sentiment and social structure together. As a disposition, habitus has both structure and propensity that are shaped by early socialization toward action. For another application of habitus to Amish society, see Reschly's *Amish on the Iowa Prairie*.

4. P. Kline, "Gelassenheit."

5. "The Big 'I,'" 6–8. For modern perspectives, see Giddens, *Modernity and Self-Identity*.

6. Letter to Emma Huyard King, April 25, 1993; emphasis added.

7. *1001 Questions*, 76–77.

8. E. Stoll, "Cheap Shirts and Shallow Reasoning," 10.

9. Quotes in this paragraph and the next are from a letter to Donald Kraybill, Oct. 12, 2009.

10. Amish parents talk about children needing to "learn to give up" and accept what comes, rather than asserting their own will. See J. Hostetler, "Anabaptist Conceptions of Child Nurture."

11. M. Smucker, "How Amish Children View Themselves," 226–29.

12. This quote and the next are from *Guidelines in Regards to Parochial Schools,* 47, 50.

13. For two Amish views that support spanking, see *1001 Questions,* 98–101, and "Cruelest Kind of Child Abuse."

14. "Rules of a Godly Life," 69, 71.

15. The few Amish church disciplines available in writing typically condemn pride and admonish members to express humility. An Ordnung of 1779 in Germany instructs ministers to serve "*not* in pride or as lords, but in humility and holiness." Clothing should display "lowliness and humility." (See *Christlicher Ordnung.*) The rejection of outward adornment is rooted in various Scriptures, including 1 Tim. 2:9 and 1 Peter 3:3–4.

16. These verses are highlighted in *1001 Questions,* 125–26.

17. *1001 Questions,* 125.

18. "Rules of a Godly Life," 99.

19. Letter, Feb. 23, 1993, in Donald Kraybill's files.

20. "Proud Look," 12–13.

21. The Pennsylvania Ordnung of 1837 and the Ohio Ordnung of 1865 both explicitly forbid mirrors (the Ohio Ordnung says "large mirrors") on the walls of houses. A late twentieth-century Daviess County, Indiana, Ordnung also eschews "large mirrors."

22. Lipovetsky, *Empire of Fashion,* 244.

23. Emphasis added.

24. Yoder and Estes, *Proceedings of the Amish Ministers' Meetings,* 218–20.

25. Ibid., 258.

26. See M. Lehman, "Amish Taboo on Photography"; D. Lehman, "Graven Images."

27. [E. Stoll], *Strangers and Pilgrims,* 4–5.

28. D. Wagler, "What Is Left to Write About?," 4.

29. "Simple Living," 18.

30. During the U.S. economic recession of 2008–2010, some other Americans turned to the Amish as exemplars of thrift and frugality. See Craker, *Money Secrets of the Amish.*

31. John K. Lapp Jr., *Social Booklet,* 2–4. For another Amish perspective, see "Scrimping: Good or Bad."

32. Letter to Donald Kraybill, Oct. 12, 2009.

33. Letter to Karen Johnson-Weiner, Nov. 23, 2010.

34. Auctioneering is not sanctioned by all Amish communities. In traditional affiliations, a member of the family will serve as an informal auctioneer for family auctions—but not in front of a public audience.

35. A & M Trustee Committee, "Plain Community Alternative," 3.

36. "The Millers," letter to Kyle Martin, April 26, 2008, in Donald Kraybill's files.

37. R. Troyer, "Selling Cut Flowers," 41. Women in the most traditional groups do not have separate flower gardens, but they delight in having well-tended flower "patches" in their vegetable gardens.

38. Women often tease men about hunting not for meat but for the "rack," or antlers. Men generally keep the rack, and some even hang it in an out-of-the way spot in a shop or barn.

39. The quotations in this paragraph and the next appeared in various reports in the December 2008 issue of the *Diary.*

40. Lancaster County Amish man, "Ask an Amishman: What do the Amish think about Jews?," *Amish America* (blog), March 16, 2009, http://amishamerica.com/ask-an-amishman-what-do-the-amish-think-about-jews/.

41. Orr, "Public Library Usage," 15.

42. When learning to read, children are told that reading for pleasure happens only after they have done all their chores.

43. Staff Notes, *Family Life*, Jan. 2010, 7.

44. Barbara Ebersol (1846–1922) made beautiful, colorful *fraktur* bookplates described by Luthy in *Amish Folk Artist Barbara Ebersol*. In *Two Amish Folk Artists*, Louise Stoltzfus provides an overview of the work of Ebersol and watercolorist and furniture maker Henry Lapp (1862–1904). For overviews of the decorative Amish arts, see Herr, *Amish Arts of Lancaster County*, and McCauley and McCauley, *Decorative Arts*.

45. Keith Elliot Greenberg, "Amish Painter Tries to Blend the Best of Both Her Worlds," *USA Today*, Jan. 29, 1991.

46. www.facebook.com/StoltzfusDigitalAbstractArt.

47. See www.amishcookonline.com; Sharon Cohen, "The Amish Cook: A Little Lifestyle, Religion—and Food," *News–Gazette* (Champaign-Urbana, IL), Aug. 3, 2000; and Eicher and Williams, *Amish Cook at Home*.

48. Other examples of Amish publishing under their own names include Enos Detweiler, father of six, a schoolteacher and part-time farmer in Van Buren County, Iowa, who writes a column, "A Week with the Amish," for *Our Iowa* magazine, and a schoolteacher, Loren Beachy, who writes a biweekly column, "The Plain Side," for the *Goshen News*.

CHAPTER 7. SYMBOLS AND IDENTITY

Epigraph: Furlong, "Research Papers." For her full story, see Furlong, *Why I Left the Amish*.

1. Our analysis of distinctions in a group's moral order rests on the classic work of Bourdieu, *Distinction*; Douglas, *Purity and Danger*; Wuthnow et al., *Cultural Analysis*; and Wuthnow, *Meaning and Moral Order*.

2. Although all Amish groups permit deer hunting, some prohibit the use of florescent orange safety clothing or traveling out of state to hunt.

3. In applying biblical principles to issues of daily life, the Ordnung operates much like Midrash in the Jewish tradition.

4. In some settlements, leaders write down portions of the Ordnung, but even in such cases the resulting document is not published and distributed as a "rule book." A written Ordnung is most common in newer settlements composed of households that have migrated from different settlements with differing Ordnung expectations. In such cases, oral tradition does not provide a common bond, so certain agreed-upon decisions in the new settlement may be written down for clarity.

5. [J. Beiler], "Ordnung," 383; See also J. Stoll, "Rule to Measure By."

6. Furlong, "Research Papers."

7. Pennsylvania "Dutch" is often considered a misnomer, that is, a mistaken English corruption of the word *Deutsch* (the German word for "German"). However, as the *Oxford English Dictionary* demonstrates, in the eighteenth century the word Dutch was the proper English word for people and places of the Rhine Valley. Thus, English sources of the 1700s spoke of Dutch immigrants where later sources spoke of Germans. Eighteenth-century English sources used the terms Holland Dutch or Low Dutch to refer to those who today would be described as residents of the Netherlands. Louden, "Pennsylvania Dutch," offers an excellent overview of the origins and formation of this language. D. Yoder, "Two Worlds in the Dutch Country," discusses the origin and evolution of the dialect. Related resources include Beam, *Revised Pennsylvania German Dictionary*, and Haag, *Pennsylvania German Reader and Grammar*. See also Louden, "Bilingualism and Syntactic Change," "Covert Prestige," "Image of the Old Order Amish," "Old Order Amish

Verbal Behavior," and "Patterns of Language Maintenance," as well as Seifert, *Word Atlas of Pennsylvania German.* Enninger's *Language and Language Use* provides a comprehensive listing of research on Pennsylvania Dutch.

8. A dialect is a variety of language "defined by both geographical factors and social factors" (Mihalicek and Wilson, *Language Files,* 689). Linguists generally use the catchall term *language variety* because the distinction between a *dialect* and a *language* is arbitrary; there is no definition of either that will adequately cover all cases. We refer to Pennsylvania Dutch as a dialect because it is a regional/social variant. It is also unstandardized, another common (though not obligatory) attribute of a dialect. At one time Pennsylvania Dutch was widely spoken; however, its use is now largely limited to sectarian groups, primarily the Amish and horse-and-buggy-driving Old Order Mennonites.

There are numerous variations of Pennsylvania Dutch; for example, the translators of *Es Nei Teshtament,* a translation of the King James Version of the New Testament into the dialect say, "In any Pennsylvania Deitsch publication, dialect variation cannot be ignored. This translation, with minor differences, is essentially the dialect spoken by the Amish in Ohio" (v–vi). Attempts have been made to document (and thus implicitly standardize) Pennsylvania Dutch vocabulary and grammar, notably by Marcus B. Lambert, whose *Pennsylvania-German Dictionary* appeared in 1924; J. William Frey, whose *Simple Grammar of Pennsylvania Dutch* first appeared in 1942; Albert F. Buffington and Preston A. Barba, authors of *Pennsylvania German Grammar;* Lee R. Thierwechter, *Das is wie mer's saagt in Deitsch;* Joshua R. Brown and Douglas J. Madenford, *Schwetz mol Deitsch;* and C. Richard Beam, an indefatigable advocate of Pennsylvania Dutch scholarship (see, e.g., his *Revised Pennsylvania German Dictionary*). Beam is also the author of *Es Pennsilfaanisch Deitsch Eck,* a column written in Pennsylvania Dutch that appears regularly in the *Budget.* Most of these works use the Buffington-Barba orthography, a sound-spelling system devised to present Pennsylvania Dutch in written form (see http://home.ptd.net/~tconrad1/dutch_pronounce_vowels.html). This system was officially adopted by the Pennsylvania German Society (see www.pgs.org/dialect_column.asp). Yet while most varieties of Pennsylvania Dutch are mutually intelligible when spoken, the Buffington-Barba orthography is often difficult for Amish Pennsylvania Dutch speakers to read. Throughout this text, when we use Pennsylvania Dutch words, we have spelled them the way they are generally spelled by Amish writers, although that varies considerably, depending on their affiliation and region. For example, although "church" appears as *Gemee* in Beam's dictionary (32), we have spelled it *Gmay.*

9. The Swiss Amish came to the United States in the 1850s and originally settled in Indiana. See Nolt and Meyers, *Plain Diversity,* 58–70, 101–20, 146–62. Representing about 6 percent of all Amish, they have 124 congregations in eight states with a total population of approximately 16,750. Swiss Amish speak *Shwitsa,* or Swiss German, which is difficult for Pennsylvania Dutch speakers to understand. A growing number of Swiss-German speakers are now learning Pennsylvania Dutch as a fourth language.

10. One study estimated that at least 256,000 people in ten traditional Anabaptist groups in 2009 spoke Pennsylvania Dutch (Kraybill, Nolt, and Scott, "Language Use among Anabaptist Groups").

11. Although the Amish originally were a small minority of the Pennsylvania Dutch–speaking population, they and the horse-and-buggy-driving Old Order Mennonites are now the primary groups using the language and passing it on to their children. See Burridge, "Separate and Peculiar"; Huffines, "Pennsylvania German" and "Strategies of Language Maintenance." For more research on Pennsylvania Dutch structure, maintenance, and sociolinguistic importance, see Enninger, "Linguistic Markers of Anabaptist Ethnicity" and "English of the Old Order Amish";

Fuller, "Sociopragmatic Values of Pennsylvania German"; Johnson-Weiner, "Keeping Dutch," "Group Identity," and "Community Identity"; and Keiser, "Pennsylvania German."

12. See *Das Leicht Büchlein.*

13. *In Meiner Jugend,* 5.

14. M. Miller, *Our Heritage, Hope, and Faith,* v. The book is handsomely designed, with parallel columns of English and German. Two essays published anonymously in the August 2011 issue of *Blackboard Bulletin* reflect the concern of leaders about the decline of German: "Preserving Our German" and "The German Dilemma."

15. *Songs of the Ausbund,* 1:iv.

16. Such translations are rarely seen in the most conservative communities because their members have a better command of the German language.

17. Johnson-Weiner, "Community Expectations," 114.

18. "What Is in a Language?," 15–16.

19. The discussion of clothing is adapted from Kraybill, *Riddle of Amish Culture,* 57–70.

20. *1001 Questions,* 130–31.

21. Ibid., 129–37.

22. The verses include 1 Tim. 2:9–10, 1 Peter 3:3–4, and Rom. 12:2. See also "Hat's a Religious Symbol?" and Luthy, "Women's Veiling."

23. "Accepting the Uniform," 18.

24. "Let's Not Be Ashamed," 2. For a contrasting perspective, see Hershberger, "Misuse of Symbols."

25. *1001 Questions,* 129, 136.

26. S. Scott, *Why Do They Dress That Way?,* 120–26.

27. "Do Bonnets Help?," 29.

28. S. Scott, *Why Do They Dress That Way?,* 38–39.

29. S. Scott, *Plain Buggies,* 44–79. *Buggy Builder's Bulletin,* published bimonthly by an Old Order Mennonite, is widely read by Amish buggy makers.

CHAPTER 8. DIVERSE AFFILIATIONS

Epigraph: Adapted from Nolt and Meyers, *Plain Diversity,* 142.

1. The affiliations are rarely identified in regional Amish directories, and although Amish historians have written accounts of particular groups, they are reluctant to make general comparisons of affiliations for fear of offending people. Some Amish historians and academic scholars have described groups in various regions and states but not at the national level. See Leroy Beachy, *Unser Leit,* vol. 2; Hurst and McConnell, *Amish Paradox;* Johnson-Weiner, *New York Amish;* Kraybill, "Plotting Social Change"; and Nolt and Meyers, *Plain Diversity.*

2. John A. Hostetler uses the term *clan* to identify Amish groups in the 1963 edition of *Amish Society,* 76, and replaces it with the label *affiliation* in the 1968 edition, 77.

3. About sixty-four districts, thirty-one of which are New Order, use tractors for field work. Settlements with four or more districts that permit tractors are Kalona, Iowa (9), Haven/Yoder, Kansas (4), Chouteau, Oklahoma (4), Meyersdale/Springs, Pennsylvania (5), New Order Fellowship in Holmes County, Ohio (4), and New Order Tobe in Holmes County, Ohio (4). Compiled by Stephen Scott from settlement directories, other documents, and informants.

4. S. Scott, "Amish Groups." Nolt and Meyers, *Plain Diversity,* 144–45, 172–74, refer to this network as the "self-consciously communal" Amish.

5. Nolt and Meyers, *Plain Diversity,* 78, 156.

6. S. Scott, "Amish Groups."

7. S. Kauffman, *Mifflin County Amish.*

8. Leroy Beachy, *Unser Leit,* 2:397.

9. Ibid., 442.

10. For more on these labels and examples, see Nolt and Meyers, *Plain Diversity,* 80–83, 142–43.

11. Nolt and Meyers, *Plain Diversity,* 13–15, 178–79; Hurst and McConnell, *Amish Paradox,* 55–57.

12. Nolt and Meyers, *Plain Diversity,* 58–70, 101–20.

13. Leroy Beachy, *Unser Leit,* 2:471; Hurst and McConnell, *Amish Paradox,* 58–95.

14. "An Alarming Concern," unpublished, undated anonymous document in Karen Johnson-Weiner's files.

15. Swartzentruber history is recounted in Leroy Beachy, *Unser Leit,* 2:398–407; Hurst and McConnell, *Amish Paradox,* 35–43; Johnson-Weiner, *New York Amish,* 52–77; E. Kline, "Letters Pertaining to the Sam Yoder Division"; Luthy, "Origin and Growth of the Swartzentruber Amish"; and R. Weaver, "Glimpses of the Amish Church."

16. A. Keim, "Military Service and Conscription."

17. For accounts of New Order origins, see Leroy Beachy, *Unser Leit,* 2:436–51; Kline and Beachy, "History and Dynamics of the New Order Amish"; and Waldrep, "New Order Amish and Para-Amish Groups."

18. Underwear is regulated by some but not all groups. Although some affiliations permit store-bought underwear, the Swartzentrubers make their own.

19. Since 1990, the Swiss Amish in Daviess County, Indiana, have had tops on their buggies.

20. Nolt and Meyers, *Plain Diversity,* 61, 115.

21. The orange emblem required by most states for slow-moving vehicles has been a contentious issue between state governments and the Swartzentrubers. See Zook, "Slow-moving Vehicles."

22. "An Alarming Concern."

23. Some groups distinguish between full fellowship (visiting minister participates in the communion service) and partial fellowship (restricted to visiting minister preaching on a regular Sunday), as noted by David Luthy in letter to Donald Kraybill, Jan. 9, 2012.

24. Leroy Beachy, *Unser Leit,* 2:439–44. See also Nolt and Meyers, *Plain Diversity,* 47.

25. Because new settlements often have small districts, groups that are starting numerous settlements may appear to be growing faster than other affiliations when church district is used as a proxy for population.

CHAPTER 9. POPULATION PATTERNS

Epigraph: Betsy Scott, "Taking Life Slower," *News-Herald* (Willoughby, OH), Oct. 1, 2006.

1. Exact population numbers are difficult to determine because some communities do not publish lists of households or members, and those that do record such information do not use consistent or comparable methods. Raber's *New American Almanac* provides an annual listing of districts by state and county but not the number of households or members. The directories of larger settlements provide detailed and fairly reliable information about districts, households, and individuals in those communities.

2. Based on the 2007 annual reports of correspondents from each settlement that appeared in the *Diary,* Jan. and Feb. 2008.

3. *Gemeinde Register,* Jan. 3, 2007, 1.

4. This estimate is similar to the 6.8 average completed family size that Ericksen et al. found in their fertility study of several Amish communities in the first half of the twentieth century ("Fertility Patterns and Trends," 258). According to the U.S. Census Bureau, Current Population Survey, June 2010, women ages 40 to 44 who had ever married had an average of 2.1 children.

5. In the 1960s, most Americans were married by their early twenties (median age was 20.3 for women and 22.8 for men), and only 9 percent of Americans ages 30 to 34 had never married. Both of these rates are similar to present-day Amish patterns.

The percent of unmarried Amish persons over 30 years is 5.7 for Elkhart–LaGrange; 4.7 for Michigan settlements; 3.6 for Jasper, New York; and 7.3 for Lancaster, Pa. Rates were calculated from samples taken from settlement directories (2007 *Indiana Amish Directory;* 2010 *Michigan Amish Directory;* 2010 *New York Amish Directory*) and Kraybill's "2010 Lancaster Demographic Study." National data is from a 2011 Pew Research Center report, "Barely Half of U.S. Adults are Married" by Cohn, Passel, and Wang, which is based on an analysis of U.S. Census data. For the Amish, the rate represents all people over age 30. The Pew report includes only those in the two age groups mentioned (30–34 and 35–39); 24 percent of Americans ages 35 to 39 had never married, up from 7 percent in 1960. Of course, some Americans marry for the first time after age 39, which would shrink the gap between all Americans and the Amish.

6. Hurst and McConnell, *Amish Paradox,* 100.

7. An exception to this pattern is the conservative Nebraska Amish in Pennsylvania's Big Valley, whose family size is limited by hereditary factors.

8. Wasao and Donnermeyer, "Analysis of Factors Related to Parity," 242; Greksa and Korbin, "Key Decisions," 389.

9. Ericksen et al., "Fertility Patterns and Trends," 269; Meyers, "Population Growth," 317; Hurst and McConnell, *Amish Paradox,* 99; and Wasao and Donnermeyer, "Analysis of Factors Related to Parity," 242.

10. Nugent, *Crossings,* 19–26. Cultural and historical factors had a bigger impact on fertility rates than urbanization or industrialization.

11. J. Stoll, "The Family under Attack," 8–10.

12. For more on this point, see Nolt and Meyers, *Plain Diversity,* 119–20.

13. This is an estimate drawn from knowledgeable insiders. A listing of some sixty converts, compiled by Robert Alexander (a convert) in 1997, includes the birth date, baptism date, spouse, and Amish settlement of each. (List in Donald Kraybill's files.) The authors are not aware of a comprehensive list of converts.

14. E-mail to Donald Kraybill, Feb. 23, 2009.

15. *Die Botschaft,* Oct. 6, 2004, 1.

16. E-mail to Donald Kraybill, Aug. 3, 2009.

17. J. Smith, "Seekers."

18. S. Scott, "Newcomers," 2.

19. Ibid.

20. Personal communication to Donald Kraybill, July 18, 2012.

21. These converts, coming from Old Colony Mennonite, plain-dressing, Low-German-dialect backgrounds in Canada and South America, needed to learn Pennsylvania Dutch. Some came from car-driving and others from horse-driving groups. A listing of these newcomers appears in a letter from David Luthy to Sam Steiner, dated September 19, 2011, in Steven Nolt's files.

22. *Ohio Amish Directory,* 611–25.

23. Since 1939, several descendants of convert Marx Jess (1867–1948) have been ordained in the Arthur, Illinois, settlement. *Illinois Directory; Diary,* Nov. 2008, 26.

24. *Diary,* July 2005, 71.

25. S. Scott, "Newcomers," 4.

26. Greksa and Korbin, "Key Decisions," 373, 383; Meyers, "Population Growth," 313. Nolt and Meyers, *Plain Diversity,* 99, report a present northern Indiana retention rate of about 95 percent compared to 80 percent in the 1920s and 1930s. Swartzentruber, "Retention Rates in Amish

Communities," also found a recent increase. Ericksen, Ericksen, and Hostetler, "Cultivation of the Soil," 56–57, used genealogical data from the *Fisher Family History* book and found defection rates to be more stable for people born between 1900 and 1930.

27. Nolt and Meyers, *Plain Diversity,* 83. For similar results from a different sample, see Meyers, "Old Order Amish," 390–91.

28. Kraybill, "2010 Lancaster Demographic Study," is the source for the Lancaster defection rate. In Lancaster County the two Amish-related car-driving alternatives are the Beachy Amish and several Amish-Mennonite churches. The Geauga County defection data was reported by Greksa and Korbin, "Key Decisions," 381.

29. One example of these organizations is MAP (Mission to Amish People), www.mapministry .org/.

30. Emma Gingerich, e-mail to Donald Kraybill, Jan. 21, 2012.

31. Greksa and Korbin, "Key Decisions," 385–89, discuss both of these factors in detail. Meyers, "Population Growth," 320, reports that farming families have a slightly higher retention rate (5 percent) than factory families, but the difference is not statistically significant.

32. Meyers, "Old Order Amish," 385, 392.

33. Ibid., 382. See also Greksa and Korbin, "Key Decisions," 394–96.

34. Hurst and McConnell, *Amish Paradox,* 84–93, describe defections in Holmes County, Ohio. For additional stories of ex-Amish leaving because of family dysfunction, see Burkholder, *Amish Confidential;* Dell, *Daring Destiny;* O. Garrett, *True Stories of the X-Amish;* and Streiker-Schmidt, *Separate God.*

35. I. Wagler, *Growing Up Amish;* W. Weaver, *Dust Between My Toes;* Wittmer, *Gentle People;* Andy Yoder's story was told in 2008 by Lee Elliott, "Doctor in Training: Amish Upbringing Fuels Area Man's Desire to Help Others," *Times-Reporter* (New Philadelphia, OH), Jan. 13, 2008. An update was published two years later: Misti Crane, "Born Amish, Student Remains on Course to Become Doctor," *Times-Reporter* (New Philadelphia, OH), April 5, 2010. Naomi Kramer, from the Jamesport, Missouri, Amish settlement, is a nursing graduate from Goshen College with a story much like Andy Yoder's. Kramer and two other formerly Amish people have started a scholarship fund for Amish-reared young adults who want to attend college (http://adsfund.weebly .com/index.html).

36. Nisly, "Community and Formerly-Amish Professionals," 61–82.

37. Sections of our discussion of shunning are adapted from Kraybill, Nolt, and Weaver-Zercher, *Amish Grace,* chap. 11. Consult that chapter for a fuller explanation of shunning as well as the distinction between forgiveness and pardon.

38. Braithwaite, "Reintegrative Shaming."

39. J. Hostetler, *Amish Society,* 85–87.

40. The primary biblical texts that support shunning include Matt. 18:15–18; Rom. 16:17; 1 Cor. 5; 2 Thess. 3:6, 14–15; 2 Tim. 3:2–5; and Titus 3:10. For an articulate Amish explanation of shunning, see *Biblical Guidelines in Shunning.*

41. Amish excommunication and shunning resemble in some ways the practices of Benedictine Orders. This same verse (1 Cor. 5:5) as well as Matt. 18:15–16 are cited in Benedictine Rules 23 through 29. See *RB 1980,* 49–53.

42. *In Meiner Jugend,* 57.

43. John A. Hostetler critiques Meidung in "Letter Concerning Shunning."

CHAPTER 10. COMMUNITY ORGANIZATION

Epigraph: Loren Beachy, "The Plain Side," *Goshen (IN) News,* Aug. 29, 2011.

1. Sections of this chapter are adapted from Kraybill, *Riddle of Amish Culture,* chap. 4.

2. Weber identified charisma as a third form of authority, and he also pointed to technology as the primary force in the process of modernization (*Theory of Social and Economic Organization*, 324–58). Weber distinguished between different types of rationality, as elucidated by Stephen Kalberg, "Max Weber's Types of Rationality."

3. "The Shop that Grew" is a two-part essay that explains the dangers of growing a big Amish business.

4. E. Hall, *Beyond Culture*, 85–128.

5. [D. Wagler], *Are All Things Lawful?*, 7.

6. Nolt and Meyers, *Plain Diversity*, 64–67, compare naming practices in several different settlements, including gendered differences in the patterns of naming children.

7. See Bell, *China's New Confucianism*, 38–55.

8. Typically, one negative vote will not stop a decision. However, two or more objections *will* derail a proposal and require additional processing.

9. A schism in a Swartzentruber Gmay divided a bishop from his married daughters, all of whom chose to go with the opposing faction. One of the married sons, a minister, also went with the opposing faction and became the bishop of the new group. A more recent schism has divided the married daughters.

10. An example is Bishop Sam Mullet Sr. in the Bergholz district in Jefferson County, Ohio. He established this one-district settlement in 1995 but spurned fraternal ties with any affiliations, including the Fredericktown (Ohio) Amish group from which he had migrated. His autocratic style of excommunicating members who disagreed with him stirred controversy among other Amish leaders, yet none of them had authority to intervene in the Bergholz district and remove him from office. On September 13, 2006, a conference of three hundred bishops and ministers from five states met to discuss their shared concerns about Mullet's activities. They unanimously agreed not to honor his excommunications and to reinstate into their own congregations the people Mullet excommunicated. Mullet's bitterness over the action of the ad hoc conference led him to reject core Amish beliefs, which further isolated his church. The Bergholz community shrank in size, discontinued church services, introduced novel rituals, and vilified Amish groups. This malice erupted in five incidents in the fall of 2011, when members of the Bergholz group attacked several Amish leaders and, in some cases, their wives, cutting the men's beards and the women's hair. Mullet and fifteen of his followers were charged with federal hate crimes, tried by jury, and found guilty in September 2012.

11. Donna Doblick, e-mail to Donald Kraybill, Jan. 19, 2011.

12. Luthy, "Amish Settlements: 1991" and "Amish Settlements: 2008." Donnermeyer and Cooksey, "Recent Growth of New Amish Settlements," trace and analyze the growth of Amish settlements from 1990 through 2009.

13. This definition, employed by Amish-owned Pathway Publishers, has generally been adopted by academic writers as well. In Pathway's definition, a mere two households could comprise a settlement if one household is that of an ordained bishop, minister, or deacon. A single household by itself is never considered a settlement—although it is hard to imagine a single household desiring to move alone or on its own.

14. Donnermeyer and Cooksey, "Recent Growth of New Amish Settlements," 195.

15. *Die Botschaft*, Dec. 5, 2005, 19, and June 26, 2006, 47. Also cited in Luthy, "Amish Settlements: 2008," 6.

16. *Diary*, June 2010, 39, and July 2010, 44.

17. Settlement failure data derived from Luthy, *Amish in America* and *Why Some Amish Communities Fail*. The story of the Honduras settlement is recounted by J. Stoll in *Sunshine and Shadow*.

18. Luthy offers nine reasons for failure in *Why Some Amish Communities Fail*. He credits John A. Hostetler for noting that a settlement needs at least eleven families to succeed (19).

19. Staff Notes, *Family Life*, Dec. 1996, 4.

20. Donnermeyer and Cooksey, "Recent Growth of New Amish Settlements."

21. Nolt and Meyers, *Plain Diversity*, 121–41.

22. L. Beiler, *Where Mountains Rise*, describes the challenges of establishing a new settlement and includes a special section thanking English van drivers who provided taxi service through the years (161–66). See also Johnson-Weiner, *New York Amish*, 117.

23. Staff Notes, *Family Life*, Dec. 1996, 4.

24. Luthy, *Amish in America*, 390.

25. Sources for these numbers tabulated by Stephen Scott include correspondents' settlement reports in various Amish publications, annual migration reports in the *Diary*, and informants in various settlements. Migration information is reported for households. The estimated number of people assumes five persons per household. For more detail on migration patterns, see www2.etown.edu/amishstudies/.

26. Luthy, *Why Some Amish Communities Fail*, 15–18; Peter Applebome, "Faraway Amish Try to Keep Faith," *New York Times*, Aug. 25, 1987.

27. "Mad about Manure: Some Residents of SD Town Upset about Droppings from Amish Settlers' Horses," *Daily Republic* (Mitchell, SD), Nov. 10, 2011; "Loyal Adopts Manure-Catching Device Rules," *Tribune Record Gleaner* (Loyal, WI), Oct. 29, 2008; and Laurie Stribling, "Road Damage, Manure and Accidents," *KSAX-TV*, Dec. 13, 2011.

28. The conflict was resolved in Pennsylvania in 2004 when the Superior Court of Pennsylvania decided in favor of the Amish and in Kentucky by legislative action in 2012.

29. Dave Tobin, "Cortland County Town of Marathon Split over Amish Community's Demand for Separate School Buses," *Post-Standard* (Syracuse, NY), Jan. 1, 2012.

30. Nolt and Meyers, *Plain Diversity*, 121–34.

31. Johnson-Weiner, *New York Amish*, chap. 5.

32. O. Gingerich, *Amish of Canada*, 65–67; G. Fisher, *Farm Life and Its Changes*, 355, 379–80.

33. Kraybill and Nolt, *Amish Enterprise*, 166–71.

CHAPTER 11. GENDER AND FAMILY

Epigraph: Adapted from Johnson-Weiner, "Katie."

1. J. Stoll, "Fireside Chats," 7.

2. Sociologist W. Bradford Wilcox argues that "religion domesticates men in ways that make them more responsive to the aspirations and needs of their immediate families." See "Soft Patriarchs, New Men," on Wilcox's website, www.wbradfordwilcox.com/book.htm. See also Wilcox, *Soft Patriarchs, New Men*.

3. *1001 Questions*, 101.

4. Kraybill and Huntington, "Amish Family," 442–45. See also Hostetler and Huntington, *Amish Children*, 19–35.

5. See "Blessings in Adoption"; "Twenty Things Adopted Children Wish Their Adoptive Parents Knew"; "Twenty Things Adoptive Parents Want Their Adopted Children to Know."

6. "Advantages of Home Birthing"; Allen, "My Birth, My Way"; Campanella, Korbin, and Acheson, "Pregnancy and Childbirth," 333–35; Hurst and McConnell, *Amish Paradox*, 222; Lucas et al., "Rural Medicine and the Closed Society," 49; and Miller et al., "Health Status," 169.

7. Menno Simons, *Complete Works of Menno Simons*, 274. See also K. Miller, "Complex Innocence."

8. Other often-cited Scriptures include Prov. 22:6; Exod. 20:12; Deut. 5:16; and Eph. 6:1–3.

9. J. Stoll, *Child Training,* 56.

10. Letter from Mrs. L. D. Miller, *Family Life,* Aug.–Sept. 1982, 3.

11. On gender and Plain dress, see Graybill, "'To Remind Us Who We Are,'" and Schmidt, "Schism."

12. R. Stevick, *Growing Up Amish,* 82–83.

13. Mackall, *Plain Secrets,* 77; J. Hostetler, *Amish Society,* 160. Many Swartzentruber Amish believe that if a woman cans vegetables when she is menstruating, the jars will not seal. Similarly, they say, cakes are more likely to fall if the baker is menstruating.

14. "Ten Rules for a Successful Marriage" appeared in the Geauga County, Ohio, *Gemeinde Brief* and was reprinted in the Lancaster County *Gemeinde Brief,* Dec. 30, 2010.

15. "Ten Rules for a Successful Marriage."

16. Esh, *Collection of Treasured Recipes and Poems,* 20.

17. *1001 Questions,* 97.

18. Huntington, "Occupational Opportunities," 115–16. See also Huntington, "Amish Family"; Johnson-Weiner, "Role of Women."

19. Huntington, "Occupational Opportunities," 116.

20. For more on gender roles, see Huntington, "Occupational Opportunities"; M. Lehman, "Writing the Everyday Self"; Olshan and Schmidt, "Amish Women and the Feminist Conundrum"; and Reschly and Jellison, "Production Patterns."

21. J. Stoll, "Fireside Chats," 9.

22. L. Stoltzfus, *Amish Women,* 64–65.

23. See Furlong, *Why I Left the Amish.*

24. M. Lehman, "Women and Their Work," 11.

25. L. Stoltzfus, personal communication to Karen Johnson-Weiner.

26. Letter to Donald Kraybill, March 7, 2012; emphasis in the original.

27. "Single's Plight," 33. For related anonymous essays in the same periodical, see "Plea for Understanding," and "Tribute to our Single Sisters."

28. Kraybill, "2010 Lancaster Demographic Study." (N=858 adults.)

29. See Cates, "Identity in Crisis."

30. "Silent Struggle."

31. For a story of one woman's Amish uncle and "aunt," who was intersex and transgender but remained Amish all her life, see Carolyn Schrock-Shenk's brief tale in her foreword to *Stumbling Toward a Genuine Conversation on Homosexuality.*

32. Letter to Donald Kraybill, Sept. 21, 2011.

33. Some of these facilities are affiliated with professional health care providers, while others are more homespun and lack professionally trained therapists.

34. Mayes, *Strong Families, Safe Children.*

35. *Healing from Sexual Sin; Walk in the Light;* Stoltzfus and Ingham, *God Moves Mountains.*

36. Five articles focusing on sexual abuse appeared in December 1999, February 2000, May 2002, November 2002, and March 2003. A series of letters regarding sexual abuse also appeared in "Can You Help Me?"

37. This essay appeared in the February 1994 issue.

38. Sewing Circle, *Doorway to Hope,* 2.

39. Miller et al., "Health Status." Amish women in the study broke taboos by admitting to using artificial birth control, so the low reported rate of domestic violence cannot automatically be considered a product of survey self-censorship.

40. Ericksen and Klein, "Women's Roles and Family Production," 284.

41. Huntington, "Occupational Opportunities," 119.

42. Ibid. See also Nolt and Meyers, *Plain Diversity,* 89–90.

43. Johnson-Weiner, "Role of Women."

44. Kraybill, *Riddle of Amish Culture,* 261.

CHAPTER 12. FROM RUMSPRINGA TO MARRIAGE

Epigraph: See D. Umble, "Wicked Truth," and Remnick, "Bad Seeds." One of the young men eventually left the Amish and joined a non-Amish church.

1. Mazie, "Consenting Adults?"

2. *Devil's Playground,* which premiered on Cinemax on May 30, 2002, was later released on DVD. Some 5.4 million viewers of the premier episode of *Amish in the City* made it the evening's second highest rated show nationally on July 28, 2004. See Eitzen, "Hollywood Rumspringa."

3. http://tlc.howstuffworks.com/tv/breaking-amish/about-breaking-amish.htm. For a thoughtful critique of the series, see Greenwood, "Shame on 'Breaking Amish.'"

4. R. Stevick, *Growing Up Amish,* provides a comprehensive guide to Rumspringa.

5. While this is literally true, parents are aware of the need to keep their children in line. In short, the church will not treat rowdy unbaptized youth as it would baptized church members, but parents and the broader church community may use other ways to control their children during this period.

6. Here we disagree with Denise Reiling, who in an otherwise cogent analysis ("'Simmie' Side of Life"), describes Rumspringa as "culturally prescribed deviance . . . constructed by adult Amish culture." Deviance during Rumspringa may be somewhat ignored by adults; however, that is quite different from a program that is intentionally designed to expose Amish youth to the outside world.

7. Letter to Donald Kraybill, Jan. 9, 2012; emphasis in original.

8. Singings from the early 1900s are described in J. Yoder, *Rosanna of the Amish,* 125–36.

9. This description of a singing is based on participant observation by the authors and R. Stevick in *Growing Up Amish,* chap. 7.

10. *Diary,* Dec. 2008, 35.

11. R. Stevick, *Growing Up Amish,* 11–13. Stevick notes that the term *gangs* is a distinctly Lancaster Amish term, whereas *crowds* is the term used in other Amish communities.

12. For mid-twentieth-century descriptions of parties, see J. Yoder, *Rosanna of the Amish,* and Rice and Steinmetz, *Amish Year,* 179–88. Goldstein, "Party On, Amos," describes one in 1997.

13. These are not options for youth in more isolated or conservative communities. Young Swartzentruber men may have to run away from home to taste such forbidden pleasures—an option far less available to young women. The overwhelming majority of runaways return to the community.

14. Reiling, "'Simmie' Side of Life," 164. See also her dissertation, "Relationship between Amish Identity and Depression."

15. Gibson, "'Gang' Prevalence."

16. "Younge Fersamlunge Liste."

17. These are fictitious names of actual gangs described in Gibson's unpublished report, "'Gang' Prevalence."

18. R. Stevick, *Growing Up Amish,* 17.

19. "Procedural Guide."

20. R. Stevick, in *Growing Up Amish,* 173–97, describes courtship. See also S. Scott, *Amish Wedding,* and Goldstein, "Party On, Amos."

21. In support of this practice, church leaders cite the Apostle Paul's words: "Be ye not unequally yoked together with unbelievers" (2 Cor. 6:14).

22. John A. Hostetler's first-person account of bed courtship appears in "Amish Beginning," 18–20. *Ein Risz in der Mauer,* a 40-page treatise against bed courtship written by New Order minister Rob Schlabach, was widely circulated among Amish groups. D. Fischer, *Albion's Seed,* includes a section on Puritan New Englanders' common practice of bundling and statistical evidence that premarital pregnancy was less common among them than among backcountry residents who did not practice bundling.

23. R. Stevick, *Growing Up Amish,* 18.

24. This quote and the one in the following paragraph are from Johnson-Weiner, *New York Amish,* 66, 113. One mother in a progressive western New York church-community noted that bed courtship was still practiced in her community, even though "it's a 'guideline rule' not to do it."

25. R. Stevick, *Growing Up Amish,* 41–58.

26. An example of the disorientation and vulnerability of runaway Amish teens was featured in the ABC News Primetime documentary "The Outsiders," June 23, 2008.

27. Weber, Cates, and Carey, "Drug and Alcohol Intervention." See also Cates and Weber, "Substance Use Survey" and "Alcohol and Drug Intervention."

28. R. Stevick, *Growing Up Amish,* 50–53.

29. Personal correspondence to Donald Kraybill, Nov. 22, 2010.

30. Ira Wagler, "Running Around," *Ira's Writings* (blog), Feb. 20, 2009, www.irawagler .com/?m=200902. Wagler's book, *Growing Up Amish,* offers a glimpse into his heart-wrenching struggle about leaving Amish society.

31. Reiling, "'Simmie' Side of Life," 156.

32. Ibid., 159.

33. See I. Wagler, *Growing Up Amish.*

34. If a Swartzentruber youth joins any Amish church other than that of his or her parents before age twenty-one, it is considered running away, dishonoring parents, and breaking the commandments ("Honor thy father and thy mother," Exod. 20:12). "If someone wants to join a different church than his parents, he has to wait until he is twenty-one," said one father.

35. *In Meiner Jugend,* 25, 27.

36. *In Meiner Jugend,* 189, and "Questions Asked at Baptism Service." The wording of the vows varies slightly by settlement. This is the wording used by the Amish in Ohio and Indiana.

37. *In Meiner Jugend,* 115–17.

38. M. Miller, *Our Heritage, Hope, and Faith,* 223.

39. Furlong, "Research Papers."

CHAPTER 13. SOCIAL TIES AND COMMUNITY RHYTHMS

Epigraph: For the father's story of this tragic event, see [A. Beiler], *Light in the Shadow of Death.*

1. Sections of this chapter are adapted from Kraybill, *Riddle of Amish Culture,* chaps. 4 and 6.

2. We view values and knowledge as *cultural* capital and social networks, rituals, and structures as *social* capital. In 1998, Tay Keong Tan, in "Silence, Sacrifice and Shoo-fly Pies," first applied social capital theory to Amish life. For recent theory and research, consult Field, *Social Capital,* and Lin and Erickson, *Social Capital.*

3. Coleman, in *Foundations of Social Theory,* 653, notes that this "primordial" social capital, rooted in an extended family system, has largely vanished in modern life.

4. For a good overview of Amish weddings, see R. Stevick, *Growing Up Amish,* 199–228, and P. Stevick, *Beyond the Plain and Simple,* 48–58. S. Scott, in *Amish Wedding,* 4–35, describes weddings in various settlements.

5. P. Stevick, *Beyond the Plain and Simple,* 50.

6. Weddings were sampled from Amish directories for Ohio, Indiana, Illinois, Wisconsin, Iowa, and Ontario. (This is not a representative national sample.) All couples under thirty-three years of age at the time of marriage were included. The mean scores for age of marriage have a standard deviation of 2.01 for women and 2.41 for men.

7. *Diary,* Dec. 2008, 85.

8. Ibid., 37.

9. In some New Order churches the couple may meet with the officiating bishop prior to the wedding to clarify the expectations.

10. Swartzentruber brides wear the crossed cape of adolescent girls.

11. *In Meiner Jugend,* 211; "Questions Asked at a Marriage Ceremony."

12. M. Miller lists the songs, prayers, and Scripture readings for weddings in *Our Heritage, Hope, and Faith,* 315–73.

13. R. Stevick describes pranks at Lancaster County weddings in *Growing Up Amish,* 223–24; Johnson-Weiner describes a Swartzentruber wedding and associated pranks in *New York Amish,* 67–69.

14. See S. Scott, *Amish Wedding,* 35, for a comparison of menus.

15. *Diary,* Dec. 2008, 85.

16. Ibid., 72–73.

17. S. Stoltzfus, "Ascension Day."

18. Reported by scribes in the December 2008 issue of the *Diary.*

19. *Die Botschaft,* March 23, 2009, 47.

20. Some midwestern Amish spend winter weeks in Arizona.

21. N. Gingerich, *History of Pinecraft,* 30; 147–50.

22. In addition to our own observations, we lean heavily and gratefully on R. Stevick, "Pinecraft Florida Notes."

23. Some of the Amish-owned bungalows have public electric service because they are temporary housing away from their home church district and because of the practical difficulty of accessing supplies for alternate forms of lighting.

24. R. Stevick, "Pinecraft Florida Notes."

25. Schwartz and Schwartz, *Schwartzs' Song-Book,* 180–91; Thompson, "Yodeling."

26. E. Lapp, *Heartland Hymns.*

27. Binford, "Values and Culture Transmitted Through Music," 1. For a detailed study of music in Holmes County, Ohio, see Elder, " 'Es Sind Zween Weg' " and "Why the Amish Sing."

28. *1001 Questions,* 165–66.

29. S. Stoltzfus, "Lancaster Counties [*sic*] Barn Raising."

30. *Die Botschaft,* Feb. 9, 2009, 68; *Budget,* March 3, 2004, 19.

31. *Die Botschaft,* Feb. 16, 2009, 64. Sunshine boxes consist of small gifts to brighten someone's day.

32. For two accounts by Amish women on death, see E. King, *Joys, Sorrows, and Shadows,* and E. Smucker, *Good Night, My Son.* Bryer, "Attitudes toward Death" and "Amish Way of Death," provides a psychological study of death among the Amish. [A. Beiler's] *Light in the Shadow of Death* is a father's lament for the death of his son. See Kraybill, Nolt, and Weaver-Zercher, *Amish Grace,* for a description of Amish grief in the aftermath of the 2006 Nickel Mines schoolhouse shooting.

33. S. Scott, *Amish Wedding,* 94–107, describes funeral customs in various affiliations.

34. Some communities designate a "funeral director" to assist the non-Amish licensed mortician with funeral logistics.

35. Communities vary in how they deal with mourners who are in the *Bann*. Illustrating the strict Swartzentruber Bann, a granddaughter of the deceased, her husband (also a former church member), and their children were not invited into the home where the mourners had gathered, and they were clearly not welcome to participate in the funeral.

36. M. Miller lists the songs, prayers, and Scripture readings for funerals in *Our Heritage, Hope, and Faith*, 407–37.

CHAPTER 14. EDUCATION

1. Although a handful of Amish communities operated private schools in the nineteenth century to provide German instruction for reading religious materials, such schools merely supplemented the education that pupils received in public schools. On German schools, see Troyer and Stoll, "Apple Grove Mennonite School." Meyers, "Education and Schooling," 294n1, identifies an Amish school built in Holmes County as early as 1815. Urie D. Byler, in a letter to Donald Kraybill dated July 8, 2006, describes several Pennsylvania schools in the nineteenth century. See also J. Stoll, "Who Shall Educate Our Children?"

2. Zimmerman, *Small Wonder*, 17. See also Fischel, *Making the Grade*.

3. For descriptions of the conflicts, see Dewalt, *Amish Education;* Huntington, "Persistence and Change in Amish Education"; Johnson-Weiner, *Train Up a Child;* A. Keim, *Compulsory Education and the Amish;* Kraybill, *Riddle of Amish Culture*, 161–87; C. Lapp, *Pennsylvania School History;* Meyers, "Education and Schooling"; and J. Stoll, *Challenge of the Child*.

4. Pratt, *Shipshewana*, 73–77, 81–85.

5. C. Lapp, *Pennsylvania School History*, 141–42.

6. D. Weaver-Zercher, *Amish in the American Imagination*, 61.

7. Huntington, "Persistence and Change in Amish Education," 78.

8. Kraybill, *Riddle of Amish Culture*, 174.

9. J. Stoll, "Who Shall Educate Our Children?," 31. See also J. Hostetler, *Amish Society;* Hostetler and Huntington, *Amish Children;* and Johnson-Weiner, *Train Up a Child*.

10. For Amish descriptions of their school history, see Hershberger, *Struggle to Be Separate;* Kinsinger, *Little History of Our Parochial Schools;* C. Lapp, *Pennsylvania School History;* J. Stoll, *Challenge of the Child;* and C. Stoltzfus, *Amish Church, School and Historical Events*.

11. Sources on this school include Troyer and Stoll, "Apple Grove Mennonite School," and Clark, *This Is Good Country*, 117–28.

12. This does not include two short-lived ones in North Carolina and Mississippi as reported by Meyers in "Education and Schooling," 89.

13. For a record of the early schools, see Huntington, "Persistence and Change in Amish Education," 84–92; Meyers, "Education and Schooling," 88–90; J. Stoll, *Challenge of the Child*, 116; and *Blackboard Bulletin* prior to 1970.

14. Editorial, *Blackboard Bulletin*, May 1963. J. Stoll's *Challenge of the Child* contains reprints of essays related to schools and teacher training from *Blackboard Bulletin*, 1957–1966.

15. Descriptions of the history and function of vocational schools appears in *Standards of Parochial and Vocational Schools*, 45–46, 52, and Kraybill, *Riddle of Amish Culture*, 171–72.

16. A. Keim, *Compulsory Education and the Amish*, 98.

17. These estimates are based on extrapolations from the 2007–2008 School Directory in *Blackboard Bulletin*, December 2007, 26. This is the last year the *Bulletin* published a school directory. Estimates for 2012 use the 2008 baseline of .85 schools per church district and 1.5 teachers per school. Estimates reflect the increase in church districts since 2008, but not any changes in the rate of private school attendance.

18. Descriptions of governance, curriculum, teacher education, and pedagogy appear in Dewalt, *Amish Education;* Fisher and Stahl, *Amish School;* Hostetler and Huntington, *Amish Children;* and Johnson-Weiner, *Train Up a Child.*

19. For a listing of regional school meetings, see "School Meetings."

20. Teachers and directors in more conservative communities rarely attend the regional meetings, which are dominated by progressive groups.

21. The private school expenses in eastern Pennsylvania were for the 2008–2009 school year. The per-pupil cost for the local public school was for 2005.

22. Johnson-Weiner, *Train Up a Child,* 206–28, provides an overview of school-related publishers and publishing.

23. Regarding special schools, see *Beginning and Development of Parochial Special Schools;* Dewalt, *Amish Education,* 135–46; Hurst and McConnell, *Amish Paradox,* 167–70; Johnson-Weiner, *Train Up a Child,* 120–21, 162–63; and Kinsinger, *Little History of Our Parochial Schools,* 111–20. A monthly newsletter, *Life's Special Sunbeams,* provides resources for the parents of "special children."

24. An Amish-authored textbook series used in some schools includes a few short stories from the Bible and Amish history.

25. Pennsylvania school leader Aaron E. Beiler, quoted in Kraybill, *Riddle of Amish Culture,* 357n25. Emphasis in the original.

26. Remarks by an Amish bishop at the fourth annual Indiana Amish parochial teachers' meeting, July 13, 2000, in Heritage Historical Library, Aylmer, ON.

27. Amish school policies vary in part because they developed at different times in various regions without national coordination and because state regulations vary.

28. See Johnson-Weiner, "Reinforcing Amish Identity" and *Train Up a Child.*

29. In Swartzentruber schools, children do not join in the morning singing until the third grade, when they begin to study German and can recognize the script.

30. Caroline Schwartz, writing from Berne, IN, *Budget,* May 2, 2007, 8.

31. Levi Borntragers, writing from Macomb, IL, *Budget,* May 2, 2007, 8.

32. Johnson-Weiner, *Train Up a Child,* 131.

33. For additional evidence of the same trends, see Dewalt, *Amish Education,* 90, and Hostetler and Huntington, *Amish Children,* 93–97. For a critique of the test scores used as evidence in *Wisconsin v. Yoder,* see Fischel, "Do Amish Schools Make the Grade?"

34. Northern Indiana Subcommittee on Testing, in a memorandum to schools, March 12, 2002, in Donald Kraybill's files.

35. *Indiana Amish Directory,* 13.

36. Based on their fieldwork in various settlements, the authors estimate that fewer than 10 percent of Amish children attend public schools.

37. Hurst and McConnell, *Amish Paradox,* 153–61; Nolt and Meyers, *Plain Diversity,* 92.

38. Johnson-Weiner, *Train Up a Child,* 164.

39. Nolt and Meyers, *Plain Diversity,* 92.

40. Johnson-Weiner, *Train Up a Child,* 164.

41. Nolt and Meyers, *Plain Diversity,* 92.

42. Johnson-Weiner, *Train Up a Child,* 164.

43. "From the Desk of Teacher Dave." Responses to Teacher Dave's essay on homeschooling appear in letters to the editor, *Blackboard Bulletin,* May 2011.

44. Hurst and McConnell found that the few Amish in the Holmes County, Ohio, area who do homeschool are New Order or New Order Fellowship. See *Amish Paradox,* 161–62, 171–72.

45. For an exception, see Hostetler and Huntington, *Amish Children*, 114–15.

46. Correspondence to Donald Kraybill, Nov. 10, 2011.

47. Guengerich, *Deutsche Gemeinde Schulen*, quoted in J. Stoll, "Who Shall Educate Our Children?," 24–25.

48. J. Stoll, "Who Shall Educate Our Children?," 28.

49. Reich, *Bridging Liberalism*, 12, 39–40, 46.

50. Johnson-Weiner, *Train Up a Child*, 239–40.

CHAPTER 15. AGRICULTURE

Epigraph: R. Schlabach, "Inroads of Industrialism," 1.

1. A. Beiler, *Vocation on the Farm*, 3. See also Ericksen, Ericksen, and Hostetler, "Cultivation of the Soil." The European practices are described by Jean Séguy in "Religion and Agricultural Success" and "Bernese Anabaptists."

2. Both quotes are from *1001 Questions*, 139.

3. For abundant examples in Amish publications, see *Family Life, Plain Interests, Truck Patch News*, and *Farming*, as well as many memoirs, published and unpublished. Additional evidence is the fourteen entries (written by non-Amish people) in Unit Eight, "Home on the Farm," in Stoll, Luthy, and Stoll, *Our Heritage*, a textbook widely used in Amish schools.

4. Reschly and Jellison, "Production Patterns."

5. See Fisher, *Farm Life and Its Changes;* Glick, *Fortunate Years;* John K. Lapp, *Remarks of By-Gone Days;* Reschly, *Amish on the Iowa Prairie;* R. Schlabach, "Amish Farming." Not every community embraced everything that was new, as evidenced by a dispute around 1900 in the Nappanee, Indiana, settlement when a group of members protested the use of hay loaders, manure spreaders, grain binders, and windmills; see *Nappanee Amish Directory*, 20.

6. Fisher, *Farm Life and Its Changes*, 9–49; Pratt, *Shipshewana*, 12–18; and Reschly, *Amish on the Iowa Prairie*, 47.

7. See R. Kline, *Consumers in the Country;* Shover, *First Majority, Last Minority*.

8. Fisher, *Farm Life and Its Changes*, 5.

9. Lancaster County Amish farm practices in the mid-twentieth century are described in Fisher, *Farm Life and Its Changes;* Glick, *Fortunate Years;* and Kollmorgen, *Culture of a Contemporary Rural Community* and "Agricultural Stability."

10. About 3 percent of Amish church districts permit the use of tractors for field work in the twenty-first century. In Kansas and Oklahoma the Amish rationale for tractor farming was that summer's intense heat was inhumane for work horses.

11. Cross, in "Restructuring America's Dairy Farms," 8, and "Expanding Role of the Amish," 12–13, describes the importance of cheese plants for Amish farmers. Deutsch Kase Haus in Middlebury, Indiana, opened in 1979, led by an Amish entrepreneur and local Mennonite investors. In 2002 it was purchased by the Canadian dairy cooperative Agropur.

12. In at least one instance, the dumping station was built on Amish land, but members of the community were quick to point out that the station itself was not Amish owned and built, so it was not the Amish who were responsible for the electricity, which would go to the building and not the land (Johnson-Weiner, *New York Amish*, 75–76, 199n28).

13. *"Lasset Uns Miteinander Rechnen"* (Come Let Us Reason Together), letter from Lancaster County dairy farmers to their bishops, March 6, 2002. Copy in Donald Kraybill's files. Emphasis in the original.

14. V. Stoltzfus, "Amish Agriculture."

15. James and James, *Changing Agricultural Community*, 19. The Grade B milk producers were mostly Amish, according to the local Ohio State University extension office.

16. R. Schlabach, "Amish Farming," 33.

17. Emma Harris, "A Horse, Two Mules and a Plough. . . . Vernon's First Year Garden Produces the Produce," *Salem (AK) News*, Sept. 3, 2009.

18. Cross, "Restructuring America's Dairy Farms," 9–11, and "Expanding Role of the Amish," 9. See also Cross's research of Amish dairy farms in Wisconsin and other states in "Change in America's Dairyland," and "Expansion of Amish Dairy Farming."

19. For a persuasive essay, see "Back to the Future."

20. *Truck Patch News* is published and distributed nationally by produce growers in Mt. Hope, Ohio.

21. "Growing Grape Tomatoes," 2005, flier in Donald Kraybill's files.

22. "Workshops Teach Amish and Mennonite Growers Ways to Improve Yields," *High Plains Journal* (Dodge City, KS), June 3, 2008.

23. *Truck Patch News*, July 15, 2008, 6. See also J. Byler, "Our Experience Growing Vegetables."

24. "Poisoning the Earth," pt. 2, 29.

25. Caroline Brock's dissertation, "Integrated Household Economics Approach," studied organic practices in two Wisconsin Amish communities.

26. Jerry L. Miller, "Change to Organic Farming," 34. Amish farmer Jerry E. Miller explains the virtues of organic farming in "Farming Practically."

27. R. Schlabach, "Organic Dairy Farming," 28–32.

28. R. Yoder, "Greenfield Farms," 28; Mariola and McConnell, "Shifting Landscape of Amish Agriculture."

29. www.lancasterfarmfresh.com.

30. *Grass-Based Dairy Farming*, v–vi.

31. See Hurst and McConnell, *Amish Paradox*, 200–204, for a discussion of new agricultural enterprises in Holmes County, Ohio.

32. See three studies of energy use and ecological impact of Amish farming: G. Foster, "Amish and the Ethos of Ecology"; Hockman-Wert, "Role of Religion in Motivating Sustainability"; and Johnson, Stoltzfus, and Craumer, "Energy Conservation."

33. Vonk, *Sustainability and Quality of Life*, 81, 96–100.

34. *Farming*, Spring 2001, 3.

35. For a sample of David Kline's writings, see *Scratching the Woodchuck, Great Possessions,* and "God's Spirit and a Theology for Living." For an academic appraisal of his approach, see the conclusion of S. Stoll, *Larding the Lean Earth.*

36. Kraybill, Nolt, and Weaver-Zercher, *Amish Way,* 150.

37. S. Stoll, *Larding the Lean Earth,* 217–18.

38. "Not Everyone Can Be a Farmer," pt. 1, 8.

39. "Not Everyone Can Be a Farmer," pt. 2, 32–34.

40. Chad Umble, "Charging Forward," *Lancaster (PA) Sunday News,* Oct. 17, 2010.

CHAPTER 16. BUSINESS

1. Sections of this chapter are adapted from Kraybill and Nolt, *Amish Enterprise,* and Kraybill, *Riddle of Amish Culture,* chap. 10.

2. Based on our interviews and review of church directories from various settlements, church districts typically have five to seven enterprises on average. With about 2,000 Amish districts, this yields a range of 10,000 to 14,000 enterprises, so 12,000 is a conservative mid-range estimate.

3. Meyers and Nolt, *Amish Patchwork,* 114; Meyers, "Lunch Pails and Factories."

4. David Dinell, "Taking Work to the Labor Pool: Precision Opens Yoder Center," *Wichita Business Journal,* April 30, 1999, 4; Greksa and Korbin, "Key Decisions."

5. Nolt and Meyers, *Plain Diversity,* 85–90.

6. Rick Farrant, "Plain Ingenuity," *Greater Fort Wayne (IN) Business Weekly,* April 22, 2011.

7. Dana, "Humility-Based Enterprising Community"; Kraybill and Kanagy, "Rise of Entrepreneurship"; Kraybill and Nolt, *Amish Enterprise;* and Olshan, "Amish Cottage Industries."

8. Kraybill, Nolt, and Wesner, "Sources of Enterprise Success," 113.

9. Kraybill and Nolt, *Amish Enterprise;* Wesner, *Success Made Simple.*

10. Of 785 men under age 65 who listed an occupation, 512 were engaged in construction and related trades; see *Adams and Jay Counties Directory.*

11. Raymond S. Lapp, Millersburg, Pennsylvania, is the publisher of *Plain Communities Business Exchange.*

12. *Lancaster County Business Directory* is published by DavCo Advertising, Kinzers, Pennsylvania. Most, but not all the businesses appearing in the directory are Amish.

13. Ola Richard Yoder, Nappanee, Indiana, is the publisher of *Amish Woodworkers of America.*

14. Gumpert, "Amish Entrepreneur's Approach."

15. Hallie Busta. "Amish Bakery Takes Root in the Loop," *Gapers Block,* Aug. 13, 2010. http://gapersblock.com/drivethru/2010/08/13/.

16. Meghan Barr, "Consumers Flock to Amish-Run Stores Selling Expired Items." *Phoenix Arizona Republic,* May 9, 2008. www.azcentral.com/arizonarepublic/business/articles/0509biz-amishstores0509.html.

17. Members of the most traditional Amish groups seldom participate in the gatherings.

18. Kraybill, Nolt, and Wesner, "Amish Enterprise," 9–10; Kraybill and Nolt, *Amish Enterprise,* 13–15.

19. U.S. Small Business Administration, Office of Advocacy, "Frequently Asked Questions," Sept. 2009. www.sba.gov/advo/stats/sbfaq.pdf.

20. Kraybill, *Riddle of Amish Culture,* 84, 261.

21. See Timothy Aeppel, "Amish Women Reap Profit in Field of Business," *Wall Street Journal,* Feb. 8, 1996. For an example in Missouri, see Hawley, "Maintaining Business While Maintaining Boundaries."

22. Kraybill and Nolt, *Amish Enterprise,* 208–10.

23. Johnson-Weiner, "Role of Women," 244. See also Bloch, "Untangling the Roots of Modern Sex Roles." For more on Anabaptist women and work, see Pederson, "She May Be Amish Now."

24. See Johnson-Weiner, "Role of Women."

25. Greksa and Korbin, "Key Decisions"; Meyers, "Old Order Amish" and "Population Growth."

26. "[Ohio] Shop Support Committee Meeting," minutes, Oct. 6, 1999, citing Steering Committee correspondence.

CHAPTER 17. TECHNOLOGY

1. "Weird" Al Yankovic, "Amish Paradise," YouTube music video, 3.25, posted by alyankovic VEVO on Oct. 9, 2009, www.youtube.com/watch?v=lOfZLb33uCg&ob=av3e.

2. Binfield, *Writings of the Luddites.*

3. The sparse research on the topic includes Kelly, *What Technology Wants,* chap. 11; Kraybill, *Riddle of Amish Culture,* chap. 8; Kraybill and Nolt, *Amish Enterprise,* chap. 7; Scott and Pellman, *Living Without Electricity;* and Wetmore, "Building Amish Community with Technology."

4. Leroy Beachy, *Unser Leit,* 2:395.

5. For discussions of this complicated issue, see Smith and Marx, *Does Technology Drive History?*

6. Kelly, *What Technology Wants,* 239.

7. [E. Stoll], *Strangers and Pilgrims,* 19, 14, 16–17.

8. An excellent account of the spread of technology in rural America and its detractors is R. Kline, *Consumers in the Country.*

9. [E. Stoll], *Strangers and Pilgrims,* 18.

10. Bijker, Hughes, and Pinch, *Social Construction of Technological Systems,* laid early groundwork for understanding the social and cultural influences on inventions and adaptations of technology.

11. Kevin Kelly's observation during a visit to Amish shops with Donald Kraybill on March 4, 2004.

12. John B. Swarey's letter in the *Diary,* March 2007, tells the story of the "self feeders" for threshing machines that were invented and manufactured by Amish man John Ebersol (1874–1950), who was born in Pennsylvania but migrated to Milverton, Ontario, where he built a factory to produce them.

13. This gas lamp and several improved models were designed and manufactured by the Midstate Lamp Co., in Arthur, Illinois.

14. A subgroup with about twenty congregations within the New Order affiliation permits its members to use public grid electrical service.

15. Harold Brubaker, "A Culture Clash in Roofing," *Philadelphia Inquirer,* Nov. 29, 2010, reports conflict between progressive Amish and English contractors.

16. See D. Umble, *Holding the Line.*

17. [D. Wagler], *Are All Things Lawful?*

18. *1001 Questions,* 141–43.

19. This occurred in these settlements: Arthur, Illinois; Nappanee, Indiana; Garnett, Kansas; and the Clinton section of the Elkhart–LaGrange, Indiana, settlement. Anecdotal evidence points to employment related to stone quarries, factories, feed mills, and even delivery trucks. See Yoder and Yoder, *Echoes of the Past.*

20. *1001 Questions,* 141.

21. [E. Stoll], *Strangers and Pilgrims,* 20.

22. Ibid.

23. Scott and Pellman, *Living Without Electricity,* 48–49.

24. *1001 Questions,* 141.

25. For more on embedded bias, see Rushkoff, *Program or Be Programmed.*

CHAPTER 18. HEALTH AND HEALING

Epigraph: Adapted from *Die Botschaft,* March 10, 2008, 6. Parts of Allgyer's letter seem like boilerplate text she reproduced, but with obvious Amish assumptions. For example, she never gives her address, assuming that any *Botschaft* reader in the Gap area would know how to find her.

1. Miller et al., "Health Status," using evidence from representative samples of Amish (N=288) and non-Amish women (N=2,002) in Central Pennsylvania, provide detailed comparisons of reproductive issues and women's health in general.

2. Wenger's work, "Cultural Context, Health and Health Care Decision Making," influenced some aspects of this chapter. See also Banks and Benchot, "Unique Aspects of Nursing Care."

3. *Die Botschaft,* Jan. 26, 2009, 28.

4. Jon Rutter, "Amish Unaffected by New Health Law: 'Religious Conscience' Covered in Legislation," *Lancaster (PA) Sunday News,* March 28, 2010; Mullen, "Religion and the PPACA."

5. Johnson-Weiner was one of those called to transport the boy to the hospital.

6. For a debate on what kinds of formalized mutual aid, if any, Amish churches should use, see "Hospital Aid Plans" and "Special Section on Hospital Aid and Insurance."

7. See, for example, E. Byler, *Plain and Happy Living* and *Home Remedies II;* Quillin, *Wisdom of Amish Folk Medicine;* and Wickey Sisters, *Amish Home Remedies.*

8. "Drawing pain," also called "pain pulling" (*shmates tsia* [or *Schmatza Zieha*] in Pennsylvania Dutch), is widely accepted among the ultraconservative Swartzentruber Amish, but they do not ascribe a magical component to it. See Johnson-Weiner, *New York Amish,* 69–70.

9. J. Hostetler, *Amish Society,* 335–42; Kriebel, *Powwowing;* L. Miller, "Role of a Braucher-Chiropractor"; and Wenger, "Phenomenon of Care."

10. Kriebel, *Powwowing,* 181.

11. Ibid., 177.

12. Wenger, "Phenomenon of Care," 69, 154.

13. Huntington, "Health Care," 170–71. See also Ron Shawgo, "Healer in DeKalb Keeps the Faith at 74," *Fort Wayne Journal-Gazette,* Sept. 9, 2012. For a self-published book by one of Wickey's supporters, see Naugle, *Solomon's Touch.*

14. Huntington, "Health Care," 171–72.

15. J. Keim, *Burn Aid* and *Comfort for the Burned;* D. Wagler, *New Concept in Treating Burns.* (The latter is a booklet containing reprints of burn articles originally published in *Plain Interests* from March 2005 to December 2006.) For a descriptive study, see Rieman et al., "Increased Risk of Burns."

16. *Die Botschaft,* May 24, 2010, 73.

17. Reiter et al., "Complementary and Alternative Medicine Use."

18. The Ohio study, conducted in 2004, involved interviews with a representative sample of Amish men (N=62) and women (N=72) living in Holmes and Tuscarawas Counties. The Amish response rate was 67 percent. The methods and results are discussed in Reiter et al., "Complementary and Alternative Medicine Use." The Pennsylvania data were gathered from a non-representative availability sample of Amish men (N=44) and women (N=68) in the Lancaster, Pa., settlement in 2011–12. Participants in various health and safety gatherings completed a questionnaire. See King and Kraybill, "Exploratory Study of Amish Health Care."

19. Graham and Cates, "Health Care and Sequestered Cultures." See also Cates and Graham, "Amish."

20. *Die Botschaft,* April 26, 2010, 68. For a lively Amish debate on the value of nutritional supplements, see "Problem Corner."

21. Examples are from *Die Botschaft* correspondents' letters between September 2009 and June 2010.

22. *1001 Questions,* 55–57.

23. See Donatelli, "Goodbye Sister," 57.

24. Currently Mississippi and West Virginia are the only states without religious exemptions from mandatory immunization. See www.childrenshealthcare.org/legal.htm.

25. Letters to the editor, *Family Life,* May 1981, 32. See also "The Choice Is Yours."

26. A writer from Union Grove, North Carolina, responding to a questionnaire circulated to *Budget* correspondents by David Wagler in 1991. The responses informed the articles on vaccination ("The Choice is Yours," pts. 1 and 2) that appeared in the November and December 1992 issues of *Family Life.* The questionnaires are in the files of Heritage Historical Library, Aylmer, Ontario.

27. From a *Budget* correspondent in Loyal, Wisconsin, also responding to the Wagler questionnaire.

28. Letters to the editor, *Family Life,* May 1981, 32.

29. Letter to the editor, *Family Life,* in Heritage Historical Library, Aylmer, ON.

30. Wenger et al., "Underimmunization in Ohio's Amish."

31. See Huntington, "Health Care," 185–89, for an extensive discussion of immunization.

32. Bobseine, "Working with Amish Communities."

33. See Huntington, "Health Care," 172–81.

34. *Diary,* Feb. 2006, 45.

35. Huntington, "Health Care," 173–75. See Amelia Reiheld's description of the Mount Eaton Care Center: "Birthing Center Serves Amish Well."

36. Showalter, "Birthing among the Amish."

37. Campanella, Korbin, and Acheson, "Pregnancy and Childbirth," 334–35.

38. Lemon, "Amish Health Care Beliefs." See especially pages 56–57 for a list of herbs used in preparation for childbirth.

39. Personal communication from Martha King, March 10, 2012.

40. Huntington, "Health Care," 166–69.

41. Family Court Act #1012 [f] [1] [A], New York State. From the decision reached in *St. Lawrence County Department of Social Services v. G. and B. Hershberger,* Dec. 8, 2008. See also Clayton and Kodish, "Baby Aaron and the Elders," 5.

42. For more on the cultural context, see Cates, "Facing Away" and "Of Course It's Confidential," and Reiling, "Boundary Maintenance." On psychological testing of Amish people, see Cates and Graham, "Psychological Assessment."

43. "Minutes of the Sixth People Helpers Meeting," 37.

44. An eight-part series of *Family Life* essays, "Brighter Days Ahead: Voices of Experience," appeared from April 1993 to January 1994. Five additional articles were published from January to April 2003.

45. Nolt, "Moving beyond Stark Options." See also minute booklets from People Helpers meetings, in Steven Nolt's files.

46. For examples, see Nolt, "Moving beyond Stark Options," 145–46.

47. Nolt, "Moving beyond Stark Options," 139–40, and "Green Pasture Report 8/8/05–5/31/10," in Steven Nolt's files.

48. For information and research publications, visit www.clinicforspecialchildren.org/.

49. Gura, "Rare Diseases." See also Strauss and Puffenberger, "Genetics, Medicine, and the Plain People."

50. Strauss, Puffenberger, and Morton, "One Community's Effort to Control Genetic Disease."

51. See www.ddcclinic.org for a detailed description and publications. Windows of Hope, in Holmes County, Ohio, also investigates and provides information on genetic disorders; see www.wohproject.org.

52. Examples include Topeka, Indiana, and Martinsburg, Pennsylvania.

53. See www.umm.edu/news/releases/amish_res_clinic.htm.

54. See the Amish Research Clinic's annual newsletters, in Donald Kraybill's files.

55. Cross and Crosby, "Amish Contributions to Medical Genetics," 465.

CHAPTER 19. GOVERNMENT AND CIVIC RELATIONS

Epigraph: From Jacob U. Gingerich, letter to "Senator," Nov. 19, 2011, copy in authors' files.

1. Roger Alford, "Amish Man's Letters Sway Lawmakers on Buggy Issue," *San Antonio Express-News,* Feb. 12, 2012; Gingerich, letter to "Senator."

2. *1001 Questions,* 156.

3. Sylvan Lapp, letter to the editor, *Lancaster (PA) Intelligencer Journal-New Era,* Jan. 19, 2012.

4. For essays on Amish views of and conflicts with the state, see Kraybill, *Amish and the State.*

5. *1001 Questions,* 156–57.

6. See Ryan Robinson, "Amish Farmers Win Battle in State Court," *Lancaster (PA) New Era,* June 2, 2009.

7. C. Lapp, *Pennsylvania School History,* 140.

8. For numerous examples, see Kidder, "Role of Outsiders."

9. *Jacob Schmucker v. David Byler et al.,* Geauga County Common Pleas No. 4399, filed Feb. 20, 1917.

10. Friedman, "Conscription and the Constitution"; Russell, "Conscientious Objector Recognition."

11. This chapter discusses Amish encounters with government in the United States; the situation in Canada bears important similarities but also key differences. See Janzen, *Limits on Liberty,* 245–71; Regehr, "Relations between the Old Order Amish and the State"; and Thomson, "Canadian Government Relations."

12. Amanda Peterka, "Amish Farmers in Chesapeake Bay Watershed Find Themselves in EPA's Sight," *New York Times,* Oct. 10, 2011, www.nytimes.com/gwire/2011/10/10/10greenwire.

13. See, for example, N. Stoltzfus, *Stories of COs in World War I Army Camps.*

14. Beechy and Beechy, *Experiences of C.O.'s.;* A. Keim, "Military Service and Conscription." The Amish in Canada faced somewhat different conditions; there was no Cold War draft, and during the few years (1940–1945) when there was conscription in Canada, it was provincially based and almost all Ontario Amish were given farm furloughs.

15. Ferrara, "Social Security and Taxes."

16. *1001 Questions,* 156–57, 158. See also J. Stoll, "Umbrella We Don't Need."

17. Hall, "Revolt of the Plain People." See also Robert Metz, "Amish and Taxes," *New York Times,* May 22, 1961; "Unto Caesar," *Time,* Nov. 3, 1958, 21; and "U.S. Sells 3 Mares for Amish Tax Debt," *New York Times,* May 2, 1961.

18. "Amish Are Granted Exclusion," *New York Times,* July 31, 1965; Ferrara, "Social Security and Taxes."

19. Bush, *Two Kingdoms, Two Loyalties,* 168–72, 196–97, 239; A. Keim, "Military Service and Conscription," 56–61.

20. *Minutes of Old Order Amish Steering Committee: First Volume,* 1.

21. Ibid., 3, 5. The meeting was held Nov. 16, 1966.

22. Ibid., 8.

23. Olshan, "National Amish Steering Committee"; Steven Nolt interview with Freeman L. Yoder (1923–2003), Middlebury, Ind., Oct. 7 and 19, 1999. Yoder, a long-time member of the original committee, reported that the founding members from the Midwest favored the name Amish Central Committee, but that Kinsinger insisted on Amish Steering Committee. "We [in the Midwest] didn't like the idea of a group 'steering' the Amish," Yoder explained.

24. For one theoretical perspective, see Olshan, "Homespun Bureaucracy."

25. *Minutes of Old Order Amish Steering Committee: Second Volume,* 13. On the continuance of the Steering Committee after the demise of the draft, see Olshan, "Homespun Bureaucracy," 3.

26. Lindholm, "National Committee for Amish Religious Freedom."

27. A. Keim, *Compulsory Education and the Amish,* 93–94.

28. The text of the decision appears in A. Keim, *Compulsory Education and the Amish,* 149–81. Recent appraisals of the case include S. Peters, *Yoder Case.*

29. The smoke detector requirement is only one of the objections raised by the Swartzentruber Amish. Also contentious, for example, is the requirement that builders submit stamped architectural drawings.

30. New York State has since mandated the installation of carbon monoxide detectors, which are also unacceptable to the Swartzentruber Amish. Settlement of the case has expanded to in-

clude these new devices. It is not simply the electrical nature of these devices: wind-up detectors are as forbidden as hard-wired and battery-operated versions.

31. Case 7:09-cv-00007-NPM-GHL Document 85, Filed 11/07/11, United States District Court, Northern District of New York, *Levi Yoder et al., v. Town of Morristown et al.* Morristown eventually dropped all the charges against the Amish.

32. See *Minutes of Old Order Amish Steering Committee: Seventh Volume; Minutes of Old Order Amish Steering Committee: Eighth Volume;* and Bontrager, "Encounters with the State."

33. Justin Quinn, "President Signs Pitts' Amish Labor Bill," *Lancaster (PA) Intelligencer Journal,* Jan. 27, 2004.

34. Diane Smith, "Amish Gain Voice on Nelson Zoning Panel." *Record-Courier* (Ravenna, OH), Jan. 6, 2012, www.recordpub.com/news/article/5143184.

35. Marlys Weaver, "Residents of Shipshewana Speak Out Against Alcohol Sales." *Elkhart (IN) Truth,* Jan. 27, 2011.

36. See, for example, Kraybill and Nolt, *Amish Enterprise,* 153.

37. *1001 Questions,* 157–59.

38. Kraybill and Kopko, "Bush Fever."

39. Jon Rutter, "Amish, Other Plain, Fill Ranks of Fire and Ambulance Companies," *Lancaster (PA) Sunday News,* July 8, 2012.

40. Poster advertising "16th Annual LaGrange County Habitat for Humanity Fundraising Auction, Shipshewana Auction Barn, Friday, August 5, 2011," Steven Nolt's files.

41. McIntyre, "Donate Blood, Win a Car!" *Cleveland Plain Dealer,* Aug. 2, 2010. Some Amish also serve as organ donors; see *Family Life,* May 1988, 30–33.

42. Janowski, "Simple Service."

43. Detweiler, *Hammer Rings Hope; Rebuilding Hope.*

44. See Stauffer, "Giant Broom of Destruction" and "By Giving, We Receive." Both articles were written by an Old Order Mennonite writer but reflect typical Amish sentiments regarding disaster work.

45. Nolt, "MCC's Relationship with 'Plain' Anabaptists."

46. Founder David N. Troyer later joined a car-driving Beachy Amish congregation.

47. Language used in various CAM publications.

48. Nolt, "MCC's Relationship with 'Plain' Anabaptists," 144–49; CAM Annual Report 2011, in Steven Nolt's files.

49. DeGeorgio-Venegas, "Conservative Anabaptist Service Program." Another organization with which some Amish have served is the Fellowship of Christian Farmers. In 2009 Amish from the Nappanee, Indiana, settlement joined this group on a trip to Texas to clean up damage in the wake of Hurricane Ike; see Cindy Horswell, "Mending Fences: Amish Offer Helping Hand in Wake of Hurricane Ike," *Goshen (IN) News,* Feb. 19, 2009. Originally published in *Houston (TX) Chronicle:* "Good Samaritans: Amish Volunteers Come to Give Ranchers a Hand in Jefferson and Chambers Counties," Feb. 16, 2009.

50. Nolt, "Mennonite Identity." The annual Haiti auction began in northern Indiana in 1978; four years later the second auction started in Ohio. The auctions spread to other communities, especially during the 1990s.

51. For an Amish critique of those who travel overseas for mission work and thus neglect their responsibility to their extended families at home, see letter to *Family Life,* June 1988, 3–4.

52. Old Colony Mennonite Support, *Called to Mexico;* Sensenig, "Old Order Amish"; issues of *Old Colony Mennonite Support Newsletter* (2000–); "History Report, Old Colony Mennonites in Mexico [1995–2008]," Steven Nolt's files; and R. Miller, *Vision for the Journey.*

53. A. Keim, *Compulsory Education and the Amish,* 163.

54. Epps, "Amish and the American Oyster," 267–68, 271.

CHAPTER 20. THE AMISH IN PRINT

Epigraph: Quotations from "Notice: Revision of Guide Lines, Effective July 1990 and Thereafter, by *Die Botschaft* Committee," reproduced in Kinsinger and Kinsinger, *Little History of Our Parochial Schools,* 232–33, and from *Die Botschaft,* Dec. 31, 2012, 2.

1. Blank, *Amazing Story of the Ausbund,* viii.

2. V. Weaver-Zercher, *Thrill of the Chaste.*

3. Kinsinger, *Family and History of Lydia Beachy's Descendants,* 119.

4. Kinsinger and Kinsinger, *Little History of Our Parochial Schools,* 164.

5. Interview with J. Stoll, Jan. 2002.

6. Some ultraconservative groups still use Strayer-Upton arithmetic textbooks in the twenty-first century.

7. "A Word about Pathway," n.d., in Heritage Historical Library, Aylmer, ON.

8. *Girl in the Mirror,* [3].

9. Ibid.

10. Staff Notes, *Family Life,* Jan. 2012, 6–7. For a collection of essays from *Family Life,* see Igou, *Amish in Their Own Words.*

11. Joseph Stoll interviews by Karen Johnson-Weiner in 2002 and 2003 on the topic of Pathway, its publishing, and the reception of Pathway materials in different communities. See Johnson-Weiner, *Train Up a Child,* chap. 8, for a discussion of the progressive influence in Pathway readers.

12. A list of seventeen new Amish publications originating between 1991 and 2001 appears in Staff Notes, *Family Life,* July 2001, 6.

13. Personal communication to Donald Kraybill, July 18, 2012.

14. Nolt, "Inscribing Community."

15. *Die Botschaft,* Dec. 5, 2011. Some communities have several regular writers.

16. *Die Botschaft,* Aug. 25, 2004, 1.

17. Nolt, "Inscribing Community," 188–89.

18. The offending ad from a Lancaster County Radio Shack appeared in *Die Botschaft* on Dec. 3, 10, 17, and 31, 2003, and on Jan. 7, 2004.

19. In fact, almost a fifth of *Die Botschaft* scribes are Old Order (horse-and-buggy) Mennonites. An Amish publisher based in Millersburg, Pennsylvania, now owns and prints *Die Botschaft.*

20. On Amish publishing and identity, see Johnson-Weiner, "Publish or Perish."

21. See D. Weaver-Zercher, *Amish in the American Imagination;* Buck, "Bloodless Theatre"; and Louden, "Image of the Old Order Amish," esp. 113–16.

22. Chase and Shaw, "Dimensions of Nostalgia," 4.

23. Keene, *Witch Tree Symbol,* 21.

24. Lasky, *Beyond the Divide,* 13, 20.

25. Keene, *Witch Tree Symbol,* 153.

26. For a discussion of the Amish and the mystified depictions of pastoral rural life, see Downing, "Witnessing the Amish," 24–41.

27. McDaniel, *Lifted Up By Angels,* 70; McDaniel, *Until Angels Close My Eyes,* 189–90.

28. Myers, *Parsley, Sage, Rosemary & Crime,* 38–39.

29. Lewis, *The Crossroad,* 42; Gaus, *Broken English,* 39.

30. Keene, *Witch Tree Symbol,* 20.

31. Lang, "Blind Man's Lantern."

32. See "Amish Science Fiction," last modified Oct. 23, 2007, www.adherents.com/lit/sf_amish.html.

33. Workinger, *In Dutch Again,* 73.

34. Gaus, *Blood of the Prodigal,* 1.

35. Picoult, *Plain Truth,* 338.

36. Gaus, *Blood of the Prodigal,* 29.

37. Lewis, *The Shunning,* 132.

38. McDaniel, *Lifted Up By Angels,* 208.

39. Lasky, *Beyond the Divide,* 6.

40. V. Weaver-Zercher, *Thrill of the Chaste,* 4–5, reports the sales numbers.

41. Personal correspondence to the authors, March 10, 2012.

42. Conversation with Donald Kraybill, Nov. 8, 2011.

43. E. Miller, "Why We Love Amish Romances."

44. Personal correspondence to Donald Kraybill, March 13, 2012.

45. V. Weaver-Zercher, *Thrill of the Chaste,* chap. 8.

46. See D. Weaver-Zercher, "An Uneasy Calling," 98–99.

47. For examples, see Furlong, *Why I Left the Amish;* R. Garrett, *Crossing Over;* Streiker-Schmidt, *Separate God,* I. Wagler, *Growing Up Amish;* and W. Weaver, *Dust Between My Toes.*

48. The number of non-English titles is based on the collection in the Heritage Historical Library in Aylmer, Ontario. In addition to books, there are dissertations, journal articles, and chapters on Amish topics that have been written in or translated into foreign languages.

CHAPTER 21. TOURISM AND MEDIA

1. Trollinger, *Selling the Amish,* 141.

2. This definition is provided by the National Trust for Historic Preservation: "Heritage Tourism," National Trust for Historic Preservation, www.preservationnation.org/information-center/economics-of-revitalization/heritage-tourism/.

3. See Chase and Shaw, "Dimensions of Nostalgia." See also Singer, "Symbolic and Historic Structure." Singer notes that "the availability and vitality of the past, in short, depends on its being embedded in living cultural traditions and on being reenacted in cultural performances" (434).

4. Graburn, "Secular Ritual," 31.

5. D. Weaver-Zercher, *Amish in the American Imagination,* 85.

6. Turco, "Tourism in Amish Communities," 142.

7. See D. Weaver-Zercher, *Amish in the American Imagination,* esp. chap. 3. See also Luthy, "Origin and Growth of Amish Tourism."

8. See Wiley, "Wilderness Theatre," esp. 124.

9. *Meet Your Amish Neighbors,* tour brochure by Alma Kaufman and Flair Travel Consultants (1961), in Heritage Historical Library, Aylmer, ON.

10. "Amish Tours for October," n.d., pamphlet in Karen Johnson-Weiner's file.

11. See Buck, "Boundary Maintenance Revisited," for a more in-depth discussion of portrayals of the Amish in tourist literature.

12. As David Weaver-Zercher points out, "The degree of Amish openness to these encounters varied" (*Amish in the American Imagination,* 92).

13. MacCannell, *The Tourist,* 98.

14. Buck, "Boundary Maintenance Revisited," 229.

15. *Hearts & Hands: The Official Travel Planner of Amish Country,* Holmes County Chamber of Commerce, 16, http://issuu.com/silenyjizda/docs/hh_2009guidebook.

16. *Amish Country Tours at Plain & Fancy Farm,* Pennsylvania Dutch Convention and Visitors Bureau, www.padutchcountry.com/members/amish_country_tours.asp.

17. Amish Impressions is no longer in business.

18. *Amish Experience Theater at Plain & Fancy Farm,* Pennsylvania Dutch Convention and Visitors Bureau, www.padutchcountry.com/members/amish_experience_theater.asp.

19. *Amish Back Roads,* LaGrange County Convention & Visitors Bureau, www.shipshewana tours.org/.

20. See www.allgetaways.com/view_destination.asp?destinationid=XGP517-007.

21. About 81,000 Amish people live in these three settlements. Tourist data provided in June 2012 by staff of the Pennsylvania Dutch Convention and Visitors Bureau, Holmes County Chamber of Commerce and Tourism Bureau, and Elkhart County Convention and Visitors Bureau.

22. Locher, "Look What Tourism's Done for Lancaster," quoted in Luthy, "Origin and Growth of Amish Tourism," 126.

23. Wiley, "Wilderness Theatre," 122. Wiley cites Walker Percy.

24. For one exception, see Meyers, "Amish Tourism."

25. For different perspectives on these issues, see Boorstin, *The Image;* Cohen, "Phenomenology of Tourist Experiences"; Holden, *Environment and Tourism;* and MacCannell, *The Tourist.*

26. http://christianhomekeeper.org.

27. For examples, see a map distributed by the Valley View Cheese Company in Conewango Valley and another for northern Chautauqua County.

28. Hurst and McConnell, *Amish Paradox,* 177.

29. Thomas, "Amishville," 117–18. David Schwartz died in a car accident in 1972; in recent years, Amishville has become a campground rather than a farming operation.

30. Letter to the editor, *Family Life,* March 1991, 2.

31. Blank, "Being a Witness to Tourists," 154.

32. O. Vernon Miller, "Shipshewana, Indiana," *Budget,* Feb. 1, 1989, 16.

33. Sarah Weaver, "Millersburg, Ohio," *Budget,* Sept. 28, 1983, 14.

34. Kraybill, *Riddle of Amish Culture,* 292.

35. Eitzen, "Hollywood Rumspringa," 151–52.

36. "The Amish," American Experience, www.pbs.org/wgbh/americanexperience/films/amish/.

37. Eitzen, "Reel Amish," 44.

38. See Downing's "Witnessing the Amish" for a discussion of these two films.

39. Laikind, "Amish Diaries: Why Do You Care About the Amish?" See his other articles, beginning April 17, 2012. Laikind's Stick Figure Productions produced *Devil's Playground, Amish in the City,* two special programs, and the ten-part series *Amish: Out of Order* for National Geographic that aired in 2012. Stick Figure Productions sent out the five teams to recruit subjects for *Amish in the City.*

40. This discussion does not include personal blogs that record a visit to an Amish settlement as part of a family vacation—the virtual equivalent of the postcard a vacationer sends to family back home.

41. *The Amish Blog,* www.lancasterpa.com/amishblog/.

42. *The Amish Cook from Oasis Newsfeatures [Blog],* www.oasisnewsfeatures.com/. The column is authored by Lovina Eicher and Kevin Williams.

43. *Amish America [Blog],* http://amishamerica.com/.

44. *Amish Internet Blog,* http://amishinternet.com/.

45. Amish Life's Facebook page, www.facebook.com/AmishLife.

46. For two examples of blogs written by ex-Amish people, see http://aboutamish.blogspot .com/ and www.irawagler.com/.

47. Eitzen, "Hollywood Rumspringa," 151.

48. Quoted in Stoneback, "Retrace Harrison Ford's Footsteps on 'Witness' Tours of Lancaster County, PA." This article for the *Morning Call (Allentown, PA)*, Sept. 4, 2010, was picked up by newspapers around the world.

49. Stoneback, "Retrace Harrison Ford's Footsteps."

50. Ibid.

51. Turco, "Tourism in Amish Communities," 143–44.

52. Trollinger, *Selling the Amish*, 77–79, 108–10.

53. J. Hostetler, *Amish Society*, 317.

54. Buck, "Boundary Maintenance Revisited," 233.

55. Chhabra, "How They See Us," 3, 11, 12.

56. D. Weaver-Zercher, *Amish in the American Imagination*, 185–89.

57. Hannah Lapp, "Labor Department vs. Amish Ways," *Wall Street Journal*, April 10, 1997.

58. S. Peters, *Yoder Case*, 152.

59. Maoz, "Mutual Gaze," 235.

CHAPTER 22. PURSUITS OF HAPPINESS

1. Diamandis and Kotler, *Abundance.*

2. Giddens, *Consequences of Modernity*, 21–45, describes this radical "disembedding" of social relationships and social mechanisms from time-space contexts as the key characteristic of late modernity.

3. Kraybill, "Amish Encounter with Modernity," 32–33.

4. Bauman, *Liquid Modernity*, 29–38; Lipovetsky, *Empire of Fashion;* and Wagner, *Modernity as Experience and Interpretation*, 24–38.

5. Jefferson Graham, "Apple Sells 3 Million New iPads," *USA Today*, March 19, 2012.

6. Igou, "Amish in the Year 2100."

7. Kathy Hedberg, "Amish Family Forges Not-So-Traditional Path in N. Idaho, Embracing Cars, Computer," *Lewistown (ID) Tribune*, Jan. 30, 2012.

8. Epps, "Amish and the American Oyster," 275.

9. "Amish Believers: A Queer Religious Sect Near an Indiana Town," *Chicago Tribune*, Feb. 2, 1888; "Odd in Many Ways," *St. Paul (MN) Globe*, April 2, 1897; and "A Queer People and Their Ways," *Odgen (UT) Standard*, Nov. 20, 1909.

10. D. Weaver-Zercher, *Amish in the American Imagination*, 51–52, 67–81.

11. Coddington, "Great Plain."

12. Cathy Horyn, "Amish Fashion Week," *New York Times*, Jan. 23, 2011, http://runway.blogs .nytimes.com/2011/01/23/amish-fashion-week/.

13. "24 Amish-Inspired Fashions," *Trend Hunter*, www.trendhunter.com/slideshow/ amish-inspired-fashions.

14. Some of the ideas in this section are adapted from Kraybill and Bowman, *On the Backroad to Heaven*, chap. 9.

15. Epps, "Amish and the American Oyster," 274.

BIBLIOGRAPHY

1001 Questions and Answers on the Christian Life. Aylmer, ON: Pathway Publishers, 1992.

A & M Trustee Committee. "A Plain Community Alternative to the Monroe Beachy Bankruptcy." Aug. 25, 2010. Photocopy, in Donald Kraybill's files.

"Accepting the Uniform." *Family Life,* Aug.–Sept. 1992, 17–18.

Adams and Jay Counties and Vicinity Amish Directory, Vol. 7. Monroe, IN: Hilty Home Sales, 2007.

"The Advantages of Home Birthing." *Family Life,* May 1993, 29–30.

Allen, Rebecca R. "My Birth, My Way: Reproductive Agency among Three Generations of Amish Women in Elkhart–LaGrange and Nappanee Settlements." Unpublished paper, Mennonite Historical Library, Goshen, IN, 2004.

The Amish: Back Roads to Heaven. DVD. Directed by Burton Buller. Massanutten, VA: Buller Films LLC, 2007.

The Amish: How They Survive. DVD. Directed by Burton Buller. Massanutten, VA: Buller Films LLC, 2005.

Ausbund: das ist, Etliche schöne Christliche Lieder. Lancaster, PA: Amish Book Committee, 1996.

"Back to the Future: Our Roots in the Soil." Pts. 1 and 2. *Family Life,* April 1997, 29–33; May 1997, 31–35.

Baecher, Robert. "1712: Investigation of an Important Date." Translated by Kevin J. Ruth. *Pennsylvania Mennonite Heritage* 21 (April 1998): 2–12.

———. "Research Note: The 'Patriarche' of Sainte-Marie-aux-Mines." *Mennonite Quarterly Review* 74 (Jan. 2000): 145–58.

Banks, Mary Jane, and Rosalie J. Benchot. "Unique Aspects of Nursing Care for Amish Children." *American Journal of Maternal/Child Nursing* 26, no. 4 (2001): 192–96.

Bates, Mary Ann Miller. "Insubordinate Anabaptists in Virtuous Clothing? Amish Anabaptists as Model Subjects in the Context of Bernese Sumptuary and Moral Mandates." *Mennonite Quarterly Review* 82 (Oct. 2008): 517–31.

Bauman, Zygmunt. *Liquid Modernity.* Malden, MA: Blackwell Publishers, 2010.

Beachy, Leroy. *Unser Leit: The Story of the Amish.* 2 vols. Millersburg, OH: Goodly Heritage Books, 2011.

Beachy, Monroe. "Decided by Lot." *Family Life,* Oct. 1969, 20–22, 24.

Beam, C. Richard. *Revised Pennsylvania German Dictionary: English to Pennsylvania Dutch.* Lancaster, PA: Brookshire Publications, 2002.

Beechy, William, and Malinda Beechy, comps. *Experiences of C.O.'s in C.P.S. Camps, in I-W Service in Hospitals, and during World War I.* LaGrange, IN: W. and M. Beechy, [1990s].

The Beginning and Development of Parochial Special Schools 1975–1996 and the S. June Smith Center 1965–1996. Gordonville, PA: Gordonville Print Shop, 1996.

Beiler, Aaron E., comp. *Vocation on the Farm: Statement of Principles of a Church Vocation in Agricultural Practice by the Old Order Amish Church of Pennsylvania.* Strasburg, PA: Homsher Printing, 1956.

[Beiler, Aaron F.] *Light in the Shadow of Death.* New Holland, PA: Aaron Beiler, 2008.

Beiler, David. *True Christianity.* Translated by Adelheide Schutzler and Isaac J. Lowry. Parkesburg, PA: Benuel S. Blank Family, 2009. Originally published as *Das Wahre Christenthum: Eine Christiche Betrachtung nach den Lehren der Heiligen Schrift* (Lancaster, PA: Johann Baers and Son, 1888).

[Beiler, Joseph F.] "Research Note: Ordnung." *Mennonite Quarterly Review* 56 (Oct. 1982): 382–84.

Beiler, Lydia Jane. *Where Mountains Rise: A History of the Amish in Perry County.* Blain, PA: L. J. Beiler, 2011.

Bell, Daniel A. *China's New Confucianism: Politics and Everyday Life in a Changing Society.* Princeton, NJ: Princeton University Press, 2008.

Bellah, Robert N., Richard Madsen, William M. Sullivan, Ann Swidler, and Steven M. Tipton. *Habits of the Heart: Individualism and Commitment in American Life.* Berkeley: University of California Press, 1985.

Bender, Harold S., trans. and ed. "Some Early American Amish Mennonite Disciplines." *Mennonite Quarterly Review* 8 (April 1934): 90–98.

Berger, Peter L. *Facing Up to Modernity: Excursions in Society, Politics, and Religion.* New York: Basic Books, 1977.

Berger, Peter L., Brigitte Berger, and Hansfried Kellner. *The Homeless Mind: Modernization and Consciousness.* New York: Vintage Books, 1974.

Berger, Peter L., and Thomas Luckmann. *The Social Construction of Reality: A Treatise in the Sociology of Knowledge.* New York: Doubleday, 1966.

"Beware of an Unbalanced Gospel." *Family Life,* July 2002, 11–13.

Beyond the Valley: Over 110 Stories of People Who Are Physically Challenged. Monroe, IN: Hilty Home Sales, 2005.

Biblical Guidelines in Shunning. Pathway Reprint Series, no. 7. LaGrange, IN: Pathway Publishers, 2008.

"The Big 'I.'" *Family Life,* Aug.–Sept. 2007, 6–8.

Bijker, Wiebe E., Thomas P. Hughes, and Trevor Pinch, eds. *The Social Construction of Technological Systems: New Directions in the Sociology and History of Technology.* Cambridge, MA: MIT Press, 1987.

Binfield, Kevin, ed. *Writings of the Luddites.* Baltimore: Johns Hopkins University Press, 2004.

Binford, Hilde. "Values and Culture Transmitted through Music in the Old Order Amish Community." Photocopy, in Donald Kraybill's files, n.d.

Birkel, Michael L., and Jeff Bach, trans. and eds. *Genius of the Transcendent: Mystical Writings of Jakob Boehme.* Boston: Shambhala, 2010.

Blank, Benuel S. *The Amazing Story of the Ausbund.* Narvon, PA: Benuel S. Blank, 2001.

———. "Being a Witness to Tourists." In *The Scriptures Have the Answers,* by Benuel Blank, 151–56. Parkesburg, PA: Blank Family, 2009.

"Blessings in Adoption." *Family Life,* July 2007, 14.

Bloch, Ruth H. "Untangling the Roots of Modern Sex Roles: A Survey of Four Centuries of Change." *Signs* 4, no. 2 (1978): 237–52.

Bobseine, Kate Rose. "Working with Amish Communities in New York State: Tips for Health Professionals." SUNY Albany School of Public Health, 2006.

Bontrager, Herman D. "Encounters with the State, 1990–2002." In *The Amish and the State,* 2nd ed., edited by Donald B. Kraybill, 235–50. Baltimore: Johns Hopkins University Press, 2003.

Boorstin, D. J. *The Image: A Guide to Pseudo Events in America.* New York: Vintage Books, 1992. First published in 1961.

Bourdieu, Pierre. *Distinction: A Social Critique of the Judgment of Taste.* Translated by Richard Nice. London: Routledge and Kegan Paul, 1984.

———. *Outline of a Theory of Practice.* Translated by Richard Nice. Cambridge: Cambridge University Press, 1977.

Braght, Thieleman J. van, comp. *The Bloody Theater or Martyrs Mirror of the Defenseless Christians, Who Baptized Only upon Confession of Faith, and Who Suffered and Died for the Testimony of Jesus, Their Savior, From the Time of Christ to the Year A.D. 1660.* 2nd English ed., 24th printing. Scottdale, PA: Herald Press, 2002. Originally published as *Der blutige Schauplatz oder Märtyrerspiegel der Taufgesinnten oder wehrlosen Christen, die um des Zeugnisses Jesu, ihres Seligmachers, willen gelitten haben und getötet worden sind, von Christi Zeit bis auf das Jahr 1600* (Dordrecht, 1660).

Braithwaite, John. "Reintegrative Shaming, Republicanism, and Policy." In *Crime and Public Policy: Putting Theory to Work,* edited by Hugh D. Barlow, 191–205. Boulder, CO: Westview Press, 1995.

Brock, Caroline. "An Integrated Household Economics Approach to Decision-Making: Dairy System Choice among Organic, Amish, Graziers and Conventional Farmers in Wisconsin." PhD diss., University of Wisconsin-Madison, 2009.

Bronner, Simon J. *Explaining Traditions: Folk Behavior in Modern Culture.* Lexington: University Press of Kentucky, 2011.

Brown, Joshua R., and Douglas J. Madenford. *Schwetz mol Deitsch.* Millersville, PA: Center for Pennsylvania German Studies, 2009.

Bryer, Kathleen B. "The Amish Way of Death: A Study of Family Support Systems." *American Psychologist* 34 (March 1979): 255–61.

———. "Attitudes toward Death among Amish Families: Implications for Family Therapy." Master's thesis, Hahnemann Medical College, 1978.

Buck, Roy C. "Bloodless Theatre: Images of the Old Order Amish in Tourism Literature." *Pennsylvania Mennonite Heritage* 2 (July 1979): 2–11.

———. "Boundary Maintenance Revisited: Tourist Experience in an Old Order Amish Community." *Rural Sociology* 43 (Summer 1978): 221–34.

Buffington, Albert F., and Preston A. Barba. *A Pennsylvania German Grammar.* Rev. ed. Allentown, PA: Schlechter's, 1965.

Burkholder, Chris. *Amish Confidential: The Bishop's Son Shatters the Silence.* Argyle, IA: Argyle Publishing, 2006.

Burridge, Kate. " 'Separate and Peculiar': The Survival of 'Pennsylvania Dutch' in Ontario, Canada." *La Trobe Working Papers in Linguistics* 1 (1988): 91–108.

Bush, Perry. *Two Kingdoms, Two Loyalties: Mennonite Pacifism in Modern America.* Baltimore: Johns Hopkins University Press, 1998.

Bushman, Richard L. *The Refinement of America: Persons, Houses, Cities.* New York: Alfred A. Knopf, 1992.

Byler, Emma. *Home Remedies II: For Farm, Garden, Lawn & House.* Millersburg, OH: Abana Books Ltd., 2003.

———. *Plain and Happy Living: Amish Recipes and Remedies.* Burton, OH: Log Cabin Press, 1991.

Byler, John J. "Our Experience Growing Vegetables." *Family Life,* Feb. 1999, 32–34.

Byler, Linda. "Mrs. Gid." *The Connection,* Nov. 2010, 55.

Byler, Uria R. *Our Better Country: A History.* Gordonville, PA: Old Order Book Society, 1963.

Campanella, Karla, Jill E. Korbin, and Louise Acheson. "Pregnancy and Childbirth among the Amish." *Social Science & Medicine* 36, no. 3 (1993): 333–42.

"Can You Help Me?" *Young Companion,* Sept.–Oct. 2011, 14–17.

Cates, James A. "Facing Away: Mental Health Treatment with the Old Order Amish." *American Journal of Psychotherapy* 59, no. 4 (2005): 371–83.

———. "Identity in Crisis: Spirituality and Homosexuality in Adolescence." *Child and Adolescent Social Work Journal* 24 (2007): 369–83.

———. "Of Course It's Confidential—Only the Community Knows: Mental Health Services with the Old Order Amish." In *Ethical Conundrums, Quandaries, and Predicaments in Mental Health Practice: A Casebook from the Files of Experts,* edited by W. Brad Johnson and Gerald P. Koocher, 309–16. New York: Oxford University Press, 2011.

Cates, James A., and Linda L. Graham. "Amish." In *The Essential Guide to Religious Traditions and Spirituality for Health Care Providers,* edited by Steven L. Jeffers, Michael E. Nelson, Vern Barnet, and Michael C. Brannigan. London: Radcliffe Publishing, 2013.

———. "Psychological Assessment of the Old Order Amish: Unraveling the Enigma." *Professional Psychology: Research and Practice* 33, no. 2 (2002): 155–61.

Cates, James A., and Chris Weber. "An Alcohol and Drug Intervention with Old Order Amish Youth: Preliminary Results of Culturally Segregated Class Participation." *Journal of Groups in Addiction and Recovery* (forthcoming). doi:10.1080/1556035X.2013.764199.

———. "A Substance Use Survey with Old Order Amish Early Adolescents: Perceptions of Peer Alcohol and Drug Use." *Journal of Child and Adolescent Substance Abuse* 21, no. 3 (2012): 193–203.

Chase, Malcolm, and Christopher Shaw. "The Dimensions of Nostalgia." In *The Imagined Past: History and Nostalgia,* edited by Christopher Shaw and Malcolm Chase, 1–17. New York: Manchester University Press, 1989.

Chhabra, Deepak. "How They See Us: Perceived Effects of Tourist Gaze on the Old Order Amish." *Journal of Travel Research* 49, no. 1 (2010): 93–105. doi:10.1177/0047287509336475.

"The Choice is Yours." Pts. 1 and 2. *Family Life,* Nov. 1992, 34–36; Dec. 1992, 33–36.

"A Christian Greeting." *Family Life,* March 2009, 6–7.

Christlicher Ordnung, or, Christian Discipline: Being A Collection and Translation of Anabaptist and Amish-Mennonite Church Disciplines (Artikel and Ordnungen) of 1527, 1568, 1607, 1630, 1668, 1688, 1779, 1809, 1837, and 1865, with Historical Explanations and Notes. Translated by William R. McGrath. Aylmer, ON: Pathway Publishing Corp., 1966.

Chupp, Lyle D., and JoAnn Chupp, comps. *Thy Will Be Done: 134 Touching Personal Stories of Fatalities among Plain People.* Shipshewana, IN: Lyle and JoAnn Chupp, 1998.

"The Church: An Earthly Refuge." *Family Life,* Nov. 1994, 12–14.

The Church and Mission Work. Pathway Reprint Series, no. 6. LaGrange, IN: Pathway Publishers, 2008.

Clark, Allen B. *This is Good Country: A History of the Amish of Delaware, 1915–1988.* Rev. ed. Gordonville, PA: Gordonville Print Shop, 1988.

Clayton, Ellen Wright, and Eric Kodish. "Baby Aaron and the Elders." *Hastings Center Report* 29, no. 5 (Sept.-Oct. 1999): 20–21.

Coddington, Grace. "The Great Plain." *Vogue,* Aug. 1993, 278–91.

Cohen, Erik. "A Phenomenology of Tourist Experiences." *Sociology* 13, no. 2 (1979): 179–201.

Cohn, D'Vera, Jeffrey S. Passel, and Wendy Wang. "Barely Half of U.S. Adults Are Married— A Record Low." Pew Research Center, Dec. 14, 2011. http://pewresearch.org/pubs/2147/ marriage-newly-weds-record-low.

Coleman, James S. *Foundations of Social Theory.* Cambridge, MA: Belknap Press of Harvard University Press, 1990.

Cooking with the Horse-and-Buggy People. 2nd ed. Sugarcreek, OH: Carlisle Press, 1994.

Craker, Lorilee. *Money Secrets of the Amish: Finding True Abundance in Simplicity, Sharing, and Saving.* Nashville, TN: Thomas Nelson, 2011.

Cronk, Sandra L. "Gelassenheit: The Rites of the Redemptive Process in Old Order Amish and Old Order Mennonite Communities." PhD diss., University of Chicago, 1977.

Cross, Harold E., and Andrew H. Crosby. "Amish Contributions to Medical Genetics." *Mennonite Quarterly Review* 82 (July 2008): 449–67.

Cross, John A. "Change in America's Dairyland." *Geographical Review* 91, no. 4 (2001): 702–14.

———. "The Expanding Role of the Amish in America's Dairy Industry." *Focus on Geography* 50, no. 3 (2007): 7–16.

———. "Expansion of Amish Dairy Farming in Wisconsin." *Journal of Cultural Geography* 21, no. 2 (2004): 77–101.

———. "Restructuring America's Dairy Farms." *Geographical Review* 96, no. 1 (2006): 1–23.

"The Cruelest Kind of Child Abuse." *Family Life,* Jan. 1995, 6–7.

Dana, Leo Paul. "A Humility-Based Enterprising Community: The Amish People in Lancaster County." *Journal of Enterprising Communities: People and Places in the Global Economy* 1, no. 2 (2007): 142–54.

Das Leicht Büchlein für die Amischen Gemeinden in Lancaster County und die Umliegenden Gegenden [The funeral booklet for the Amish Church in Lancaster County and the outlying regions]. N.p.: 2002.

Dawley, Richard Lee. *Amish in Wisconsin: An Anecdotal Journal.* New Berlin, WI: Amish Insight, 2003.

DeGeorgio-Venegas, Ramona. "Conservative Anabaptist Service Program (CASP) Volunteers Complete Projects on the Manistee District." USDA Forest Service. Nov. 11, 2011. www.fs.fed.us/r9/ssrs/story?id=6401.

Dell, Emma. *Daring Destiny.* Alpine, TX: Special Delivery Books, 2006.

Detweiler, Lowell. *The Hammer Rings Hope: Photos and Stories from Fifty Years of Mennonite Disaster Service.* Scottdale, PA: Herald Press, 2000.

Devil's Playground. DVD. Directed by Lucy Walker. Stick Figure Productions. [New York]: Wellspring Media, 2002.

A Devoted Christian's Prayer Book. Aylmer, ON: Pathway Publishers, 1995.

Dewalt, Mark W. *Amish Education in the United States and Canada.* Lanham, MD: Rowman & Littlefield Education, 2006.

Diamandis, Peter H., and Steven Kotler. *Abundance: The Future is Better Than You Think.* New York: Free Press, 2012.

Die Ernsthafte Christenpflicht. Lancaster County, PA: Amischen Gemeinden, 1996.

"Do Bonnets Help?" *Family Life,* Feb. 1976, 29.

Donatelli, Nancy Stephens. "Goodbye Sister." *Journal of Emergency Nursing* 33, no. 1 (Feb. 2007): 57–60.

Donnermeyer, Joseph F., and Elizabeth C. Cooksey. "On the Recent Growth of New Amish Settlements." *Mennonite Quarterly Review* 84 (April 2010): 181–206.

Douglas, Mary. *Purity and Danger: An Analysis of Concepts of Pollution and Taboo.* London: Routledge & Kegan Paul, 1966.

Downing, Crystal. "Witnessing the Amish: Plain People on Fancy Film." In *The Amish and the Media,* edited by Diane Zimmerman Umble and David L. Weaver-Zercher, 25–41. Baltimore: Johns Hopkins University Press, 2008.

Durnbaugh, Hedwig T. "The Amish Singing Style: Theories of Its Origin and Description of Its Singularity." *Pennsylvania Mennonite Heritage* 22 (April 1999): 24–31.

Eicher, Lovina, and Kevin Williams. *The Amish Cook at Home: Simple Pleasures of Food, Family, and Faith.* Kansas City, MO: Andrews McMeel Publishing, 2008.

Eine Unparteiische Lieder-Sammlung zum Gebrauch beim oeffentlichen Gottesdienst und der häuslichen Erbauung [Baer book]. Lancaster, PA: Johann Bär's Söhne, 1860 and reprints.

Eitzen, Dirk. "Hollywood Rumspringa: Amish in the City." In *The Amish and the Media,* edited by Diane Zimmerman Umble and David L. Weaver-Zercher, 133–53. Baltimore: Johns Hopkins University Press, 2008.

———. "Reel Amish: The Amish in Documentaries." In *The Amish and the Media,* edited by Diane Zimmerman Umble and David L. Weaver-Zercher, 43–64. Baltimore: Johns Hopkins University Press, 2008.

Elder, D. R. " 'Es Sind Zween Weg': Singing Amish Children into the Faith Community." *Cultural Analysis* 2 (2001): 39–67.

———. "Why the Amish Sing." Unpublished manuscript, 2012.

Enninger, Werner. "The English of the Old Order Amish of Delaware: Phonological, Morpho-Syntactical and Lexical Variation of English in the Language Contact Situation of a Trilingual Speech Community." *English World-Wide* 5, no. 1 (1984): 1–24.

———, et al. *Language and Language Use of the Amish and of Mennonite Groups of Swiss-German Origin: An Annotated Bibliography.* Essen, Germany: LAUD/Linguistic Agency University Essen, 2002.

———. "Linguistic Markers of Anabaptist Ethnicity through Four Centuries." In *Language and Ethnicity,* edited by James R. Dow, 23–60. Philadelphia: John Benjamins Publishing, 1991.

Epps, Garrett. "The Amish and the American Oyster." In *The Amish and the State,* 2nd ed., edited by Donald B. Kraybill, 267–75. Baltimore: Johns Hopkins University Press, 2003.

Ericksen, Eugene P., Julia A. Ericksen, and John A. Hostetler. "The Cultivation of the Soil as a Moral Directive: Population Growth, Family Ties, and the Maintenance of Community among the Old Order Amish." *Rural Sociology* 45, no. 1 (Spring 1980): 49–68.

Ericksen, Julia A., Eugene P. Ericksen, John A. Hostetler, and Gertrude E. Huntington. "Fertility Patterns and Trends among the Old Order Amish." *Population Studies* 33, no. 2 (July 1979): 255–76.

Ericksen, Julia A., and Gary L. Klein. "Women's Roles and Family Production among the Old Order Amish." *Rural Sociology* 46, no. 2 (Summer 1981): 282–96.

Esh, Mrs. Jerre S. [Ruthie], comp. *A Collection of Treasured Recipes and Poems from the Esh Family.* Christiana, PA: Mrs. Jerre S. [Ruthie] Esh, n.d.

Es Nei Teshtament. South Holland, IL: Bible League, n.d.

Ferrara, Peter J. "Social Security and Taxes." In *The Amish and the State,* 2nd ed., edited by Donald B. Kraybill, 125–43. Baltimore: Johns Hopkins University Press, 2003.

Field, John. *Social Capital.* 2nd ed. New York: Routledge, 2008.

Fischel, William A. "Do Amish One-Room Schools Make the Grade? The Dubious Data of *Wisconsin v. Yoder.*" Working paper, March 3, 2011.

———. *Making the Grade: The Economic Evolution of American School Districts.* Chicago: University of Chicago Press, 2009.

Fischer, Claude S. *Made In America: A Social History of American Culture and Character.* Chicago: University of Chicago Press, 2010.

Fischer, David Hackett. *Albion's Seed: Four British Folkways in America.* New York: Oxford University Press, 1989.

Fisher, Gideon L. *Farm Life and Its Changes.* Gordonville, PA: Pequea Publishers, 1978.

Fisher, Sara E., and Rachel K. Stahl. *The Amish School.* Intercourse, PA: Good Books, 1997.

Foster, Charles I. *An Errand of Mercy: The Evangelical United Front, 1790–1837.* Chapel Hill: University of North Carolina Press, 1960.

Foster, George M. "The Amish and the Ethos of Ecology." *Ecologist* 10 (Dec. 1980): 331–35.

Frey, J. William. *A Simple Grammar of Pennsylvania Dutch.* 3rd ed. Lancaster, PA: Brookshire Publications, 2002. Originally published in 1942.

Friedman, Leon. "Conscription and the Constitution: The Original Understanding." *Michigan Law Review* 67 (June 1969): 1493–552.

"From the Desk of Teacher Dave." *Blackboard Bulletin,* March 2011, 15–16.

Fuller, Janet M. "The Sociopragmatic Values of Pennsylvania German ("Dutch"): Change across Time, Place and Anabaptist Sect." In *ISB4: Proceedings of the 4th International Symposium on Bilingualism,* edited by James Cohen, Kara T. McAlister, Kellie Rolstad, and Jeff MacSwan, 800–7. Somerville, MA: Cascadilla Press, 2005.

Furlong, Saloma Miller. "Research Papers." Unpublished papers, Young Center for Anabaptist and Pietist Studies, Elizabethtown College, Elizabethtown, PA, 2006.

———. *Why I Left the Amish: A Memoir.* East Lansing: Michigan State University Press, 2011.

Furner, Mark. "The Repression and Survival of Anabaptism in the Emmental, 1659–1743." PhD diss., Cambridge University, 1998.

———. "Research Note: On the Trail of Jacob Ammann." *Mennonite Quarterly Review* 74 (April 2000): 326–28.

Garrett, Ottie. *True Stories of the X-Amish.* Horse Cave, KY: Neu Leben, 1998.

Garrett, Ruth Irene. *Crossing Over: One Woman's Escape from Amish Life.* With Rick Farrant. New York: HarperCollins, 2003.

Gaus, P. L. *Blood of the Prodigal.* Athens: Ohio University Press, 1999.

———. *Broken English.* Athens: Ohio University Press, 2000.

"The German Dilemma." *Blackboard Bulletin,* Aug. 2011, 20–23.

Gibbons, Phebe Earle. *Pennsylvania Dutch and Other Essays.* Mechanicsburg, PA: Stackpole Books, 2001. Originally published in 1882 by J. B. Lippincott.

Gibson, Seth A. " 'Gang' Prevalence and Involvement among Old Order Amish Youth in the Elkhart–LaGrange Settlement: An Interview Project of the Amish Youth Vision Project." Unpublished paper, Shipshewana, IN, 2006.

Giddens, Anthony. *The Consequences of Modernity.* Stanford, CA: Stanford University Press, 1990.

———. *Modernity and Self-Identity: Self and Society in the Late Modern Age.* Stanford, CA: Stanford University Press, 1991.

Gingerich, Melvin. *Mennonite Attire through Four Centuries.* Breinigsville, PA: Pennsylvania German Society, 1970.

———. *The Mennonites in Iowa.* Iowa City, IA: State Historical Society, 1939.

Gingerich, Noah M. *The History of Pinecraft, 1925–1960: A Historical Album of the Amish and Mennonites in Pinecraft, Florida.* Sugarcreek, OH: Carlisle Press, 2006.

Gingerich, Orland. *The Amish of Canada.* Waterloo, ON: Conrad Press, 1972.

Girl in the Mirror. Aylmer, ON: Pathway Publishing Corp., 1972.

Glick, Aaron S. *The Fortunate Years: An Amish Life.* Intercourse, PA: Good Books, 1994.

Goldstein, Michael A. "Party On, Amos." *Philadelphia Magazine,* Aug. 1997, 137–44.

Graburn, Nelson H. H. "Secular Ritual: A General Theory of Tourism." In *Tourists and Tourism: A Reader,* edited by Sharon B. Gmelch, 23–34. Long Grove, IL: Waveland Press, 2004.

Graham, Linda, and James Cates. "Health Care and Sequestered Cultures: A Perspective from the Old Order Amish." *Journal of Multicultural Nursing & Health* 12, no. 3 (2006): 60–66.

Grass-Based Dairy Farming: 15 Farmers Share Considerations for Starting Your Own Grass-Based Dairy. Sugarcreek, OH: Carlisle Press, 2008.

Graybill, Beth. "'To Remind Us Who We Are': Multiple Meanings of Conservative Women's Dress." In *Strangers at Home: Amish and Mennonite Women in History,* edited by Kimberly D. Schmidt, Diane Zimmerman Umble, and Steven D. Reschly, 53–77. Baltimore: Johns Hopkins University Press, 2002.

Greenwood, Elizabeth. "Shame on 'Breaking Amish.'" *The Atlantic,* Sept. 18, 2012. www.theatlantic.com/entertainment/archive/2012/09/shame-on-breaking-amish/262530/.

Gregory, Brad S. *Salvation at Stake: Christian Martyrdom in Early Modern Europe.* Cambridge, MA: Harvard University Press, 1999.

Greksa, Lawrence P., and Jill E. Korbin. "Key Decisions in the Lives of the Old Order Amish: Joining the Church and Migrating to Another Settlement." *Mennonite Quarterly Review* 76 (Oct. 2002): 373–98.

Gross, Leonard, trans. and ed. *Prayer Book for Earnest Christians.* Scottdale, PA: Herald Press, 1997.

Guengerich, Samuel D. *Deutsche Gemeinde Schulen.* Amisch, IA: printed by author, 1897.

Guidelines in Regards to the Old Order Amish or Mennonite Parochial Schools. Gordonville, PA: Gordonville Print Shop, 1978. Fourth printing 1981.

Gumpert, David E. "An Amish Entrepreneur's Old-Fashioned Approach." *Business Week,* Jan. 5, 2010. www.businessweek.com/print.small biz/content.jan2010/sb2010014.

Gura, Trisha. "Rare Diseases: Genomics, Plain and Simple; A Pennsylvania Clinic Working with Amish and Mennonite Communities Could Be a Model for Personalized Medicine." *Nature* 483 (March 1, 2012): 20–22.

Haag, Earl C. *A Pennsylvania German Reader and Grammar.* University Park: Pennsylvania State University Press, 1982.

Handbuch für Bischof [Handbook for bishops]. Translated by Noah G. Good. Gordonville, PA: Gordonville Print Shop, 1978. First published in 1935.

Hall, Clarence W. "The Revolt of the Plain People." *Reader's Digest,* Nov. 1962, 74–78.

Hall, Edward T. *Beyond Culture.* New York: Anchor Books, 1977.

Harvey, David. *The Condition of Postmodernity.* Malden, MA: Blackwell Publishers, 1990.

"The Hat's a Religious Symbol?" *Family Life,* Aug.–Sept. 1996, 11–12.

Hawley, Jana M. "Maintaining Business While Maintaining Boundaries: An Amish Woman's Entrepreneurial Experience." *Entrepreneurship, Innovation, and Change* 4 (Dec. 1995): 315–28.

Healing from Sexual Sin. Topeka, IN: Healing Journey, 2011.

Herr, Patricia T. *Amish Arts of Lancaster County.* Atglen, PA: Schiffer Publishing, 1998.

Hershberger, Noah. "Misuse of Symbols." *Family Life,* April 1990, 24.

———. *A Struggle to Be Separate: A History of the Ohio Amish Parochial School Movement.* Orville, OH: N. L. Hershberger, 1985.

Hockman-Wert, David Patrick. "The Role of Religion in Motivating Sustainability: The Case of the Old Order Amish in Kishacoquillas Valley, PA." Master's thesis, University of Oregon, 1998.

Holden, Andrew. *Environment and Tourism.* 2nd ed. New York: Routledge, 2008.

"Hospital Aid Plans." *Family Life,* Dec. 1989, 7–9.

Hostetler, Beulah Stauffer. "The Formation of the Old Orders." *Mennonite Quarterly Review* 66 (Jan. 1992): 5–25.

Hostetler, John A. "The Amish as a Redemptive Community." In *The Amish: Origin and Characteristics, 1693–1993,* edited by Lydie Hege and Christoph Wiebe, 346–54. Ingersheim, France: Association Française d'Histoire Anabaptiste-Mennonite, 1996.

———. "An Amish Beginning." In *Writing the Amish: The Worlds of John A. Hostetler,* edited by David L. Weaver-Zercher, 5–35. State College: Pennsylvania State University Press, 2005.

———, ed. *Amish Roots: A Treasury of History, Wisdom, and Lore.* Baltimore: Johns Hopkins University Press, 1989.

———. *Amish Society.* 4th ed. Baltimore: Johns Hopkins University Press, 1993. First published in 1963.

———, ed. "Anabaptist Conceptions of Child Nurture and Schooling: A Collection of Source Materials Used by the Old Order Amish." Typescript, Temple University, Philadelphia, 1968.

———. "Letter to Amish Bishops Concerning Shunning (1944)." In *Writing the Amish: The Worlds of John A. Hostetler,* edited by David L. Weaver-Zercher, 154–60. State College: Pennsylvania State University Press, 2005.

———. "Old World Extinction and New World Survival of the Amish: A Study of Group Maintenance and Dissolution." *Rural Sociology* 20, nos. 3/4 (1955): 212–19.

———. "Silence and Survival Strategies among the New and Old Order Amish." In *Internal and External Perspectives on Amish and Mennonite Life,* edited by Werner Enninger, 81–91. Essen, Germany: Unipress, 1984.

Hostetler, John A., and Gertrude Enders Huntington. *Amish Children: Education in the Family, School, and Community.* 2nd ed. New York: Harcourt Brace Jovanovich, 1992.

Huffines, Marion Lois. "Pennsylvania German: Maintenance and Shift." *International Journal of the Sociology of Language* 25 (1980): 43–57.

———. "Strategies of Language Maintenance and Ethnic Marking among the Pennsylvania Germans." *Language Sciences* 8 (1986): 1–16.

Hughes, Robert. *American Visions: The Epic History of Art in America.* New York: Alfred A. Knopf, 1997.

Huntington, Gertrude Enders. "The Amish Family." In *Ethnic Families in America: Patterns and Variations,* edited by Charles H. Mindel and Robert W. Habenstein, 295–322. New York: Elsevier Scientific Publishing Company, 1976.

———. *Amish in Michigan.* East Lansing: Michigan State University Press, 2001.

———. "Health Care." In *The Amish and the State,* 2nd ed., edited by Donald B. Kraybill, 163–89. Baltimore: Johns Hopkins University Press, 2003.

———. "Occupational Opportunities for Old Order Amish Women." *Pennsylvania Folklife* 43, no. 3 (Spring 1994): 115–20.

———. "Persistence and Change in Amish Education." In *The Amish Struggle with Modernity,* edited by Donald B. Kraybill and Mark A. Olshan, 77–95. Hanover, NH: University Press of New England, 1994.

Hüppi, John. "Research Note: Identifying Jacob Ammann." *Mennonite Quarterly Review* 74 (April 2000): 329–39.

Hurst, Charles E., and David L. McConnell. *An Amish Paradox: Diversity and Change in the World's Largest Amish Community.* Baltimore: John Hopkins University Press, 2010.

Igou, Brad. *The Amish in Their Own Words: Amish Writings from 25 Years of Family Life Magazine.* Scottdale, PA: Herald Press, 1999.

———. "The Amish in the Year 2100 A.D." *Amish Country News.* www.amishnews.com/amisharticles/Amish%202001.htm.

Illinois Directory of Amish Communities 2003. Tuscola, IL: LaVerne and Dorothy Schlabach, 2003.

Indiana Amish Directory: Elkhart, LaGrange, and Noble Counties, 2007. Middlebury, IN: Jerry E. Miller, 2007.

In Meiner Jugend: A Devotional Reader in German and English. Translated by Joseph Stoll. Aylmer, ON: Pathway Publishers, 2000.

International Encyclopedia of the Social and Behavioral Sciences. 26 vols. Editors in chief: Neil J. Smelser, Paul B. Baltes. New York: Elsevier, 2001.

James, Randall E., and Barbara H. James. *The Changing Agricultural Community in Geauga County, Ohio, 1990–1997.* Columbus: Ohio State University, 1997.

Janowski, Kelly. "Simple Service." *Lion: Lion's Club International,* May 2010, 38–39.

Janzen, William. *Limits on Liberty: The Experience of Mennonite, Hutterite and Doukhobor Communities in Canada.* Toronto: University of Toronto Press, 1990.

Johnson, Curtis D. *Redeeming America: Evangelicals and the Road to Civil War.* Chicago: Ivan R. Dee, 1993.

Johnson, Warren A., Victor Stoltzfus, and Peter Craumer. "Energy Conservation in Amish Agriculture." *Science* 198 (Oct. 28, 1977): 373–78.

Johnson-Weiner, Karen M. "Community Expectations and Second Language Acquisition: English as a Second Language in a Swartzentruber Amish School." *Yearbook of German-American Studies* 28 (1993): 107–17.

———. "Community Identity and Language Change in North American Anabaptist Communities." *Journal of Sociolinguistics* 2, no. 3 (1998): 375–94.

———. "Group Identity and Language Maintenance: The Survival of Pennsylvania German in Old Order Communities." In *Diachronic Studies on the Languages of the Anabaptists,* edited by Kate Burridge and Werner Enninger, 26–42. Bochum, Germany: Universitatsverlag Dr. N. Brockmeyer, 1992.

———. "Katie." In *Living North Country: Essays on Life and Landscapes in Northern New York,* edited by Natalia Rachel Singer and Neil Burdick, 207–20. Utica, NY: North Country Books, 2001.

———. "Keeping Dutch: Linguistic Heterogeneity and the Maintenance of Pennsylvania German in Two Old Order Amish Communities." In *Studies on the Languages and Verbal Behavior of the Pennsylvania Germans,* edited by Werner Enninger, Joachim Raith, and Karl-Heinz Wandt, 95–101. Stuttgart: Franz Steiner Verlag, 1989.

———. *New York Amish: Life in the Plain Communities of the Empire State.* Ithaca, NY: Cornell University Press, 2010.

———. "Publish or Perish: Amish Publishing and Old Order Identity." In *The Amish and the Media,* edited by Diane Zimmerman Umble and David L. Weaver-Zercher, 201–19. Baltimore: Johns Hopkins University Press, 2008.

———. "Reinforcing a Separate Amish Identity: English Instruction and the Preservation of Culture in Old Order Amish Schools." In *Languages and Lives: Essays in Honor of Werner Enninger,* edited by James R. Dow and Michele Wolff, 67–78. New York: Peter Lang, 1997.

————. "The Role of Women in Old Order Amish, Beachy Amish and Fellowship Churches." *Mennonite Quarterly Review* 75 (April 2001): 231–56.

————. *Train Up a Child: Old Order Amish and Mennonite Schools.* Baltimore: Johns Hopkins University Press, 2006.

Kalberg, Stephen. "Max Weber's Types of Rationality: Cornerstones for the Analysis of Rationalization Processes in History." *American Journal of Sociology* 85, no. 5 (March 1980): 1145–79.

Kauffman, Cephas. "Staying Awake in Church." *Family Life,* March 1993, 7–9.

Kauffman, S. Duane. *Mifflin County Amish and Mennonite Story, 1791–1991.* Belleville, PA: Mifflin County Mennonite Historical Society, 1991.

Keene, Carolyn. *The Witch Tree Symbol.* Nancy Drew Mystery Stories. New York: Grosset & Dunlap, 1975.

Keim, Albert N., ed. *Compulsory Education and the Amish: The Right Not to Be Modern.* Boston: Beacon Press, 1975.

————. "Military Service and Conscription." In *The Amish and the State,* 2nd ed., edited by Donald B. Kraybill, 43–64. Baltimore: Johns Hopkins University Press, 2003.

Keim, John W. *Burn Aid: Self-Applied Prevention/Treatment.* Millersburg, OH: School of Self-Applied Prevention, 2006.

————. *Comfort for the Burned and Wounded.* Quakertown, PA: Philosophical Publishing Company, 1999.

Keiser, Steven Hartman. "Pennsylvania German and the 'Lunch Pail Threat': Language Shift and Cultural Maintenance in Two Amish Communities." In *When Languages Collide: Perspectives on Language Conflict, Language Composition, and Language Coexistence,* edited by Brian D. Joseph, Johanna Destaphano, Neil D. Jacobs, and Ilse Lehiste, 3–20. Columbus: Ohio State University Press, 2003.

Kelly, Kevin. *What Technology Wants.* New York: Viking, 2010.

Kidder, Robert L. "The Role of Outsiders." In *The Amish and the State,* 2nd ed., edited by Donald B. Kraybill, 213–33. Baltimore: Johns Hopkins University Press, 2003.

King, Amos M., comp. *Hidden Treasures (Repeated History) Handed Down from Our Ancestors Since 1600.* Gordonville, PA: Amos M. King, 1995.

King, Emma. *Joys, Sorrows, and Shadows, by One Who Experienced the Joys, Sorrows, and Shadows.* Elverson, PA: Olde Springfield Shoppe, 1992.

King, Martha, and Donald B. Kraybill. "An Exploratory Study of Amish Health Care Practices among the Lancaster Amish." Unpublished study, 2012.

Kinsinger, Andrew S., and Susan A. Kinsinger, comps. *A Little History of Our Parochial Schools and Steering Committee from 1956–1994.* Gordonville, PA: Gordonville Print Shop, 1997.

Kinsinger, Susan, comp. *Family and History of Lydia Beachy's Descendants 1889 to 1989.* Gordonville, PA: Gordonville Print Shop, 1988.

Kline, David. "God's Spirit and a Theology for Living." In *Creation and the Environment: An Anabaptist Perspective on a Sustainable World,* edited by Calvin Redekop, 61–69. Baltimore: Johns Hopkins University Press, 2000.

————. *Great Possessions: An Amish Farmer's Journal.* San Francisco: North Point Press, 1990.

————. *Scratching the Woodchuck: Nature on an Amish Farm.* Athens: University of Georgia Press, 1997.

Kline, Edward A. "Research Notes: Letters Pertaining to the Sam Yoder Division." *Heritage Review* 16 (Jan. 2007): 11–13.

———. *A Theology of the Will of Man and Some Practical Applications for the Christian Life: Being a Discussion of the Part and Responsibility of Man in the Process of Salvation.* Baltic, OH: Amish Brotherhood Publications, 1992.

Kline, Edward A., and Monroe L. Beachy. "History and Dynamics of the New Order Amish of Holmes County, Ohio." *Old Order Notes* 18 (Fall–Winter 1998): 7–19.

Kline, Paul. "Gelassenheit." Unpublished notes, Holmes County, OH, n.d.

Kline, Ronald R. *Consumers in the Country: Technology and Social Change in Rural America.* Baltimore: Johns Hopkins University Press, 2000.

Kollmorgen, Walter M. "The Agricultural Stability of the Old Order Amish and Old Order Mennonites of Lancaster County, Pennsylvania." *American Journal of Sociology* 49 (Nov. 1943): 233–41.

———. *Culture of a Contemporary Rural Community: The Old Order Amish of Lancaster County, Pennsylvania.* Washington, DC: US Department of Agriculture, Bureau of Agricultural Economics, 1942.

Kraybill, Donald B. "2010 Lancaster Demographic Study." Unpublished study, 2010.

———. *The Amish and the State.* 2nd ed. Baltimore: Johns Hopkins University Press, 2003.

———. "The Amish Encounter with Modernity." In *The Amish Struggle with Modernity,* edited by Donald B. Kraybill and Marc A. Olshan, 21–33. Hanover, NH: University Press of New England, 1994.

———. "Plotting Social Change across Four Affiliations." In *The Amish Struggle with Modernity,* edited by Donald B. Kraybill and Marc A. Olshan, 53–74. Hanover, NH: University Press of New England, 1994.

———. "The Redemptive Community: An Island of Sanity and Silence." In *Writing the Amish: The Worlds of John A. Hostetler,* edited by David L. Weaver-Zercher, 36–55. State College: Pennsylvania State University Press, 2004.

———. *The Riddle of Amish Culture.* Rev. ed. Baltimore: Johns Hopkins University Press, 2001.

Kraybill, Donald B., and Carl F. Bowman. *On the Backroad to Heaven: Old Order Hutterites, Mennonite, Amish, and Brethren.* Baltimore: Johns Hopkins University Press, 2001.

Kraybill, Donald B., and Gertrude Enders Huntington. "The Amish Family." In *Ethnic Families in America: Patterns and Variations,* 5th ed., edited by Roosevelt H. Wright Jr., Charles H. Mindel, Thanh Van Tran, and Robert W. Habenstein, 437–60. Boston: Pearson, 2012.

Kraybill, Donald B., and Conrad L. Kanagy. "The Rise of Entrepreneurship in Two Old Order Amish Communities." *Mennonite Quarterly Review* 70 (July 1996): 263–79.

Kraybill, Donald B., and Kyle C. Kopko. "Bush Fever: Amish and Old Order Mennonites in the 2004 Presidential Election." *Mennonite Quarterly Review* 81 (April 2007): 165–205.

Kraybill, Donald B., and Steven M. Nolt. *Amish Enterprise: From Plows to Profits.* 2nd ed. Baltimore: Johns Hopkins University Press, 2004.

Kraybill, Donald B., Steven M. Nolt, and Stephen E. Scott. "Language Use among Anabaptist Groups." Unpublished paper, 2010.

Kraybill, Donald B., Steven M. Nolt, and David Weaver-Zercher. *Amish Grace: How Forgiveness Transcended Tragedy.* San Francisco: Jossey-Bass, 2007.

———. *The Amish Way: Patient Faith in a Perilous World.* San Francisco: Jossey-Bass, 2010.

Kraybill, Donald B., Steven M. Nolt, and Erik J. Wesner. "Amish Enterprise: The Collective Power of Ethnic Entrepreneurship." *Global Business and Economics Review* 12, nos. 1/2 (2010): 3–20.

———. "Sources of Enterprise Success in Amish Communities." *Journal of Enterprising Communities: People and Places in the Global Economy* 5, no. 2 (2011): 112–30.

Kraybill, Donald B., and Marc A. Olshan. *The Amish Struggle with Modernity.* Hanover, NH: University Press of New England, 1994.

Kriebel, David W. *Powwowing among the Pennsylvania Dutch: A Traditional Medical Practice in the Modern World.* University Park: Pennsylvania State University Press, 2007.

Labi, Nadya. "The Gentle People." *Legal Affairs,* Jan.–Feb. 2005. www.legalaffairs.org/issues/January-February-2005/feature_labi_janfeb05.msp.

Ladd, Brian. *Autophobia: Love and Hate in the Automotive Age.* Chicago: University of Chicago Press, 2008.

Laikind, Daniel. "The Amish Diaries: Why Do You Care About the Amish?" *Faster Times,* May 15, 2012. www.thefastertimes.com/tv/2012/05/15/the-amish-diaries-why-do-you-care -about-the-amish/.

Lambert, Marcus B. *Pennsylvania-German Dictionary.* Exton, PA: Schiffer Ltd, 1977. Reprinted from the Publications of the Pennsylvania-German Society, vol. 30, 1924.

Lang, Allen Kim. "Blind Man's Lantern." *Analog: Science Fact–Science Fiction* 70 (Dec. 1962): 6–34.

Lapp, Christ S. *Pennsylvania School History: 1690–1990.* Edited by Mark L. Louden, Howard Martin, and Joseph C. Salmons. Gordonville, PA: Christ S. Lapp, 1991.

Lapp, Esther, comp. *Heartland Hymns.* Rosenort, MB: PrairieView Press, 2005.

Lapp, John K. *Remarks of By-Gone Days: A Few Remarks of Old Times.* Gordonville, PA: Gordonville Print Shop, 1986.

Lapp, John K., Jr. *The Social Booklet: Principles for Everyday Living.* New Holland, PA: Lapp Family, 2008.

Lasky, Kathryn. *Beyond the Divide.* New York: Aladdin Paperbacks, 1995.

Lears, Jackson. *No Place of Grace: Antimodernism and the Transformation of American Culture, 1880–1920.* New York: Pantheon, 1981.

———. *Rebirth of a Nation: The Making of Modern America, 1877–1920.* New York: HarperCollins, 2009.

Lee, Douglas. "The Plain People of Pennsylvania." *National Geographic* 165, no. 4 (April 1984): 492–519.

Lehman, Daniel W. "Graven Images and the (Re)presentation of Amish Trauma." *Mennonite Quarterly Review* 72 (Oct. 1998): 577–87.

Lehman, Marilyn E. "The Amish Taboo on Photography: Its Historical and Social Significance." *Pennsylvania Folklife* 43, no. 3 (Spring 1994): 121–23.

———. "Women and Their Work: Reflections on the Amish Church Tradition." *Mennonite Historical Bulletin,* Oct. 2005, 10–12.

———. "Writing the Everyday Self: Identity and Self-Consciousness in Amish Women's Diaries." In *What Mennonites are Thinking, 2002,* edited by Merle Good and Phyllis Pellman Good, 212–31. Intercourse, PA: Good Books, 2002.

Leith, John H., ed. *Creeds of the Churches: A Reader in Christian Doctrine from the Bible to the Present.* 3rd ed. Louisville, KY: John Knox Press, 1982.

Lemon, Betty Spencer. "Amish Health Care Beliefs and Practices in an Obstetrical Setting." *Journal of Multicultural Nursing & Health* 12, no. 3 (2006), 54–59.

"Let's Not Be Ashamed." *Family Life,* Nov. 1992, 2.

Levine, Neil Ann Stuckey, Ursula Roy, and David J. Rempel Smucker. "The View of Louis C. Jüngerich (1803–1882) in 1826: It is Best to Come to This Country Well Prepared." *Pennsylvania Mennonite Heritage* 20 (July 1997): 2–15.

Lewis, Beverly. *The Crossroad.* Minneapolis, MN: Bethany House Publishers, 1999.

———. *The Shunning.* Minneapolis, MN: Bethany House Publishers, 1997.

Lin, Nan, and Bonnie H. Erickson, eds. *Social Capital: An International Research Program.* New York: Oxford University Press, 2008.

Lindholm, William C. "The National Committee for Amish Religious Freedom." In *The Amish and the State,* 2nd ed., edited by Donald B. Kraybill, 109–23. Baltimore: Johns Hopkins University Press, 2003.

Lipovetsky, Gilles. *The Empire of Fashion: Dressing Modern Democracy.* Translated by Catherine Porter. Princeton, NJ: Princeton University Press, 1994.

———. *Hypermodern Times.* With Sébastien Charles. Translated by Andrew Brown. Cambridge, UK: Polity Press, 2005.

Loewen, Royden. "To the Ends of the Earth: An Introduction to the Conservative Low German Mennonites in the Americas." *Mennonite Quarterly Review* 82 (July 2008): 427–48.

Louden, Mark L. "Bilingualism and Syntactic Change in Pennsylvania German." PhD diss., Cornell University, 1988.

———. "Covert Prestige and the Role of English in Plain Pennsylvania German Sociolinguistics." Paper presented at the Annual Meeting of the Linguistic Society of America, Chicago, 1991.

———. "The Image of the Old Order Amish: General and Sociolinguistic Stereotypes." *National Journal of Sociology* 5, no. 2 (1991): 111–41.

———. "Old Order Amish Verbal Behavior as a Reflection of Cultural Convergence." In *Diachronic Studies on the Languages of the Anabaptists,* edited by Kate Burridge and Werner Enninger, 264–78. Bochum, Germany: Universitatsverlag Dr. N. Brockmeyer, 1992.

———. "Patterns of Language Maintenance in German-American Speech Islands." In *Studies in Contact Linguistics: Essays in Honor of Glenn G. Gilbert,* edited by Linda L. Thornburg and Janet M. Fuller, 127–45. New York: Peter Lang, 2006.

———. "Pennsylvania Dutch: The Story of an American Language." Unpublished manuscript, 2011.

Lowry, James W. *The Martyrs' Mirror Made Plain: A Study Guide and Further Studies.* Aylmer, ON: Pathway Publishers, 2000.

Lucas, Cheryl A., Robert M. O'Shea, Maria A. Zielezny, Jo L. Freudenheim, and James F. Wild. "Rural Medicine and the Closed Society: Pregnancy Outcomes among Amish and Non-Amish Women." *New York State Journal of Medicine* 91, no. 2 (Feb. 1991): 49–52.

"The Lunch Pail Problem." Pts. 1, 2, and 3. *Family Life,* April 1982, 12–16; May 1982, 10–14; June 1982, 11–16.

Luthy, David. *The Amish in America: Settlements That Failed, 1840–1960.* Aylmer, ON: Pathway Publishers, 1986.

———. *Amish Folk Artist Barbara Ebersol: Her Life, Fraktur, and Death Record Book.* Lancaster, PA: Lancaster Mennonite Historical Society, 1995.

———. "Amish Meetinghouses." *Family Life,* Aug.–Sept. 1981, 17–22.

———. "Amish Settlements across America: 1991." *Family Life,* April 1992, 19–24.

———. "Amish Settlements across America: 2008." *Family Life,* Aug.–Sept. 2008, 17–23.

———. *Amish Settlements across America: 2008.* Aylmer, ON: Pathway Publishers, 2009.

———. "Bibliographical and Research Notes: A History of Raber's Bookstore." *Mennonite Quarterly Review* 58 (April 1984): 168–78.

———. "Clothing and Conduct in Swiss Laws: 1450–1700." *Family Life,* July 1994, 23–26.

———. *Dirk Willems: His Noble Deed Lives On.* Aylmer, ON: Pathway Publishers, 2011.

———."A History of the *Lust-Gärtlein* Prayerbook." *Family Life,* July 1981, 21–24.

———. "The Origin and Growth of Amish Tourism." In *The Amish Struggle with Modernity,* edited by Donald B. Kraybill and Marc A. Olshan, 113–29. Hanover, NH: University Press of New England, 1994.

———."The Origin and Growth of the Swartzentruber Amish." *Family Life,* Aug.–Sept. 1998, 19–22.

———. "A Survey of Amish Ordination Customs." *Family Life,* March 1975, 13–17.

———. *Why Some Amish Communities Fail: Extinct Settlements, 1961–1999.* Rev. ed. Aylmer, ON: Pathway Publishers, 2000.

———. "Women's Veiling." *Family Life,* Sept. 1969, 18–20.

MacCannell, Dean. *The Tourist: A New Theory of the Leisure Class.* New York: Schocken Books, 1999. First published in 1976.

Mackall, Joe. *Plain Secrets: An Outsider among the Amish.* Boston: Beacon Press, 2007.

Maoz, Darya. "The Mutual Gaze." *Annals of Tourism Research* 33, no. 1 (2005): 221–39. doi:10.1016/j.annals.2005.10.010.

Mariola, Matt J., and David L. McConnell. "The Shifting Landscape of Amish Agriculture: Balancing Tradition and Modernity in an Organic Farming Cooperative." Unpublished paper, 2012.

Martin, Donald. *Distinctive Teachings of the Old Order People.* Wallenstein, ON: Vineyard Publications, 2007.

Mast, Daniel E. *Lessons in the Sermon on the Mount.* Weatherford, OK: John B. Mast, [1953]. Reprint, Gordonville, PA: Gordonville Print Shop, 1999.

———. *Salvation Full and Free.* Edited by John B. Mast. Partridge, KS: Daniel Nisly, 1994. Originally published as *Anweisungen zur Seligkeit* (Baltic, OH: J. A. Raber, [1933]).

Mayes, Mary. *Strong Families, Safe Children: An Amish Family Resource Book.* LaGrange, IN: Pathway Press, 2002.

Mazie, Steven V. "Consenting Adults? Amish *Rumspringa* and the Quandary of Exit in Liberalism." *Perspectives on Politics* 33, no. 4 (Dec. 2005): 745–59.

McCauley, Daniel, and Kathryn McCauley. *Decorative Arts of the Amish of Lancaster County.* Intercourse, PA: Good Books, 1988.

McConnell, David L., and Charles E. Hurst. "No 'Rip Van Winkles' Here: Amish Education since *Wisconsin v. Yoder.*" *Anthropology and Education Quarterly* 37 (Sept. 2006): 236–54.

McDaniel, Lurlene. *Angels Watching Over Me.* New York: Bantam Books, 1996.

———. *Lifted Up By Angels.* New York: Bantam Books, 1997.

———. *Until Angels Close My Eyes.* New York: Bantam Books, 1998.

McDannell, Colleen. *Material Christianity: Religion and Popular Culture in America.* New Haven, CT: Yale University Press, 1995.

Meier, Marcus. *The Origin of the Schwarzenau Brethren.* Translated by Dennis L. Slabaugh. Philadelphia: Brethren Encyclopedia, 2008.

———. "Research Note: *Golden Apples in Silver Bowls* and the Relationship of Swiss Anabaptism to Pietism." *Mennonite Quarterly Review* 82 (Oct. 2008): 591–602.

Menno Simons. *The Complete Works of Menno Simons.* Aylmer, ON: Pathway Publishers, 1983.

Meyers, Thomas J. "Amish Tourism: 'Visiting Shipshewana Is Better than Going to the Mall.'" *Mennonite Quarterly Review* 77 (Jan. 2003): 109–26.

———. "Education and Schooling." In *The Amish and the State,* 2nd ed., edited by Donald B. Kraybill, 87–106. Baltimore: Johns Hopkins University Press, 2003.

——. "Lunch Pails and Factories." In *The Amish Struggle with Modernity,* edited by Donald B. Kraybill and Marc A. Olshan, 165–81. Hanover, NH: University Press of New England, 1994.

——. "The Old Order Amish: To Remain in the Faith or to Leave." *Mennonite Quarterly Review* 68 (July 1994): 378–95.

——. "Population Growth and Its Consequences in the Elkhart–LaGrange Old Order Amish Settlement." *Mennonite Quarterly Review* 65 (July 1991): 308–21.

Meyers, Thomas J., and Steven M. Nolt. *An Amish Patchwork: Indiana's Old Orders in the Modern World.* Bloomington, IN: Quarry Books, 2005.

Michigan Amish Directory, 2010. Millersburg, OH: Abana Books, 2010.

Mihalicek, Vedrana, and Christin Wilson, eds. *Language Files: Materials for an Introduction to Language and Linguistics.* 11th ed. Columbus: Ohio State University Press, 2011.

Miller, Eric. "Why We Love Amish Romances." *Christianity Today,* April 2011, 38–41.

Miller, Jerry E. "Farming Practically." *Family Life,* Oct. 1992, 27–31.

Miller, Jerry L. "The Change to Organic Farming." *Family Life,* Jan. 2007, 34.

Miller, Joseph S. "The Peculiar Beauty of *Gelassenheit:* An Interview with Amos B. Hoover." In *The Measure of My Days: Engaging the Life and Thought of John L. Ruth,* edited by Reuben Z. Miller and Joseph S. Miller, 201–27. Telford, PA: Cascadia Publishing House, 2004.

Miller, Keith Graber. "Complex Innocence, Obligatory Nurturance, and Parental Vigilance: 'The Child' in the Work of Menno Simons." In *The Child in Christian Thought,* edited by Marcia J. Bunge, 194–226. Grand Rapids, MI: Wm. B. Eerdmans, 2001.

Miller, Kirk, Berwood Yost, Sean Flaherty, Marianne M. Hillemeier, Gary A. Chase, Carol S. Weisman, and Anne-Marie Dyer. "Health Status, Health Conditions, and Health Behaviors among Amish Women: Results from the Central Pennsylvania Women's Health Study (CePAWHS)." *Women's Health Issues* 17 (2007): 162–71.

Miller, Levi. "The Role of a Braucher-Chiropractor in an Amish Community." *Mennonite Quarterly Review* 55 (April 1981): 157–71.

Miller, Mary M. *Our Fervent Prayers: Translated Prayers from the Ernsthafte Christenpflicht.* Topeka, IN: Mary M. Miller, 2004.

——, comp. *Our Heritage, Hope, and Faith.* Rev. ed. Topeka, IN: Mary M. Miller, 2008.

Miller, Rachel. *A Vision for the Journey.* Sugarcreek, OH: Carlisle Printing, 2008.

Minutes of Old Order Amish Steering Committee from September 12, 2001 to September 21, 2005: Seventh Volume. N.p., 2005.

Minutes of Old Order Amish Steering Committee from September 20, 2006 to September 17, 2008: Eighth Volume. N.p., 2008.

Minutes of Old Order Amish Steering Committee from Oct. 20, 1966 to Oct. 25, 1972: First Volume. [Gordonville, PA]: Gordonville Print Shop, 1972.

Minutes of Old Order Amish Steering Committee from Oct. 24, 1973 to Oct. 22, 1980: Second Volume. [Gordonville, PA]: Gordonville Print Shop, 1980.

"Minutes of the Sixth People Helper's Meeting of Lancaster County." In *People Helpers Meetings, May 1998 to July 2000,* 36–44. N.p., n.d.

"The Most Humble Position?" *Family Life,* Jan. 1988, 12.

Mullen, Jeffery. "Religion and the PPACA: An Analysis of Non-Secular Line Drawing within the Health Insurance Mandate." *Rutgers Journal of Law and Religion* 14, no. 1 (Fall 2012).

Müller, Ernst. *History of the Bernese Anabaptists: According to Documentation Presented by Ernst Müller, Minister in Langnau.* Translated by John A. Gingerich. Edited by Joseph Stoll. Aylmer, ON: Pathway Publishers, 2010.

Myers, Tamar. *Parsley, Sage, Rosemary & Crime.* New York: Signet Books, 1996.

Nappanee Amish Directory including Rochester, Kokomo and Milroy Communities, 2008. Compiled by the Owen E. Borkholder family. Nappanee, IN: Owen E. Borkholder, 2008.

Naugle, June. *Solomon's Touch: The Life and Work of Solomon J. Wickey.* Bloomington, IN: AuthorHouse, 2005.

Neu vermehrtes geistliches Lust-Gärtlein frommer Seelen. Lancaster County, PA: Amischen Gemeinden, 2008.

New York Amish Directory of the Jasper-Woodhull Settlement, 1983–2010. Compiled by Chester Byler. Woodhull, NY: Chester Byler, 2010.

Nisly, Paul W. "Community and Formerly-Amish Professionals: An Introductory Survey and Reflective Study." *Mennonite Quarterly Review* 80 (Jan. 2006): 61–82.

Nolt, Steven M. "The Amish 'Mission Movement' and the Reformulation of Amish Identity in the Twentieth Century." *Mennonite Quarterly Review* 75 (Jan. 2001): 7–36.

———. *A History of the Amish.* Rev. ed. Intercourse, PA: Good Books, 2003.

———. "Inscribing Community: *The Budget* and *Die Botschaft* in Amish Life." In *The Amish and the Media,* edited by Diane Zimmerman Umble and David L. Weaver-Zercher, 181–98. Baltimore: Johns Hopkins University Press, 2008.

———. "MCC's Relationship with 'Plain' Anabaptists in Historical Perspective." In *A Table of Sharing: Mennonite Central Committee and the Expanding Networks of Mennonite Identity,* edited by Alain Epp-Weaver, 135–66. Telford, PA: Cascadia Publishing House, 2011.

———. "Mennonite Identity and the Writing on the 'New Giving' Since 1945." *Journal of Mennonite Studies* 23 (2005): 59–76.

———. "Moving beyond Stark Options: Old Order Mennonite and Amish Approaches to Mental Health." *Journal of Mennonite Studies* 29 (2011): 133–51.

Nolt, Steven M., and Thomas J. Meyers. *Plain Diversity: Amish Cultures and Identities.* Baltimore: Johns Hopkins University Press, 2007.

"Not Everyone Can Be a Farmer." Pts. 1 and 2. *Family Life,* Jan. 2002, 8; March 2002, 32–34.

Nugent, Walter. *Crossings: The Great Transatlantic Migrations, 1870–1914.* Bloomington: Indiana University Press, 1992.

Ohio Amish Directory: Geauga County and Vicinity, 2009 Edition. Compiled by John J. Miller. Sugarcreek, OH: Schlabach Printers, 2010.

Old Colony Mennonite Support. *Called to Mexico: Bringing Hope and Literacy to the Old Colony Mennonites.* Nappanee, IN: Old Colony Mennonite Support, 2011.

Olshan, Marc A. "Amish Cottage Industries as Trojan Horse." In *The Amish Struggle with Modernity,* edited by Donald B. Kraybill and Marc A. Olshan, 133–46. Hanover, NH: University Press of New England, 1994.

———. "Homespun Bureaucracy: A Case Study in Organizational Evolution." In *The Amish Struggle with Modernity,* edited by Donald B. Kraybill and Marc A. Olshan, 199–213. Hanover, NH: University Press of New England, 1994.

———. "Modernity, the Folk Society, and the Old Order Amish." In *The Amish Struggle with Modernity,* edited by Donald B. Kraybill and Marc A. Olshan, 185–96. Hanover, NH: University Press of New England, 1994.

———. "The National Amish Steering Committee." In *The Amish and the State,* 2nd ed., edited by Donald B. Kraybill, 67–84. Baltimore: Johns Hopkins University Press, 2003.

Olshan, Marc A., and Kimberly D. Schmidt. "Amish Women and the Feminist Conundrum." In *The Amish Struggle with Modernity,* edited by Donald B. Kraybill and Marc A. Olshan, 215–29. Hanover, NH: University Press of New England, 1994.

Orr, Monica St. Clair. "Public Library Usage among the Old Order Amish." Paper presented at the Amish in America conference, Young Center for Anabaptist and Pietist Studies, Elizabethtown College, Elizabethtown, PA, June 2007.

Oyer, John S. "Is There an Amish Theology? Some Reflections on Amish Religious Thought and Practice." In *The Amish: Origin and Characteristics, 1693–1993,* edited by Lydie Hege and Christoph Wiebe, 278–302. Ingersheim, France: Association Française d'Histoire Anabaptiste-Mennonite, 1996.

"PA School Meetings." *The Diary,* July 1999, 61–62.

Patterson, James T. *Grand Expectations: The United States, 1945–1974.* New York: Oxford University Press, 1996.

Pederson, Jane Marie. " 'She May Be Amish Now, but She Won't Be Amish Long': Anabaptist Women and Antimodernism." In *Strangers at Home: Amish and Mennonite Women in History,* edited by Kimberly D. Schmidt, Diane Zimmerman Umble, and Steven D. Reschly, 339–63. Baltimore: Johns Hopkins University Press, 2002.

Peters, Galen A., ed. *The Earliest Hymns of the Ausbund: Some Beautiful Christian Songs Composed and Sung at the Prison at Passau, Published in 1564.* Translated by Robert A. Riall. Kitchener, ON: Pandora Press, 2003.

Peters, Shawn Francis. *The Yoder Case: Religious Freedom, Education, and Parental Rights.* Lawrence: University Press of Kansas, 2003.

"Petition: 'To Our Men in Authority,' November 17, 1937." Reprinted in *Report of Committee of Plain People Making Pleas for Leniency from Depressive School Laws,* compiled by Aaron E. Beiler and Eli M. Shirk, 86–87. New Holland, PA: Aaron E. Beiler and Eli M. Shirk, 1939.

Picoult, Jodi. *Plain Truth.* New York: Pocket Books, 2000.

"A Plea For Understanding." *Family Life,* Feb. 2005, 7–8.

"Poisoning the Earth." Pts. 1, 2, and 3. *Family Life,* April 1990, 16–20; May 1990, 29–33; June 1990, 29–33.

Pratt, Dorothy O. *Shipshewana: An Indiana Amish Community.* Bloomington: Indiana University Press, 2004.

"Preserving Our German." *Blackboard Bulletin,* Aug. 2011, 12–14.

"The Problem Corner." *Family Life,* Aug.–Sep. 1994, 25–29.

"Procedural Guide." Unpublished guidelines for the Eagles youth group in Lancaster County, Pa.

"A Proud Look." *Family Life,* July 1994, 11–14.

"Public Alms." *Family Life,* March 1988, 8.

"Questions Asked at a Marriage Ceremony." *Family Life,* Feb. 1988, 16–17.

"Questions Asked at Baptism Service." *Family Life,* Feb. 1988, 16.

Quillin, Patrick. *The Wisdom of Amish Folk Medicine.* North Canton, OH: Leader, 1993.

Raber, John Paul. "Following Christ in Truth." *Family Life,* June 2002, 10–13.

RB 1980: The Rule of St. Benedict in English. Collegeville, MN: Liturgical Press, 1981.

Rebuilding Hope: Disaster Response Services. Millersburg, OH: Christian Aid Ministries, 2002.

Regehr, T. D. "Relations between the Old Order Amish and the State in Canada." *Mennonite Quarterly Review* 69 (April 1995): 151–77.

Reich, Rob. *Bridging Liberalism and Multiculturalism in American Education.* Chicago: University of Chicago Press, 2002.

Reiheld, Amelia T. "Birthing Center Serves Amish Well." In *The Amish of Holmes County: A Culture, a Religion, a Way of Life,* edited by Jon Kinney, 87–94. Orrville, OH: Spectrum Publications, 1996.

Reiling, Denise M. "Boundary Maintenance as a Barrier to Mental Health Help-Seeking for Depression among the Old Order Amish." *Journal of Rural Health* 18, no. 3 (June 2002): 428–36.

———. "An Exploration of the Relationship between Amish Identity and Depression among the Old Order Amish." PhD diss., Michigan State University, 2000.

———. "The 'Simmie' Side of Life: Old Order Amish Youths' Affective Response to Culturally Prescribed Deviance." *Youth and Society* 34, no. 2 (Dec. 2002): 146–71.

Reiter, Paul L., Mira L. Katz, Amy K. Ferketich, Electra D. Paskett, Steven K. Clinton, and Clara D. Bloomfield. "Complementary and Alternative Medicine Use among Amish and Non-Amish Residents of Ohio Appalachia." *Online Journal of Rural Nursing and Health Care* 9, no. 2 (Fall 2009): 33–44.

Remnick, David. "Bad Seeds: Letter from Lancaster County." *New Yorker,* July 20, 1998, 28–33.

Reschly, Steven D. *The Amish on the Iowa Prairie, 1840 to 1910.* Baltimore: Johns Hopkins University Press, 2000.

Reschly, Steven D., and Katherine Jellison. "Production Patterns, Consumption Strategies, and Gender Relations in Amish and Non-Amish Farm Households in Lancaster County, Pennsylvania, 1935–1936." *Agricultural History* 67, no. 2 (Spring 1993): 134–62.

Rheingold, Howard. "Look Who's Talking," *Wired,* Jan. 1999. www.wired.com/wired/archive/7.01/amish.html.

Rice, Charles Scott, and Rollin C. Steinmetz. *The Amish Year.* New Brunswick, NJ: Rutgers University Press, 1956.

Rieman, Mary T., Melissa Hunley, Lori Woeste, and Richard J. Kagan. "Is There an Increased Risk of Burns to Amish Children?" *Journal of Burn Care & Research* 29, no. 5 (2008): 742–49.

Roth, John D., trans. and ed. *Letters of the Amish Division: A Sourcebook.* Goshen, IN: Mennonite Historical Society, 1993.

"Rules of a Godly Life." In *In Meiner Jugend: A Devotional Reader in German and English,* translated by Joseph Stoll, 65–103. Aylmer, ON: Pathway Publishers, 2000.

Rushkoff, Douglas. *Program or Be Programmed: Ten Commands for a Digital Age.* New York: OR Books, 2010.

Russell, R. R. "Development of Conscientious Objector Recognition in the United States." *George Washington Law Review* 20 (March 1952): 409–48.

Schlabach, Gracia. *Now Thank We All Our God: A Guide to Six German Hymnals.* Medina, NY: Lilting Leaf, 2011.

Schlabach, Mary, comp. *Message Mem'ries.* Millersburg, OH: Emanuel and Mary Schlabach, 2007.

[Schlabach, Rob R.] *Ein Risz in der Mauer: Treatise on Courtship.* Sugarcreek, OH: Schlabach Printers, n.d.

Schlabach, Rob R. "Amish Farming: Past, Present, and Future." *Family Life,* June 2010, 30.

———. "The Inroads of Industrialism." *Plain Interests* 1, no.1 (Jan. 2001): 1.

———. "Organic Dairy Farming." *Family Life,* Feb. 2007, 28–32.

Schlabach, Theron F. *Peace, Faith, Nation: Mennonites and Amish in Nineteenth-Century America.* Mennonite Experience in America, vol. 2. Scottdale, PA: Herald Press, 1988.

Schmidt, Kimberly D. "Schism: Where Women's Outside Work and Insider Dress Collided." In *Strangers at Home: Amish and Mennonite Women in History,* edited by Kimberly D. Schmidt, Diane Zimmerman Umble, and Steven D. Reschly, 208–33. Baltimore: Johns Hopkins University Press, 2002.

Schmidt-Lange, Anne Augspurger. "Roast Bear? No Thank You!—An 1821 Letter from Kurhessen, Germany, to Daniel and Christian Schwartzentruber in Somerset County, Pennsylvania." *Pennsylvania Mennonite Heritage* 25 (Oct. 2002): 9–20.

"School Meetings." *Blackboard Bulletin,* May 2010, 11–12.

Schrock-Shenk, Carolyn. Foreword to *Stumbling Toward a Genuine Conversation on Homosexuality,* edited by Michael A. King, 13–18. Telford, PA: Cascadia Publishing House, 2007.

Schwartz, Christian, and Elizabeth N. Schwartz, comps. *Schwartzs' Song-Book.* Gordonville, PA: Gordonville Print Shop, 1980.

Schwieder, Elmer, and Dorothy Schwieder. *A Peculiar People: Iowa's Old Order Amish.* Ames: Iowa State University Press, 1975.

Scott, Stephen. "Amish Groups, Affiliations, and Categories." Unpublished paper, Sept. 2011.

———. *The Amish Wedding and Other Special Occasions of the Old Order Communities.* Intercourse, PA: Good Books, 1988.

———. "Newcomers: English Converts to the Amish." Paper presented at the Amish in America conference, Young Center for Anabaptist and Pietist Studies, Elizabethtown College, Elizabethtown, PA, June 2007.

———. *Plain Buggies: Amish, Mennonite, and Brethren Horse-Drawn Transportation.* Intercourse, PA: Good Books, 1981.

———. *Why Do They Dress That Way?* Intercourse, PA: Good Books, 1986.

Scott, Stephen, and Kenneth Pellman. *Living Without Electricity.* Intercourse, PA: Good Books, 1990.

"Scrimping: Good or Bad." *Family Life,* Aug.–Sept. 1991, 29–32.

Séguy, Jean. "The Bernese Anabaptists in Sainte-Marie-aux-Mines." Translated by Mervin Smucker. *Pennsylvania Mennonite Heritage* 3 (July 1980): 2–9.

———. "The French Anabaptists: Four and One-Half Centuries of History." *Mennonite Quarterly Review* 58 (July 1984): 206–17.

———. "Religion and Agricultural Success: The Vocational Life of the French Anabaptists from the Seventeenth to the Nineteenth Centuries." Translated by Michael Shank. *Mennonite Quarterly Review* 47 (July 1973): 179–224.

Seifert, Lester W. J. *A Word Atlas of Pennsylvania German.* Edited by Mark L. Louden, Howard Martin, and Joseph C. Salmons. Madison, WI: Max Kade Institute for German-American Studies, 2001.

Seiler, Cotton. *Republic of Drivers: A Cultural History of Automobility in America.* Chicago: University of Chicago Press, 2008.

Sensenig, Kenneth. "Old Order Amish: MCC's Invisible Partner, 1990–2010." Unpublished paper, 2010.

Sewing Circle. *The Doorway to Hope for the Hurting, Struggling and Discouraged.* Fort Wayne, IN: Sewing Circle, 2009.

"The Shop that Grew." Pts. 1 and 2. *Family Life,* Aug.–Sept. 2002, 10–15; Nov. 2002, 13–16.

Shover, John L. *First Majority, Last Minority: The Transforming of Rural Life in America.* DeKalb: Northern Illinois University Press, 1976.

Showalter, Anita. "Birthing among the Amish." *International Journal of Childbirth Education* 15, no. 4 (2000): 10–11.

"The Silent Struggle." *Family Life,* May 1988, 32–33.

"Simple Living: How Can We Keep It?" *Family Life,* May 1997, 18–19.

Singer, Milton. "On the Symbolic and Historic Structure of an American Identity." *Ethos* 5, no. 4 (Winter 1977): 431–54.

"A Single's Plight." *Family Life,* May 2009, 33.

Smith, Christian. *Moral, Believing Animals: Human Personhood and Culture.* New York: Oxford University Press, 2003.

Smith, Jeff. "The Seekers: Why This Grosse Pointe Family Went Amish." *Traverse,* Nov. 2009, 23–29.

Smith, Merritt Roe, and Leo Marx, eds. *Does Technology Drive History? The Dilemma of Technological Determinism.* Cambridge, MA: MIT Press, 1994.

Smucker, Esther F. *Good Night, My Son: A Treasure in Heaven.* Elverson, PA: Olde Springfield Shoppe, 1995.

Smucker, Janneken. *Amish Quilts: Crafting an American Icon.* Baltimore: Johns Hopkins University Press, 2013.

———. "Destination Amish Quilt Country: The Consumption of Quilts in Lancaster County, Pennsylvania." *Mennonite Quarterly Review* 80 (April 2006): 184–206.

Smucker, Mervin R. "How Amish Children View Themselves and Their Families: The Effectiveness of Amish Socialization." *Brethren Life and Thought* 33 (Summer 1988): 218–36.

Snyder, C. Arnold. *Anabaptist History and Theology: An Introduction.* Kitchener, ON: Pandora Press, 1995.

———. *Following in the Footsteps of Christ: The Anabaptist Tradition.* Maryknoll, NY: Orbis Books, 2004.

"Some Questions about Baptism." *Family Life,* July 1993, 12–16.

Songs of the Ausbund: History and Translations of Ausbund Hymns. 2 vols. Millersburg, OH: Ohio Amish Library, 1998 and 2011.

"Special Section on Hospital Aid and Insurance." *Family Life,* Feb. 1990, 28–33.

Standards of the Old Order Amish and Old Order Mennonite Parochial and Vocational Schools of Penna. Gordonville, PA: Gordonville Print Shop, 2003.

Stauffer, J. "By Giving, We Receive." *Family Life,* Feb. 2007, 22–23.

———. "Giant Broom of Destruction." *Family Life,* Jan. 2006, 15–19.

Stevick, Pauline. *Beyond the Plain and Simple: A Patchwork of Amish Lives.* Kent, OH: Kent State University Press, 2006.

Stevick, Richard A. *Growing Up Amish: The Teenage Years.* Baltimore: Johns Hopkins University Press, 2007.

———. "Pinecraft Florida Notes." Unpublished notes, Oct. 10, 2006.

Stoll, Christian. "According to the Title Deed." *Family Life,* Jan. 1997, 6–9.

[Stoll, Elmo]. *Strangers and Pilgrims: Why We Live Simply.* Aylmer, ON: Pathway Publishers, 2008.

———. "Cheap Shirts and Shallow Reasoning." *Family Life,* Jan. 1972, 11–12.

———. "Ordaining by Lot." *Family Life,* March 1986, 10–12.

———. "Preparing for an Ordination." *Family Life,* Feb. 1986, 9–11.

Stoll, Joseph. *The Amish in Daviess County, Indiana.* Aylmer, ON: Joseph Stoll, 1997.

———, ed. *The Challenge of the Child: Selections from "The Blackboard Bulletin" 1957–1966.* Aylmer, ON: Pathway Publishing Corporation, 1967.

———. *Child Training.* Aylmer, ON: Pathway Publishing Corporation, 1976.

———. "The Family under Attack." *Family Life,* Feb. 2012, 8–10.

———. "Fireside Chats: Men and Women." *Family Life,* Oct. 1971, 7–9.

———. *How the Dordrecht Confession Came Down to Us.* Aylmer, ON: Pathway Publishers, 2000.

———. "A Rule to Measure By." *Family Life,* Jan. 1992, 7–10.

———. *Sunshine and Shadow: Our Seven Years in Honduras.* Aylmer, ON: Joseph Stoll, 1996.

———. "An Umbrella We Don't Need." *Family Life,* Jan. 1993, 7–10.

———. "Who Shall Educate Our Children?" In *Compulsory Education and the Amish: The Right Not to Be Modern,* edited by Albert N. Keim, 16–42. Boston: Beacon Press, 1975.

Stoll, Joseph, David Luthy, and Elmo Stoll, eds. *Our Heritage.* Reprint, LaGrange, IN: Pathway Publishers, 2007. Originally published in 1968.

Stoll, Steven. *Larding the Lean Earth: Soil and Society in Nineteenth-Century America.* New York: Hill and Wang, 2002.

Stoltzfus, Christian P., comp. *Amish Church, School and Historical Events.* 2nd ed. Morgantown, PA: Masthof Press, 2010.

Stoltzfus, Louise. *Amish Women: Lives and Stories.* Intercourse, PA: Good Books, 1994.

———. *Two Amish Folk Artists: The Story of Henry Lapp and Barbara Ebersol.* Intercourse, PA: Good Books, 1995.

Stoltzfus, Naomi, and Linda S. Ingham. *God Moves Mountains One Pebble at a Time: The Healing Journey of Naomi Stoltzfus.* Morgantown, PA: Masthof Press, 2005.

Stoltzfus, Nicholas, comp. *Stories of COs in World War I Army Camps.* Reprint, [Millersburg, Ohio]: Robert Yoder, 2005.

Stoltzfus, Samuel S. "Ascension Day." Unpublished notes, in Donald Kraybill's files.

———. "Going in with the Boys." *Pennsylvania Mennonite Heritage* 31, no. 1 (Jan. 2008): 31–32.

———. "Lancaster Counties *[sic]* Barn Raising in 1991." Unpublished essay, in Donald Kraybill's files.

Stoltzfus, Victor E. "Amish Agriculture: Adaptive Strategies for Economic Survival of Community Life." *Rural Sociology* 38 (Summer 1973): 196–206.

Strauss, Kevin A., and Erik G. Puffenberger. "Genetics, Medicine, and the Plain People." *Annual Review of Genomics and Human Genetics* 10 (Sept. 2009): 513–36. doi: 10.1146/annurev-genom-082908-150040.

Strauss, Kevin A., Erik G. Puffenberger, and D. Holmes Morton. "One Community's Effort to Control Genetic Disease." *American Journal of Public Health.* Published online ahead of print May 17, 2012. doi:10.2105/AJPH.2011.300569.

Streiker-Schmidt, Lucinda. *A Separate God: Journal of an Amish Girl.* Mustang, OK: Tate Publishing, 2008.

Swartz, David. *Culture and Power: The Sociology of Pierre Bourdieu.* Chicago: University of Chicago Press, 1997.

Swartzentruber, Mara S. "Retention Rates in Amish Communities, with Special Reference to Nappanee, Indiana." Unpublished paper, Goshen College, Goshen, IN, 2011.

Tan, Tay Keong. "Silence, Sacrifice and Shoo-fly Pies: An Inquiry into the Social Capital and Organizational Strategies of the Amish Community in Lancaster County, Pennsylvania." PhD diss., Harvard University, 1998.

Taylor, Charles. *Modern Social Imaginaries.* Durham, NC: Duke University Press, 2004.

"Ten Rules for a Successful Marriage." Reprinted in *Lancaster (PA) Gemeinde Brief,* December 30, 2010, 11. Originally published in the Geauga County, Ohio, *Gemeinde Brief.*

Thierwechter, Lee R. *Das is wie mer's saagt in Deitsch: Lee R. Thierwechter's Responses to Dr. Ellsworth Kyger's Word Lists.* Millersville, PA: Center for Pennsylvania German Studies at Millersville University, 2002.

Thomas, Bill. "Amishville." *Indiana History Bulletin* 46, no. 9 (1969): 117–18.

Thompson, Chad L. "Yodeling of the Indiana Swiss Amish." *Anthropological Linguistics* 38 (Fall 1996): 495–520.

Thomson, Dennis L. "Canadian Government Relations." In *The Amish and the State,* edited by Donald B. Kraybill, 235–50. Baltimore: Johns Hopkins University Press, 1993.

"A Tribute to our Single Sisters." *Family Life,* Dec. 2005, 13.

Trollinger, Susan L. *Selling the Amish: The Tourism of Nostalgia.* Baltimore: Johns Hopkins University Press, 2012.

Troyer, David A. *The Writings of David A. Troyer Published after His Death: An English Translation.* Compiled and translated by Paton Yoder. Edited and translated by Joseph Stoll. Aylmer, ON: Pathway Publishers, 1998.

Troyer, Effie Mast, and Joseph Stoll. "Apple Grove Mennonite School, First of its Kind." *Blackboard Bulletin,* Oct. 1965, 37–49.

Troyer, Rebecca. "Selling Cut Flowers." *Farming Magazine,* Fall 2002, 41.

The Truth in Word and Work: A Statement of Faith by Ministers and Brethren of Amish Churches of Holmes Co., Ohio, and Related Areas. Baltic, OH: Amish Brotherhood Publications, 1983.

Turco, Douglas M. "Tourism in Amish Communities." *Parks & Recreation* 35 (2000): 138–44.

"Twenty Things Adopted Children Wish Their Adoptive Parents Knew." *Family Life,* June 2004, 24.

"Twenty Things Adoptive Parents Want Their Adopted Children to Know." *Family Life,* Aug.– Sept. 2004, 17–18.

Umble, Diane Zimmerman. *Holding the Line: The Telephone in Old Order Amish and Mennonite Life.* Baltimore: Johns Hopkins University Press, 1996.

———. " 'Wicked Truth': The Amish, the Media, and Telling the Truth." In *The Amish and the Media,* edited by Diane Zimmerman Umble and David L. Weaver-Zercher, 221–41. Baltimore: Johns Hopkins University Press, 2008.

Umble, Diane Zimmerman, and David L. Weaver-Zercher, eds. *The Amish and the Media.* Baltimore: Johns Hopkins University Press, 2008.

Umble, John, trans. and ed. "Memoirs of an Amish Bishop." *Mennonite Quarterly Review* 22 (April 1948): 94–115.

Unparteiische Liedersammlung zum Gebrauch beim oeffentlichen Gottesdienst und zur häuslichen Erbauung. Elkhart, IN: Mennonitische Verlagsanstalt, 1892 and reprints.

Vaisey, Stephen. "Motivation and Justification: A Dual-Process Model of Culture in Action." *American Journal of Sociology* 114, no. 6 (May 2009): 1675–715.

Vincent, John Martin. *Costume and Conduct in the Laws of Basel, Bern, and Zurich, 1370–1800.* Baltimore: John Hopkins University Press, 1953.

Vonk, Martine. *Sustainability and Quality of Life: A Study on the Religious Worldviews, Values and Environmental Impact of Amish, Hutterite, Franciscan and Benedictine Communities.* Amsterdam: Vrije Universiteit, 2011.

[Wagler, David]. *Are All Things Lawful?* Aylmer, ON: Pathway Publishers, n.d.

Wagler, David, comp. *The New Concept in Treating Burns.* Millersburg, PA: Plain Interests Research, 2007.

———. "Ordinations in the Church." *Family Life,* Oct. 1996, 40, 34–36.

———. "What Is Left to Write About?" *Plain Interests,* Dec. 2010, 4–6.

Wagler, Ira. *Growing Up Amish: A Memoir.* Carol Stream, IL: Tyndale House Publishers, 2011.

Wagner, Peter. *Modernity as Experience and Interpretation: A New Sociology of Modernity.* Cambridge, UK: Polity Press, 2008.

Waldrep, G. C. "The New Order Amish and Para-Amish Groups: Spiritual Renewal within Tradition." *Mennonite Quarterly Review* 83 (July 2008): 395–426.

Walk in the Light. Millersburg, PA, n.d. Originally published as *A Fence or an Ambulance* (Aylmer, ON, n.d).

Wasao, Samson W., and Joseph F. Donnermeyer. "An Analysis of Factors Related to Parity among the Amish in Northeast Ohio." *Population Studies* 50 (1996): 235–46.

Watters, Ethan. *Urban Tribes: A Generation Redefines Friendship, Family, and Commitment.* New York: Bloomsbury, 2003.

Weaver, J. Denny. *Becoming Anabaptist: The Origin and Significance of Sixteenth-Century Anabaptism.* 2nd ed. Scottdale, PA: Herald Press, 2005.

———. *Keeping Salvation Ethical: Mennonite and Amish Atonement Theology in the Late Nineteenth Century.* Scottdale, PA: Herald Press, 1997.

Weaver, Roy M. "Glimpses of the Amish Church in Holmes County, Ohio, 1917–1922, and Report of a Ministers' Meeting in 1922." *Heritage Review* 16 (Jan. 2007): 9–11.

Weaver, Wayne M. *Dust Between My Toes: An Amish Boy's Journey.* Sugarcreek, OH: Carlisle Press, 1997.

Weaver-Zercher, David. *The Amish in the American Imagination.* Baltimore: Johns Hopkins University Press, 2001.

———. "An Uneasy Calling: John A. Hostetler and the Work of Cultural Mediation." In *Writing the Amish: The Worlds of John A. Hostetler,* edited by David L. Weaver-Zercher, 98–149. State College: Pennsylvania State University Press, 2005.

Weaver-Zercher, Valerie. *Thrill of the Chaste: The Allure of Amish Romance Novels.* Baltimore: Johns Hopkins University Press, 2013.

Weber, Chris, James A. Cates, and Shirley Carey. "A Drug and Alcohol Intervention with Old Order Amish Youth: Dancing on the Devil's Playground." *Journal of Groups in Addiction and Recovery* 5, no. 2 (2010): 97–112.

Weber, Max. *The Theory of Social and Economic Organization.* Translated by A. M. Henderson and Talcott Parsons. New York: Free Press, 1964. First published in 1947 by Oxford University Press.

Wenger, Anna Frances Zimmerman. "Cultural Context, Health and Health Care Decision Making." *Journal of Transcultural Nursing: Official Journal of the Transcultural Nursing Society* 7, no. 1 (Summer 1995): 3–14.

———. "The Phenomenon of Care in a High Context Culture: The Old Order Amish." PhD diss., Wayne State University, 1988.

Wenger, Olivia K., Mark D. McManus, John R. Bower, and Diane L. Langkamp. "Underimmunization in Ohio's Amish: Parental Fears Are a Greater Obstacle than Access to Care." *Pediatrics* 128 (2011): 79–85.

Wesner, Erik. *Success Made Simple: An Inside Look at Why Amish Businesses Thrive.* San Francisco: Jossey-Bass, 2010.

Wetmore, Jameson M. "Building Amish Community with Technology: Regulating Machines and Techniques to Forward Social Goals." *IEEE Technology and Society Magazine* 26 (Summer 2007): 10–21.

"What is in a Language?" *Family Life,* Feb. 1986, 12–16.

Wickey Sisters. *Amish Home Remedies.* Gordonville, PA: Gordonville Print Shop, 1991.

Wilcox, W. Bradford. *Soft Patriarchs, New Men: How Christianity Shapes Fathers and Husbands.* Chicago: University of Chicago Press, 2004.

Wiley, Eric. "Wilderness Theatre: Environmental Tourism and Cajun Swamp Tours." *The Drama Review* 46 (2002): 118–31.

Wittmer, Joe. *The Gentle People: An Inside View of Amish Life.* 4th ed. N.p.: Wittmer Books, 2010.

Workinger, Barbara. *In Dutch Again: An Amish Country Mystery.* Bloomington, IN: 1st Books Library, 2002.

Wuthnow, Robert. *Meaning and Moral Order: Explorations in Cultural Analysis.* Berkeley: University of California Press, 1989.

Wuthnow, Robert, James Davison Hunter, Albert Bergesen, and Edith Kurzweil. *Cultural Analysis: The Work of Peter L. Berger, Mary Douglas, Michel Foucault, and Jürgen Habermas.* Boston: Routledge & Kegan Paul, 1984.

Yoder, Don. "Two Worlds in the Dutch Country." *Pennsylvania Folk Life* 46, no. 3 (Spring 1997): 102–8.

Yoder, Elmer S. *The Beachy Amish Mennonite Fellowship Churches.* Hartville, OH: Diakonia Ministries, 1987.

Yoder, Freeman L., and Lizzie Yoder, comps. *Echoes of the Past: Experiences of the Plain People 1920's through 1940's, during the Depression Years and More.* Middlebury, IN: F. L. and L. Yoder, 1998.

Yoder, John Howard, ed. and trans. *The Schleitheim Confession.* Scottdale, PA: Herald Press, 1977.

Yoder, Joseph W. *Rosanna of the Amish: The Restored Text.* Scottdale, PA: Herald Press, 2008. First published in 1940 by Yoder Publishing Company, Huntingdon, NY.

Yoder, Paton. *Tradition and Transition: Amish Mennonites and Old Order Amish, 1800–1900.* Scottdale, PA: Herald Press, 1991.

Yoder, Paton, and Steven R. Estes, eds. and trans. *Proceedings of the Amish Ministers' Meetings, 1862–1878.* Goshen, IN: Mennonite Historical Society, 1999.

Yoder, Raymond J. "Greenfield Farms." *Family Life,* Nov. 2006, 28–30.

"Younge Fersamlunge Liste." Unpublished list, Gordonville, PA, 2006.

Zimmerman, Jonathan. *Small Wonder: The Little Red Schoolhouse in History and Memory.* New Haven, CT: Yale University Press, 2009.

Zook, Lee J. "Slow-Moving Vehicles." In *The Amish and the State,* 2nd ed., edited by Donald B. Kraybill, 145–60. Baltimore: Johns Hopkins University Press, 2003.

INDEX

ABC (TV network), 396

Abe Miller affiliation, 138, 139

abortion, 205, 337, 362

Abstract Design in American Quilts (exhibition), 53–54

Abundance: The Future Is Better Than You Think (Diamandis and Kotler), 403

abuse, 167; alcohol, 96, 217, 224, 395; child, 51, 54; domestic violence, 206–9; drug, 54, 212–13, 224, 395; sexual, 164, 190, 207–8

acceptance. See *Gelassenheit*

Adams County, Indiana, 139, 153, 157–58, 186, 243, 282

adaptation, 9, 117, 211, 311, 405, 407–8, 412–13; and technology, 168, 170, 278, 290, 313, 315–16, 332–33, 406

addiction, 96, 190, 207–8

affiliations, 12, 137–54, 336–37; and church-communities, 138–39; and dress, 126, 128–29; growth rate of, 153–54; high vs. low, 12–13, 103, 143–44; relations between, 151–52; sizes of, 138, 139, 146

agriculture. See farming

airplane travel, 149, 324, 366

Alabama, 180

alcohol, 96, 217, 224, 395

Allen County, IN, 139, 153, 157, 186

Allgyer, Liz, 335

almsgiving, 89–90, 176

Alsace, France, 27–32

Amana Colonies, 422

Amazing Story of the Ausbund, The (Blank), 369–70

American Girl book series, 112

Amish: Out of Order (National Geographic Channel), 396

Amish, The (PBS documentary), 394, 395

Amish: The World's Squarest Teens (Channel Four, British TV), 213, 396

Amish Acres (IN), 53, 389

Amish America (blog), 397

Amish and Mennonite Heritage Center (OH), 393

Amish at the Altar (National Geographic Channel), 396

Amish Backroads (travel guide), 389

Amish Blog, 397

Amish brand, 52, 305, 416–17

"Amish Cook, The" (Coblenz), 114, 397

Amish Cook from Oasis Newsfeatures, The (blog), 397

Amish Country Tours (Lancaster County), 389

Amish Experience Tour and Theater at Plain and Fancy Farm (Lancaster County), 389, 398

Amish Farm and House (Lancaster County), 53

Amish Grace (Lifetime TV), 396

Amish Impressions (Lancaster County), 389

Amish in America, The (Luthy), 373

Amish Internet Blog, 397

Amish in the City (reality series), 213, 396

"Amish Life" (Facebook page), 397

Amish Mennonites (19th century), 31, 35. See also Beachy Amish Mennonite affiliations

Amish Outlaws (band), 165

"Amish Paradise" (Yankovic), 312

Amish Research Clinic, 350

Amish Society (Hostetler), xi–xii

Amishville (IN), 389, 393

Amish Woodworkers of America, 298

Amish Youth Vision Project, 224

Ammann, Anna (Rupp), 27

Ammann, Jakob, 4, 27–33

Ammann, Michael, 27

Ammann, Uli, 27

Anabaptists, 23–35, 62–68, 73–74, 77, 147–48, 366, 396, 415, 421–22; and Amish heritage, 227, 244, 275, 370, 372, 392

Andy Weaver affiliation, 13, 108, 139, 141, 152, 157, 163, 223, 290

Angels Watching Over Me (McDaniel), 378

animal husbandry, 275, 282, 287, 336

apprenticeship, 267–70

Arkansas, 178, 185

art, 112–13

Arthur, IL, 44, 157, 186, 248, 266, 277

Arthur affiliation, 139, 153, 280–82

Ascension Day. *See* holidays

Ashland affiliation, 139, 183, 282

Asimov, Isaac, 379

auctions, 241, 284–85

Ausbund (hymnbook), 22–24, 60–62, 73, 80, 82, 87, 124, 244, 370

authority, 99, 171–72, 263; of church, 39–40, 68, 79, 170, 177–78, 213–15, 227, 309, 410; of church-communities, 20, 68–69, 71, 138, 147, 152, 270, 314, 333; divine, 68–69, 85; of government, 352–53; moral, 13, 69, 71–72, 411; of parents, 39–40, 213

automobiles, 52, 224, 315, 324–26, 404, 406; and other Plain groups, 421–22; and ownership vs. access, 9–10, 46, 117, 307, 317, 407

Aylmer affiliation, 139

Ball, William Bentley, 359

bankruptcy, 97, 108–9

Bann. See excommunication

baptism, 4–5, 42, 60, 63–64, 149, 164, 199, 225–29; and church authority, 39, 68, 214–15, 227; service for, 227–28

barn raising, 137, 239–40, 395

Bates, Mary Ann Miller, 33

Bauman, Zygmunt, 10–11

BBC (British Broadcasting Corporation), 396

Beachy, Leroy, 146

Beachy, Monroe, 97

Beachy, Moses M., 46

Beachy Amish Mennonite affiliations, 46, 48, 165–66, 365–66, 411, 422

Bear, Greg, 379

beards, 16, 34, 59, 69, 119–20, 128, 421–22, 441n10

Becket Fund for Religious Liberty, 359

bed courtship, 222–23, 412

Beiler, David, 40–41

Beiler, Elam, 290

Beiler, Manny, 80

Beiler family, 231

beliefs, 62–66

benevolence. *See* almsgiving; charitable work

Benjie and Becky books, 373

Bergholz settlement, 441n10

Bernese Swiss German, 122

Berry, Wendell, 289

Beside the Still Waters, 64

Beyond the Divide (Lasky), 378

Bible, iv, 84, 87, 118, 123–25, 166, 200; study of, 48–49, 60–61, 75, 149, 257–58

Big Decisions (Byler), 114

Binford, Hilde, 244

bird watching, 116, 190

birth, 194–95, 346–47

birth control, 157–58, 222

birth rates, 156–59

bishops, 42, 44, 79–80, 85, 88–89, 91–95, 143, 152, 202; and leadership, 102, 120, 140, 147, 186; and National Amish Steering Committee, 358–59; role of, 175–78

Blackboard Bulletin, 254, 257, 374

Blank, Nicholas, 32

"Blind Man's Lantern" (Lang), 379

blogs, 396–97

Blood of the Prodigal (Gaus), 380

Bloomfield, IA, 282

born again. *See* salvation

Borntreger, Ida, 282

Borntreger, Vernon, 282

Botschaft, Die (correspondence newspaper), 340, 369, 375–77

branding. *See* Amish brand

brauchers (folk healers), 340

Breaking Amish (reality series), 213, 396
Brennemann, Jacob, 35
Brennemann, Samuel, 35
Brethren, 15, 160, 422
Brunstetter, Wanda, 381
Buchanan County, IA, 157, 282
Buchanan/Medford affiliation, 139, 141, 146
Budget. See *Sugarcreek Budget*
buggies, 131–32, 150–51. *See also* horse-
    drawn transportation
building codes, 9, 355, 359–60
bundling. *See* bed courtship
bureaucracy, 140, 171, 186, 191–92, 358; and
    religion, 14, 75, 79, 406. *See also* decentral-
    ization
Burger, Warren, 51, 359, 367, 400
Burn Aid (Keim), 341
business, 291–311; and the church, 97, 186,
    410; and informality, 108, 188, 267; manu-
    facturing, 292, 298, 327–28
businesses, Amish, 49, 117, 185–87, 192,
    270, 291, 294–307, 410–11; and church-
    communities, 109, 152, 174; and comput-
    ers, 120, 155, 297, 301, 316–17, 322–23;
    and economic factors, 52, 107, 169–70,
    188, 310; and English language, 123; fail-
    ure of, 109, 302–4; and family, 158–59;
    and farming, 283–84, 290; small scale of,
    191, 304, 407; and technology, 75, 118,
    149, 304, 322; and tourism, 391–93; and
    women, 13, 210–11, 305–7
Byler, Linda, 114
Byler, Valentine Y., 357
Byler Amish affiliation, 12, 139, 150

California, 180
Calvin, John, 23
Canada, 4, 6, 39, 43, 140, 178, 180, 185, 406
capital. *See* social capital
capitalism, 292–96. *See also* industrialization
carriages. *See* buggies
cars. *See* automobiles
Catholic Church, 23–24
cell phones, 11, 17, 315, 324, 363
Channel Four (British TV), 396
charitable work, 241, 365–67, 411
Chase, Malcolm, 378
Chhabra, Deepak, 399
child labor, 355, 360, 399, 412

children, Amish, 18, 39, 101–2, 105–7, 116,
    195–98, 221, 347; and infancy, 194–95, 337
choice, freedom of, 4, 17–18, 20, 100–101,
    230, 406, 417
Christian Aid Ministries (CAM), 365–66
Christian Homekeeper Blog, 391
Christmas. *See* holidays
church-communities (*Gmays*), 5, 39, 99, 101,
    156, 164, 201–2, 246; and affiliations,
    138–39; and Amish businesses, 109, 152,
    174; and Amish diversity, 290; and Amish
    identity, 77, 193, 332; authority of, 20,
    68–69, 71, 138, 147, 152, 270, 314, 333;
    and education, 253–56, 264–65, 270; and
    harmony, 86–88; and health care, 344–45,
    351; leadership of, 175–78; membership
    in, 20, 70; North American location of, 6;
    publications of, 376; small scale of, 68, 404;
    and social structure, 174–76; and technol-
    ogy, 313–14; and weddings, 233–34
church district (*Gmay*), 5, 78, 172, 174–76
churches, 14, 63, 77–80, 84–85; authority of,
    39–40, 68, 79, 170, 177–78, 213–15, 227,
    309, 410; and business, 97, 186, 410; and
    church buildings, 44, 68; and discipline,
    92–96, 165–67; leadership of, 79, 90; mem-
    bership in, 4–5, 20, 68, 95; Sunday services
    of, 77–79
circle letters, 237–38, 344
citizenship, 353–54
civic participation, 66, 116, 360–65, 411
Clear Valley School (PA), 250–51
clergy. *See* bishops; deacons; ministers
Clinic for Special Children (PA), 246, 349
clothing. *See* dress, Amish
Clymer, NY, 280–82, 391–92
Coblenz, Elizabeth, 114
collective society: and autonomy, 223–24;
    and communal support, 97, 165, 173, 229,
    231–32, 236–38, 245–49, 303–4, 308, 339,
    351; and individualism, 20, 60, 65, 71,
    99–101, 333, 406, 418–19
Colorado, 180, 185
committees, local, 186–87
communion, 28, 60, 66, 68, 86, 88–90
computers, 18, 116–17, 188, 242, 313–19,
    327–34, 349; for business, 120, 155, 297,
    301, 316–17, 322–23; in schools, 266, 318
confession, 85, 87, 92–96, 166–68, 348

congregation. *See* church district

conscientious objection, 47–48, 148, 189, 355–58, 366, 406

Conservative Anabaptist Service Program (CASP), 366

consumerism, 41, 43, 308, 333, 395, 406–7; and Amish brand, 52, 305, 416–17; and Amish culture, 106, 126, 131, 386

converts, 159–61

Cooking with the Horse and Buggy People, 370

Cooksey, Elizabeth, 180

Cooper, Anderson, 396

Council Meeting (*Ordnungs Gmay*), 86–88

courtship, 49, 213, 216, 221–23

crafts, 52, 100, 112–13, 245, 298, 300, 306, 414

creativity, 112–13, 370

crime, 354–55

Cross, John A., 283

Crossing Over: One Woman's Escape from Amish Life (Garrett), 164

cultural analysis, x, 115–18

cultural capital. *See* social capital

culture, American, 16–18, 41–43, 48, 53, 209, 415

culture, Amish, 48, 97–114, 168–70, 301–2, 307–13, 367–68, 372–74; and American identity, 16–18; and community, 231–32, 245, 249; and consumerism, 106, 126, 131, 386; and education, 257, 264–65, 269–71; and *Gelassenheit*, 98–101; and health care, 335–37, 342, 347; and high context, 173–74; popularity of, 52, 305, 385–400, 415–19; and religion, 59–60, 77; and technology, 52, 232, 312–13, 332–33; and tourism, 398–400. *See also* identity, Amish

Das Deutsch Center (OH), 350

Daviess Amish affiliation, 139, 141–42, 153

Daviess County, IN, 37, 186

Dawdyhaus, 203

deacons, 42, 79, 81, 83, 85, 90, 93, 176, 178

de Angeli, Marguerite, 387

death, 246–49, 344–45

decentralization, 99, 147, 168, 172, 180, 191–92, 358

defection, 162–65, 307. *See also* ex-Amish

Delaware, 182, 185, 254, 282

Delaware Amish, 151

Delegation for Common Sense Schooling, 252

democracy, 176, 251, 354, 367–68, 380, 400

demographics, 6, 155–58, 178–86. *See also* population, Amish

Devil's Playground (documentary), 54, 213, 395

Devoted Christian's Prayer Book, 124

Diary of the Old Order Churches (*Diary*; periodical), 374, 376

"*dien*," 151

Dior Homme, 416

disabilities, 120, 257, 351

disaster aid, 189

Disaster Response Services (DRS), 365

discipleship, 64–66

discipline: and members, 85, 92–96, 165–67; and parents, 196. *See also* excommunication; shunning

diversity, Amish, x–xii, 8–14, 44, 49, 118, 137–54, 368, 405, 411–13; and church-communities, 290; and economic factors, 211; and health care, 336–37; and modernity, 11–12, 409–11; and print culture, 377; and religion, 149, 151–52; and *Rumspringa*, 216–21; and schools, 258–63; and technology, 314–18, 411

divorce, 199, 406

Dobson, James, 64

doctrine, religious. *See* beliefs

documentaries, 394–96

domestic violence, 206–9. *See also* abuse

Donnermeyer, Joseph, 180

Dordrecht Confession of Faith, 14–15, 30, 60, 62–63, 89, 124, 166, 191, 227

Dover affiliation, 139

dress, Amish, 8, 14, 33–34, 69, 99, 105, 120, 150, 197–98; vs. dress of other Plain groups, 421–22; and humility, 103–4; and identity, 125–30; and Sunday services, 77, 85; and weddings, 233, 235

drugs, 54, 212–13, 217, 224, 395

Dust between My Toes (Weaver), 165

Dutch, 427n4, 435n7. *See also* Pennsylvania Dutch

Easter. *See* holidays

East Lampeter Township (PA), 252

Echoes of the Past (Yoder and Yoder), 23

ecology. *See* environmental concerns

economic factors, 9, 39, 41–42, 229, 281–82, 298, 407; and Amish businesses, 52, 107, 169–70, 188, 310; and Amish diversity, 211; and apprenticeship, 267–69; and education, 256, 262; and farming, 182–84, 276–90; and labor costs, 156, 158, 209, 283, 285, 293, 304; local, 291–92, 310; and migration, 182–83; and recession (2008–9), 293, 303, 381; regional, 305, 390, 405; and technology, 331; and tourism, 390, 394; and women, 306–7. *See also* business

education, 14, 17, 48, 75, 164, 250–71; and Amish culture, 257, 264–65, 269–71; and church-communities, 253–56, 264–65, 270; and economic factors, 256, 262; higher, 4, 75, 98, 116, 138, 165, 170, 253, 307, 406; and homeschooling, 267; and teachers, 254, 256–57. *See also* high school; schools, Amish; schools, public

Eicher, Jacob, 372

Eicher, Lovina, 114

Eighteen Articles. *See* Dordrecht Confession of Faith

Eitzen, Dirk, 394

electricity, public grid, 8–9, 52, 314–15; alternatives to, 7, 279, 315–16, 320–21, 326–31

Elkhart County, IN, 374, 390

Elkhart–LaGrange affiliation, 139, 141, 146, 153, 157–58, 186, 282, 292, 323

Empire of Fashion (Lipovetsky), 126

endogamy, 170, 221, 232

English, the, xiii, 5, 414–15. *See also* outsiders

English language, 43, 60, 121–25, 243, 261, 309, 371, 408

entertainment. *See* recreation

environmental concerns, 52, 288–89

Epps, Garrett, 367, 415

ER (TV series), 213

Ernsthafte Christenpflicht, Die (The Prayer Book for Earnest Christians), 63, 84, 88, 124

Esprit clothing company, 54

Essentials of English Spelling (1919), 259

Eucharist. *See* communion

Europe, 4, 16, 22–36, 145, 353, 421–22

evangelism, 48, 74, 155, 262, 366, 381–82, 411. *See also* mission movement, Amish

evolution, 116

ex-Amish, 206, 383, 394, 396, 398. *See also* defection

excommunication (*Bann*), 30, 63, 68, 85–87, 94–95, 152, 165–68, 353, 380. *See also* shunning

Facebook, 376, 396–97, 404

family, 109–11, 183, 193–211, 201, 376, 404, 406, 413–14; extended, 172, 198, 203–4, 207, 232, 237–39; and farming, 156, 158–59, 275–76, 285, 289–90; and religion, 39, 158–59; and *Rumspringa*, 214; size of, 153–54, 156–58; and social structure, 172; and technology, 319, 326, 333; and work, 102, 158–59, 209, 294–95, 307

Family Helpers, 189, 348

Family Life (periodical), 112, 208, 374

farmers' markets, 183, 284–85, 296–97, 309

farming, 13, 164, 275–90, 358, 407–8; dairy, 7, 184, 279–80, 283; decline of, 49, 281, 291; and economic factors, 182–84, 276–90; and European Anabaptists, 26, 28, 31–32; and family, 156, 158–59, 275–76, 285, 289–90; organic, 285–87; produce, 284–85; small scale of, 43, 52, 276–77; and sustainability, 288–89; and technology, 52, 144, 276–80, 316–17, 320–21

Farming: People, Land, and Community (magazine), 289

Farmwald, Delbert, 372

Farmwald, Linda, 372

fasting (*Fastdag*), 64, 88, 239

fiction, Amish. *See* publishing about Amish

Fisher, Annie, 3

Fisher, Gideon, 277

Fisher, Levi, 3

fishing, 239, 242

Flair Travel Consultants, 387

Florida, 179, 185

foods, 85, 105

footwashing, 28–30, 63, 89, 98

Ford, Harrison, 54

Ford, Henry, 11

forgiveness, 55, 63, 66–67, 87, 95–96

For Richer or Poorer (film), 395

Foundation's Edge (Asimov), 379

Fourth of July. *See* holidays

Fredericktown affiliation, 139
freedom: of choice, 4, 17–18, 20, 100–101, 230, 406, 417; individual, 20, 39, 269–70, 333, 406; religious, 18, 35, 39, 255, 353–54, 405, 415
frolics ("work parties"), 239–41
frugality, 106–8
funerals, 28, 247–49
Furlong, Saloma Miller, 115, 164, 230
furniture: and Amish brand, 4, 37, 52, 305, 414; and Amish business, 117, 199, 268, 284, 297–301, 391

"gangs," 217–21. See also *Rumspringa*
gardening, 109, 113, 116
Garrett, Ruth Irene, 164
Gaus, P. L., 378, 380, 415
Geauga County, OH, 44, 161–63, 186, 251, 281–82, 292, 346, 354
Geauga I affiliation, 139, 146, 153
Geauga II affiliation, 139
Gelassenheit, 62, 65–67, 77, 85, 96, 157, 211, 370; and Amish culture, 98–101; and death, 247, 249; and dress, 129; and education, 270; and health care, 336; and the *Ordnung*, 121
gender, 193–211, 239–40; and Amish businesses, 305–7; and the church, 79–80, 202; and marriage, 200–201; and work, 201, 209–10, 307. See also women, Amish
genealogy, 23, 349, 370
genetics, 336, 349–50
Georgia, 180
German language, xiii, 14–15, 38, 60, 62, 79, 121–25, 243, 260–61, 421–22. See also Pennsylvania Dutch
Germany, 23, 26, 31, 35–36, 421
Gingerich, Jacob U., 352, 355
Girl in the Mirror, The, 373
Gmay. See church-communities; church district
God's will, 11, 65, 80–81, 87, 100, 114–15, 192, 352–53, 361–63, 366
Good Friday. *See* holidays
Gordonville Print Shop, 371–72
government, 352–68; assistance from, 165, 338, 356, 406; authority of, 352–53; local, 265, 360–61; negotiation with, 354, 357–59, 368, 408; regulation by, 8–9, 51,

192, 279–81, 355–56, 407; relations with, 50–51, 232, 353–54, 411; and religion, 352–53; state, 251, 254–55
Grass-Based Dairy Farming, 287
"Great Plain, The" (*Vogue*), 416
Green Field Farms (OH), 20, 286, 289
Green Pastures (PA), 349
Greksa, Lawrence, 307

Habitat for Humanity, 362
Haiti Benefit Auctions, 366
Haslibacher, Hans, 24
Hazleton, IA, 252
head covering, 128-29
Healing from Sexual Sin, 208
health care, 245–46, 335–51; alternative, 336, 341–43; and Amish culture, 335–37, 342, 347; and Amish diversity, 336–37; and birthing, 346–47; Canadian, 406; centers for, 346–50; and church-communities, 344–45, 351; and death, 344–45; and drawing pain, 340, 453n8; and folk resources, 339–41, 370; and immunization, 51, 345–46; insurance for, 14, 188, 293, 308, 337–38; for mental illness, 189–90, 348–49; and mutual aid, 187–88, 338–39, 351, 356; providers of, 195, 337, 340–41, 343, 346–47; and refusal of treatment, 336, 347; and religion, 336, 342–44, 350. *See also* Patient Protection and Affordable Care Act
Heartland Hymns (Lapp, comp.), 244
Heartland Mattress LLC, 293–94
Hearts and Hands: The Official Travel Planner of Amish Country, 389
Heaven, 17, 39, 58, 70–72, 82–86, 90, 101, 112, 121, 125–27, 132, 226, 242, 330, 360
Helmuth, Joseph W., 341
Henner's Lydia (de Angeli), 387
Heritage Historical Library, 161, 190
Herold der Wahrheit (periodical), 370–71
Hertzler, Aaron, 291
Hidden Treasures Handed Down from Our Ancestors Since 1600 (King), 23
Higgins, Orrin, 184
high school, 8, 170, 257, 262–63, 406, 418; and compulsory attendance, 3, 48, 51, 251–55, 355–56, 359, 399; and work, 292–93, 302, 304, 307, 311
holidays, 86, 238–39

Holmes County, OH, 53, 63, 142, 157, 162–63, 186, 223, 266, 362; and farming, 282, 286; health care in, 342–43; and internal division, 146, 148–49; and tourism, 390, 392

Holmes Old Order affiliation, 139, 146, 149, 153, 157, 163, 221

holy kiss, 89, 92

homes, Amish, 106–7, 209, 318–20; worship in, 14, 78

homosexuality, 206, 362

Honduras, 180

honesty, 108–9

horse-drawn transportation, 3, 8, 14–15, 46, 52, 67–69, 138, 184, 325–26, 413; buggies for, 131–32, 150–51

Horse Progress Days, 187, 190–91

horses, 130–31, 183–84

hospice care, 345, 362

Hostetler, John A., xi, 399

Hostetler, Tobe, 141

How the Dordrecht Confession Came Down to Us (Stoll), 373

humility, 60, 67, 77, 85, 89, 103–4, 116, 270, 295, 419; and children, 102; and *Gelassenheit*, 98–99

hunting, 110–11, 118

Huntington, Gertrude Enders, ix–x, 194

Hurst, Charles, 157, 392

Hutterites, 422

hypermodernity, 11, 130, 159, 381–82, 395, 403, 409–11, 419

Hypermodern Times (Lipovetsky), 11

Idaho, 185

identity, Amish, x–xi, 3–21, 38, 115–33, 232, 238, 315, 375–77; and American identity, 16–18; and Amish literature, 370–72; and Amish schools, 265; and church-community, 77, 193, 332; and dress, 125–30; and language, 121–25; nineteenth-century, 313; and public image, 55, 386, 414; and *Rumspringa*, 223–24; symbols of, 99, 125–26, 130–33, 138, 149–51, 168, 171–72, 191–92, 332, 414; and tourism, 399; twenty-first century, 55, 312, 386, 413–14; and work, 293, 307, 311. *See also* culture, Amish

Igou, Brad, 398, 413

Illinois, 39, 141, 178, 182, 185. *See also* particular locations

immigration, North American, 4, 16, 34–36, 38–39, 421

immunization, 51, 345–46

Indiana, 4, 39, 163, 185, 264. *See also* particular locations

Indiana County, PA, 186

individualism, 49, 113, 170, 232, 302, 308, 417; American, 4, 17, 38, 42, 368; and Amish dress, 126–27; and collective society, 20, 60, 65, 71, 99–101, 333, 406, 418–19; and modernity, 5, 11, 406; and religion, 71, 75, 95

industrialization, 7, 41, 158–59, 209, 275, 294, 302, 313, 404

In Dutch Again (Workinger), 379–80

informality, 61, 99, 112, 217, 236, 337–38, 342; and business, 108, 188, 267; and social structure, 140, 172–73, 177, 190–91

In Meiner Jugend, 124

innovation. *See* invention

insurance, 165, 232, 245–46, 356; health, 14, 188, 293, 308, 337–38

Internal Revenue Service, 356, 395

Internet, 3, 8–9, 17, 170, 266, 314–16, 409

invention, 316–17

Iowa, 39, 178, 185, 264, 359. *See also* particular locations

Iowa Tests of Basic Skills, 263–64

Jamesport/Bloomfield affiliation, 139

Jasper, NY, 282

Jay County, IN, 282

Joe Troyer (Swartzentruber) Amish affiliation, 106

Johnson County, IA, 39, 43, 276

Judging Amy (CBS TV), 213

Jüngerich, Louis, 39

Kalona, IA, 157, 366, 389

Kalona affiliation, 139

Kansas, 182, 185, 359

Kansas/Oklahoma affiliation, 139

Kapp (head covering), 128–29

Kaufman, Alma, 387

Keene, Carolyn, 415

Keim, John, 341

Kelly, Kevin, 313

Kelly, Sheryl, 361

Kenton affiliation, 139, 141

Kentucky, 4, 178, 182, 185

Kingsbury, Karen, 112

Kinsinger, Andrew S., 358, 371

Kline, Paul, 98, 289

Kokomo affiliation, 138–39

Korbin, Jill, 307

Korean War, 148

Labor Day. *See* holidays

labor unions, 292–93

Ladies Journal, 374

LaGrange County, IN, 361, 389

Laikind, Daniel, 396

Lancaster affiliation, 12, 138–39, 146, 150–53, 163, 184, 219, 282, 396

Lancaster County, PA, 46, 50, 157, 161, 183, 186, 305, 362, 371, 374; farming in, 280, 284–85, 286; health care in, 342–43; and tourism, 52, 53–54, 389, 390

Lancaster Farm Fresh Cooperative, 286–87

Lang, Allen Kim, 379

language, 121–25, 136, 165, 249. *See also particular languages and dialects*

Lapp, Hannah, 399

Lasky, Kathryn, 378, 380–81

Lawrence County, PA, 282

law suits. *See* litigation

leadership, 79, 90, 148, 158, 173, 175–78, 193–94, 202. *See also* bishops; deacons; ministers

Leaving Amish Paradise (BBC), 396

legal issues, 8, 10, 111, 354–60, 441n10; and bankruptcy, 97, 108–9; and child labor, 355, 360, 399, 412; and education, 51, 251–52, 255, 359, 367, 399; and health care, 338, 341, 347; and litigation, 66, 338, 353, 355–57, 359–60, 407; and nonresistance, 353, 357

Lehman, Marilyn, 202

Lehman, Mervin, 293

leisure. *See* recreation

Lewis, Beverly, 378, 380, 415

libraries, 112, 190, 257

Life's Special Sunbeams (periodical), 374

Lifetime Movie Network, 396

Lifted Up By Angels (McDaniel), 378

Lindholm, William C., 252, 359

Lions Club International, 363–65

Lipovetsky, Gilles, 11, 126

Liquid Modernity (Bauman), 10–11

literature, Amish, 369–84, 387; popular fiction, 377–84. *See also* writing

litigation, 66, 338, 353, 355–57, 359–60, 407

Living with the Amish (BBC), 396

Loblied, Das ("The Praise Song"), 82–83

Lord's Prayer, 61–62, 65, 66, 84

Lord's Supper. *See* communion

Louis XIV, 32

Lucado, Max, 64, 112, 262

Luddites, xi, 52, 312, 333, 407

Lust-Gärtlein (prayer book), 63

Luther, Martin, 23, 26, 60, 123

Lutheran Church, 23, 26, 30

Luthy, David, 161, 180, 373

Madison, James, 367

Maine, 141, 178–80, 185

Maoz, Darya, 400

marriage, 189, 199–201, 214, 221

Martin, Helen Reimensnyder, 381

martyrdom, 22, 24–26, 62

Martyrs Mirror (Braght), 25, 60, 66, 73, 84, 253, 370

Maryland, 185. *See also particular locations*

Master's International Ministries, 366

McConnell, David, 157, 392

McDaniel, Lurlene, 378, 380

McGuffey's Readers, 259

McKusick, Victor A., 349

media, popular, 54, 114, 212–13, 262, 360, 361, 394–400

Medicaid, 406

Medicare, 357, 406

medicine. *See* health care

meetinghouses, 43, 44

Meet Your Amish Neighbors (Kaufman and Flair Travel Consultants), 387

Meidung. See shunning

members' meetings, 85–86

Memorial Day. *See* holidays

Menno-Hof (IN), 393

Mennonite Central Committee (MCC), 365

Mennonite Disaster Service (MDS), 365

Mennonites, 15, 34–35, 42, 148, 166, 377, 392; and charitable work, 365–67, 411; and conscientious objection, 357–58; Dutch, 26, 30, 62; and European Amish, 35–36; and farming, 285–86; merging

of Amish with, 43, 48, 180; Old Colony,
366–67, 421; Old Order, 122, 265, 286,
371, 421

Mennonite Voluntary Service, 47

Menno Simons, 26, 195

mental illness, 189–90, 348–49

Mexico, 337, 339, 342–43, 366–67

Meyers, Thomas J., 163, 307

Michigan, 4, 182, 185, 282. *See also particular locations*

Michigan-related affiliation, 139

Middlefield Care Center (OH), 346

Midwest Conservative churches, 141

Midwest Mainstream churches, 141

midwives, 195, 341, 343, 346–47

Mifflin County, PA, 186

Mighty Whirlwind, The (Wagler), 373

migration, 145, 181–83

military service, 4, 14, 20, 35–36, 39, 66, 162,
353; and conscientious objection, 47–48,
148, 189, 355–58, 366, 406; and National
Amish Steering Committee, 189

Miller, Emma, 363

Miller, Jacob K. ("Oregon Jake"), 181

Miller, Mary M., 124

Miller, Naomi, 363

Milroy / West Union affiliation, 139

Milverton affiliation, 139, 153

ministers, 14, 49, 61, 68–69, 102, 120,
161, 170, 202; and Amish diversity, 149,
151–52; and church services, 79–84; and
confession, 93–94; and excommunication,
94–95; and leadership, 186; meetings of,
42–44; and National Amish Steering Committee, 359; and ordination, 28, 68, 90–92,
158, 164, 170; and the *Ordnung*, 88–89;
and social structure, 173, 176–80, 186

Minnesota, 141, 178, 185

missionary work, 75, 366–67, 411

mission movement, Amish, 47–49, 149

Mississippi, 185

Missouri, 4, 140–41, 178, 185, 282, 285, 287

Missouri/Illinois affiliation, 139

mobile phones. *See* cell phones

mobility, 181, 232, 406; and higher education,
170; and transportation, 117, 130, 132,
158, 314, 324, 325

modernity, xi, 5–12, 191–92, 400; and fragmentation, 160, 173–74, 404; liquid vs.
solid, 11, 311, 334, 404, 408–9, 416; negotiation with, 8–10, 331–32, 405–8; resistance to, 8–9, 114, 133, 211, 249. *See also*
hypermodernity

modernization, 425n6

Mohawk Valley, NY, 183, 184

Montana, 179, 185

moral neutrality, 314–15

moral objects, 116–18

Moravians, 422

Morton, D. Holmes, 349

Moser, Bill, 160

Moser, Tricia, 160

Mount Eaton Care Center (OH), 346

Moving Mars (Bear), 379

Muller, Ulrich, 30

multiculturalism, 261, 269

music. *See* singing

mutual aid, 187–88, 245, 338–39, 351, 356

Myer, Tamar, 378

names, 161, 174–75

Nancy Drew (character), 378–79, 380

Nappanee affiliation, 39, 53, 139, 157, 186,
292

National Amish Steering Committee, 20, 189,
357–60, 408, 411

National Committee for Amish Religious
Freedom (NCARF), 252, 359

National Federation of Independent Businesses, 361

National Geographic Channel, 396

nature, 109–11, 130–31, 379–80

Nebraska, 178, 185

Nebraska affiliation, 139, 141, 150–51, 157,
282, 320

negotiation. *See* adaptation; modernity

New American Almanac, The (*Der Neue
Amerikanische Calendar*; Raber), 46

New Birth Sunday, 86

New Eden Care Center (IN), 346

New Mexico, 180

New Order affiliation, 12, 49, 139–43, 146–49,
153, 221–22, 242, 282; Holmes County,
157, 163

New Wilmington affiliation, 139, 186

New York, 4, 182, 185. *See also particular
locations*

New York Times, ix, 50, 252, 387, 416

Nickel Mines school shooting, 55, 65, 67, 381, 396
Niemeyer, Lucian, 250
Nolt, Steven M., 163
nonconformity. *See* world, separation from
nonresistance, 353, 356–57, 373
nonviolence, 66, 208, 399, 422
North Carolina, 185
"Not Everyone Can Be a Farmer" (*Family Life*), 289
Nugent, Walter, 158

oaths, 63, 116
obedience, 17, 60, 67, 85, 98–99, 101–2, 116, 232; and children, 101, 195–97; and government, 354; and religion, 26, 64–65, 72, 95
Occupational Safety and Health Act, 50, 359
Ohio, 4, 39, 182, 185, 393. *See also particular locations*
Ohio Amish Library, 124
Oke, Janette, 112
Oklahoma, 185
old age, 120, 203, 337, 351
Old German Baptist Brethren, 422
Old Order Amish, xiii, 42–47, 143, 429n20. *See also* Holmes Old Order affiliation
Old Order Book Society of Pennsylvania, 371
Old Order River Brethren, 160, 422
Ontario, Canada, 4, 39, 43, 140, 178, 185
"On the Beutiful [*sic*] Country Days," 369–70
oral tradition, 44, 62–63, 118, 172–73, 371
ordination, 28, 68, 90–92, 158, 164, 170
Ordnung, the, 41–42, 69–70, 78, 85–89, 118–21, 145, 277–81, 297–98, 355; and technology, 69, 110, 332
Ordnungs Gmay, 86–88
Oregon, 180
"Oregon Jake" (Jacob K. Miller), 181
organizations, Amish, 186–87
Otsego County, NY, 184
Our Daily Bread, 64
Our Heritage, Hope, and Faith (Miller), 124
outsiders: economic relations with, 118, 407–8; and education, 261, 265, 372; interaction with, 37, 123, 310–11, 407–8, 412, 414; local relations with, 183–84, 412. *See also* English, the

pacifism. *See* conscientious objection; military service; nonresistance; nonviolence
Paraguay, 180
parents, Amish, 18, 214–15, 220–21, 228, 347; authority of, 39–40, 213
Parke County, IN, 184
Parsley, Sage, Rosemary, and Crime (Myers), 378–79
Pathway Publishers, 49, 124, 141, 161, 257, 261, 372–74
Pathway Readers, 372
patience, 67, 77, 85, 130–31
Patient Protection and Affordable Care Act (2010), 337, 360
patriarchy, 193–94, 201–2, 307
PBS (Public Broadcasting System), 394
peer groups, 212–21, 223, 228–29, 241
Penn, William, 34
Pennsylvania, 4, 34, 38–39, 43, 182, 185. *See also particular locations*
Pennsylvania Dutch, 38, 79, 121–25, 137, 145, 249, 421–22, 428n3, 429n20, 435n7, 436n8, 436n9, 436n10, 436n11, 439n21, 453n8; and Pennsylvania German, 428n3, 435n7, 436n9, 439n29; and Swiss German, 145, 432n5, 436n9
Pentecost. *See* holidays
People Helpers, 189, 348
Peters, Shawn F., 400
photographs, 104, 355, 360, 394, 404
Picoult, Jodi, 378, 380, 415
Pietism, 30, 35, 63
Pinecraft, FL, 241–43
Plain and Fancy (musical), 53
Plain Buggies (Stephen Scott), 131
Plain Communities Business Exchange (newspaper), 298, 374
Plain Interests (periodical), 374
plainness, 98–99, 105–9
Plain Truth (Picoult), 378, 380
pluralism, 38, 406
"Poisoning the Earth" (*Family Life*), 286
politics, 361–62
population, Amish, 155–70, 185–86; growth of, 4, 19, 153–56, 168–70, 281, 411
postmodern, the, 103, 416–17. *See also* modernity
Powwowing. See *brauchers*

prayer, 59, 61–63, 81, 84, 88, 92, 121

preaching, 81–84

pride, 72, 100, 103–4, 113, 116, 310

"Primetime: The Outsiders" (ABC), 396

products, Amish, 52–54, 296–301

progressivism, 153–55, 157–58, 163, 297, 315, 318; and affiliation, 143–44, 147–51

Protestants, 23–24, 148

publications, 49, 63–64, 374–76. *See also particular publications*

public image, Amish, ix–x, 4, 50–55, 133, 212–13, 385–86, 415–19; and Amish literature, 377–84; and tourism, 399–400

publishing, Amish, 369–84; and English language, 371; history of, 370–80; and periodicals, 374–75; and schoolbooks, 371–73

publishing about Amish, 377–84

"puppy mills," 288

Purpose-Driven Life, The (Warren), 64

Quakers, 34, 422

quality of life, 21, 232, 418–19

quilts, 53–54, 113

Raber, John A., 46

radio, 314, 315, 326–27

Rapinz, David, 155

rationality, 171–72, 192, 263, 309. *See also* thought, analytical

Reader's Digest (periodical), 50

reading, 112, 116, 122–23, 369

recession (2008–9), 293, 303, 381

recreation, 109–13, 237–43

Reformation (Protestant), 23, 35, 423; and literature, 370, 373

Reformed Church, 23, 27, 30

Reformist Amish affiliation, 140–41

Reiling, Denise, 225–26

Reist, Hans, 30

religion, 4–5, 7, 15, 59–76, 100, 191–92, 247; and Amish culture, 59–60, 77; and Amish diversity, 149, 151–52; and Amish schools, 257–58; and bureaucracy, 14, 75, 79, 406; and the devil, 72–74, 116; and family, 158–59; freedom of, 18, 35, 39, 255, 353–54, 405, 415; and German language, 123–25; and government, 352–53; and

health care, 336, 342–44, 350; and heaven, 17, 68–70, 74, 105, 116, 127, 226, 314, 344, 405; and prayer, 59, 61–63, 81, 84, 88, 92, 121; and technology, 314, 333. *See also* churches; rituals

remarriage, 199

Renno affiliation, 139, 150

responsibility, 165, 194, 198, 200–202, 253, 355; and children, 102, 195, 270; to community, 45, 72, 167, 339

Rest Haven (IN), 348–49

restoration, 95–96

retention, 156, 162–65

retirement, 203

reunions, 152, 161, 171, 187, 190, 202, 236–38, 301, 317

revivalism, Protestant, 41–43

Rice, Antoine, 33

Riehl, Susie, 113

rituals, 8, 70, 77–96, 99; footwashing, 28–30, 63, 89, 98; funeral, 247–49; social, 232. *See also* baptism; communion; holy kiss; ordination

Rivers, Francine, 112

romance novels, 381–82

"Rules of a Godly Life" (*Lust-Gärtlein*), 63–64, 75–76, 124

Rumspringa, 54, 199, 212–30; and future, 225–26, 229–30, 307; myths regarding, 212–16; and parental supervision, 214–15, 220–21

Rumspringa (off-Broadway play), 213

Running Around (and Such) (Byler), 114

rural residence, 14, 131, 158–59, 168, 178, 182

Sabina: A Story of the Amish (Reimensnyder), 381

safety, 189, 386

Sainte-Marie-aux-Mines (Alsace), 27–28, 31–32

salvation, 70–72

Salvation Army, 365

Samels, Mark, 394

Schlabach, Rob, 275–76

Schlabbach, Peter, 36

Schmucker, Jacob, 354

School Echoes (periodical), 374

schoolhouses, 258–61

schools, Amish, 49, 162, 170, 189, 202, 250–51, 254–65, 269–70, 371–73; and Amish diversity, 258–63; curriculum of, 254, 257, 259–60, 261–63, 266; and religion, 257–58; and technology, 266, 318. *See also* education

schools, public, 252–54, 265–66, 269–70; and busing, 184, 252; consolidation of, ix, 20, 48, 251–52, 254, 387. *See also* education

Schwartz, David, 393

Schwartzentruber, Christian, 35

science, 7, 17, 43, 75, 98; and health care, 336, 345, 349–51; in schools, 251, 253, 263

Scott, Stephen, 128–29, 131, 140, 160

Scripture. *See* Bible

self-denial, 67, 72, 89, 98–100, 104, 127, 232, 270

Selling the Amish (Trollinger), 390

separateness. *See* world, separation from

settlements, 5, 45, 138, 142–43, 157, 178–84, 217–20; abandoned, 180

sex education, 199, 207, 253

sexuality, 204–6, 222

Shakers, 422

Shaw, Christopher, 378

Shipshewana, IN, 346, 361, 366, 393

Shuldiner, Alan R., 350

shunning (*Meidung*), 30–31, 33, 63, 95, 148, 152, 154, 165–68, 380. *See also* excommunication

Shunning, The, 380–81

silence, 67, 77, 99, 319

"Silent Struggle, The," 206

Simons, Menno. *See* Menno Simons

simplicity, 40–41, 79, 102, 105, 247; American search for, 386–88

singing, 14, 80–83, 216–17, 222, 243–44, 262, 426n3

single status, 204

slow-moving vehicle (SMV) emblem, 46, 352–53, 356

slow pace, 263, 333, 382, 386–87, 409–10, 416; and transportation, 130–31, 232, 315, 325

small scale, 68, 99, 173, 186, 232, 314, 418–19; and Amish businesses, 191, 304, 407; and farming, 43, 52, 276–77

smartphones, 11, 315

Smith, Christian, 15

snowbirds, 241–43

social capital, 231–32, 240, 245

socialization, 196–97, 264–65, 267, 270

social life, 109, 130, 171, 186–87, 190, 204, 231–49, 344, 364, 407. See also *Rumspringa*

social media, 222, 376–77, 391, 396–98, 404

social organization, 171–76, 190–92, 231

Social Security, 10, 50, 293, 304, 308, 356–57, 406

social structure, 77, 132, 172–92, 308–10, 407; and decentralization, 99, 147, 168, 172, 180, 191–92

solar power, 328–31

Somerset affiliation, 44, 139

Somerset County, PA, 46

South Carolina, 180

South Dakota, 178, 185

Spartansburg, PA, 282

spirituality, 60–68, 75

sports, 111, 217, 218, 220

St. Joseph County, MI, 265–66

St. Mary's County, MD, 157

state. *See* government

Steering Committee. *See* National Amish Steering Committee

Stephenville, TX, 183

Stevick, Richard, 198–99, 217, 223–24, 243

Stick Figure Productions, 396

Stoll, Joseph, 180, 181, 194, 269, 371–74

Stoll, Steven, 289

Stoltzfus, Louise, 201, 202

Stoltzfus, Sam, 80

Strayor-Upton Arithmetic Series (1930s), 259–60, 372

Strong Families, Safe Children, 208

Stüdler, Verena, 27

Study Time (publisher), 372

submission, 4, 62, 82, 95, 100, 260. See also *Gelassenheit*

Sugarcreek Budget (*Budget*; correspondence newspaper), 46–47, 375–77

Sunday schools, 43, 48, 79, 149

Supreme Court, U.S., 51, 252, 255, 359, 367, 399

sustainability, 288–89

Swartzentruber, Jacob F., 43

Swartzentruber Amish affiliation, 12, 141, 147–48, 157, 163, 180, 352, 405; and Amish schools, 258–60; buggies of, 151; and building codes, 359–60; and courtship, 222; dress of, 150; and farming, 282, 290; growth of, 153; size of, 139, 146; weddings of, 234

Swiss Amish, 12, 122, 145–46, 151, 153, 157, 177, 297, 360; Adams County affiliation, 243–44; Allen County affiliation, 139

Swiss German (language), 122, 137, 145

Switzerland, 23, 26–32, 421

Tagliches Manna, 64

taxes, 9, 256, 353, 356, 407

taxi service. *See* transportation: non-Amish taxi

teachers, 254, 256–57

technology, 7, 14, 17, 49, 113, 165, 312–34, 407–8; and adaptation, 168, 170, 278, 290, 313, 315–16, 332–33, 406; and Amish businesses, 75, 118, 149, 304, 322; and Amish culture, 52, 232, 312–13, 332–33; and Amish diversity, 314–18, 411; and changing work patterns, 297, 309, 322; and family, 319, 326, 333; and farming, 52, 144, 276–80, 316–17, 320–21; household, 319–20; and hypermodernity, 403, 409; and innovation, 316–17; and the *Ordnung*, 69, 110, 332; and other Plain groups, 421–22; and ownership vs. access, 317–18, 323, 325–26; and schools, 266, 318. *See also particular items*

teenagers. *See* youth, Amish (*die Youngie*)

telephones, 3, 43, 52, 149, 314, 319, 323, 327, 404; location of, 118, 309, 333; and ownership vs. access, 317. *See also* cell phones

television, 3, 8–9, 170, 314–15, 326–27, 377, 404, 406; and Amish reality shows, 213, 395–96

Tennessee, 138, 148, 185

Texas, 179, 185

texting, 222, 410

Thanksgiving Day. *See* holidays

theology. *See* beliefs

Thormann, Georg, 27

thought, analytical, 62, 67, 70, 98, 149, 170, 260, 263

Thrill of the Chaste (Weaver-Zercher), 381

Thy Will Be Done (Chupp and Chupp), 66

TLC (The Learning Channel), 396

Tobe Hostetler affiliation, 139, 157, 163

Tompkins, Doug, 54

tourism, 52–54, 113, 305, 310, 383, 385–400, 416; and Amish culture, 398–400; Amish participation in, 391–96, 398–99; benefits of, 391–93; virtual, 394–400

tractors, 140, 149, 277

tractor-using churches, 153

traditionalism, 41–42, 69–70, 113–14, 163, 183, 315, 318, 418–19; and affiliation, 143–44, 147–51; and family, 157–58; and farming, 277–81; and *Gelassenheit*, 98–99; high *vs.* low, 12–13, 103, 143–44; and population growth, 153–55, 413; and work, 297–98

transportation: horse-drawn, 3, 8, 14–15, 46, 52, 67–69, 131–32, 138, 150–51, 184, 325–26, 413; non-Amish taxi, 10, 317, 322–23, 325–26; public, 10, 14–15, 118, 317, 324, 326

travel, 14–15, 110–11, 196, 237

Trend Hunter (website), 416

Trollinger, Susan, 390–91, 399

Trouble in Amish Paradise (BBC), 396

Troyer affiliation, 139, 279, 282

Truck Patch News, 285

Turbotville affiliation, 139

Turco, Douglas, 398

2012 Holmes County Map and Visitors' Guide, 387

Ukraine, 366

unity, 43, 61, 69, 79, 83, 85–89, 160, 267

Until Angels Close My Eyes (McDaniel), 378

vacations, 111, 241–42

values, Amish, 60, 67, 98–109, 267. *See also* culture, Amish; *particular values*

van Beckum, Maria, 25

Vermont, 180

Vietnam War, 148

Virginia, 182, 185

visiting, 109, 236–37, 243, 344

Vogue, 416

Von das Schlacht Haus (*From the Slaughter House;* periodical), 374

Vonk, Martine, 288
Vorsinger (song leader), 77, 82
voting, 361–62

Wagler, David, 371–72
Wagler, Ezra, 369
Wagler, Ira, 164, 225
Wagler, Peter, 37
Walker, Lucy, 213
Walk in the Light, 208
Wang, Heng, 350
Warren, Rick, 64
Wayne County, OH, 43, 157
Weaver, Wayne, 165
Weaver-Zercher, David, 55, 386
Weaver-Zercher, Valerie, 381–82
Weber, Max, 171
weddings, 28, 232–36
Weir, Peter, 395
Wesner, Erik, 295, 397
West Virginia, 185
When Strawberries Bloom (Byler), 114
Whitney Museum of American Art, 53
Why Do They Dress That Way? (Scott), 128–29
Why I Left the Amish (Furlong), 164
Wickey, Solomon J., 341
Willems, Dirk, 22, 25
Winfrey, Oprah, 213, 396
Wisconsin, 4, 157, 182, 185, 279, 282
Wisconsin v. Yoder et al., 51, 255, 359, 367, 399
Witch Tree Symbol, The (Keene), 378
Witness (film), 54, 395, 398, 399, 416
Wittmer, Joe, 37
women, Amish, 201–3, 224, 230; and work, 13, 210–11, 293, 305–7. *See also* gender
Woodhull, NY, 282
Woodsmall, Cindy, 381
work, 116, 165, 182, 297–98, 317, 322–23; and Amish culture, 301–2, 307–11; changing patterns of, 162, 209–10, 292, 297, 299, 302, 304, 307–11, 322; and children, 197, 199; and family, 102, 209, 294–95, 307; and gender, 201, 209–10, 307; and higher education, 292–93, 302, 304, 307, 311; and identity, 293, 307, 311; and local factors, 292–93, 299, 310; and women, 13, 210–11, 293, 305–7. *See also* business; businesses, Amish; farming
workers' compensation, 304, 355
Workinger, Barbara, 379–80
world, separation from, xi–xii, 13, *33*, 72–74, 100, 116–18, 397, 409; and Amish diversity, 147, 154; and changing work patterns, 292, 302, 311; and dress, 125–30; and education, 253, 261, 265, 269–70; and European Anabaptists, 28–31; and population growth, 168–70; and technology, 314, 323, 332; and tourism, 385, 388–89
World War II, 47, 148, 356
World Wide Web (www). *See* Internet
Worth Dying For (Stoltzfus), 373
writers, 376–84
writing, 112, 122–23, 237–38, 369–84
Wyoming, 185

Yankovic, "Weird Al," 312
yieldedness, 100–102. See also *Gelassenheit*
Yoder, Andy, 165
Yoder, Samuel E., 141, 148
You Are Special (Lucado), 262
Young Companion (periodical), 374
youth, Amish (*die Youngie*), 18, 120, 131–32, 156, 170, 198–99, 243, 383, 396; freedom of, 40, 47–49. See also *Rumspringa*
YouTube, 377, 396

Zondervan, 397
zoning laws, 310, 355–56, 408
Zwingli, Ulrich, 23